Computer Accounting with QuickBooks® Online: A Cloud-Based Approach

Second Edition

Carol Yacht, MA
Software Consultant

Susan Crosson, MS, CPA
Emory University

COMPUTER ACCOUNTING WITH QUICKBOOKS ONLINE: A CLOUD-BASED APPROACH, SECOND EDITION

This book is printed on acid-free paper.

4 5 6 7 8 9 QVS 23 22 21 20 19

ISBN 978-1-260-04082-1
MHID 1-260-04082-8

Portfolio Manager: *Steve Schuetz*
Product Developer: *Allie Kukla*
Marketing Manager: *Michelle Williams*
Content Project Manager: *Dana M. Pauley*
Buyer: *Susan K. Culbertson*
Design: *Egzon Shaqiri*
Content Licensing Specialist: *Melissa Homer*
Cover Image: *(Sky/clouds)©Evgeny Karandaev/Shutterstock; (Fiber Optic Cables/sky)©John Lund/Getty Images*
Compositor: *SPi Global*

mheducation.com/highered

Table of Contents

The Timetable for Completion is a guideline for lecture/discussion/ demonstration and hands-on work. In most Accounting classes, students can expect to spend approximately two hours outside of class for every hour in class.

A typical 3-credit course is 45 hours (15 weeks X 3 hours per week). Forty-five hours is the approximate time to complete the textbook within the classroom hours. Work <u>not</u> completed within the hours shown is homework.

TIMETABLE FOR COMPLETION		**Hours**
Chapter 1	QuickBooks Online Test-drive	3.0
Chapter 2	New Company Setup and Chart of Accounts	3.0
Chapter 3	Beginning Balances and October Transaction Register	3.0
Chapter 4	Vendors and Inventory	3.0
Chapter 5	Customers and Sales	3.0
Chapter 6	December Source Documents	3.0
Chapter 7	Analysis and Reports—End of Fourth Quarter and Year	3.0
Chapter 8	January Source Documents	4.0
Chapter 9	February Source Documents	4.0
Chapter 10	March Source Documents and End of First Quarter	4.0
Chapter 11	Certification, Report Customization and QB Labs	2.0
Chapter 12	Apps, Updates, QB Blog and Tips	2.0
Case Problem 1	Payroll and Importing Excel Data	2.0
Case Problem 2	Budgeting	2.0
Case Problem 3	Your Name Accounting	4.0
TOTAL HOURS		**45.0**

Preface

Computer Accounting with QuickBooks Online: A Cloud-Based Approach, Second Edition, teaches you how to use QuickBooks Online (***QBO***[1]) software which is accessed via an internet connection. Using the sign-on information provided in this textbook, QBO can be used for 12 months.

Being "in the cloud" means data is stored on web servers instead of your computer. Cloud software is *always* accessible, up-to-date and has similar features to QuickBooks desktop or other accounting software installed locally on computers. QB desktop files can be converted to QB Online.

Join over 2.2 million small business owners who use QuickBooks Online. Globally, 4.3 million customers use QuickBooks products. QuickBooks Online is the **number one cloud-based accounting software** for small businesses. QuickBooks Online is available from Intuit.

> At Intuit, we believe we are in a unique position to use technology to tip the odds in favor of entrepreneurs. With more than two million subscribers, QuickBooks Online is the largest global platform for small businesses and the self-employed. It is their global village, the community where they come together with trusted advisors and partners to unlock their collective power. *More new customers choose QuickBooks Online than QuickBooks desktop.*

QBO provides an easy-to-understand interface for students to grasp accounting concepts while honing cloud computing skills.

---

[1]Words that are boldfaced and italicized are defined in Appendix B, Glossary.

NEW With this textbook, students use the Access Card's license and product numbers for **12** months of use with QuickBooks Online Plus. Educators register for unlimited use. To learn more, go online to www.mhhe.com/qbo2e > Access Card.

When customers buy QBO, they pay monthly or yearly subscription fees. QuickBooks Online includes full use of the version's features, secure storage of data, automatic upgrades and support at no extra cost. At any time, features can be added for additional fees (http://quickbooks.intuit.com/online/ > Pricing.)

As of this writing, subscription costs for customers are:

- QuickBooks Online Simple Start, $10 per month
- QuickBooks Online Essentials, $21 per month
- QuickBooks Online Plus, $35 per month

NEW *Students receive 12 months of QuickBooks Online Plus access. Chapter 2 includes sign-in information for setting up a products and services company. Educators receive unlimited use.*

With the ***cloud***, you are a click away from seeing your work. Information is available wherever you are and with whatever device you use – smart phones, tablets, desktop or laptop computers. All you need is an internet connection. Here is why businesses use QuickBooks Online for their accounting needs.

NEW *Computer Accounting with QuickBooks Online: A Cloud-Based Approach, 2e,* includes **access to the software for 12 months.**

NEW There are three exercises at the end of each chapter. Two end-of-chapter exercises focus on transactions and reports. The **new third exercise** is a problem-solving activity. Using the result of business processes, transactions, or financial reporting, students explain why and how the result occurred. The goal of the problem-solving exercise is to improve critical thinking skills.

NEW Using Spreadsheet Compare, compare two versions of Excel files. Requires Microsoft Office 2016 Professional. (Refer to Appendix A, Troubleshooting.)

- **Always up-to-date:** The cloud automatically updates to the latest version so you always have the most current features.
- **Always secure:** The cloud uses the same encryption as leading financial institutions so your data is safe. For example, QBO uses the same technology used by banks and brokerage firms to transmit your private data over the internet. Intuit trusts the same system to submit millions of TurboTax returns every year.
- **Always backed up:** The cloud keeps your data backed on Intuit's web server. This means even if your computer has problems, your data is still there. All you need to do is start an internet browser to access your company.
- **Always accessible:** The cloud lets you sign in from any place at any time so you can define your own schedule.
- **No software installation hassles:** Simply sign in and get to work.

ACCESS THE CLOUD

A high-speed Internet connection is recommended, such as DSL or cable modem. You can use a slower connection, but it will take longer to process data. For more information, go online to www.mhhe.com/qbo2e > System Requirements.

Compatibility
QuickBooks Online works on your PC, Mac, tablet, and smart phone.
System Requirements
Internet connection required (high-speed connection recommended)
Supported browsers: Google Chrome, Mozilla Firefox, Internet Explorer 10 and higher, Safari 6.1 and higher.
Also accessible via Chrome or Android on Safari iOS
QuickBooks Online mobile app works with iPhone, iPad, and Android phones and tablets, Surface tablet.

TEXTBOOK FEATURES

- Start your **Internet browser** to use the software. No desktop or hard-drive installation hassles.
- Use software **anywhere/anytime** from devices with Internet access.
- Complete the QuickBooks Online test-drive (Chapter 1).
- Sign in to QuickBooks Online with a unique user ID (valid email address) and password (Chapter 2).
- Set up a products and services company, chart of accounts, enter beginning balances (Chapter 3).
- Journalize and post transactions and complete the accounting cycle for the fourth quarter (Chapters 4 through 6).
- Journalize and post adjusting entries, print financial statements, and complete the closing process (Chapter 7).
- Start the New Year, analyze source documents, and complete the accounting cycle for the first quarter. (Chapters 8 through 10).
- Complete Chapter 11, Certification, Report Customization and QB Labs. Go online to www.mhhe.com/qbo2e > Student Edition > Certification Multiple-Choice Test and take the practice 100-question Certification Test.

- Chapter 12, Apps, Updates, QB Blog and Tips. Learn about Apps, updates, the QB Blog and 5 essential tips.
- Complete Case Problem 1, Payroll and Importing Excel Data; CP2, Budgeting, and CP3, Your Name Accounting.
- Appendix A, Troubleshooting, includes information about how to resolve QBO issues.
- Appendix B, Glossary, incudes definitions for words that are italicized and boldface within the chapters.

NEW **Check Your Data:** Chapters begin with Expense Transactions, Sales Transactions, and a Trial Balance so you can make sure you are starting with transactions entered and correct account balances. *Read and follow the Stop sign information.*

- **Check Your Progress** assignments review accounting processes *and* software features. These assignments can be turned in for a grade. They are available online at www.mhhe.com/qbo2e > Student Edition > select the appropriate chapter > Check Your Progress.
- **Check Your Figures:** After the chapter exercises, key figures are shown to make sure you have completed the work accurately.

NEW **Third Exercise, Problem Solving:** Each chapter includes work within the chapter and **three** exercises at the end of the chapter. The third exercise is a Problem-Solving activity.

- Each chapter ends with an index with keywords and chapter sections.
- The Online Learning Center at www.mhhe.com/qbo2e includes additional chapter resources, videos, interactive multiple-choice and true/false quizzes, analysis questions, going to the net exercises, check your progress assignments, narrated PowerPoints, and QBO certification.

In *Computer Accounting with QuickBooks Online: A Cloud-Based Approach, 2e*, you learn about the relationship between the software and the accounting cycle. The diagram below illustrates the QuickBooks Online accounting system.

Business processes are completed in this order.

- Start your Internet browser and sign into QuickBooks Online.
- Set up the products and services company, QB Cloud_Student Name.
- Record transactions, post to the general ledger and subsidiary ledgers, and prepare reports.
- Complete the accounting cycle for the fourth quarter and end the fiscal year. Complete the accounting cycle for the first quarter of the next year.

Once entries are recorded and checked for accuracy, posting is a click of the mouse. All entries are posted to the correct accounts in the general ledger and account balances are calculated — fast, easy, and accurate. Think of it as a process where journalizing and posting is the first step, then ledgers and financial statements are next. The diagram below illustrates this ***workflow*** — the sequence of processes through which work passes from initiation to completion.

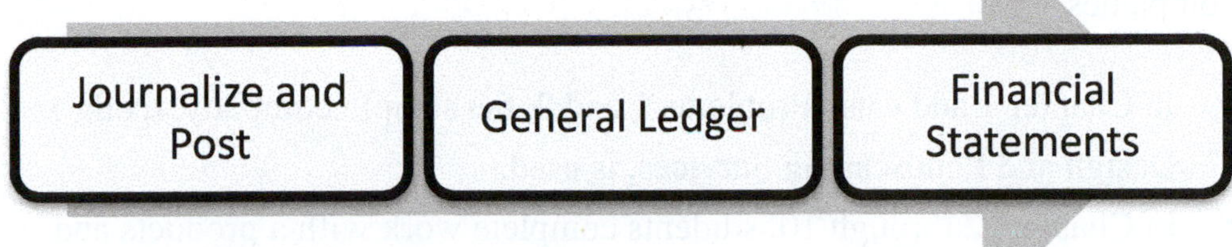

FAVORITE QBO FEATURES

- ✓ Access on multiple devices
- ✓ Online access anytime, anywhere
- ✓ Backup data automatically on Intuit's web server
- ✓ Track income and expenses
- ✓ Create estimates and send invoices
- ✓ Export data to Excel; import data from Excel into QBO
- ✓ Save reports as PDF files
- ✓ Email reports.
- ✓ Access data from tablet or Smartphone
- ✓ Invite two accountants to access your data
- ✓ Manage and pay bills from vendors
- ✓ Enter bills and schedule payments
- ✓ Control what users can access
- ✓ Create and send purchase orders
- ✓ Track inventory
- ✓ Create budgets
- ✓ Categorize income and expenses
- ✓ More than 65 built-in reports

✓ Accept online and mobile payments
✓ Convert data from QB desktop to QB Online

Computer Accounting with QuickBooks Online: A Cloud-Based Approach, 2e, includes 12 chapters and 3 case problems. Students work with three companies.

- In Chapter 1 and Case Problems 1 and 2, the sample company, Craig's Design and Landscaping Services, is used.
- In Chapters 2 through 10, students complete work with a products and services business, QB Cloud_Student Name.
- In Chapter 11, Certification, Report Customization and QB Labs, learn about QuickBooks Online User Certification, and how to customize reports.
- In Chapter 12, Apps, Updates, QB Blog and Tips, learn about third-party apps, automatic software updates, and 5 essential tips.
- In Case Problem 3, Your Name Accounting. There are two ways to complete CP3.

    - Use the free 30-day trial version of QBO. Textbook pages 589-605 show how to set up Your Name Accounting.
    - If you have QuickBooks Desktop software available, go online to www.mhhe.com/qbo2e > Student Edition > CP3. Steps are included for converting a QuickBooks Desktop company file to QuickBooks Online.

Included with *Computer Accounting with QuickBooks Online: A Cloud-Based Approach, 2e,* is 12 months of access to the internet-delivered software, QuickBooks Online Plus. In Chapters 2 through 10, students set up a products and services company, QB Cloud_Student Name (students use their first and last name).

After the company is set up and beginning balances are entered, the accounting cycle is completed for the fourth-quarter and first quarter of the next year. Source documents are used for real-world accounting practice. For 12 months, students can sign in to their company from any device with Internet access.

For QuickBooks Online retail versions, monthly or yearly subscription fees are paid for access to one company. No additional fee is required for accountant access to their clients' QBO companies.

NEW **SCENARIOS:** Each chapter begins with a scenario. The chapter scenarios are descriptions of the work that is completed. The Chapter 2 scenario is shown as an example.

> **Scenario:** In Chapter 2, you set up a new company, QB Cloud_Student Name. After changing QB Online's settings or preferences, you complete a chart of accounts, save your work, and learn how to provide your professor access to your QBO company. To see the work accomplished, you display an Audit Log. The objectives specify the work that is completed in Chapter 2.

CHAPTERS, CASE PROBLEMS AND APPENDICES

NEW Each chapter includes a third exercise which emphasizes problem-solving skills.

Chapter 1: QuickBooks Online Test-drive

In Chapter 1, you take a QBO test-drive. The sample company, Craig's Design and Landscaping Services, is used to show you the QuickBooks Online interface. To start the sample company, go online to https://qbo.intuit.com/redir/testdrive.

Using the sample company, you complete company settings, add account numbers to the chart of accounts, use Quick Links to record entries, and look at reports.

The sample company is used to explore the software rather that to test accounting knowledge. The subsequent chapters in the book show you how to set up a products and services company called QB Cloud_Student Name: use your first and last name after QB_Cloud.

Chapter 2: New Company Setup and the Chart of Accounts

To begin, you go online to https://quickbooks.intuit.com/signup/retail/. After setting up your account and completing information about your company, you start using QuickBooks Online.

NEW In Chapter 2, you set up a products and services company called QB Cloud_ Student Name (type your first and last name after QB Cloud). After navigating the Dashboard (or Home page) and learning about its features, you complete company settings and a Chart of Accounts. The Chart of Accounts is saved as a PDF file and exported to Excel.

Chapter 3: Beginning Balances and October Transaction Register

In Chapter 3, you continue using QB Cloud. After entering beginning balances, you record cash sales, write checks, and display reports, financial statements, and the audit log. Reports are saved as PDF files and exported to Excel.

Chapter 4: Vendors and Inventory

In Chapter 4, you add vendors and inventory and complete accounts payable transactions for November. You record vendor purchases of inventory on account, make vendor payments, display accounts payable reports, display financial statements, filter the audit log, and complete account reconciliation. Reports are saved as PDF files and exported to Excel.

Chapter 5: Customers and Sales

In Chapter 5, you add customers and complete accounts receivable transactions. You record customer sales on account, receive payments from customers, display accounts receivable reports and financial statements, and complete account reconciliation. Reports are saved as PDF files and exported to Excel.

NEW Use Advanced Search to search by date, transaction and amount.

Chapter 6: December Source Documents

In Chapter 6, you analyze source documents, then record transactions. The source documents trigger transaction analysis for accounts payable (vendors), inventory, accounts receivable (customers), cash and credit card sales, checks for expenses, and account reconciliation. Reports are saved as PDF files and exported to Excel.

NEW Comparative financial reports: Custom Balance Sheet and Profit and Loss by month.

Chapter 7: Analysis and Reports -- End-of-Fourth Quarter and Year

In Chapter 7, you complete transactions for the end of the fourth quarter and the end of the year. At the end of December, you complete adjusting entries, print financial statements, and close the fiscal year. Reports are saved as PDF files and exported to Excel.

Chapter 8: January Source Documents

January source documents are analyzed for transaction entry. The source documents prompt transaction analysis for issuing checks, accounts payable, inventory, accounts receivable and cash and credit card sales. You also use the January 31 bank statement to reconcile Account 101 Checking. The general ledger accounting cycle is completed for the first month of the new year.

Chapter 9: February Source Documents

After analyzing source documents, you complete transactions. You also use February's bank statement to reconcile the checking account.

Chapter 10: March Source Documents and End of First Quarter

Using March's source documents, you analyze source documents, complete account reconciliation, record first-quarter adjusting entries, and prepare financial statements. You also use March's bank statement to reconcile the Account 101 Checking.

Chapter 11: Certification, Report Customization and QB Labs

In this chapter, QBO User Certification and the Online Learning Center's practice tests are explained. Students learn about report customization and learn how to send feedback to Intuit.

Chapter 12: Apps, Updates, QB Blog and Tips

Students learn about additional applications for QuickBooks Online, software updates. Using the QB Blog and tips.

Computer Accounting in the Cloud with QuickBooks Online: A Cloud-Based Approach, 2e, ends with three case problems:

- **Case Problem 1: Payroll and Importing Excel Data**. Using the sample company, Craig's Design and Landscaping Services, payroll settings and employee transactions are shown. Case Problem 1 also includes importing data from an Excel file to QBO.
- **Case Problem 2: Budgeting**. Using the sample company, Craig's Design and Landscaping Services, QBO's budgeting feature is shown.
- **Case Problem 3**: **Your Name Accounting**. You can complete CP3 either using the free trial version (textbook pages 589-605), *or* convert a QB Desktop company file to QBO. Conversion steps are at www.mhhe.com/qbo2e > Student Edition > CP3.

Appendix A: Troubleshooting – Tips and suggestions for workarounds are shown in the Troubleshooting appendix.

Appendix B: Glossary – Words that are italicized and boldfaced in the textbook are defined in the glossary.

Index: At the end of each chapter as well as at the end of the textbook.

ONLINE LEARNING CENTER: www.mhhe.com/qbo2e

NEW Each chapter includes additional resources at www.mhhe.com/qbo2e. These resources include:

- ❖ Narrated PowerPoints
- ❖ Going to the Net Exercises
- ❖ Interactive multiple-choice and true or false questions
- ❖ Analysis questions
- ❖ Videos
- ❖ Glossary of terms
- ❖ **NEW:** Problem Solving
- ❖ QuickBooks Online Support at https://help.quickbooks.intuit.com/

QUICKBOOKS ONLINE UPDATES

Each time you sign into QBO, the most recently updated version of the software displays. To read about What's New in QBO, go to http://quickbooks.intuit.com/blog/. When changes are being made, messages appear on the QBO screen. For example, if a message appears that says "Alert. Your navigation is getting a refresh to help you run your business more efficiently. Link to Take Action. Follow the link and read the information.

The Online Learning Center at www.mhhe.com/qbo2e also includes Text Updates for checking major QB Online updates. Remember, as you work through the textbook, screen images may not match exactly. Changes are part of internet-delivered software.

CONVENTIONS USED

As you work through *Computer Accounting in the Cloud with QuickBooks Online: A Cloud-Based Approach, 2e*, you should read and follow the step-by-step instructions.

Numerous screen illustrations help you to check your work. The following conventions are used in this textbook.

1. Dates are shown with XXs, for example, 10/1/20XX. Substitute the current year for the XXs.
2. Information that you type appears in boldface; for example, Type **Prepaid Insurance** in the ACCOUNT field.
3. Keys on the keyboard that should be pressed appear in angle brackets, for example, <Tab>.
4. Buttons and icons are shown as they appear.

Examples:

 Gear icon to go to company settings

 Create transactions

 Search transactions *and* recent transactions

 Help

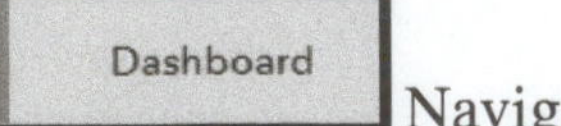

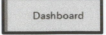

Navigation bar selection for Dashboard or Home page

5. Step sequences are separated by a greater-than sign. Examples:

   Click  > Chart of Accounts

   Go to 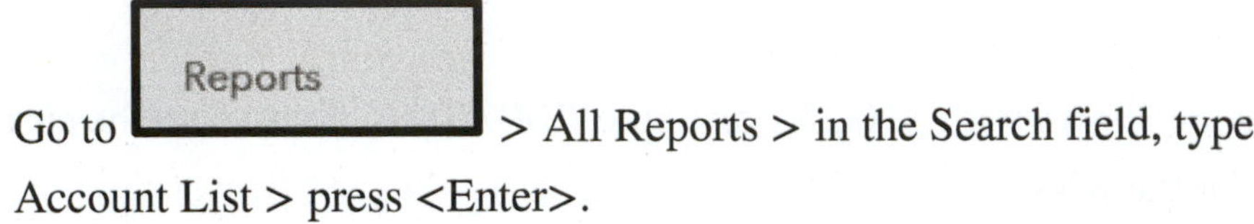

 > All Reports > in the Search field, type Account List > press <Enter>.

6. To remind you to check data, a cloud icon is used. Make sure you are starting with the correct trial balance amounts.

7. Read the information next to the stop sign. For example, in Chapter 4, the stop sign information says the following:

   Make sure your Expense and Sales transactions match what is shown. Work accumulates in Chapters 2, 3 and 4. You need to check your work so far. The Expenses and Sales shown help you check the data stored to this point.

8. When inputting data for a transaction, this image is shown next to the date and description.

Analyze transaction

Transaction date

Input transaction

Date	*Description of Transaction*
10/1/20XX	The owner invested $50,000 cash along with $10,000 in computer equipment in the company in exchange for common stock.

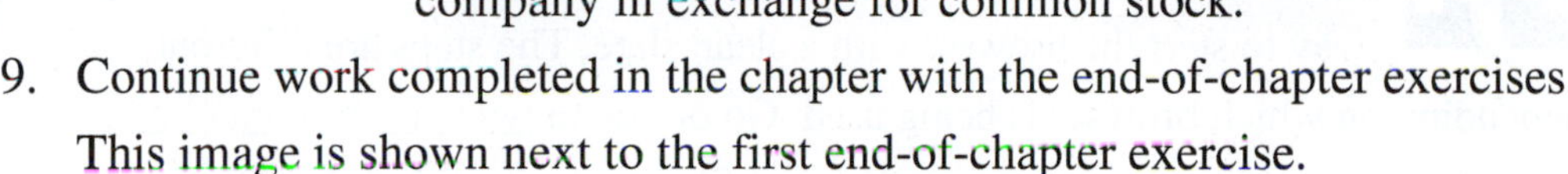

9. Continue work completed in the chapter with the end-of-chapter exercises. This image is shown next to the first end-of-chapter exercise.

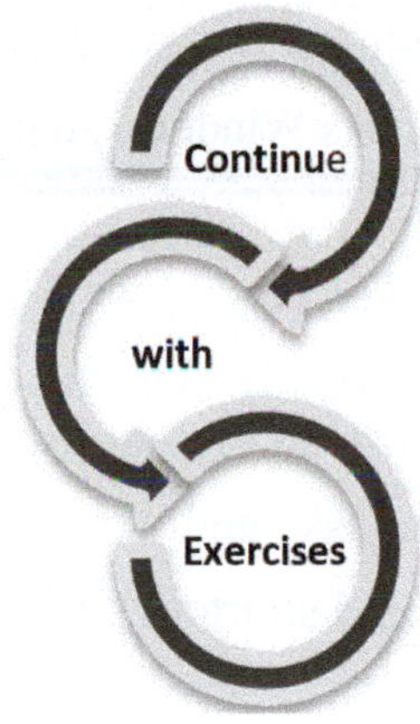

10. Indicates the third end-of-chapter exercise, Problem Solving activities.

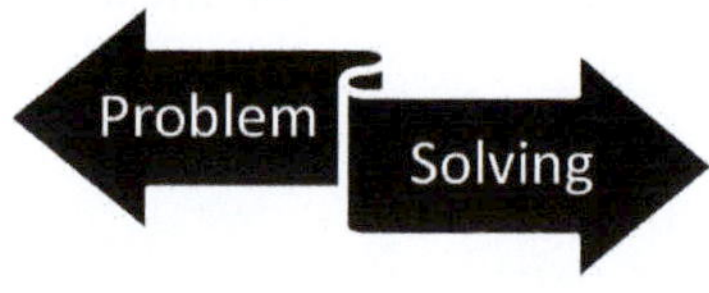

FYI, COMMENTS, AND TROUBLESHOOTING

In each chapter, there are FYI boxes, comments and troubleshooting tips. The end-of-chapter index includes the page numbers where FYIs, comments and troubleshooting appear within the chapter. An example of an FYI box follows. Read the information.

> **fyi** **CLEARING TEMPORARY INTERNET FILES/CACHE**
> Deleting temporary internet files or clearing the browser cache is a good way to start the browser with a clean slate. The steps are different depending on which browser is being used. Go online to www.mhhe.com/qbo2e > Troubleshooting. Clearing temporary internet files/cache is included for these browsers: Internet Explorer, Firefox, Google Chrome, Safari, Safari (for iPad/iPhone) and the QuickBooks Windows App.

KEYBOARD SHORTCUTS

You can use the keyboard instead of a mouse or trackpad to save time. To help speed you through common tasks and workflows, QBO has many ***keyboard shortcuts***. To see the keyboard shortcuts, from any QBO page, press <Ctrl>+<Alt>+</>.

One of the first decisions is whether to use the mouse or keyboard. The instructions in this book assume that you are using a mouse. When the word click or select is used, it means to use the mouse, but you can also use the keyboard.

Go To:

To quickly go to...	Press
*Customers page	<Ctrl + Alt + C>
*Vendors page	<Ctrl + Alt + V>
*Lists page	<Ctrl + Alt + L>
*Chart of Accounts page	<Ctrl + Alt + A>
*Search transaction window	<Ctrl + Alt + F>
*Help window	<Ctrl + Alt + H>

Work with forms:

To...	Press
*Start a new invoice	<Ctrl + Alt + I>
*Start a new check	<Ctrl + Alt + W>
*Start a new estimate	<Ctrl + Alt + E>
*Start a new expense	<Ctrl + Alt + X>
*Receive a payment	<Ctrl + Alt + R>
*Save current form and start a new one	<Ctrl + Alt + S>
Save current form and send it	<Ctrl + Alt + M>

*Unavailable when a form is onscreen (any form from the Create (+) menu)

Move between fields:

1. Press <Tab> to move forward from one field to the next.
2. Press <Shift-Tab> to move backward through fields.

- ➢ Mac users: You can control whether the Tab key lets you move through text boxes and lists only or through all controls.

To change this setting:

a) From the Apple menu, click System Preferences.
b) Choose Keyboard, and then click the Keyboard Shortcuts tab.
c) At the bottom of the dialog box, in the Full Keyboard Access section, choose All controls.

Enter dates in fields:

To Change the Date to...	Press
Next day	+ (plus key)
Previous day	- (minus key)
Today	T
First day of the **w**eek	W
Last day of the wee**k**	K
First day of the **m**onth	M
Last day of the mont**h**	H
First day of the **y**ear	Y
Last day of the yea**r**	R

You can also Press <Alt + down arrow> to open the popup calendar icon at the right of a Date field.

Change dates in a calendar:

To Change the Date to...	Press
Any surrounding date	Left, Right, Up, Down arrow keys
Same day next month	Page Down
Same day previous month	Page Up
Same day next year	<Ctrl + Page Down>
Same day previous year	<Ctrl + Page Up>

First day of the **m**onth	M
Last day of the mont**h**	H
First day of the **w**eek	W
Last day of the wee**k**	K
First day of the **y**ear	Y
Last day of the yea**r**	R
Select data	<Enter>

Calculate amounts and rates:

In any Amount or Rate field, you can enter a calculation. When you press <Tab>, QuickBooks calculates the result.

You can...	Using	Example
Add	+	1256.94+356.50
Subtract	-	48.95-15
Multiply	*	108*1.085
Divide	/	89.95/.33
Group	( )	13.95+(25.95*.75)

Choose items in drop-down lists

1. Press <Tab> until you reach the field.
2. Press <Alt + down arrow> to open the list.
3. Press <up arrow> or <down arrow> to move through the items in the list.
4. Press <Tab> to select the item you want and move to the next field.

If you don't want to open the whole list, but just want to scroll through the items in the text box, press <Ctrl + down arrow> or <Ctrl + up arrow>.

If the list has sub-items:

1. Type the first few characters of the parent item until it is selected.
2. Then you can:
   - Type **:** (colon) to jump to the list of sub-items, and then type the first few characters of the sub-item until it is selected.
   - Press <Alt + down arrow> to open the list of sub-items, and then press <down arrow> or <up arrow> to scroll through the sub-items.
3. Press **Tab** to select the item you want and move to the next field.

Respond to messages:

When a message pops up and the button names have underlined letters, type the letter to select the button you want.

Enter transactions in an account register:

To select a transaction type:

1. In a new, yellow transaction row, press <Shift + Tab> to select the transaction type field.
2. Press <Alt + down arrow> to open the list.
3. Press <up arrow> or <down arrow> to move through the list, or type the first letter of the transaction type you want.

   If there are two types that start with the same letter, you can type the letter twice to select the second one. For example, type **C** once to select Check, and type **C** the second time to select Cash Purchase.

4. Press <Tab> to select the type you want and move to the next field.

Once you're familiar with the transaction types available, you can tab to the field and type the first letter to select the one you want without opening the list.

When the Ref No. field is selected:

- Press **+** to increase the Ref No.
- Press **-** to decrease the Ref No.
- Type **T** to enter To Print in the Ref No. field for a bill payment (from a checking account), check, or paycheck.

To save or edit the selected transaction:

- Press <Shift + Alt + S> to save.
- Press <Ctrl + S> to save.
- Press <Shift + Alt + E> to edit a saved transaction. This opens the transaction form.
- Press <Ctrl + E> to edit a saved transaction. This opens the transaction form.

To move between transactions within the register, selecting the Date field as you go:

- Press <up arrow> to select the transaction above.
- Press <down arrow> to select the transaction below

Adjust print alignment:

When aligning checks, invoices, deposit slips, payroll forms, or 1099-MISC forms (QuickBooks Plus only):

- Select the Vertical or Horizontal field and press + to raise the number and - to lower it. (You must use the keys on the numeric keypad instead of the regular + and - keys.)

Move around in journal entries:

In a Journal Entry, press <up arrow> to move to the distribution line above and <down arrow> to move to the one below.

Carol Yacht, carol@carolyacht.com, is an educator and author of technology-based accounting textbooks. Carol authors QuickBooks Online (2/e), QuickBooks Desktop (9/e), and Sage Peachtree (20/e), textbooks. Carol taught on the faculties of California State University-Los Angeles, West Los Angeles College, Yavapai College, and Beverly Hills High School. She started using accounting software in her classes in 1980. Carol's teaching career includes first and second year accounting courses, accounting information systems, and computer accounting.

Since 1989, Carol's textbooks have been published by McGraw-Hill. She contributes regularly to professional journals and is the Editor of the American Accounting Association's Teaching, Learning, and Curriculum section's *The Accounting Educator*.

Carol Yacht was an officer of AAA's Two-Year College section and recipient of its Lifetime Achievement Award. She is a board member of the Microsoft Dynamics Academic Alliance; worked for IBM Corporation as an education instruction specialist; serves on AAA's Teaching, Learning, and Curriculum section's research, instructional, and hall of honor award committees; and works for Intuit and Sage as a consultant. Carol earned her MA degree from California State University-Los Angeles, BS degree from the University of New Mexico, and AS degree from Temple University.

Susan V. Crosson is an Adjunct Senior Lecturer at Emory University and the Director of the Center for Advancing Accounting Education for the American Accounting Association. Previously she was a Professor and Coordinator of Accounting at Santa Fe College in Gainesville, FL. She has also taught on the faculties of University of Florida, Washington University in St. Louis, University of Oklahoma, Johnson County Community College, and Kansas City Kansas Community College.

Susan continues to be guided by her mission to create a learning process as individual as each student requires to master the course content and actively apply with confidence what's learned. She is pleased to be able to speak and write on the effective use of technology throughout the accounting curriculum. In addition to her over 300 YouTube videos, she has co-authored several accounting textbooks including the *Computer Accounting Essentials* series. Susan earned her Master of Science in Accounting from Texas Tech University and her undergraduate degree in accounting and economics from Southern Methodist University. She is a CPA.

Acknowledgments

I would like to thank the following colleagues for their help in the preparation of this book: Steve Schuetz, Michelle Williams, and Matt Lowenkron. A special thank you to the following professors.

James Adkins, Missouri Western State University
Richard Andrews, Sinclair Community College
Julia Angel, North Arkansas College
Gary Becker, Casper College
Jeanne Bedell, Keiser University
Edward Bennett, University of Alaska Anchorage-Mat-Su College
J. Britt Blackwell, Central Community College
Angi Bruns, Baton Rouge Community College
Shifei Chung, Rowan University
Erin Dischler, Milwaukee Area Technical College
Brad Fader, Shoreline Community College
Bonny Herndon, Southwest Texas Junior College
Adrian Jarrell, Forsyth Technical College
Christine Kloezeman, Glendale College
Amber Lamadrid, Mt. Hood Community College
Steve Loflin, Augusta University
Margarita Maria Lenk, Colorado State University
Jennifer Lyons, National Park College
Sarah Mathews, Cowley College
Paul H. McLester, Florida State College at Jacksonville
Julie Miller Millmann, Chippewa Valley Technical College

Susan Minke, Purdue University-Fort Wayne
Barry Palatnik, Stockton University
Paige Paulsen, Salt Lake Community College
Joel Peralto, Hawaii Community College
Jeffrey Pullen, Strayer University
Michelle Randall, Schoolcraft College
Joe Reeves, Edgecombe Community College
Silvia Romero, Montclair State University
Anne Shawver, Radford University
Regina Shea, Community College of Baltimore County
Noema Santos, State College of Florida
Melanie Thomas, Wake Technical College
William Van Glabek, Florida SouthWestern College

Chapter 1 QuickBooks Online Test-drive

Scenario: In Chapter 1, you use the test drive's sample company, Craig's Design and Landscaping Services. The test drive company sells landscaping products, purchases inventory from vendors, and provides customers with landscaping services. In this chapter, you learn how to navigate the QuickBooks Online user interface, enter journal transactions, and display and save reports. The objectives that follow specify the work completed.

OBJECTIVES

1. Start the sample company, Craig's Design and Landscaping Services.
2. Tour QuickBooks Online (QBO).
3. Explore the User Interface.
4. Export the Chart of Accounts to Excel.
5. View recent transactions and reports.
6. Create an invoice, sales receipt, bill, and write check.
7. Complete Check Your Progress.
8. Go to the Online Learning Center at www.mhhe.com/qbo2e for additional resources.
9. Complete Exercises 1-1, 1-2 and 1-3.

The screens that are shown in the textbook may differ from what you see. Each time you sign into QBO, the software is the most current version. If you notice updates to Chapter 1, go online to www.mhhe.com/qbo2e > Text Updates. Updates occur on a regular basis. That is the nature of internet-delivered software.

SYSTEM REQUIREMENTS: https://community.intuit.com/articles/1145516-system-requirements-for-quickbooks-online

To use QuickBooks Online (QBO), sign in with a web browser. You can access QBO from any PC or Mac with an Internet connection. For more information, go online to www.mhhe.com/qbo2e > System Requirements. Internet connection is required (high-speed connection recommended).

Supported Browsers

- Google Chrome, recommended (updates automatically), Mozilla Firefox (updates automatically), Internet Explorer 10 or 11, Apple Safari 6.1 or later
- Also accessible via Chrome on Android and Safari on iOS
- QuickBooks Online mobile app works with the iPhone, iPad and Android phones and tablets, Surface tablet
- Not all features are available on mobile devices

Other

For exporting reports to Excel, Microsoft Excel 97 or later. The author used Excel 2007 and 2013. Adobe for saving PDF files. The free Adobe Acrobat Reader is available at https://get.adobe.com/reader/

GETTING STARTED

To access the sample company, Craig's Design and Landscaping Services, follow these steps.

Sample Company Sign In

In Chapter 1, you use the sample company, Craig's Design and Landscaping Services. Follow these steps to start the sample company.

1. Start your Internet browser. Refer to Supported Browsers on the previous page.
2. Go online to https://qbo.intuit.com/redir/testdrive. (*Hint:* Chapter 1 is online at www.mhhe.com/qbo2e > Chapter 1.) **Each time you start the test drive, a new session begins. Data is <u>not</u> saved.**

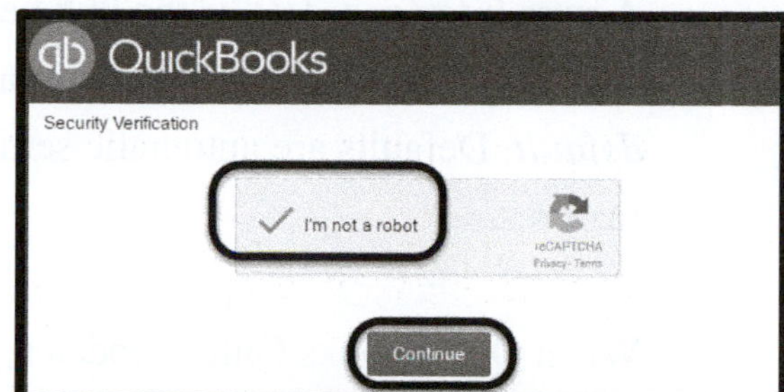

3. Complete the Security Verification I'm not a robot > click <Continue>. Select images and verify.
4. The ***Dashboard***, also called the ***Home page***, appears for the sample company, Craig's Design and Landscaping Services. Depending on what day you signed in your screen may differ. As of this writing, the author's Dashboard looks like the one below.

   The Dashboard shows profit and loss, how much was spent, the income and sales summary, and bank accounts for Craig's Design and Landscaping Services. The dashboard is a current snapshot of the business as of the day you signed in. A partial Dashboard is shown.

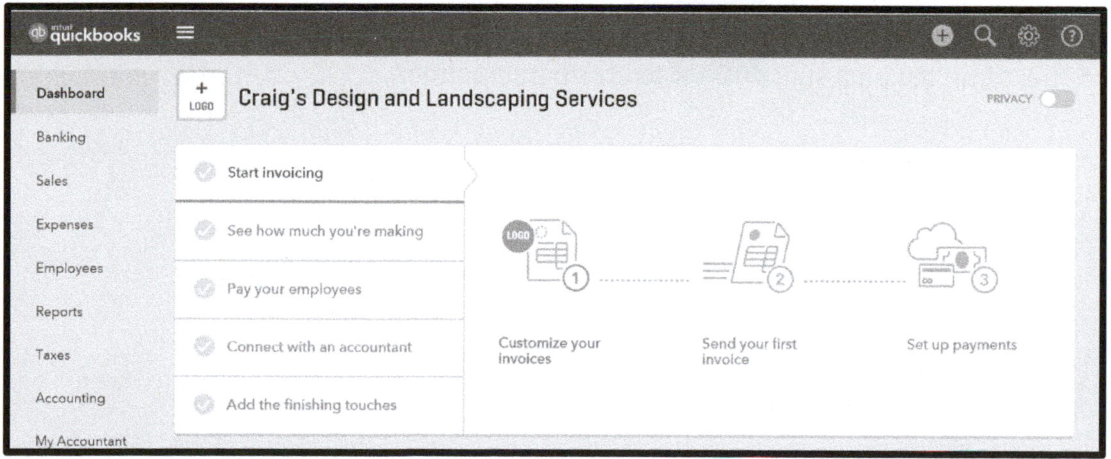

USER INTERFACE

A ***user interface (UI)***[1] is the link between a user and the software. On the left side, QuickBooks Online includes a ***Navigation bar***. The Dashboard is the ***default***. Defaults are automatic settings. The Navigation bar lists QBO's main features.

When QuickBooks Online updates, the Navigation bar may change. As of this writing, the test drive's Navigation bar includes these selections–Dashboard, Banking, Sales, Expenses, Employees, Reports, Taxes, Accounting, and My Accountant.

Regularly check QBO changes at www.mhhe.com/qbo2e > Text Updates. Another way to learn about updates is the QuickBooks blog at http://quickbooks.intuit.com/blog/ > What's New in QBO.

QBO Navigation

1. Use the Navigation bar to access pages within QBO.
2. Use the plus sign to create transactions.

[1]Words that are boldfaced and italicized are defined in the Glossary, Appendix B.

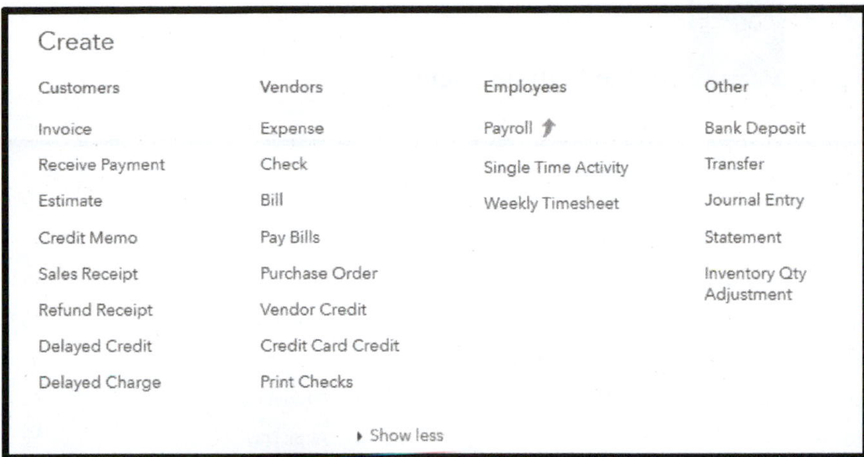

3. The magnifying-glass for Search and Recent Transactions.

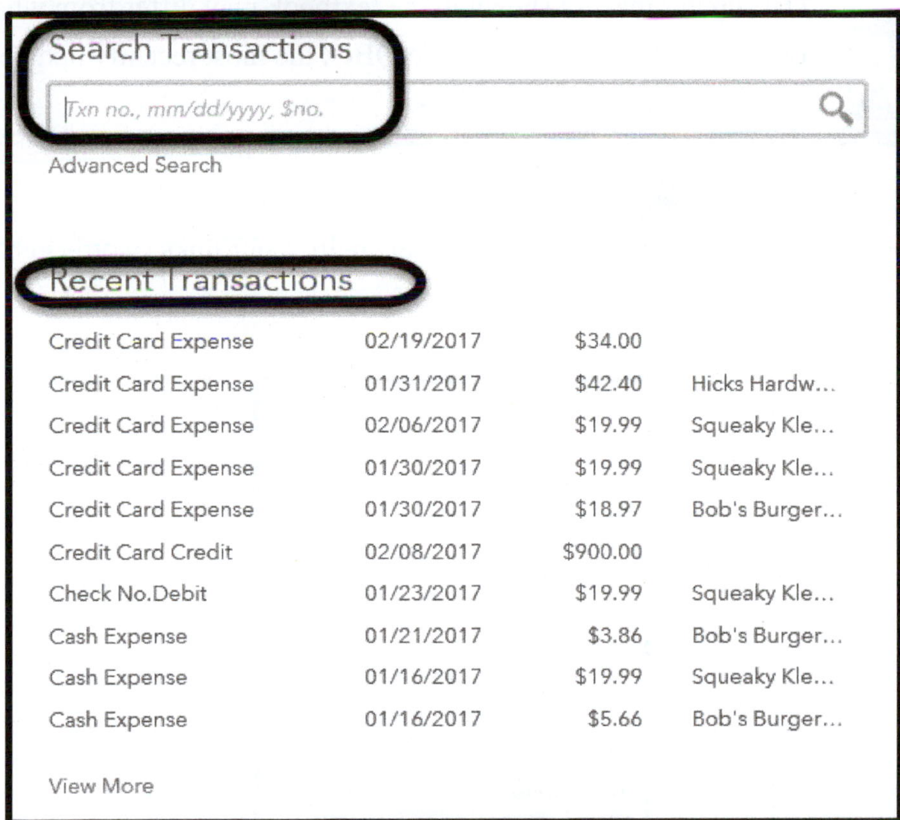

4. The gear  for the Settings menu.

The screens that are shown in the textbook may differ from what you see. Each time you sign into QBO, the most recently updated version of the software displays.

5. The question mark is for QBO self-help. Your links (words in blue) may differ.

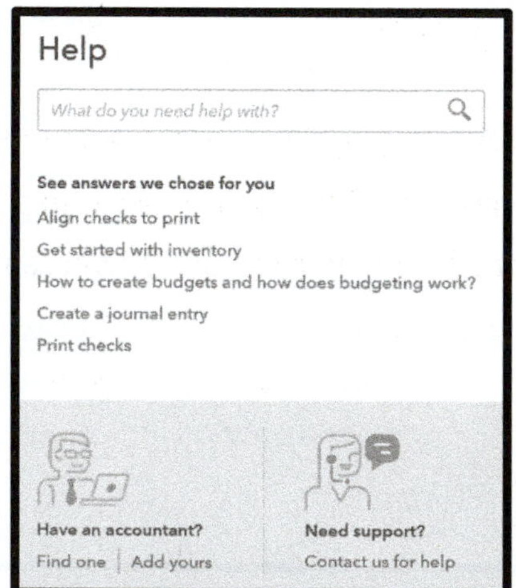

DASHBOARD

When you sign into QuickBooks Online, the Dashboard appears. The Dashboard provides a starting point that allows you to access all the features of QBO. The Dashboard includes a picture of the current status of Profit and Loss, Expenses, Income, Sales, Banking activities and Tips. When you enter transactions, the values change, displaying a real-time overview of your company.

The Dashboard includes information about Craig's Design and Landscaping Services. In the steps that follow, you link to various parts of the Dashboard.

Checklist

1. On the top of the page, the dashboard shows a checklist: Start invoicing, See how much you're making, Pay your employees, Connect with an accountant.
2. Click on Customize your invoices (if available). The Create invoices that turn heads and open wallets page appears. Design is the default. You may want to click on a few links: Content, Emails, Payments.
3. Click on the back-arrow 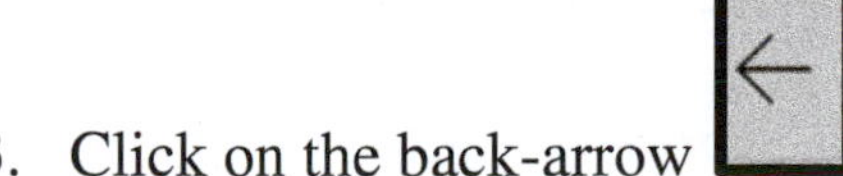.

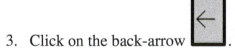

Comment: Since QBO regularly updates, some sections of the Dashboard may change. For example, the author's Dashboard has a link that says "Your navigation is getting a refresh to help run your business more efficiciently." To read about the QBO changes, link to Learn more .

4. If necessary, click <Dashboard>. Review the Bank accounts section. Mastercard, checking, savings, Visa and the number of QuickBooks

transactions to review. (*Hint:* This information reflects the day the author signed in. Your amounts may differ.)

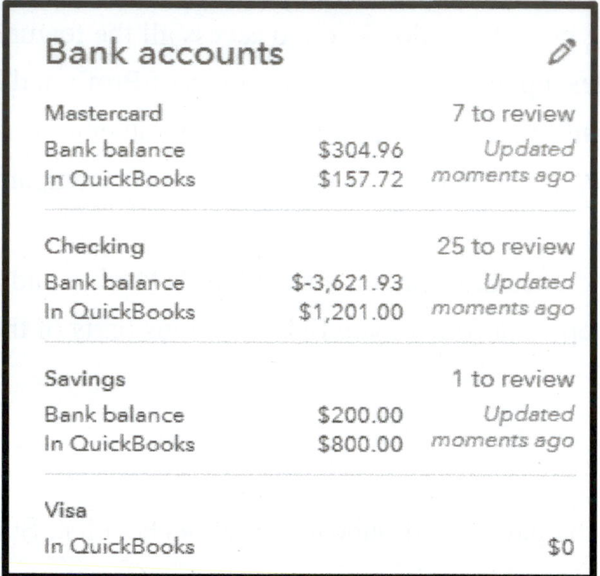

5. In the Bank accounts section of the Dashboard, click Checking 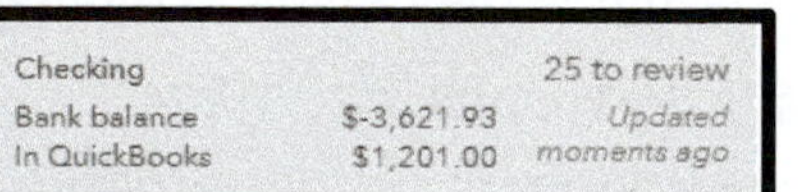

. The Bank and Credit Cards | Checking page appears. (*Hint:* Your amounts may differ.)

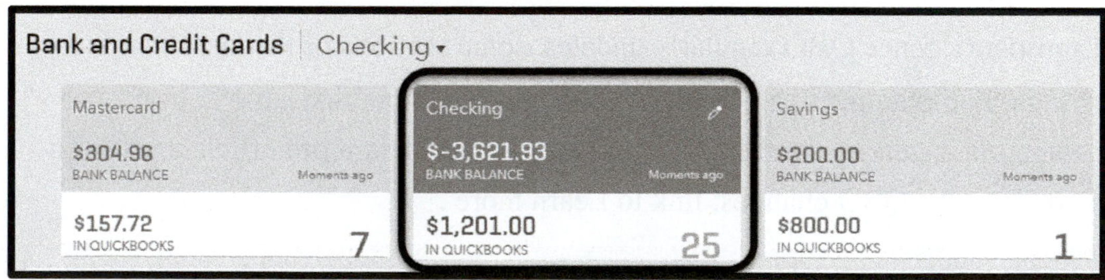

Craig's Design and Landscaping Services

For Review

Date	Description	Payee	Category or match	Spent	Received
06/21/2017	Books By Bessie	Books by Bessie	Uncategorized Income		$55.00
05/22/2017	A Rental		Uncategorized Income		$200.00
05/22/2017	A Rental		Uncategorized Expense	$1,200.00	
04/29/2017	A Rental		Uncategorized Expense	$800.00	
04/26/2017	Pam Seitz	Pam Seitz	MATCH Expense 76 04/26/2017 $75.00 Pam Seitz	$75.00	
04/26/2017	undefined		MATCH Deposit 04/26/2017 $868.15		$868.15
04/26/2017	Hicks Hardware	Hicks Hardware	MATCH Check 75 04/26/2017 $228.75 Hicks Hardware	$228.75	
04/25/2017	Pg E	PG&E	MATCH Bill Payment 6 04/25/2017 $114.09 PG&E	$114.09	
04/25/2017	undefined		MATCH Deposit 04/25/2017 $408.00		$408.00
04/24/2017	Travis Waldron	Travis Waldron	MATCH Payment 2064 04/24/2017 $103.55 Travis Waldron		$103.55
04/24/2017	Pye's Cakes	Pye's Cakes	MATCH Refund 04/24/2017 $87.50 Pye's Cakes	$87.50	
04/24/2017	undefined	Freeman Sporting Goods:55 Twin Lane	MATCH Payment 04/24/2017 $50.00 Freeman Sporting Goods:55 Twin Lane		$50.00
04/24/2017	Squeaky Kleen Car	Squeaky Kleen Car Wash	MATCH Check Debit 04/24/2017 $19.99 Squeaky Kleen Car Wash	$19.99	
04/24/2017	undefined		MATCH Deposit 04/24/2017 $218.75		$218.75
04/24/2017	Books By Bessie	Pam Seitz	MATCH Expense 76 04/26/2017 $75.00 Pam Seitz	$75.00	
04/23/2017	Brosnahan Insurance Agency	Brosnahan Insurance Agency	MATCH Bill Payment 1 04/23/2017 $2,000.00 Brosnahan Insurance Agency	$2,000.00	
04/21/2017	Dylan Sollfrank	Dylan Sollfrank	MATCH Sales Receipt 10264 04/21/2017 $337.50 Dylan Sollfrank		$337.50

6. Select Savings.

Profit and Loss

To see the ***Profit and Loss*** statement for Craig's Design and Landscaping Services, go to the Dashboard.

1. The Profit and Loss area includes Net Profit for Last month. If not, click on the down-arrow > select Last month.

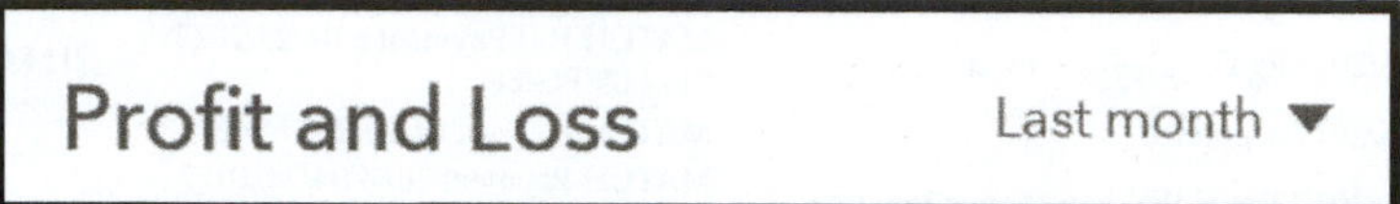

2. Click on the Income bar. A Customize reports instantly pop-up message appears. Read the information, click <Next> to read the pages. When through, click I'm done.

   Another way to go to the P&L is to select <Reports> from the Navigation bar > type **Profit and Loss** in the Search field > press <Enter>. For the Report period, select This month > click <Run report>. Since the author's current month/year is January 2017, that month is shown. A partial P&L is shown on the next page.

   The Profit and Loss report shows money you earned (income) and money you spent (expenses) so you can see how profitable you are. The P&L is also called an income statement. The P&L includes income and expense accounts, also called temporary accounts.

Craig's Design and Landscaping Services

PROFIT AND LOSS

January 2017

	TOTAL
INCOME	
Design income	1,275.00
Discounts given	-89.50
Landscaping Services	797.50
Job Materials	
Fountains and Garden Lighting	1,501.50
Plants and Soil	2,220.72
Sprinklers and Drip Systems	30.00
Total Job Materials	**3,752.22**
Labor	
Installation	250.00
Total Labor	**250.00**
Total Landscaping Services	**4,799.72**
Pest Control Services	-30.00
Sales of Product Income	912.75
Services	503.55
Total Income	**$7,371.52**
COST OF GOODS SOLD	
Cost of Goods Sold	405.00
Total Cost of Goods Sold	**$405.00**

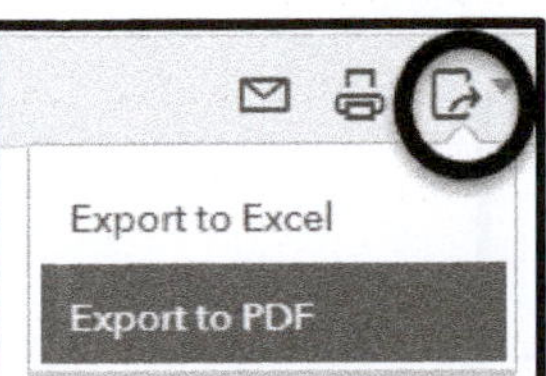

Export to PDF was selected to display the partial P&L report. Your totals may differ.

> **fyi** QuickBooks Online updates automatically. When you sign into the test drive, the latest version of the sample company, Craig's Design and Landscaping Services, is being used. Software updates improve QBO's features and functions. Some screen images may change but differences are minor. Regularly check the Online Learning Center's Text Updates link at www.mhhe.com/qbo2e > Text Updates.

When you are through reviewing the P&L, click 

logo.

Start Invoicing

1. The Dashboard includes 3 selections: Customize your invoices, Send your first invoice, Set up payments. Select Customize your invoices. To change the font, do this:

   a. Click 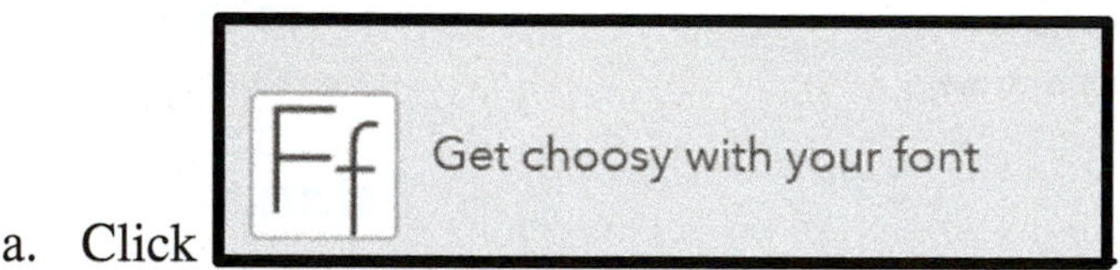

   b. Helvetica 10pt is the default. Select 12 pt. to enlarge the fonts on the invoice.

   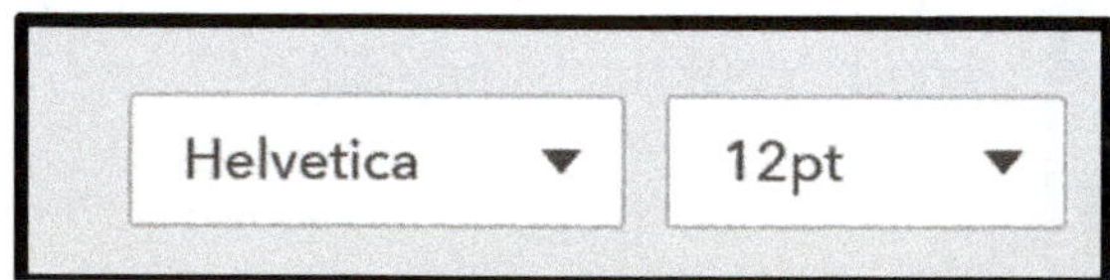

   Observe that the fonts on the Invoice increased. Depending on the day you logged in, your Invoice may differ.

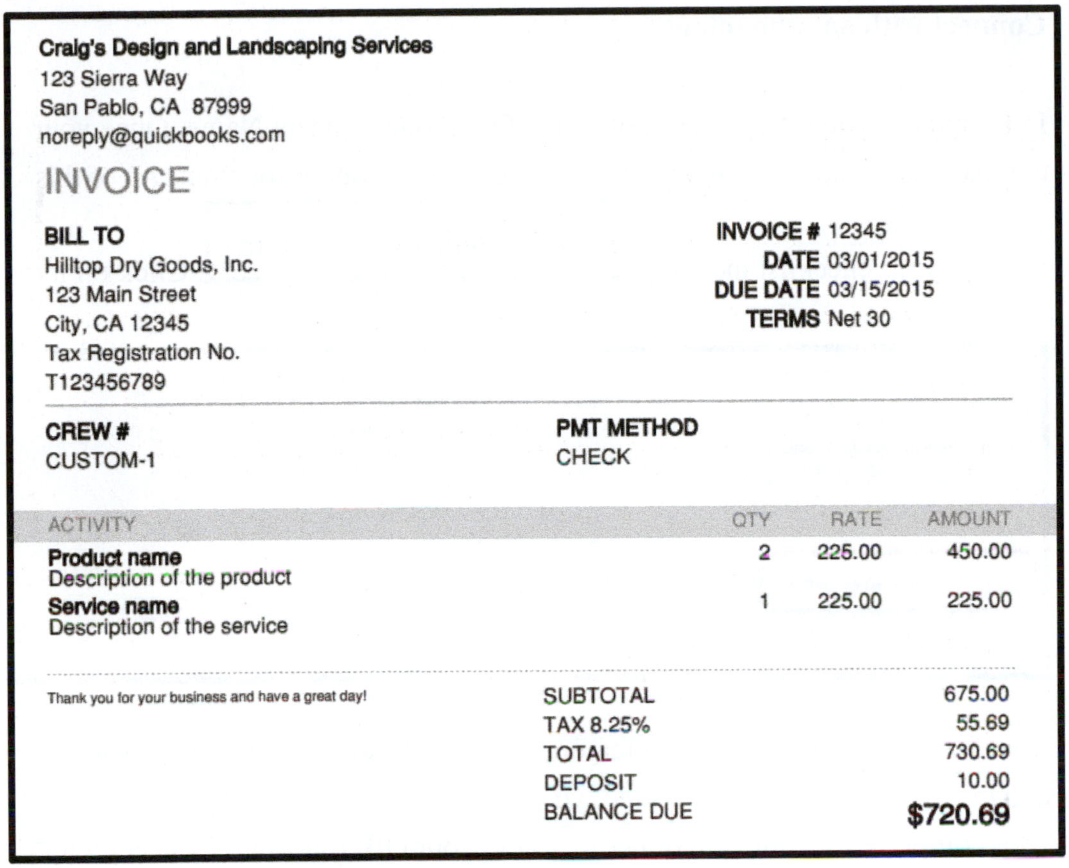

Craig's Design and Landscaping Services
123 Sierra Way
San Pablo, CA 87999
noreply@quickbooks.com

INVOICE

BILL TO
Hilltop Dry Goods, Inc.
123 Main Street
City, CA 12345
Tax Registration No.
T123456789

INVOICE # 12345
DATE 03/01/2015
DUE DATE 03/15/2015
TERMS Net 30

CREW #
CUSTOM-1

PMT METHOD
CHECK

ACTIVITY	QTY	RATE	AMOUNT
Product name Description of the product	2	225.00	450.00
Service name Description of the service	1	225.00	225.00

Thank you for your business and have a great day!

SUBTOTAL	675.00
TAX 8.25%	55.69
TOTAL	730.69
DEPOSIT	10.00
BALANCE DUE	**$720.69**

c. To close, click Done.

2. There are two more selections on the Start invoicing page – Send your first invoice and Set up payments. Link to both to review the information. To move between pages, click on the back arrow. When necessary, click <X> to close pages.

Connect with an accountant

In Chapter 2, you set up a new company, QB Cloud_Student Name. Once your company is set up, you can invite your professor as your accountant. As of this writing, your checklist includes **Connect with an accountant**. Click on it.

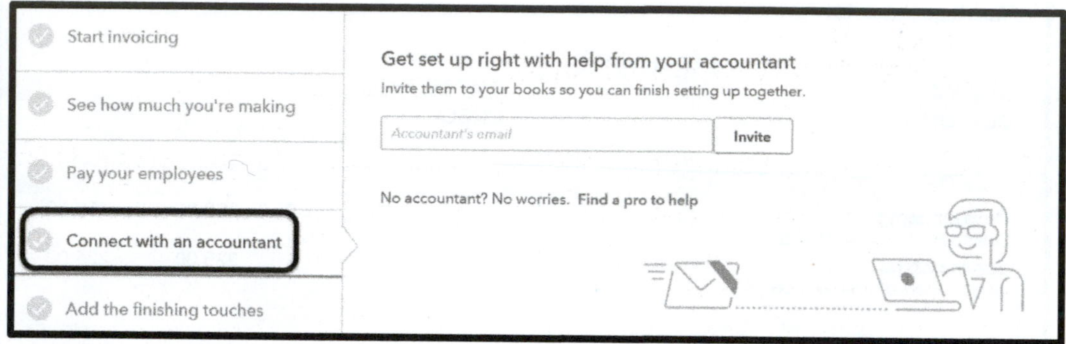

Connect with an accountant is a feature that allows you and your professor to collaborate. In QuickBooks Online, you can invite an accountant as a user in your company allowing him or her to access your QBO account. Connect with an accountant will be shown in Chapter 2.

Troubleshooting: If a sign-in screen appears, what should I do?

If QBO is not being used, you are automatically signed out. The default is one hour. If that happens, restart the sample company by going online to https://qbo.intuit.com/redir/testdrive. Each time you start the sample company, it is a new session. Data is not saved.

ACCOUNT AND SETTINGS

The gear icon at the top right includes settings and preferences for your company. This is where you can change your Settings, Manage Your Account, Import Data, access lists, import data, reconcile accounts, and go to the audit log.

1. Click > Account and Settings.
2. The Account and Settings page shows Company as the default. This includes the Company name, Company type, Contact info, Address, and Communications with Intuit.
3. Click Advanced. Review the information about the company.
4. In the Chart of accounts area, select the pencil icon. To include account numbers, put a checkmark in the Enable account numbers and Show account numbers boxes. Observe that On is shown.

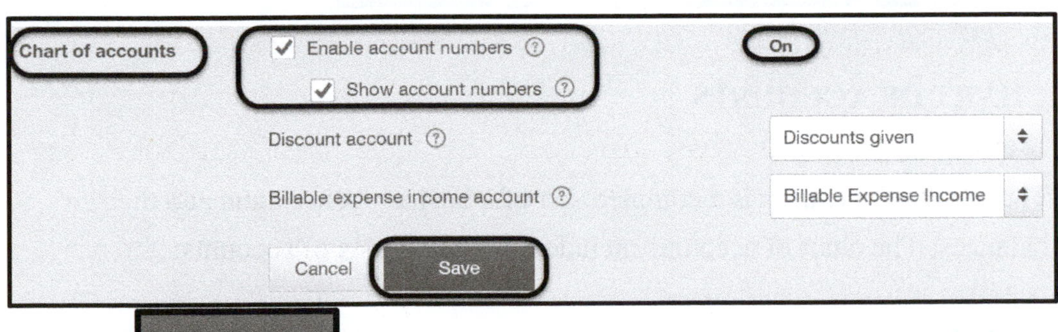

5. Click Save.

6. Select Advanced. In the Other preferences area, you can increase the number of hours your company is active. The default is one hour.

7. Click on the pencil icon to edit. In the Sign me out if inactive for field, select 3 hours.

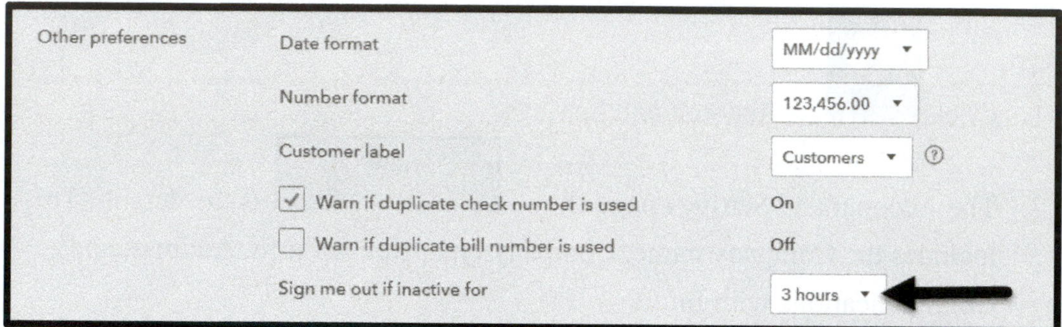

Comment: If you plan to spend time working on Chapter 1, make this selection. Otherwise, you are automatically signed out. Each time you sign into the sample company, the populated data starts fresh. Data is <u>not</u> saved between sign ins.

8. Click 

> then click .

CHART OF ACCOUNTS

The ***chart of accounts*** is a complete list of a business's accounts and their balances. The chart of accounts includes two categories of accounts:

- ***Balance Sheet*** accounts: In QBO, these types of accounts reflect what you own and what you owe, like Bank, Credit Card, Assets, Liabilities, Accounts Receivable, Accounts Payable and Equity. The Balance Sheet includes permanent accounts.

- ***Income and expense accounts***: These are categories for tracking how money flows in and out of your company. QBO's Profit and Loss statement (also called the Income Statement) includes income and expense accounts. Temporary accounts appear on QBO's P&L.

In accounting textbooks, the term Chart of Accounts is defined as a list of all the accounts used in the General Ledger. Accounts are used to classify transaction information for reporting purposes. QBO includes the Account name, Type (for financial statement classification), Detail Type, QuickBooks Balance, and Bank Balance. The Chart of Accounts usually includes account numbers using the following system:

Numbers	Type
1000s	Assets
2000s	Liabilities
3000s	Equity
4000s	Income
5000s	Cost of Sales
6000s	Expenses

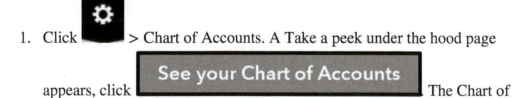

1. Click > Chart of Accounts. A Take a peek under the hood page appears, click 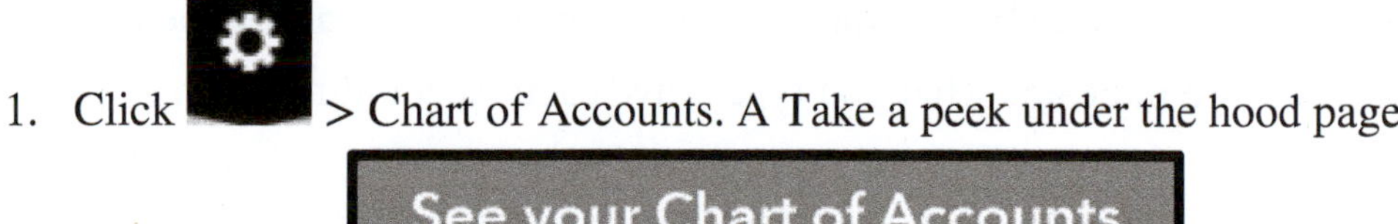

The Chart of Accounts page appears. The Chart of Accounts should have a Number column.

Troubleshooting: Refer to Settings, steps 3 and 4. > Account and Settings > Advanced > Chart of Accounts > > Enable account numbers and Show account numbers should be selected > Save.)

There are two balance columns – QuickBooks Balance and Bank Balance. What is the difference between the QuickBooks Balance and the Bank Balance? The QuickBooks Balance represents the check register balance. The Bank Balance shows the balance at the bank that is linked to your QBO account. For example, if you entered a check for $100 and the checking account balance is $1,000, $900 will be shown as the QuickBooks Balance on the Chart of Accounts. The Bank Balance will continue to be $1,000 since the $100 check has not cleared the bank. In other words, the QuickBooks Balance represents all transactions entered. The Bank Balance is different because not every bank account transaction has cleared the bank.

2. To add the account numbers shown on the table, select the pencil icon to batch edit . A Number column appears on the Chart of Accounts page. Add account numbers to the accounts shown in the chart on the next page. Boldface indicates what you type. Save each Account number.

Number	Name	Category Type	Detail Type
1000	Checking	Bank	Checking
1010	Savings	Bank	Savings
1020	Accounts Receivable	Accounts receivable (A/R)	Accounts Receivable (A/R)
1025	Inventory Asset	Other Current Assets	Inventory
1030	Prepaid Expenses	Other Current Assets	Prepaid Expenses
1035	Uncategorized Asset	Other Current Assets	Other Current Assets
1040	Undeposited Funds	Other Current Assets	Undeposited Funds
1050	Truck	Fixed Assets	Vehicles
1051	Depreciation	Fixed Assets	Accumulated Depreciated
1052	Original Cost	Fixed Assets	Vehicles
2000	Accounts Payable	Accounts payable (A/P)	Accounts Payable (A/P)
2005	Mastercard	Credit Card	Credit Card
2010	Visa	Credit Card	Credit Card
2013	Board of Equalization Payable	Other Current Liabilities	Sales Tax Payable
2015	Loan Payable	Other Current Liabilities	Other Current Liabilities
2200	Notes Payable	Long Term Liabilities	Other Long Term Liabilities
3000	Opening balance equity	Equity	Opening Balance Equity

3900	Retained Earnings	Equity	Retained Earnings

3. Scroll down to the bottom of the page, click .

   Examine the chart of accounts:

   a. The account number is shown in the first column.
   b. The account number is shown next to the Name.
   c. The account Type is shown. The Type column categories the accounts for the Balance Sheet or Profit and Loss (also called the ***Income Statement***).
   d. The Detail Type assigns the account into a subcategory in order to have it appear in the correct place according to the ***Generally Accepted Accounting Principles (GAAP)***. For example, all cash or cash equivalents are grouped together on the Balance Sheet under assets, and subcategorized as Current Assets. Choosing the correct categories places the accounts in the correct positions on the Balance Sheet or Profit & Loss Statement.

What is the difference between the View register accounts and Run report accounts? The View register accounts show their Chart of Accounts balances. They are also called permanent accounts and appear on the Balance Sheet. The Run report accounts do not show balances and are called temporary accounts. Temporary accounts appear on the Profit and Loss statement. The Run report accounts are closed at the end of the year. The chart of accounts appears with account numbers next to the name of each account.

Chart of Accounts

Craig's Design and Landscaping Services

Chart of Accounts

Number	Name	Type	Detail Type	Balance	Bank Balance
1000	1000 Checking	Bank	Checking	1,201.00	-3,621.93
1010	1010 Savings	Bank	Savings	800.00	200.00
1020	1020 Accounts Receivable (A/R)	Accounts receivable (A/R)	Accounts Receivable (A/R)	5,281.52	
1025	1025 Inventory Asset	Other Current Assets	Inventory	596.25	
1030	1030 Prepaid Expenses	Other Current Assets	Prepaid Expenses	0.00	
1035	1035 Uncategorized Asset	Other Current Assets	Other Current Assets	0.00	
1040	1040 Undeposited Funds	Other Current Assets	Undeposited Funds	2,062.52	
1050	1050 Truck	Fixed Assets	Vehicles	13,495.00	
1051	1051 Depreciation	Fixed Assets	Accumulated Depreciation	0.00	
1052	1052 Original Cost	Fixed Assets	Vehicles	13,495.00	
2000	2000 Accounts Payable (A/P)	Accounts payable (A/P)	Accounts Payable (A/P)	1,602.67	
2005	2005 Mastercard	Credit Card	Credit Card	157.72	-304.96
2010	2010 Visa	Credit Card	Credit Card	0.00	
2013	2013 Board of Equalization Payable	Other Current Liabilities	Sales Tax Payable	370.94	
2015	2015 Loan Payable	Other Current Liabilities	Other Current Liabilities	4,000.00	
	Arizona Dept. of Revenue Payable	Other Current Liabilities	Sales Tax Payable	0.00	
2200	2200 Notes Payable	Long Term Liabilities	Other Long Term Liabilities	25,000.00	
3000	3000 Opening Balance Equity	Equity	Opening Balance Equity	-9,337.50	
3900	3900 Retained Earnings	Equity	Retained Earnings	0.00	

Export the Chart of Accounts to Excel

To export Craig's Design and Landscaping Services to Excel, follow these steps.

1. Go to Reports > in the Search field, type **Account List**. (*Hint:* There are a couple ways to display the Account List: Gear > Chart of Accounts (which is also the Account List) > Run Report.)
2. Craig's Design and Landscaping Services Account List page appears. Click on the down-arrow next to the Export icon > Export to Excel.

Export to Excel
Export to PDF

3. On the taskbar at the bottom of the screen, double-click on the Excel button.

4. If necessary, select Enable Editing. Save as **Chapter 1_CofA_sample company_Student Name** (use your first and last name). A partial Account List is shown as an Excel file.
5. Exit Excel.

Save the Chart of Accounts as a PDF file

1. The Account List should be displayed. If necessary, go to Reports > type **Account List** in the Search field. Select the Export icon, Export to PDF.

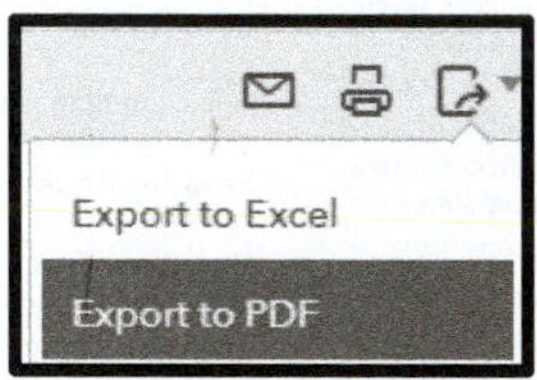

If a page appears that says Couldn't open PDF, click to close it. Another way to save Adobe PDFs, is to Export to Excel, then save as a PDF file. Refer to Appendix A, Troubleshooting, or go to www.mhhe.com/qbo2e > Troubleshooting.

2. The Print, email, or save as PDF page appears. Select Save as PDF.
3. On the taskbar at the bottom of your screen, double-click AccountList.pdf

4. Click on the download icon (right side of AccountList.pdf title bar). Go to the location where you want to save. Use the file name **Chapter 1_CofA_sample company_Student Name** (use your first and last name).

5. On title bar, click <x> on the qb Craig's Design and Landscaping tab Craig's Design and Lanc ×.

6. On the Print, email, or save as PDF page, click <X>.

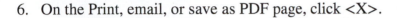

The Account List page displays.

SIGN OUT

To sign out, click > Sign Out. The numbers added to the Chart of Accounts are *not* saved. If you want to continue your work without losing data, do not sign out at this time. When you sign out, a Sign In page appears. Close your browser.

RECENT TRANSACTIONS

If you signed out, go online to https://qbo.intuit.com/redir/testdrive to start the sample company. Type the security verification to begin. At the top of the Dashboard, there are four icons — .

The plus icon allows you to add transactions and complete typical Customer, Vendor, Employee, and Other tasks. You have the option to Show More or Show Less depending on your preference.

Search transactions and view recent transactions.

The Gear icon takes you to settings for Your Company, Lists, Tools, and Profile.

QuickBooks Online self-help. Complete help searches online, submit questions to the QuickBooks Community, or contact Intuit.

Follow these steps to view recent transactions.

1. Click . Recent Transactions appear. Depending on when you selected Recent Transactions, yours may differ from the ones shown on the next page.

   In the example that follows, on 2/07/2017 (your date may differ), a $19.99 Squeaky Kleen Car Wash credit card expense transaction is shown. The dates on the sample company pages default to the month/year you are using QBO. For example, if you are using the sample company, Craig's Design and Landscaping Services, during the month of February 2017, the pages will default to that month and year.

   The purpose of using the sample company is to explore QB Online. Setting up a company, journalizing and posting transactions, account reconciliation, viewing financial reports, completing the accounting cycle, and starting a new fiscal year is done in Chapters 2 through 10.

   To see how a credit card transaction is entered, double-click on Credit Card Expense.

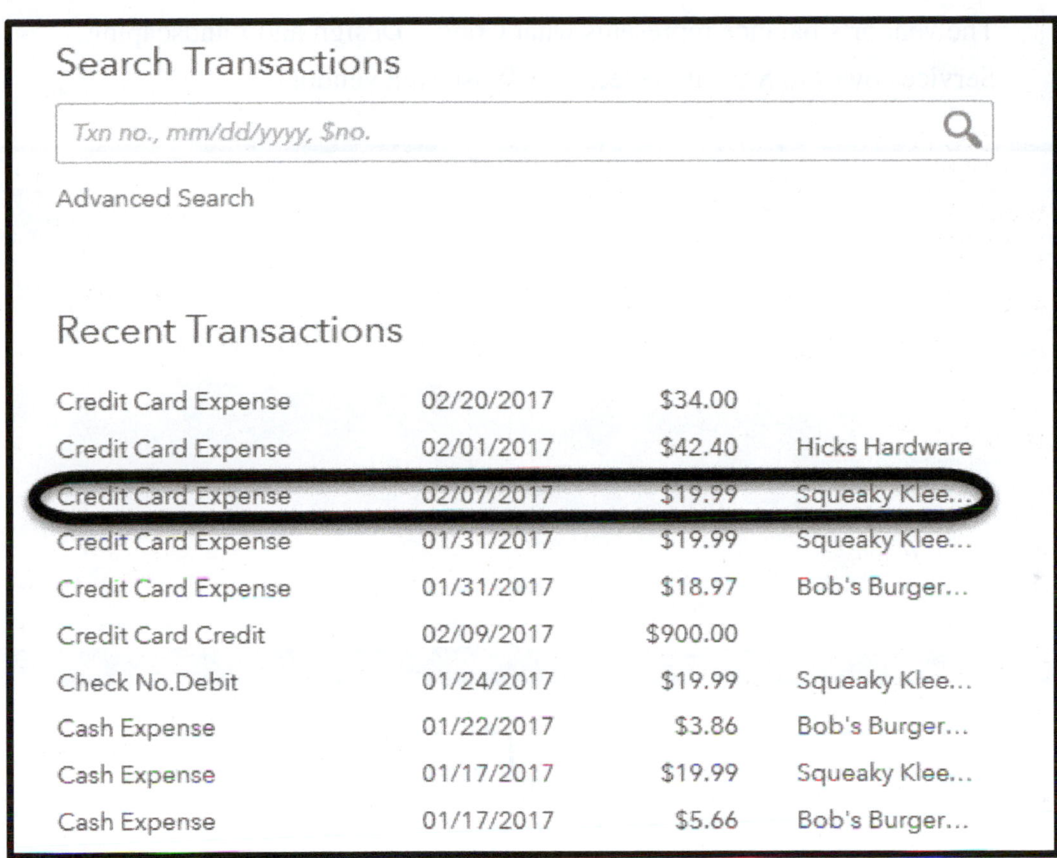
Search Transactions

Txn no., mm/dd/yyyy, $no.

Advanced Search

Recent Transactions

Credit Card Expense	02/20/2017	$34.00	
Credit Card Expense	02/01/2017	$42.40	Hicks Hardware
Credit Card Expense	02/07/2017	$19.99	Squeaky Klee...
Credit Card Expense	01/31/2017	$19.99	Squeaky Klee...
Credit Card Expense	01/31/2017	$18.97	Bob's Burger...
Credit Card Credit	02/09/2017	$900.00	
Check No.Debit	01/24/2017	$19.99	Squeaky Klee...
Cash Expense	01/22/2017	$3.86	Bob's Burger...
Cash Expense	01/17/2017	$19.99	Squeaky Klee...
Cash Expense	01/17/2017	$5.66	Bob's Burger...

2. In this example, Credit Card Expense is shown for 02/07/2017 (your date will differ), Squeaky Kleen Car Wash. The Expense page on the next page shows that the vendor, Squeaky Kleen Car Wash (**1**) was paid with a Mastercard (**2**). The vendor's balance is $157.72 (**3**). The account debited is Automobile (**4**). The total amount is $19.99 (**5** and **6**).

The vendor's balance represents what Craig's Design and Landscaping Services owes to Squeaky Kleen Car Wash (the vendor).

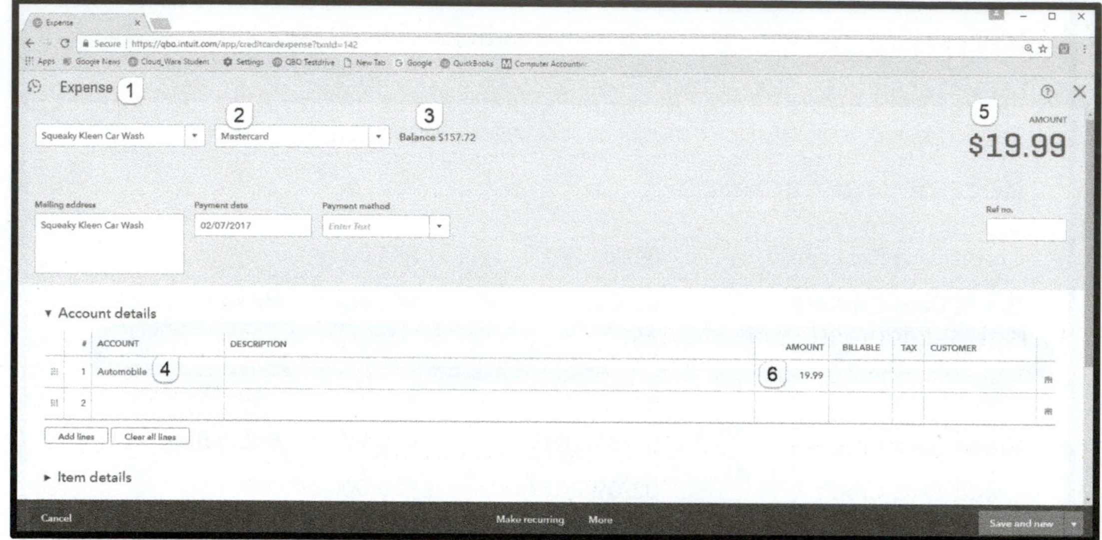

3. On the Expense page's title bar, click X to close.

REPORTS

Use reports to view the company's financial information. Generate important financial statements, transaction details, employee information, etc. The top half of the Reports page shows a snapshot of your business based on QuickBooks transactions. The bottom half of the page lists the reports that are available.

Reports are divided into five sections:

- Recommended: Reports that QuickBooks recommends you run.
- Frequently Run: Reports that you run most frequently, and are easy to access in this section.

- My Custom Reports: Reports that you have customized and saved.
- Management Reports: Professional, ready-to-use templates that contain reports and other customizable content, consolidated into a single document. Management reports present information in a polished package that can be printed, emailed, or exported.
- All Reports: A list of all available reports, categorized by subject.

Journal

To look at a journal report, do this:

1. From the Navigation Bar, select Reports > type **Journal** in the search field.

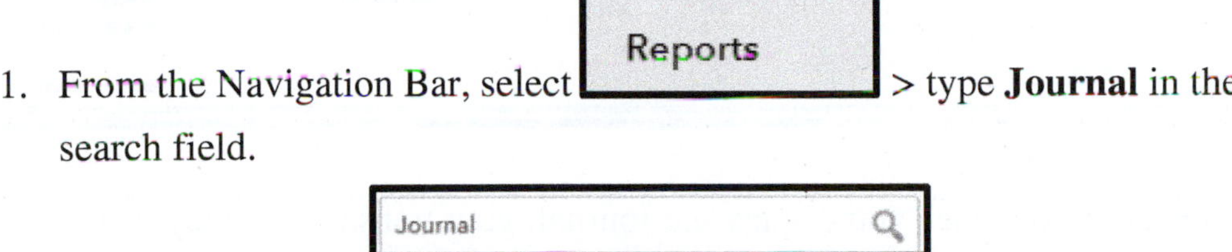

2. Press <Enter>. The Journal report appears. The Report period defaults to This Month-to-date. Since the author is viewing this report on February 21, 2017, 02/01/2017 to 02/21/2017 is shown. The Squeaky Kleen Car Wash transaction is shown on the next page. Your dates will differ.

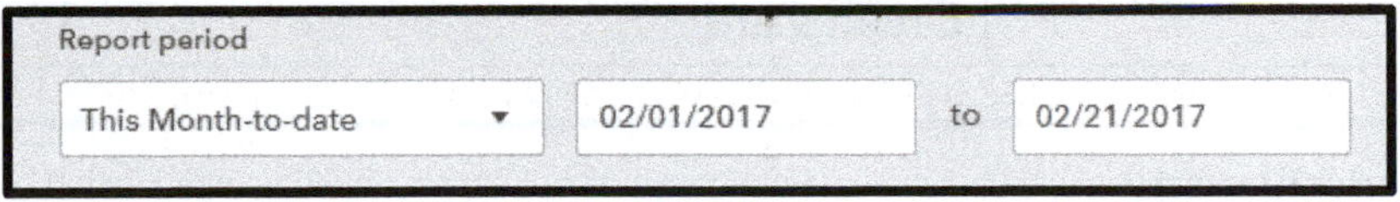

Craig's Design and Landscaping Services

JOURNAL

February 1-21, 2017

DATE	TRANSACTION TYPE	NUM	NAME	MEMO/DESCRIPTION	ACCOUNT	DEBIT	CREDIT
02/01/2017	Credit Card Expense		Hicks Hardware		Mastercard		$42.40
					Job Expenses:Job Materials:Decks and Patios	$42.40	
						$42.40	**$42.40**
02/07/2017	Credit Card Expense		Squeaky Kleen Car Wash		Mastercard		$19.99
					Automobile	$19.99	
						$19.99	**$19.99**
02/09/2017	Credit Card Credit			Monthly Payment	Mastercard	$900.00	
					Checking		$900.00
						$900.00	**$900.00**
02/20/2017	Credit Card Expense				Mastercard		$34.00
					Automobile	$34.00	
						$34.00	**$34.00**
TOTAL						**$996.39**	**$996.39**

Depending on when you display the Journal, your transactions may differ from what is shown. The account distribution for the Squeaky Kleen Car wash is:

Account	Account Type	Debit	Credit
Automobile	Expense	19.99	
Mastercard	Credit Card		19.99

Troubleshooting

If you are not using Craig's Design and Landscaping Services, QBO closes automatically. Remember if you exit or sign out, your chart of account numbers will not be saved. Each time you start the sample company, it begins again.

CHECK YOUR PROGRESS

In subsequent chapters, Check Your Progress questions are at the end of the chapter and do not include answers. For purposes of showing how to complete Check Your Progress, answers are included in Chapter 1. The Online Learning Center at www.mhhe.com/qbo2e includes Check Your Progress files for Chapters 2 through 12. They can be completed online and emailed to your instructor.

1. What are Balance Sheet accounts?

   Answer: Balance Sheet accounts show what you own and what you owe.

2. List two accounts and their balances that show what you own; list two accounts and their balances that show what you owe.

   Answer:

Craig's Design and Landscaping Services

ACCOUNT LIST

ACCOUNT	TYPE	DETAIL TYPE	DESCRIPTION	BALANCE
Checking	Bank	Checking		1,201.00
Savings	Bank	Savings		800.00

Accounts Payable (A/P)	Accounts payable (A/P)	Accounts Payable (A/P)		-1,602.67
Mastercard	Credit Card	Credit Card		-157.72

3. What are income and expense accounts?

   Answer: Income and expense accounts are categories for tracking how money flows in and out of your company.

4. List the first two income accounts and the first two expense accounts.

   Answer:

   Income: Billable Expense Income and Design Income
   Expenses: Advertising and Automobile

5. In this chapter, what account numbering system is suggested for Assets, Liabilities, Equity, Income, Cost of Sales, and Expenses?

Assets:	1000s
Liabilities:	2000s
Equity	3000s
Income:	4000s
Cost of Sales:	5000s
Expenses:	6000s

CREATE AN INVOICE

Every invoice is automatically tracked, so you know who owes you money and who has paid. Use invoices when the customer pays you later.

Customer Invoice

Complete the following sales invoice.

Date	*Description of Transaction*
Current Date	Sold a Rock Fountain to Dukes Basketball Camp, $275 plus 8% California tax of $22; total $297.

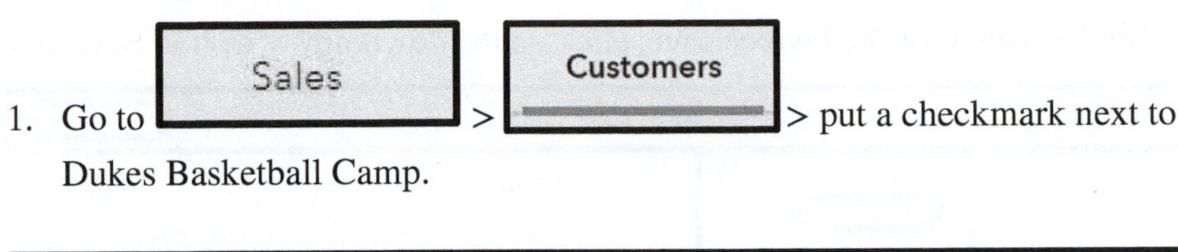

1. Go to Sales > Customers > put a checkmark next to Dukes Basketball Camp.

2. Select Create invoice. The Invoice page appears with Dukes Basketball Camp selected. The Invoice date field shows the current date.
3. Click PRODUCT/SERVICE > Rock Fountain *Design: Fountains*. The description, quantity, rate, and amount fields are automatically completed. If necessary, in the Tax field, select California (8%). The Balance due is $297.

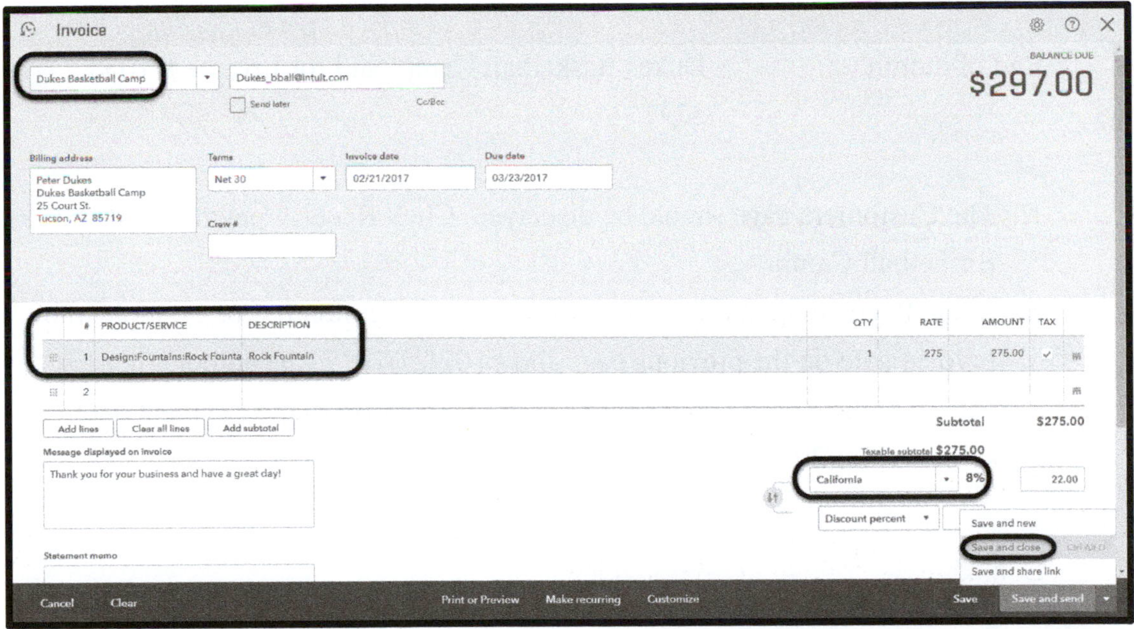

4. On the bottom of the Invoice page, click on the down-arrow next to Save and

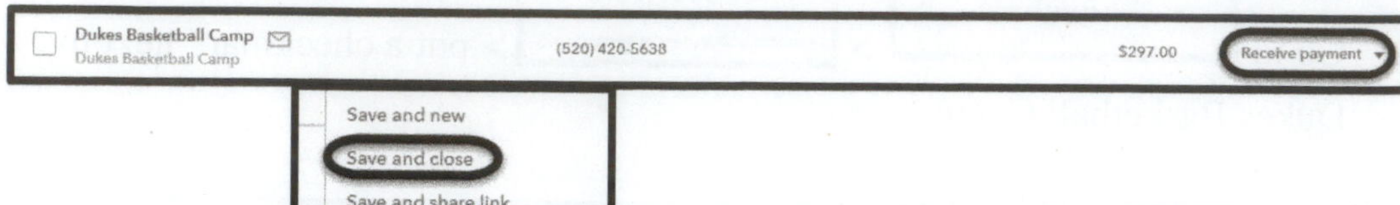

Send. Click [Save and close]. A screen prompts that Invoice 1038 was saved. The Customers page shows Receive payment next to Dukes Basketball Camp. (If necessary, click on Dukes to put a checkmark next to it.)

Receive Payment

Date	*Transaction*
End of month	Dukes Basketball Camp paid for Invoice # 1038, $297.

1. The Customers page should be displayed. Click Receive payment for Dukes Basketball Camp.
2. In the Payment date field, type the last day of the month. For example, the Invoice date on the previous page shows 02/21/2017 (the author's current date). On the Receive Payment page on the next page, the Payment date shows 02/28/2017. In the Deposit to field, select Checking.

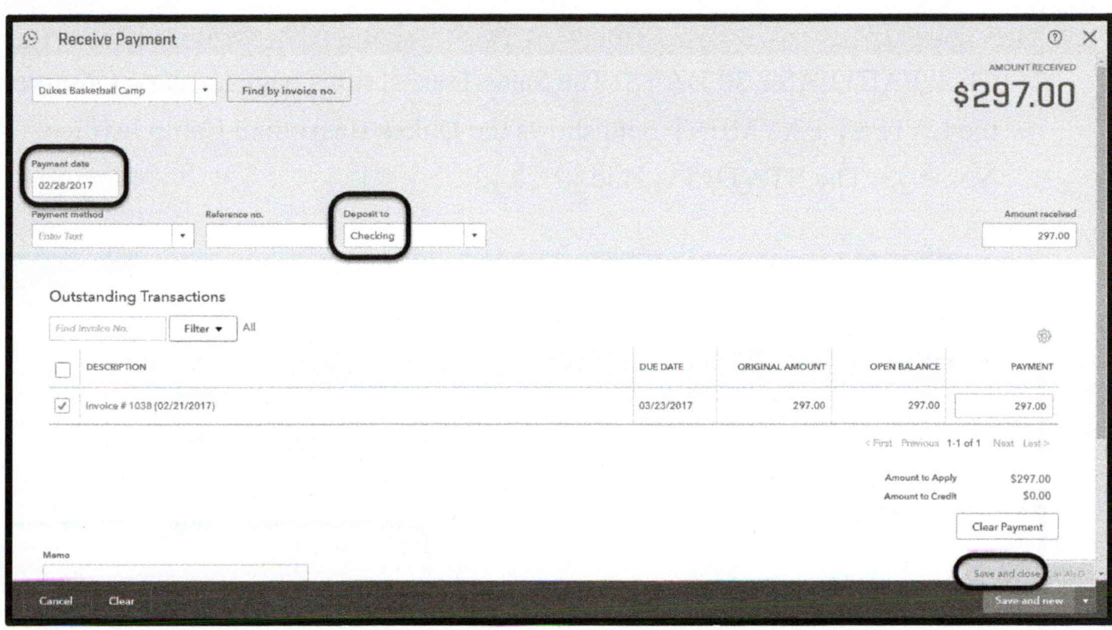

3. Review the Receive Payment page. Select Save and close. The page prompts Receive payment $297.00 saved.

Income

From the Dashboard you can quickly see what has been paid in the last 30 days. (*Hint:* Click on the qb intuit quickbooks icon to go to the Dashboard.)

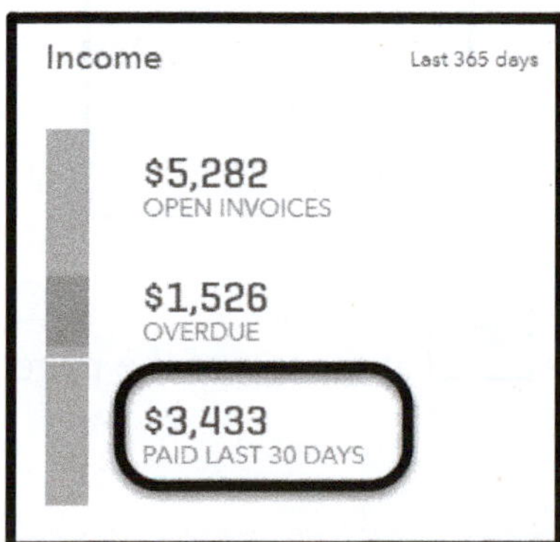

1. Click PAID LAST 30 DAYS. The Sales Transactions page appears. Observe the LATEST PAYMENT field shows the Dukes Basketball Camp Invoice No. 1038. The STATUS is Paid.

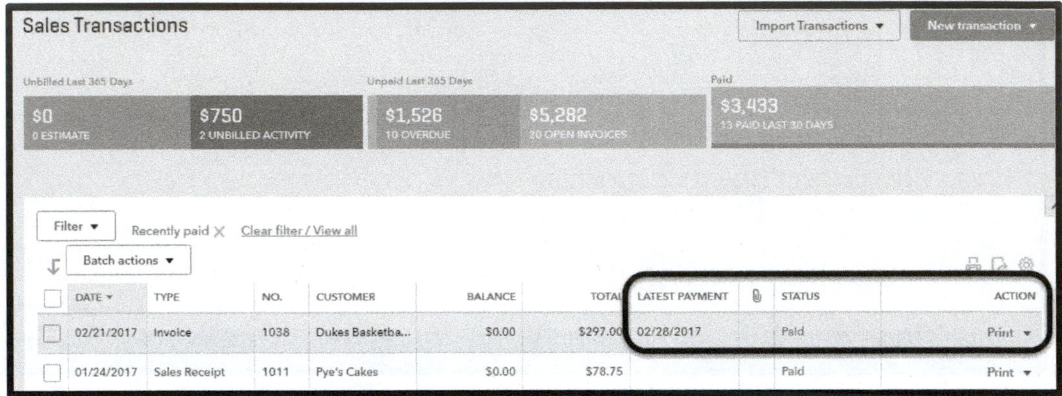

2. On the right side of the Sales Transactions page, three icons are included — — Print, Export to Excel, and Settings (for editing columns).
3. From the Sales Transactions page, go to the Payment page by clicking on Invoice 1038. Invoice # 1038 shows PAID. A partial page is shown. The information on this page agrees with the payment completed previously.

PAYMENT STATUS
PAID
1 payment made on 02/28/2017

4. Click on the left arrow at the top of the page to return to the Sales Transactions page.

A/R Aging Summary

1. From the Navigation bar, go to Reports > Recommended. Link to A/R Aging Summary, which shows unpaid invoices for the current period and for the last 30, 60, 90+ days.
2. In the as of field, type the last day of the month > Run Report. Observe that the TOTAL shows $5,281.52 (your amount may differ). This is the amount of Accounts Receivable the Craig's Design and Landscaping Services can expect to receive from its customers.

Your A/R Summary report will differ. For example, the As of field shows February 28, 2017.

Craig's Design and Landscaping Services

A/R AGING SUMMARY

As of February 28, 2017

	CURRENT	1 - 30	31 - 60	61 - 90	91 AND OVER	TOTAL
Amy's Bird Sanctuary		239.00				$239.00
Bill's Windsurf Shop			85.00			$85.00
Freeman Sporting Goods						$0.00
0969 Ocean View Road		477.50				$477.50
55 Twin Lane		4.00	81.00			$85.00
Total Freeman Sporting Goods		**481.50**	**81.00**			**$562.50**
Geeta Kalapatapu		629.10				$629.10
Jeff's Jalopies		81.00				$81.00
John Melton		450.00				$450.00
Kookies by Kathy			75.00			$75.00
Mark Cho		314.28				$314.28
Paulsen Medical Supplies		954.75				$954.75
Red Rock Diner		70.00		156.00		$226.00
Rondonuwu Fruit and Vegi		78.60				$78.60
Shara Barnett						$0.00
Barnett Design		274.50				$274.50
Total Shara Barnett		**274.50**				**$274.50**
Sonnenschein Family Store		362.07				$362.07
Sushi by Katsuyuki		160.00				$160.00
Travis Waldron		414.72				$414.72
Weiskopf Consulting		375.00				$375.00
TOTAL	**$0.00**	**$4,884.52**	**$241.00**	**$156.00**	**$0.00**	**$5,281.52**

3. Compare the total, $5,281.52, to the Accounts Receivable balance by selecting Reports > then type **Trial Balance** in the search field > type the last day of the month in the to field (*or* select This Month in the Report period field). The Trial Balance Account Receivable (AR) balance shows $5,281.52. (*Hint:* This Month-to-date is the default. Your As of date will differ.) A partial ***Trial Balance*** is shown below.

Craig's Design and Landscaping Services

TRIAL BALANCE

As of February 28, 2017

	DEBIT	CREDIT
Checking	1,498.00	
Savings	800.00	
Accounts Receivable (A/R)	5,281.52	
Inventory Asset	471.25	
Undeposited Funds	2,062.52	
Truck:Original Cost	13,495.00	
Accounts Payable (A/P)		1,602.67
Mastercard		157.72
Arizona Dept. of Revenue Payable		0.00
Board of Equalization Payable		392.94

Transaction Detail by Account

This report lists transactions subtotaled by each account on the chart of accounts. It is like the General Ledger without opening balances.

1. Go to Reports > All Reports > Accountant Reports > Transaction Detail by Account.
2. In the Report period field, select All Dates > Run Report. Scroll down the screen to look at the last entry for the Checking account which shows the payment from Dukes Basketball Camp. Remember, your dates will differ.

02/28/2017	Payment	Dukes Basketball Camp	Accounts Receivable (A/R)	297.00	1,498.00
Total for Checking				$1,498.00	

3. Scroll down to see the Accounts Receivable (A/R) balance. Dukes Basketball Camp Invoice and payment is shown, and the balance is $5,281.52.

02/21/2017	Invoice	1038	Dukes Basketball Camp	Sales of Product Income	297.00	5,578.52
02/28/2017	Payment		Dukes Basketball Camp	Checking	-297.00	5,281.52
Total for Accounts Receivable (A/R)					$5,281.52	

COMPANY SNAPSHOT

The Company Snapshot displays your income and expenses in year-over-year comparisons using pie charts and bar graphs. Follow these steps to see the Company Snapshot. (*Hint:* If you signed out some of your balances will differ. Remember, these balances are as of the author's current date. Your current date is different.)

1. Go to Reports > Recommended > Company Snapshot. The Company Snapshot shows graphs for My Income, My Expenses, Previous Year Income Comparison, and Previous Year Expense Comparison. Tables are shown for Who Owes Me, Whom I Owe. This Year-to-date is the default, 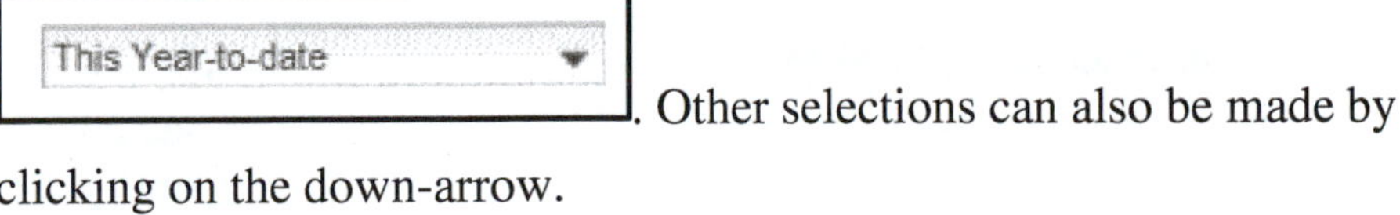

. Other selections can also be made by clicking on the down-arrow.
2. In the My Income area, the graph shows Income accounts. The My Expenses Profit and Loss shows expense accounts. Link to Profit and Loss. The Profit and Loss statement for Craig's Design and Landscaping Services is shown. The Transaction Date field shows This Year-to-date so the dates are from January 1 to your current date. In this example, that's January 1 – February 21, 2017. Your ending date will differ.

A partial Profit and Loss is shown. Observe, you can Print, Email, export to Excel, and customize. Scroll down to see all of it.

Craig's Design and Landscaping Services

PROFIT AND LOSS

January 1 - February 21, 2017

	TOTAL
INCOME	
Design income	2,250.00
Discounts given	-89.50
Landscaping Services	797.50
Job Materials	
Fountains and Garden Lighting	1,501.50
Plants and Soil	2,220.72
Sprinklers and Drip Systems	30.00
Total Job Materials	**3,752.22**
Labor	
Installation	250.00
Total Labor	**250.00**
Total Landscaping Services	**4,799.72**
Pest Control Services	-30.00
Sales of Product Income	1,187.75
Services	503.55
Total Income	**$8,621.52**
COST OF GOODS SOLD	
Cost of Goods Sold	530.00
Total Cost of Goods Sold	**$530.00**

3. To go back to the Company Snapshot, click .

CHECK YOUR PROGRESS 2

How is the Accounts Receivable balance checked?

Answer:

Go to the Trial Balance report (Reports > Frequently Run > Trial Balance or This Year-to-date on the Transaction Detail by Account report.). On the Trial Balance and Transaction Detail by Account report, the balance for Accounts Receivable (A/R) is shown. To make sure it agrees with the customer balance, display the A/R aging summary (Reports > Recommended > AR Aging Summary; Transaction Date is Today). The Accounts Receivable balance on the Trial Balance and the Total on the A/R Aging Summary are the same.

SIGN OUT

Select Gear > Sign Out. When you sign out, transactions entered are not saved. If you prefer to continue, the Journal shown with Check Your Progress 3 will differ.

SALES RECEIPT

Use sales receipts when the customer pays you at the time of the sale. To record this transaction, follow the steps on the next page.

Date	*Description of Transaction*
Current Date	Completed three hours of custom design work for cash for the customer, Cool Cars, $225.00

1. If necessary, start the test drive at https://qbo.intuit.com/redir/testdrive. Click  > Sales Receipt. Complete these fields.

Customer:	Select Cool Cars
Sales Receipt Date:	Current date automatically completed
Payment method:	Check
Deposit to:	Select Checking
Product/Service:	Select Design (Custom Design, *Design*)
Qty:	Type **3**

Hint: Depending on when you entered the Sales Receipt, the date field will differ. QBO defaults to the current date.

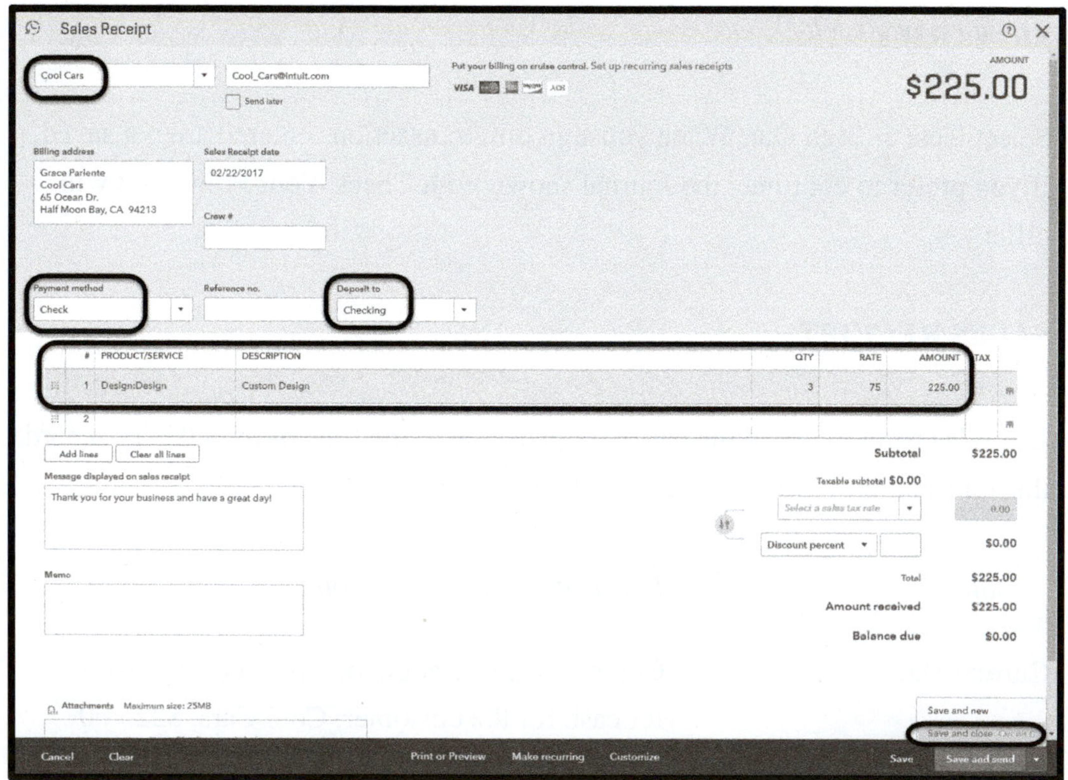

2. Save and close. The screen prompts your sales receipt was saved.

ENTER A BILL

To enter bills that you received but pay later, use the Bill page. Entering a bill helps you track how much money you owe and control your cash flow. Bills are entered for vendors or suppliers.

Date	*Transaction*
Current date	Craig's Design and Landscaping Services received a bill for $250 from Lee Advertising.

1. Go to ⊕ > Bill. The Bill page appears. Complete these fields

Vendor:	Select Lee Advertising
Bill date:	Current date automatically completed
Account:	Advertising
Amount:	250.00

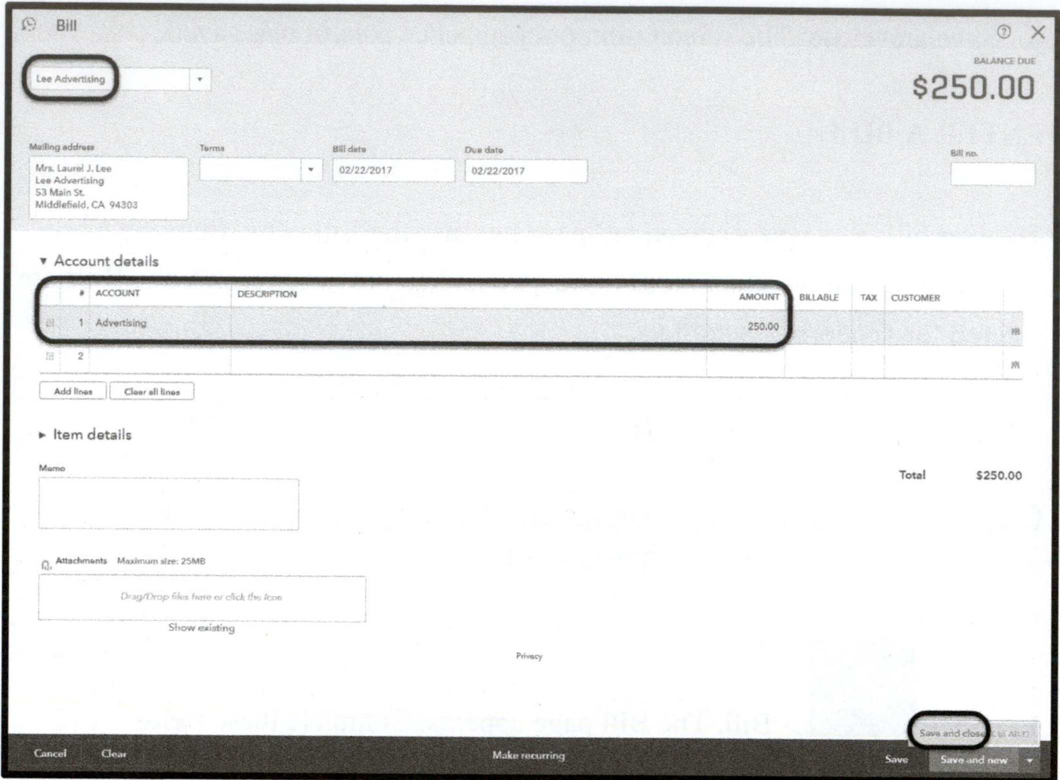

2. Save and close. A page appears saying the bill was saved.

WRITE CHECK

Enter the following check.

Date	*Transaction*
Current date	Check No. 71, from the Checking account was issued to Computers by Jenni in the amount of $650.

1. Go to > Check (in the Vendors list). Complete these fields:

Payee:	Select Computers by Jenni
	Checking is automatically selected
Check no.:	71 is automatically completed
Account:	Select Supplies – Expenses
Description:	Type **Purchased tablet computer**
Amount:	Type **650**

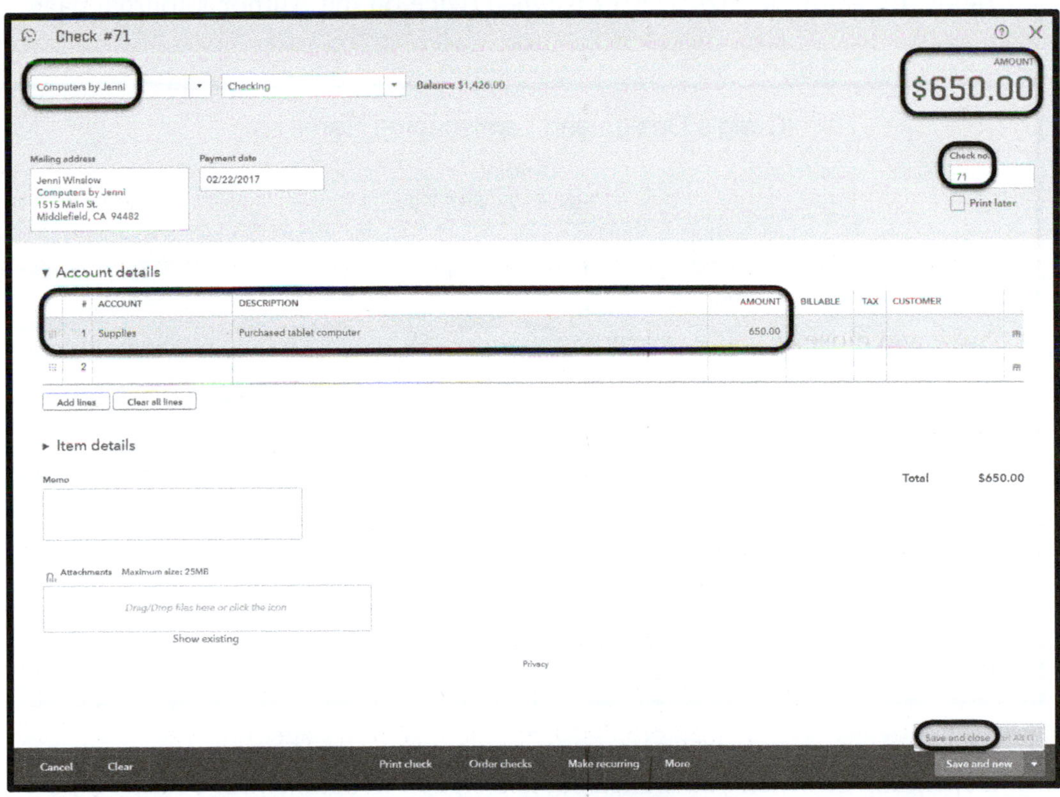

➢ *Hint: Your Balance field may differ depending on when you started the sample company.*

2. Save and close.

JOURNAL REPORT

The Journal report breaks down every transaction during a period of time into debits and credits and displays them chronologically. Transaction List by Date also lists transactions chronologically, but not as debits and credits.

1. Go to Reports > type **Journal** in the search field > press Enter.
2. In the Report period field, select Custom > type today's date in both date fields; for example, 02/22/2017 is typed twice on the Author's Journal page.

Craig's Design and Landscaping Services

JOURNAL

February 22, 2017

DATE	TRANSACTION TYPE	NUM	NAME	MEMO/DESCRIPTION	ACCOUNT	DEBIT	CREDIT
02/22/2017	Sales Receipt	1038	Cool Cars		Checking	$225.00	
				Custom Design	Design income		$225.00
						$225.00	**$225.00**
02/22/2017	Bill		Lee Advertising		Accounts Payable (A/P)		$250.00
					Advertising	$250.00	
						$250.00	**$250.00**
02/22/2017	Check	71	Computers by Jenni		Checking		$650.00
				Purchased tablet computer	Supplies	$650.00	
						$650.00	**$650.00**
TOTAL						**$1,125.00**	**$1,125.00**

Depending on when you signed out and signed in again, your Journal report will differ.

CHECK YOUR PROGRESS 3

My journal shows more transactions listed for today's date. Why?

ANSWER: Your Journal shows the transactions recorded today. Each time QBO's sample company is started by typing the security verification, Craig's Design and Landscaping Services starts over. (*Hint:* If you did not sign out after Check Your Progress 2, your Journal will differ.)

- The author entered three transactions shown on the previous page's Journal report: Sales Receipt, Bill, and Check.
- Another way to check whether you signed out is to look at the ***Audit Log***.

  (Go to [gear icon] > Audit Log. The Audit Log shows when you logged out and when you logged back in.)

  The Audit Log contains a list of all the changes that have ever been made to your company data. By default, the Audit Log displays 200 of the most recent events. Dates and times in the Audit Log and Audit History reflect when events occurred, displayed in your local time.

When you work with QB Cloud_Student Name, the company set up in Chapter 2, and continued in Chapters 3-10, data is stored online when you sign out. In Chapters 2 through 10, you work with QB Cloud_Student Name to create the company, enter beginning balances, set up a chart of accounts, record transactions, complete the accounting cycle, and sign in each time you want to continue work. Once you set up your account and company, QB Online data will not be lost when you sign out because it is stored online.

In Chapter 1, you use the sample company to learn about the interface and how QB Online is used. In other words, you practice using QBO. The sample company used in Chapter 1, Craig's Design and Landscaping Services, includes populated data (accounts, balances, customers, vendors, employees, etc). In Chapter 2, when you set up QB Cloud_ Student Name, you create the data within QuickBooks Online.

SIGN OUT

Go to the Settings menu and Sign Out – Gear > Sign Out. Close your browser.

ONLINE LEARNING CENTER (OLC): www.mhhe.com/qbo2e

The OLC includes additional resources. Go online to www.mhhe.com/qbo2e > link to Student Edition > Chapter 1.

1. Narrated PowerPoints.
2. Online quizzes: 10 multiple-choice and 10 True or False questions. The Online Quizzes are graded and can be emailed to your instructor.
3. Analysis question: Answer the analysis question, then email to your instructor.
4. Going to the Net: Go online to compare QuickBooks Desktop (QBD) to QuickBooks Online (QBO).
5. Videos: QuickBooks Online for iPad and Navigate in QuickBooks. The links for the videos are included in the Chapter 1 narrated PowerPoints and the Video link at www.mhhe.com/qbo2e > Student Edition.
6. Glossary of terms: Words that are italicized and boldfaced are defined in the glossary. The Glossary is also Appendix B.
7. Problem solving link includes Exercise 1-3.

Exercise 1-1: Follow the instructions below to complete Exercise 1-1:

1. If you have not signed out, do that now. For Exercise 1-1, start the test drive again. Go online to https://qbo.intuit.com/redir/testdrive. Type the security verification. Craig's Design and Landscaping Services Dashboard appears.
2. Go to Gear > Account and Settings > Advanced. In the Other preferences area, increase Sign me out if inactive to 3 hours > Save.

Sign me out if inactive for	3 hours

3. After saving, click <Done>.
4. Enter the following transactions. Use your current date and year.

- Sold 3 rock fountains on account to the customer, Amy's Bird Sanctuary, $825 plus 8% sales tax; total $891.
- Sold 20 sprinkler heads on account to the customer, Sushi by Katsuyuki, $40 plus 8% sales tax; total $43.20. (*Hint:* For sales tax, select California.)
- Completed 4 hours of installation of landscape design for Kookies by Kathy; received $200. (*Hint:* + > Sales Receipt. Payment method, Check; Deposit to, Checking; Product/Service, Installation; no sales tax charged for installation.)
- Completed 3 hours of custom design work for Cool Cars; received $225. (*Hint:* Payment method, Check; Deposit to, Checking; Product/Service, Design; No sales tax.)
- Completed 10 hours of custom design work on account for the customer, John Melton, $750.
- Received a bill from Lee Advertising, $250, for local paper advertising.
- Received a bill from Cal Telephone for $56.50, for telephone expense.

- Received a bill from PG&E for $86.44, for utilities (gas and electric) expense.
- Received a bill from Hall Properties for $900, for building lease.
- Issued Check No. 71 from the Checking account to Chin's Gas and Oil, $48.05, for Automobile:Fuel. (*Hint:* In the Account field, select Automobile:Fuel. Type the Amount, $48.05. Since you restarted the sample company, the default check number is 71.)
- Issued Check No. 72 to Ellis Equipment Rental, from the Checking account, $115, for equipment rental expense. (*Hint:* In the Account field, select Equipment Rental, an Expenses account.)
- Issued Check No. 73 to Red Rock Diner, from the Checking account, for $23.37, for Meals and Entertainment.

5. Do **not** sign out. Continue with Exercise 1-2.

Exercise 1-2: Follow the instructions below to complete Exercise 1-2:

1. Display the Journal for the date you entered Exercise 1-1 transactions. (*Hint:* This Month-to-date is the default. The From and To fields should show the current date; for example, select Today in the Transaction Date field. Go to Reports > All Reports > Accountant Reports > Journal > Today > Run Report.) Check that you entered Exercise 1-1's transactions.
2. Export the Journal to Excel and save as a PDF file. The suggested file name is **Exercise 1-2_Journal**. Type the date that you entered the Journal transactions. (*Hint:* Since you started QBO's sample company in Exercise 1-1, scroll down to see that the Exercise 1-1 transactions were entered.)

3. Display the Transaction Detail by Account report. Export the report to Excel and save as a PDF file. In the Report period field, select All dates. Use the file name **Exercise 1-2_Transaction Detail by Account**.
4. Display the Trial Balance. In the Transaction Date field, select All Dates. Export to Excel and save as a PDF file. Use the file name **Exercise 1-2_Trial Balance.**

Check Your Figures:

Checking	1,439.58
Accounts Receivable	6,965.72
Accounts Payable	2,895.61
Design Income	3,225.00
Advertising	324.86

These account balances are based on starting the sample company with Exercise 1-1. If you did not sign in for a new session with the required security verification, your balances will differ.

5. Continue with Exercise 1-3.

Exercise 1-3: Problem Solving, www.mhhe.com/qbo2e > Student Edition > Chapter 1 > Problem Solving.

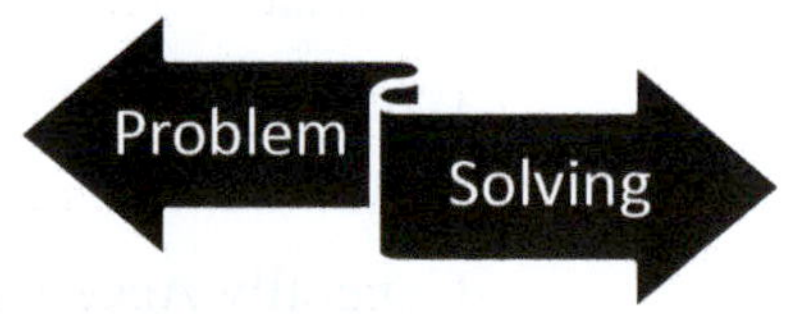

1. Display the Chart of Accounts.
2. How do the View register accounts differ from the Run report accounts? Include information about financial statements in your answer.
3. When through, sign out.

CHAPTER 1 INDEX

Chapter 2 New Company Setup and Chart of Accounts

Scenario: In Chapter 2, you set up a new company, QB Cloud_Student Name. After changing QB Online's settings or preferences, you complete a chart of accounts, save your work, and learn how to provide your professor access to your QBO company. To see the work accomplished, you display an Audit Log. The objectives that follow specify the work that is completed in Chapter 2.

OBJECTIVES

1. Start QuickBooks Online with your User ID and Password.
2. Set up the company, QB Cloud_Student Name (your first and last name).
3. Watch Explore the Power of QuickBooks videos.
4. Complete account and settings.
5. Create a Chart of Accounts.
6. Save Chart of Accounts as PDF file.
7. Export the Chart of Accounts to Excel.
8. Invite accountant and learn about user roles and access rights.
9. View the Audit Log.
10. Complete Check Your Progress assignments within the chapter.
11. Go to the Online Learning Center at www.mhhe.com/qbo2e for additional resources.
12. Complete Exercises 2-1, 2-2 and 2-3.

Cloudware refers to software that is built, installed, delivered and accessed entirely from a remote Web server, also called the "cloud." Cloudware is a software delivery method that provides software over the Internet.

QuickBooks Online is an example of ***cloud computing***, or ***Software as a Service*** (or **SaaS**). ***SaaS*** is a way of delivering applications over the Internet — as a service. Instead of installing and maintaining software, you access it via the Internet, freeing you from complex software installation and hardware management. For a complete definition of cloudware, cloud computing and software as a service, refer to Appendix B, Glossary.

The company set up in this chapter is called QB Cloud_Student Name. To identify your company, you add your first and last name after QB Cloud. The products and services company, QB Cloud, provides hosting services for retail businesses, schools, and medical and legal offices.

GETTING STARTED: Set Up Your Account

In Chapter 2, you start QBO and set up a company, QB Cloud_Student Name. Start your Internet browser. Go online to https://quickbooks.intuit.com/signup/retail/. The Set Up Your Account page appears.

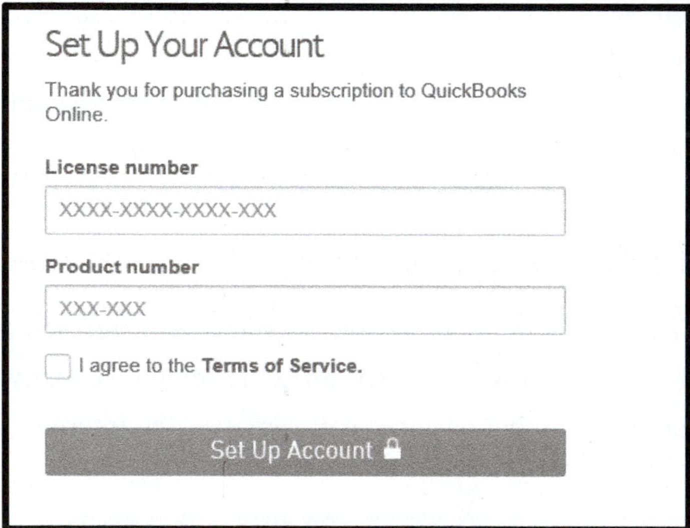

1. Type your License Number and Product Number. Refer to the access card that came with your textbook for the License and Product Numbers.
2. Click on the box next to I agree to the Terms of Service > click Set Up Account.

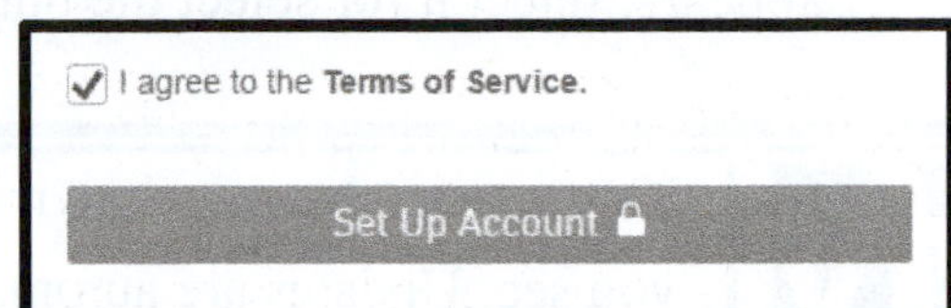

3. Complete the form shown. In the Email Address field, type a *valid* Email address. (*Hint:* You may want to set up a new email address for use with QBO.) Then, type your first and last name. Type a Password that is 8 or more characters, a mix of upper and lowercase letters, and includes a symbol. Each time you sign into QBO, you need your User ID and Password.

   IMPORTANT: Do not use the *same* User ID and Password associated with another Intuit QuickBooks account. The QB Online User ID and Password must be unique. If you have a QuickBooks account, do not use that information. **Write down your User ID and Password**. You will need it each time to sign into QuickBooks Online.

   User ID____

   Password____

4. After clicking Set Up Account, complete the fields on the pages that appear. As of this writing the first screen includes fields for the name of business and length of time for the business .

   - The business is called: **QB Cloud_Student Name** (use your first and last name)
   - How long have you been in business: select Less than 1 year.

5. Click **Next** to go to the next page. Read the information. If **All set** appears, select it (or select the button on your page).

> The screens that are shown in the textbook may differ from what you see. Updates are automatic and may change the user interface. Regularly go online to www.mhhe.com/qbo2e > Text Updates.

6. The QB Cloud_Student Name Dashboard appears. If a message pops-up, read it. A partial Dashboard is shown. Your Dashboard may look different. This is okay.

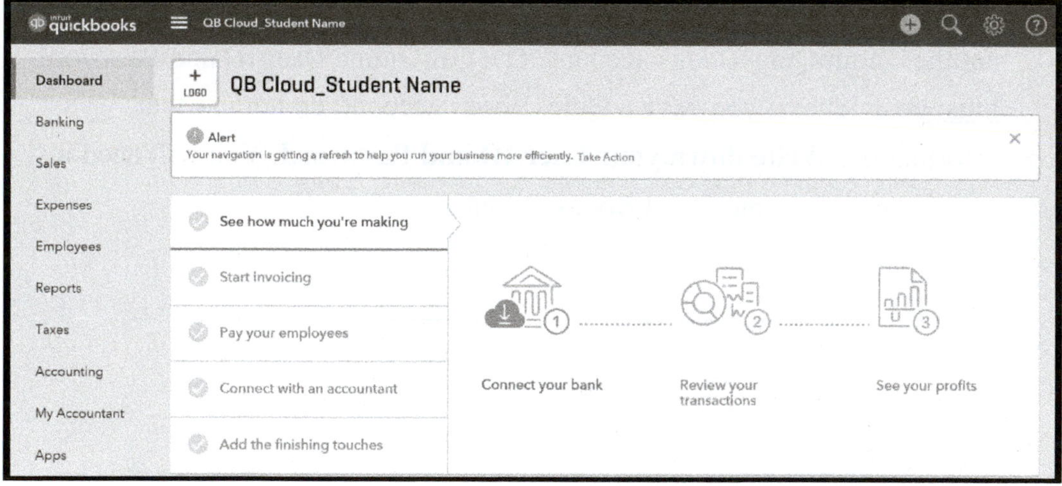

7. Your QBO access is for 12 months. There is NO CHARGE during this time.

   You can check your subscription by clicking ⚙ > Account and Settings > Billing & Subscription. Observe that a Company ID is shown, along with your Subscription status, and when your subscription ends. (*Hint:* At the top of your screen, there may be a green bar showing your subscription status. Continue with step 8.)

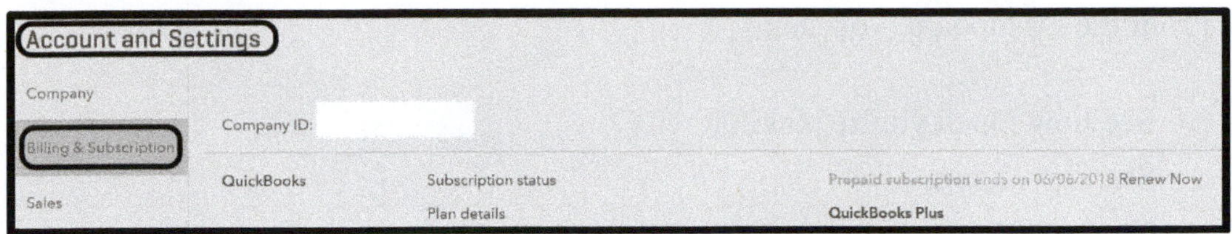

8. To close the Account and Settings page, click X on its title bar. You are returned to the Dashboard. (If not, click Dashboard.)

> **fyi** Some of the screens that follow may differ from what you see. Each time you sign in to QBO, the most recently updated version of the software will display. Regularly check www.mhhe.com/qbo2e > Text Updates.

DASHBOARD OR HOME PAGE

The Dashboard, also called the Home page, shows Profit and Loss, how much was spent, and the income and sales summary. As you add transactions, the dashboard changes.

From the Dashboard, you can:

- See how much you're making.
- Start invoicing.
- Connect with an accountant.
- Add the finishing touches.

When you are ready to go beyond the basics, you can:

- Configure settings or preferences.
- Search for transactions.

Based on user access rights, QuickBooks Online controls the information it displays. This chapter includes a section about Company Administrator access.

Navigation Bar

The Navigation bar is on the left side. This is where you access different pages. As of this writing, the selections are Dashboard, Banking, Sales, Expenses, Employees, Reports, Taxes, Accounting, and Apps. The Dashboard is the default. When a Navigation bar selection is made, a vertical green bar appears next to the selection.

When QuickBooks Online updates, sometimes the Navigation bar changes. Go to www.mhhe.com/qbo2e > Text Updates regularly. Another way to learn about updates is the QuickBooks blog at http://quickbooks.intuit.com/blog/ > What's New in QBO.

Comment: If a message appears on your screen, for example "Alert. Your navigation is getting a refresh to help you run your business more efficiently." Link to Take Action and read the message.

Create Menu

The plus sign (+) allows you to add various types of transactions. The Create menu is organized by module: Customers, Vendors, Employees, Other. You have the option to Show less or Show more.

Create

Customers	Vendors	Employees	Other
Invoice	Expense	Payroll	Bank Deposit
Receive Payment	Check	Single Time Activity	Transfer
Estimate	Bill	Weekly Timesheet	Journal Entry
Credit Memo	Pay Bills		Statement
Sales Receipt	Purchase Order		Inventory Qty Adjustment
Refund Receipt	Vendor Credit		
Delayed Credit	Credit Card Credit		
Delayed Charge	Print Checks		

▸ Show less

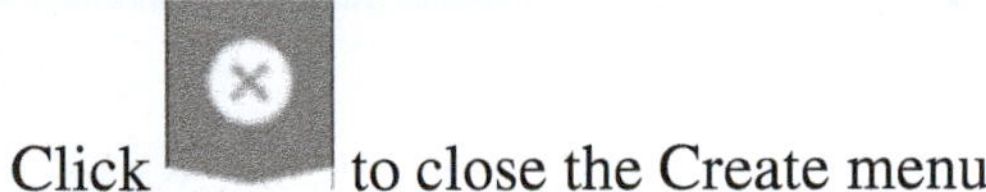

Click to close the Create menu.

Search

The magnifying-glass icon is next to the plus sign. You can Search Transactions or go to Recent Transactions.

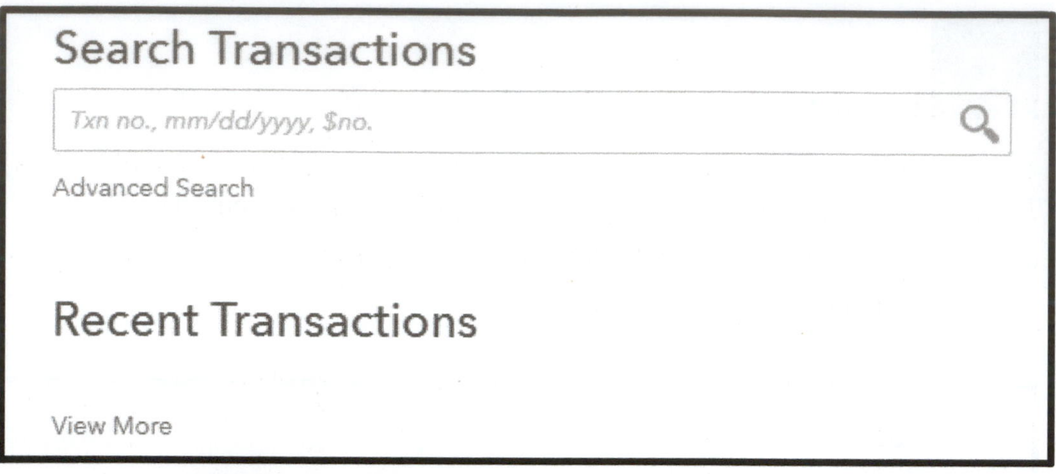

To close, click .

Settings Menu

The gear icon accesses the Settings menu. You can access Your Company, Lists, and Tools. The last column includes your name, User Profile, Feedback, Refer a Friend, Privacy, and Sign Out.

QB Cloud_Student Name

Your Company	Lists	Tools	Carol Yacht
Account and Settings	All Lists	Import Data	User Profile
Manage Users	Products and Services	Import Desktop Data	Feedback
Custom Form Styles	Recurring Transactions	Export Data	Refer a Friend
Chart of Accounts	Attachments	Reconcile	Privacy
QuickBooks Labs		Budgeting	
		Audit Log	Sign Out
		Order Checks	

Help

The question mark is used for self-help. If you have a question about QBO, type keyword(s) into the search field. (*Hint:* Your Help page may differ.)

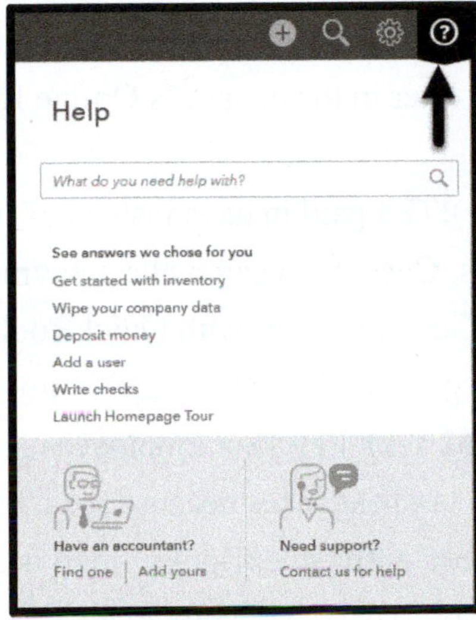

QBO ***updates*** interface elements, and may add accounting features and user functions. Intuit tests changes on specific companies or groups of users so they can collect feedback. If users like the update, it is changed. Be flexible and ready for changes. If you have an issue, use QBO's self-help 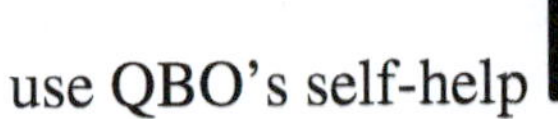.

> Easily assign or edit account numbers and names. This replaces "Assign Account Numbers" from the previous version.

VIDEOS: EXPLORE THE POWER OF QUICKBOOKS

If Help information includes a link to Videos: Explore the power of QuickBooks, click on it. If you do not have the Videos link on the Help page, the YouTube websites are shown on the next page. You can also link to QBO videos at https://community.intuit.com/quickbooks-online > link to videos within the

Browse Topics areas. Chapter videos are also included at www.mhhe.com/qbo2e > Student Edition > Videos.

- Stay organized with QuickBooks (60 sec): Watch how to track invoices, keep an eye on expenses, and stay up to date and organized. Stay organized with QuickBooks is at https://www.youtube.com/watch?v=bSea0itap-Q. This video is included later in the chapter's Online Learning Center. Watch now or later.
- Get paid faster (52 sec): Get paid in days instead of months with QuickBooks Payments. Customers can make a payment as soon as they receive your invoice. Get paid faster with QuickBooks video is at https://www.youtube.com/watch?v=49oEZNNv-uo.
- Pay your employees (62 sec): Pay your employees in under 5 minutes with easy payroll setup. No tax headaches because we handle e-file and e-pay for you. Pay your employees with QuickBooks video is at https://www.youtube.com/watch?v=bRJpGtHexYc.

ACCOUNT AND SETTINGS

One of the first things you want to do is complete Account and Settings. Each setting configures QuickBooks to work the way you want. As you work through the chapters, settings are selected or edited.

1. Click  > Account and Settings.

When Account and Settings are changed, the selections add accounts to the Chart of Accounts or Account List. Settings also impact the user interface. For example, making product and services changes (step 4), also changes fields that are available on QBO transaction pages (bills, sales receipts, invoices, etc.).

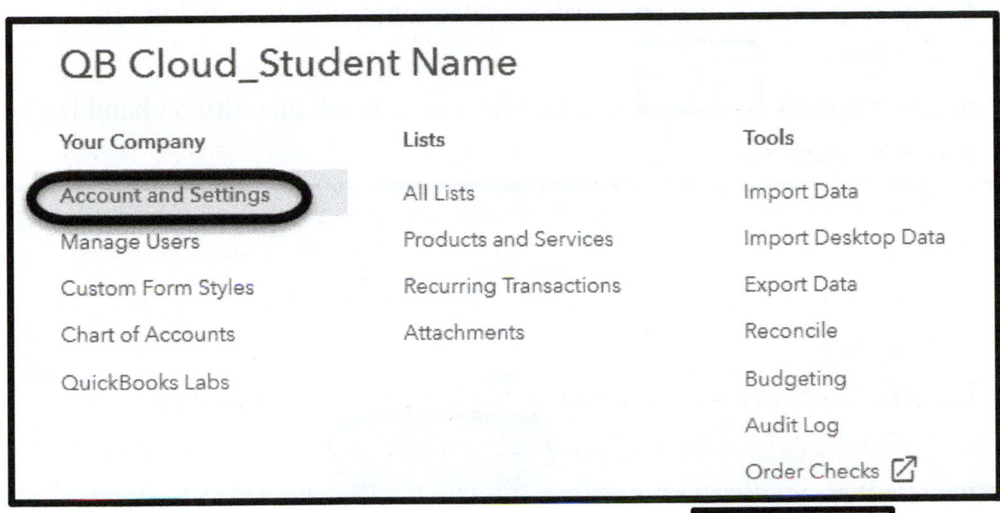

2. The Account and Settings page appears. Company is the default. To make changes, click on the pencil icon.

   Company Name: QB Cloud_Student Name. Your first and last name should appear after QB Cloud. If *not*, click to edit the Company name. Review the information within each section. When necessary, edit.

   Troubleshooting: If you do not have a Company selection, continue with step 3.

3. Click . In the Sales form content area, click to edit. Click on the box next to Custom transaction numbers to turn them on . Make sure the Custom transaction numbers shows On. Click .

4. Compare your Products and services selections to the ones below. If necessary, click [pencil icon] to edit. Make sure Track quantity on hand is checked. Then, save.

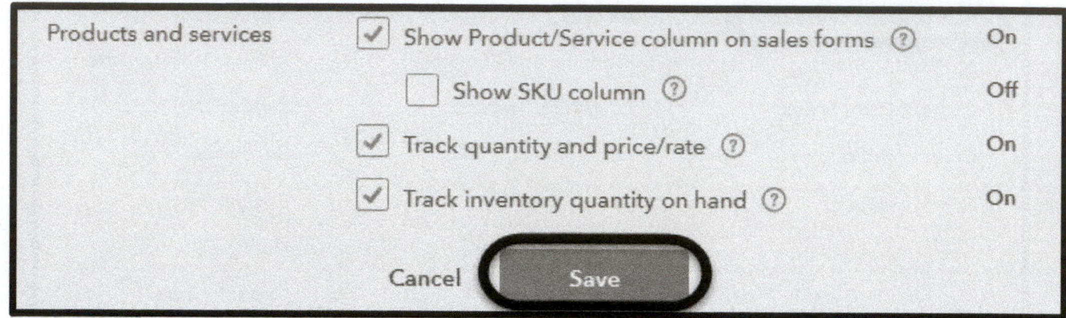

Read the information that explains "Turning on Track inventory quantity on hand will also turn on Show items table on expense and purchase forms." In order to track inventory, click <OK>.

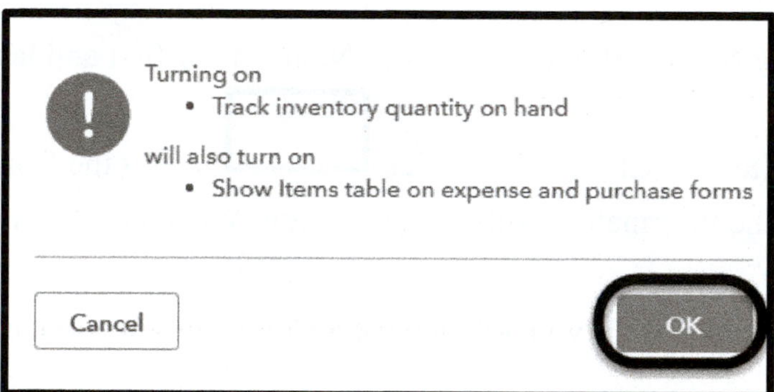

5. Compare your Sales, Account and Settings page to the one shown on the next page. Make the necessary changes. For example, in the Sales form content area, the Preferred delivery method is Print later and Shipping is checked.

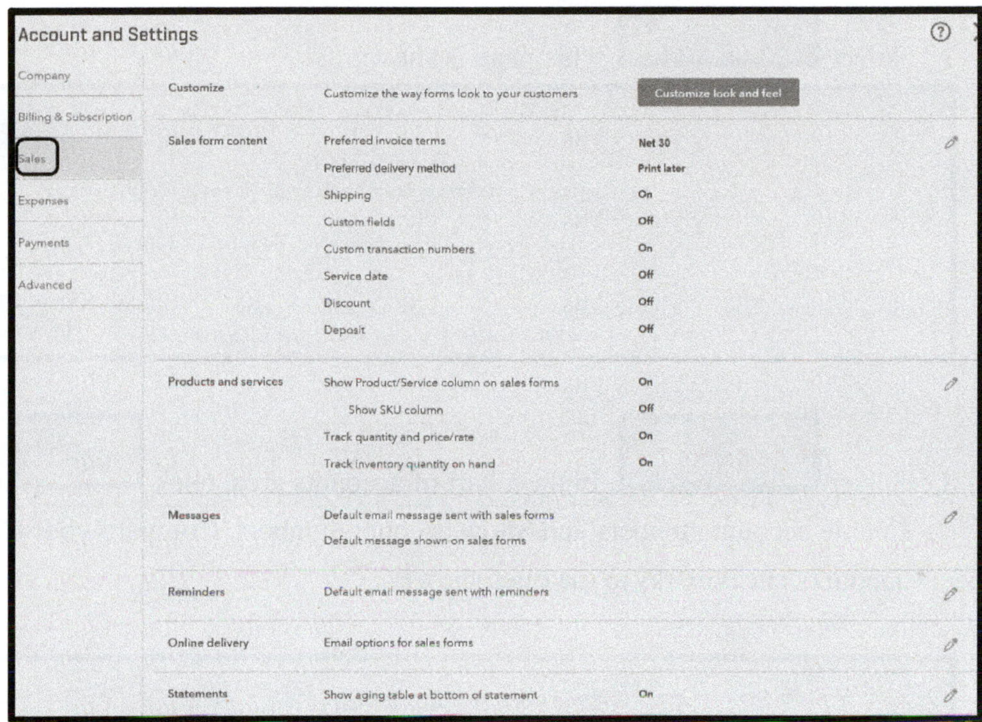

6. Select Expenses. Make sure the Show Items table on expense and purchase forms is On. Purchase Orders should say on. If needed, edit and save.

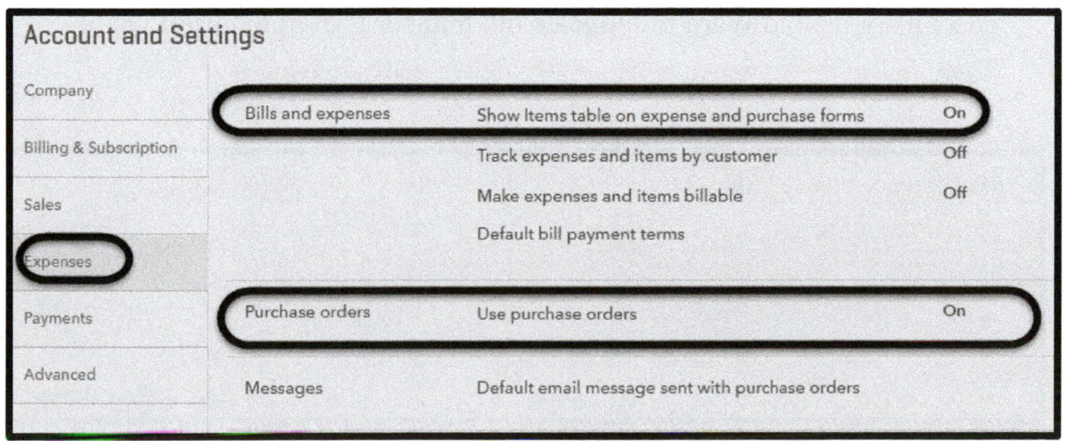

7. Select Payments. This page is shown.

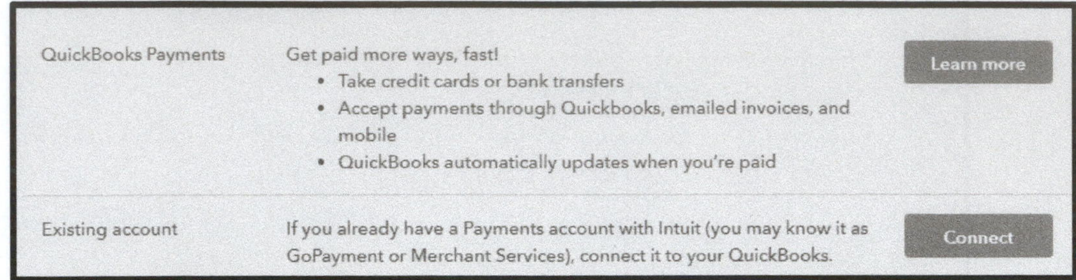

8. Select Advanced. In the Chart of accounts area, click [edit] to Enable account numbers and Show account numbers. Compare your Chart of accounts checkmarks to the ones shown.

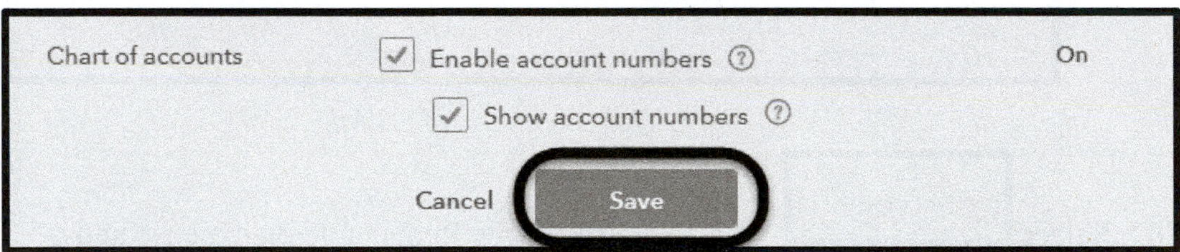

9. On the Advanced page, in the Other preferences area, click [edit]. Put a checkmark next to Warn if duplicate bill number is used to turn it On > Save.

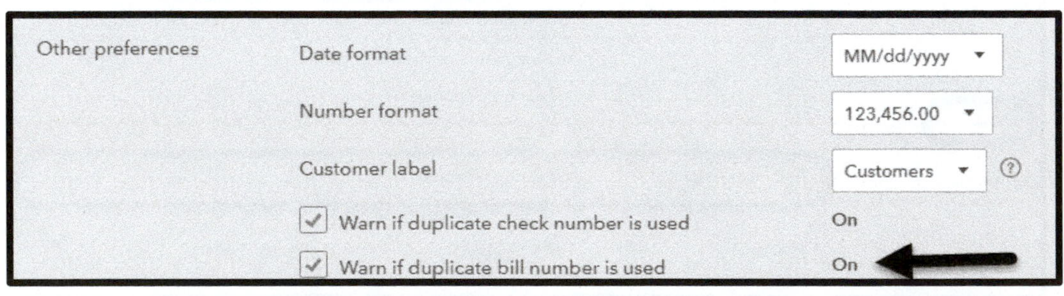

10. After clicking <Save>, compare your Advanced settings with the ones shown below. Edit when necessary, then <Save>.

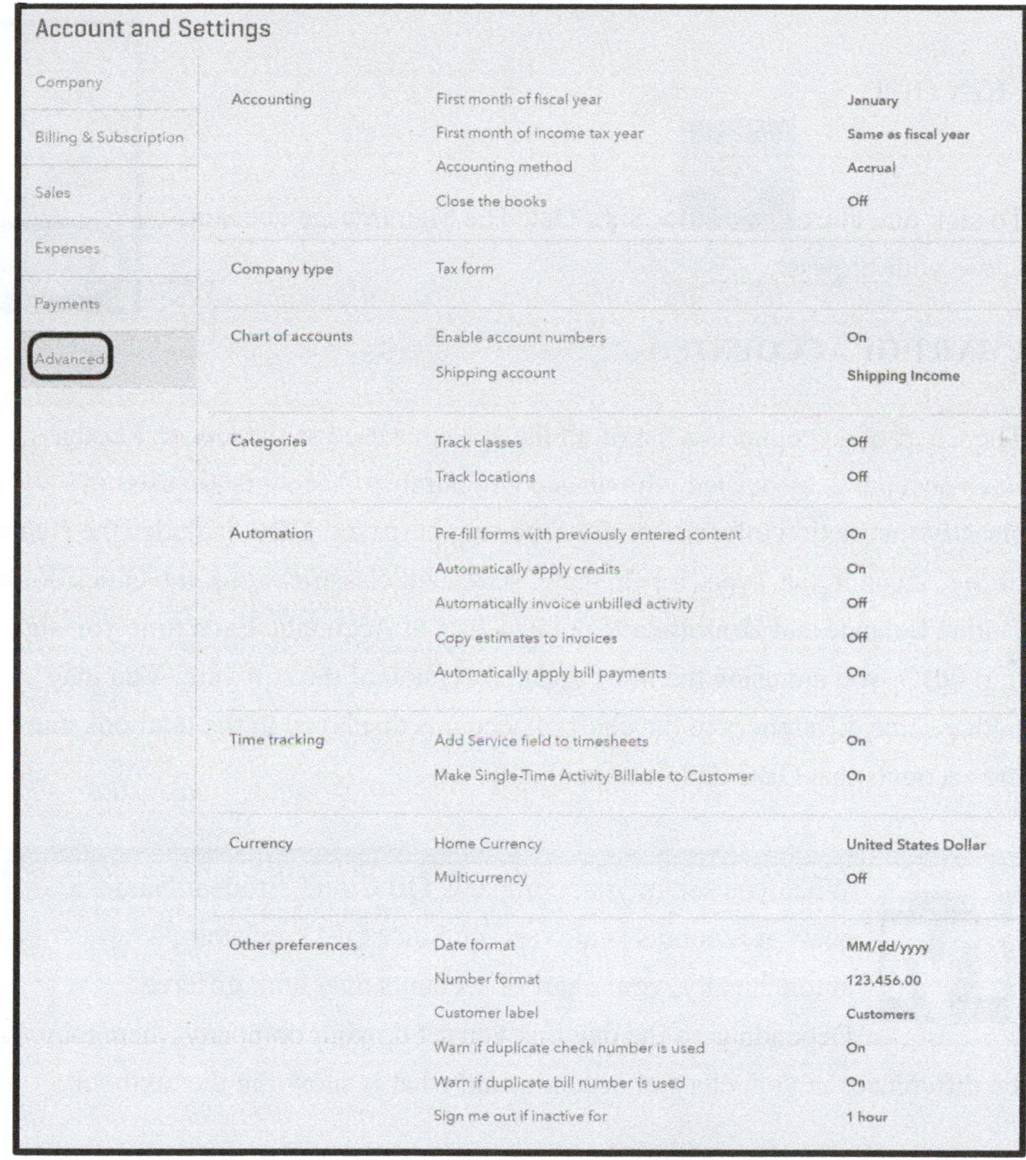

11. Make sure that fields that are turned <On> agree with your settings. If needed, edit section(s). When finished, click Done.

The Account and Settings pages include QBO preferences. To accommodate accounts payable, inventory, and accounts payable tasks, settings will be checked, and sometimes changed, in subsequent chapters.

SIGN OUT

To sign out, click > Sign Out. The Sign in page appears. Close your browser.

CHART OF ACCOUNTS

The Chart of Accounts is a list of all the accounts used in the General Ledger. Each account is associated with an account number. Accounts are used to classify transaction information for reporting purposes. QBO includes the Name of the Account, the Type (for financial statement classification), the QuickBooks Online Balance and Bank Balance in its Chart of Accounts. Each time you sign into QBO, you are using the most updated version of the software. You may notice some differences in the chart of accounts displayed in the textbook and the accounts that QBO adds automatically.

> fyi When you set up your company, QB Cloud_Student Name, a chart of accounts is also set up. Since QBO updates automatically, your chart of accounts may look different. Depending on the day that you set up your company, there may be differences in your chart of accounts and what is shown in the textbook.
>
> *Using internet-delivered software, requires flexibility.*

Sign In

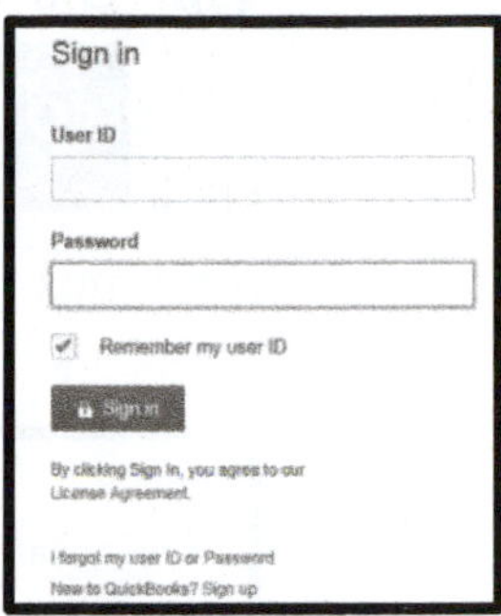

1. Start your browser. Go online to http://qbo.intuit.com. Type your User ID and Password.
2. After typing your User ID and Password, click on the box next to Remember my User ID > Sign In. The Dashboard appears.

If a page appears, like the one shown below, read the information.

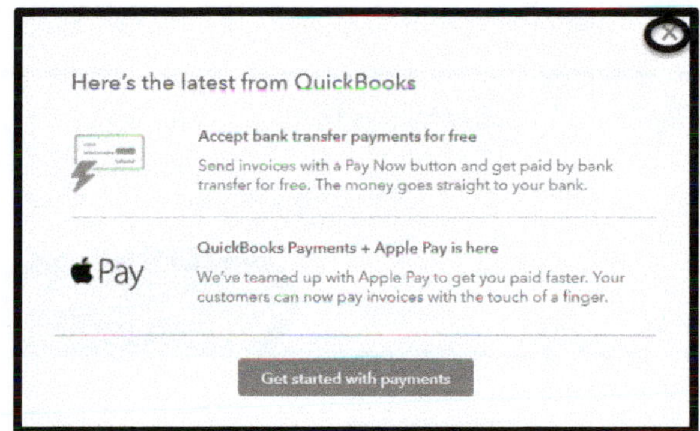

Click ✕ within the dialog box to close it. *Remember, QBO updates automatically. Some screen messages may differ from what is shown in the textbook.*

Add Accounts

QBO automatically sets up a chart of accounts. Steps 1 through 5 show you how to add two new accounts: 101 Checking, 105 Accounts Receivable.

1. Select ⚙ > Chart of Accounts. A Take a peek under the hood message appears > click See your Chart of Accounts. The first column shows NUMBER. If not, read the tip.

Tip: Did you set up the preference for enabling account numbers? To check click [gear icon] > Account and Settings > Advanced. The Chart of accounts field <u>must</u> show On.

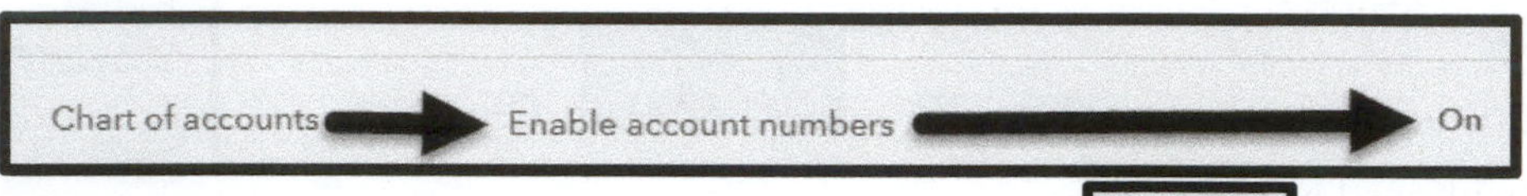

To make sure accounts numbers are enabled, click [pencil icon]. Put a checkmark next to Enable account numbers *and* Show account numbers

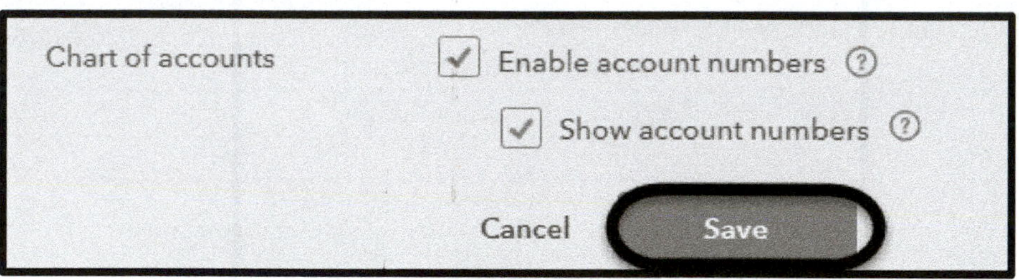

Click [Save] > [Done]. You are returned to the Chart of Accounts page. The first column shows NUMBER.

2. On the Chart of Accounts page, click [New] to add the Bank account. Complete these fields.

Category Type:	Select Bank
Detail Type:	Select Checking
Name:	Checking automatically completes
Number:	Type **101**
Description:	Leave blank
as of:	Defaults to today's date

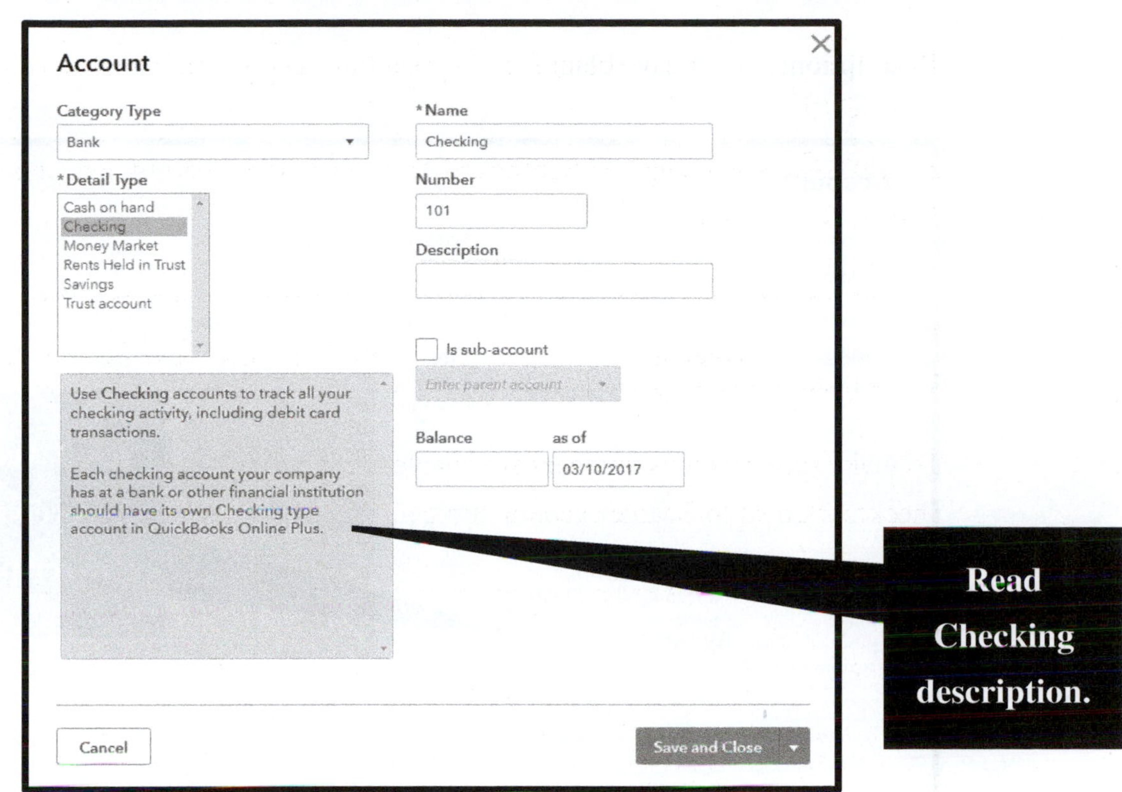

3. Compare the Bank account information to the one shown above > 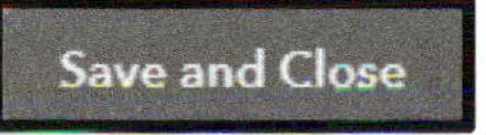

. 101 is added to the Number field.

NUMBER	NAME	TYPE ▲	DETAIL TYPE
101	101 Checking	Bank	Checking

4. To add an Accounts Receivable account, click **New**. Complete these fields:

Category Type:	Accounts receivable (A/R) completed
Detail Type:	Accounts Receivable (A/R) completed
Name:	Accounts Receivable (A/R) completed
Number:	Type **105**

Description: Leave blank

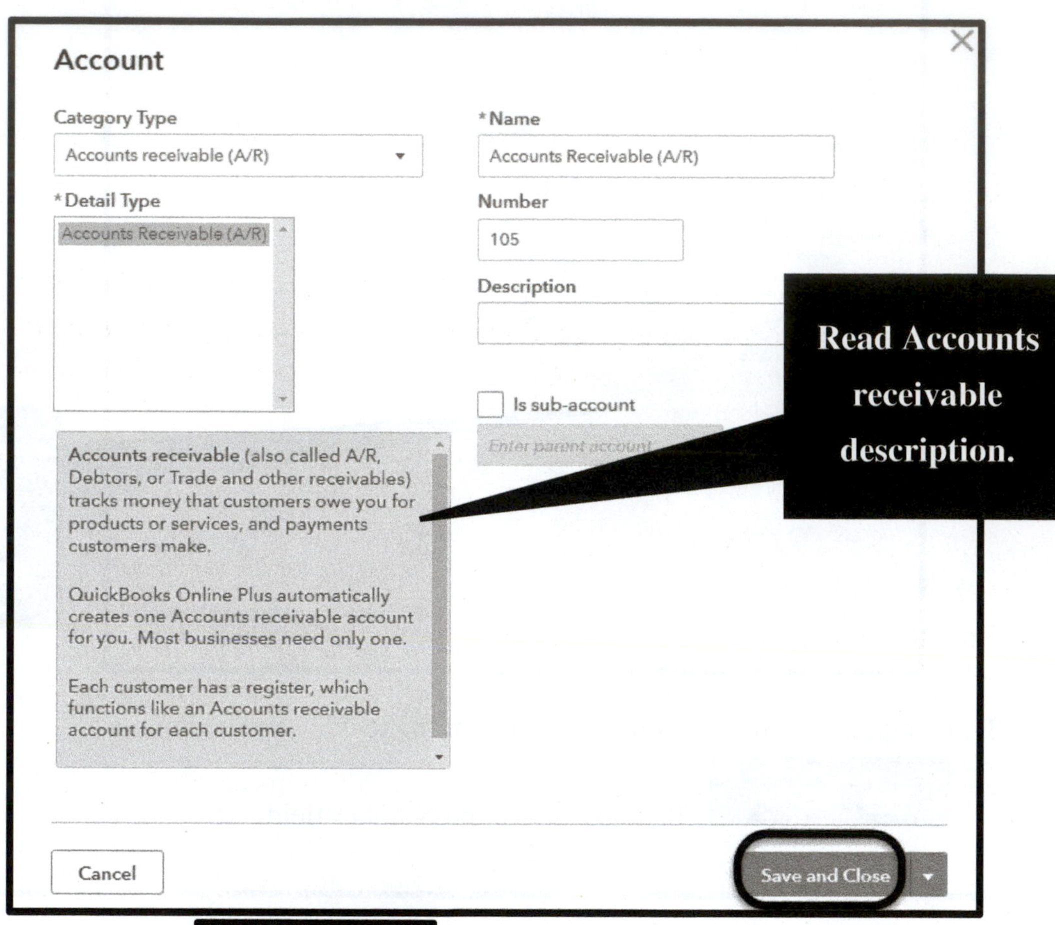

5. After clicking **Save and Close**, you are returned to the Chart of Accounts page.

NUMBER	NAME	TYPE ▲	DETAIL TYPE
101	101 Checking	Bank	Checking
105	105 Accounts Receivable (A/R)	Accounts receivable (A/R)	Accounts Receivable (A/R)

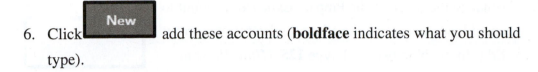

6. Click New add these accounts (**boldface** indicates what you should type).

Comment: You may notice some differences in account names. QBO updates accounts automatically. In some cases, you may need to add only the account number. As of this writing, it was necessary to add the account names that are boldfaced. *Make sure the Detail Type is correct for each account. The Detail Type assigns the account into a subcategory in order to have it appear on the financial statements according to Generally Accepted Accounting Principles (GAAP).*

Category Type	*Detail Type*	Name	Number
Other current assets	Inventory	**Merchandise Inventory**	**115**
To add the next account, select <Save and New>.			
Fixed Assets	Machinery & Equipment	**Computer Equipment**	**135**
Fixed Assets	Accumulated Depreciation	**Accumulated Depreciation**	**137**
Accounts Payable	Accounts Payable (A/P)	**Accounts Payable (A/P)**	**201**
Equity	Common Stock	**Common Stock**	**301**
Expenses	Office/General Administrative	**Depreciation Expense**	**607**
Expenses	Office/General Administrative	**Telephone Expense**	**633**

Edit Accounts

Prepaid Expenses is used as an editing example. If your chart of accounts does not include Account 125 Prepaid Insurance, click <New> to add it.

7. To change the name of the Prepaid Expenses account to Prepaid Insurance, click the View Register down-arrow > Edit. In the Number field, type **125**. (*Hint:* Prepaid Expenses is shown in the Detail Type field. The as of field shows today's date.)

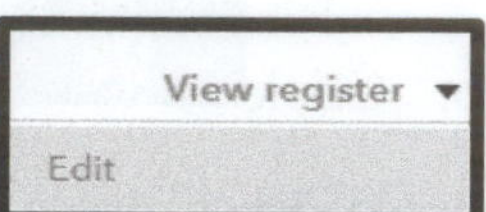

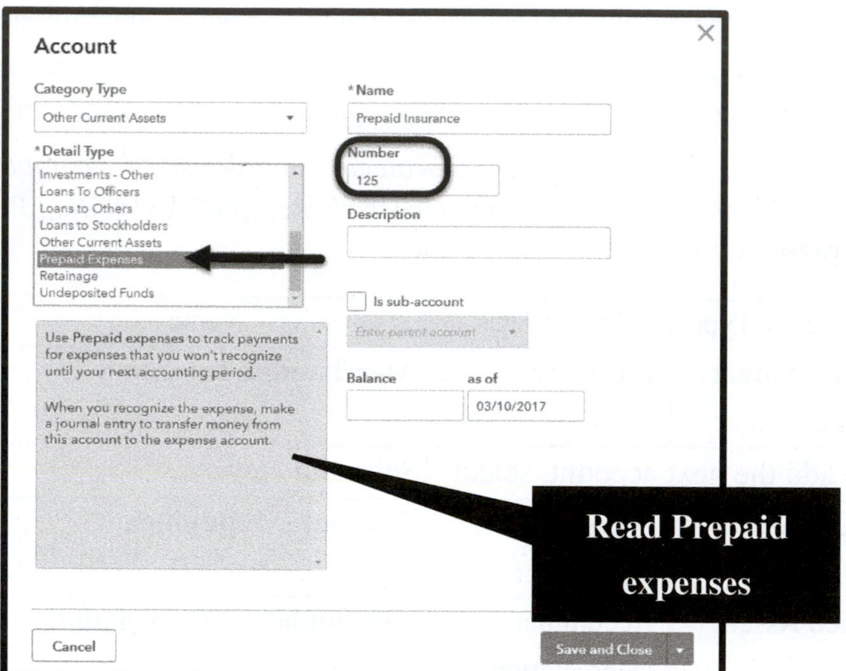

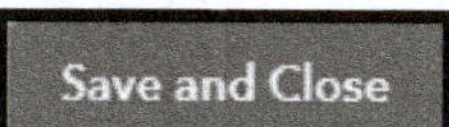

8. On the Supplies & Material – COGS row, select Run report down-arrow > Edit. Type **Cost of Goods Sold** in the Name field, type **501** as the account number.

   Save and Close.

9. On the Office Supplies & Software row, select the Run Report down-arrow > Edit. Type **Office Supplies** in the Name field, type **621** in the Number field. (The Detial Type is already selected – Office/General Administrative Expenses > Save and Close.

Comment: What is the difference between View register and Run report? View register are Balance Sheet accounts (bank, current and fixed assets, liabilities and equity, *except* Retained Earnings). Run report accounts are on the Profit and Loss statement (income, cost of goods sold, and expenses). Registers display transactions in a traditional ledger format.

Batch Edit

The Chart of Accounts page includes batch edit. This means that a bunch of account numbers can be added. Scroll over the pencil icon and Batch edit is shown.

Use Batch Edit to add an account number and, if needed, change the account name for these accounts. In Batch Edit, accounts are in alphabetic order.

305 Opening Balance Equity
318 Retained Earnings
401 Sales
601 Advertising & Marketing, *change to* **Advertising**
603 Bank Charges & Fees, *change to* **Bank Charges**
611 Insurance
613 Interest Paid, *change to* **Interest Expense**
615 Job Supplies, *change to* **Job Materials**
617 Legal & Professional Services, *change to* Legal & Professional Fees
619 Meals & Entertainment, *change to* Meals and Entertainment
621 Office Supplies & Software, *change to* **Office Supplies**
623 Rent & Lease, *change to* **Rent or Lease**
625 Repairs & Maintenance, *change to* **Repair & Maintenance**
635 Utilities

When finished, click <Save>.

The table below and on the next page, shows the Chart of Accounts category types, detail types, names, and numbers. The detail type is important. Once the detail type is selected, it places the account in the correct place on financial statements. The first two accounts are italicized because they were already added. To add accounts, click <New>. To resort in number order, click NUMBER.

Category Type	Detail Type	Name	Number
Bank	*Checking*	*Checking*	*101*
Accounts receivable (A/R)	*Accounts Receivable (A/R)*	*Accounts Receivable (A/R)*	*105*
Other Current Assets	Inventory	Merchandise Inventory	115
Other Current Assets	Prepaid Expenses	Prepaid Insurance	125
Other Current Assets	Undeposited Funds	Undeposited Funds	130
Fixed Assets	Machinery & Equipment	Computer Equipment	135
Fixed Assets	Accumulated Depreciation	Accumulated Depreciation	137
Accounts payable (A/P)	Accounts Payable (A/P)	Accounts Payable (A/P)	201
Equity	Common Stock	Common Stock	301
Cost of Goods Sold	Supplies & Material - COGS	Cost of Goods Sold	501

Category Type	Detail Type	Name	Number
Cost of Goods Sold	Shipping, Freight & Delivery - COS	Freight & delivery – COS	503
Expenses	Dues & subscriptions	Dues & Subscriptions	605
Expenses	Office/General Administrative Expenses	Depreciation Expense	607
Expenses	Shipping, Freight & Delivery	Freight & Delivery	609
Expenses	Shipping, Freight & Delivery	Shipping and delivery expense	627
Expenses	Office/General Administrative Expenses	Stationery & Printing	629
Expenses	Supplies & Materials	Supplies	631
Expenses	Office/General Administrative	Telephone Expense	633

When you set up QB Cloud_Student Name, a default chart of accounts was also set up. Some of QBO's default accounts do not have account numbers. Accounts are added automatically. You may also notice accounts with similar account names. This is okay.

To make sure you have the accounts used in the textbook, make sure your accounts agree with the table shown on pages 76-77 *and* with the Account List shown on pages 80-81. The FYI box on page 68 explains more.

Double-check that these accounts are included: 115 Merchandise Inventory (Detail Type, Inventory), 401 Sales (Detail Type, Sales of Product Income), 501 Cost of Goods Sold (Detail Type, Supplies & Materials – COGS). In Chapter 4, when inventory is added these accounts are used. Compare your chart of accounts to the Account List shown on pages 80-81. The Type and Detail Type columns are important. They classify your accounts for the financial statements.

Troubleshooting: What if the Detail Type is incorrect? For example, what if 115 Merchandise Inventory does not show it's Detail Type as Inventory. Do this: On the 115 Merchandise Inventory row, click View Register > Edit. Make sure the Detail Type shows Inventory. The Detail Type, Inventory, tracks quantity, sales revenue and cost of goods sold for inventory items.

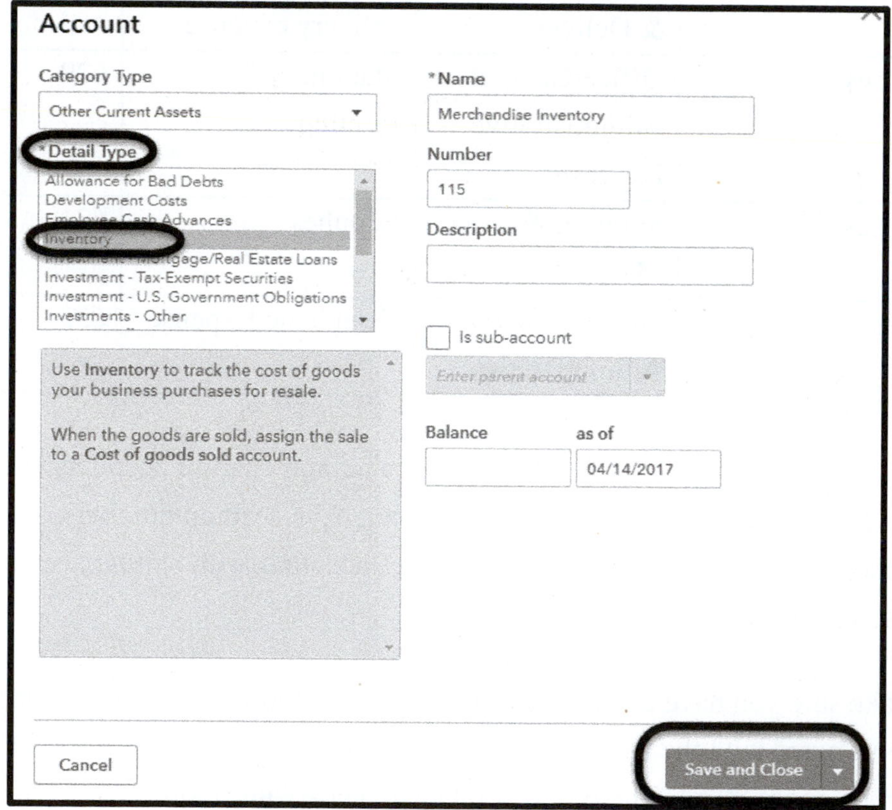

SAVE THE ACCOUNT LIST (Chart of Accounts) AS A PDF FILE

To save your Chart of Accounts as a PDF file, follow these steps. (*Hint:* If needed, download the free Adobe Reader at https://get.adobe.com/reader.)

1. Click [gear icon] > Chart of Accounts > Run Report. The Account List appears. A message may appear that explains how to customize reports instantly. Read the information. Click <X> on the message to close.
2. Click on the Export icon > select Export to PDF.

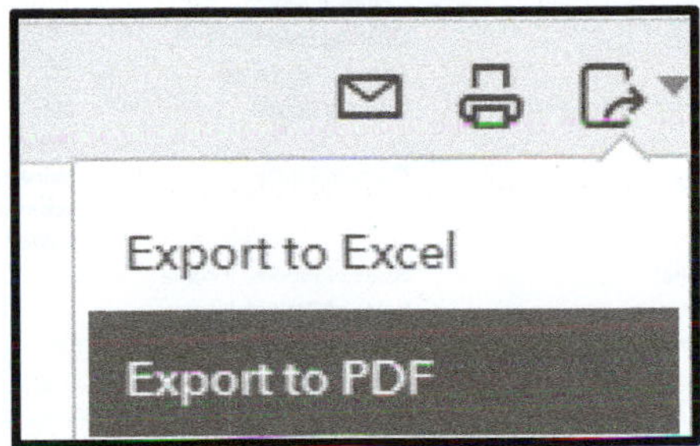

Compare your Account List with the one shown on the next two pages.

Page 1 of 2

QB Cloud_Student Name

ACCOUNT LIST

ACCOUNT #	ACCOUNT	TYPE	DETAIL TYPE	DESCRIPTION	BALANCE
101	Checking	Bank	Checking		0.00
105	Accounts Receivable (A/R)	Accounts receivable (A/R)	Accounts Receivable (A/R)		0.00
115	Merchandise Inventory	Other Current Assets	Inventory		0.00
125	Prepaid Insurance	Other Current Assets	Prepaid Expenses		0.00
130	Undeposited Funds	Other Current Assets	Undeposited Funds		0.00
	Uncategorized Asset	Other Current Assets	Other Current Assets		0.00
135	Computer Equipment	Fixed Assets	Machinery & Equipment		0.00
137	Accumulated Depreciation	Fixed Assets	Accumulated Depreciation		0.00
201	Accounts Payable (A/P)	Accounts payable (A/P)	Accounts Payable (A/P)		0.00
301	Common Stock	Equity	Common Stock		0.00
305	Opening Balance Equity	Equity	Opening Balance Equity		0.00
318	Retained Earnings	Equity	Retained Earnings		0.00
	Owner's Investment	Equity	Owner's Equity	Money you invested in your business	0.00
	Owner's Pay & Personal Expenses	Equity	Owner's Equity	Money you took out of your business to pay yourself (not payroll expenses)	0.00
401	Sales	Income	Sales of Product Income		
	Billable Expense Income	Income	Sales of Product Income		
	Shipping Income	Income	Sales of Product Income		
	Uncategorized Income	Income	Sales of Product Income		
501	Cost of Goods Sold	Cost of Goods Sold	Supplies & Materials - COGS		
503	Freight & delivery - COS	Cost of Goods Sold	Shipping, Freight & Delivery - COS		
601	Advertising	Expenses	Advertising/Promotional	Ads, business cards, and other marketing costs	
603	Bank Charges	Expenses	Bank Charges	Fees or charges from your bank or credit card	
605	Dues & Subscriptions	Expenses	Dues & subscriptions		
607	Depreciation Expense	Expenses	Office/General Administrative Expenses		
609	Freight & Delivery	Expenses	Shipping, Freight & Delivery		
611	Insurance	Expenses	Insurance	Liability, fire, theft, and other insurance for your business (not health)	
613	Interest Expense	Expenses	Interest Paid	Interest paid on loans, credit cards, and business vehicles	
615	Job Materials	Expenses	Supplies & Materials	Supplies you bought to complete a job (not products you sell to customers)	
617	Legal & Professional Fees	Expenses	Legal & Professional Fees	Professional services including legal, financial, accounting, and payroll	
619	Meals and Entertainment	Expenses	Entertainment Meals	Client meals and entertainment and travel meals (business-related only)	
621	Office Supplies	Expenses	Office/General Administrative Expenses	Office, kitchen, and bathroom supplies, including software under $2,500	
623	Rent or Lease	Expenses	Rent or Lease of Buildings	Office space, storage, vehicle, machinery, and equipment rentals and leases (short or	

QBO adds the descriptions automatically.

Troubleshooting: You may notice some difference on your Account List. Match the Account #, Account name, Type, and Detail Type with your Account List. Accounts *without* account numbers may be different. This is okay.

Page 2 of 2

ACCOUNT #	ACCOUNT	TYPE	DETAIL TYPE	DESCRIPTION	BALANCE
				long-term)	
625	Repair & Maintenance	Expenses	Repair & Maintenance	Repairs, maintenance, and cleaning for office space and equipment	
627	Shipping and delivery expense	Expenses	Shipping, Freight & Delivery		
629	Stationery & Printing	Expenses	Office/General Administrative Expenses		
631	Supplies	Expenses	Supplies & Materials		
633	Telephone Expense	Expenses	Office/General Administrative Expenses		
635	Utilities	Expenses	Utilities	Phone, gas, electric, water, internet, and other utilities for your business	
	Ask My Accountant	Expenses	Utilities	Flagged to review with your accountant.	
	Car & Truck	Expenses	Auto	Gas, repairs, insurance, and other costs for your business-only vehicle (not loan payments)	
	Contractors	Expenses	Payroll Expenses	Services provided by 1099 contractors, such as landscapers, electricians, and web designers	
	Other Business Expenses	Expenses	Office/General Administrative Expenses	Other expenses for your business, including training and conferences	
	Reimbursable Expenses	Expenses	Supplies & Materials	Purchases you made for a customer that they will reimburse	
	Taxes & Licenses	Expenses	Taxes Paid	Property and business taxes, licenses, memberships, and permits (not sales tax)	
	Travel	Expenses	Travel	Business travel including transportation, hotels, and tips (not meals)	
	Uncategorized Expense	Expenses	Other Miscellaneous Service Cost		

3. The Print, email, or save as PDF page appears. Select Save as PDF. On the taskbar, double-click AccountList.pdf.

4. Click on the download icon (right side of AccountList.pdf title bar). Go to the location where you want to save. Use the file name **Chapter 2_Chart of Accounts**.

5. On QBO title bar, click <x> on the AccountList.pdf tab
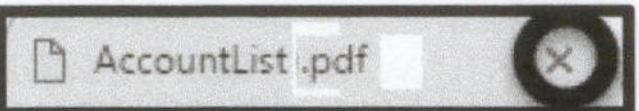

.

6. On the Print, email, or save as PDF page, click <X>.

Print, email, or save as PDF

7. You are returned to the Account List.

Comment: There are three ways to display the chart of accounts: 1) Gear > Chart of Accounts > Run Report; 2) Navigation bar > Accounting > Run Report; (3) Navigation Bar > Reports > in the search field, type **Account List**.

EXPORT THE ACCOUNT LIST TO EXCEL

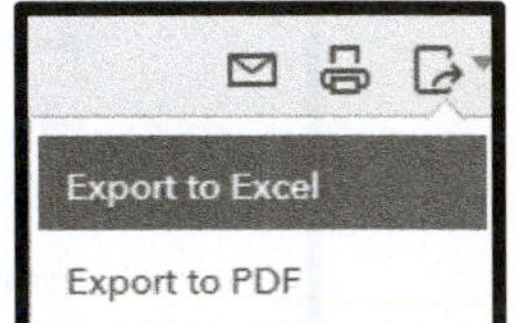

1. The Account List should be displayed. On the export icon, select Export to Excel.
2. On the taskbar, double-click QB Cloud_Student…xlsx. Excel starts. Click Enable Editing. (*Hint:* The Author used Excel 2013 and 2016. Depending on your Excel version, steps may differ.)
3. File > Save As. Go to the location to save the file. Save as **Chapter 2_Chart of Accounts**. When through, exit Excel.

COMPANY ADMINISTRATOR

A ***Company Administrator*** has access rights within QuickBooks Online. There are three ways to provide your professor with access to your company. Ask your professor for his or her preference.

1. Invite Accountant

    - The student signs in to their QBO account.
    - Click Gear > Manage Users.

- On the Manage Users page in the Accounts section, click Invite Accountant. (*Or,* from the Dashboard, select Connect with an accountant > Accountant's email > Invite.)
- Enter the professor's email address and name. Your professor will be sent an email that contains a link for signing in to your company.
- Your professor will be asked to create a User ID before signing in the first time. Until your professor signs in, their status on the Manage Users page is "Invited." After accepting the invitation, their status changes to "Active." (*Hint:* Once the professor clicks the link, they should create an entirely new user ID that will be associated with their email address for the purpose of accessing student accounts. This helps keep things organized while attached to the professor's email address.)
- Click <Next> and <Finish>.

2. Email the professor your User ID and Password. If using this step, the professor should set up a time with their student to receive the emailed ***Confirmation code***. To sign in using a different computer or browser, *or* to sign in to student accounts with their User ID and password, ***multi-factor authentication*** is required. (Refer to the Appendix B, for the glossary's definition of multi-factor authentication for more information.)

   - The Professor, using their student's User ID and Password, signs in at https://qbo.intuit.com. A Let's make sure it's you message appears.
   - Click <Continue> to send an email to your student's email account. **Do <u>not</u> close your browser.**

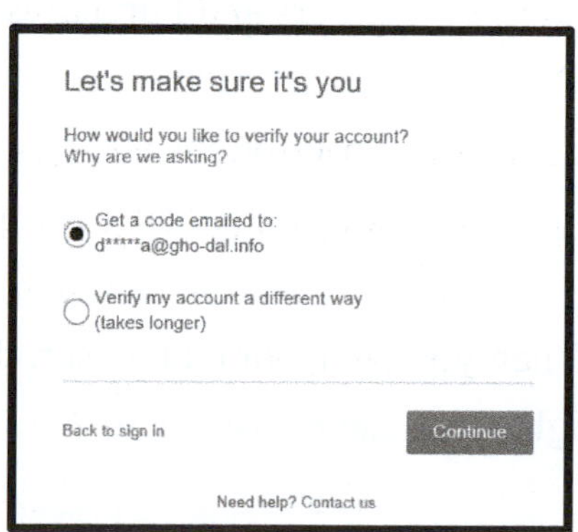

Let's make sure it's you
How would you like to verify your account?
Why are we asking?
Get a code emailed to:
d*****a@gho-dal.info
Verify my account a different way
(takes longer)
Back to sign in
Continue
Need help? Contact us

- ➢ The student receives an email from Intuit with a Confirmation code, then forwards that email to their professor.
- ➢ The professor types the 6-digit code, then clicks <Continue>. (*Hint:* If different computers or browsers are used to sign in, another code is emailed for account access. Each sign-in is authenticated via the computer's ***IP address***.)

3. Company Administrator

- The student signs in to their QBO account.
- Click Gear > Manage Users.
- On the Manage Users page, click New.
- Select Company administrator as the user type.
- Click <Next>.
- Enter the professor's email address and name.
- Click <Next>.
- Click <Finish>.

User Roles and Access Rights

You can limit users' access to different parts of QBO, such as Customers and Sales, or Vendors and Purchases. You can also limit a user's ability to perform administrative functions such as adding users, changing company information, managing subscriptions and billing. If you are a Company Administrator, or if you have management access rights, access changes can be made.

When you create or edit a user, the following list shows the types of access rights that can be assigned.

Company Administrator	Access to all features and capabilities of QBO.
Regular or custom user	Ordinary user. May have access to all QBO features, *or* you can limit access to Customers and Sales, and Vendors and Purchases. You may also choose to give this user some administration capabilities.
Master Administrator	All access rights of a company administrator. You cannot delete or change the access rights for the Master Administrators. There is only one Master Administrator. Initially, it's the user who created the company. To edit or delete the user with Master Administrator rights, you must first transfer the Master Administrator to another user.
Time Tracking Online	Access to timesheets-and-time reports only version of QBO. Time-tracking-only users do not count toward the current user limit.
Reports Only	Access to a reports-only version of QBO. Reports-only users can access all reports, except payroll reports and those listing the contact information of employees, customers, or vendors. Reports-only users do not count toward the current user limit.

Accountant User

You can also identify one user as your accountant. You can have one user identified as your accountant, but you can invite another accountant to access your company. To do this, under Accounting Firms, click Invite Accountant. This user doesn't count toward your user limit.

AUDIT LOG

The ***Audit Log*** contains a list of all the changes that have ever been made to your company data and by whom. By default, the Audit Log displays the 200 most recent events. Dates and times in the Audit Log and Audit History reflect when events occurred, displayed in your local time.

Many accountants use the audit log to review client activity. A business owner may want to check the audit log on a regular basis as part of the company's ***internal controls*** and fraud prevention procedures.

The steps for opening the Audit Log are shown next.

1. Click Gear > Audit Log. (*Hint:* The Audit Log is also available from the Navigation bar. Select Reports > All Reports > Business Overview > Audit Log.)

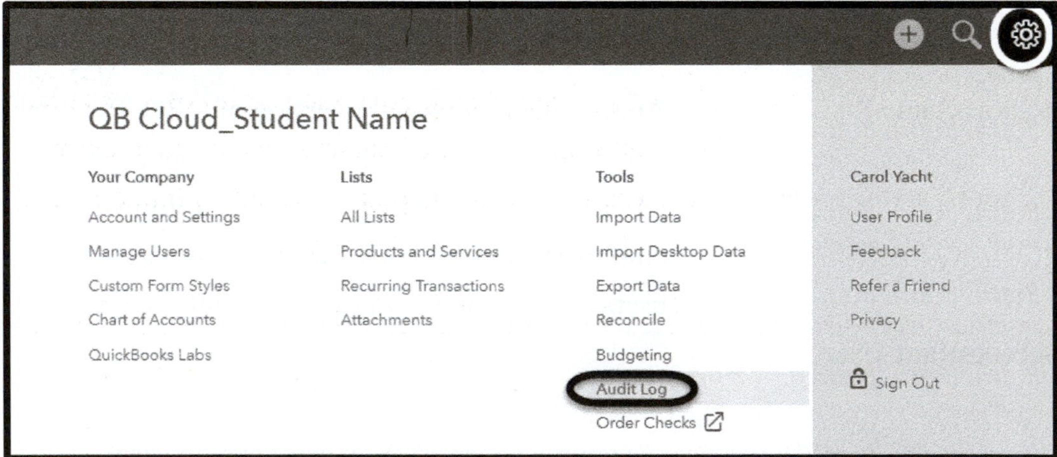

2. There are several ways to view the Audit Log.

    - To limit the view to specific users, dates, or type of events, click Filter.
    - To control which columns are shown and printed, click the gear icon.
    - To open a transaction noted in the Event column, click its link.
    - To see a history of the event, select View in the History column.
    - To view more events, scroll to the bottom of the screen and click <Next>.

A partial Audit Log is shown. The first column shows your current date, time, and time zone. Where the author's name is shown, your name will appear. Your dates and time will differ.

DATE CHANGED	USER	EVENT	NAME	DATE	AMOUNT	HISTORY
Mar 10, 5:49 pm US Mount...	Carol Yacht	Logged in.				
Mar 10, 5:37 pm US Mount...	Carol Yacht	Edited Account: Prepaid Insurance				View
Mar 10, 5:12 pm US Mount...	Carol Yacht	Added Account: Telephone Expense				View
Mar 10, 5:09 pm US Mount...	Carol Yacht	Edited Account: Depreciation Expense				View
Mar 10, 5:08 pm US Mount...	Carol Yacht	Edited Account: Opening Balance Equity				View
Mar 10, 5:08 pm US Mount...	Carol Yacht	Edited Account: Shipping and delivery expense				View

fyi

To see the work that you completed, go to the Audit Log — ⚙ > Audit Log. The Audit Log shows the date and time of your logins, logouts, and work completed. The work you complete is saved on Intuit's web server. To start where you left off after signing out, go to http://qbo.intuit.com. Sign in with your User ID and Password.

CHECK YOUR PROGRESS

Check Your Progress assignments are included on the Online Learning Center at www.mhhe.com/qbo2e > Student Edition > Chapter 2 > Check Your Progress.

1. The Account No. for Checking is ______________________________.
2. The Category Type for Checking is ____________________________.
3. The Account No. for Accounts Payable is_______________________.
4. The Category Type for Accounts Payable is_____________________.
5. The Account Number for Common Stock is ______________________.
6. The Category Type for Common Stock is________________________.

ONLINE LEARNING CENTER (OLC): www.mhhe.com/qbo2e

The OLC includes additional Chapter 2 resources. Go online to www.mhhe.com/qbo2e >Student Edition >Chapter 2.

1. Narrated PowerPoints.
2. Online quizzes: 10 True or False and 10 multiple-choice questions. The Online quizzes are graded and can be emailed to your professor.
3. Analysis question: Answer the analysis question, then email it to your instructor.
4. Going to the Net: Go online to http://quickbooks.intuit.com/products > link to Try it Free. What Online products are available for independent contractors and small business? What version of QBO is included with the textbook? Explain the difference between each product.

5. Video: Watch the Stay Organized with QuickBooks video at https://www.youtube.com/watch?v=oU6BGWHg5As#t=36. (Also shown earlier in the chapter.)
6. Glossary of terms: Words that are italicized and boldfaced are defined in the glossary. The Glossary is also Appendix B.
7. Problem solving link includes Exercise 2-3.

Exercise 2-1: Follow the instructions below to complete Exercise 2-1:

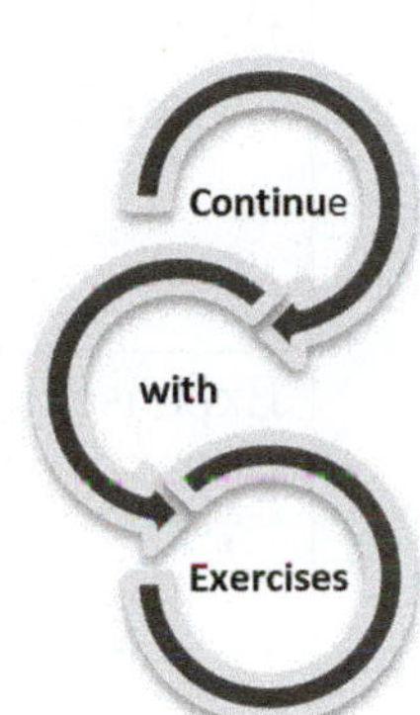

1. If necessary start QBO.
2. Complete the following Chart of Accounts edits.

- Add these accounts:

Category Type	Detail Type	Name	Number
Other Current Assets	Prepaid Expenses	**Prepaid Rent**	**123**
Other Current Liabilities	Loan Payable	Loan Payable	**205**
Income	Service/Fee Income	**Professional Fees**	**403**

- Edit these accounts:

Category Type	*Detail Type	*Name	Number
Other Current Assets	Other Current Assets	Uncategorized Asset	**133**
Income	Service/Fee Income (*Yes to changing the detail type.*)	Uncategorized Income	**455**
Expenses	Travel	**Conventions**	**604**
Expenses	Other Miscellaneous Service Cost	Uncategorized Expense	**701**

Exercise 2-2: Follow the instructions below to complete Exercise 2-2:

1. Save the Chart of Accounts as a PDF file. Use the file name **Exercise 2-2_Chart of Accounts.**
2. Export the Chart of Accounts to Excel. Use the file name **Exercise 2-2_Chart of Accounts.xlsx**. (*Hint:* Your chart of accounts may show some default accounts *without* account numbers.)

Check Your Chart of Accounts:

- Account 101 Checking; Bank; Detail Type, Checking.
- Account 123 Prepaid Rent; Other Current Assets; Detail Type, Prepaid Expenses
- Account 133 Uncategorized Asset; Other Current Assets; Detail Type, Other Current Assets

- Account 205 Loan Payable; Other Current Liabilities; Detail Type, Loan Payable
- Account 403 Professional Fees; Income; Detail Type, Service/Fee Income
- Account 455 Uncategorized Income; Income; Detail Type, Service Fee/Income
- Account 604 Conventions; Expenses; Detail Type, Travel
- Account 701 Uncategorized Expenses; Expenses; Detail Type, Other Miscellaneous Service Cost

2. Continue with Exercise 2-3.

Exercise 2-3: Problem Solving

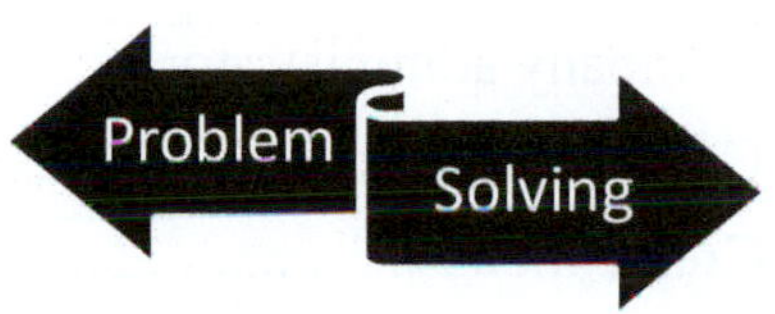

The Online Learning Center includes Exercise 2-3 at www.mhhe.com/qbo2e > Student Edition > Chapter 2 > Problem Solving.

1. If necessary, go to www.mhhe.com/qbo2e > Student Edition > Chapter 2 > Problem Solving.
2. On the Chart of Accounts, why are the category and detail type selections important? To explain the category and detail types, use 3 accounts – one asset, one liability, and one expense account. Identify the Category Type, Detail Type, Name, Number and financial statement.

CHAPTER 2 INDEX

Chapter 3

Beginning Balances and October Transaction Register

Scenario: In Chapter 3, you start by checking the work completed so far. The stop sign reminds you to check your data. After recording the journal entry for the owner's investment in the business, checks and deposits are entered from a Transaction Register. You also display the bank register, reports, and the audit log. The objectives that follow specify the work that is completed in Chapter 3.

OBJECTIVES

1. Start QuickBooks Online and sign in to QB Cloud_Student Name (your first and last name).
2. Enter the owner's investment in the business.
3. Use a transaction register to write checks.
4. Record cash sales and complete a transfer of funds.
5. Display the Bank Register, Journal, Trial Balance, Balance Sheet, Income Statement, and Audit Log.
6. Save PDF files and export reports to Excel.
7. Complete Check Your Progress.
8. Watch QBO video.
9. Go to the Online Learning Center at www.mhhe.com/qbo2e for additional resources.
10. Complete Exercises 3-1, 3-2 and 3-3.

In Chapter 2, you set up the company QB Cloud_Student Name (your first and last name), and completed a Chart of Accounts. In this chapter, you use those accounts to record transactions for October 20XX, the first month of the fourth quarter.

In Chapter 3, the owner invests cash and computer equipment in the business. The owner's investment is recorded in the Journal. Once that's completed, use the transaction register to issue checks, ATMs, and make deposits.
October is the month that QB Cloud started. For recording transactions, a ***transaction register*** is used. The transaction register shows checking account activity. In later chapters, vendors, inventory, and customers are added. The transaction register is the ***source document*** for analyzing each entry. Source documents are used to show written evidence of a business transaction.

GETTING STARTED

1. Start your browser. Go online to http://qbo.intuit.com.
2. Sign in with your User ID and Password. (*Hint:* You can save your User ID.)

ACCOUNT LIST OR CHART OF ACCOUNTS

To check that you are starting in the correct place, display the Chart of Accounts.

1. Select [Reports] > in the search field, type **Account List** > press <Enter>. The Account List is also called the Chart of Accounts. There are also two other ways to display the Chart of Accounts.

   a. From the Navigation bar, select [Accounting], the Chart of Accounts displays > Run Report.

   Or,

   b. Click Gear > Chart of Accounts.

The Account List or Chart of Accounts shows accounts that you set up and accounts QBO sets up automatically. When QBO updates, accounts may be added and some may not have account numbers. In Exercise 2-2, the Chart of Accounts was completed. Compare your Account List with the one shown.

QB Cloud_Student Name
Account List

Account #	Account	Type	Detail type
101	Checking	Bank	Checking
105	Accounts Receivable (A/R)	Accounts receivable (A/R)	Accounts Receivable (A/R)
115	Merchandise Inventory	Other Current Assets	Inventory
123	Prepaid Rent	Other Current Assets	Prepaid Expenses
125	Prepaid Insurance	Other Current Assets	Prepaid Expenses
130	Undeposited Funds	Other Current Assets	Undeposited Funds
133	Uncategorized Asset	Other Current Assets	Other Current Assets
135	Computer Equipment	Fixed Assets	Machinery & Equipment
137	Accumulated Depreciation	Fixed Assets	Accumulated Depreciation
201	Accounts Payable (A/P)	Accounts payable (A/P)	Accounts Payable (A/P)
205	Loan Payable	Other Current Liabilities	Loan Payable
301	Common Stock	Equity	Common Stock
305	Opening Balance Equity	Equity	Opening Balance Equity
318	Retained Earnings	Equity	Retained Earnings
	Owner's Investment	Equity	Owner's Equity
	Owner's Pay & Personal Expenses	Equity	Owner's Equity
401	Sales	Income	Sales of Product Income
403	Professional Fees	Income	Service/Fee Income
455	Uncategorized Income	Income	Service/Fee Income
	Billable Expense Income	Income	Sales of Product Income
	Shipping Income	Income	Sales of Product Income
501	Cost of Goods Sold	Cost of Goods Sold	Supplies & Materials - COGS
503	Freight & delivery - COS	Cost of Goods Sold	Shipping, Freight & Delivery - COS
601	Advertising	Expenses	Advertising/Promotional
603	Bank Charges	Expenses	Bank Charges
604	Conventions	Expenses	Travel
605	Dues & Subscriptions	Expenses	Dues & subscriptions
607	Depreciation Expense	Expenses	Office/General Administrative Expenses
609	Freight & Delivery	Expenses	Shipping, Freight & Delivery
611	Insurance	Expenses	Insurance
613	Interest Expense	Expenses	Interest Paid
615	Job Materials	Expenses	Supplies & Materials
617	Legal & Professional Fees	Expenses	Legal & Professional Fees
619	Meals and Entertainment	Expenses	Entertainment Meals
621	Office Supplies	Expenses	Office/General Administrative Expenses
623	Rent or Lease	Expenses	Rent or Lease of Buildings
625	Repair & Maintenance	Expenses	Repair & Maintenance

Make sure the Account #, Account name, Type, and Detail Type agree with your Account List.

Account #	Account	Type	Detail Type
627	Shipping and delivery expense	Expenses	Shipping, Freight & Delivery
629	Stationery & Printing	Expenses	Office/General Administrative Expenses
631	Supplies	Expenses	Supplies & Materials
633	Telephone Expense	Expenses	Office/General Administrative Expenses
635	Utilities	Expenses	Utilities
701	Uncategorized Expense	Expenses	Other Miscellaneous Service Cost
	Ask My Accountant	Expenses	Utilities

2. The Chart of Accounts was set up in Chapter 2 and completed in Exercises 2-1 and 2-2. If some of your accounts need to be edited, do that before continuing. To edit, select 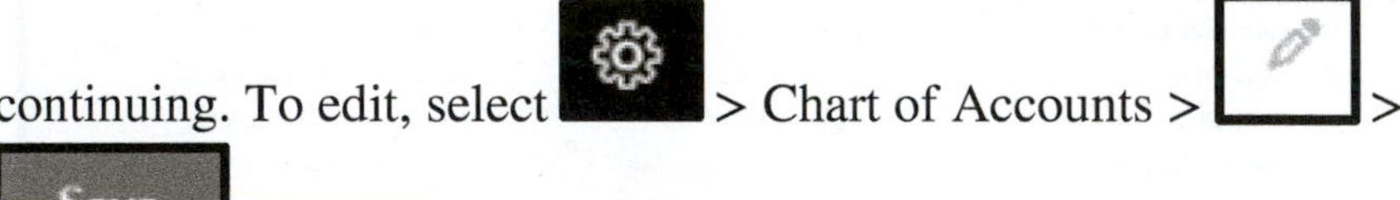 > Chart of Accounts > > Save.

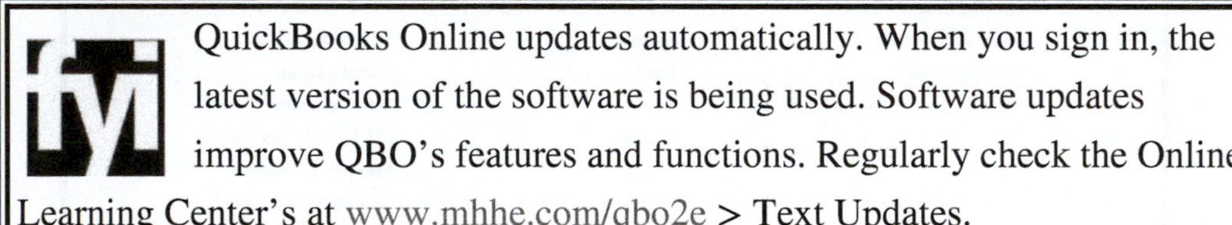

QuickBooks Online updates automatically. When you sign in, the latest version of the software is being used. Software updates improve QBO's features and functions. Regularly check the Online Learning Center's at www.mhhe.com/qbo2e > Text Updates.

JOURNAL ENTRY

A ***journal entry*** is a transaction in which:

- There are at least two parts: a Debit and Credit called distribution lines.
- Each distribution line includes an account from the Chart of Accounts.
- The total of the Debit column equals the total of the Credit column.

When you record a Journal Entry, QBO labels the transaction Journal in a register and Journal Entry on reports that list transactions. You can also enter other types of transactions in QBO using ***specialized screens***, such as Check, Receive Payment, Bill, Bank Deposit, and Transfer.

The following transaction is the initial capital out to establish QB Cloud_Student Name (your first and last name).

Analyze transaction → **Transaction date** → **Input transaction**

Date	*Description of Transaction*
10/1/20XX	The owner invested $50,000 cash along with $10,000 in computer equipment in the company in exchange for common stock.

1. From the Dashboard or Home page, click [+] > the Create menu appears. If necessary, select ► Show more.

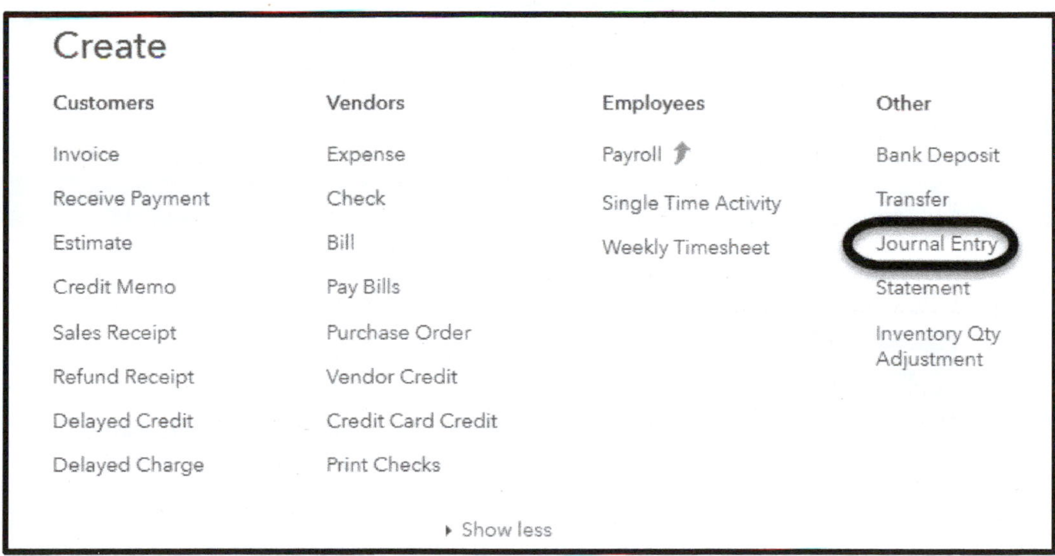

2. Click Journal Entry (in the Other list). Complete these fields:

Journal date:	Type **10/1/20XX** (type the current year)
	Journal no. 1 is completed automatically
ACCOUNT:	Select 101 Checking (*Hint:* You can also type **101**)
DEBITS:	Type **50000**
ACCOUNT:	Select 135 Computer Equipment
DEBITS:	Type **10000**
ACCOUNT:	Select 301 Common Stock
CREDITS:	60,000.00 is completed automatically
DESCRIPTION:	Type **Owner invested cash and computer equipment for stock**

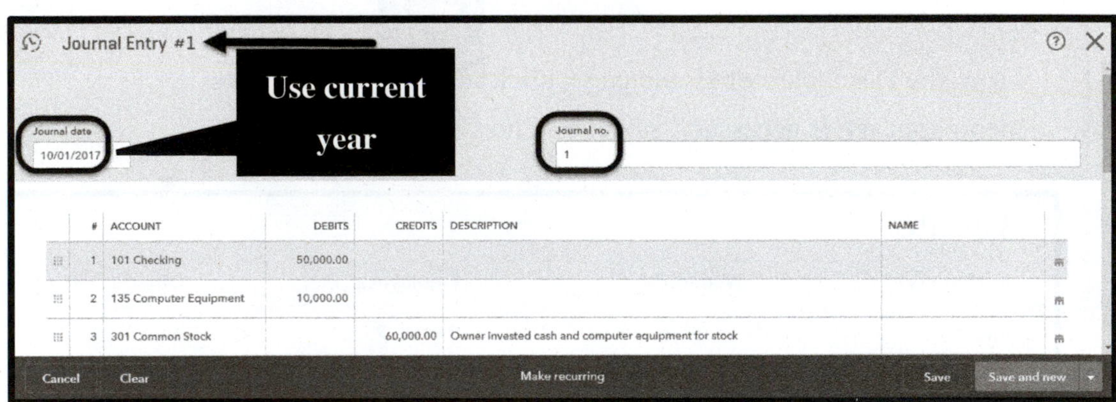

3. Click on the down-arrow▼next to Save and New. Select Save and close 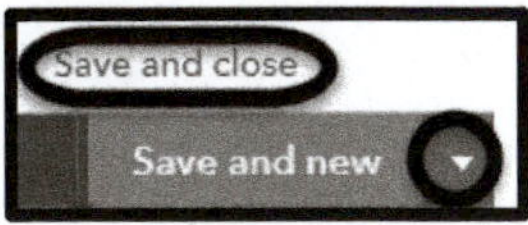

. The screen prompts Journal entry #1 1010saved.

ACCOUNT LIST

After recording the owner investment, look at the Account List.

1. From the Navigation bar, select Reports > in the Search box, type **Account List >** press <Enter>. Observe that Checking, Computer Equipment, and Common Stock show a balance. The minus sign in front of Common Stock means it is a credit balance.

QB Cloud_Student Name

ACCOUNT LIST

ACCOUNT #	ACCOUNT	TYPE	DETAIL TYPE	DESCRIPTION	BALANCE
101	Checking	Bank	Checking		50,000.00
105	Accounts Receivable (A/R)	Accounts receivable (A/R)	Accounts Receivable (A/R)		0.00
115	Merchandise Inventory	Other Current Assets	Inventory		0.00
123	Prepaid Rent	Other Current Assets	Prepaid Expenses		0.00
125	Prepaid Insurance	Other Current Assets	Prepaid Expenses		0.00
130	Undeposited Funds	Other Current Assets	Undeposited Funds		0.00
133	Uncategorized Asset	Other Current Assets	Other Current Assets		0.00
135	Computer Equipment	Fixed Assets	Machinery & Equipment		10,000.00
137	Accumulated Depreciation	Fixed Assets	Accumulated Depreciation		0.00
201	Accounts Payable (A/P)	Accounts payable (A/P)	Accounts Payable (A/P)		0.00
205	Loan Payable	Other Current Liabilities	Loan Payable		0.00
301	Common Stock	Equity	Common Stock		-60,000.00

2. Return to the Dashboard, also called the Home page. Observe that the Bank accounts area shows 101 Checking In QuickBooks $50,000.00.

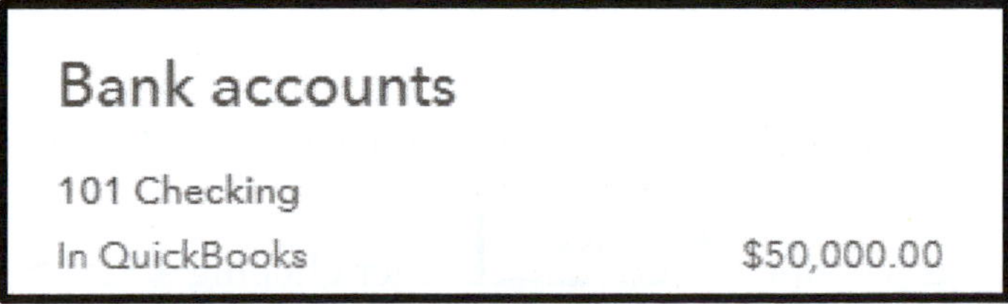

OCTOBER TRANSACTION REGISTER

The transaction register, similar to a checkbook register, shows QB Cloud's checking account activity. The transaction register has the information necessary to record entries for the month of October. Within Chapter 3, you record October 1-17, 20XX transactions. In Exercise 3-1, entries for the rest of October are shown.

Ck. No.	Date	Description of Transaction	Payment	Deposit	Balance
	10/1	*Balance*			*50,000.00*
1010	10/2	River Insurance (Insurance for one year)	3,000.00		47,000.00

CHECK

To record Check No. 1010, follow these steps.

1. Go to the Create menu. Click > select Check (in Vendors list). (*Hint:* For purposes of verifying check numbers and Transaction Register balances, the Check page is used. In QBO, another way to record checks is the Expense page.) Complete these fields on the Check page:

   Choose a payee: Type **River Insurance**, click + Add River Insurance > the Type is Vendor > Save. After clicking <Save> River Insurance is shown.

   Payment date: Type **10/2/20XX** (use current year)

Check no.:	Type **1010**
ACCOUNT:	Select or type **125** Prepaid Insurance
DESCRIPTION:	Type **Paid insurance for one year**
AMOUNT:	Type **3000**

2. Compare Check #1010 page with the one shown. Before saving the check, the **Balance** field shows $50,000.00, which is the 10/1 balance on the Transaction Register. That's the owner's investment.
3. On the top right of the page, $3,000.00 is shown as the amount. Compare your Check to the one shown below.

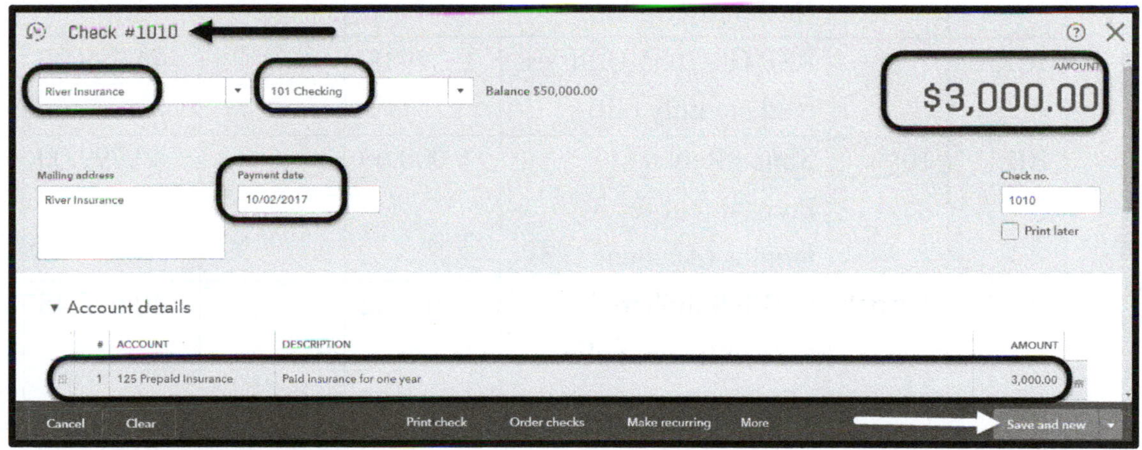

4. Click Save and new. After selecting <Save and new>, the Balance field shows $47,000 and the Check No. field is ready for Check no. 1011.

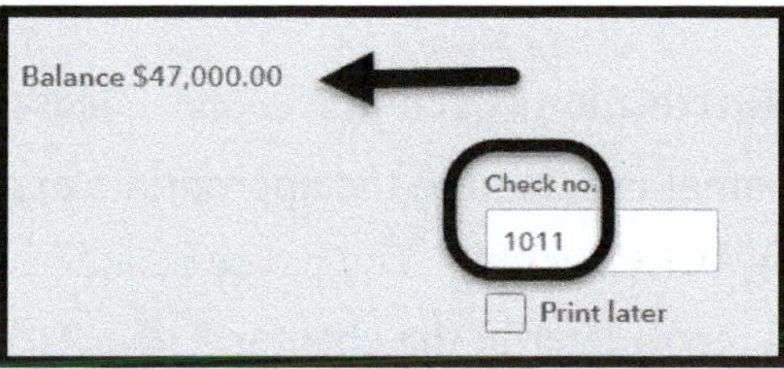

Using the transaction register, enter Check Nos. 1011 to 1017. Start with Check No. 1011 and use the current year. Add payee names as Vendors.

Ck. No.	Date	Description of Transaction	Payment	Deposit	Balance
	10/1	*Balance*			*50,000.00*
1010	*10/2*	*River Insurance*	*3,000.00*		*47,000.00*
1011	**10/3**	**U.S. Post Office** (627 Shipping and delivery expense)	**47.00**		46,953.00
1012	10/3	Valley News (605 Subscription)	75.00		46,878.00
1013	10/4	RSP Gas (635 Utilities; paid monthly bill)	79.00		46,799.00
1014	10/5	Simon Rentals Prepaid rent for 3 months (Account 123)	6,000.00		40,799.00
1015	10/10	Office Suppliers (621 Office Supplies; bought office supplies)	106.52		40,692.48
1016	10/12	County Telephone (633 Paid monthly bill)	76.19		40,616.29
1017	10/15	Albert Benson (625 Repair & Maintenance)	140.00		40,476.29

Expense Account Distribution: Each time a check is issued, the account distribution in the Journal is a debit to the appropriate expense account and a credit to Account No. 101 Checking. The payee is added as a vendor. This is shown in the Journal report later in the chapter.

ACCOUNT AND SETTINGS

Before you continue with Sales Receipts in the next section, check your account settings or preferences. Some of these settings were completed in Chapter 2, but to make sure you have them selected, complete 1 through 5. When needed, click on the pencil icon to edit.

1. If the Check page is shown, click <X> next to the ? to close it. Then, select Gear > Account and Settings > Company. In the Company type field, select > Tax form down-arrow > Corporation, one or more shareholders (Form 1120) > click <Save>. The Industry field can be left blank. (*Hint:* If you do not have a company selection, continue with step 2.)

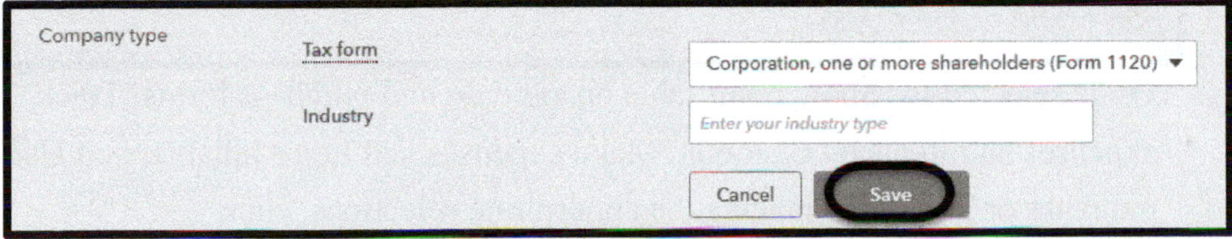

NOTE TO INSTRUCTOR: If you are using QuickBooks Online Accountant, you may notice some user interface differences. More information about QB Online Accountant and Educator Registration is available at www.mhhe.com/qbo2e > Instructor Edition > Educator Registration. Refer to Appendix A, Troubleshooting, for a comparison of QB Online Plus (version with textbook) and QB Online Accountant (requires educator registration).

2. In the Account and Settings list, select Sales. Check the Sales form content area and Products and services. If needed, click on the pencil icon to edit. For example, for Custom fields, select each box. This turn custom fields On.

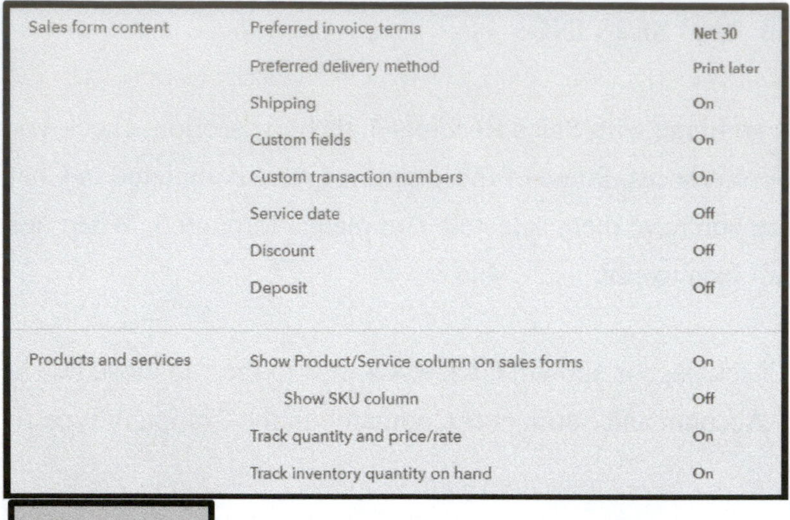

3. Select Expenses. Check the Bills and expenses area and Purchase orders. Edit to set the Default bill payment terms to Net 30.

On is selected for Show Items table on expense and purchase forms, Track expenses and items by customer, Make expenses and Items billable, and Use purchase orders. After making the apporpirate selections, click

.

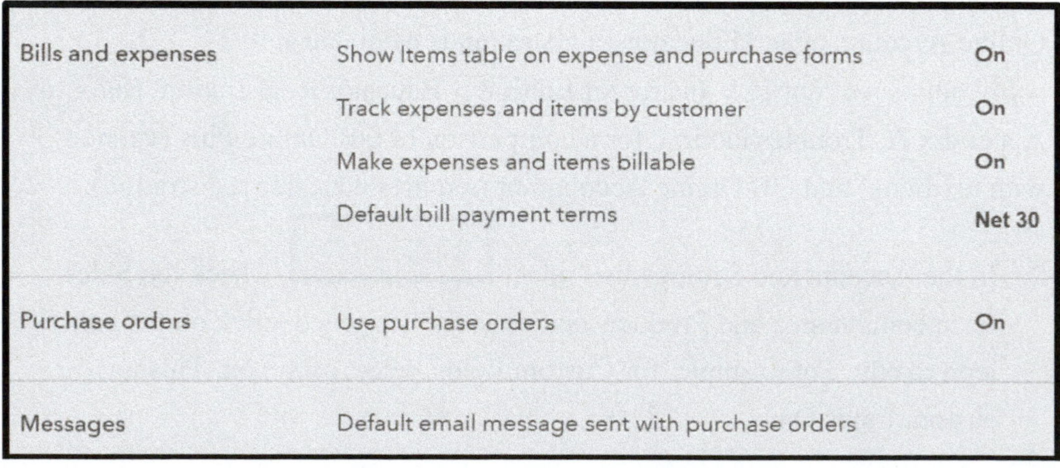

4. Select Advanced. You may want to change Sign me out if inactive for to 3 hours > then <Save>. Check each area.

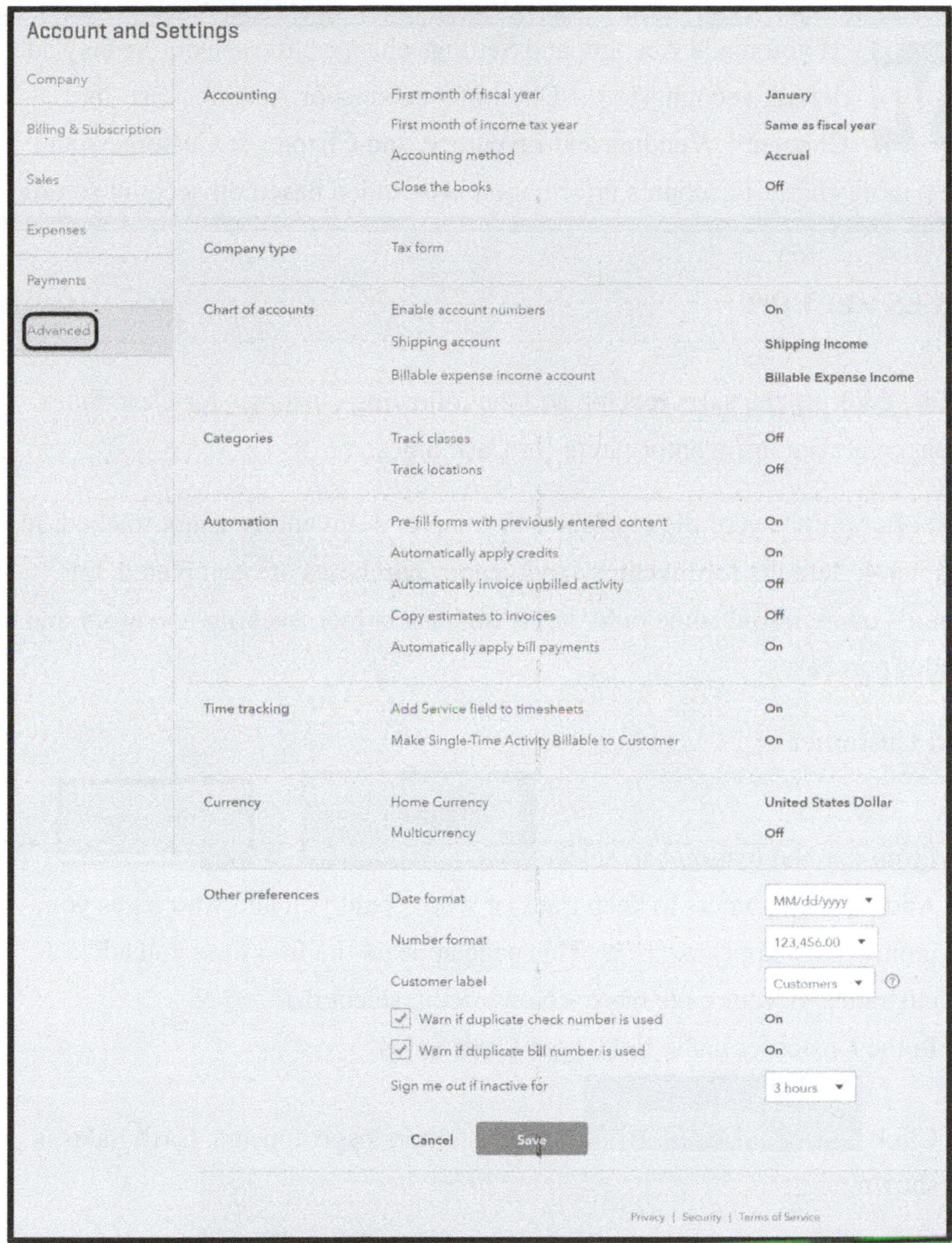

5. When through, click .

> If you made Account and Settings changes, the selections may add default accounts to the Chart of Accounts or Account List. In Chapter 4, Vendors and Inventory, and Chapter 5, Customers and Sales, more chart of accounts information is included based on account settings.

SALES RECEIPT

Before entering the sales receipt, add the following customer for Cash Sales. Then, create a non-inventory item for Cash Sales.

Note: For purposes of the cash sales in Chapter 3, inventory is <u>not</u> tracked. In Chapter 4, defaults for inventory and vendor purchases are completed. QB Cloud's owners sold some older items for cash before tracking inventory and vendor purchases.

Add Customer

1. From the Navigation bar, select Sales > Customers. The Add your customers to keep track of who's paid you and who owes you money page appears. (*Hint:* This page appears the first time you add a customer. If your page has a <New> icon, select it.)
2. In the Customer name field, type **Cash Sales**.
3. Click Add a customer. The Customers page appears. Cash Sales is shown.

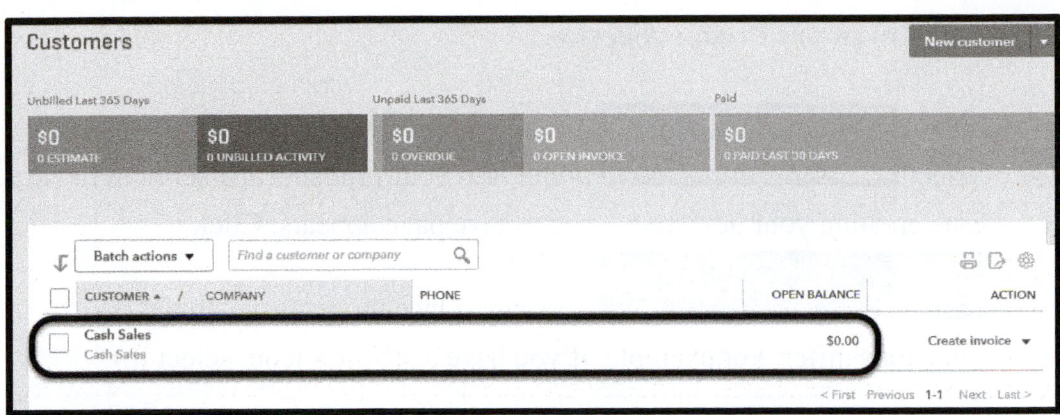

Troubleshooting: If you make a selection and the page does not display, select Help (?). In the Search field, type **I click a button or link**. Link to the I click a button or link, but pop-up window doesn't appear / nothing happens. Read the information and make the necessary changes.

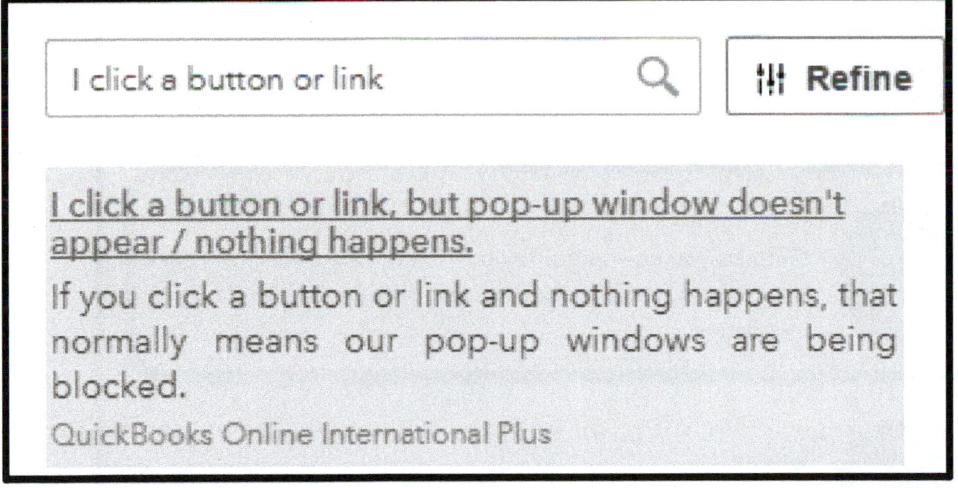

Add Non-Inventory Product/Service

1. Select Products and Services > the Add your products and services to save time creating your next invoice or receive page appears. Click Add a product or service. (*Hint:* Once products are added, selections differ. For example, if you have a <New> icon, select it.)

2. The Product/Service information page appears. Select Non-inventory.

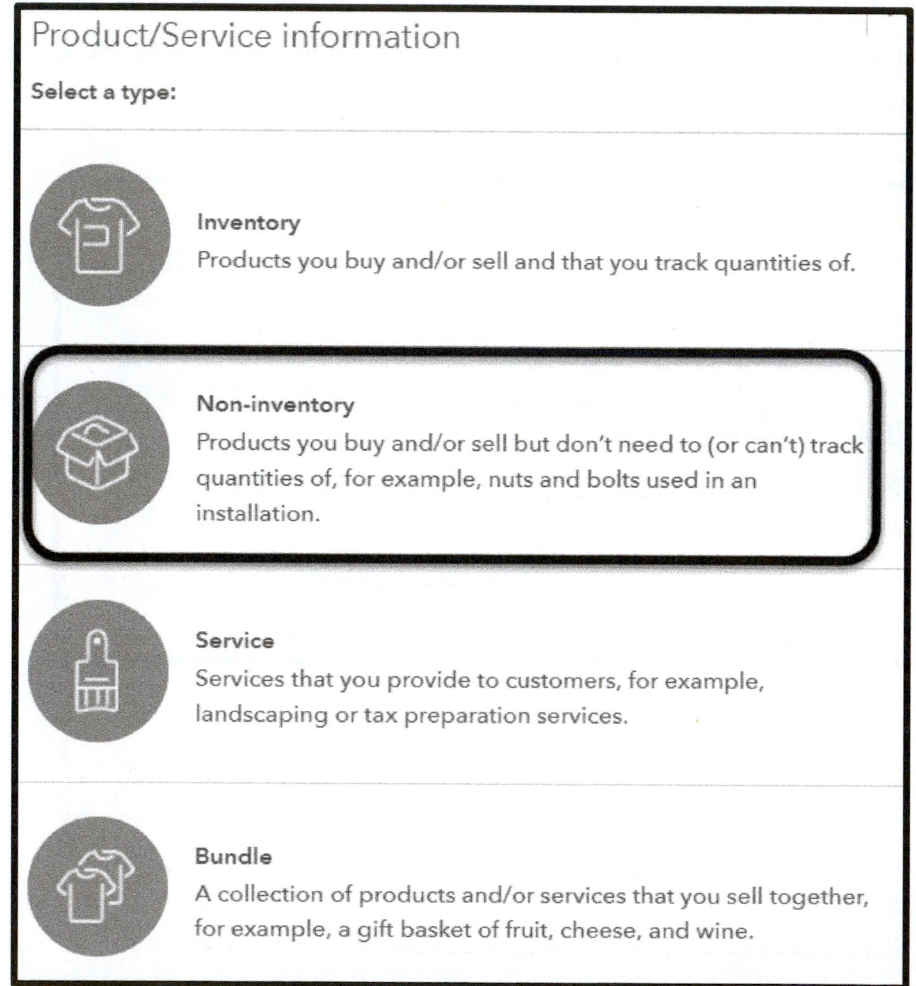

3. The Non-inventory page appears. Complete these fields:

   Name: **Cash Sales**
   Sales information: ✓ I sell this product/service to my customers should be checked.
   Income Account: Make sure 401 Sales is selected.

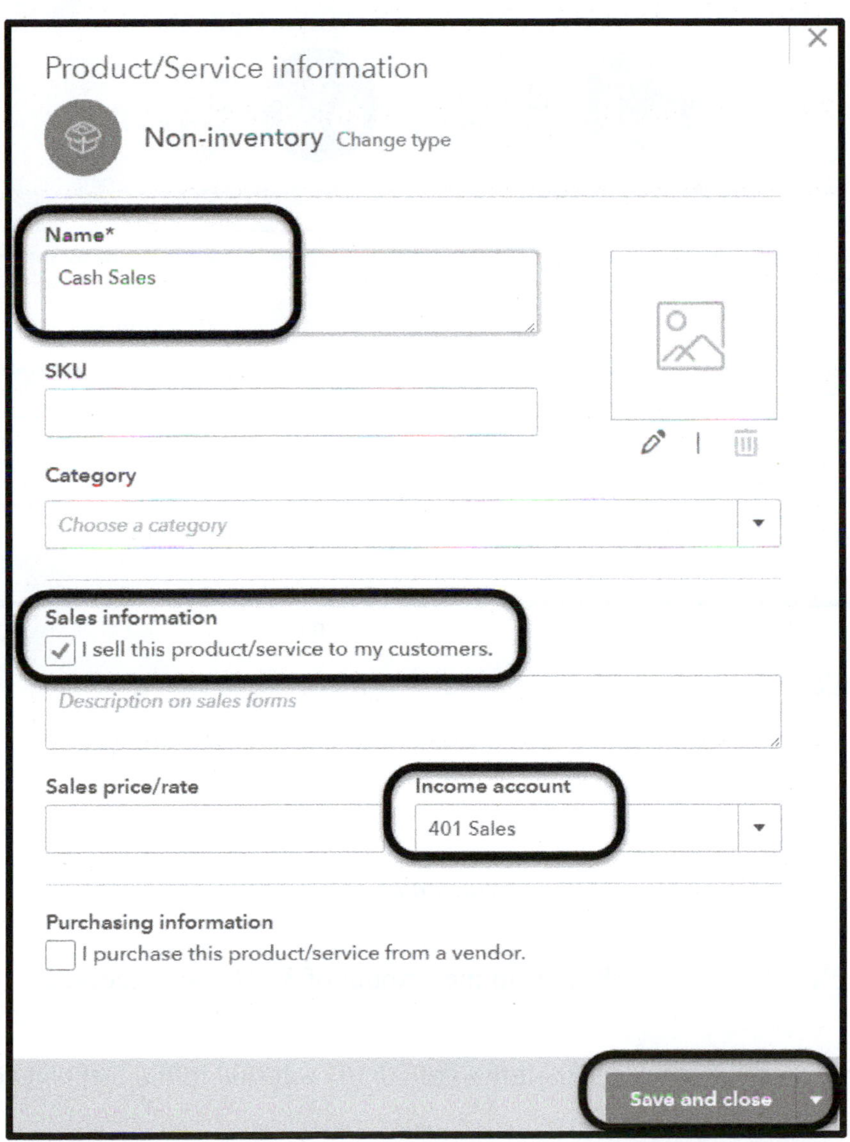

4. After selecting <Save and close>, a screen prompt says that Cash Sales non-inventory product was saved.
5. To make sure Cash Sales was added as a Non-inventory item, display the Products and Services page. If necessary, click Gear > Products and Services.

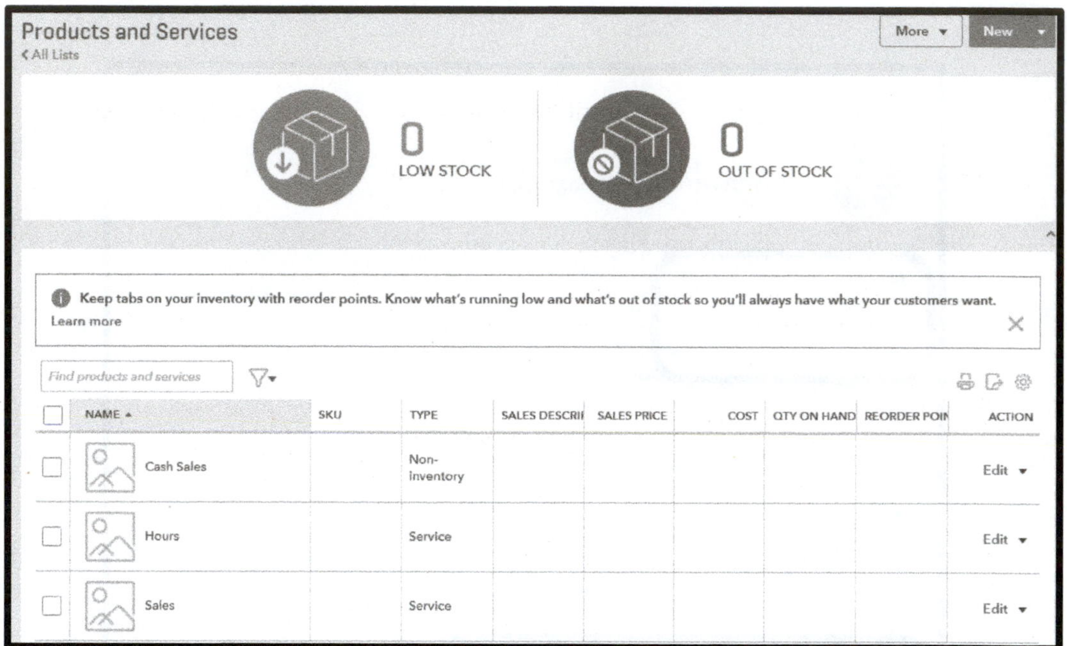

Cash Sales

The transaction for cash sales is:

Date	*Description of Transaction*
10/16/20XX	Cash sales in the amount of $2,500 are received.

The partial transaction register shows the 10/16 cash sale in the Deposit column.

Ck. No.	Date	Description of Transaction	Payment	Deposit	Balance
1017	*10/15*	*Albert Benson (Repair & Maintenance)*	*140.00*		*40,476.29*
	10/16	**Cash Sales**		**2,500.00**	42,976.29

6. Click [+] > Sales Receipt (in the Customers list). The Sales Receipt page appears. Complete these fields.

Choose a customer: Select Cash Sales

Cash Sales

Billing address:	Cash Sales completed automatically
Sales Receipt date:	Type **10/16/XXXX** (use current year)
Sales Receipt no.	1001 completed automatically
Payment method:	Select Check
Deposit to:	101 Checking automatically selected
PRODUCT/SERVICE:	Select Cash Sales.
DESCRIPTION:	Type **Cash sales**
QTY:	1 automatically completed
RATE:	Type **2500**
AMOUNT:	2,500.00 automatically completed

Troubleshooting: If you do not have a Product/Service field, check account settings for Sales and Expenses are on pages 105-106, steps 2 and 3.

Compare your Sales Receipt #1001 to the one shown on the next page.

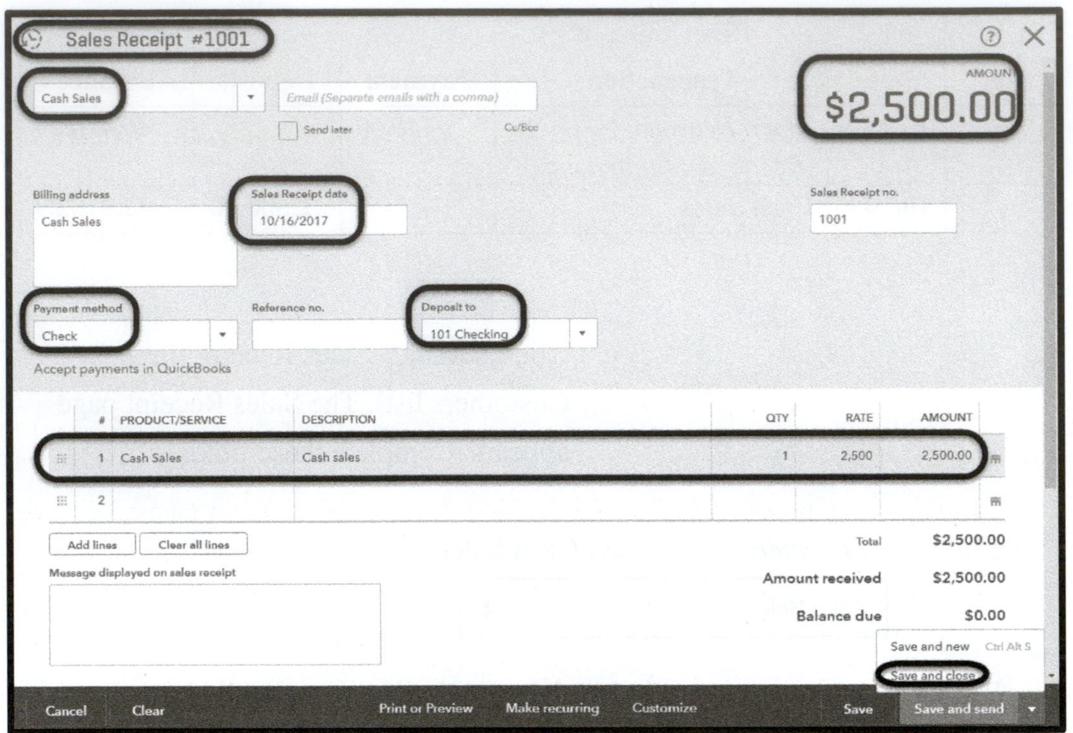

7. Click <Save and close> Save and new / Save and close Ctrl Alt D / Save and send. The screen prompts Sales receipt 1001 saved.

Sales Receipt Account Distribution: Each time a cash sale is recorded, Account No. 101 Checking is debited and Account No. 401 Sales is credited. The account distribution is shown on the Journal report. Reports are displayed later in the chapter. Here's how the Journal report shows the 10/16 Sales Receipt. The 10/16 Sales Receipt is displayed in the Journal report below.

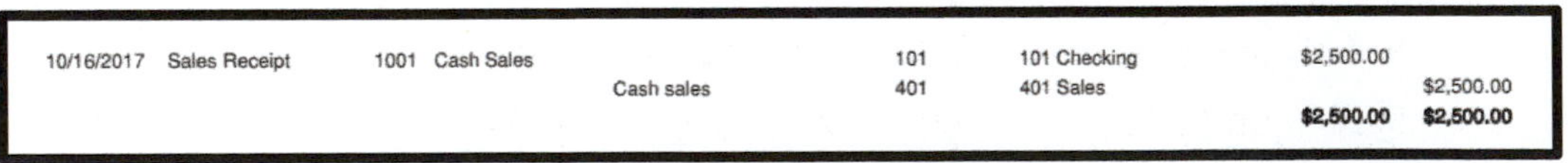

10/16/2017	Sales Receipt	1001	Cash Sales		101	101 Checking	$2,500.00	
				Cash sales	401	401 Sales		$2,500.00
							$2,500.00	**$2,500.00**

TRANSFER

You can transfer funds between most balance sheet accounts in your Chart of Accounts *except* between Accounts Payable (A/P) and Accounts Receivable (A/R). In this transaction, funds are transferred from the Checking Account to Loan Payable.

Date	*Description of Transaction*
10/17/20XX	After completing the transfer, Account 205 Loan Payable has a balance of $5,000. The Loan is owed to First Trust Bank.

The partial transaction register shows the Transfer.

Ck. No.	Date	Description of Transaction	Payment	Deposit	Balance
1017	*10/15*	*Albert Benson (Repair & Maintenance)*	*140.00*		*40,476.29*
	10/16	*Cash Sales*		*2,500.00*	*42,976.29*
	10/17	**First Trust Bank** (Loan Payable)		**5,000.00**	47,976.29

The steps that follow show how to record a transfer.

1. Click [+] > Transfer. The Transfer page appears. Complete the following fields.

   Transfer Funds From: Select Account 205 Loan Payable
   Transfer Funds To: Select or type 101 Checking

Transfer Amount:	Type **5000**
Memo:	Type **First Trust Bank**
Date:	Type **10/17/20XX** (use current year)

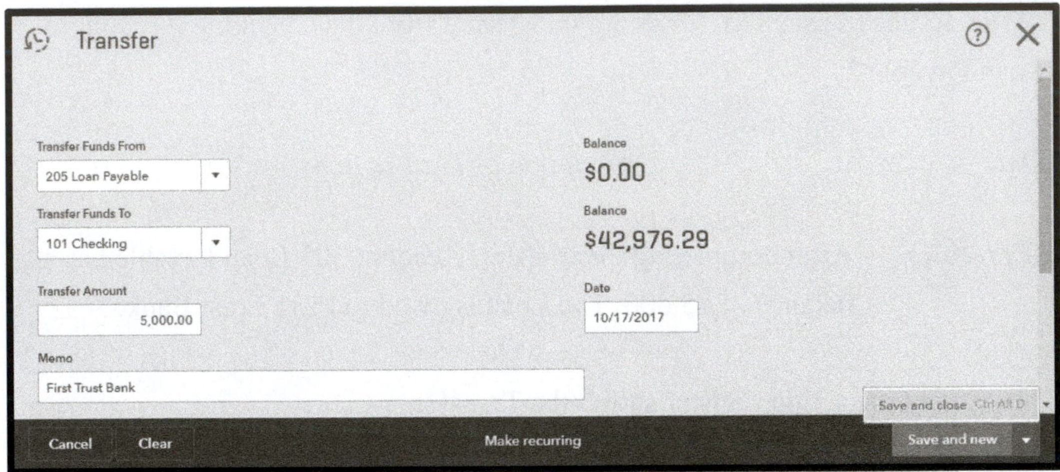

2. Click . The screen prompts Transfer saved.

Transfer Account Disbribution: When this transfer is recorded, the account distribution in the Journal report is a debit to Account No. 101, Checking and a credit to Account No. 205 Loan Payable. The account distribution is shown on the Journal report. The Journal is displayed later in this chapter.

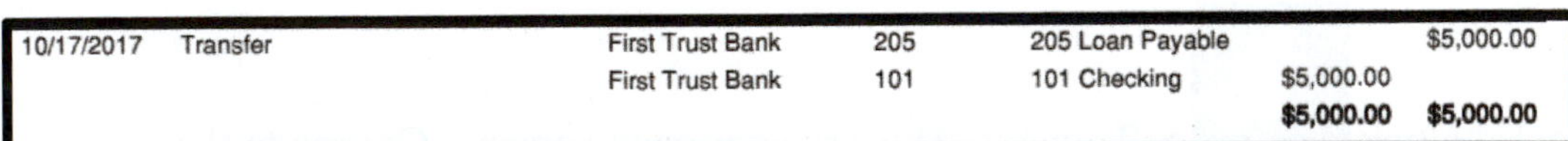

10/17/2017	Transfer	First Trust Bank	205	205 Loan Payable		$5,000.00
		First Trust Bank	101	101 Checking	$5,000.00	
					$5,000.00	**$5,000.00**

Comment: The Loan Payable will be paid in a later chapter. When that's done, the vendor, First Trust Bank, will be added. For this transaction, the Memo includes the vendor name. *Or*, if preferred, you could add First Trust Bank as the vendor now.

DASHBOARD OR HOME PAGE

Let's examine how QBO populated data based on the cash sale recorded and expenses from the transaction register. (*Hint:* For your Dashboard to show Income and Expense balances, transactions need to be entered within the last 30 days. Your Expenses area may show $0.)

The dashboard includes a managerial reporting focus that displays the same data in a different way than a standard Profit and Loss financial report. The display totals include both Reviewed and To Review transactions while the P&L report only shows Reviewed transactions.

If you would like to dig deeper and compare the two different reports, an understanding of the following differences is helpful:

- Dashboard P&L Income and Expense Totals use the Company default setting for cash or accrual basis.
- Dashboard Expenses = Total of COGS + Expenses + Other Expenses
- Dashboard Income = Total of Income + Other Income

Float your mouse pointer over the solid portion of the display bar to see the Reviewed value. Alternatively, accept all To Review transactions before attempting to compare the dashboard to the P&L report.

Bank Accounts

The Bank accounts area of the Dashbaord shows the balance in Account 101 Checking, $47,976.29.

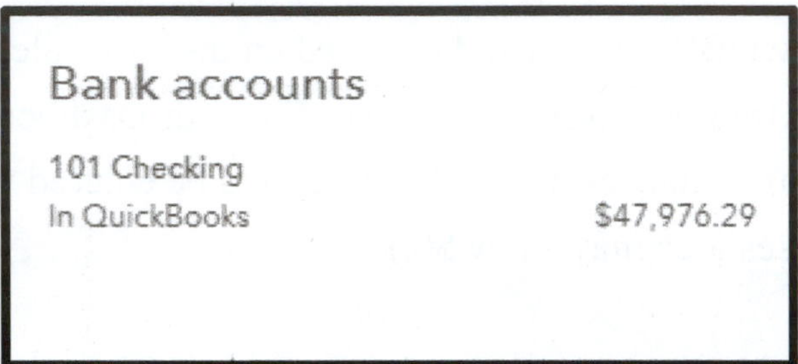

Profit and Loss

The Profit and Loss, Expenses, Income, and Sales default to the current month. To see the Profit and Loss shown below, the author clicked on the down-arrow and selected This year. Depending on the month and year you recorded transactions, you may need to make another selection. (*Hint:* Amounts are rounded up or down.) Scroll over the graphs to see that Income and Expenses of $2,500 was Reviewed.

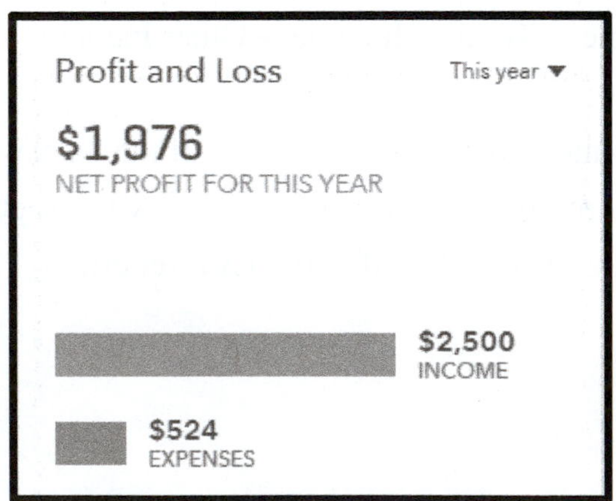

Expenses

When This year was selected for Profit and Loss, Expenses also changed to This year. Balances are rounded up. Scroll over the circle to see individual expenses; for example, $140 for Account 625 Repair & Maintenance, $107 for Account 621 Office Supplies, etc.

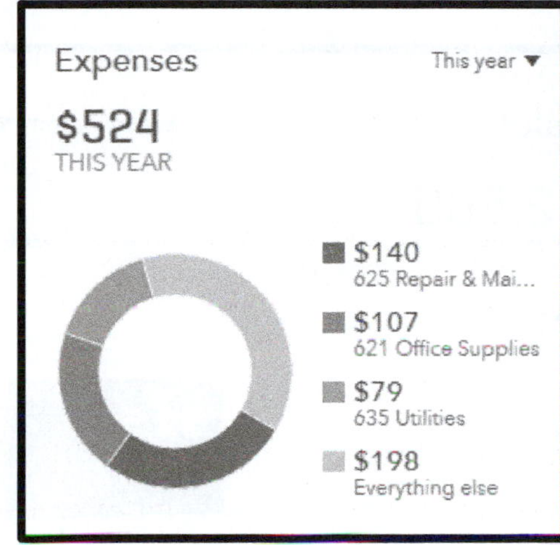

Income

The Income area defaults to the Last 365 days. Since there are no open invoices, invoices within the last 365 days, zeroes are shown. Depening on your current month, the Income graph may differ.

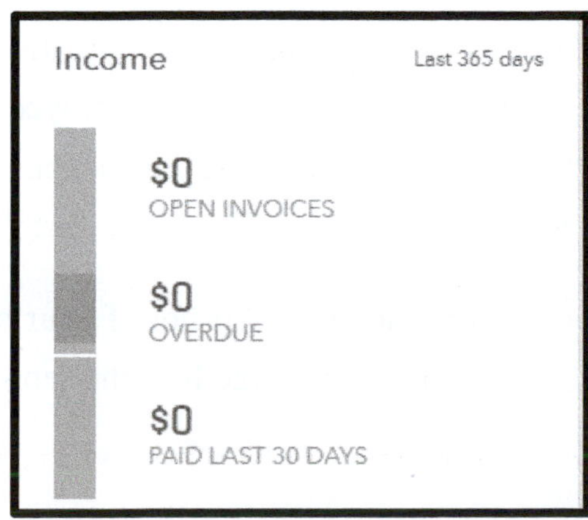

Sales

Click on the down arrow and make the appropriate selection. The author selected This year by month. When you click on the high-point, $2,500 Oct 2017 appears. In Chapter 3, sales transactions were entered in October 20XX (your current year).

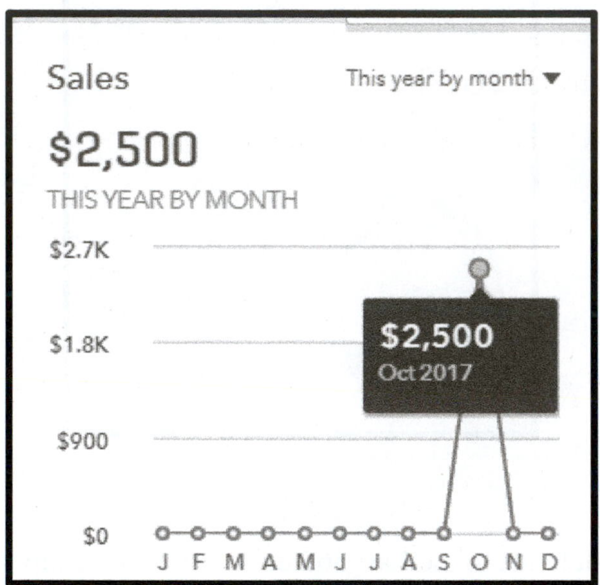

REPORTS

Use reports to view your company and financial information at a glance. Reports generate financial statements, transaction details, employee information, and more. If you don't see the report that you want, you can customize an existing report and memorize it to use again later.

The top half of the Reports page shows a snapshot of your business based on your transactions. The bottom half of the page lists the reports that are available.

Reports are divided into five sections:

- Recommended: Reports that QuickBooks recommends you run.
- Frequently Run: Reports that you run most frequently, and are easy to access in this section.
- My Custom Reports: Reports that you have customized and saved.
- Management Reports: Management reports include a cover page, table of contents, preliminary pages, reports, and end notes. There are three ready-to-use report templates:
    - Company Overview: Contains the Profit and Loss and Balance Sheet reports.
    - Sales Performance: Contains the Profit and Loss, A/R Aging Detail, and Sales by Customer Summary reports.
    - Expense Performance: Profit and Loss, A/P Aging Detail, and Expenses by Vendor Summary reports. All Reports: A list of all available reports, categorized by subject.
- All Reports: A list of all available reports, categorized by subject.

Journal

To see the transactions that you have entered, display the Journal report.

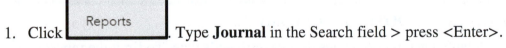

1. Click Reports. Type **Journal** in the Search field > press <Enter>.
2. Type **10/1/XX** in the From field. Type **10/17/XX** in the To field. (*Hint:* Use the current year. Type either four characters or two for the year.)

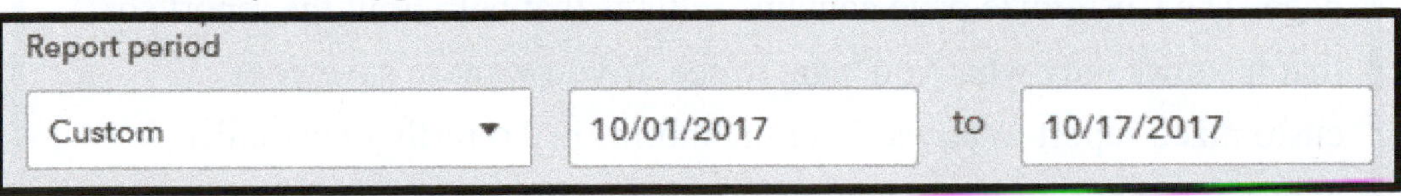

3. After typing the date range, press <Tab> . A partial Journal is shown below. Scroll down to see all of it.

QB Cloud_Student Name

JOURNAL

October 1-17, 2017

DATE	TRANSACTION TYPE	NUM	NAME	MEMO/DESCRIPTION	ACCOUNT #	ACCOUNT	DEBIT	CREDIT
10/01/2017	Journal Entry	1			101	101 Checking	$50,000.00	
					135	135 Computer Equipment	$10,000.00	
				Owner invested cash and computer equipment for stock	301	301 Common Stock		$60,000.00
							$60,000.00	**$60,000.00**
10/02/2017	Check	1010	River Insurance		101	101 Checking		$3,000.00
				Paid insurance for one year	125	125 Prepaid Insurance	$3,000.00	
							$3,000.00	**$3,000.00**
10/03/2017	Check	1011	U.S. Post Office		101	101 Checking		$47.00
				Shipping and delivery	627	627 Shipping and delivery expense	$47.00	
							$47.00	**$47.00**
10/03/2017	Check	1012	Valley News		101	101 Checking		$75.00
				Subscription	605	605 Dues & Subscriptions	$75.00	
							$75.00	**$75.00**

In the NUM column, observe that the Cash sales transaction on 10/16 automatically added 1001.

3. Save the Journal as an Excel file. Use the file name **Chapter 3_Oct 1 to Oct 17_Journal**. If your instructor would like a PDF file, select <Save as PDF>.

TROUBLESHOOTING: CUSTOMIZE

By default, each report shows data as of today's date. To limit the report to a different set of dates, choose a Transaction Date range in the Customize page. The Customize page contains settings that help limit the report so that it shows only what you want to see. If you want to save your customized report to access later, memorize it. To further customize, export the report to Excel and make changes.

Trial Balance

1. The ***Trial Balance*** report shows the debit and credit balances of each account in your chart of accounts during a period of time. Type **Trial Balance** in the Search field > from **10/1/XX** to **10/17/XX** > Run report. If needed, edit balances that do not agree. Editing transactions is shown on page 127.

QB Cloud_Student Name

TRIAL BALANCE

As of October 17, 2017

	DEBIT	CREDIT
101 Checking	47,976.29	
123 Prepaid Rent	6,000.00	
125 Prepaid Insurance	3,000.00	
135 Computer Equipment	10,000.00	
205 Loan Payable		5,000.00
301 Common Stock		60,000.00
401 Sales		2,500.00
605 Dues & Subscriptions	75.00	
621 Office Supplies	106.52	
625 Repair & Maintenance	140.00	
627 Shipping and delivery expense	47.00	
633 Telephone Expense	76.19	
635 Utilities	79.00	
TOTAL	**$67,500.00**	**$67,500.00**

IMPORTANT: If your trial balance does not agree with the one shown, make the needed changes. The work continues in the end-of-chapter exercises. Your Trial Balance should be the same *before* adding additional transactions in the exercises.

2. Export to Excel and save as a PDF file. Use the file name **Chapter 3_Oct 1 to Oct 17_Trial Balance.**

Profit and Loss

The Profit and Loss report shows money you earned (income) and money you spent (expenses) so you can see how profitable your company is. The P&L is also called an income statement.

1. Go to the Reports page, type **Profit and Loss** in the search field. The date range is 10/1/XX to 10/17/XX > Run report.

QB Cloud_Student Name

PROFIT AND LOSS

October 1-17, 2017

	TOTAL
INCOME	
401 Sales	2,500.00
Total Income	**$2,500.00**
GROSS PROFIT	**$2,500.00**
EXPENSES	
605 Dues & Subscriptions	75.00
621 Office Supplies	106.52
625 Repair & Maintenance	140.00
627 Shipping and delivery expense	47.00
633 Telephone Expense	76.19
635 Utilities	79.00
Total Expenses	**$523.71**
NET INCOME	**$1,976.29**

2. Export the Profit and Loss report to Excel and save as a PDF file. Use the file name **Chapter 3_Oct 1 to Oct 17_Profit and Loss**. (*Hint:* When the Excel report display, click Enable Editing.)

Balance Sheet

The Balance Sheet lists what you own (assets), what your debts are (liabilities), and what you've invested in your company (equity).

1. Go to the Reports page > Balance Sheet > from 10/1/XX to 10/17/XX > Run report. Compare your Balance Sheet with the one shown on the next page.

QB Cloud_Student Name

BALANCE SHEET

As of October 17, 2017

	TOTAL
ASSETS	
Current Assets	
Bank Accounts	
101 Checking	47,976.29
Total Bank Accounts	**$47,976.29**
Other Current Assets	
123 Prepaid Rent	6,000.00
125 Prepaid Insurance	3,000.00
Total Other Current Assets	**$9,000.00**
Total Current Assets	**$56,976.29**
Fixed Assets	
135 Computer Equipment	10,000.00
Total Fixed Assets	**$10,000.00**
TOTAL ASSETS	**$66,976.29**
LIABILITIES AND EQUITY	
Liabilities	
Current Liabilities	
Other Current Liabilities	
205 Loan Payable	5,000.00
Total Other Current Liabilities	**$5,000.00**
Total Current Liabilities	**$5,000.00**
Total Liabilities	**$5,000.00**
Equity	
301 Common Stock	60,000.00
318 Retained Earnings	
Net Income	1,976.29
Total Equity	**$61,976.29**
TOTAL LIABILITIES AND EQUITY	**$66,976.29**

2. Export the Balance Sheet to Excel and save as a PDF file. Use the file name **Chapter 3_Oct 1 to Oct 17_Balance Sheet**.

Audit Log

There are a couple ways to view the Audit Log. It is available in the Tools list (click on the Gear icon) *or* within the Reports page. You may want to look at all the changes that you made to QBO. The Audit Log is a good way to do that. You can also drill down to the original entry from the Audit Log. For example, let's say you want to look at the customer you added.

Comment: The author's Audit Log is shown. Your audit log may differ.

1. From the Audit Log, drill down on Sales Receipt No. 1001

Added Sales Receipt No. 1001 .

2. The Sales Receipt #1001 page appears.

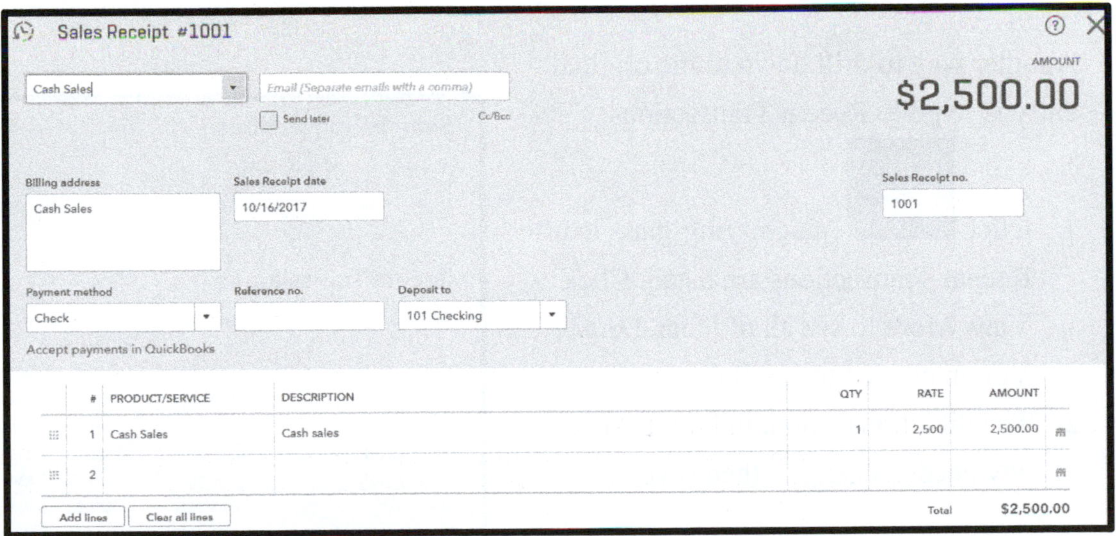

3. Continue with Editing a Transaction.

EDITING A TRANSACTION

With the Audit Log shown, drill down to a transaction that needs editing. The original entry is shown. Make the needed corrections, then <Save and Close>. When you view the Audit Log again, the edited transaction is shown.

The Audit Log shows everything that was entered. The example is from the author's audit log, yours will differ.

Example: The Author changed the date from 10/15/20XX to 10/16/20XX for Sales Receipt No. 1001. The Audit Log shows that the sales receipt was edited.

Edited Sales Receipt No. 1001	Cash Sales	10/15/2017	$2,500.00
Edited Sales Receipt No. 1001	Cash Sales	10/16/2017	$2,500.00

Recent Transactions

Another way to drill down to the original entry is to go to Recent Transactions.

1. Click (magnifying-glass icon). Recent Transactions are listed. Click View More to see all of them. (*Hint:* You may need to scroll down.)
2. To edit a transaction, link to it. Make any needed changes, then save.

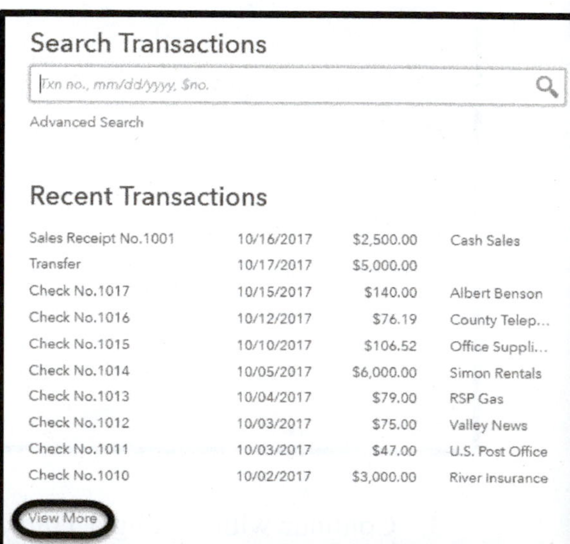
Search Transactions

Txn no., mm/dd/yyyy, $no.

Advanced Search

Recent Transactions

Sales Receipt No.1001	10/16/2017	$2,500.00	Cash Sales
Transfer	10/17/2017	$5,000.00	
Check No.1017	10/15/2017	$140.00	Albert Benson
Check No.1016	10/12/2017	$76.19	County Telep...
Check No.1015	10/10/2017	$106.52	Office Suppli...
Check No.1014	10/05/2017	$6,000.00	Simon Rentals
Check No.1013	10/04/2017	$79.00	RSP Gas
Check No.1012	10/03/2017	$75.00	Valley News
Check No.1011	10/03/2017	$47.00	U.S. Post Office
Check No.1010	10/02/2017	$3,000.00	River Insurance

View More

REGISTERS

There are a variety of accounts in QuickBooks — assets, liabilities, etc. Registers are a useful way to look at transactions and amounts associated with a particular account.

1. From the Navigation bar > select Accounting. The Chart of Accounts appears.
2. In the 101 Checking row, link to View register. If a pop-up appears about Register basics read the information. To move between pages, click <Next: Filter and find>.
3. The Bank Register appears. Observe that the balance is $47,976.29. This agrees with the transaction register. A partial bank register is shown.

CHECK YOUR PROGRESS

Check Your Progress assignments are included on the Online Learning Center at www.mhhe.com/qbo2e > Student Edition > Chapter 3 > Check Your Progress.

1. What is the account balance as of 10/17/XX in these accounts? Indicate whether the accounts have a debit (dr.) or credit (cr.) balance.

   Account 101 Checking ____________________

   Account 205 Loan Payable ____________________

Account 401 Sales ____________________

Account 621 Office Supplies ____________________

Account 633 Telephone Expense ____________________

Account 635 Utilities ____________________

2. What is the 10/17/XX Net Income? ____________________

3. What are the total Liabilities and Equity? ____________________

4. What report(s) show the Net Income? ____________________

5. What report(s) shows all work completed? ____________________

WATCH VIDEO

Watch the Get paid 2x faster YouTube video at https://www.youtube.com/watch?v=-ruACVAWvkw. (*Hint:* The video link is also included on the Online Learning Center at www.mhhe.com/qbo2e > Student Edition > Chapter 3 > Videos or Narrated PowerPoints.)

SIGN OUT

To sign out of QBO, go Gear > Sign Out. *Or,* continue.

ONLINE LEARNING CENTER (OLC): www.mhhe.com/qbo2e

The OLC includes additional Chapter 3 resources. Go online to www.mhhe.com/qbo2e > Student Edition > select Chapter 3.

1. Narrated PowerPoints.
2. Online quizzes: 10 True or False and 10 multiple-choice questions. The Online quizzes are graded and can be emailed to your instructor.
3. Analysis question: Answer the analysis question, then email to your instructor.
4. Going to the Net

    a. Go online to the QuickBooks Learn & Support website at https://community.intuit.com/questions.
    b. Type a Search word; for example, type **Export a report list to Excel**. Answer these questions.

        1) What version of QuickBooks Online can be used to export to Excel.
        2) Do the changes you make in Excel affect the Excel report? Explain.

5. Video: Watch the Navigating QuickBooks on video at https://www.youtube.com/watch?v=48QBRQdyRmU.
6. Glossary of terms: Words that are italicized and boldfaced are defined in the glossary. The Glossary is also Appendix B.
7. Problem solving link includes Exercise 3-3.

QuickBooks Online updates on a regular basis. To read about new features and improvements, go to the QuickBooks blog, http://quickbooks.intuit.com/blog/ > Release notes. The Release notes are organized by month.

Exercise 3-1: Follow the instructions below to complete Exercise 3-1:

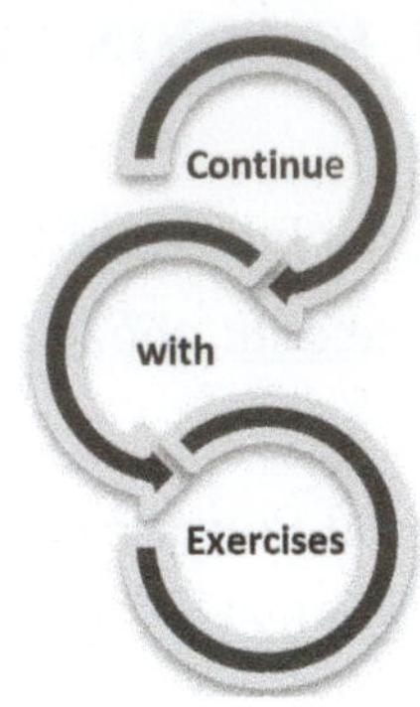

1. If necessary start QBO.
2. Use the transaction register to enter the following checks and cash sales.

   Tip: In the Bank accounts area of the Dashboard, 101 Checking shows $47,976.29. That's the same balance as the Transaction Register.

101 Checking In QuickBooks	$47,976.29

Ck. No.	Date	Description of Transaction	Payment	Deposit	Balance
	10/17	*Balance*			*47,976.29*
1018	10/19	Office Suppliers[1]	100.34		47,875.95
1019	10/20	Cays Advertising	125.00		47,750.95
	10/20	Cash Sales Sales Receipt 1002		2,000.00	49,750.95
1020	10/23	Best Cellular (Cell phone service; Telephone expense)	82.13		49,668.82
1021	10/25	Journal of Accounting (Dues & Subscriptions)	75.00		49,593.82

[1]QBO remembers the last Office Suppliers previous transaction amount. Type the 10/19 amount.

1022	10/29	Hour Deliveries (Freight & Delivery Expense)	42.40		49,551.42
ATM[2]	10/30	Cottage Restaurant[3] (Meal with clients)	126.40		49,425.02
	10/30	Cash Sales Sales Receipt 1003		1,500.00	50,925.02
1023	10/30	Barber's Paper Supply (Stationery & Printing)	425.22		50,499.80
1024	10/30	Hour Deliveries	22.25		50,477.55
1025	10/30	Office Suppliers	19.99		50,457.56

Hint: To compare your work to the Transaction Register, click Gear > Recent Transactions > View More. If necessary, edit transactions. Check the ending balance.

3. Display the Register for Account 101 Checking. (*Hint:* From the Navigation bar, select Accounting. On the Chart of Accounts, the 101 Checking row > click View register.) Make sure your ending balance is $50,457.56. If not, edit transaction(s).

Tip: If a Register basics prompt appears, click Next: Filter and find to read more. You can resort the register by clicking on the down-arrow next to DATE.

10/30/2017	1003	Cash Sales			$1,500.00		$50,457.56

4. Sign out or continue with Exercise 3-2.

[2]Debit card used so there is no check number.

[3]Add Cottage Restaurant as a Vendor. Type **ATM** in the Check No. field.

Exercise 3-2: Follow the instructions below to complete Exercise 3-2:

1. Export the Journal, Trial Balance, Profit and Loss and Balance Sheet as Excel and Adobe PDFs. The date range is 10/1/20XX to 10/30/20XX.
2. Use these file names:

Exercise 3-2_October Journal
Exercise 3-2_October Trial Balance
Exercise 3-2_October Profit and Loss
Exercise 3-2_October Balance Sheet

Hint: Another way to save Adobe PDF files is to Export to Excel and save the file. Then, on Excel's file menu, click File > Save as Adobe PDF > Convert to PDF > go to the location to save the PDF file. Steps are included in Appendix A, Troubleshooting.

Troubleshooting:

1) If exporting to Excel is not working, exit Excel and try again. *Or*, sign out and sign back in.
2) If your Journal shows a blank ***Undeposited Funds*** entry for the current date with a zero balance, refer to Appendix A, Undeposited Funds. This is a default entry and is okay.

Check Your Figures:

- Account No. 101 Checking, $50,457.56
- Account No. 401 Sales, $6,000.00
- Account No. 601 Advertising, $125.00
- Account No. 605 Dues & Subscriptions, $150.00
- Account No. 619 Meals and Entertainment, $126.40
- Account No. 621 Office Supplies, $226.85
- Account No. 627 Shipping and delivery expense, $47.00
- Net income, $4,457.56
- Total Liabilities and Equity, $69,457.56

Exercise 3-3: Problem Solving

The Online Learning Center includes Exercise 3-3 at www.mhhe.com/qbo2e > Student Edition > Chapter 4 > Problem Solving.

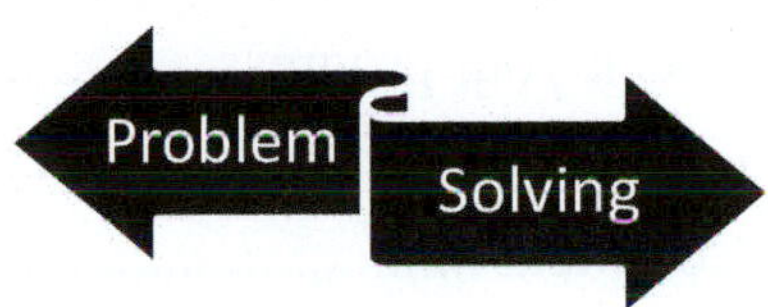

1. What is the date of the beginning balance?
2. Describe the beginning balance transaction type and the account distribution.
3. What are the steps for accessing the report that shows the beginning balance?

CHAPTER 3 INDEX

Chapter 4 Vendors and Inventory

Scenario: In this chapter, you start by checking your data. Remember to read the information next to the stop sign, then check the data entered so far. In Chapter 4, you use a bank statement to reconcile the checking account, enter vendors and inventory, record transactions, and display reports. You also display reports, financial statements, and the audit log. The objectives specify the work that is completed in Chapter 4.

OBJECTIVES

1. Start QuickBooks Online and sign in to QB Cloud_Student Name (your first and last name).
2. To check data, display Expense and Sales transactions and the October 30 Trial Balance.
3. Complete bank reconciliation with the October bank statement.
4. Enter new vendors.
5. Enter inventory products and services.
6. Record vendor transactions.
7. Print reports and financial statements.
8. Filter the audit log.
9. Save PDF files and export reports to Excel.
10. Complete Check Your Progress.
11. Go to the Online Learning Center at www.mhhe.com/qbo2e for additional resources.
12. Complete Exercises 4-1, 4-2 and 4-3.

In Chapter 4, you make sure your data is ready for adding new ***vendors*** who offer QB Cloud 30 days to pay for merchandise purchased. The Vendors page is where the company keeps track of suppliers. Vendors are people or companies that you pay money to, such as a store, utility, landlord, or subcontractor.

Before adding vendors, reconcile Account 101 Checking from the October 31 bank statement. Once you've reconciled the checking account, the October 31 Trial Balance is displayed. Then, you're ready to add vendors and learn about QBO's accounts payable system.

GETTING STARTED

1. Start your browser. Go online to http://qbo.intuit.com.
2. Sign in with your User ID and Password. (*Hint:* You can save your User ID. When you sign in, sometimes a pop-up may appear. Read the information, click X to close the pop-up.)

IMPORTANT: To verify your work so far, complete the next section, Check Your Data. If you notice any differences with the Sales and Expense transactions or the Trial Balance, make the necessary edits *before* adding transactions.

CHECK YOUR DATA

The purpose of Check Your Data is to make sure you have completed QB_Cloud Student Name work correctly. To do that, check Expenses, Sales, and the October 30 Trial Balance. If needed, drill down on transactions that need editing, then <Save>. Transactions are added in Chapter 4 and continued in Exercise 4-1. *Do not skip these steps.*

Make sure your Expense and Sales transactions match what is shown. Work accumulates in Chapters 2, 3 and 4. You need to check your work so far. The Expenses and Sales shown help you check the data stored to this point.

1. From the Navigation bar, select Expenses > Expenses tab. In Chapter 3 and Exercise 3-1, these Expense transactions were completed. Drill down and edit if needed. Compare your Expense transactions with the ones shown below. (*Hint:* The date order may be different on your Expense Transactions page. Click DATE to resort.) The total Expense Transactions are $10,542.44.

QB Cloud_Student Name

Date	Type	No.	Payee	Category	Total
10/02/2017	Check	1010	River Insurance	Prepaid Insurance	$3,000.00
10/03/2017	Check	1012	Valley News	Dues & Subscriptions	$75.00
10/03/2017	Check	1011	U.S. Post Office	Shipping and delivery expense	$47.00
10/04/2017	Check	1013	RSP Gas	Utilities	$79.00
10/05/2017	Check	1014	Simon Rentals	Prepaid Rent	$6,000.00
10/10/2017	Check	1015	Office Suppliers	Office Supplies	$106.52
10/12/2017	Check	1016	County Telephone	Telephone Expense	$76.19
10/15/2017	Check	1017	Albert Benson	Repair & Maintenance	$140.00
10/19/2017	Check	1018	Office Suppliers	Office Supplies	$100.34
10/20/2017	Check	1019	Cays Advertising	Advertising	$125.00
10/23/2017	Check	1020	Best Cellular	Telephone Expense	$82.13
10/25/2017	Check	1021	Journal of Accounting	Dues & Subscriptions	$75.00
10/29/2017	Check	1022	Hour Deliveries	Freight & Delivery	$42.40
10/30/2017	Check	1023	Barber's Paper Supply	Stationery & Printing	$425.22
10/30/2017	Check	ATM	Cottage Restaurant	Meals and Entertainment	$126.40
10/30/2017	Check	1024	Hour Deliveries	Freight & Delivery	$22.25
10/30/2017	Check	1025	Office Suppliers	Office Supplies	$19.99

2. From the Navigation bar, select Sales > All Sales. Sales Transactions are shown on the next page. Ignore the Sales Receipt for

today's date. It is a default entry to Undeposited Funds. Refer to Appendix A, Troubleshooting, or Appendix B, the Glossary for an explanation of Undeposited Funds. The total Sales Transactions are $6,000.00.

QB Cloud_Student Name

Date	Type	No.	Customer	Due date	Balance	Total	Status
10/16/2017	Sales Receipt	1001	Cash Sales		$0.00	$2,500.00	Paid
10/20/2017	Sales Receipt	1002	Cash Sales		$0.00	$2,000.00	Paid
10/30/2017	Sales Receipt	1003	Cash Sales		$0.00	$1,500.00	Paid

Edit if any of your Expense and Sales Transactions are incorrect.

October 30 Trial Balance

Display the October 30, 20XX Trial Balance. In Chapter 3, the account balances include the October 1 through 30 transactions entered in the chapter and in Exercise 3-2.

QB Cloud_Student Name

TRIAL BALANCE

As of October 30, 2017

	DEBIT	CREDIT
101 Checking	50,457.56	
123 Prepaid Rent	6,000.00	
125 Prepaid Insurance	3,000.00	
135 Computer Equipment	10,000.00	
205 Loan Payable		5,000.00
301 Common Stock		60,000.00
401 Sales		6,000.00
601 Advertising	125.00	
605 Dues & Subscriptions	150.00	
609 Freight & Delivery	64.65	
619 Meals and Entertainment	126.40	
621 Office Supplies	226.85	
625 Repair & Maintenance	140.00	
627 Shipping and delivery expense	47.00	
629 Stationery & Printing	425.22	
633 Telephone Expense	158.32	
635 Utilities	79.00	
TOTAL	**$71,000.00**	**$71,000.00**

Do your debit and credit balances agree? Make sure your Expense transactions, Sales transactions, and Trial Balance agree with the one shown. Drill down and edit if needed. Display the 10/1 thru 10/30 Trial Balance again.

QuickBooks Online updates automatically. When you sign in, the latest version of the software is being used. Some screen images may change but differences are usually minor. Regularly check the Online Learning Center's Text Updates link at www.mhhe.com/qbo2e.

ACCOUNT RECONCILIATION

QB Cloud receives a bank statement every month for their checking account, Account 101 Checking. The bank statement shows which checks, ATMs, and deposits cleared the bank. QBO's reconcile feature allows you to reconcile the bank statement. QB Cloud's bank statement is shown on the next two pages.

Statement of Account Checking Account October 1 to October 31, 20XX			QB Cloud_Student Name Your address, city, state, Zip Account No. 7731-2256
	REGULAR CHECKING		
Previous Balance	10/1/XX	$ 50,000.00	
4 Deposits (+)		11,000.00	
16 checks (-)		10,416.04	
1 Other Deductions (-)		126.40	
Service Charge		20.00	
Ending Balance	10/31/XX	**$50,437.56**	*Continued*

DEPOSITS				
		10/17/XX	2,500.00	
		10/18/XX	5,000.00	
		10/21/XX	2,000.00	
		10/30/XX	1,500.00	
CHECKS (Asterisk * indicates break in check number sequence)				
	10/3/XX	1010	3,000.00	
	10/4/XX	1011	47.00	
	10/4/XX	1012	75.00	
	10/6/XX	1013	79.00	
	10/7/XX	1014	6,000.00	
	10/17/XX	1015	106.52	
	10/16/XX	1016	76.19	
	10/16/XX	1017	140.00	
	10/24/XX	1018	100.34	
	10/26/XX	1019	125.00	
	10/26/XX	1020	82.13	
	10/26/XX	1021	75.00	
	10/31/XX	1022	42.40	
	10/31/XX	1023	425.22	
	10/31/XX	1024	22.25	
	10/31/XX	1025	19.99	
OTHER DEDUCTIONS (ATM's)				
	10/20/XZ	ATM	126.40	

Bank Reconciliation is the process of bringing the balance of the bank statement and the balance of the checking account into agreement. The Reconcile feature can be used with other accounts too.

Checking Account Register

1. From the Navigation bar, select . The Chart of Accounts All Lists page appears.
2. Double-click 101 Checking. The Bank Register 101 Checking page appears.

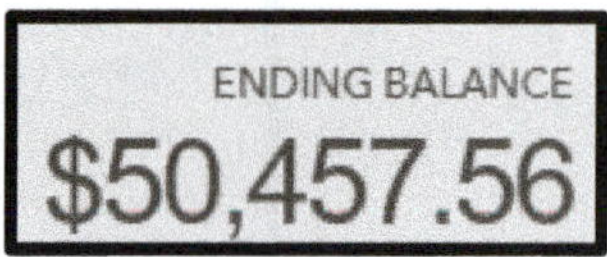

A list of all the transactions entered from 10/1/20XX through 10/30/20XX is shown. The Check register Ending Balance is $50,457.56 and does not include the service charge.

The bank statement balance on the previous page includes the $20 service charge: $50,457.56 – 20.00 = $50,437.56. Each check and each deposit has cleared the bank. Refer to the transaction registers in Chapter 3 and Exercise 3-1. Follow these steps to reconcile.

1. From the Bank Register page, click . Complete these fields.

Statement Ending Date:	type **10/31/20XX** (current year)
Ending Balance:	type **50437.56**
Service Charge:	type **20.00**
Date:	type **10/31/20XX** (current year)
Account:	603 Bank Charges completed automatically.

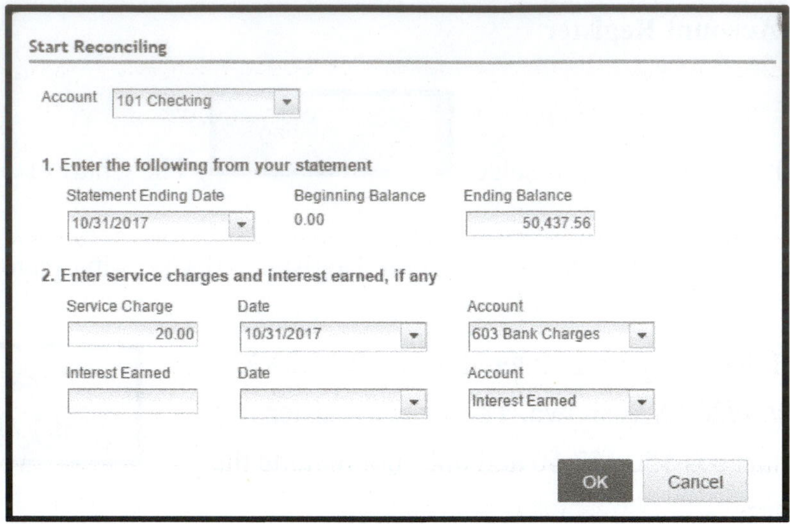

Before clicking <OK> check each field. Use the current year.

2. Click OK. The Reconcile - Checking page appears. Place checkmark next to each check and deposit (including the $50,000 owner investment). The bottom of the Reconcile – Checking page is shown below. (*Hint:* If you click on the box next to the Date in *both* the Checks and Payments and Deposits and Other Credits fields, checkmarks will be places in all the boxes.)

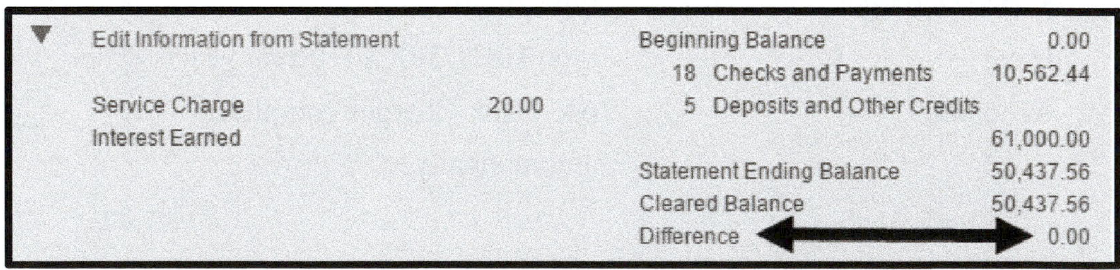

Observe the Cleared Balance shows 50,437.56 which is the same as the Ending Balance on the Bank Statement. Also, the Difference shows 0.00.

3. Click Finish Now. The Reconcile page appears and the Ending Balance, 50,437.56, is shown. (*Hint:* The Reconciled On column shows the current date.)

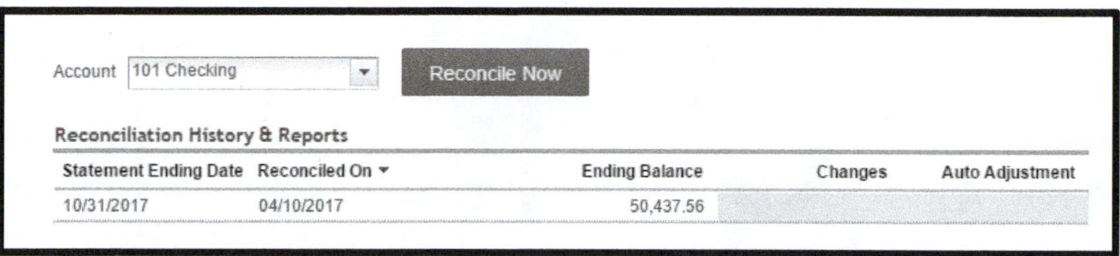

Statement Ending Date	Reconciled On	Ending Balance	Changes	Auto Adjustment
10/31/2017	04/10/2017	50,437.56		

Trial Balance

1. Go to the Reports page. Display the 10/1/20XX to 10/31/20XX Trial Balance. Compare your October 31 Trial Balance with the one shown.

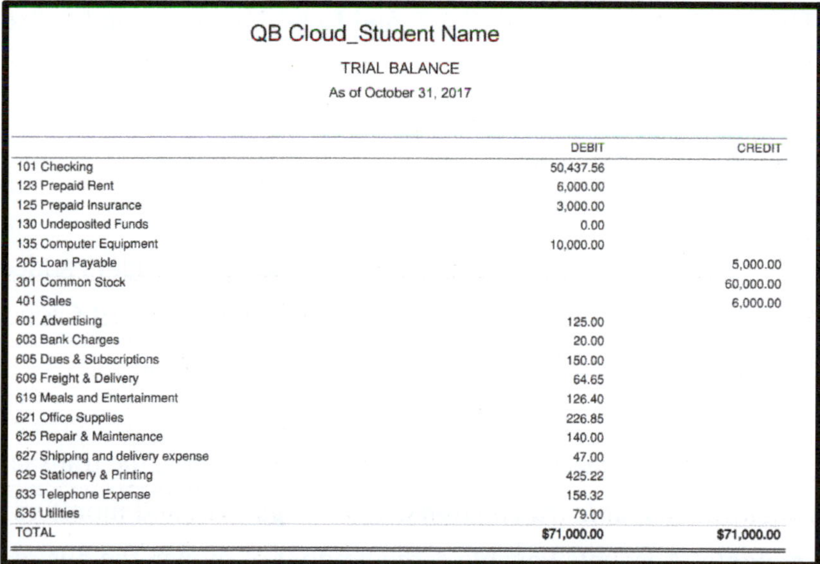

QB Cloud_Student Name

TRIAL BALANCE

As of October 31, 2017

	DEBIT	CREDIT
101 Checking	50,437.56	
123 Prepaid Rent	6,000.00	
125 Prepaid Insurance	3,000.00	
130 Undeposited Funds	0.00	
135 Computer Equipment	10,000.00	
205 Loan Payable		5,000.00
301 Common Stock		60,000.00
401 Sales		6,000.00
601 Advertising	125.00	
603 Bank Charges	20.00	
605 Dues & Subscriptions	150.00	
609 Freight & Delivery	64.65	
619 Meals and Entertainment	126.40	
621 Office Supplies	226.85	
625 Repair & Maintenance	140.00	
627 Shipping and delivery expense	47.00	
629 Stationery & Printing	425.22	
633 Telephone Expense	158.32	
635 Utilities	79.00	
TOTAL	$71,000.00	$71,000.00

Account 101 Checking shows the same balance as the bank statement, 50,437.56. Account 603 Bank Charges shows a balance of 20.00.

2. Save the October 31 Trial Balance as a PDF file and export to Excel. Use the file name **Chapter 4_October 31_Trial Balance**.
3. Return to the Dashboard or Home page. If you selected This year for the Dashboard's Profit and Loss, Expenses and Sales, these graphs are shown.

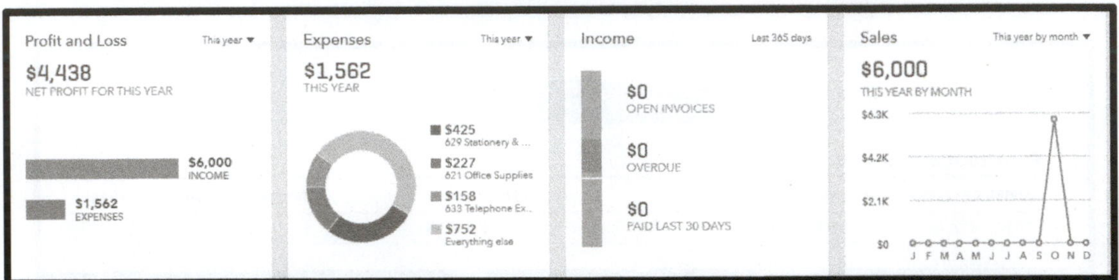

Why is the Income graph blank? The author completed work in April 2017. The Income area defaults to the Last 365 days. Since April 2017 is not within the last 365 days, the Income graph is empty.

Because This year can be selected, Profit and Loss, Expenses, and Sales show results.

ACCOUNTS PAYABLE: VENDORS

In Chapter 3, vendors that paid by check were added. The vendors added in Chapter 4 are paid later. Vendors are the businesses that offer QB Cloud credit to buy merchandise and/or assets, or credit for expenses incurred.

When QB Cloud makes purchases on account from vendors, the transactions are known as ***accounts payable transactions***. QBO organizes and monitors ***accounts payable***. Accounts Payable is the amount of money the business owes.

The next section shows how to set up new vendors. The Vendors page shows information about vendors who offer credit to QB Cloud. Since QB Cloud buys on credit from various vendors, the business wants to keep track of the amount owed and the due dates of bills. QBO's accounts payable system does that.

Vendors Page

To go to the Vendors page, from the Navigation bar, select Expenses > Vendors. The vendors added in Chapter 3 are shown below.

QB Cloud_Student Name

Vendor	Phone	Email	Open Balance
Albert Benson			$0.00
Barber's Paper Supply			$0.00
Best Cellular			$0.00
Cays Advertising			$0.00
Cottage Restaurant			$0.00
County Telephone			$0.00
Hour Deliveries			$0.00
Journal of Accounting			$0.00
Office Suppliers			$0.00
River Insurance			$0.00
RSP Gas			$0.00
Simon Rentals			$0.00
U.S. Post Office			$0.00
Valley News			$0.00

In Chapter 3, when checks were entered, these vendors were added on-the-fly. No addresses or other information was included.

Create New Checks

The transaction register shows checks that are issued on November 1, 20XX. **Note:** The date entered is **11/1/XXXX** (the current year). (*Hint:* QBO stores payment information. When needed, change the amount.)

Before entering 11/1/20XX transactions, verify the 10/31 balance of $50,437.56, select Accounting > Chart of Accounts appears > 101 Checking. The Bank Register for 101 Checking appears. The 10/31/20XX balance is $50,437.56.

ENDING BALANCE
$50,437.56

Ck. No.	Date	Description of Transaction	Payment	Deposit	Balance
	10/31	*Balance*			*50,437.56*
1026	11/1	RSP Gas	84.32		50,353.24
1027	11/1	County Telephone	76.19		50,277.05
1028	11/1	Hour Deliveries	46.90		50,230.15
1029	11/1	Cays Advertising	125.00		50,105.15
1030	11/1	Barber's Paper Supply (QB Cloud envelopes)	127.96		49,977.19

1. From the Navigation bar, select Expenses > Vendors
2. In the box next to RSP Gas, click on the box to put a checkmark in it. Click on the down-arrow next to Create bill > select Write check.

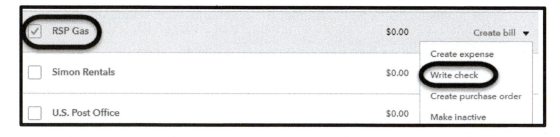

3. Using the transaction register on the previous page, complete the appropriate fields. *(Hint:* Type the date, **11/1/20XX**, amount, **$84.32,** and, if necessary, **1026** in the Check no. field). QBO stores the amount paid on 10/4.

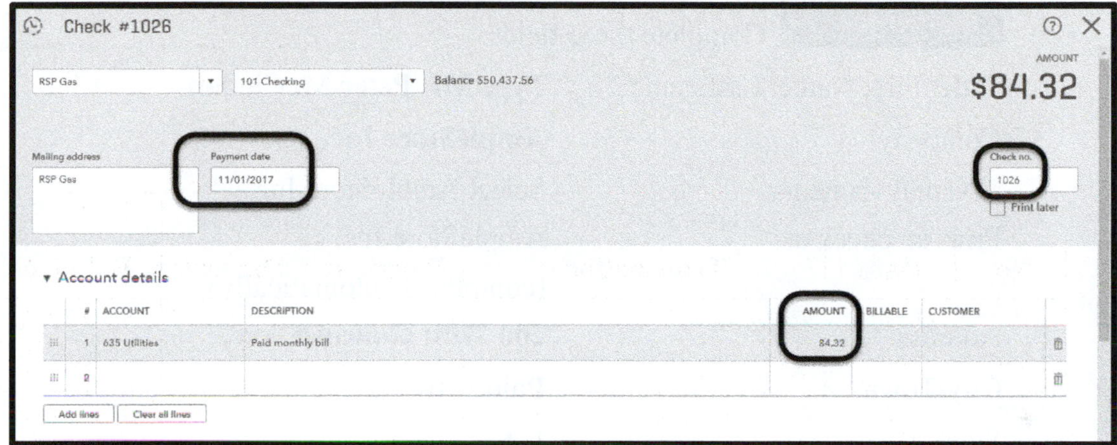

4. Save and close Ctrl Alt D. Go to the Vendors page. Complete checks 1027-1030. *Hint:* There are a couple ways to enter vendor checks.

   1) + > Check > select the appropriate vendor > type the Payment date > Check no., if necessary > Amount > click <Save and new>.
   2) From the Check page > select the vendor (payee) and enter the check information > click <Save and new>.

Verify the 11/1/20XX checking account balance of $49,977.19. (*Hint:* Select <Accounting>. On the Chart of Accounts, 101 Checking shows:

New Vendors

1. From the Navigation bar, select **Expenses** > **Vendors** > **New vendor**. Complete these fields.

Title, First Name, Last name:	Type **Mr. Peter McClellan**
Company:	**AmpleStore Inc.**
*Display name as:	Select AmpleStore Inc.
Print on check as:	AmpleStore Inc. (completed automatically)
Address:	**200 West Concord Ave.**
City/Town	**Palo Alto**
State	**CA**
ZIP:	**94301**
Country:	**USA**
Phone:	**650-555-8527**
Terms:	Select Net 30
as of:	Type **11/1/20XX**

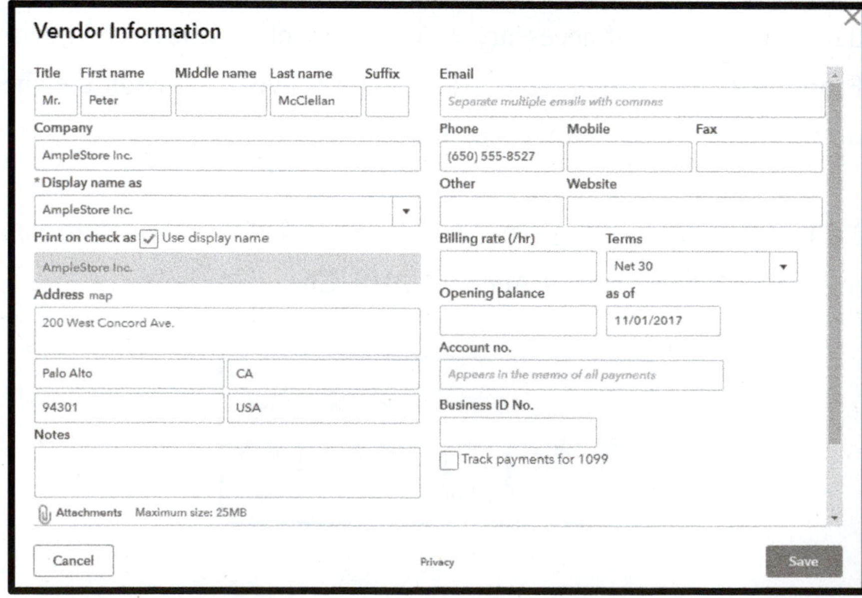

2. Click Save. Add the following vendors.

Title, First Name, Last name:	**Ms. Linda Rios**
Company:	**Any Time Deployment**
*Display name as:	Select Any Time Deployment
Print on check as:	Any Time Deployment (completed automatically)
Address:	**1189 W. Burnside**
City/Town	**Lexington**
State	**MA**
ZIP:	**02421**
Country:	**USA**
Phone:	**781-555-4671**
Terms:	Select Net 30
as of:	Type **11/1/20XX**

Save

Title, First Name, Last name:	**Mr. Jon Chen**
Company:	**CloudZ Channel**
*Display name as:	Select CloudZ Channel
Print on check as:	CloudZ Channel (completed automatically)
Address:	**110 Merit Street**
City/Town	**Menlo Park**
State	**CA**
ZIP:	**94025**

Country:	**USA**
Phone:	**650-555-3250**
Terms:	Select Net 30
as of:	Type **11/1/20XX**

Save

Title, First Name, Last name:	**Ms. Geraldine Harrison**
Company:	**Conf/Call**
*Display name as:	Select Conf/Call
Print on check as:	Conf/Call (completed automatically)
Address:	**700 North Prince Street**
City/Town	**Tempe**
State	**AZ**
ZIP:	**85008**
Country:	**USA**
Phone:	**480-555-2411**
Terms:	Select Net 30
as of:	Type **11/1/20XX**

Save

Vendor Contact List

To view all of the vendors added in Chapters 3 and 4, do this.

1. From the Navigation bar, select Reports > type **Vendor Contact List** in the search field.

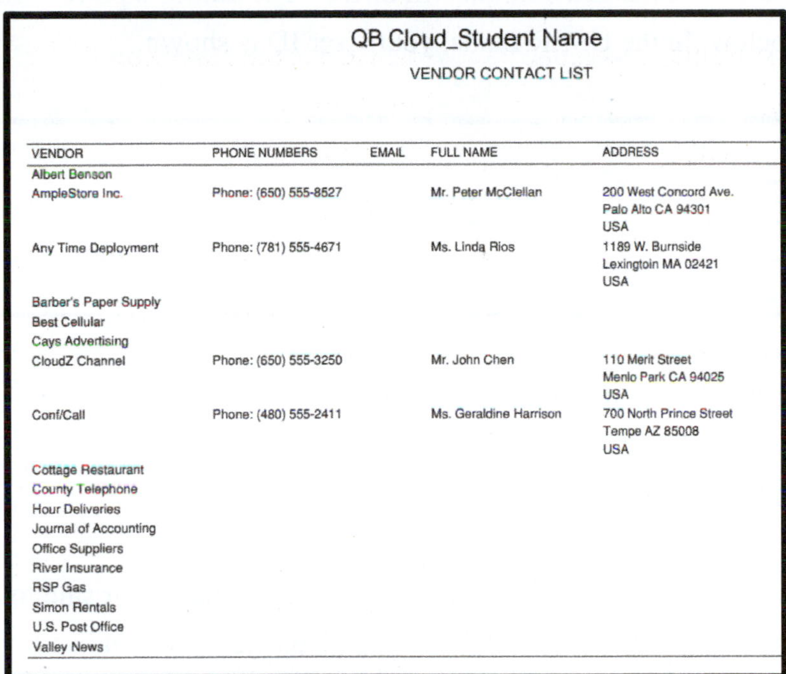

QB Cloud_Student Name

VENDOR CONTACT LIST

VENDOR	PHONE NUMBERS	EMAIL	FULL NAME	ADDRESS
Albert Benson				
AmpleStore Inc.	Phone: (650) 555-8527		Mr. Peter McClellan	200 West Concord Ave. Palo Alto CA 94301 USA
Any Time Deployment	Phone: (781) 555-4671		Ms. Linda Rios	1189 W. Burnside Lexingtoin MA 02421 USA
Barber's Paper Supply				
Best Cellular				
Cays Advertising				
CloudZ Channel	Phone: (650) 555-3250		Mr. John Chen	110 Merit Street Menlo Park CA 94025 USA
Conf/Call	Phone: (480) 555-2411		Ms. Geraldine Harrison	700 North Prince Street Tempe AZ 85008 USA
Cottage Restaurant				
County Telephone				
Hour Deliveries				
Journal of Accounting				
Office Suppliers				
River Insurance				
RSP Gas				
Simon Rentals				
U.S. Post Office				
Valley News				

The four vendors added in this chapter show the vendor name, phone numbers, full name, and address. In Chapter 3, vendors were added on-the-fly with only the vendor name.

2. Save the Vendor Contact List as a PDF file and export to Excel. Use the file name **Chapter 4_Vendor Contact List**.

When you enter bills for a vendor, Accounts Payable and the vendor, are credited. The asset account or expense account is debited.

AUDIT LOG

The Audit Log shows all the work completed.

1. Select  > Audit Log. All the work you have completed is shown. (*Hint:* Your Date Changed column will differ.) The author's partial Audit Log is shown below. In the USER fields, your User ID is shown.

DATE CHANGED	USER ▲	EVENT	NAME	DATE	AMOUNT	HISTORY
Apr 18, 12:51 pm US Mountain S...		Added Vendor: Conf/Call				View
Apr 18, 12:44 pm US Mountain S...		Added Vendor: AmpleStore Inc.				View
Apr 18, 2:23 pm US Mountain St...		Added Bill No. AS7	AmpleStore Inc.	11/02/2017	$300.00	View
Apr 18, 12:47 pm US Mountain S...		Added Vendor: CloudZ Channel				View

2. To edit work, click View. If necessary drill down.

INVENTORY PRODUCTS AND SERVICES

An ***inventory item*** is a product that is purchased from vendors for sale to customers. Inventory is tracked within Account No. 115 Merchandise Inventory on the balance sheet. Because the Merchandise Inventory account is increased or decreased for every purchase, sale or return, its balance in the general ledger is current. In QBO when QB Cloud purchases and receives inventory items, they are added to inventory. When those items are sold, they are subtracted from inventory.

Key points about inventory:

- The value of an inventory item is the amount the company paid for it.
- Recording the purchase of an inventory item increases the Inventory Asset account on the Balance Sheet by the cost of the item and increases the Quantity on Hand units for that item.
- Recording the sale of an inventory item decreases the Inventory Asset account by the original cost of the item and decreases the Quantity on hand for that item.
- Recording a sale also increases the Cost of Goods Sold account by the original cost of the item and increases the Sales or Product Income account by the amount the customer paid for that item. The difference between the income amounts and the COGS amount is the gross profit on that item.

Products and Services

Use ***products and services*** to enter transaction descriptions and prices or rates. Products and services can also be added on a purchase form (such as a bill or purchase order) or a sales form (such as an invoice, sales receipt, or estimate).

Inventory items, also called products, are tracked both at their purchase cost and sales price. To make sure the Account #, Account name, Type, and Detail Type are correct, go to the Account List (Reports > type **Account List**.) QBO tracks purchases and sales using these classifications. Make sure your account list agrees. If necessary, drill down on the account to edit.

Account #	Account	Type	Detail Type
105	Accounts Receivable (A/R)	Accounts receivable (A/R)	Account Receivable (A/R)
115	Merchandise Inventory	Other Current Assets	Inventory
401	Sales	Income	Sales of Product Income
501	Cost of Goods Sold	Cost of Goods Sold	Supplies & Materials - COGS

When you add inventory, the Products or Service Information page includes these fields for inventory costing (shown on page 163).

Fields	Account used
Inventory Asset Account	115 Merchandise Inventory
Income Account	401 Sales
Expense Account	501 Cost of Goods Sold

In this chapter, Vendors and Inventory, and then in Chapter 5, Customers and Sales, these account distributions are recorded when purchases and sales are posted.

Purchase inventory on account

Account	Debit	Credit
115 Merchandise Inventory	300.00	
201 Accounts Payable/AmpleStore Inc.		300.00
Bill No. AS7 received from AmpleStore Inc. for the purchase of 20 data storage products, $15 each, for a total of $300.		

Sold inventory on account

Account	Debit	Credit
105 Accounts Receivable/eBiz	150.00	
501 Cost of Goods Sold	75.00	
401 Sales		150.00
115 Merchandise Inventory		75.00
Sold 5 data storage products on account to eBiz for a total of $150, Invoice 1007. (*Hint:* Data storage is purchased from the vendor for a cost of $15 each. The sales price to customers is $30 each.)		

Observe that when inventory is purchased on account, the cost of the product increases Merchandise Inventory (account debited) and Accounts Payable/vendor is credited. When inventory is sold on account, Account Receivable/customer is debited for the sales price and Cost of Goods Sold is debited for the cost of inventory. Sales is credited for the sales price and Merchandise Inventory is credited for the cost of inventory.

When products are set up, general ledger accounts are updated when purchases and sales are recorded. QBO tracks cost of goods sold, stock levels, sales prices, and vendors. This is an example of a ***perpetual inventory*** system. In a perpetual inventory system, an up-to-date record of inventory is maintained and the inventory account is revised each time a purchase or sale is made.

QBO's inventory tracking has specific effects on the Balance Sheet and Profit & Loss reports. On the Balance Sheet, the inventory account is associated with the inventory-enabled Product/Service item. Inventory is grouped under Other Current Assets. The asset balance shows the cost of your current (unsold) inventory.

The P&L report shows the Sales of Product Income accounts and the Cost of Goods Sold accounts that are associated with your inventory-enabled Product/Service items. COGS accounts are displayed in a separate section of the P&L report between the Income and Expense sections. The difference between your Total Income amount and your Total COGS amount is shown on the Gross Profit line.

Make sure that your Sales settings for Products and services are On. Select Gear > Account and Settings > Sales. Edit if necessary.

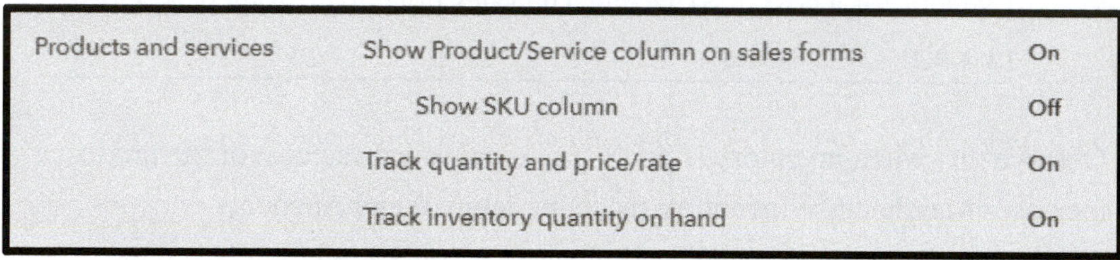

Check Account and Settings for Expenses. If necessary, place a checkmark next to Track billable expenses and items as income. The default bill payment terms are Net 30. Check the Bills and expenses selections then <Save>.

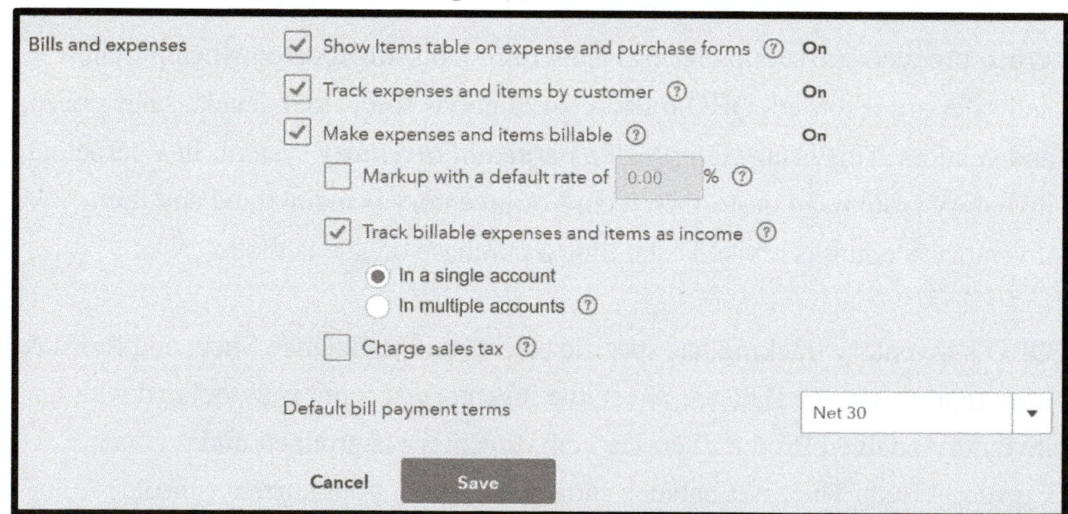

After saving, Bills and expenses shows:

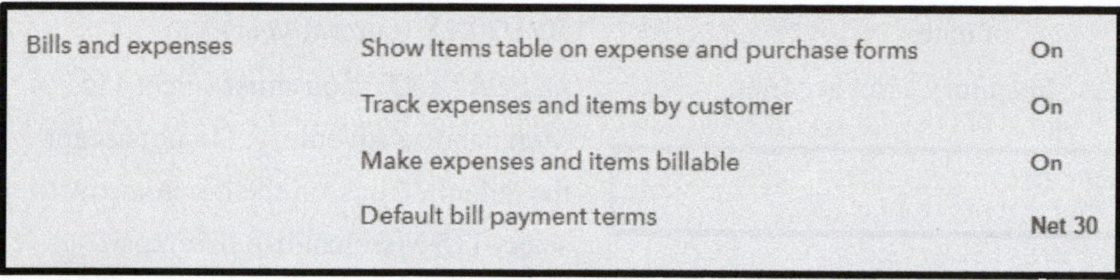

Done

Follow these steps to add inventory.

1. From the Navigation bar, 

.
2. The Products and Services page appears. Click New. The Product/Service Information page appears. Select Inventory.

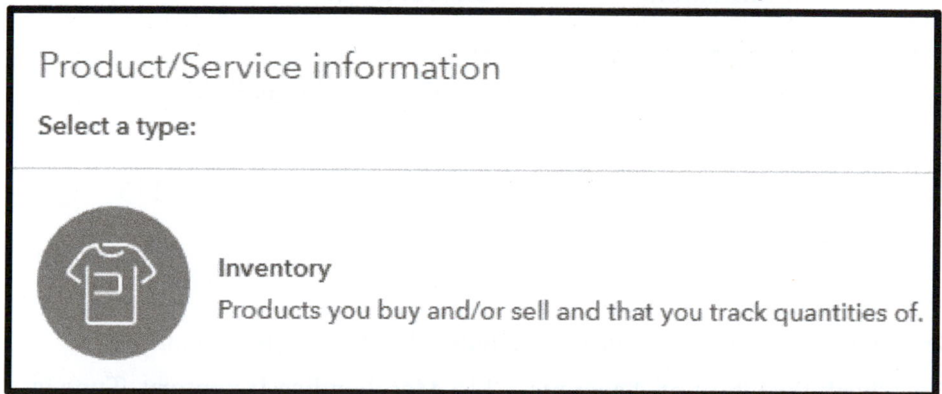

After selecting Inventory, complete these fields. (*Hint:* An asterisk * indicates field that must be completed.)

*Name: Type **Data storage**

Initial quantity on hand: **0** (you *must* type a zero)

As of date: **10/1/20XX** (current year)

Inventory asset account: *IMPORTANT*: You **must** select 115 Merchandise Inventory. Do not accept the default. Click on the down-arrow to select 115 Merchandise Inventory.

Sales information: **Data storage**

Sales price/rate: **30**

Income account:

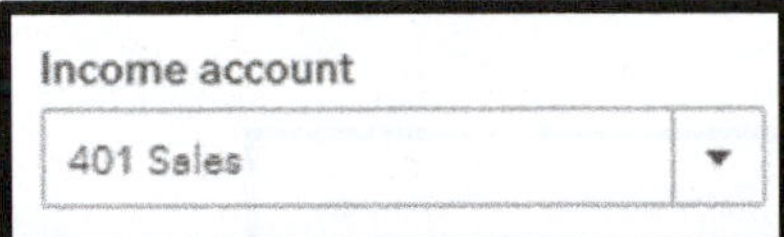

You **must** select 401 Sales. Do not accept the default. Click on the down-arrow to select 401 Sales. If necessary, scroll up.

If necessary, select SHOW MORE.

Purchasing information: **Data storage**

Cost: **15**

Expense account: 501 Cost of Goods Sold

Troubleshooting: If you do not have selections for Account 115 Merchandise Inventory or 401 Sales, do this:

- Check Account and Settings, pages 105-107, steps 2, 3 and 4.
- Check the Chart of Accounts – 115 Merchandise Inventory, Type is Other Current Assets, Detail Type is Inventory; 401 Sales, Type is Income, Detail Type is Sales of Product Income. Refer to pages 80-81 for the Chart of Accounts (or Account List).

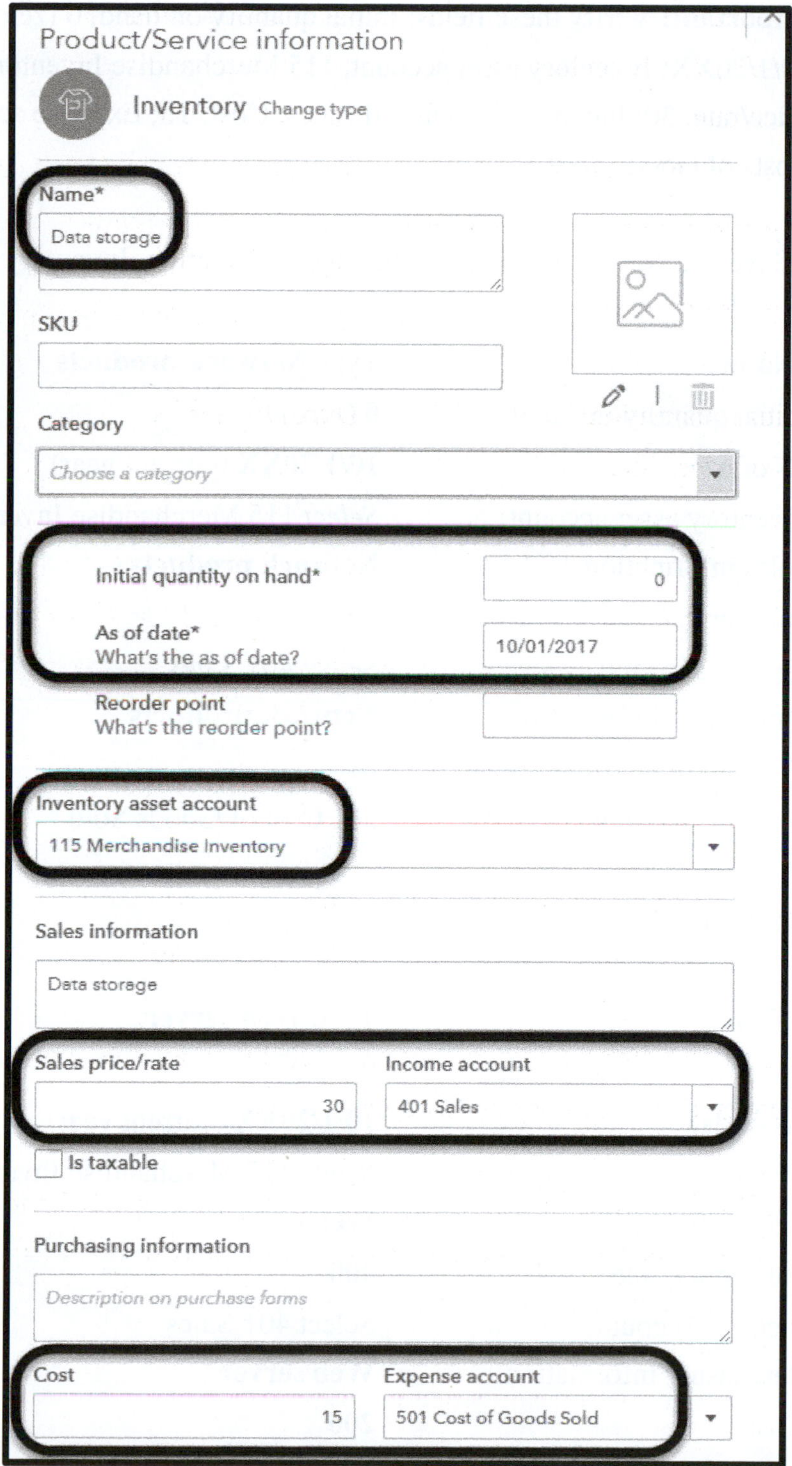
Product/Service information
Inventory Change type
Name*
Data storage
SKU
Category
Choose a category
Initial quantity on hand*
0
As of date*
What's the as of date?
10/01/2017
Reorder point
What's the reorder point?
Inventory asset account
115 Merchandise Inventory
Sales information
Data storage
Sales price/rate
30
Income account
401 Sales
Is taxable
Purchasing information
Description on purchase forms
Cost
15
Expense account
501 Cost of Goods Sold

Important: Verify these fields: Initial quantity on hand, 0 (zero); As of date, 10/1/20XX; Inventory asset account, 115 Merchandise Inventory; Sales price/rate, 30; Income account, 401 Sales; Cost, 15; Expense account, 501 Costs of Goods Sold.

3. <Save and New>. The Product/Service information, Inventory page appears.

***Name**:	Type **Network products**
Initial quantity on hand:	**0** (zero)
As of date:	**10/1/20XX** (current year)
Inventory asset account:	*Select* 115 Merchandise Inventory
Sales information:	**Network products**
Sales price/rate	**50**
Income account:	Select 401 Sales
Purchasing information:	**Network products**
Cost:	**25**
Expense Account:	501 Cost of Goods Sold

4. <Save and New>.

***Name**:	Type **Web server**
Initial quantity on hand:	**0** (zero)
As of date:	**10/1/20XX** (current year)
Inventory asset account:	*Select* 115 Merchandise Inventory
Sales information:	**Web server**
Sales price/rate:	**400**
Income Account:	Select 401 Sales
Purchasing information:	**Web server**
Cost:	**200**

Expense Account: 501 Cost of Goods Sold

5. <Save and New>. Select Inventory item.

***Name**:	Type **Webinars**
Initial quantity on hand:	**0** (zero)
As of date:	**10/1/20XX** (current year)
Inventory asset account:	Select 115 Merchandise Inventory
Sales information:	**Webinars**
Sales price/rate:	**90**
Income account:	Select 401 Sales
Purchasing information:	**Webinars**
Cost:	**45**
Expense account:	501 Cost of Goods Sold

6. Save and close.

Products and Services List

7. After entering inventory items, the Products and Services page appears. The Products and Services list shows the name, type, sales description, sales price, and cost. To see individual product costs, link to the item.

8. From the Navigation bar, select Reports > in the Search field, type **Product/Service List** > press <Enter>.

QB Cloud_Student Name

PRODUCT/SERVICE LIST

PRODUCT/SERVICE	TYPE	DESCRIPTION	PRICE	COST	QTY ON HAND
Cash Sales	Noninventory		0.00		
Data storage	Inventory	Data storage	30.00	15.00	
Hours	Service		0.00		
Network products	Inventory	Network products	50.00	25.00	
Sales	Service		0.00		
Web server	Inventory	Web server	400.00	200.00	
Webinars	Inventory	Webinars	90.00	45.00	

Save the Product/Service List as a PDF file and export to Excel. Use the file name **Chapter 4_Product Service List**. (*Hint:* Your Product/Service List may include additional accounts that QBO adds automatically. This is okay.)

VENDOR TRANSACTIONS

In QBO, information about a purchase can be recorded on the Vendors page *or* by selecting the Create button (+) > Bill. A ***bill*** posts to Accounts Payable and the vendor with the appropriate expense or asset account. You enter a bill (payable to a vendor) to record an expense or purchase of assets.

Enter Bills

Analyze transaction → Transaction date → Input transaction

Date	*Description of Transaction*
11/2/20XX	Bill no. AS7 received from AmpleStore Inc. for the purchase of 20 data storage products, $15 each, for a total of $300.

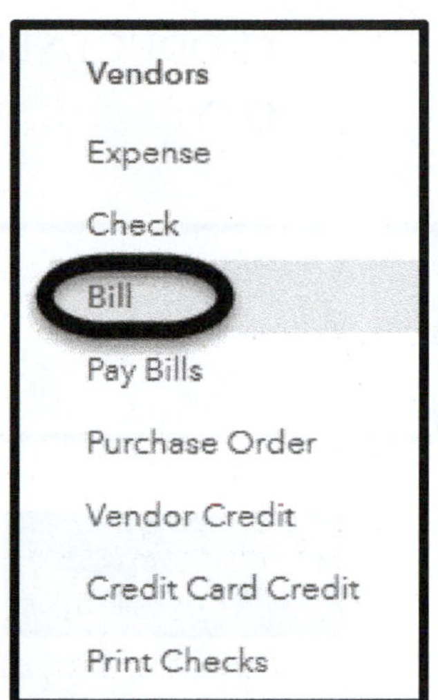

1. After clicking > select Bill. (*Hint:* You may need to ► Show more to see the Bill selection.) The Bill page appears.
2. Complete these fields.

Choose a vendor:	Select AmpleStore Inc.
Bill date:	Type **11/2/20XX** (Due date automaitcally completed.)
Bill No.	**AS7**

In the Item details section, click on the right-arrow to expand it

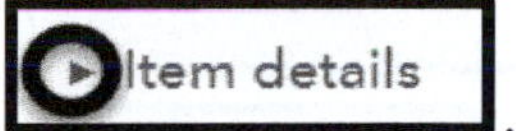

. (*Hint:* If you do not have an Item details section, read Troubleshooting.)

Troubleshooting: My Bill page does <u>not</u> show an Item Details area? What should I do? Click <Yes> to close the Bill page without saving. Go to > Account and Settings > Expenses. Make sure Show Items table on expense and purchase forms is On. To edit, click . Return to step 1 above to enter Bill no. AS7.

Bills and expenses	Show Items table on expense and purchase forms	On
	Track expenses and items by customer	On
	Make expenses and items billable	On
	Default bill payment terms	Net 30

PRODUCT/SERVICE: select Data storage
QTY: **20** (The Item details section is shown below)

▾ Item details

#	PRODUCT/SERVICE	DESCRIPTION	QTY	RATE	AMOUNT
1	Data storage	Data storage	20	15	300.00

Save and new

Additional transactions

Analyze transaction → Transaction date → Input transaction

Date	*Description of Transaction*
11/3/20XX	Bill no. ATD90 received from Any Time Deployment for the purchase of 10 network products, $25 each, for a total of $250. (*Hint:* In the ▼ Item details section Product/Service field, select Network products.)
11/3/20XX	Bill No. CZ33 received from CloudZ Channel for the purchase of 8 web servers, $200 each, for a total of $1,600. (*Hint:* In the ▼ Item details area Product/ Service, select Web server.)
11/3/20XX	Bill No. 78CC received from Conf/Call for the purchase of 6 webinars, $45 each, for a total of $270. (*Hint:* In the ▼ Item details area, Product/Service field, select Webinars.)

REPORTS

Display the following reports. Your instructor may require additional reports.

Journal

To see the transactions that you have entered, display the Journal report.

1. If necessary, close the Bill page by clicking [X] on the right side of the Bill page.
2. Click [Reports]. Type **Journal** in the Search field. Press <Enter>.
3. Type **11/1/XX** to **11/3/XX** > press <Tab>. (*Hint:* Use the current year. Type either four characters or two characters for the year.)

QB Cloud_Student Name

JOURNAL

November 1-3, 2017

DATE	TRANSACTION TYPE	NUM	NAME	MEMO/DESCRIPTION	ACCOUNT #	ACCOUNT	DEBIT	CREDIT
11/01/2017	Check	1030	Barber's Paper Supply		101	101 Checking		$127.96
					629	629 Stationery & Printing	$127.96	
							$127.96	**$127.96**
11/01/2017	Check	1026	RSP Gas		101	101 Checking		$84.32
					635	635 Utilities	$84.32	
							$84.32	**$84.32**
11/01/2017	Check	1027	County Telephone		101	101 Checking		$76.19
					633	633 Telephone Expense	$76.19	
							$76.19	**$76.19**
11/01/2017	Check	1028	Hour Deliveries		101	101 Checking		$46.90
					609	609 Freight & Delivery	$46.90	
							$46.90	**$46.90**
11/01/2017	Check	1029	Cays Advertising		101	101 Checking		$125.00
					601	601 Advertising	$125.00	
							$125.00	**$125.00**
11/02/2017	Bill	AS7	AmpleStore Inc.		201	201 Accounts Payable (A/P)		$300.00
				Data storage	115	115 Merchandise Inventory	$300.00	
							$300.00	**$300.00**
11/03/2017	Bill	ATD90	Any Time Deployment		201	201 Accounts Payable (A/P)		$250.00
				Network products	115	115 Merchandise Inventory	$250.00	
							$250.00	**$250.00**
11/03/2017	Bill	CZ33	CloudZ Channel		201	201 Accounts Payable (A/P)		$1,600.00
				Web server	115	115 Merchandise Inventory	$1,600.00	
							$1,600.00	**$1,600.00**
11/03/2017	Bill	78CC	Conf/Call		201	201 Accounts Payable (A/P)		$270.00
				Webinars	115	115 Merchandise Inventory	$270.00	
							$270.00	**$270.00**
TOTAL							**$2,880.37**	**$2,880.37**

Did you notice some of the checks are out of order, 1030, then 1026? The author may have recorded the checks out of order.

4. Save the Journal as a PDF file and export to Excel. Use the file name **Chapter 4_Journal**. (*Hint:* If you did not type a description, the memo/description column will be blank or show a different description. This is okay.)

Transaction Detail by Account

1. Go to the Reports page. In the Search field > type **Transaction Detail by Account** > from 11/1/2017 to 11/3/2017 > Run report. Compare your Transaction Detail by Account report with the one shown on the next page

QB Cloud_Student Name

TRANSACTION DETAIL BY ACCOUNT

November 1-3, 2017

DATE	TRANSACTION TYPE	NUM	NAME	MEMO/DESCRIPTION	SPLIT	AMOUNT	BALANCE
101 Checking							
11/01/2017	Check	1030	Barber's Paper Supply		629 Stationery & Printing	-127.96	-127.96
11/01/2017	Check	1029	Cays Advertising		601 Advertising	-125.00	-252.96
11/01/2017	Check	1026	RSP Gas		635 Utilities	-84.32	-337.28
11/01/2017	Check	1027	County Telephone		633 Telephone Expense	-76.19	-413.47
11/01/2017	Check	1028	Hour Deliveries		609 Freight & Delivery	-46.90	-460.37
Total for 101 Checking						**$ -460.37**	
115 Merchandise Inventory							
11/02/2017	Bill	AS7	AmpleStore Inc.	Data storage	201 Accounts Payable (A/P)	300.00	300.00
11/03/2017	Bill	CZ33	CloudZ Channel	Web server	201 Accounts Payable (A/P)	1,600.00	1,900.00
11/03/2017	Bill	78CC	Conf/Call	Webinars	201 Accounts Payable (A/P)	270.00	2,170.00
11/03/2017	Bill	ATD90	Any Time Deployment	Network products	201 Accounts Payable (A/P)	250.00	2,420.00
Total for 115 Merchandise Inventory						**$2,420.00**	
201 Accounts Payable (A/P)							
11/02/2017	Bill	AS7	AmpleStore Inc.		115 Merchandise Inventory	300.00	300.00
11/03/2017	Bill	78CC	Conf/Call		115 Merchandise Inventory	270.00	570.00
11/03/2017	Bill	ATD90	Any Time Deployment		115 Merchandise Inventory	250.00	820.00
11/03/2017	Bill	CZ33	CloudZ Channel		115 Merchandise Inventory	1,600.00	2,420.00
Total for 201 Accounts Payable (A/P)						**$2,420.00**	
601 Advertising							
11/01/2017	Check	1029	Cays Advertising		101 Checking	125.00	125.00
Total for 601 Advertising						**$125.00**	
609 Freight & Delivery							
11/01/2017	Check	1028	Hour Deliveries		101 Checking	46.90	46.90
Total for 609 Freight & Delivery						**$46.90**	
629 Stationery & Printing							
11/01/2017	Check	1030	Barber's Paper Supply		101 Checking	127.96	127.96
Total for 629 Stationery & Printing						**$127.96**	
633 Telephone Expense							
11/01/2017	Check	1027	County Telephone		101 Checking	76.19	76.19
Total for 633 Telephone Expense						**$76.19**	
635 Utilities							
11/01/2017	Check	1026	RSP Gas		101 Checking	84.32	84.32
Total for 635 Utilities						**$84.32**	

2. Save the Transaction Detail by Account as a PDF file and export to Excel. Use the file name **Chapter 4_Transaction Detail by Account.**

Trial Balance

1. Go to the Reports page. In the Search field, select or type **Trial Balance** from 10/1/XX to 11/3/XX > Run report.

QB Cloud_Student Name

TRIAL BALANCE

As of November 3, 2017

	DEBIT	CREDIT
101 Checking	49,977.19	
115 Merchandise Inventory	2,420.00	
123 Prepaid Rent	6,000.00	
125 Prepaid Insurance	3,000.00	
130 Undeposited Funds	0.00	
135 Computer Equipment	10,000.00	
201 Accounts Payable (A/P)		2,420.00
205 Loan Payable		5,000.00
3000 Opening Balance Equity		0.00
301 Common Stock		60,000.00
401 Sales		6,000.00
601 Advertising	250.00	
603 Bank Charges	20.00	
605 Dues & Subscriptions	150.00	
609 Freight & Delivery	111.55	
619 Meals and Entertainment	126.40	
621 Office Supplies	226.85	
625 Repair & Maintenance	140.00	
627 Shipping and delivery expense	47.00	
629 Stationery & Printing	553.18	
633 Telephone Expense	234.51	
635 Utilities	163.32	
TOTAL	**$73,420.00**	**$73,420.00**

Comment: Make sure your November 3 Trial Balance agrees with this one. If your Trial Balance does not show Account 130 Undeposited Funds or Account 3000 Opening Balance Equity, that is okay. Depending on when QBO updates, accounts with zero balances may be shown on your Trial Balance. Reports can be filtered so that zero balances do not display. (This is shown in Chapter 5 on page 201).

2. Export to Excel and save as a PDF file. Use the file name **Chapter 4_Trial Balance.**

Observe that Account 101 Checking's balance, $49,977.19 is the same as the Bank Register balance – select **Accounting** > the Chart of Accounts appears.

Inventory Valuation Summary

1. Go to the Reports page > in the Search field, type **Inventory Valuation Summary** as of **11/3/XX** > **Run report**.

QB Cloud_Student Name

INVENTORY VALUATION SUMMARY

As of November 3, 2017

	SKU	QTY	ASSET VALUE	CALC. AVG
Data storage		20.00	300.00	15.00
Network products		10.00	250.00	25.00
Web server		8.00	1,600.00	200.00
Webinars		6.00	270.00	45.00
TOTAL			**$2,420.00**	

Observe that the Asset Value, $2,420.00, is the same as Account No. 115, Merchandise Inventory, and Account No. 201 Accounts Payable, on the Trial Balance.

2. Export to Excel and save as a PDF file. Use the file name **Chapter 4_Inventory Valuation Summary.**

Vendor Balance Summary as of 11/3/20XX

1. Go to the Report page. In the Search field, select or type **Vendor Balance Summary** > As of 11/3/20XX.

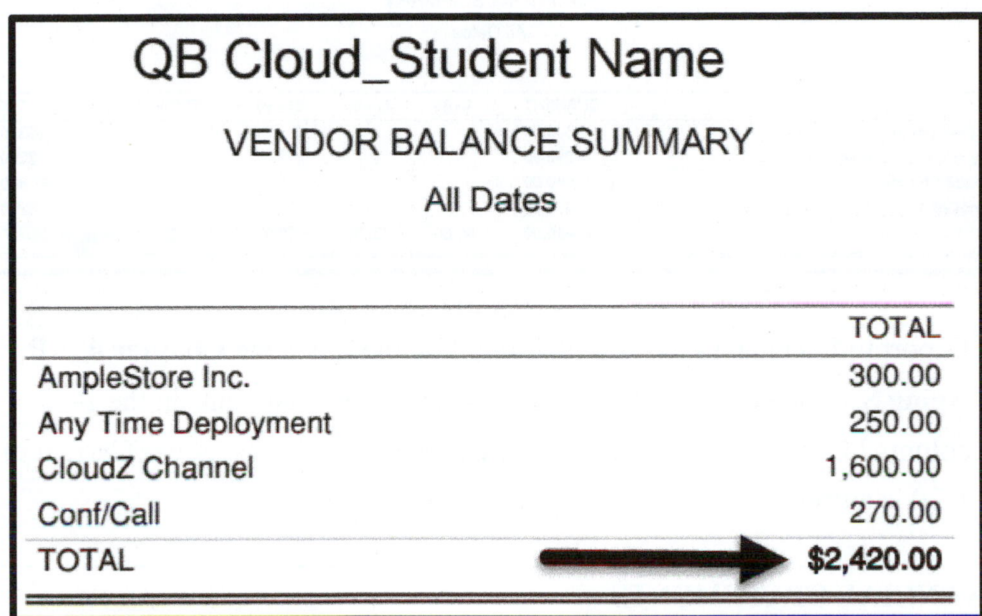

QB Cloud_Student Name

VENDOR BALANCE SUMMARY

All Dates

	TOTAL
AmpleStore Inc.	300.00
Any Time Deployment	250.00
CloudZ Channel	1,600.00
Conf/Call	270.00
TOTAL	**$2,420.00**

2. Observe that the Vendor Total, $2,420.00, is the same as Account 201 Accounts Payable, on the Trial Balance. Export to Excel and save as a PDF file. Use the file name **Chapter 4_Vendor Balance Summary.**

A/P Aging Summary

1. Go to the Reports page. In the Search field, select or type **A/P Aging Summary**. In the Report period field, select All Dates [Report period: All Dates] > [Run report]. (*Hint:* Select all dates so that the current date does not

affect the report.) Observe that the Total is also $2,420.00 which matches the balances of Account 115 Merchandise Inventory and Account 201 Accounts Payable on the Trial Balance.

QB Cloud_Student Name

A/P AGING SUMMARY

All Dates

	CURRENT	1 - 30	31 - 60	61 - 90	91 AND OVER	TOTAL
AmpleStore Inc.	300.00					$300.00
Any Time Deployment	250.00					$250.00
CloudZ Channel	1,600.00					$1,600.00
Conf/Call	270.00					$270.00
TOTAL	**$2,420.00**	**$0.00**	**$0.00**	**$0.00**	**$0.00**	**$2,420.00**

2. Export to Excel and save as a PDF file. Use the file name **Chapter 4_AP Aging Summary.** (*Hint:* Why does my report show amounts in the 1-30 column? Depending on the date your entered transactions, *either* Current or 1-30 is correct.)

FINANCIAL STATEMENTS

In QBO, the ***financial statements*** report economic information about the business. In QBO, the financial statements include:

- Profit and Loss: The P&L is also called an income statement. It summarizes income and expenses for the year or other period of time so you can tell whether you are operating at a profit or loss. The report shows subtotals for each income or expense account in your chart of accounts. The last line shows your net income (or loss) for the year or other period of time.

- Balance Sheet: The Balance Sheet summarizes the financial position of a business. It shows the value of the company's assets, liability, and equity as of a particular day. It is called a Balance Sheet because the value of the assets is always exactly equal to the combined value of the liabilities and equity. The balance sheet shows the ***accounting equation***.

Assets = Liabilities + Equity

- ***Statement of Cash Flows***: A report that shows how changes in the balance sheet accounts and income affect cash and cash equivalents, and breaks the analysis down to operating, investing, and financial activities.

1. **Profit and Loss** from 10/1/20XX to 11/3/20XX. Go to Reports > Recommended Reports > in the Profit and Loss section, click Run > Run report. Compare your P&L with the one shown on the next page.

QB Cloud_Student Name

PROFIT AND LOSS

October 1 - November 3, 2017

	TOTAL
INCOME	
401 Sales	6,000.00
Total Income	**$6,000.00**
GROSS PROFIT	**$6,000.00**
EXPENSES	
601 Advertising	250.00
603 Bank Charges	20.00
605 Dues & Subscriptions	150.00
609 Freight & Delivery	111.55
619 Meals and Entertainment	126.40
621 Office Supplies	226.85
625 Repair & Maintenance	140.00
627 Shipping and delivery expense	47.00
629 Stationery & Printing	553.18
633 Telephone Expense	234.51
635 Utilities	163.32
Total Expenses	**$2,022.81**
NET OPERATING INCOME	**$3,977.19**
NET INCOME	**$3,977.19**

Export the Profit and Loss to Excel and save as a PDF file. Use the file name **Chapter 4_Profit and Loss**.

2. **Balance Sheet** from 10/1/20XX to 11/3/20XX. Go to Reports > in the Balance Sheet section, click Run > Run report. (*Hint:* If necessary, on the Reports page select Recommended Reports.) Compare your Balance sheet with the one shown on the next page.

QB Cloud_Student Name

BALANCE SHEET

As of November 3, 2017

	TOTAL
ASSETS	
Current Assets	
Bank Accounts	
101 Checking	49,977.19
Total Bank Accounts	**$49,977.19**
Other Current Assets	
115 Merchandise Inventory	2,420.00
123 Prepaid Rent	6,000.00
125 Prepaid Insurance	3,000.00
130 Undeposited Funds	0.00
Total Other Current Assets	**$11,420.00**
Total Current Assets	**$61,397.19**
Fixed Assets	
135 Computer Equipment	10,000.00
Total Fixed Assets	**$10,000.00**
TOTAL ASSETS	**$71,397.19**
LIABILITIES AND EQUITY	
Liabilities	
Current Liabilities	
Accounts Payable	
201 Accounts Payable (A/P)	2,420.00
Total Accounts Payable	**$2,420.00**
Other Current Liabilities	
205 Loan Payable	5,000.00
Total Other Current Liabilities	**$5,000.00**
Total Current Liabilities	**$7,420.00**
Total Liabilities	**$7,420.00**
Equity	
3000 Opening Balance Equity	0.00
301 Common Stock	60,000.00
318 Retained Earnings	
Net Income	3,977.19
Total Equity	**$63,977.19**
TOTAL LIABILITIES AND EQUITY	**$71,397.19**

Export the Balance Sheet to Excel and save as a PDF file. Use the file name **Chapter 4_Balance Sheet**.

3. **Statement of Cash Flows:** Go to Reports > search for **Statement of Cash Flows** > 10/1/20XX to 11/3/20XX > Run report. Compare your Statement of Cash Flows with the one shown on the next page.

QB Cloud_Student Name

STATEMENT OF CASH FLOWS

October 1 - November 3, 2017

	TOTAL
OPERATING ACTIVITIES	
Net Income	3,977.19
Adjustments to reconcile Net Income to Net Cash provided by operations:	
115 Merchandise Inventory	-2,420.00
123 Prepaid Rent	-6,000.00
125 Prepaid Insurance	-3,000.00
201 Accounts Payable (A/P)	2,420.00
205 Loan Payable	5,000.00
Total Adjustments to reconcile Net Income to Net Cash provided by operations:	**-4,000.00**
Net cash provided by operating activities	**$ -22.81**
INVESTING ACTIVITIES	
135 Computer Equipment	-10,000.00
Net cash provided by investing activities	**$ -10,000.00**
FINANCING ACTIVITIES	
3000 Opening Balance Equity	0.00
301 Common Stock	60,000.00
Net cash provided by financing activities	**$60,000.00**
NET CASH INCREASE FOR PERIOD	**$49,977.19**
CASH AT BEGINNING OF PERIOD	0.00
CASH AT END OF PERIOD	**$49,977.19**

Save as a PDF file and export to Excel. Use the file name **Chapter 4_Statement of Cash Flows**. The Cash at end of period agrees with Account 101 Checking on the Balance Sheet.

Does your taskbar at the bottom of the screen show a list of the PDF and Excel files saved? Click <X> to close it.

FILTER THE AUDIT LOG

The Audit Log contains a list of all the changes that have ever been made to your company data and by whom. By default, the Audit Log displays the 200 most recent events. Dates and times in the Audit Log and Audit History reflect when events occurred, displayed in your local time. To see a history of the events, click View in the History columns.

There are several ways to view the Audit Log:

- To limit the view to specific users, dates, or types of events, click Filter.
- To control which columns are shown and printed, click the Gear icon.
- To open a transaction in the Event column, click its link.
- To see a history of the event, click View in the History column. See View the history of list items below.
- To view more events, scroll to the bottom of the screen and click <Next>.

To print the current view of the Audit Log (except that the History column doesn't print), click Print. For best results, select Landscape orientation from your browser's Print dialog box.

Audit a Transaction

1. Go to Gear > Audit Log. The Audit Log displays.

2. On the Filter button, click on the down-arrow [Filter ▾]. In the User field, select your email address or User ID. In the Date field, select All dates. In the Events section, select the radio button for Show only these events. Put a checkmark next to Transactions > click <Apply>.

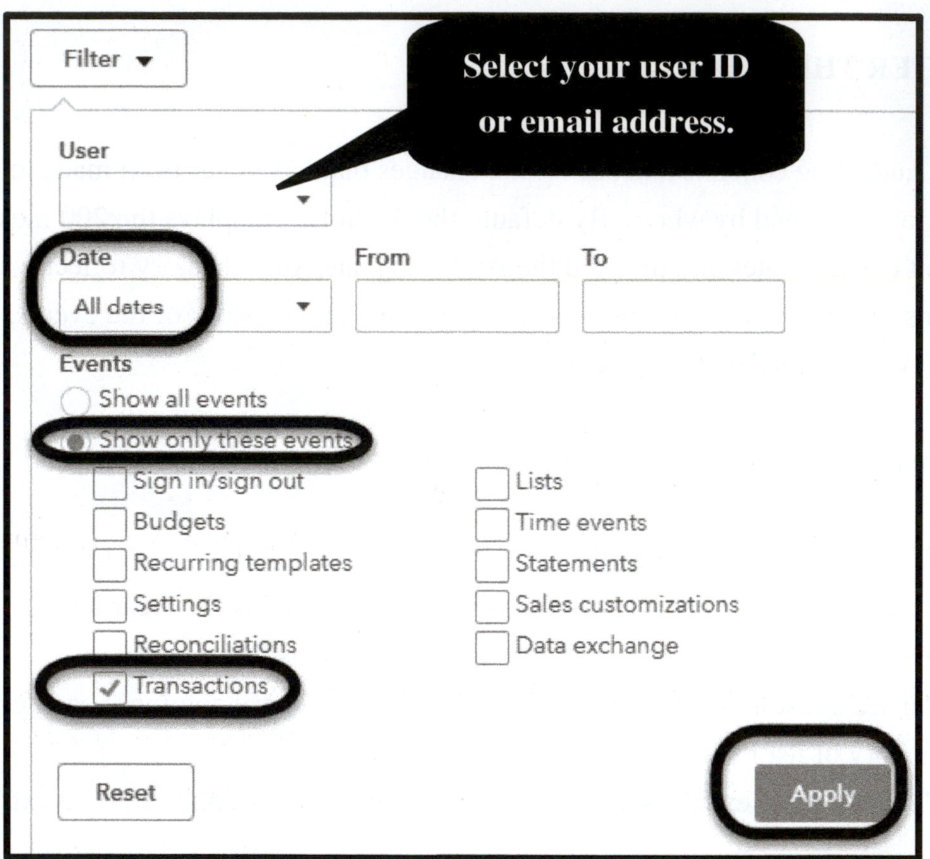

3. After clicking <Apply>, the Audit Log shows a list of the Transactions entered. The Audit Log includes these columns —— Date Changed, User ID

(or your email address), Event, Name, Date, Amount, History with a link to View.

4. In the History column link to View. For example, choose View for Bill No. 78CC. If necessary, select the right arrow to expand the view. The Audit History, and the date Bill No. 78CC was entered, is shown.

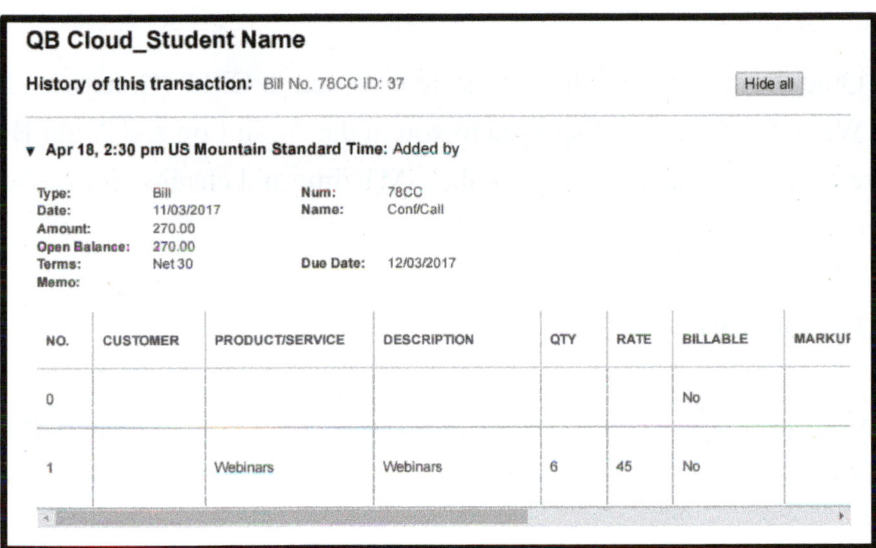

QB Cloud_Student Name

History of this transaction: Bill No. 78CC ID: 37 Hide all

▾ **Apr 18, 2:30 pm US Mountain Standard Time:** Added by

Type: Bill **Num:** 78CC
Date: 11/03/2017 **Name:** Conf/Call
Amount: 270.00
Open Balance: 270.00
Terms: Net 30 **Due Date:** 12/03/2017
Memo:

NO.	CUSTOMER	PRODUCT/SERVICE	DESCRIPTION	QTY	RATE	BILLABLE	MARKUP
0						No	
1		Webinars	Webinars	6	45	No	

5. Drill down on Bill No. 78CC to see the original entry. The Bill page is shown. After reviewing the transaction, close the Bill page. You are returned to the Dashboard.

In the History column, you can view a transaction to see when the transaction was entered. To more conveniently monitor when events occurred, you can filter the Audit Log. For example, select Sign in/sign out to see when log-ins and log-outs occurred.

Some Audit Log events are not transactions (perhaps they are actions taken on vendors or employees). For these types of events, you can click View to see the history, but you can't audit exactly what data changed.

If you see nothing in the History column, this is the type of event that has no history. This could be a login or logout event, a setting changed, or so on. To more conveniently monitor when these types of events happened, you can filter the Audit Log to show only certain types of events.

How does the Audit Log work?

On the QuickBooks servers, the events are recorded in GMT (Greenwich Mean Time). When the times are displayed to you in the Audit Log and Audit History, software on your computer interprets the GMT time and changes it to reflect your time zone.

CHECK YOUR PROGRESS

Check Your Progress assignments are included on the Online Learning Center at www.mhhe.com/qbo2e > Student Edition > Chapter 4 > Check Your Progress.

1. What is the account balance as of 11/3/20XX in each of these accounts? Indicate whether these accounts have debit (dr.) or credit (cr.) balances.

   Account 101 Checking ____________________

   Account 115 Merchandise Inventory ____________________

   Account 201 Accounts Payable ____________________

   Account 601 Advertising ____________________

   Account 603 Bank Charges ____________________

Account 629 Stationery & Printing ____________

2. What is 11/3 Net Income? ____________

3. What is the 11/3 total Liabilities and Equity? ____________

4. What is the quantity and asset value of data storage?

____

5. What is the quantity and asset value of network products?

____

6. What is the quantity and asset value of web servers?

____

7. What is the quantity and asset value of webinars?

____

SIGN OUT

To sign out of QBO, go to the company settings (click on the company name), link to Sign Out. *Or,* continue.

ONLINE LEARNING CENTER (OLC): www.mhhe.com/qbo2e

The OLC includes additional Chapter 4 resources. Go online to www.mhhe.com/qbo2e > Student Edition > Chapter 4.

1. Narrated PowerPoints.
2. Online quizzes: 10 True or False and 10 multiple-choice questions. The Online quizzes are graded and can be emailed to your instructor.
3. Analysis question: Answer the analysis question, then email to your instructor.
4. Going to the Net

    a. Go to the QuickBooks Learn & Support website at https://community.intuit.com/.
    b. Type a Search word; for example, type **Inventory**.
    c. Link to articles of interest.

5. Videos:

    a. Watch an Inventory video at http://quickbooks.intuit.com/tutorials/lessons/inventory/.
    b. Watch the Create Bills and Expense Reports in QuickBooks video at https://www.youtube.com/watch?v=NmUyBRE8sxc. .

6. Glossary of terms: Words that are italicized and boldfaced are defined in the glossary. The Glossary is also Appendix B.
7. Problem solving link includes Exercise 4-3.

Exercise 4-1: Complete Exercise 4-1.

Continue with Exercises

1. If necessary start QBO.

2. Add the following vendor.

Title, First Name, Last name:	**Ms. Sherry Milton**
Company:	**Computers 2 You**
*Display name as:	Select Computers 2 You
Print on check as:	Computers 2 You
Address:	**2006 East 14 Avenue**
City/Town	**Los Angeles**
State	**CA**
ZIP:	**90046**
Country:	**USA**
Phone:	**213-555-2300**
Terms:	Select Net 30
as of:	Type **11/1/20XX**

3. Add the following Inventory item:

***Name**:	**Computers**
Initial quantity on hand:	**0** (zero)
As of date:	**10/1/20XX** (current year)
Inventory asset account:	Select 115 Merchandise Inventory
Sales information:	**Computers**
Sales price/rate:	**1000**
Income account:	Select 401 Sales
Purchasing information:	**Computers**

Cost: **500**

Expense account: 501 Cost of Goods Sold

4. Use the transaction register below to enter the following checks.

Ck. No.	Date	Description of Transaction	Payment	Deposit	Balance
	11/1	*Balance*			*49,977.19*
1031	11/4	Office Suppliers[1]	90.82		49,886.37
1032	11/4	Cays Advertising	125.00		49,761.37
1033	11/5	Best Cellular	82.13		49,679,24
ATM	11/5	Cottage Restaurant	46.40		49,632.84
1034	11/6	Hour Deliveries	42.25		49,590.59
1035	11/6	Office Suppliers	21.00		49,569.59

5. Display the Register for Account 101 Checking. (*Hint:* From the Navigation bar, select Accounting > double-click 101 Checking.) Make sure your ending balance is $49,569.59. If not, edit checks.
6. Complete the following transactions. (*Hint:* QBO stores quantities and amounts from earlier Bills. Before saving, make sure the QTY field is correct.)

[1]If necessary, type **1031** in the Check no. field.

Date	*Description of Transaction*
11/8/20XX	Bill no. 80C2U received from Computers 2 You for the purchase of 20 computers, $500 each, for a total of $10,000.
11/8/20XX	Bill no. ATD131 received from Any Time Deployment for the purchase of 11 network products, $25 each, for a total of $275.
11/8/20XX	Bill No. CZ40 received from CloudZ Channel for the purchase of 7 web servers, $200 each, for a total of $1,400.
11/8/20XX	Bill No. 91CC received from Conf/Call for the purchase of 5 webinars, $45 each, for a total of $225.
11/8/20XX	Bill No. AS12 received from AmpleStore Inc. for the purchase of 25 data storage devices, $15 each, for a total of $375.
11/9/20XX	Sold three computers for cash, $1,000 each, for a total of $3,000, Sales Receipt no. 1004.[2] (*Hint:* Click + > Sales Receipt. In the Product/Service field, select Computers.)
11/10/20XX	Sold four computers for cash, $1,000 each, for a total of $4,000, Sales Receipt no. 1005.
11/11/20XX	Bill no. 112C2U received from Computers 2 You for the purchase of 6 computers, $500 each, for a total of $3,000.
11/11/20XX	Bill No. 115CC received from Conf/Call for the purchase of 5 webinars, $45 each, for a total of $225.

Analyze transaction
Transaction date
Input transaction

[2]If necessary, type **1004** in the Sales Receipt no. field.

11/12/20XX Sold three computers for cash, $1,000 each, for a total of $3,000, Sales Receipt no. 1006.

7. Continue with Exercise 4-2.

Exercise 4-2: Follow the instructions below to complete Exercise 4-2:

1. Save these reports as PDF files and export to Excel. Run reports from 10/1/20XX to 11/12/20XX. When necessary, in the Report period field select Custom, then type the appropriate date

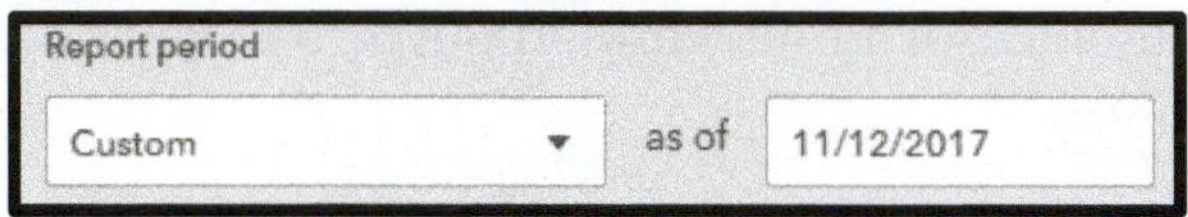

.

- Exercise 4-2_Vendor Contact List
- Exercise 4-2_Product/Service List
- Exercise 4-2_Journal
- Exercise 4-2_Transaction Detail by Account
- Exercise 4-2_Trial Balance
- Exercise 4-2_Inventory Valuation Summary
- Exercise 4-2_Vendor Balance Summary
- Exercise 4-2_AP Aging Summary
- Exercise 4-2_Profit and Loss
- Exercise 4-2_Balance Sheet
- Exercise 4-2_Statement of Cash Flows

2. **Check Your Figures** (from 10/1/20XX to 11/12/XX):

   - Account 101 Checking, $59,569.59
   - Account 115 Merchandise Inventory, $12,920.00
   - Account 201 Accounts Payable, $17,920.00

- Account 401 Sales, $16,000.00
- Account 501, Cost of Goods Sold, $5,000.00
- Account 621 Office Supplies, $338.67
- Total Liabilities and Equity, $91,489.59

Exercise 4-3: Problem Solving

The Online Learning Center includes Exercise 4-3 at www.mhhe.com/qbo2e > Student Edition > Chapter 5 > Problem Solving.

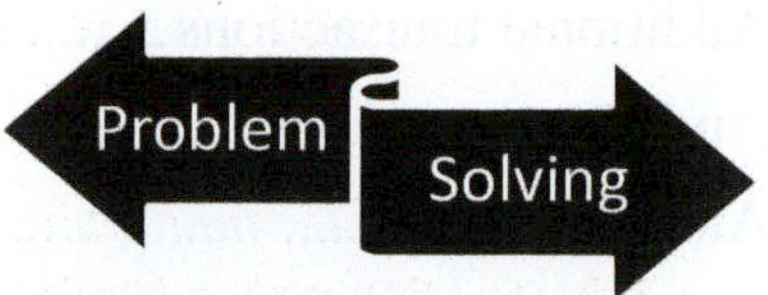

1. What report lists the debits and credits for each transaction? Show the final report balance.
2. Identify the report that shows revenues and expenses. Explain how to display this report and the final balance.
3. Identify the report that shows assets, liabilities, and equity. Show the steps for displaying that report, and the final balance(s).

CHAPTER 4 INDEX

Chapter 5 Customers and Sales

Scenario: In this chapter, start by checking the work that you have completed. The stop sign reminds you to make sure your expense transactions, sales transactions, and 11/30 trial balance are correct. If any of your totals do not agree, drill down to the original transaction and make the needed changes. After checking your data, enter customer defaults, record transactions for customer sales and cash sales, learn how to do an advanced search, and display reports. The objectives specify the work that is completed in Chapter 5.

OBJECTIVES

1. Start QuickBooks Online and sign in to QB Cloud_Student Name (your first and last name).
2. To check data, display Expense and Sales transactions and the November 12 Trial Balance.
3. Enter customer settings.
4. Enter new customers and record customer sales and cash sales.
5. Complete an advanced search.
6. Display financial statements.
7. Display the audit log.
8. Export reports to Excel and Adobe PDF.
9. Complete Check Your Progress.
10. Go to the Online Learning Center at www.mhhe.com/qbo2e for additional resources.
11. Complete Exercises 5-1, 5-2 and 5-3.

In Chapter 5, you start by making sure data is ready for adding new ***customers***. The Customers page manages your customer list and transactions. On the Customers page you can:

- View and update a complete list of your customers and their contact information.
- Add notes to any customer record.
- Search for a customer by name or company.
- Sort customers by name, company, open balance, or overdue balance.
- Track existing customer transactions, including overdue status.
- Create new customer transactions.

GETTING STARTED

1. Start your browser. Go online to http://qbo.intuit.com.

2. Sign in to QuickBooks Online with your User ID and Password. (*Hint:* You can save your User ID.)

CHECK YOUR DATA

To make sure you are starting in the correct place, display Expense Transactions, Sales Transactions, and the 10/1/20XX to 11/12/20XX Trial Balance. This Trial Balance was completed in Exercise 4-2.

> **fyi** Have you selected a Navigation bar button or other selection and nothing happens, meaning the screen seems frozen? You may need to clear temporary internet files/cache. The Online Learning Center at www.mhhe.com/qbo2e > Troubleshooting includes information for Internet Explorer, Firefox, Google Chrome, Safari, and the Windows App.

Expense Transactions

To verify Expense Transactions go to Expenses > Expenses tab > click on the Filter's down-arrow > in the Date field, select Custom > From 11/1/20XX to 11/12/20XX > click <Apply>. The total Expense Transactions from 11/1 to 11/12 are $18,787.97.

QB Cloud_Student Name

Date	Type	No.	Payee	Category	Total
11/01/2017	Check	1030	Barber's Paper Supply	Stationery & Printing	$127.96
11/01/2017	Check	1029	Cays Advertising	Advertising	$125.00
11/01/2017	Check	1028	Hour Deliveries	Freight & Delivery	$46.90
11/01/2017	Check	1027	County Telephone	Telephone Expense	$76.19
11/01/2017	Check	1026	RSP Gas	Utilities	$84.32
11/02/2017	Bill	AS7	AmpleStore Inc.	Merchandise Inventory	$300.00
11/03/2017	Bill	ATD90	Any Time Deployment	Merchandise Inventory	$250.00
11/03/2017	Bill	CZ33	CloudZ Channel	Merchandise Inventory	$1,600.00
11/03/2017	Bill	78CC	Conf/Call	Merchandise Inventory	$270.00
11/04/2017	Check	1031	Office Suppliers	Office Supplies	$90.82
11/04/2017	Check	1032	Cays Advertising	Advertising	$125.00
11/05/2017	Check	1033	Best Cellular	Telephone Expense	$82.13
11/05/2017	Check	ATM	Cottage Restaurant	Meals and Entertainment	$46.40
11/06/2017	Check	1034	Hour Deliveries	Freight & Delivery	$42.25
11/06/2017	Check	1035	Office Suppliers	Office Supplies	$21.00
11/08/2017	Bill	80C2U	Computers 2 You	Merchandise Inventory	$10,000.00
11/08/2017	Bill	ATD131	Any Time Deployment	Merchandise Inventory	$275.00
11/08/2017	Bill	CZ40	CloudZ Channel	Merchandise Inventory	$1,400.00
11/08/2017	Bill	91CC	Conf/Call	Merchandise Inventory	$225.00
11/08/2017	Bill	AS12	AmpleStore Inc.	Merchandise Inventory	$375.00
11/11/2017	Bill	112C2U	Computers 2 You	Merchandise Inventory	$3,000.00
11/11/2017	Bill	115CC	Conf/Call	Merchandise Inventory	$225.00

Sales Transactions

To verify Sales Transactions, go to Sales > All Sales > Filter > Custom > Date, 11/1/2017 to 11/12/2017 > click <Apply>. The total Sales Transactions from 11/1 to 11/12 are $10,000.00.

QB Cloud_Student Name

Date	Type	No.	Customer	Due date	Balance	Total	Status
11/09/2017	Sales Receipt	1004	Cash Sales		$0.00	$3,000.00	Paid
11/10/2017	Sales Receipt	1005	Cash Sales		$0.00	$4,000.00	Paid
11/12/2017	Sales Receipt	1006	Cash Sales		$0.00	$3,000.00	Paid

Trial Balance

To make sure your accounts have the correct balances, display the 10/1/20XX to 11/12/20XX Trial Balance. This Trial Balance was also completed in Exercise 4-2.

QB Cloud_Student Name

TRIAL BALANCE

As of November 12, 2017

	DEBIT	CREDIT
101 Checking	59,569.59	
115 Merchandise Inventory	12,920.00	
123 Prepaid Rent	6,000.00	
125 Prepaid Insurance	3,000.00	
130 Undeposited Funds	0.00	
135 Computer Equipment	10,000.00	
201 Accounts Payable (A/P)		17,920.00
205 Loan Payable		5,000.00
3000 Opening Balance Equity		0.00
301 Common Stock		60,000.00
401 Sales		16,000.00
501 Cost of Goods Sold	5,000.00	
601 Advertising	375.00	
603 Bank Charges	20.00	
605 Dues & Subscriptions	150.00	
609 Freight & Delivery	153.80	
619 Meals and Entertainment	172.80	
621 Office Supplies	338.67	
625 Repair & Maintenance	140.00	
627 Shipping and delivery expense	47.00	
629 Stationery & Printing	553.18	
633 Telephone Expense	316.64	
635 Utilities	163.32	
TOTAL	**$98,920.00**	**$98,920.00**

What if my account balances do not agree? Check the Expense transactions, Sales transactions, and Trial Balance. If any of your totals do not agree, drill down to the original transaction and make the needed changes. Then, <Save>. Display the 10/1 to 11/12 Trial Balance again.

Show non-zero or active only
Non-zero Rows/Non-zero C
Show rows
Active
All
Non-zero
Show columns
Active
All
Non-zero

If needed, you can remove accounts with zero balances from the Trial Balance. In the Show non-zero or active only field, select Non-zero > Run report. On the previous page Account 3000 was shown with a zero balance.

CUSTOMER SETTINGS

Before adding customers, check QB Cloud's Account and Settings.

1. Go to > Account and Settings > Advanced. In the Other preferences area, the Customer label shows Customers. If not, to edit click 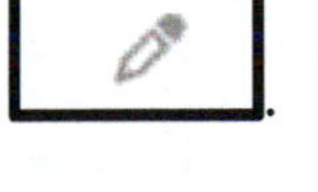.

Warn if duplicate check number or bill number is On.

Warn if duplicate check number is used	On
Warn if duplicate bill number is used	On

If necessary, to edit click [edit].

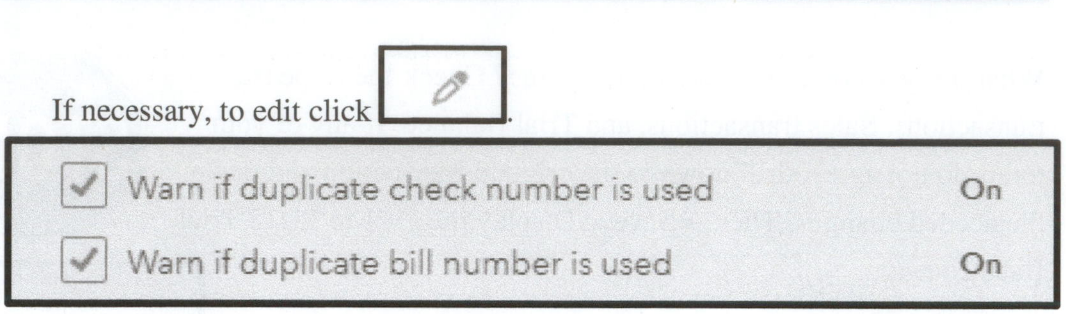

Oberve that *both* Warn if duplicate check number is used *and* Warn if duplicate bill number is used is On. When through, click [Save].

2. Go to [gear] > Account and Settings > Sales. In the Sales form content area, click [edit] to edit. If necessary, place a checkmark next to Custom transaction numbers to turn it On.

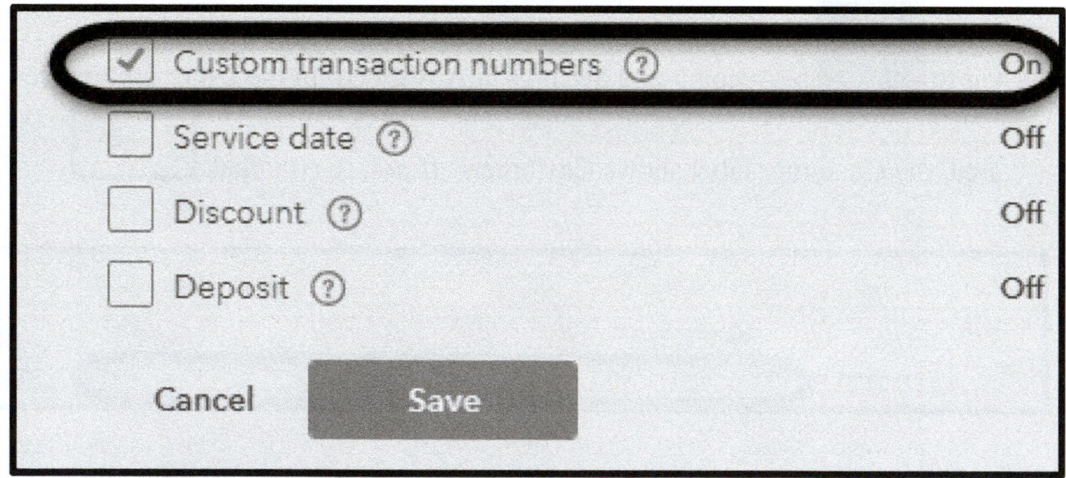

3. Click [Save]. To check Sales, compare your Settings window with the one shown on the next page. Observe that Custom transaction numbers are On. If any selections need editing, click [edit].

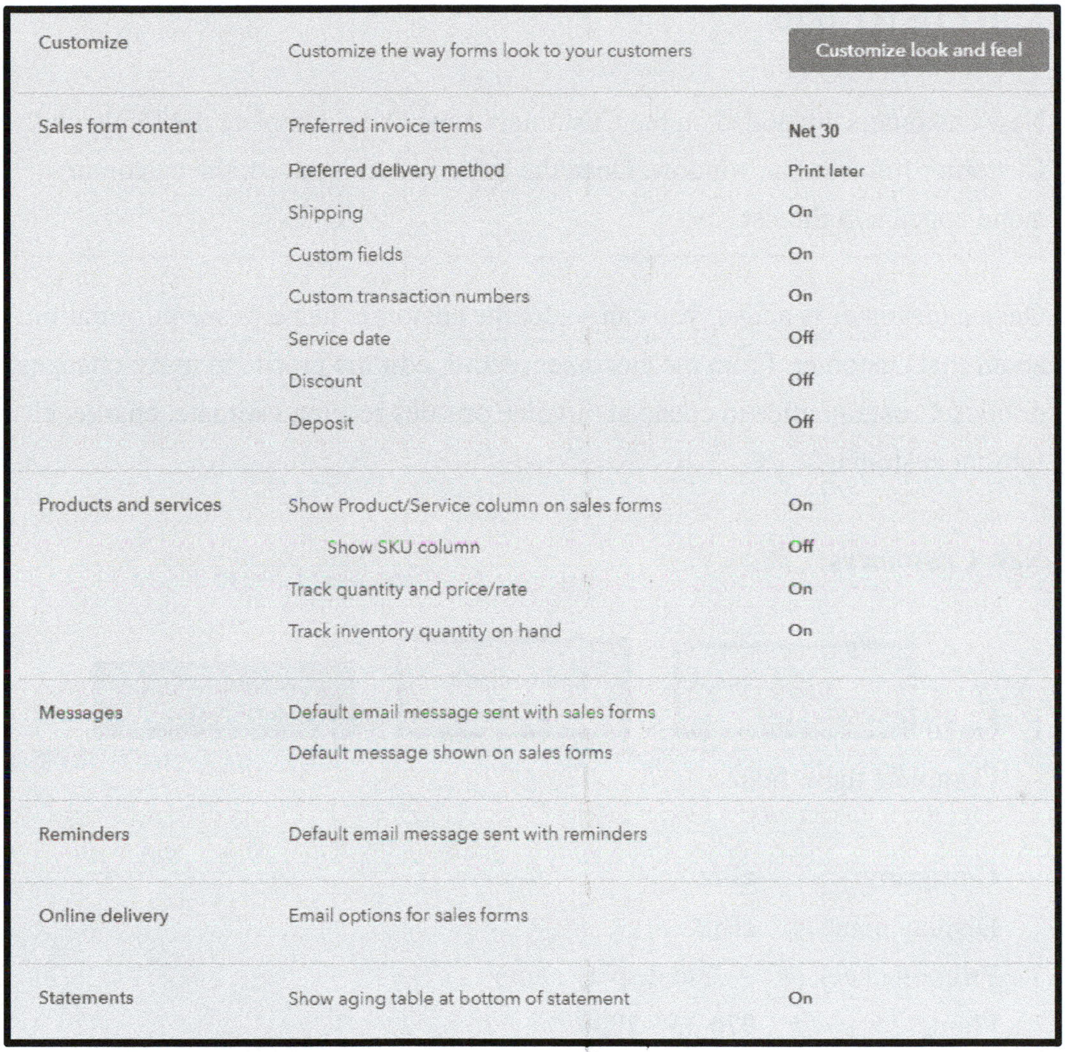

Customize	Customize the way forms look to your customers	Customize look and feel
Sales form content	Preferred invoice terms	Net 30
	Preferred delivery method	Print later
	Shipping	On
	Custom fields	On
	Custom transaction numbers	On
	Service date	Off
	Discount	Off
	Deposit	Off
Products and services	Show Product/Service column on sales forms	On
	Show SKU column	Off
	Track quantity and price/rate	On
	Track inventory quantity on hand	On
Messages	Default email message sent with sales forms	
	Default message shown on sales forms	
Reminders	Default email message sent with reminders	
Online delivery	Email options for sales forms	
Statements	Show aging table at bottom of statement	On

4. Click Done. Observe that the Dashboard shows the Bank accounts balance in Account 101 Checking, $59,569.59. This agrees with the 11/12/20XX trial balance.

101 Checking	
In QuickBooks	$59,569.59

ADD CUSTOMERS

New customers are added on the Customers page. You complete the fields on the Customer Information window. Once the information is saved, the customer name appears in the list.

Once a customer is added, you can select the customer name to see information about that customer. From the customer record, edit the profile to make changes, or click Create invoice to create an invoice or sales receipt, estimate, charge, etc. for that customer.

New Customers

1. Go to Sales > Customers > New customer.

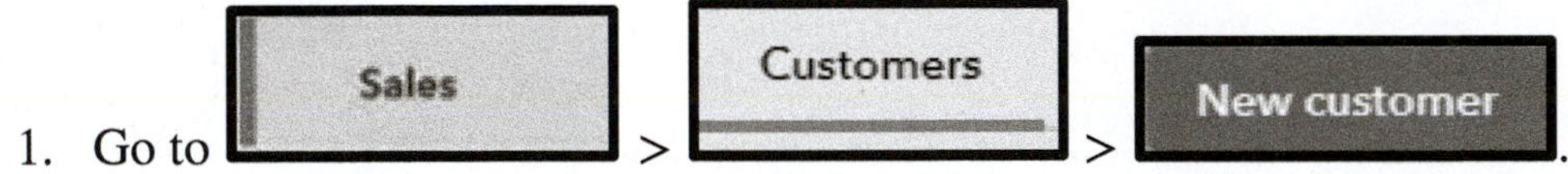

   Complete these fields:

Company:	**eBiz**
Display name as:	eBiz
Print on check as	✓ Use display name
Phone:	**970-555-2000**
Street:	**800 West Second Ave.**
City/Town:	**Durango**
State:	**CO**
ZIP:	**81301**
Country:	**USA**
Shipping address	✓ Same as billing address

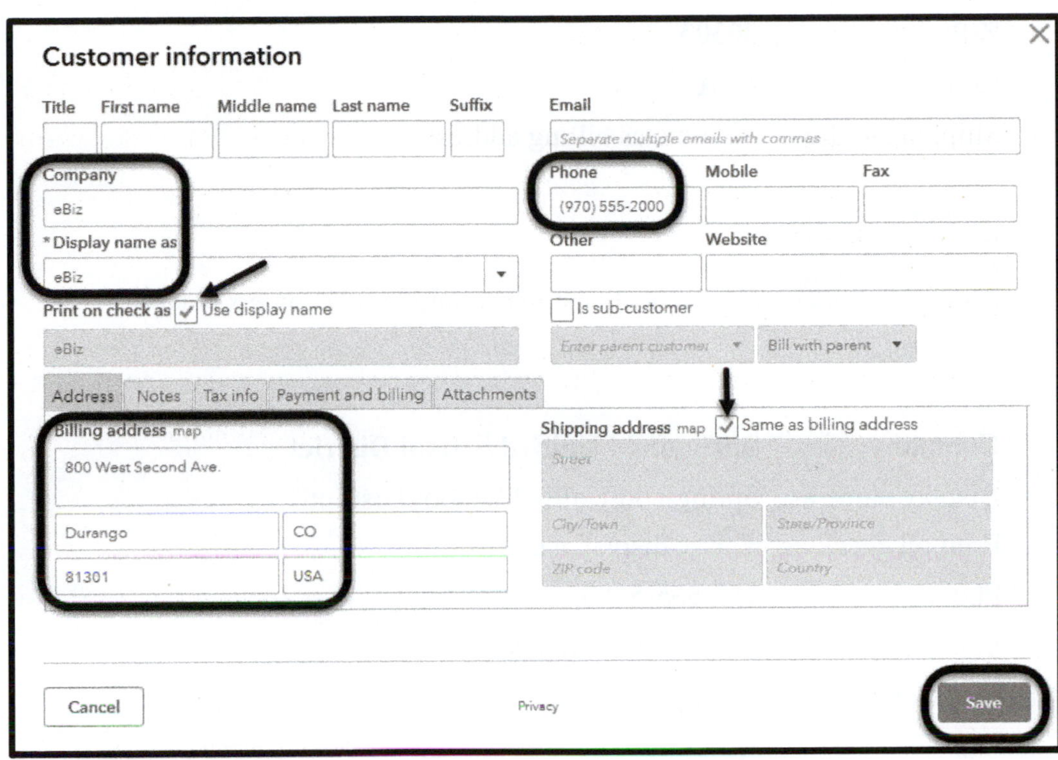

2. 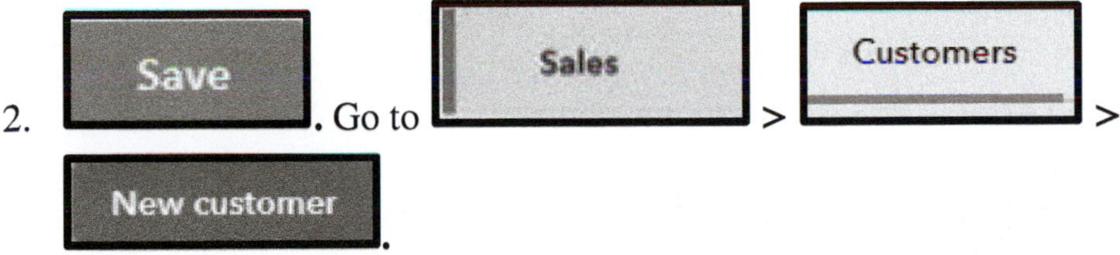

. Go to > > .

Company: **Law Offices of Williamson, Gallagher & Katz**
Display name as: Law Offices of Williamson, Gallagher & Katz
Print on check as ✓ Use display name
Phone: **404-555-8134**
Street: **18 Piedmont Ave. NW**
City/Town: **Atlanta**
State: **GA**

ZIP: **30303**
Country: **USA**
Shipping address ✓ Same as billing address)

Save. Add the next customer: Sales > Customers > New customer.

Company: **Springfield Unified School District**
Display name as: Springfield Unified School District
Print on check as ✓ Use display name
Phone: **217-555-5500**
Street: **4892 Clear Lake Ave.**
City/Town: **Springfield**
State: **IL**
ZIP: **62703**
Country: **USA**
Shipping address ✓ Same as billing address

Save. Add the next customer.

Company: **Permanente Medical Services**
Display name as: Permanente Medical Services
Print on check as ✓ Use display name
Phone: **808-555-9000**
Street: **18771 Ala Moana Blvd.**
City/Town: **Honolulu**
State: **HI**

ZIP: **96815**

Country: **USA**

Shipping address ✓ Same as billing address

Customer Contact List

To view the cusomters added in Chapter 5, do this.

1. Go to Reports > in the Search field, type **Customer Contact List**. The Customer Contact List shows the Customer name, Phone Numbers, Billing Address and Shipping Address.

QB Cloud_Student Name

CUSTOMER CONTACT LIST

CUSTOMER	PHONE NUMBERS	EMAIL	FULL NAME	BILLING ADDRESS	SHIPPING ADDRESS
Cash Sales					Cash Sales
eBiz	Phone: (970) 555-2000			800 West Second Ave. Durango CO 81301 USA	800 West Second Ave. Durango CO 81301 USA
Law Offices of Williamson, Gallagher & Katz	Phone: (404) 555-8134			18 Piedmont Ave. NW Atlanta GA 30303 USA	18 Piedmont Ave. NW Atlanta GA 30303 USA
Permanente Medical Services	Phone: (808) 555-9000			18771 Ala Moana Blvd. Honolulu HI 96815 USA	18771 Ala Moana Blvd. Honolulu HI 96815 USA
Springfield Unified School District	Phone: (217) 555-5500			4892 Clear Lake Ave. Springfield IL 62703 USA	4892 Clear Lake Ave. Springfield IL 62703 USA

Troubleshooting: To edit, drill down on the customer > select Edit > Save.

2. Save the Customer Contact List as an Excel and PDF file. Use the file name **Chapter 5_Customer Contact List**. (*Hint:* After saving the Excel file > Save as an Adobe PDF.)

Customer Invoices

If customers are billed after the sale is made, create an invoice so QB Cloud can be paid later. If the customer pays you at the time of the sale, enter a sales receipt.

When the customer pays the invoice, you can record the payment from the Customers or Receive Payment pages. To see a list of invoices and their due dates, run the A/R Aging Summary. For invoices that you need to send regularly, set up a recurring transaction to be reminded to enter the invoice. ***Accounts receivable*** are what customers owe your business. Credit transactions from customers are called ***accounts receivable transactions***.

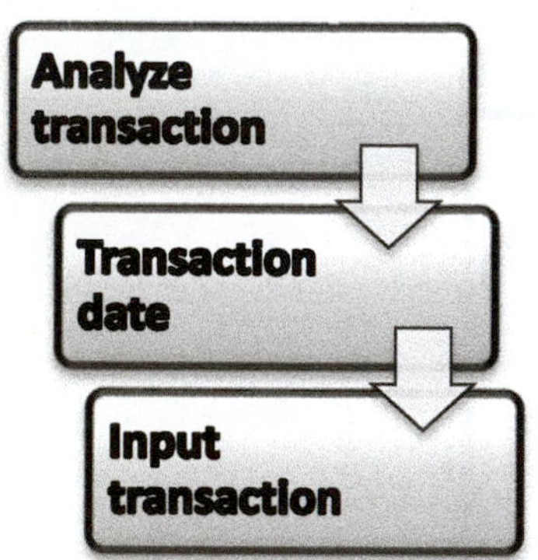

The transaction you are going to work with is:

Date	*Description of Transaction*
11/15/XX	Sold 5 data storage products on account to eBiz for a total of $150, Invoice 1007.

1. From the Sales page, select eBiz > Create invoice.

Or, select [+] > Invoice > eBiz. If It shouldn't take a detective to track down payments pop-up appears, click <Send your first invoice>. Read the information on Take our invoicing for a spin screen > click <No thanks>.

1. Complete these fields:

Invoice date:	**11/15/20XX**
Invoice No.	1007 completed automatically (or type it)
PRODUCT/SERVICE:	Select Data storage
QTY:	**5**
RATE:	30 completed automatically
AMOUNT:	150.00 completed automatically

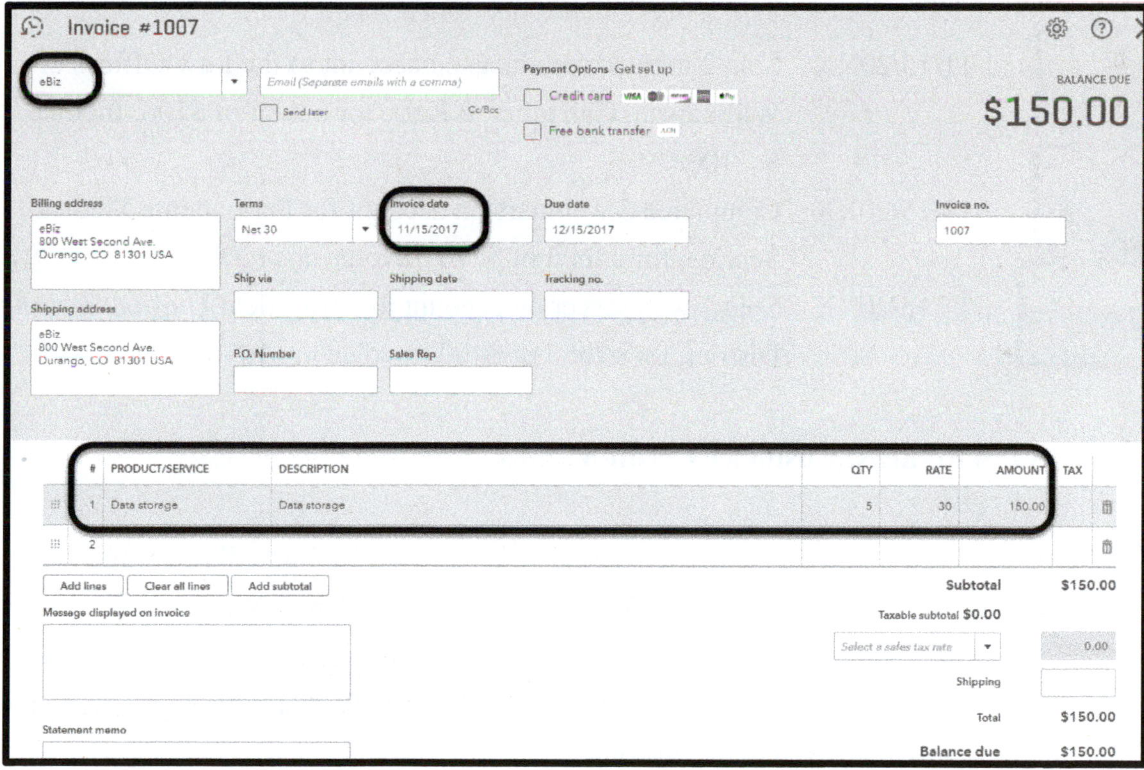

2. Select the down-arrow next to Save and send > then click <Save and new>. Invoice 1007 saved. The account distribution for Invoice 1007 is shown on the next page. (*Hint:* To see the account distribution, go to Reports > Journal > report period is 11/15/20XX to 11/15/20XX).

Account	Debit	Credit
105 Accounts Receivable/eBiz	150.00	
401 Sales/Data storage		150.00
501 Cost of Goods Sold/Data storage	75.00	
115 Merchandise Inventory/Data storage		75.00

3. Complete these transactions.

Analyze transaction
Transaction date
Input transaction

Date	*Description of Transaction*
11/15/20XX	Sold 2 network products on account to the Law Offices of Williamson, Gallagher & Katz, for a total of $100, Invoice no. 1008.
11/15/20XX	Completed 3 webinars on account for Permanente Medical Service, for a total of $270, Invoice no. 1009.
11/15/20XX	Sold 1 web server on account to Springfield Unified School District, for a total of $400, Invoice no. 1010.

Sales Returns: Customer Credit Memos

When credit customers are dissatisfied, you can issue an immediate refund or credit memo. A ***credit memo*** affects the customer's balance. What is the difference between a credit memo or ***refund***? With credits, you hold the amount in the customer's account and apply it to a sale later. With a refund, you write a check or payout cash to the customer.

For the transaction shown, you are going to issue a credit memo so that the customer balance is affected. After the transaction's description, steps are shown for recording it.

Date	*Description of Transaction*
11/16/20XX	eBiz returned one USB flash drive (data storage) and received a $30 reduction in their balance, Credit Memo 1011.

Analyze transaction

Transaction date

Input transaction

1. If the Invoice window is displayed, click on its title bar.

   Then, 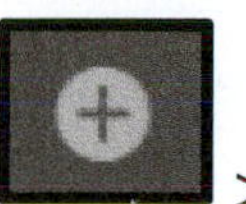 > Credit Memo. Complete these fields.

Choose a customer:	Select eBiz
Credit Memo date:	**11/16/20XX**
Credit Memo no.	1011 completed automatically (or type it)
PRODUCT/SERVICE:	select Data storage
DESCRIPTION:	Data storage (automatically shown)
QTY:	1 (automatically shown)
RATE:	30 (automatically shown)
AMOUNT:	30.00 (automatically shown)

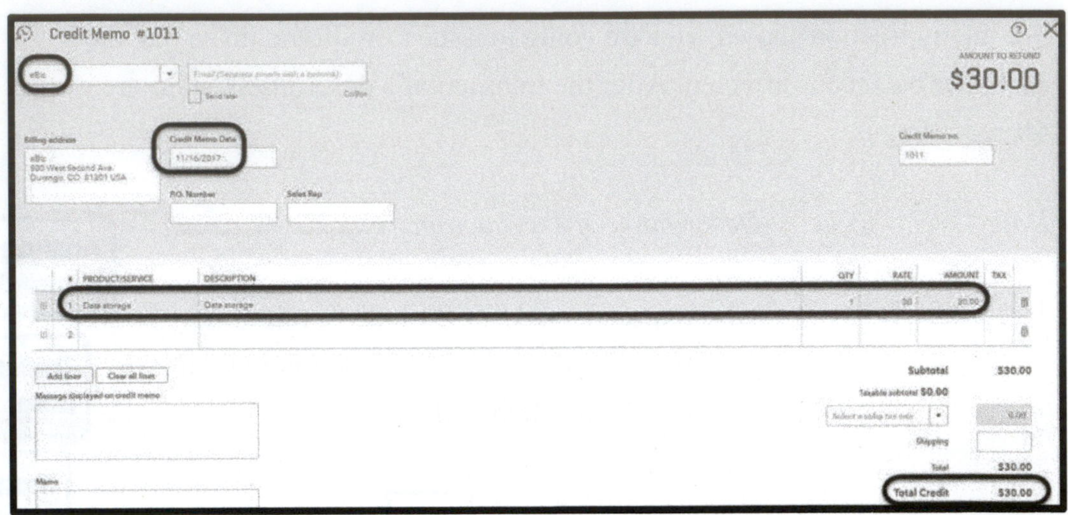

2. Click on the down arrow next to <Save and Send> select <Save and Close>. Credit memo 1011 saved. The account distribution for the return is shown below.

Account	Debit	Credit
105 Accounts Receivable (A/R)		30.00
401 Sales/Data storage	30.00	
501 Cost of Goods Sold/Data storage		15.00
115 Merchandise Inventory/Data storage	15.00	

Accounts Receivable Register

To see that your customer transactions and refunds that have been recorded, display the Accounts Receivable (A/R) register.

1. From the Navigation bar, select Accounting. Account 105 Accounts Receivable (A/R) shows a QuickBooks Balance of $890.00.
2. On the 105 Accounts Receivable row, double-click View Register. Remember, QBO updates regularly; for example, the author recorded transactions in 2017. Your year will differ. These differences are minor and do not affect the software's functions.

QB Cloud_Student Name

105 Accounts Receivable (A/R) Ending Balance: $890.00

Date	Ref No. Type	Payee Memo	Charge / Credit	Payment Due Date	Open Balance
11/16/2017	1011 Credit Memo	eBiz		$30.00	$0.00
11/15/2017	1010 Invoice	Springfield Unified School District	$400.00	12/15/2017	$400.00
11/15/2017	1009 Invoice	Permanente Medical Services	$270.00	12/15/2017	$270.00
11/15/2017	1008 Invoice	Law Offices of Williamson, Gallagher & Katz	$100.00	12/15/2017	$100.00
11/15/2017	1007	eBiz	$150.00		$120.00

There are a variety of accounts in QBO–bank, asset, liability, equity, income, and expenses. Registers are a useful way to look at transactions and amounts associated with a particular account. The A/R Register shows all customer invoices (1007 thru 1010) and the customer credit memo (1011) by date.

> **fyi** Some of the screens may differ from what you see. Each time you sign on to QBO, the software is the most current version and this could change some of the screens. Refer to www.mhhe.com/qbo2e > Text Updates.

3. The A/R Aging Detail also shows the Accounts Receivable balance. Go to Reports > type **A/R Aging Summary** (Search field) > All dates

(Report period) > Run report. At this point in the data, the total customer balance is $890.00.

QB Cloud_Student Name

A/R AGING SUMMARY

All Dates

	CURRENT	1 - 30	31 - 60	61 - 90	91 AND OVER	TOTAL
eBiz	120.00					$120.00
Law Offices of Williamson, Gallagher & Katz	100.00					$100.00
Permanente Medical Services	270.00					$270.00
Springfield Unified School District	400.00					$400.00
TOTAL	**$890.00**	**$0.00**	**$0.00**	**$0.00**	**$0.00**	**$890.00**

Receive Payments from Customers

Once you issue an invoice to a customer, that customer owes your business money. It is easy to apply customer payments in QBO.

From the Customers page, select the customer, then Receive payment. *Or,* from the Create menu (+), select Receive Payment.

Date	*Description of Transaction*
11/29/20XX	Received a $120.00 check from eBiz in payment of the November 15 invoice, less the November 16 credit memo, Check no. 9346.

1. Go to the Customers page > eBiz > Receive payment. Complete these fields.

Customer:	eBiz (automatically shown)
Payment date:	**11/29/20XX**
Payment method:	Check
Reference no.	Type **9346**
Deposit to:	101 Checking (automatically shown)
Amount received:	120.00 (automatically shown)

Place a checkmark next to Invoice 1007. The payment is $120.00. The November 16 credit memo of $30 is automatically applied.

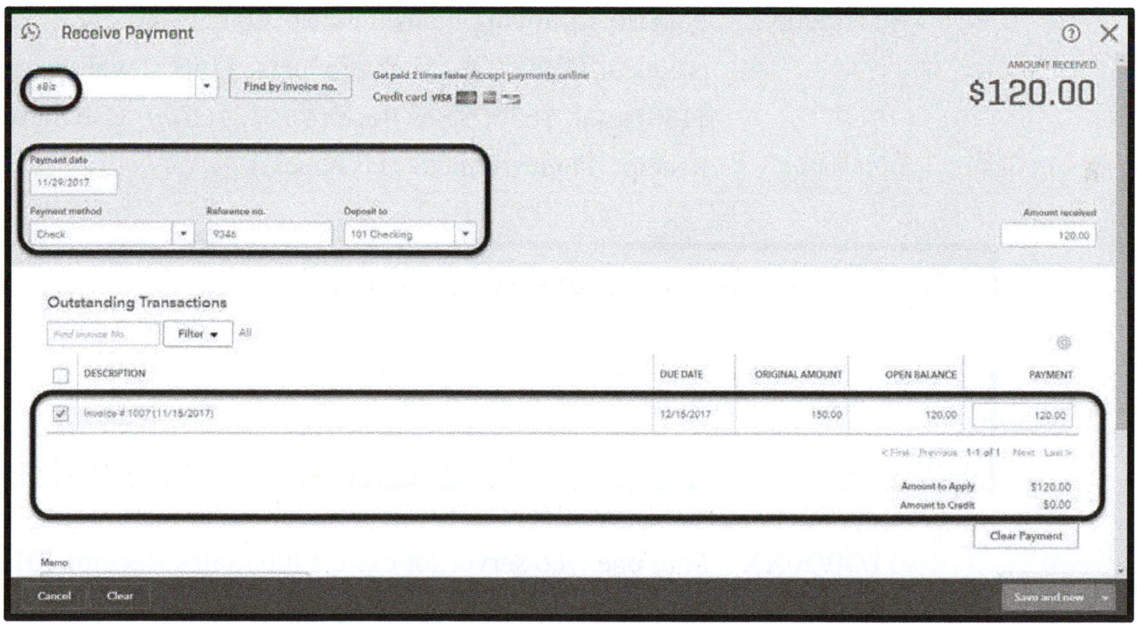

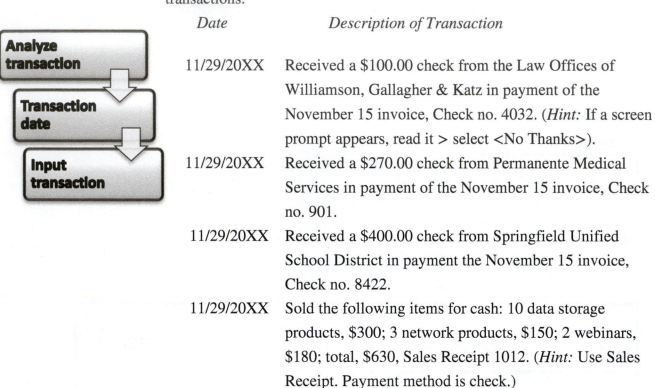

2. Save and new. Received payment 9346 saved. Complete the following transactions.

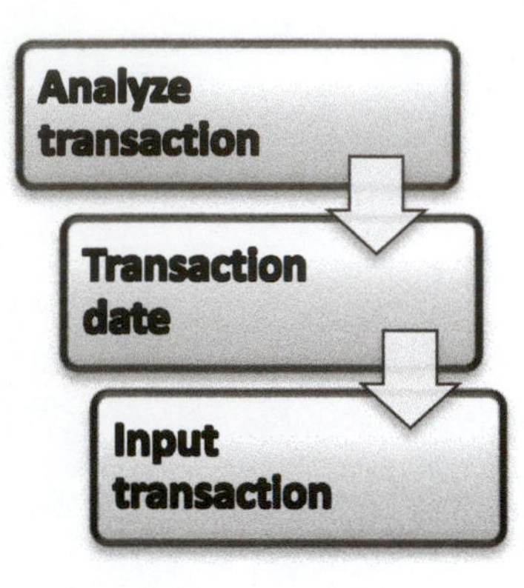

Date	*Description of Transaction*
11/29/20XX	Received a $100.00 check from the Law Offices of Williamson, Gallagher & Katz in payment of the November 15 invoice, Check no. 4032. (*Hint:* If a screen prompt appears, read it > select <No Thanks>).
11/29/20XX	Received a $270.00 check from Permanente Medical Services in payment of the November 15 invoice, Check no. 901.
11/29/20XX	Received a $400.00 check from Springfield Unified School District in payment the November 15 invoice, Check no. 8422.
11/29/20XX	Sold the following items for cash: 10 data storage products, $300; 3 network products, $150; 2 webinars, $180; total, $630, Sales Receipt 1012. (*Hint:* Use Sales Receipt. Payment method is check.)

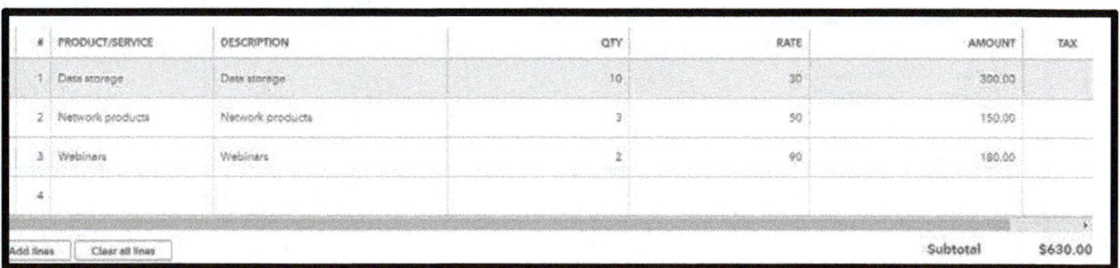

#	PRODUCT/SERVICE	DESCRIPTION	QTY	RATE	AMOUNT	TAX
1	Data storage	Data storage	10	30	300.00	
2	Network products	Network products	3	50	150.00	
3	Webinars	Webinars	2	90	180.00	
4						

Add lines | Clear all lines | Subtotal $630.00

11/30/20XX	Sold one web server for cash, $400, Sales Receipt 1013. (*Hint:* For the check number, type 3001 in the Reference no. field.)

ACCOUNT RECONCILIATION: NOVEMBER 20XX

QB Cloud receives a bank statement every month for the checking account. The Bank Statement shows the checks and deposits that cleared that bank from November 1 through November 30. To reconcile, use the bank statement.

Checking Account Register

1. Go to Accounting > double-click 101 Checking. The Bank Register window appears.

   The Bank Register shows the newest transactions first, unless changed. To change the order, click on the Date column. (*Hint:* Scroll down to see November and October transactions.) The Check register balance is $61,489.59 and does not include the service charge. The Ending Balance is shown.

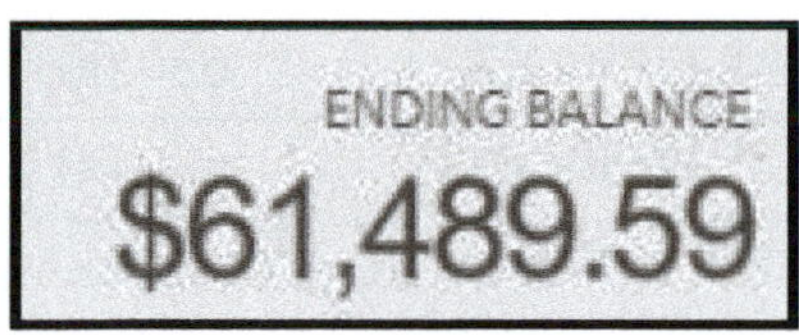

   The bank statement balance includes the $20 service charge: $61,489.59 – 20.00 = $61,469.59.

2. From the Bank Register page, select Reconcile. Use the November 30 bank statement to reconcile the checking account balance.

Statement of Account Checking Account November 1 to November 30, 20XX		QB Cloud_Student Name Your address, city, state, Zip Account No. 7731-2256	
REGULAR CHECKING			
Previous Balance	10/31/XX	$ 50,437.56	
7 Deposits (+)		11,920.00	
10 checks (-)		821.57	
1 Other Deductions (-)		46.40	
Service Charge		20.00	
Ending Balance	11/30/XX	**$61,469.59**	
DEPOSITS			
	11/10//XX	3,000.00	
	11/11/XX	4,000.00	
	11/13/XX	3,000.00	
	11/30/XX	270.00	
	11/30/XX	100.00	
	11/30/XX	400.00	
	11/30/XX	120.00	
	11/30/XX	630.00	
	11/30/XX	400.00	

CHECKS (Asterisk * indicates break in check number sequence)				
	11/3/XX	1026	84.32	
	11/4/XX	1027	76.19	
	11/4/XX	1028	46.90	
	11/5/XX	1029	125.00	
	11/5/XX	1030	127.96	
	11/6/XX	1031	90.82	
	11/6/XX	1032	125.00	
	11/10/XX	1033	82.13	*continued*

	11/10/XX	1034	42.25	
	11/10/XX	1035	21.00	
OTHER DEDUCTIONS (ATM's)				
	11/5/XX	ATM	46.40	

3. Complete these fields.

Statement Ending Date:	type **11/30/20XX** (current year)
Ending Balance:	type **61,469.59**
Service Charge:	type **20.00**
Date:	type **11/30/20XX** (current year)
Account:	603 Bank charges

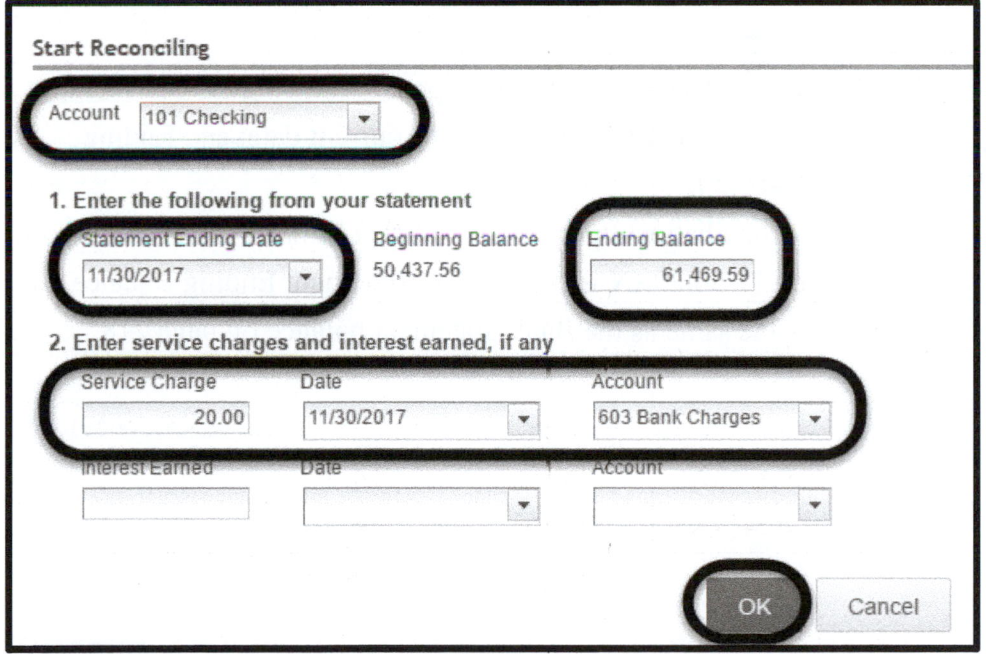

4. OK. The Reconcile – Checking window appears. The bank statement shows that all checks and deposits cleared. *Make sure your Difference shows*

0.00. (*Hint:* You can select all Checks and Payments and all Deposits and Other Credits by clicking on the box to the left of Date.)

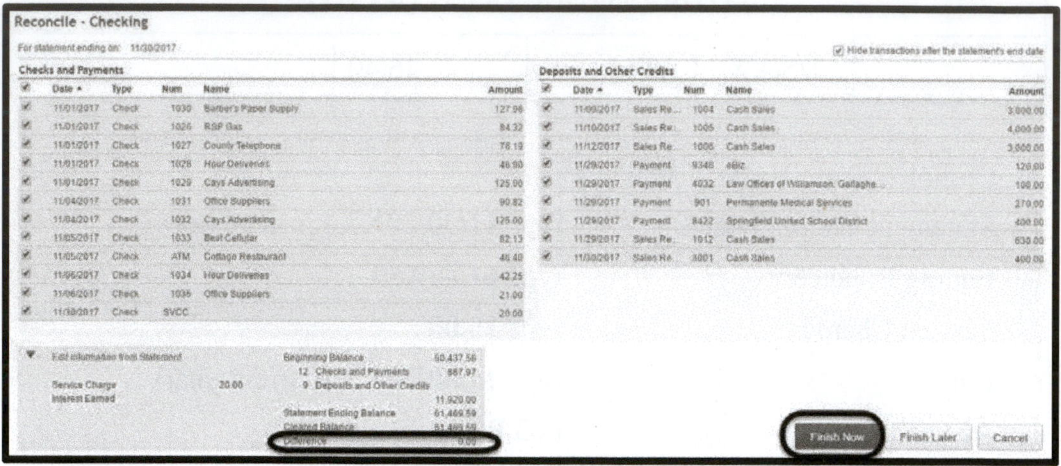

5. Finish Now. The Reconcile page appears showing the Statement Ending Date, 11/30/20XX, Reconciled On, current date; and Ending Balance, $61,469.59.
6. To see the Reconciliation report, double-click 11/30/20XX. The Checking, Period Ending 11/30/20XX is shown. The Statement Ending Balance $61,469.59 is the same as the Bank Statement balance on page 218.

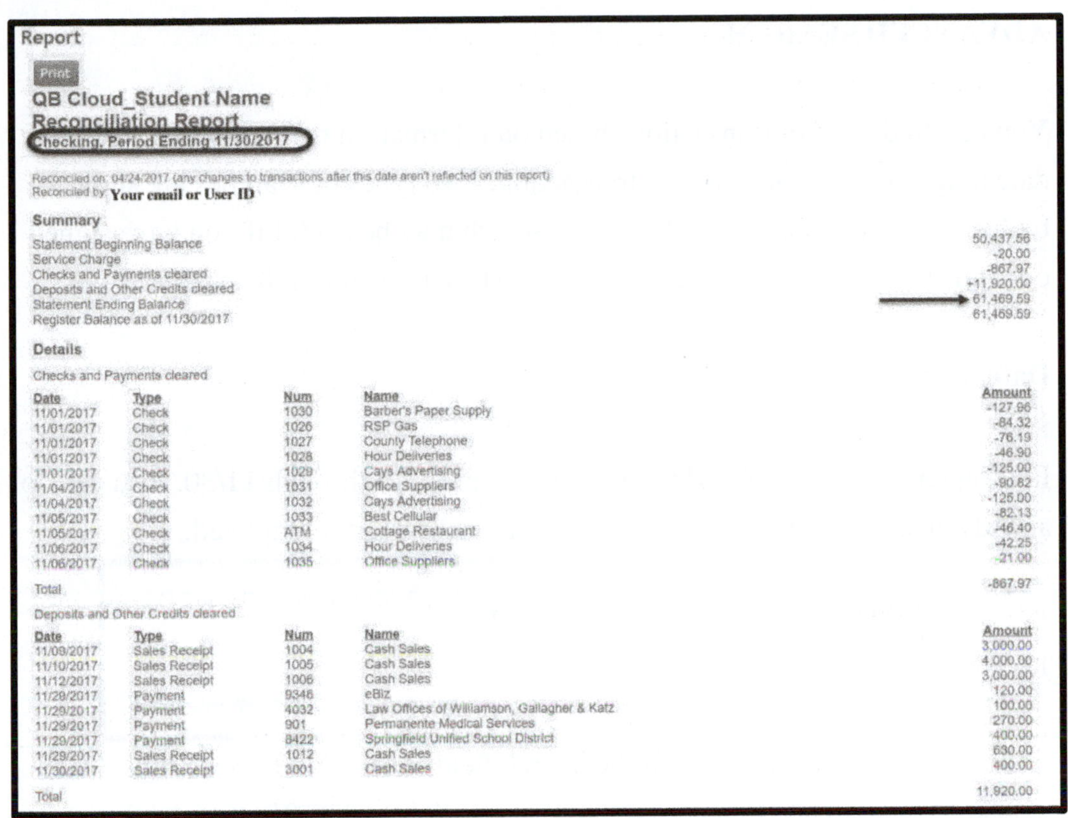

Report

Print

QB Cloud_Student Name

Reconciliation Report

Checking, Period Ending 11/30/2017

Reconciled on: 04/24/2017 (any changes to transactions after this date aren't reflected on this report)

Reconciled by: **Your email or User ID**

Summary

Statement Beginning Balance	50,437.56
Service Charge	-20.00
Checks and Payments cleared	-867.97
Deposits and Other Credits cleared	+11,920.00
Statement Ending Balance	61,469.59
Register Balance as of 11/30/2017	61,469.59

Details

Checks and Payments cleared

Date	Type	Num	Name	Amount
11/01/2017	Check	1030	Barber's Paper Supply	-127.96
11/01/2017	Check	1026	RSP Gas	-84.32
11/01/2017	Check	1027	County Telephone	-76.19
11/01/2017	Check	1028	Hour Deliveries	-46.90
11/01/2017	Check	1029	Cays Advertising	-125.00
11/04/2017	Check	1031	Office Suppliers	-90.82
11/04/2017	Check	1032	Cays Advertising	-125.00
11/05/2017	Check	1033	Best Cellular	-82.13
11/05/2017	Check	ATM	Cottage Restaurant	-46.40
11/06/2017	Check	1034	Hour Deliveries	-42.25
11/06/2017	Check	1035	Office Suppliers	-21.00
Total				-867.97

Deposits and Other Credits cleared

Date	Type	Num	Name	Amount
11/09/2017	Sales Receipt	1004	Cash Sales	3,000.00
11/10/2017	Sales Receipt	1005	Cash Sales	4,000.00
11/12/2017	Sales Receipt	1006	Cash Sales	3,000.00
11/28/2017	Payment	9346	eBiz	120.00
11/29/2017	Payment	4032	Law Offices of Williamson, Gallagher & Katz	100.00
11/29/2017	Payment	901	Permanente Medical Services	270.00
11/29/2017	Payment	8422	Springfield Unified School District	400.00
11/29/2017	Sales Receipt	1012	Cash Sales	630.00
11/30/2017	Sales Receipt	3001	Cash Sales	400.00
Total				11,920.00

7. Go to the Dashboard. The 101 Checking In QuickBooks shows $61,469.59.

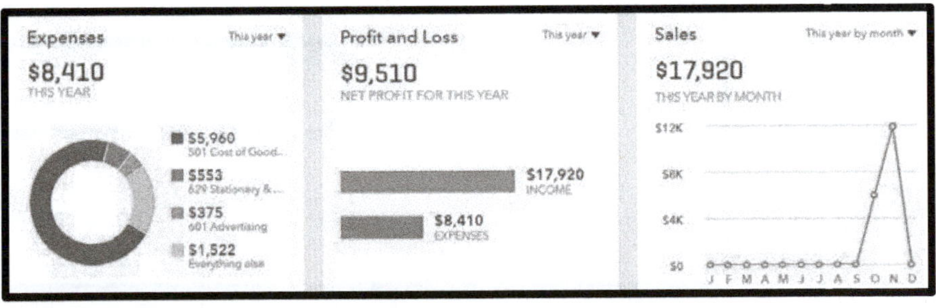

This year's Expenses are $8,410; Profit and Loss, $9,510. Sales, This year by month, $17,920. If you look at the Profit and Loss statement, Total Expenses are $2,450.41 and total Cost of Goods Sold are $5,960.00. The Dashboard's Expenses of $8,410 are the P&L's Total Expenses plus Cost of Goods Sold: $5,960.00 + $2,450.41 = $8,410.41 (amounts are rounded).

ADVANCED SEARCH

You can find a list of transactions based on information that you enter, such as date range, amount, and type of transaction. Two types of searches are shown – by Date and by Transaction. Advanced search may be useful if you have signed out and aren't sure when you sign in where to start again in the chapter.

Date Search

In Chapter 5, you completed transactions from 11/15 through 11/30. You can do an Advanced Search to make sure these transactions are completed.

1. Click > Advanced Search.

2. The Search page appears. In the Search field, select All Transactions. Click Add Filter > Date Filter > type from 11/15/XX to 11/30/XX > Apply.

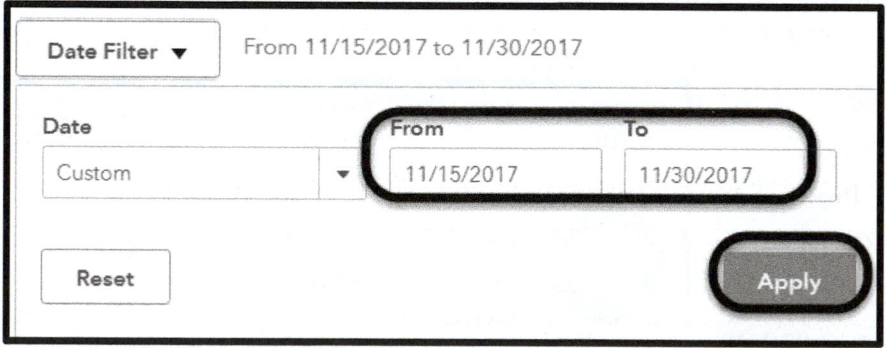

Twelve matches are found. Observe that the Last Modified Date shows when the transactions were entered. The Results for All Transactions on the next page shows a search completed for 11/15 thru 11/30.

Search for QB Cloud_Student Name

Results for All Transactions

Date	Type	No.	Contact	Amount	Last Modified Date
11/30/2017	Sales Receipt	1013	Cash Sales	$400.00	04/24/2017, 03:13 PM
11/30/2017	Check	SVCCHRG		$20.00	04/24/2017, 03:23 PM
11/29/2017	Payment	4032	Law Offices of Williamson, Gallagher & Katz	$100.00	04/24/2017, 03:06 PM
11/29/2017	Sales Receipt	1012	Cash Sales	$630.00	04/24/2017, 03:12 PM
11/29/2017	Payment	8422	Springfield Unified School District	$400.00	04/24/2017, 03:07 PM
11/29/2017	Payment	9346	eBiz	$120.00	04/24/2017, 03:05 PM
11/29/2017	Payment	901	Permanente Medical Services	$270.00	04/24/2017, 03:07 PM
11/16/2017	Credit Memo	1011	eBiz	$30.00	04/24/2017, 02:42 PM
11/15/2017	Invoice	1008	Law Offices of Williamson, Gallagher & Katz	$100.00	04/24/2017, 03:06 PM
11/15/2017	Invoice	1007	eBiz	$150.00	04/24/2017, 03:05 PM
11/15/2017	Invoice	1009	Permanente Medical Services	$270.00	04/24/2017, 03:07 PM
11/15/2017	Invoice	1010	Springfield Unified School District	$400.00	04/24/2017, 03:07 PM

Transaction Type

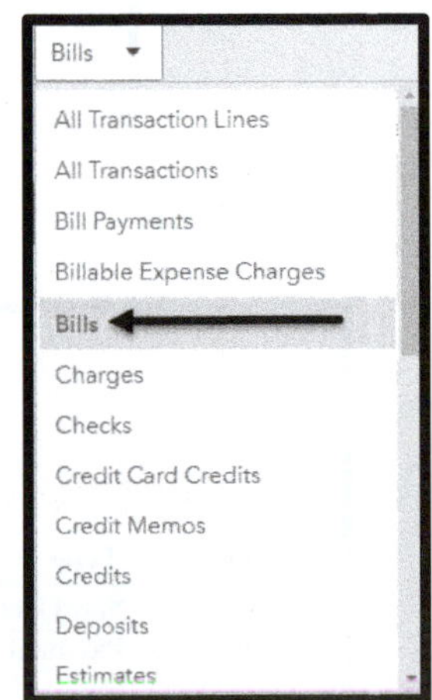

The Search page includes other criteria. For example, click on the down-arrow next to All Transactions > select Bills > in the Vendor field, select AmpleStore, Inc. > Search.

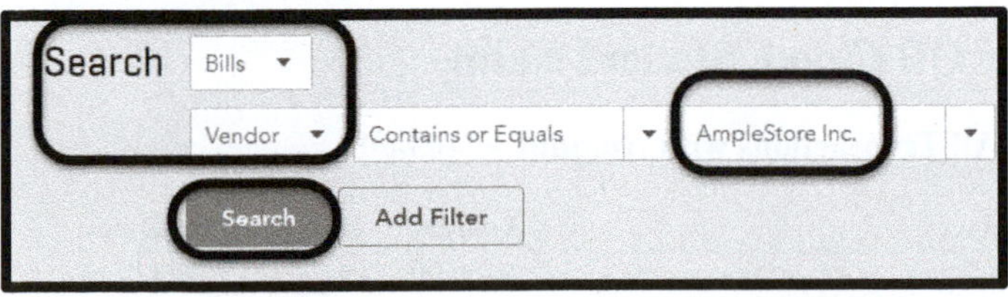

Two matches appear. (*Hint:* You may need to select dates.)

Search for QB Cloud_Student Name

Results for Bills with Vendor = 'AmpleStore Inc.'

Date	Type	No.	Contact	Amount	Last Modified Date
11/08/2017	Bill	AS12	AmpleStore Inc.	$375.00	04/19/2017, 01:32 PM
11/02/2017	Bill	AS7	AmpleStore Inc.	$300.00	04/18/2017, 02:23 PM

Amount

Select All Transations > in the Reference no. field, select Amount > type **400** in the Enter Amount field > Add Filter > Date Filter is from 10/1/XX to 11/30/XX > Apply.

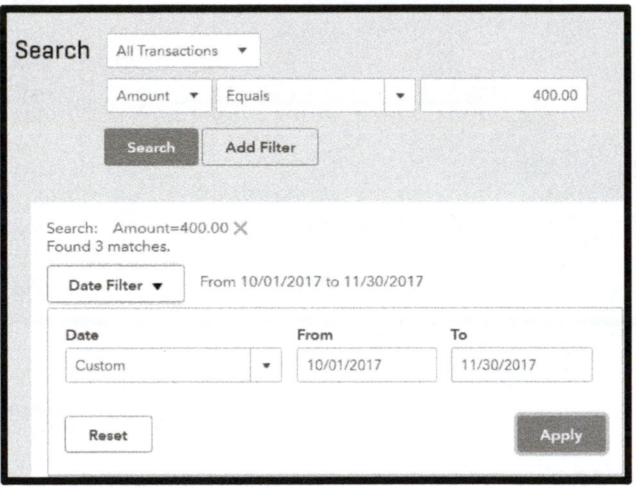

Three matches are found.

Search for QB Cloud_Student Name

Results for All Transactions with Amount = '400.00'

Date	Type	No.	Contact	Amount	Last Modified Date
11/30/2017	Sales Receipt	1013	Cash Sales	$400.00	04/24/2017, 03:13 PM
11/29/2017	Payment	8422	Springfield Unified School District	$400.00	04/24/2017, 03:07 PM
11/15/2017	Invoice	1010	Springfield Unified School District	$400.00	04/24/2017, 03:07 PM

PRODUCTS AND SERVICES

On invoices and other sales transactions, you don't choose income accounts directly. Instead, you choose products or services, which are associated with income accounts. Choosing a product or service determines where the transaction is categorized on your Profit and Loss report.

1. To check QB Cloud's products and services, go to ⚙ > Products and Services > More > Run Report. The Product/Service List is shown below.

QB Cloud_Student Name

PRODUCT/SERVICE LIST

PRODUCT/SERVICE	TYPE	DESCRIPTION	PRICE	COST	QTY ON HAND
Cash Sales	Noninventory				
Computers	Inventory	Computers	1,000.00	500.00	16.00
Data storage	Inventory	Data storage	30.00	15.00	31.00
Hours	Service				
Network products	Inventory	Network products	50.00	25.00	16.00
Sales	Service				
Web server	Inventory	Web server	400.00	200.00	13.00
Webinars	Inventory	Webinars	90.00	45.00	11.00

Comment: Now that you have completed customer transactions, the Price/Rate and Quantity fields differ from the Chapter 4 Products and Services List.

2. Save the Product List/Service List as Excel and Adobe PDF files. Use the file name **Chapter 5_Products and Services List**.

REPORTS

Display the following reports. Your instructor may require additional reports.

Journal

The journal entry is a transaction in which:

- There are at least two parts: a Debit and a Credit. These are called distribution lines.
- Each distribution line has an account from the Chart of Accounts.
- The total of the Debit column equals the total of the Credit column.

Use the Journal entry if:

- You need to transfer money between income and expense accounts.
- You need to transfer money from an asset, liability, or equity account to an income or expense account.
- You prefer the traditional system of accounting – entering debits and credits in a general journal or ledger.

You can also enter transactions using specialized screens, such as Invoice, Receive Payment, Credit Memo, Sales Receipt, Check, Bill, Transfer, Bank Deposit.

To see the transactions that you entered in Chapter 5, display the 11/15/20XX to 11/30/20XX journal.

1. Click 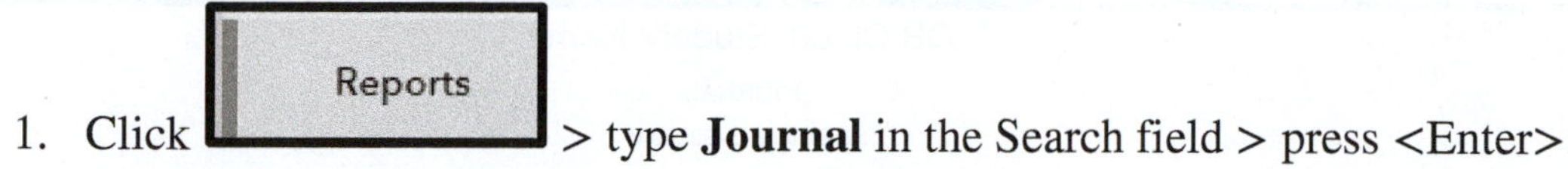

> type **Journal** in the Search field > press <Enter>.

2. Type **11/15/XX** To **11/30/XX** > press <Tab>. (*Hint:* Use the current year. Type either four characters or two for the year.) The Journal is shown on the next two pages.

QB Cloud_Student Name

JOURNAL

November 15-30, 2017

DATE	TRANSACTION TYPE	NUM	NAME	MEMO/DESCRIPTION	ACCOUNT #	ACCOUNT	DEBIT	CREDIT
11/15/2017	Invoice	1007	eBiz		105	105 Accounts Receivable (A/R)	$150.00	
				Data storage	401	401 Sales		$150.00
				Data storage	115	115 Merchandise Inventory		$75.00
				Data storage	501	501 Cost of Goods Sold	$75.00	
							$225.00	**$225.00**
11/15/2017	Invoice	1008	Law Offices of Williamson, Gallagher & Katz		105	105 Accounts Receivable (A/R)	$100.00	
				Network products	115	115 Merchandise Inventory		$50.00
				Network products	401	401 Sales		$100.00
				Network products	501	501 Cost of Goods Sold	$50.00	
							$150.00	**$150.00**
11/15/2017	Invoice	1009	Permanente Medical Services		105	105 Accounts Receivable (A/R)	$270.00	
				Webinars	115	115 Merchandise Inventory		$135.00
				Webinars	501	501 Cost of Goods Sold	$135.00	
				Webinars	401	401 Sales		$270.00
							$405.00	**$405.00**
11/15/2017	Invoice	1010	Springfield Unified School District		105	105 Accounts Receivable (A/R)	$400.00	
				Web server	501	501 Cost of Goods Sold	$200.00	
				Web server	401	401 Sales		$400.00
				Web server	115	115 Merchandise Inventory		$200.00
							$600.00	**$600.00**
11/16/2017	Credit Memo	1011	eBiz		105	105 Accounts Receivable (A/R)		$30.00
				Data storage	501	501 Cost of Goods Sold		$15.00
				Data storage	401	401 Sales	$30.00	
				Data storage	115	115 Merchandise Inventory	$15.00	
							$45.00	**$45.00**
11/29/2017	Payment	9346	eBiz		101	101 Checking	$120.00	
					105	105 Accounts Receivable (A/R)		$120.00
							$120.00	**$120.00**
11/29/2017	Payment	4032	Law Offices of Williamson, Gallagher & Katz		101	101 Checking	$100.00	
					105	105 Accounts Receivable (A/R)		$100.00
							$100.00	**$100.00**
11/29/2017	Payment	901	Permanente Medical Services		101	101 Checking	$270.00	
					105	105 Accounts Receivable (A/R)		$270.00
							$270.00	**$270.00**

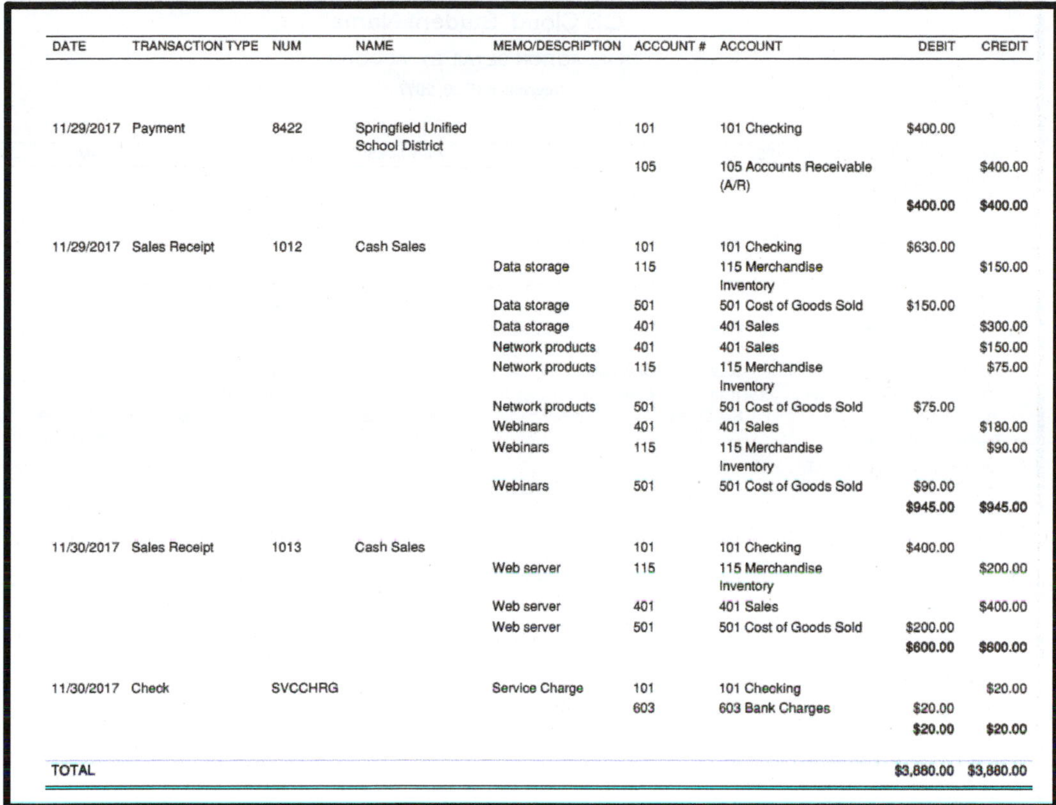

DATE	TRANSACTION TYPE	NUM	NAME	MEMO/DESCRIPTION	ACCOUNT #	ACCOUNT	DEBIT	CREDIT
11/29/2017	Payment	8422	Springfield Unified School District		101	101 Checking	$400.00	
					105	105 Accounts Receivable (A/R)		$400.00
							$400.00	**$400.00**
11/29/2017	Sales Receipt	1012	Cash Sales		101	101 Checking	$630.00	
				Data storage	115	115 Merchandise Inventory		$150.00
				Data storage	501	501 Cost of Goods Sold	$150.00	
				Data storage	401	401 Sales		$300.00
				Network products	401	401 Sales		$150.00
				Network products	115	115 Merchandise Inventory		$75.00
				Network products	501	501 Cost of Goods Sold	$75.00	
				Webinars	401	401 Sales		$180.00
				Webinars	115	115 Merchandise Inventory		$90.00
				Webinars	501	501 Cost of Goods Sold	$90.00	
							$945.00	**$945.00**
11/30/2017	Sales Receipt	1013	Cash Sales		101	101 Checking	$400.00	
				Web server	115	115 Merchandise Inventory		$200.00
				Web server	401	401 Sales		$400.00
				Web server	501	501 Cost of Goods Sold	$200.00	
							$600.00	**$600.00**
11/30/2017	Check	SVCCHRG		Service Charge	101	101 Checking		$20.00
					603	603 Bank Charges	$20.00	
							$20.00	**$20.00**
TOTAL							**$3,880.00**	**$3,880.00**

Save the Journal as an Excel File and an Adobe PDF file. Use the file name **Chapter 5_Journal**.

Transaction Detail by Account

1. Go to the Reports page. In the Search field, select or type **Transaction Detail by Account**. Run report from from 11/15/20XX to 11/30/20XX > Run report. The Transaction Detail by Account report is shown on the next two pages.

QB Cloud_Student Name

TRANSACTION DETAIL BY ACCOUNT

November 15-30, 2017

DATE	TRANSACTION TYPE	NUM	NAME	MEMO/DESCRIPTION	SPLIT	AMOUNT	BALANCE
101 Checking							
11/29/2017	Payment	9346	eBiz		105 Accounts Receivable (A/R)	120.00	120.00
11/29/2017	Payment	901	Permanente Medical Services		105 Accounts Receivable (A/R)	270.00	390.00
11/29/2017	Payment	8422	Springfield Unified School District		105 Accounts Receivable (A/R)	400.00	790.00
11/29/2017	Payment	4032	Law Offices of Williamson, Gallagher & Katz		105 Accounts Receivable (A/R)	100.00	890.00
11/29/2017	Sales Receipt	1012	Cash Sales		-Split-	630.00	1,520.00
11/30/2017	Sales Receipt	1013	Cash Sales		401 Sales	400.00	1,920.00
11/30/2017	Check	SVCCHRG		Service Charge	603 Bank Charges	-20.00	1,900.00
Total for 101 Checking						$1,900.00	
105 Accounts Receivable (A/R)							
11/15/2017	Invoice	1009	Permanente Medical Services		401 Sales	270.00	270.00
11/15/2017	Invoice	1007	eBiz		401 Sales	150.00	420.00
11/15/2017	Invoice	1008	Law Offices of Williamson, Gallagher & Katz		401 Sales	100.00	520.00
11/15/2017	Invoice	1010	Springfield Unified School District		401 Sales	400.00	920.00
11/16/2017	Credit Memo	1011	eBiz		401 Sales	-30.00	890.00
11/29/2017	Payment	4032	Law Offices of Williamson, Gallagher & Katz		101 Checking	-100.00	790.00
11/29/2017	Payment	9346	eBiz		101 Checking	-120.00	670.00
11/29/2017	Payment	901	Permanente Medical Services		101 Checking	-270.00	400.00
11/29/2017	Payment	8422	Springfield Unified School District		101 Checking	-400.00	0.00
Total for 105 Accounts Receivable (A/R)						$0.00	
115 Merchandise Inventory							
11/15/2017	Invoice	1010	Springfield Unified School District	Web server	105 Accounts Receivable (A/R)	-200.00	-200.00
11/15/2017	Invoice	1009	Permanente Medical Services	Webinars	105 Accounts Receivable (A/R)	-135.00	-335.00
11/15/2017	Invoice	1007	eBiz	Data storage	105 Accounts Receivable (A/R)	-75.00	-410.00
11/15/2017	Invoice	1008	Law Offices of Williamson, Gallagher & Katz	Network products	105 Accounts Receivable (A/R)	-50.00	-460.00
11/16/2017	Credit Memo	1011	eBiz	Data storage	105 Accounts Receivable (A/R)	15.00	-445.00
11/29/2017	Sales Receipt	1012	Cash Sales	Webinars	101 Checking	-90.00	-535.00
11/29/2017	Sales Receipt	1012	Cash Sales	Network products	101 Checking	-75.00	-610.00
11/29/2017	Sales Receipt	1012	Cash Sales	Data storage	101 Checking	-150.00	-760.00
11/30/2017	Sales Receipt	1013	Cash Sales	Web server	101 Checking	-200.00	-960.00
Total for 115 Merchandise Inventory						$ -960.00	
401 Sales							
11/15/2017	Invoice	1008	Law Offices of Williamson, Gallagher & Katz	Network products	105 Accounts Receivable (A/R)	100.00	100.00
11/15/2017	Invoice	1007	eBiz	Data storage	105 Accounts Receivable (A/R)	150.00	250.00
11/15/2017	Invoice	1009	Permanente Medical Services	Webinars	105 Accounts Receivable (A/R)	270.00	520.00
11/15/2017	Invoice	1010	Springfield Unified School District	Web server	105 Accounts Receivable (A/R)	400.00	920.00
11/16/2017	Credit Memo	1011	eBiz	Data storage	105 Accounts Receivable	-30.00	890.00

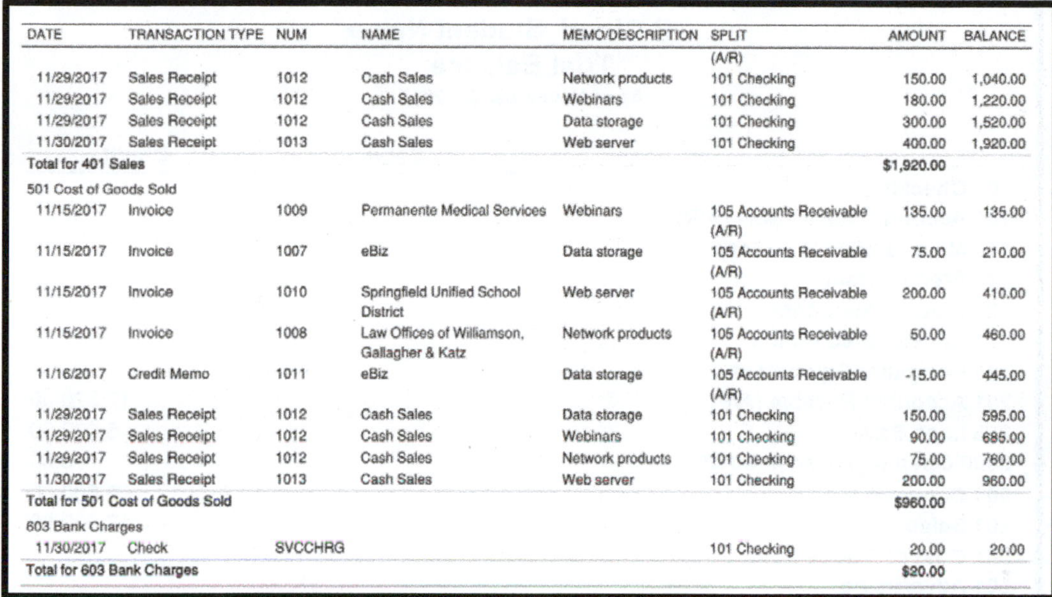

DATE	TRANSACTION TYPE	NUM	NAME	MEMO/DESCRIPTION	SPLIT	AMOUNT	BALANCE
					(A/R)		
11/29/2017	Sales Receipt	1012	Cash Sales	Network products	101 Checking	150.00	1,040.00
11/29/2017	Sales Receipt	1012	Cash Sales	Webinars	101 Checking	180.00	1,220.00
11/29/2017	Sales Receipt	1012	Cash Sales	Data storage	101 Checking	300.00	1,520.00
11/30/2017	Sales Receipt	1013	Cash Sales	Web server	101 Checking	400.00	1,920.00
Total for 401 Sales						$1,920.00	
501 Cost of Goods Sold							
11/15/2017	Invoice	1009	Permanente Medical Services	Webinars	105 Accounts Receivable (A/R)	135.00	135.00
11/15/2017	Invoice	1007	eBiz	Data storage	105 Accounts Receivable (A/R)	75.00	210.00
11/15/2017	Invoice	1010	Springfield Unified School District	Web server	105 Accounts Receivable (A/R)	200.00	410.00
11/15/2017	Invoice	1008	Law Offices of Williamson, Gallagher & Katz	Network products	105 Accounts Receivable (A/R)	50.00	460.00
11/16/2017	Credit Memo	1011	eBiz	Data storage	105 Accounts Receivable (A/R)	-15.00	445.00
11/29/2017	Sales Receipt	1012	Cash Sales	Data storage	101 Checking	150.00	595.00
11/29/2017	Sales Receipt	1012	Cash Sales	Webinars	101 Checking	90.00	685.00
11/29/2017	Sales Receipt	1012	Cash Sales	Network products	101 Checking	75.00	760.00
11/30/2017	Sales Receipt	1013	Cash Sales	Web server	101 Checking	200.00	960.00
Total for 501 Cost of Goods Sold						$960.00	
603 Bank Charges							
11/30/2017	Check	SVCCHRG			101 Checking	20.00	20.00
Total for 603 Bank Charges						$20.00	

Comment: It is okay if your transactions are in a different order. For example, if you edited transactions, the order may be changed. If needed, you can drill down to entries from the Transaction Detail by Account report.

2. Save the Transaction Detail by Account as a PDF file and export to Excel. Use the file name **Chapter 5_Transaction Detail by Account**.

Trial Balance

1. Go to the Reports page. In the Search field, select or type **Trial Balance** from **11/1/XX** to **11/30/XX** > Run report.

   Compare your trial balance with the one shown on the next page. (*Hint:* If your trial balance does not show Opening Balance Equity this is okay.)

QB Cloud_Student Name
Trial Balance
As of November 30, 2017

	Debit	Credit
101 Checking	61,469.59	
105 Accounts Receivable (A/R)	0.00	
115 Merchandise Inventory	11,960.00	
123 Prepaid Rent	6,000.00	
125 Prepaid Insurance	3,000.00	
130 Undeposited Funds	0.00	
135 Computer Equipment	10,000.00	
201 Accounts Payable (A/P)		17,920.00
205 Loan Payable		5,000.00
3000 Opening Balance Equity		0.00
301 Common Stock		60,000.00
401 Sales		17,920.00
501 Cost of Goods Sold	5,960.00	
601 Advertising	375.00	
603 Bank Charges	40.00	
605 Dues & Subscriptions	150.00	
609 Freight & Delivery	153.80	
619 Meals and Entertainment	172.80	
621 Office Supplies	338.67	
625 Repair & Maintenance	140.00	
627 Shipping and delivery expense	47.00	
629 Stationery & Printing	553.18	
633 Telephone Expense	316.64	
635 Utilities	163.32	
TOTAL	$ 100,840.00	$ 100,840.00

If your Trial Balance does not show Account 130 Undeposited Funds and Account 3000 Opening Balance Equity, that is okay. Depending on when QBO updates, accounts with zero balances may be shown on your Trial Balance. Reports can also be filtered so that only non-zero account balances appear (refer to page 201).

2. Export to Excel and save as a PDF file. Use the file name **Chapter 5_Trial Balance.** Observe that Account 101 Checking's balance, $61,469.59 is the same as the bank statement balance.

A/R Register

1. Go to Accounting > on the Chart of Accounts, double-click 105 Accounts Receivable (A/R) *or* select View Register. The Ending Balance is 0.00. This is the same as Account 105 Accounts Receivable on the Trial Balance, and the A/R balance on the Transaction Detail by Account report. (*Hint:* The last line shows a zero balance for payment created by QB Online to link credits to charges. The author's date is shown, your date will differ. Ignore the last line. It is a default entry.)

QB Cloud_Student Name

105 Accounts Receivable (A/R) Ending Balance: $0.00

Date	Ref No.	Payee	Charge / Credit	Payment	Open Balance
	Type	**Memo**		**Due Date**	
11/29/2017	8422	Springfield Unified School District		$400.00	$0.00
	Payment				
11/29/2017	901	Permanente Medical Services		$270.00	$0.00
	Payment				
11/29/2017	4032	Law Offices of Williamson, Gallagher & Katz		$100.00	$0.00
	Payment				
11/29/2017	9346	eBiz		$120.00	$0.00
	Payment				
11/16/2017	1011	eBiz		$30.00	$0.00
	Credit Memo				
11/15/2017	1010	Springfield Unified School District	$400.00		$0.00
	Invoice			Paid	
11/15/2017	1009	Permanente Medical Services	$270.00		$0.00
	Invoice			Paid	
11/15/2017	1008	Law Offices of Williamson, Gallagher & Katz	$100.00		$0.00
	Invoice			Paid	
11/15/2017	1007	eBiz	$150.00		$0.00
	Invoice			Paid	
04/24/2017		eBiz	$0.00		$0.00
	Payment	Created by QB Online to link credits to charges.			

2. Go to the Reports page.

Inventory Valuation Summary

1. Go to the Reports page. In the Search field, select or type **Inventory Valuation Summary** > Report period is Custom > As of **11/30/XX** > Run report.

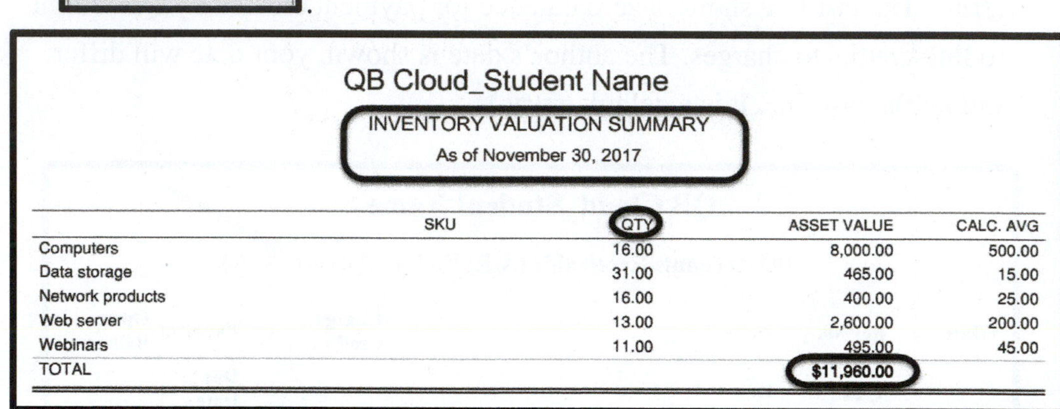

QB Cloud_Student Name

INVENTORY VALUATION SUMMARY

As of November 30, 2017

	SKU	QTY	ASSET VALUE	CALC. AVG
Computers		16.00	8,000.00	500.00
Data storage		31.00	465.00	15.00
Network products		16.00	400.00	25.00
Web server		13.00	2,600.00	200.00
Webinars		11.00	495.00	45.00
TOTAL			$11,960.00	

Observe that the total, $11,960.00, is the same as Account 115 Merchandise Inventory on the Trial Balance. The quantity of each inventory item agrees with the Products and Services list.

2. Export to Excel and save as a PDF file. Use the file name **Chapter 5_Inventory Valuation Summary.**

Vendor Balance Summary

1. Go to the Reports page. In the Search field, select or type **Vendor Balance Summary**. You can select all dates *or* select Custom > type **11/30/20XX** in the As of field.

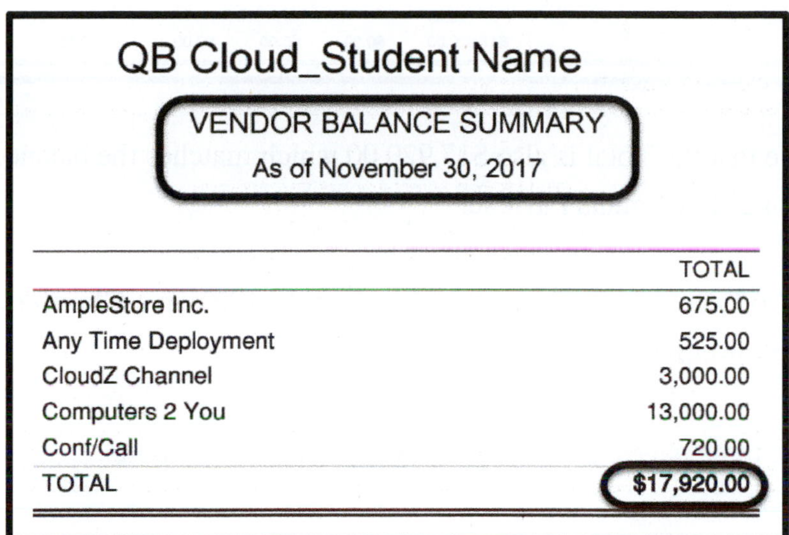

QB Cloud_Student Name

VENDOR BALANCE SUMMARY

As of November 30, 2017

	TOTAL
AmpleStore Inc.	675.00
Any Time Deployment	525.00
CloudZ Channel	3,000.00
Computers 2 You	13,000.00
Conf/Call	720.00
TOTAL	$17,920.00

Observe that the total, $17,920.00, is the same Account 201 Accounts Payable on the Trial Balance.

2. Export to Excel and save as a PDF file. Use the file name **Chapter 5_Vendor Balance Summary.**

A/P Aging Summary

1. Go to the Reports page. In the Search field, select or type **A/P Aging Summary**. You can select all dates *or* type **11/30/20XX** in the As of field > Run Report.

QB Cloud_Student Name

A/P AGING SUMMARY

As of November 30, 2017

	CURRENT	1 - 30	31 - 60	61 - 90	91 AND OVER	TOTAL
AmpleStore Inc.	675.00					$675.00
Any Time Deployment	525.00					$525.00
CloudZ Channel	3,000.00					$3,000.00
Computers 2 You	13,000.00					$13,000.00
Conf/Call	720.00					$720.00
TOTAL	$17,920.00	$0.00	$0.00	$0.00	$0.00	$17,920.00

Observe that the Total is also $17,920.00 which matches the balance in Account 201 Accounts Payable.

2. Export to Excel and save as a PDF file. Use the file name **Chapter 5_AP Aging Summary.**

On the next three pages, continue displaying and saving reports.

Profit and Loss from 10/1/20XX to 11/30/20XX

QB Cloud_Student Name

PROFIT AND LOSS

October - November, 2017

	TOTAL
INCOME	
401 Sales	17,920.00
Total Income	**$17,920.00**
COST OF GOODS SOLD	
501 Cost of Goods Sold	5,960.00
Total Cost of Goods Sold	**$5,960.00**
GROSS PROFIT	**$11,960.00**
EXPENSES	
601 Advertising	375.00
603 Bank Charges	40.00
605 Dues & Subscriptions	150.00
609 Freight & Delivery	153.80
619 Meals and Entertainment	172.80
621 Office Supplies	338.67
625 Repair & Maintenance	140.00
627 Shipping and delivery expense	47.00
629 Stationery & Printing	553.18
633 Telephone Expense	316.64
635 Utilities	163.32
Total Expenses	**$2,450.41**
NET OPERATING INCOME	**$9,509.59**
NET INCOME	**$9,509.59**

Export the Profit and Loss to Excel and save as a PDF file. Use the file name **Chapter 5_Profit and Loss.**

Balance Sheet from 10/1/20XX to 11/30/20XX

QB Cloud_Student Name
Balance Sheet
As of November 30, 2017

		Total
ASSETS		
Current Assets		
Bank Accounts		
101 Checking		61,469.59
Total Bank Accounts	$	61,469.59
Accounts Receivable		
105 Accounts Receivable (A/R)		0.00
Total Accounts Receivable	$	0.00
Other Current Assets		
115 Merchandise Inventory		11,960.00
123 Prepaid Rent		6,000.00
125 Prepaid Insurance		3,000.00
130 Undeposited Funds		0.00
Total Other Current Assets	$	20,960.00
Total Current Assets	$	82,429.59
Fixed Assets		
135 Computer Equipment		10,000.00
Total Fixed Assets	$	10,000.00
TOTAL ASSETS	$	92,429.59
LIABILITIES AND EQUITY		
Liabilities		
Current Liabilities		
Accounts Payable		
201 Accounts Payable (A/P)		17,920.00
Total Accounts Payable	$	17,920.00
Other Current Liabilities		
205 Loan Payable		5,000.00
Total Other Current Liabilities	$	5,000.00
Total Current Liabilities	$	22,920.00
Total Liabilities	$	22,920.00
Equity		
3000 Opening Balance Equity		0.00
301 Common Stock		60,000.00
318 Retained Earnings		
Net Income		9,509.59
Total Equity	$	69,509.59
TOTAL LIABILITIES AND EQUITY	$	92,429.59

Export the Balance Sheet to Excel and save as a PDF file. Use the file name **Chapter 5_Balance Sheet**.

Statement of Cash Flows from 10/1/20XX to 11/30/20XX

QB Cloud_Student Name

STATEMENT OF CASH FLOWS

October - November, 2017

	TOTAL
OPERATING ACTIVITIES	
Net Income	9,509.59
Adjustments to reconcile Net Income to Net Cash provided by operations:	
105 Accounts Receivable (A/R)	0.00
115 Merchandise Inventory	-11,960.00
123 Prepaid Rent	-6,000.00
125 Prepaid Insurance	-3,000.00
201 Accounts Payable (A/P)	17,920.00
205 Loan Payable	5,000.00
Total Adjustments to reconcile Net Income to Net Cash provided by operations:	**1,960.00**
Net cash provided by operating activities	**$11,469.59**
INVESTING ACTIVITIES	
135 Computer Equipment	-10,000.00
Net cash provided by investing activities	**$ -10,000.00**
FINANCING ACTIVITIES	
3000 Opening Balance Equity	0.00
301 Common Stock	60,000.00
Net cash provided by financing activities	**$60,000.00**
NET CASH INCREASE FOR PERIOD	**$61,469.59**
CASH AT BEGINNING OF PERIOD	0.00
CASH AT END OF PERIOD	**$61,469.59**

Export the Statement of Cash Flows to Excel and save as a PDF file. Use the file name **Chapter 5_Statement of Cash Flows**. (*Hint:* If your instructor prefers the November SCF only, change the dates to 11/1/20XX to 11/30/20XX).

Filtering the Audit Log

By default, the Audit Log displays the 200 most recent events. Dates and times in the Audit Log and Audit History reflect when events occurred, displayed in your local time. To see a history of the event, click View in the History columns.

1. Select [gear icon] > Audit Log > in the Filter box, click on the down-arrow > User, select your User ID or name > Date, All dates > Events > check Transactions.

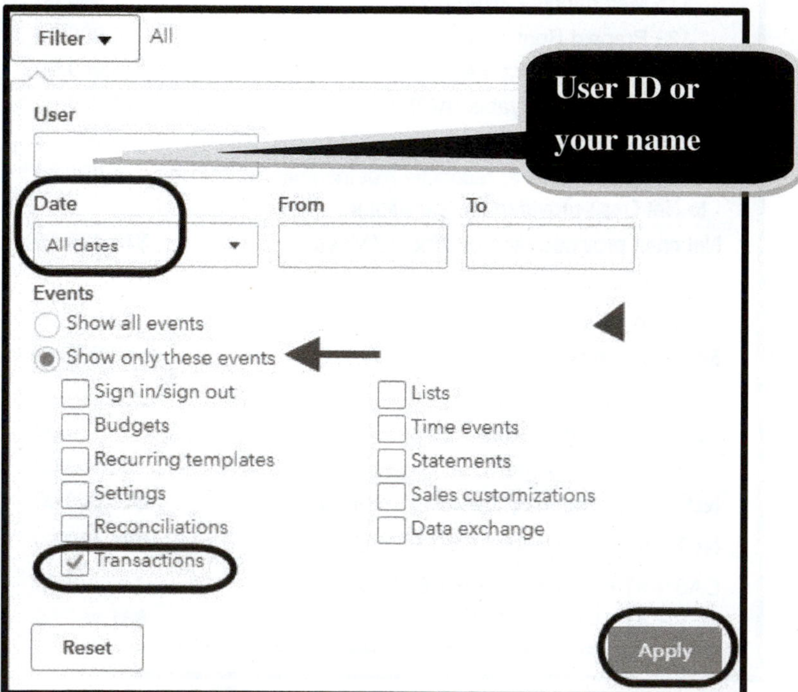

2. After clicking <Apply>, the Audit Log shows transactions.

Audit a Transaction

To see a detailed history, do this.

1. To see the work completed, scroll down the Audit Log page.
2. Blue font indicates links. In the History column, click View.
3. From the Audit Log page, you can drill down to transactions.
4. Click the back arrow to return to the Audit Log. To see more, go to other filter selections.

CHECK YOUR PROGRESS

Check Your Progress assignments are included on the Online Learning Center at www.mhhe.com/qbo2e > Student Edition > Chapter 5 > Check Your Progress.

1. What is account balance from 10/1/20XX to 11/30/20XX in these accounts? Indicate whether these accounts have debit (dr.) or credit (cr.) balances.

   Account 101 Checking ____________________

   Account 105 Accounts Receivable ____________________

   Account 115 Merchandise Inventory ____________________

   Account 401 Sales ____________________

Account 501 Cost of Goods Sold __________________

Account 603 Bank Charges __________________

2. What is Net Income? __________________

3. What are the total Liabilities and Equity? __________________

4. What is the quantity, asset value, and average cost of computers?

____

5. What is the quantity, asset value, and average cost of data storage?

____

6. What is the quantity, asset value, and average cost of network products?

____

7. What is the quantity, asset value, and average cost of web servers?

____

8. What is the quantity, asset value, and average cost of webinars?

____

SIGN OUT

To sign out of QBO, go to the company settings (click on the company name), link to Sign Out. *Or,* continue.

ONLINE LEARNING CENTER (OLC): www.mhhe.com/qbo2e

The OLC includes additional Chapter 5 resources. Go online to www.mhhe.com/qbo2e > Student Edition > Chapter 5.

1. Narrated PowerPoints.
2. Online quizzes: 10 True or False and 10 multiple-choice questions. The Online quizzes are graded and can be emailed to your instructor.
3. Analysis question: Answer the analysis question, then email to your instructor.
4. Going to the Net

    a. Go to the QuickBooks blog at http://quickbooks.intuit.com/blog/.
    b. What are the QuickBooks Blog selections and links on its Home page? Make a selection, then read an article of interest. Describe each section of the Home page.

5. Videos:

    a. Watch the Create an Invoice in QuickBooks video at https://www.youtube.com/watch?v=k3-j0mmqoZA
    b. Go to RadioFreeQB at www.youtube.com/RadioFreeQB. Watch a QBO video of interest.

6. Glossary of terms: Words that are italicized and boldfaced are defined in the glossary. The Glossary is also Appendix B.
7. Problem Solving link includes Exercise 5-3.

Continue with Exercises

Exercise 5-1: Follow the instructions below to complete Exercise 5-1:

1. If necessary start QBO.

2. Add the following customers

Company:	**Main Office Depot**
Display name as:	Main Office Depot
Print on check as	(Use display name)
Phone:	**312-555-8911**
Street:	**4123 Broadway**
City/Town:	**Chicago**
State:	**IL**
ZIP:	**60290**
Country:	**USA**
Shipping address	(Same as billing address)

Company:	**WebPro**
Display name as:	WebPro
Print on check as	(Use display name)
Phone:	**505-555-5311**
Street:	**18 Alameda Road**
City/Town:	**Santa Fe**
State:	**NM**

ZIP: **87501**

Country: **USA**

Shipping address (Same as billing address)

3. To enter the 12/1 checks and ATM, use the transaction register. Before entering checks, make sure your Checking account register shows the same 11/30 balance, $61,469.59, as the transaction register. (*Hint:* Accounting Chart of Accounts displays > 101 Checking.) When necessary, type the appropriate payment amounts, ATM, and check number.

Transaction Register					
Ck. No.	**Date**	**Description of Transaction**	**Payment**	**Deposit**	**Balance**
	11/30	*Balance*			*61,469.59*
1036	**12/1**	**Office Suppliers**	**100.75**		61,368.84
1037	12/1	Cays Advertising	155.00		61,213.84
1038	12/1	Best Cellular	82.13		61,131.71
ATM	12/1	Cottage Restaurant	56.90		61,074.81
1039	12/1	Hour Deliveries	52.65		61,022.16
1040	12/1	Office Suppliers	21.00		61,001.16

4. After recording the 12/1 transactions, display the Bank Register for Account 101 Checking. (*Hint:* From the Navigation bar, select Accounting > on the Chart of Accounts double-click 101 Checking.) Make sure your ending balance is $61,001.16. If not, edit checks.

   Before entering the transactions on the next page, make sure the Checking account register shows $61,001.16.

If needed, Checks can be edited by drilling down from the Vendors Page *or* Audit Log.

> **Comment:** Payments to vendors are similar to receiving payments from customers. Go to the Vendor's page, select the appropriate bill and then make a payment.

Date	*Description of Transaction*
12/1/20XX	Paid the vendor, AmpleStore Inc. for Bill No. AS7, $300, Ref no. 1041. (*Hint:* Expenses > Vendors > AmpleStore > Make payment. When you uncheck Bill # AS12, the bill you want to pay, AS7, is checked.)

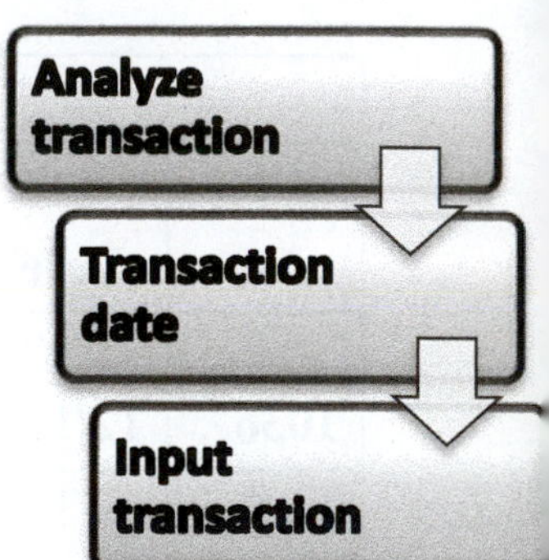

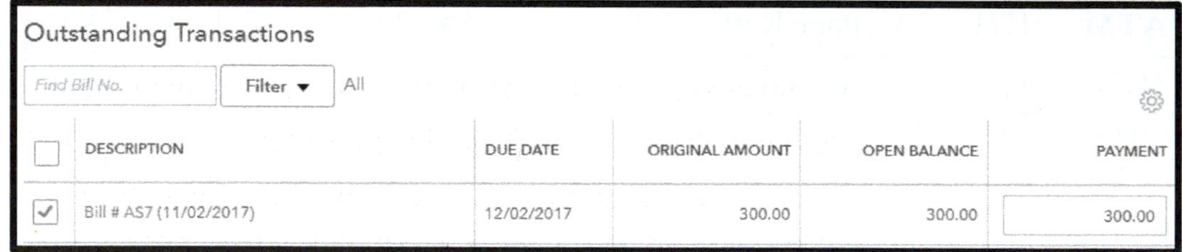

Outstanding Transactions

Find Bill No. | Filter | All

	DESCRIPTION	DUE DATE	ORIGINAL AMOUNT	OPEN BALANCE	PAYMENT
✓	Bill # AS7 (11/02/2017)	12/02/2017	300.00	300.00	300.00

Click <Save and new>.

12/1/20XX	Paid the vendor, Any Time Deployment, Bill No. ATD90, $250, Ref no. 1042.

12/1/20XX	Paid the vendor, Conf/Call, Bill No. 78CC, $270, Ref no. 1043.
12/1/20XX	Bill no. ATD288 received from Any Time Deployment for the purchase of 11 network products, $25 each, for a total of $275. (*Hint:* You may want to prefill the bill. Then, verify these Item details–product/service, quantity, rate, and amount.)
12/1/20XX	Bill No.CZ92 received from CloudZ Channel for the Purchase of 3 web servers, $200 each, for a total of $600. (*Hint:* If the Bill prefills, verify these Item details–quantity, rate, and amount.)
12/1/20XX	Bill No. 121CC received from Conf/Call for the purchase of 5 webinars, $45 each, for a total of $225.
12/1/20XX	Bill No. AS23 received from AmpleStore Inc. for the purchase of 20 data storage devices, $15 each, for a total of $300.
12/1/20XX	Sold 2 computers for cash for a total of $2,000, Sales Receipt 1014.
12/1/20XX	Sold 1 web server on account to WebPro, $400, Invoice 1015.
12/1/20XX	Completed 2 webinars on account to Permanente Medical Services, for a total of $180, invoice 1016.
12/1/20XX	Sold 2 network products on account to the Law Offices of Williamson, Gallagher & Katz, for a total of $100, Invoice 1017.
12/1/20XX	Sold 5 data storage devices to eBiz on account, for a total of $150, Invoice 1018.
12/1/20XX	Sold 3 computers for cash for a total of $3,000, Sales Receipt 1019.

12/1/20XX	Sold 1 web server on account to WebPro for a total of $400, Invoice 1020.
12/1/20XX	Sold 6 data storage products on account to Main Office Depot, for a total of $180, Invoice 1021.
12/1/20XX	Paid the vendor, CloudZ Channel, Bill No. CZ33, $1,600, Ref no. 1044.

5. Continue with Exercise 5-2.

Exercise 5-2: Follow the instructions below to complete Exercise 5-2:

1. Export these reports to Excel and PDF. Run most of the reports from **10/1/20XX to 12/1/20XX**, *or* as shown below. (*Hint:* When the report needs as As of date, use 12/1/20XX)

   - Exercise 5-2_Vendor Balance Summary (Report period > Custom > as of 12/1/20XX.)
   - Exercise 5-2_AP Aging Summary
   - Exercise 5-2_Customer Contact List
   - Exercise 5-2_ Journal (In Exercise 4-2, the Journal was printed from 10/1/20XX through 11/12/20XX. For Exercise 5-2, use 11/13/20XX through 12/1/20XX.)
   - Exercise 5-2_Transaction Detail by Account
   - Exercise 5-2_Trial Balance
   - Exercise 5-2_Inventory Valuation Summary
   - Exercise 5-2_Customer Balance Summary
   - Exercise 5-2_AR Aging Summary
   - Exercise 5-2_Profit and Loss
   - Exercise 5-2_Balance Sheet
   - Exercise 5-2_Statement of Cash Flows

2. **Check Your Figures** (from 10/1/20XX to 12/1/XX):

    - Account 101 Checking, $63,581.16
    - Account 105 Accounts Receivable, $1,410.00
    - Account 115 Merchandise Inventory, $10,155.00
    - Account 201 Accounts Payable, $16,900.00
    - Account 401 Sales, $24,330.00
    - Account 501, Cost of Goods Sold, $9,165.00
    - Account 621 Office Supplies, $460.42
    - Total Liabilities and Equity, $94,146.16
    - Net Income, $12,246.16

Exercise 5-3: Problem Solving

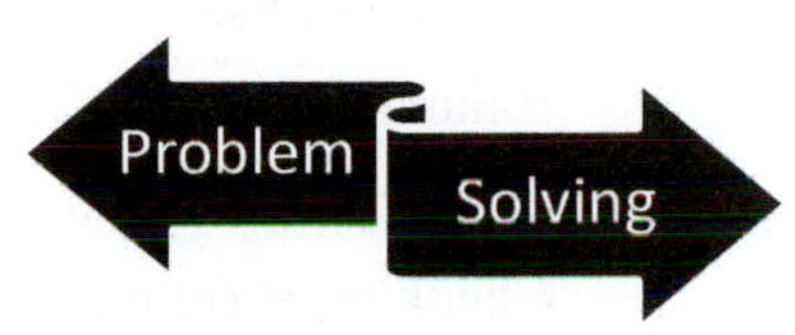

The Online Learning Center includes Exercise 5-3 at www.mhhe.com/qbo2e > Student Edition > Chapter 5 > Problem Solving.

List three, or more, ways to show account balances for an asset and expense account. Include the QBO steps for each method. Specify the account and balance in your answer. What is the difference between View Register accounts and Run report accounts?

CHAPTER 5 INDEX

Chapter 6 December Source Documents

Scenario: In Chapter 6, start by checking the work completed in Chapters 2 through 5. Read the information next to the stop sign. Then, compare your expenses, sales, and the 12/1 trial balance to the ones shown. In this chapter, you analyze source documents used by businesses. For example, memos remind you to make customer payments and vendor payments, sales receipts show cash and credit card sales, bills are used for recording purchases on account, and invoices for sales on account. You also display financial statements that compare fourth quarter information. The objectives specify the work completed in Chapter 6.

OBJECTIVES

1. Start QuickBooks Online and sign in to QB Cloud_Student Name.
2. To check data, display expense and sales transactions and the December 1 Trial Balance.
3. Analyze source documents.
4. Record vendor, customer, cash, and credit card transactions.
5. Complete financial statement comparisons.
6. Export reports to Excel and save as PDF files.
7. Complete Check Your Progress.
8. Use the Online Learning Center, www.mhhe.com/qbo2e, for additional resources.
9. Complete Exercises 6-1, 6-2 and 6-3.

In Chapter 6, you complete business processes for QB Cloud_Student Name. QB Cloud sells computers, data storage, network products, web servers, and webinars.

The purpose of Chapter 6 is to review what you have learned in the previous chapters. In this chapter, you analyze source documents, then record transactions. The documents shown trigger transaction analysis for accounts payable (vendors), inventory, accounts receivable (customers), cash and credit card sales. You also use a bank statement to prepare bank reconciliation.

The source documents that you analyze include:

- Vendor bills for purchasing inventory.
- Memos include customer payments, vendor payments and ***remittances***. A remittance is the action of sending money in payment of a bill.
- Transaction register for issuing checks for expenses and recording ATM withdrawals.
- Sales invoices for credit customers.
- Sales receipts for cash and credit card sales.

GETTING STARTED

1. Start your browser. Go online to http://qbo.intuit.com.
2. Sign in to QuickBooks Online with your User ID and Password. (*Hint:* You can save your User ID.)

CHECK YOUR DATA

To make sure you are starting in the correct place, display Expense Transactions, Sales Transactions, the 10/1/20XX to 12/1/20XX Trial Balance.

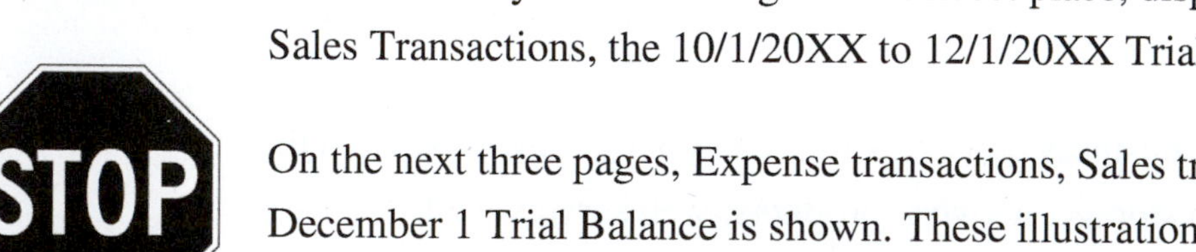

On the next three pages, Expense transactions, Sales transactions, and the December 1 Trial Balance is shown. These illustrations show the work completed within Chapters 2, 3, 4 and 5, including the end-of-chapter exercises. If you see differences with your work, drill down to edit.

Expense Transactions

To verify Expense Transactions, go to Expenses > Expenses tab > click on the Filter's down-arrow > in the Date field, select Custom > From 11/13/20XX to 12/1/20XX > click <Apply>. The total Expense Transactions from 11/13 to 12/1 are $531.57.

QB Cloud_Student Name

Type: All transactions · Status: All statuses · Delivery method: Any · Date: 11/13/2017 - 12/01/2017

Date	Type	No.	Payee	Category	Total
12/01/2017	Check	1036	Office Suppliers	Office Supplies	$100.75
12/01/2017	Check	1037	Cays Advertising	Advertising	$155.00
12/01/2017	Check	1038	Best Cellular	Telephone Expense	$82.13
12/01/2017	Check	1039	Hour Deliveries	Freight & Delivery	$52.65
12/01/2017	Check	1040	Office Suppliers	Office Supplies	$21.00
12/01/2017	Bill Payment (Check)	1041	AmpleStore Inc.		$300.00
12/01/2017	Bill Payment (Check)	1042	Any Time Deployment		$250.00
12/01/2017	Bill Payment (Check)	1043	Conf/Call		$270.00
12/01/2017	Bill Payment (Check)	1044	CloudZ Channel		$1,600.00
12/01/2017	Bill	121CC	Conf/Call	Merchandise Inventory	$225.00
12/01/2017	Bill	AS23	AmpleStore Inc.	Merchandise Inventory	$300.00
12/01/2017	Bill	ATD288	Any Time Deployment	Merchandise Inventory	$275.00
12/01/2017	Check	ATM	Cottage Restaurant	Meals and Entertainment	$56.90
12/01/2017	Bill	CZ92	CloudZ Channel	Merchandise Inventory	$600.00
11/30/2017	Check	SVCCHRG		Bank Charges	$20.00

Sales Transactions

To verify Sales Transactions, go to Sales > All Sales > Filter > Custom > Date, 11/13/20XX to 12/1/20XX > click <Apply>. The total Sales Transactions are $7,440.00

QB Cloud_Student Name

Type: All transactions · Status: All statuses · Delivery method: Any · Date: 11/13/2017 - 12/01/2017

Date	Type	No.	Customer	Due date	Balance	Total	Status
11/15/2017	Invoice	1008	Law Offices of Williamson, Gallagher & Katz	12/15/2017	$0.00	$100.00	Paid
11/15/2017	Invoice	1009	Permanente Medical Services	12/15/2017	$0.00	$270.00	Paid
11/15/2017	Invoice	1010	Springfield Unified School District	12/15/2017	$0.00	$400.00	Paid
11/15/2017	Invoice	1007	eBiz	12/15/2017	$0.00	$150.00	Paid
11/16/2017	Credit Memo	1011	eBiz	11/16/2017	$0.00	$-30.00	Closed
11/29/2017	Payment	901	Permanente Medical Services	11/29/2017	$0.00	$-270.00	Closed
11/29/2017	Payment	9346	eBiz	11/29/2017	$0.00	$-120.00	Closed
11/29/2017	Payment	4032	Law Offices of Williamson, Gallagher & Katz	11/29/2017	$0.00	$-100.00	Closed
11/29/2017	Payment	8422	Springfield Unified School District	11/29/2017	$0.00	$-400.00	Closed
11/29/2017	Sales Receipt	1012	Cash Sales		$0.00	$630.00	Paid
11/30/2017	Sales Receipt	1013	Cash Sales		$0.00	$400.00	Paid
12/01/2017	Invoice	1016	Permanente Medical Services	12/31/2017	$180.00	$180.00	Open
12/01/2017	Invoice	1020	WebPro	12/31/2017	$400.00	$400.00	Open
12/01/2017	Invoice	1018	eBiz	12/31/2017	$150.00	$150.00	Open
12/01/2017	Invoice	1021	Main Office Depot	12/31/2017	$180.00	$180.00	Open
12/01/2017	Invoice	1017	Law Offices of Williamson, Gallagher & Katz	12/31/2017	$100.00	$100.00	Open
12/01/2017	Invoice	1015	WebPro	12/31/2017	$400.00	$400.00	Open
12/01/2017	Sales Receipt	1014	Cash Sales		$0.00	$2,000.00	Paid
12/01/2017	Sales Receipt	1019	Cash Sales		$0.00	$3,000.00	Paid

Trial Balance

To make sure your accounts have the correct balances, display the 10/1/20XX to 12/1/20XX Trial Balance. This Trial Balance was completed in Exercise 5-2.

QB Cloud_Student Name

TRIAL BALANCE

As of December 1, 2017

	DEBIT	CREDIT
101 Checking	63,581.16	
105 Accounts Receivable (A/R)	1,410.00	
115 Merchandise Inventory	10,155.00	
123 Prepaid Rent	6,000.00	
125 Prepaid Insurance	3,000.00	
130 Undeposited Funds	0.00	
135 Computer Equipment	10,000.00	
201 Accounts Payable (A/P)		16,900.00
205 Loan Payable		5,000.00
3000 Opening Balance Equity		0.00
301 Common Stock		60,000.00
401 Sales		24,330.00
501 Cost of Goods Sold	9,165.00	
601 Advertising	530.00	
603 Bank Charges	40.00	
605 Dues & Subscriptions	150.00	
609 Freight & Delivery	206.45	
619 Meals and Entertainment	229.70	
621 Office Supplies	460.42	
625 Repair & Maintenance	140.00	
627 Shipping and delivery expense	47.00	
629 Stationery & Printing	553.18	
633 Telephone Expense	398.77	
635 Utilities	163.32	
TOTAL	$106,230.00	$106,230.00

How do I show the Trial balance *without* zero balances?

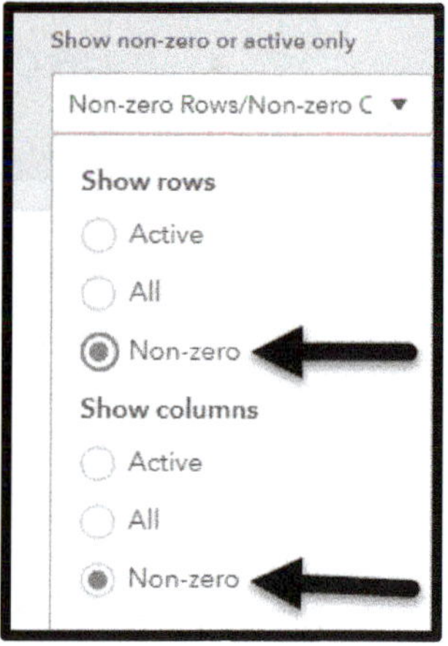

1. If needed, go to Reports > Trial Balance > Custom, from 10/1/20XX to 12/1/XX.
2. In the Active rows/active columns field, click on the down-arrow to select non-zero Rows/Non-zero Columns.
3. The Trial Balance displays *without* Account 130 Undeposited Funds and Account 3000 Opening Balance Equity because they have zero balances. A partial Trial Balance is shown below.

125 Prepaid Insurance	3,000.00	
135 Computer Equipment	10,000.00	
201 Accounts Payable (A/P)		16,900.00
205 Loan Payable		5,000.00
301 Common Stock		60,000.00
401 Sales		24,330.00

SOURCE DOCUMENT ANALYSIS

After analyzing each source document, record the appropriate transaction. All transactions occurred during December of your current year.

QB Cloud_Student Name

Memo

Date: 12/2 current year

Re: Customer Payments

QB Cloud_Student Name received the following customer payments.

1. Received payment from eBiz, Invoice 1018, $150, customer check 9951. (*Hint:* Use the Reference no. field for the check number.)
2. Received payment from the Law Offices of Williamson, Gallagher & Katz, Invoice 1017, $100, customer check 5103.
3. Received payment from Main Office Depot, Invoice 1021, $180, customer check 3788.
4. Received payment from Permanente Medical Services, Invoice 1016, $180.00, customer check 1211.
5. Received payment from WebPro, Invoice 1015, and Invoice 1020, $800, customer check 628. (There are two open invoices.)

QB Cloud_Student Name

Memo

Date: 12/2 current year

Re: Credit Card Receipts

The bank sent verification of credit card receipts in the amount of $2,530.00. Refer to the sales receipts on the next three pages for the products sold and credit cards used.

Checking Account Bank Statement		**Checks**	**Credit Card**	**Amount**
Date: December 5		1	American Express	$350.00
List of Deposits:		2	MasterCard	$1,000.00
Coin	**Totals**	3	Visa	$1,180.00
Quarters:	$	4		
Dimes:	$	5		
Nickels:	$	6		
Pennies	$			
$1	$			
$5	$			
$10	$			
$20	$			
$50	$			
$100	$			
Total	$		**Totals**	$2,530.00
Total Cash			**Total Deposit**	$2,530.00

Hint: Add the customer, Credit Card Sales. If needed, on the Sales Receipt page, add the appropriate credit card type in the Payment Method field. Credit Card Sales are deposited to Account 101 Checking.

Comment: If the Payment method field does not include the credit card type (American Express, MasterCard, or Visa), add it.

SALES RECEIPT

QB Cloud_Student Name

Date: 12/2

RECEIPT # 1022

For: **Credit Card**

Payment Method	Type
CREDIT CARD	American Express

Qty	Description	Rate	Amount
5	Data storage	$30.00	$150.00
4	Network products	$50.00	200.00
		Subtotal	350.00
		Total	$350.00

Thank you for your business!

SALES RECEIPT

QB Cloud_Student Name

Date: 12/2
RECEIPT # 1023
For: **CREDIT CARD**

Payment Method	Type
CREDIT CARD	MasterCard

Qty	Description	Rate	Amount
4	Network products	$50.00	$200.00
2	Web server	400.00	800.00
		Subtotal	1,000.00
		Total	$1,000.00

Thank you for your business!

SALES RECEIPT

QB Cloud_Student Name

Date: 12/2

RECEIPT # 1024

For: **CREDIT CARD**

Payment Method	Type
CREDIT CARD	Visa

Qty	Description	Rate	Amount
1	Computer	$1,000.00	$1,000.00
2	Webinars	90.00	180.00
		Subtotal	1,180.00
		Total	$1,180.00

Thank you for your business!

BILL #: CZ132 **DATE: 12/3** Customer:
QB Cloud_
Student Name

CloudZ Channel
110 Merit Street
Menlo Park, CA 94025
650-555-3250

Date	Quantity	Description	Unit Price	Amount
12/3	4	Web server	$200.00	$800.00

Remittance

Bill #	CZ132
Date	12/3
Amount Due	$800.00

Thank you for your business!

Make all checks payable to CloudZ Channel.

Sales Invoice

TO:

eBiz
800 W. Second Ave.
Durango, CO 81301
(970) 555-2000

SHIP TO: **SAME**

Date	Invoice Number	Payment Terms	Due Date
12/3	1025	Net 30	1/2

Qty	Product	Description	Rate	Amount
6	Data storage	Data storage	$30.00	$180.00

Make all checks payable to QB Cloud_Student Name

Thank you for your business!

QB Cloud_Student Name

Memo

Date: 12/4 current year

Re: Vendor Payments

QB Cloud_Student Name pays the following vendors:

Vendor ID	Bill #	Check No.	Amount
AmpleStore	AS12	1045	$375.00
Any Time Deployment	ATD131	1046	$275.00
CloudZ Channel	CZ40	1047	$1,400.00
Computers 2 You	80C2U	1048	$10,000.00
Conf/Call	91CC	1049	$225.00

REMITTANCE	
Bill #	AS12
Customer ID	QB Cloud_Student Name
Date	12/4
Amount Enclosed	$375.00
	AmpleStore Inc. 200 West Concord Ave. Palo Alto, CA 94301 650-555-8527

REMITTANCE	
Bill #	ATD131
Customer ID	QB Cloud_Student Name
Date	12/4
Amount Enclosed	$275.00
	Any Time Deployment 1189 W. Burnside Lexington, MA 02421 781-555-4671

REMITTANCE	
Bill #	CZ40
Customer ID	QB Cloud_Student Name
Date	12/4
Amount Enclosed	$1,400.00
	CloudZ Channel 110 Merit Street Menlo Park, CA 94025 650-555-3250

REMITTANCE	
Bill #	80C2U
Customer ID	QB Cloud_Student Name
Date	12/4
Amount Enclosed	$10,000.00
	Computers 2 You 2006 East 14 Avenue Los Angeles, CA 90046 213-555-2300

REMITTANCE	
Bill #	91CC
Customer ID	QB Cloud_Student Name
Date	12/4
Amount Enclosed	$225.00
	Conf/Call 700 North Prince Street Tempe, AZ 85008 (480) 555-2411

Bill: AS42

AmpleStore Inc.

Bill to: QB Cloud_Student Name

Date	Quantity	Description	Unit Price	Amount
12/6	20	Data storage	$15.00	$300.00

Remittance

Bill #	AS42
Date	12/6
Amount Due	$300.00

AmpleStore Inc. 200 West Concord Ave. Palo Alto, CA 94301
(650) 555-8527

Bill: 143CC

Conf/Call
700 North Prince Street
Tempe, AZ 85008 USA
480-555-2411

Bill to: QB Cloud
Student Name

Date	Quantity	Description	Unit Price	Amount
12/6	2	Webinars	$45	$90

Remittance

Bill #	143CC
Date	12/6
Amount Due	$90

Make all checks payable to Conf/Call.
Thank you for your business!

Sales Invoice

TO: **Law Offices of Williamson, Gallagher & Katz**
18 Piedmont Ave. NW
Atlanta, GA 30303
(404) 555-8134

SHIP TO: **SAME**

Date	Invoice Number	Payment Terms	Due Date
12/9	1026	Net 30	1/8

Qty	Product	Description	Rate	Amount
6	Network Products	Network products	$50.00	$300.00

Make all checks payable to QB Cloud_Student Name

Thank you for your business!

Sales Invoice

TO: **Permanente Medical Services**
18771 Ala Moana Blvd.
Honolulu, HI 96815
(808) 555-555-9000

SHIP TO: **SAME**

Date	**Invoice Number**	**Payment Terms**	**Due Date**
12/9	1027	Net 30	1/8

Qty	**Product**	**Description**	**Rate**	**Amount**
3	Webinars	Webinars	$90	$270.00

Make all checks payable to QB Cloud_Student Name

Thank you for your business!

Bill: AS99

AmpleStore Inc.

Bill to: QB Cloud_
Student Name

Date	Quantity	Description	Unit Price	Amount
12/10	12	Data storage	$15.00	$180.00

Remittance

Bill #	AS99
Date	12/10
Amount Due	$180.00

AmpleStore Inc. 200 West Concord Ave. Palo Alto, CA 94301
(650) 555-8527

Sales Invoice

TO: **WebPro**
18 Alameda Road
Santa Fe, NM 87501
(505) 555-5311

SHIP TO: **SAME**

Date	Invoice Number	Payment Terms	Due Date
12/10	1028	Net 30	1/9

Qty	Product	Description	Rate	Amount
1	Web server	Web server	$400.00	$400.00

Make all checks payable to QB Cloud_Student Name

Thank you for your business!

QB Cloud_Student Name

Memo

Date: 12/10 current year

Re: Vendor Payments

QB Cloud_Student Name pays the following vendors:

Vendor ID	Bill #	Check No.	Amount
Computers 2 You	112C2U	1050	$3,000.00
Conf/Call	115CC	1051	$225.00

REMITTANCE	
Bill #	112C2U
Customer ID	QB Cloud_Student Name
Date	12/10
Amount Enclosed	$3,000.00
	Computers 2 You 2006 East 14 Avenue Los Angeles, CA 90046 (213) 555-2300

REMITTANCE	
Bill #	115CC
Customer ID	QB Cloud_Student Name
Date	12/10
Amount Enclosed	$225.00
	Conf/Call 700 North Prince Street Tempe, AZ 85008 (480) 555-2411

Transaction Register

Check No.	Date	Description of Transaction	Debit (-)	Credit (+)	Balance
	12/10	*Balance*			$52,021.16
1052	12/13	Best Cellular	82.13		51,939.03
1053	12/13	Valley News	125.00		51,814.03
1054	12/13	County Telephone	76.19		51,737.84
1055	12/14	Office Suppliers	78.36		51,659.48
1056	12/15	Cays Advertising	175.00		51,484.48
1057	12/15	RSP Gas	85.33		51,399.15
ATM	12/15	Cottage Restaurant	52.81		51,346.34
1058	12/16	U.S. Post Office	47.00		51,299.34
1059	12/16	Albert Benson	150.00		51,149.34
1060	12/16	Barber's Paper Supply	115.82		51,033.52

Hint: When the Auto Recall Dialog window appears, select <Yes>. When necessary, change the AMOUNT field on the Check page.

Date:

12/17 **BILL #: 190C2U**

Computers 2 You
2006 East 14 Avenue
Los Angeles, CA 90046
(213) 555-2300

BILL TO:
QB Cloud_
Student Name

quantity	description	Unit Price	amount
3	Computers	$500.00	$1,500.00

Remittance

Bill #	190C2U
Date	12/17
Amount Due	$1,500.00

Any Time Deployment
1189 W. Burnside
Lexington, MA 02421
(781) 555-4681

Bill Number: ATD460

Date: 12/17

Ship To:
QB Cloud_Student Name

SHIPPED VIA	TERMS
UPS	Net 30

QTY	DESCRIPTION	UNIT PRICE	TOTAL
10	Network products	25.00	$250.00
		SUBTOTAL	$250.00
		TOTAL	$250.00

Remittance

Bill #	ATD460
Date	12/17
Amount Due	$250.00

QB Cloud_Student Name

Memo

Date: 12/22 current year

Re: Customer Payments

QB Cloud_Student Name received the following customer payments.

1. Received payment from eBiz, Invoice 1025, $180, customer check 10248.
2. Received payment from the Law Offices of Williamson, Gallagher & Katz, Invoice 1026, $300, customer check 5521.
3. Received payment from Permanente Medical Services, Invoice 1027, $270, customer check 1483.
4. Received payment from WebPro, Invoice 1028, $400, customer check 731.

Sales Invoice

TO: **Springfield Unified School District**
4892 Clear Lake Ave.
Springfield, IL 62703
(217) 555-555-5500

SHIP TO: **SAME**

Date	Invoice Number	Payment Terms	Due Date
12/24	1029	Net 30	1/23

Qty	Product	Description	Rate	Amount
1	Web server	Web server	$400.00	$400.00

Make all checks payable to QB Cloud_Student Name

Thank you for your business!

SALES RECEIPT

QB Cloud_Student Name

Date: 12/24
RECEIPT # 1030
For: **Cash Sales**

Payment Method	Type
Check	Check 80761

Qty	Description	Rate	Amount
1	Computer	$1,000.00	$1,000.00
		Subtotal	$1,000.00
		Total	$1,000.00

Thank you for your business!

Hint: The Payment method is check. In the Reference no. field, use the check number.

QB Cloud_Student Name

Memo

Date: 12/27 current year

Re: Credit Card Receipts

The bank sent verification of credit card receipts in the amount of $1,730. Refer to the sales receipts on the next three pages for the products sold and credit cards used.

Checking Account Bank Statement		**Checks**	**Credit Card**	**Amount**
Date: December 5		1	American Express	$1,150.00
List of Deposits:		2	MasterCard	150.00
Coin	**Totals**	3	Visa	430.00
Quarters:	$	4		
Dimes:	$	5		
Nickels:	$	6		
Pennies	$			
Total				
Cash	**Totals**			
$1	$			
$5	$			
$10	$			
$20	$			
$50	$			
$100	$			
Total	$		**Totals**	$1,730.00
Total Cash			**Total Deposit**	$1,730.00

Hint: On the Sales Receipts page, select the appropriate credit card.

SALES RECEIPT

QB Cloud_Student Name

Date: 12/27
RECEIPT #1031
For: **CREDIT CARD**

Payment Method	Type
CREDIT CARD	American Express

Qty	Description	Rate	Amount
5	Data storage	$30.00	$150.00
1	Computer	$1,000.00	$1,000.00
		Subtotal	$1,150.00
		Total	$1,150.00

Thank you for your business!

SALES RECEIPT

QB Cloud_Student Name

Date: 12/27
RECEIPT #1032
For: **CREDIT CARD**

Payment Method	Type
CREDIT CARD	MasterCard

Qty	Description	Rate	Amount
3	Network products	$50.00	$150.00
		Subtotal	$150.00
		Total	$150.00

Thank you for your business!

SALES RECEIPT

QB Cloud_Student Name

Date: 12/27
RECEIPT #1033
For: **CREDIT CARD**

Payment Method	Type
CREDIT CARD	Visa

Qty	Description	Rate	Amount
5	Data storage	$30.00	$150.00
2	Network products	$50.00	$100.00
2	Webinars	$90.00	$180.00
		Subtotal	$430.00
		Total	$430.00

Thank you for your business!

QB Cloud_Student Name

Memo

Date: 12/30 current year

Re: Vendor Payments

QB Cloud_Student Name pays the following vendors:

Vendor ID	Bill #	Check No.	Amount
AmpleStore Inc.	AS23	1061	$300.00
Any Time Deployment	ATD288	1062	$275.00
CloudZ Channel	CZ92	1063	$600.00
Conf/Call	121CC	1064	$225.00

REMITTANCE	
Bill #	AS23
Customer ID	QB Cloud_Student Name
Date	12/30
Amount Enclosed	$300.00
	AmpleStore Inc. 200 West Concord Ave. Palo Alto, CA 94301 (650) 555-8527

REMITTANCE	
Bill #	ATD288
Customer ID	QB Cloud_Student Name
Date	12/30
Amount Enclosed	$275.00
	Any Time Deployment 1189 W. Burnside Lexington, MA 02421 (781) 555-4781

REMITTANCE	
Bill #	CZ92
Customer ID	QB Cloud_Student Name
Date	12/30
Amount Enclosed	$600.00
	CloudZ Channel 110 Merit Street Menlo Park, CA 94025 (650) 555-3250

REMITTANCE	
Bill #	121CC
Customer ID	QB Cloud_Student Name
Date	12/30
Amount Enclosed	$225.00
	Conf/Call 700 North Prince Street Tempe, AZ 85008 480-555-2411

REPORTS

Display the following reports. The suggested date range is shown for each report. Ask your instructor if he or she would prefer different dates.

1. Journal: 12/2/20XX thru 12/30/20XX. For this date range, the Journal shows a TOTAL of $33,782.64.

   Troubleshooting: When you display the journal, make sure the current year is shown for each transaction. If necessary, drill down from the QBO Journal to the original entry to make any necessary changes.

QB Cloud_Student Name

JOURNAL

December 2-30, 2017

DATE	TRANSACTION TYPE	NUM	NAME	MEMO/DESCRIPTION	ACCOUNT #	ACCOUNT	DEBIT	CREDIT
12/02/2017	Payment	9951	eBiz		101	101 Checking	$150.00	
					105	105 Accounts Receivable (A/R)		$150.00
							$150.00	**$150.00**
12/02/2017	Payment	5103	Law Offices of Williamson, Gallagher & Katz		101	101 Checking	$100.00	
					105	105 Accounts Receivable (A/R)		$100.00
							$100.00	**$100.00**
12/02/2017	Payment	3788	Main Office Depot		101	101 Checking	$180.00	
					105	105 Accounts Receivable (A/R)		$180.00
							$180.00	**$180.00**
12/02/2017	Payment	1211	Permanente Medical Services		101	101 Checking	$180.00	
					105	105 Accounts Receivable (A/R)		$180.00
							$180.00	**$180.00**
12/02/2017	Payment	628	WebPro		101	101 Checking	$800.00	
					105	105 Accounts Receivable (A/R)		$800.00
							$800.00	**$800.00**
12/02/2017	Sales Receipt	1022	Credit Card Sales		101	101 Checking	$350.00	
				Data storage	115	115 Merchandise Inventory		$75.00
				Data storage	501	501 Cost of Goods Sold	$75.00	
				Data storage	401	401 Sales		$150.00
				Network products	115	115 Merchandise Inventory		$75.00
				Network products	115	115 Merchandise Inventory		$25.00
				Network products	501	501 Cost of Goods Sold	$75.00	
				Network products	501	501 Cost of Goods Sold	$25.00	
				Network products	401	401 Sales		$200.00
							$525.00	**$525.00**
12/02/2017	Sales Receipt	1023	Credit Card Sales		101	101 Checking	$1,000.00	
				Network products	501	501 Cost of Goods Sold	$100.00	
				Network products	401	401 Sales		$200.00
				Network products	115	115 Merchandise Inventory		$100.00
				Web server	401	401 Sales		$800.00
				Web server	115	115 Merchandise Inventory		$400.00
				Web server	501	501 Cost of Goods Sold	$400.00	
							$1,500.00	**$1,500.00**
12/02/2017	Sales Receipt	1024	Credit Card Sales		101	101 Checking	$1,180.00	
				Computers	401	401 Sales		$1,000.00
				Computers	115	115 Merchandise Inventory		$500.00
				Computers	501	501 Cost of Goods Sold	$500.00	
				Webinars	115	115 Merchandise Inventory		$90.00
				Webinars	501	501 Cost of Goods Sold	$90.00	
				Webinars	401	401 Sales		$180.00
							$1,770.00	**$1,770.00**
12/03/2017	Bill	CZ132	CloudZ Channel		201	201 Accounts Payable (A/P)		$800.00
				Web server	115	115 Merchandise Inventory	$800.00	
							$800.00	**$800.00**

1/5

DATE	TRANSACTION TYPE	NUM	NAME	MEMO/DESCRIPTION	ACCOUNT #	ACCOUNT	DEBIT	CREDIT
12/03/2017	Invoice	1025	eBiz		105	105 Accounts Receivable (A/R)	$180.00	
				Data storage	501	501 Cost of Goods Sold	$90.00	
				Data storage	115	115 Merchandise Inventory		$90.00
				Data storage	401	401 Sales		$180.00
							$270.00	**$270.00**
12/04/2017	Bill Payment (Check)	1045	AmpleStore Inc.		101	101 Checking		$375.00
					201	201 Accounts Payable (A/P)	$375.00	
							$375.00	**$375.00**
12/04/2017	Bill Payment (Check)	1046	Any Time Deployment		101	101 Checking		$275.00
					201	201 Accounts Payable (A/P)	$275.00	
							$275.00	**$275.00**
12/04/2017	Bill Payment (Check)	1047	CloudZ Channel		101	101 Checking		$1,400.00
					201	201 Accounts Payable (A/P)	$1,400.00	
							$1,400.00	**$1,400.00**
12/04/2017	Bill Payment (Check)	1048	Computers 2 You		101	101 Checking		$10,000.00
					201	201 Accounts Payable (A/P)	$10,000.00	
							$10,000.00	**$10,000.00**
12/04/2017	Bill Payment (Check)	1049	Conf/Call		101	101 Checking		$225.00
					201	201 Accounts Payable (A/P)	$225.00	
							$225.00	**$225.00**
12/06/2017	Bill	AS42	AmpleStore Inc.		201	201 Accounts Payable (A/P)		$300.00
				Data storage	115	115 Merchandise Inventory	$300.00	
							$300.00	**$300.00**
12/06/2017	Bill	143CC	Conf/Call		201	201 Accounts Payable (A/P)		$90.00
				Webinars	115	115 Merchandise Inventory	$90.00	
							$90.00	**$90.00**
12/09/2017	Invoice	1026	Law Offices of Williamson, Gallagher & Katz		105	105 Accounts Receivable (A/R)	$300.00	
				Network products	115	115 Merchandise Inventory		$150.00
				Network products	401	401 Sales		$300.00
				Network products	501	501 Cost of Goods Sold	$150.00	
							$450.00	**$450.00**
12/09/2017	Invoice	1027	Permanente Medical Services		105	105 Accounts Receivable (A/R)	$270.00	
				Webinars	501	501 Cost of Goods Sold	$90.00	
				Webinars	501	501 Cost of Goods Sold	$45.00	
				Webinars	401	401 Sales		$270.00
				Webinars	115	115 Merchandise Inventory		$90.00
				Webinars	115	115 Merchandise Inventory		$45.00
							$405.00	**$405.00**
12/10/2017	Bill	AS99	AmpleStore Inc.		201	201 Accounts Payable (A/P)		$180.00
				Data storage	115	115 Merchandise Inventory	$180.00	
							$180.00	**$180.00**
12/10/2017	Invoice	1028	WebPro		105	105 Accounts Receivable (A/R)	$400.00	

2/5

DATE	TRANSACTION TYPE	NUM	NAME	MEMO/DESCRIPTION	ACCOUNT #	ACCOUNT	DEBIT	CREDIT
				Web server	401	401 Sales		$400.00
				Web server	501	501 Cost of Goods Sold	$200.00	
				Web server	115	115 Merchandise Inventory		$200.00
							$600.00	**$600.00**
12/10/2017	Bill Payment (Check)	1050	Computers 2 You		101	101 Checking		$3,000.00
					201	201 Accounts Payable (A/P)	$3,000.00	
							$3,000.00	**$3,000.00**
12/10/2017	Bill Payment (Check)	1051	Conf/Call		101	101 Checking		$225.00
					201	201 Accounts Payable (A/P)	$225.00	
							$225.00	**$225.00**
12/13/2017	Check	1052	Best Cellular		101	101 Checking		$82.13
				Cell phone service	633	633 Telephone Expense	$82.13	
							$82.13	**$82.13**
12/13/2017	Check	1053	Valley News		101	101 Checking		$125.00
				Subscription	605	605 Dues & Subscriptions	$125.00	
							$125.00	**$125.00**
12/13/2017	Check	1054	County Telephone		101	101 Checking		$76.19
				Paid monthly bill	633	633 Telephone Expense	$76.19	
							$76.19	**$76.19**
12/14/2017	Check	1055	Office Suppliers		101	101 Checking		$78.36
				Bought office supplies	621	621 Office Supplies	$78.36	
							$78.36	**$78.36**
12/15/2017	Check	1056	Cays Advertising		101	101 Checking		$175.00
				Advertising expense	601	601 Advertising	$175.00	
							$175.00	**$175.00**
12/15/2017	Check	1057	RSP Gas		101	101 Checking		$85.33
				Paid monthly bill	635	635 Utilities	$85.33	
							$85.33	**$85.33**
12/15/2017	Check	ATM	Cottage Restaurant		101	101 Checking		$52.81
				Paid for meal with clients	619	619 Meals and Entertainment	$52.81	
							$52.81	**$52.81**
12/16/2017	Check	1058	U.S. Post Office		101	101 Checking		$47.00
				Shipping and delivery	627	627 Shipping and delivery expense	$47.00	
							$47.00	**$47.00**
12/16/2017	Check	1059	Albert Benson		101	101 Checking		$150.00
				Repair and maintenance	625	625 Repair & Maintenance	$150.00	
							$150.00	**$150.00**
12/16/2017	Check	1060	Barber's Paper Supply		101	101 Checking		$115.82
					629	629 Stationery & Printing	$115.82	
							$115.82	**$115.82**
12/17/2017	Bill	190C2U	Computers 2 You		201	201 Accounts Payable (A/P)		$1,500.00
				Computers	115	115 Merchandise Inventory	$1,500.00	
							$1,500.00	**$1,500.00**
12/17/2017	Bill	ATD460	Any Time Deployment		201	201 Accounts Payable (A/P)		$250.00
				Network products	115	115 Merchandise Inventory	$250.00	

3/5

DATE	TRANSACTION TYPE	NUM	NAME	MEMO/DESCRIPTION	ACCOUNT #	ACCOUNT	DEBIT	CREDIT
							$250.00	**$250.00**
12/22/2017	Payment	10248	eBiz		101	101 Checking	$180.00	
					105	105 Accounts Receivable (A/R)		$180.00
							$180.00	**$180.00**
12/22/2017	Payment	5521	Law Offices of Williamson, Gallagher & Katz		101	101 Checking	$300.00	
					105	105 Accounts Receivable (A/R)		$300.00
							$300.00	**$300.00**
12/22/2017	Payment	1483	Permanente Medical Services		101	101 Checking	$270.00	
					105	105 Accounts Receivable (A/R)		$270.00
							$270.00	**$270.00**
12/22/2017	Payment	731	WebPro		101	101 Checking	$400.00	
					105	105 Accounts Receivable (A/R)		$400.00
							$400.00	**$400.00**
12/24/2017	Invoice	1029	Springfield Unified School District		105	105 Accounts Receivable (A/R)	$400.00	
				Web server	401	401 Sales		$400.00
				Web server	115	115 Merchandise Inventory		$200.00
				Web server	501	501 Cost of Goods Sold	$200.00	
							$600.00	**$600.00**
12/24/2017	Sales Receipt	1030	Cash Sales		101	101 Checking	$1,000.00	
				Computers	115	115 Merchandise Inventory		$500.00
				Computers	401	401 Sales		$1,000.00
				Computers	501	501 Cost of Goods Sold	$500.00	
							$1,500.00	**$1,500.00**
12/27/2017	Sales Receipt	1031	Credit Card Sales		101	101 Checking	$1,150.00	
				Data storage	501	501 Cost of Goods Sold	$75.00	
				Data storage	115	115 Merchandise Inventory		$75.00
				Data storage	401	401 Sales		$150.00
				Computers	501	501 Cost of Goods Sold	$500.00	
				Computers	115	115 Merchandise Inventory		$500.00
				Computers	401	401 Sales		$1,000.00
							$1,725.00	**$1,725.00**
12/27/2017	Sales Receipt	1032	Credit Card Sales		101	101 Checking	$150.00	
				Network products	401	401 Sales		$150.00
				Network products	115	115 Merchandise Inventory		$75.00
				Network products	501	501 Cost of Goods Sold	$75.00	
							$225.00	**$225.00**
12/27/2017	Sales Receipt	1033	Credit Card Sales		101	101 Checking	$430.00	
				Data storage	401	401 Sales		$150.00
				Data storage	115	115 Merchandise Inventory		$15.00
				Data storage	115	115 Merchandise Inventory		$45.00
				Data storage	115	115 Merchandise Inventory		$15.00
				Data storage	501	501 Cost of Goods Sold	$45.00	
				Data storage	501	501 Cost of Goods Sold	$15.00	
				Data storage	501	501 Cost of Goods Sold	$15.00	
				Network products	501	501 Cost of Goods Sold	$50.00	
				Network products	401	401 Sales		$100.00
				Network products	115	115 Merchandise Inventory		$50.00
				Webinars	501	501 Cost of Goods Sold	$90.00	
				Webinars	115	115 Merchandise Inventory		$90.00

4/5

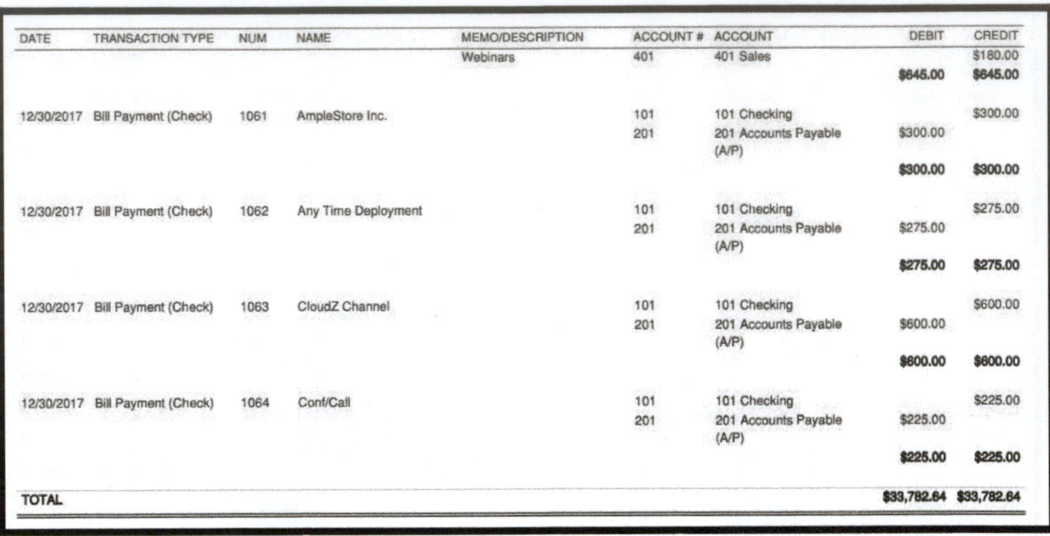

DATE	TRANSACTION TYPE	NUM	NAME	MEMO/DESCRIPTION	ACCOUNT #	ACCOUNT	DEBIT	CREDIT
				Webinars	401	401 Sales		$180.00
							$645.00	**$645.00**
12/30/2017	Bill Payment (Check)	1061	AmpleStore Inc.		101	101 Checking		$300.00
					201	201 Accounts Payable (A/P)	$300.00	
							$300.00	**$300.00**
12/30/2017	Bill Payment (Check)	1062	Any Time Deployment		101	101 Checking		$275.00
					201	201 Accounts Payable (A/P)	$275.00	
							$275.00	**$275.00**
12/30/2017	Bill Payment (Check)	1063	CloudZ Channel		101	101 Checking		$600.00
					201	201 Accounts Payable (A/P)	$600.00	
							$600.00	**$600.00**
12/30/2017	Bill Payment (Check)	1064	Conf/Call		101	101 Checking		$225.00
					201	201 Accounts Payable (A/P)	$225.00	
							$225.00	**$225.00**
TOTAL							**$33,782.64**	**$33,782.64**

➤ Export the Journal to Excel and save as a PDF file. Use the file name, **Chapter 6_Journal**.

2. Trial Balance: 10/1/20XX to 12/30/20XX. Display the Trial Balance without zero account balances. (*Hint:* To remove accounts with zero balances, select Non-zero > Run report.)

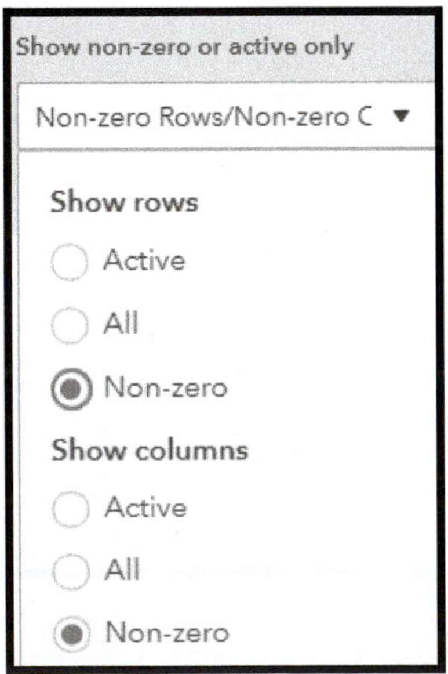

QB Cloud_Student Name

TRIAL BALANCE

As of December 30, 2017

	DEBIT	CREDIT
101 Checking	53,513.52	
105 Accounts Receivable (A/R)	400.00	
115 Merchandise Inventory	9,870.00	
123 Prepaid Rent	6,000.00	
125 Prepaid Insurance	3,000.00	
135 Computer Equipment	10,000.00	
201 Accounts Payable (A/P)		3,120.00
205 Loan Payable		5,000.00
301 Common Stock		60,000.00
401 Sales		31,140.00
501 Cost of Goods Sold	12,570.00	
601 Advertising	705.00	
603 Bank Charges	40.00	
605 Dues & Subscriptions	275.00	
609 Freight & Delivery	206.45	
619 Meals and Entertainment	282.51	
621 Office Supplies	538.78	
625 Repair & Maintenance	290.00	
627 Shipping and delivery expense	94.00	
629 Stationery & Printing	669.00	
633 Telephone Expense	557.09	
635 Utilities	248.65	
TOTAL	**$99,260.00**	**$99,260.00**

- Export the Trial Balance to Excel and save as a PDF file. Use the file name, **Chapter 6_Trial Balance**.

3. Customer Balance Summary: 12/30/20XX. In the Report period field, select Custom > as of 12/30/20XX > Run report.)

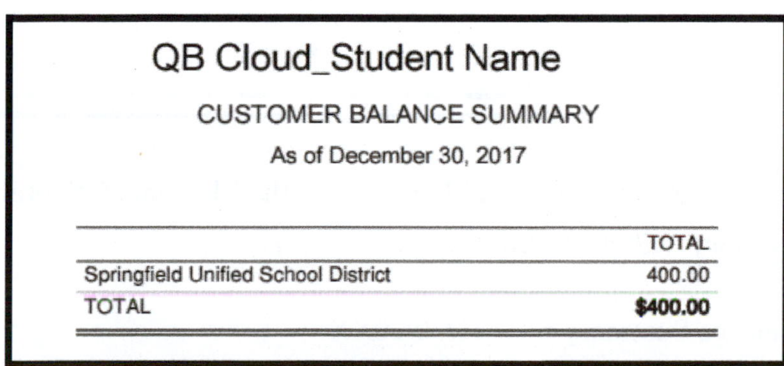

QB Cloud_Student Name

CUSTOMER BALANCE SUMMARY

As of December 30, 2017

	TOTAL
Springfield Unified School District	400.00
TOTAL	**$400.00**

➢ Export the Customer Balance Summary to Excel and save as a PDF file. Use the f name, **Chapter 6_Customer Balance Summary.**

4. A/R Aging Summary**:** As of 12/30/20XX

QB Cloud_Student Name

A/R AGING SUMMARY

As of December 30, 2017

	CURRENT	1 - 30	31 - 60	61 - 90	91 AND OVER	TOTAL
Springfield Unified School District	400.00					$400.00
TOTAL	**$400.00**	**$0.00**	**$0.00**	**$0.00**	**$0.00**	**$400.00**

➢ Export the A/R Aging Summary to Excel and save as a PDF file. Use the file name, **Chapter 6_AR Aging Summary.**

5. Inventory Valuation Summary: As of 12/30/20XX

QB Cloud_Student Name

INVENTORY VALUATION SUMMARY

As of December 30, 2017

	SKU	QTY	ASSET VALUE	CALC. AVG
Computers		11.00	5,500.00	500.00
Data storage		51.00	765.00	15.00
Network products		16.00	400.00	25.00
Web server		14.00	2,800.00	200.00
Webinars		9.00	405.00	45.00
TOTAL			**$9,870.00**	

➢ Export to Excel and save as a PDF file. Use the file name **Chapter 6_Inventory Valuation Summary.**

6. Vendor Balance Summary as of 12/30/20XX

QB Cloud_Student Name

VENDOR BALANCE SUMMARY

As of December 30, 2017

	TOTAL
AmpleStore Inc.	480.00
Any Time Deployment	250.00
CloudZ Channel	800.00
Computers 2 You	1,500.00
Conf/Call	90.00
TOTAL	**$3,120.00**

- Export to Excel and save as a PDF file. Use the file name **Chapter 6_Vendor Balance Summary.**

7. A/P Aging Summary: As of 12/30/20XX

QB Cloud_Student Name

A/P AGING SUMMARY

As of December 30, 2017

	CURRENT	1 - 30	31 - 60	61 - 90	91 AND OVER	TOTAL
AmpleStore Inc.	480.00					$480.00
Any Time Deployment	250.00					$250.00
CloudZ Channel	800.00					$800.00
Computers 2 You	1,500.00					$1,500.00
Conf/Call	90.00					$90.00
TOTAL	**$3,120.00**	**$0.00**	**$0.00**	**$0.00**	**$0.00**	**$3,120.00**

- Export to Excel and save as a PDF file. Use the file name **Chapter 6_AP Aging Summary.**

8. Profit and Loss from 10/1/20XX to 12/30/20XX.

QB Cloud_Student Name

PROFIT AND LOSS

October 1 - December 30, 2017

	TOTAL
INCOME	
401 Sales	31,140.00
Total Income	**$31,140.00**
COST OF GOODS SOLD	
501 Cost of Goods Sold	12,570.00
Total Cost of Goods Sold	**$12,570.00**
GROSS PROFIT	**$18,570.00**
EXPENSES	
601 Advertising	705.00
603 Bank Charges	40.00
605 Dues & Subscriptions	275.00
609 Freight & Delivery	206.45
619 Meals and Entertainment	282.51
621 Office Supplies	538.78
625 Repair & Maintenance	290.00
627 Shipping and delivery expense	94.00
629 Stationery & Printing	669.00
633 Telephone Expense	557.09
635 Utilities	248.65
Total Expenses	**$3,906.48**
NET OPERATING INCOME	**$14,663.52**
NET INCOME	**$14,663.52**

➢ Export the Profit and Loss to Excel and save as a PDF file. Use the file name **Chapter 6_Profit and Loss**.

Customize Reports: Adding Comparison Columns

Sometimes it's helpful to compare different aspects of your business. Some reports have the ability to add a subcolumn for comparison. When customizing, this can be found in the Rows/Columns section. Look for: Add Subcolumns for comparison.

Reports with subcolumns option for comparison:

- Profit & Loss
- Balance Sheet
- Budget vs. Actuals
- Majority of summary reports (Reports with summary in the title)

To customize and add a comparison column:

1. Go to Reports.
2. Find the desired report and run it.
3. Open the customize tab, click Rows/Columns on the left.
4. Find the Add Subcolumns for comparison area and click to select the name of each subcolumn desired.

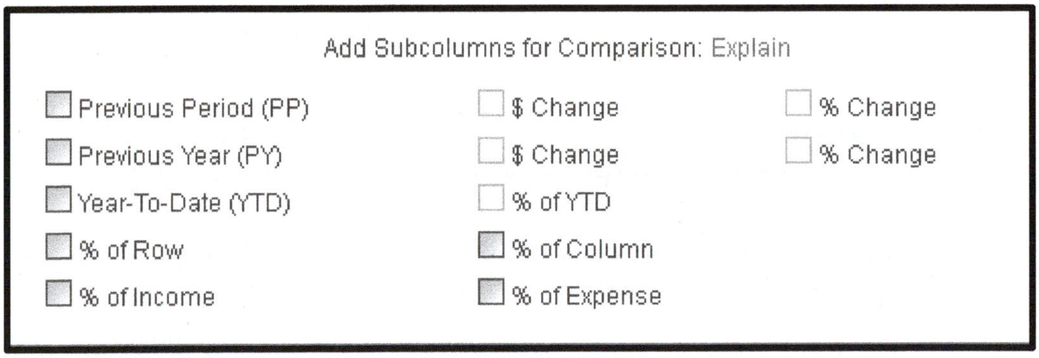

Add Subcolumns for Comparison: Explain

☐ Previous Period (PP)	☐ $ Change	☐ % Change
☐ Previous Year (PY)	☐ $ Change	☐ % Change
☐ Year-To-Date (YTD)	☐ % of YTD	
☐ % of Row	☐ % of Column	
☐ % of Income	☐ % of Expense	

5. Click Run Report.

Comment: Not all reports have the option to add a comparison column. For purposes of example, complete a Profit and Loss by Month report and customize it to include a percent of income column.

Profit and Loss By Month

1. Go to Reports > in the search field, type **Profit and Loss By Month** > press <Enter>. In the Report period field, select custom > 10/1/20XX to 12/30/20XX > Run report. Observe that the columns are displayed by month--Oct 20XX, Nov 20XX, and Dec 1-30, 20XX. The total column agrees with the P&L on page 296.
2. To show the percent of income, select <Customize>. The Customize report page appears. Click Rows/Columns > select % of Income. There are also other options.

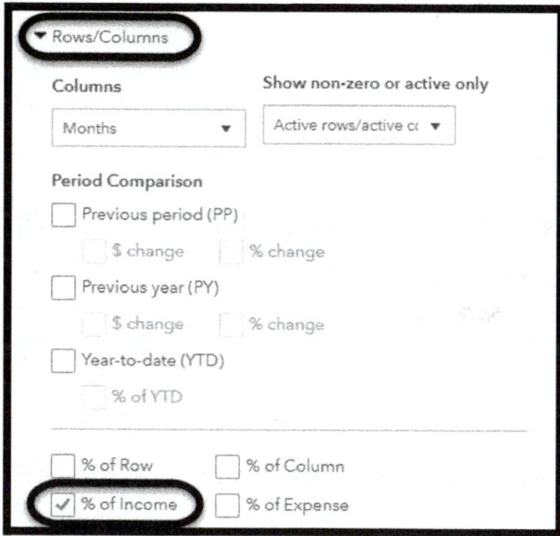

3. After selecting % of Income, click <Run report>. A % of Income column is added for each month.

QB Cloud_Student Name

PROFIT AND LOSS BY MONTH

October 1 - December 30, 2017

	OCT 2017		NOV 2017		DEC 1-30, 2017		TOTAL	
	CURRENT	% OF INCOME	CURRENT	% OF INCOME	CURRENT	% OF INCOME	CURRENT	% OF INCOME
INCOME								
401 Sales	6,000.00	100.00 %	11,920.00	100.00 %	13,220.00	100.00 %	$31,140.00	100.00 %
Total Income	**$6,000.00**	**100.00 %**	**$11,920.00**	**100.00 %**	**$13,220.00**	**100.00 %**	**$31,140.00**	**100.00 %**
COST OF GOODS SOLD								
501 Cost of Goods Sold			5,960.00	50.00 %	6,610.00	50.00 %	$12,570.00	40.37 %
Total Cost of Goods Sold	**$0.00**	**0.00%**	**$5,960.00**	**50.00 %**	**$6,610.00**	**50.00 %**	**$12,570.00**	**40.37 %**
GROSS PROFIT	**$6,000.00**	**100.00 %**	**$5,960.00**	**50.00 %**	**$6,610.00**	**50.00 %**	**$18,570.00**	**59.63 %**
EXPENSES								
601 Advertising	125.00	2.08 %	250.00	2.10 %	330.00	2.50 %	$705.00	2.26 %
603 Bank Charges	20.00	0.33 %	20.00	0.17 %			$40.00	0.13 %
605 Dues & Subscriptions	150.00	2.50 %			125.00	0.95 %	$275.00	0.88 %
609 Freight & Delivery	64.65	1.08 %	89.15	0.75 %	52.65	0.40 %	$206.45	0.66 %
619 Meals and Entertainment	126.40	2.11 %	46.40	0.39 %	109.71	0.83 %	$282.51	0.91 %
621 Office Supplies	226.85	3.78 %	111.82	0.94 %	200.11	1.51 %	$538.78	1.73 %
625 Repair & Maintenance	140.00	2.33 %			150.00	1.13 %	$290.00	0.93 %
627 Shipping and delivery expense	47.00	0.78 %			47.00	0.36 %	$94.00	0.30 %
629 Stationery & Printing	425.22	7.09 %	127.96	1.07 %	115.82	0.88 %	$669.00	2.15 %
633 Telephone Expense	158.32	2.64 %	158.32	1.33 %	240.45	1.82 %	$557.09	1.79 %
635 Utilities	79.00	1.32 %	84.32	0.71 %	85.33	0.65 %	$248.65	0.80 %
Total Expenses	**$1,562.44**	**26.04 %**	**$887.97**	**7.45 %**	**$1,456.07**	**11.01 %**	**$3,906.48**	**12.54 %**
NET OPERATING INCOME	**$4,437.56**	**73.96 %**	**$5,072.03**	**42.55 %**	**$5,153.93**	**38.99 %**	**$14,663.52**	**47.09 %**
NET INCOME	**$4,437.56**	**73.96 %**	**$5,072.03**	**42.55 %**	**$5,153.93**	**38.99 %**	**$14,663.52**	**47.09 %**

To calculate the % of Income, divide an individual amount by total income. F or example, October Bank Charges, 20/6,000 = .33%.

- Export the Profit and Loss to Excel and save as a PDF file. Use the file name **Chapter 6_Profit and Loss by Month**

4. Balance sheet from 10/1/20XX to 12/30/20XX.

QB Cloud_Student Name

BALANCE SHEET

As of December 30, 2017

	TOTAL
ASSETS	
Current Assets	
Bank Accounts	
101 Checking	53,513.52
Total Bank Accounts	**$53,513.52**
Accounts Receivable	
105 Accounts Receivable (A/R)	400.00
Total Accounts Receivable	**$400.00**
Other Current Assets	
115 Merchandise Inventory	9,870.00
123 Prepaid Rent	6,000.00
125 Prepaid Insurance	3,000.00
130 Undeposited Funds	0.00
Total Other Current Assets	**$18,870.00**
Total Current Assets	**$72,783.52**
Fixed Assets	
135 Computer Equipment	10,000.00
Total Fixed Assets	**$10,000.00**
TOTAL ASSETS	**$82,783.52**
LIABILITIES AND EQUITY	
Liabilities	
Current Liabilities	
Accounts Payable	
201 Accounts Payable (A/P)	3,120.00
Total Accounts Payable	**$3,120.00**
Other Current Liabilities	
205 Loan Payable	5,000.00
Total Other Current Liabilities	**$5,000.00**
Total Current Liabilities	**$8,120.00**
Total Liabilities	**$8,120.00**
Equity	
3000 Opening Balance Equity	0.00
301 Common Stock	60,000.00
318 Retained Earnings	
Net Income	14,663.52
Total Equity	**$74,663.52**
TOTAL LIABILITIES AND EQUITY	**$82,783.52**

- Export the Balance Sheet to Excel and save as a PDF file. Use the file name **Chapter 6_Balance Sheet**.

Customize Balance Sheet

1. The 10/1/20/XX to 12/30/XX balance sheet should be displayed. Click

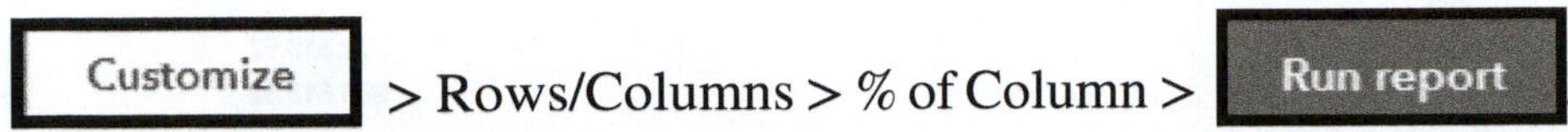

2. The Balance Sheet includes % of Column. Each row is divided by $82,783.52, the total assets and total liabilities and equity amount. For example, the calculation for 101 Checking is $53,513.52/$82,783.52 = 64.64%.

QB Cloud_Student Name

BALANCE SHEET

As of December 30, 2017

	TOTAL	
	AS OF DEC 30, 2017	% OF COLUMN
ASSETS		
Current Assets		
Bank Accounts		
101 Checking	53,513.52	64.64 %
Total Bank Accounts	**$53,513.52**	**64.64 %**
Accounts Receivable		
105 Accounts Receivable (A/R)	400.00	0.48 %
Total Accounts Receivable	**$400.00**	**0.48 %**
Other Current Assets		
115 Merchandise Inventory	9,870.00	11.92 %
123 Prepaid Rent	6,000.00	7.25 %
125 Prepaid Insurance	3,000.00	3.62 %
130 Undeposited Funds	0.00	0.00 %
Total Other Current Assets	**$18,870.00**	**22.79 %**
Total Current Assets	**$72,783.52**	**87.92 %**
Fixed Assets		
135 Computer Equipment	10,000.00	12.08 %
Total Fixed Assets	**$10,000.00**	**12.08 %**
TOTAL ASSETS	**$82,783.52**	**100.00 %**
LIABILITIES AND EQUITY		
Liabilities		
Current Liabilities		
Accounts Payable		
201 Accounts Payable (A/P)	3,120.00	3.77 %
Total Accounts Payable	**$3,120.00**	**3.77 %**
Other Current Liabilities		
205 Loan Payable	5,000.00	6.04 %
Total Other Current Liabilities	**$5,000.00**	**6.04 %**
Total Current Liabilities	**$8,120.00**	**9.81 %**
Total Liabilities	**$8,120.00**	**9.81 %**
Equity		
3000 Opening Balance Equity	0.00	0.00 %
301 Common Stock	60,000.00	72.48 %
318 Retained Earnings		
Net Income	14,663.52	17.71 %
Total Equity	**$74,663.52**	**90.19 %**
TOTAL LIABILITIES AND EQUITY	**$82,783.52**	**100.00 %**

➢ Export the Custom Balance Sheet to Excel and save as a PDF file. Use the file name **Chapter 6_Custom Balance Sheet.**

9. Statement of Cash Flows from 10/1/20XX to 12/30/20XX. Some instructors may prefer a Statement of Cash Flows for the month of December only. .

QB Cloud_Student Name

STATEMENT OF CASH FLOWS

October 1 - December 30, 2017

	TOTAL
OPERATING ACTIVITIES	
Net Income	14,663.52
Adjustments to reconcile Net Income to Net Cash provided by operations:	
105 Accounts Receivable (A/R)	-400.00
115 Merchandise Inventory	-9,870.00
123 Prepaid Rent	-6,000.00
125 Prepaid Insurance	-3,000.00
201 Accounts Payable (A/P)	3,120.00
205 Loan Payable	5,000.00
Total Adjustments to reconcile Net Income to Net Cash provided by operations:	**-11,150.00**
Net cash provided by operating activities	**$3,513.52**
INVESTING ACTIVITIES	
135 Computer Equipment	-10,000.00
Net cash provided by investing activities	**$ -10,000.00**
FINANCING ACTIVITIES	
3000 Opening Balance Equity	0.00
301 Common Stock	60,000.00
Net cash provided by financing activities	**$60,000.00**
NET CASH INCREASE FOR PERIOD	**$53,513.52**
CASH AT BEGINNING OF PERIOD	0.00
CASH AT END OF PERIOD	**$53,513.52**

- Export the Statement of Cash Flows to Excel and save as a PDF file. Use the file name **Chapter 6_Statement of Cash Flows.**

CHECK YOUR PROGRESS

Check Your Progress assignments are included on the Online Learning Center at www.mhhe.com/qbo2e > Student Edition > Chapter 6 > Check Your Progress.

1. What are the account balance from 10/1/20XX to 12/30/20XX in these accounts? Indicate whether these accounts have debit (dr.) or credit (cr.) balances.

   Account 101 Checking ____________________

   Account 105 Accounts Receivable ____________________

   Account 115 Merchandise Inventory ____________________

   Account 201 Accounts Payable ____________________

   Account 401 Sales ____________________

   Account 501 Cost of Goods Sold ____________________

2. What Total is shown on the 12/30 Trial Balance? ____________________

3. What is Net Income? ____________________

4. What are the total Liabilities and Equity? ________________

5. What is the quantity, asset value, and average cost of computers?

____

6. What is the quantity, asset value, and average cost of data storage?

____

7. What is the quantity, asset value, and average cost of network products?

____

8. What is the quantity, asset value, and average cost of web servers?

____

9. What is the quantity, asset value, and average cost of webinars?

____

10. What is the cash at the end of the period?

____

SIGN OUT

To sign out of QBO, go to the company settings (click on the company name), link to Sign Out. *Or,* continue.

ONLINE LEARNING CENTER (OLC): www.mhhe.com/qbo2e

The OLC includes additional Chapter 6 resources. Go online to www.mhhe.com/qbo2e > Student Edition > Chapter 6.

1. Narrated PowerPoints.
2. Online quizzes: 10 True or False and 10 multiple-choice questions. The Online quizzes are graded and can be emailed to your instructor.
3. Analysis question: Answer the analysis question, then email to your instructor.
4. Going to the Net

    a. Go to the QuickBooks Learn & Support website at https://community.intuit.com.
    b. In the Search field, type **what is reconciliation**. Answer these questions:

        1) What account types can be reconciled?
        2) What amounts should match on both the bank statement and reconcile window? What if amounts do not match; what should you do?

5. Videos: Watch the Create and Send Invoices video at https://www.youtube.com/watch?v=931MTKUQiuY.
6. Glossary of terms: Words that are italicized and boldfaced are defined in the glossary. The Glossary is also Appendix B.
7. Problem Solving link includes Exercise 6-3.

Exercise 6-1: Follow the instructions below to complete Exercise 6-1:

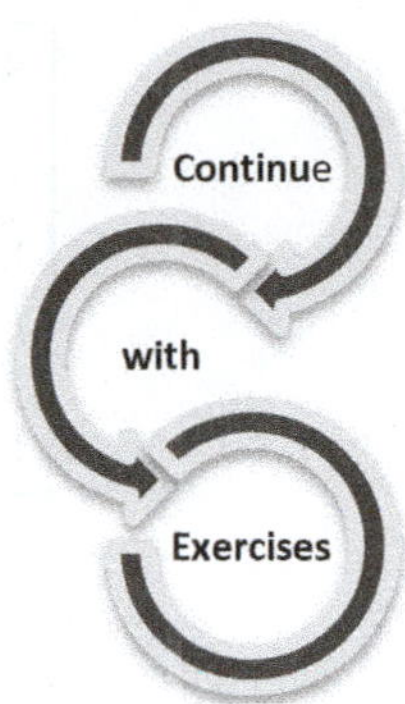

1. Start QBO. Log into QB Cloud_Student Name.

2. To reconcile Account 101 Checking, use the December 31 bank statement on the next three pages. *Hint:* Use your current year> Reconcile > Account 101 Checking > Reconcile Now .)

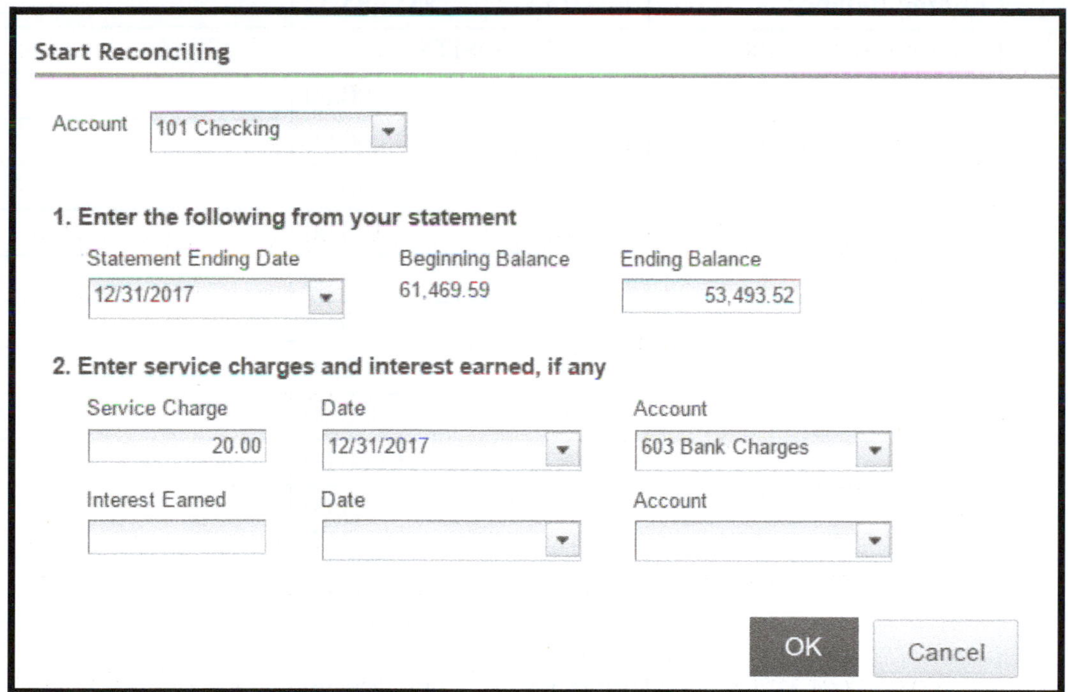

Statement of Account Checking Account December 1 to December 31, 20XX			QB Cloud_Student Name Your address, city, state, Zip Account No. 7731-2256
REGULAR CHECKING			
Previous Balance	11/30/XX	$61,469.59	
18 Deposits (+)		12,820.00	
29 checks (-)		20,666.36	
2 Other Deductions (-)		109.71	
Service Charge		20.00	
Ending Balance	12/31/XX	**$53,493.52**	
DEPOSITS			
	12/2/XX	2,000.00	
	12/2/XX	3,000.00	
	12/3/XX	150.00	
	12/3/XX	100.00	
	12/3/XX	180.00	
	12/3/XX	180.00	
	12/3/XX	800.00	
	12/3/XX	350.00	
	12/3/XX	1,000.00	
	12/3/XX	1,180.00	
	12/23/XX	180.00	
	12/23/XX	300.00	
	12/23/XX	270.00	
	12/23/XX	400.00	
	12/24/XX	1,000.00	
	12/27/XX	1,150.00	
	12/27/XX	150.00	
	12/27/XX	430.00	

Continued

CHECKS (Asterisk * indicates break in check number sequence)				
	12/4/XX	1036	100.75	
	12/4/XX	1037	155.00	
	12/4/XX	1038	82.13	
	12/5/XX	1039	52.65	
	12/5/XX	1040	21.00	
	12/6/XX	1041	300.00	
	12/6/XX	1042	250.00	
	12/6/XX	1043	270.00	
	12/6/XX	1044	1,600.00	
	12/10/XX	1045	375.00	
	12/10/XX	1046	275.00	
	12/10/XX	1047	1,400.00	
	12/11/XX	1048	10,000.00	
	12/11/XX	1049	225.00	
	12/15/XX	1050	3,000.00	
	12/15/XX	1051	225.00	
	12/16/XX	1052	82.13	
	12/16/XX	1053	125.00	
	12/16/XX	1054	76.19	
	12/20/XX	1055	78.36	
	12/20/XX	1056	175.00	
	12/20/XX	1057	85.33	
	12/22/XX	1058	47.00	
	12/22/XX	1059	150.00	
	12/22/XX	1060	115.82	
	12/31/XX	1061	300.00	
	12/31/XX	1062	275.00	
	12/31/XX	1063	600.00	
	12/31/XX	1064	225.00	

Continued

OTHER DEDUCTIONS (ATM's)				
	12/1/XX	ATM	56.90	
	12/15/XX	ATM	52.81	

Comment: To select All Checks and Payments and all Deposits and Other Credits, click on the box next to date.

3. Print the Reconciliation Report. After completing reconciliation, the Reconcile window appears. Link to the 12/31/20XX report > Print. Save as a PDF file. Use the file name **Exercise 6-1_Reconciliation Report**. The report shows Reconciled by: Student first and last name. (*Hint:* From the Reconciliation Report, you can drill down to the original entry.)

Exercise 6-2: Follow the instructions below to complete Exercise 6-2:

1. Export these reports to Excel and save as PDF files. Refer to the date ranges for each report. The dates are not included in the file names; for example, use Exercise 6-2_Journal as the file name.

   - Exercise 6-2_Journal (from 12/31/20XX to 12/31/20XX)
   - Exercise 6-2_Transaction Detail by Account (from 12/2/20XX to 12/31/20XX)
   - Exercise 6-2_General Ledger (from 10/1/20XX to 12/31/20XX)
   - Exercise 6-2_Trial Balance (from 10/1/20XX to 12/31/20XX)
   - Exercise 6-2_Profit and Loss (from 10/1/20XX to 12/31/10XX)
   - Exercise 6-2_Profit and Loss by Month (10/1/20XX to 12/31/20XX, % of income)
   - Exercise 6-2_Balance Sheet (from 10/1/20XX to 12/31/20XX)
   - Exercise 6-2_Custom Balance Sheet (10/1/20XX to 12/31/20XX, % of column)

- Exercise 6-2_Statement of Cash Flows (from 10/1/20XX to 12/31/20XX)

2. **Check Your Figures** (from 10/1/201XX to 12/31/XX):

    - Account 101 Checking, $53,493.52
    - Account 621 Office Supplies, $538.78
    - Account 625 Repair & Maintenance, $290.00
    - Account 633 Telephone, $557.09
    - Net Income, $14,643.52
    - Total Liabilities and Equity, $82,763.52

Exercise 6-3

The Online Learning Center includes Exercise 6-3 at www.mhhe.com/qbo2e > Student Edition > Chapter 6 > Problem Solving.

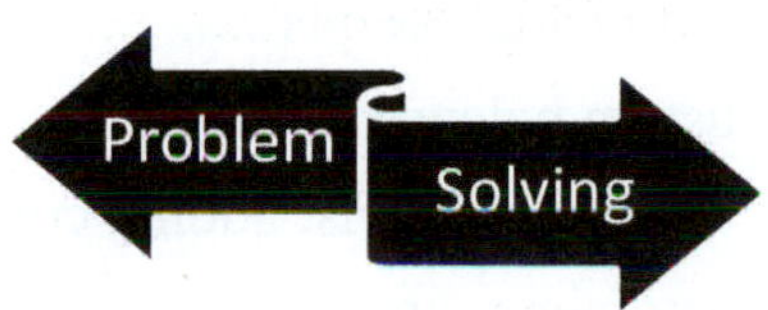

1. On the Profit and Loss report, describe how to compare October, November and December. Show calculations for determining percent of income for an expense account.
2. Describe how the Balance Sheet can be customized. Show an example and two calculations – one for an asset and one for a liability.

CHAPTER 6 INDEX

Chapter 7 Analysis and Reports–End of Fourth Quarter and Year

Scenario: The end of the fourth quarter includes October, November and December ***record keeping***. At this point in your work, fourth quarter transactions and reports have been completed, *except* for the adjusting entries. To make sure your account balances are correct, the December 31 trial balance should be checked carefully. QB Cloud records adjusting entries on December 31, prepares an adjusted trial balance and financial statements, then closes its books for the year and prepares a postclosing trial balance. QuickBooks Online organizes reports by ***module***–accounts payable (expenses and purchases), accounts receivable (customers and sales), general ledger (accountant reports). To learn more about Chapter 7, read the objectives.

OBJECTIVES

1. Start QuickBooks Online and sign in to QB Cloud_Student Name.
2. To check data, display the December 31 Trial Balance.
3. Record end-of-quarter adjusting entries.
4. Display the adjusted trial balance and financial statements.
5. Complete the closing process and display the postclosing trial balance.
6. Export reports to Excel and save as PDF files.
7. Complete Check Your Progress.
8. Go to the Online Learning Center at www.mhhe.com/qbo2e for additional resources.
9. Complete Exercises 7-1, 7-2, and 7-3.

In Chapter 7, you continue recording financial information for QB Cloud_ Student Name. You complete transactions for the end of the fourth quarter and the end of the year. At the end of December, which is also the end of the fourth quarter, you complete ***adjusting entries***, print financial statements, and close the ***fiscal year***.

The fiscal year is a period that a company (or government) uses for accounting purposes and preparing financial statements. The fiscal year may or may not be the same as the calendar year. For tax purposes, companies can choose to be calendar-year taxpayers or fiscal-year taxpayers. The default Internal Revenue Service system is based on the calendar year.

ADJUSTING ENTRIES

Adjusting journal entries are recorded to correct account balances. They are created for a variety of reasons, including booking depreciation, reallocating accruals, and reversing accruals of prepaid income or expenses.

Adjusting entries are usually made on the last day of an accounting period, end of the year, quarter or month. This is done so that the financial statements reflect the revenues that have been earned and the expenses that were incurred during the accounting period.

The reasons for adjusting entries include:

- Revenue has been earned, but it has not yet been recorded.
- An expense has been incurred, but it has not been recorded.
- A company may have prepaid for three months of insurance coverage or rent, but the accounting period is only one month. This means that three months of insurance and rent expense is prepaid and should not be reported as an expense on the current, or monthly, Profit and Loss statement. The prepaid expense needs to be adjusted.

- A customer paid a company in advance of receiving goods or services. Until the goods or services are delivered, the amount is reported as a liability. After the goods or services are delivered, an entry is needed to reduce the liability and to report the revenues.

A common characteristic of an adjusting entry is that it will involve one Profit and Loss statement account and one Balance Sheet account. The purpose of each adjusting entry is to get both the Profit and Loss statement and Balance Sheet to be accurate.

CLOSE THE BOOKS

The purpose of closing the books is so that the Net Income balance is transferred to the equity account Retained Earnings. The Profit and Loss statement accounts all have zero balances until the new period starts. QuickBooks Online makes the following changes automatically on the first day of your next fiscal year.

- On the Balance Sheet, the previous year's Net Income amount appears as the Retained Earnings balance. This way you know how much profit was made for the year.
- Income, cost of goods sold, and expense accounts are reset to zero amounts. This allows the next year's Net Income account to accumulate new totals for the new year's profits.

In Chapter 7, when the Balance Sheet's date is changed to January 1 of the next year, the Retained Earnings account will show the previous year's Net Income; and the Profit and Loss accounts will have zero balances. For example, if you've been entering transactions for October, November and December of 2015, the next year's transactions start on January 1, 2016.

GETTING STARTED

1. Start your browser. Go online to http://qbo.intuit.com.

2. Sign in to QuickBooks Online with your User ID and Password.

CHECK YOUR DATA

To make sure you are starting in the correct place, display the 10/1/20XX to 12/31/20XX Trial Balance.

QB Cloud_Student Name

TRIAL BALANCE

As of December 31, 2017

	DEBIT	CREDIT
101 Checking	53,493.52	
105 Accounts Receivable (A/R)	400.00	
115 Merchandise Inventory	9,870.00	
123 Prepaid Rent	6,000.00	
125 Prepaid Insurance	3,000.00	
135 Computer Equipment	10,000.00	
201 Accounts Payable (A/P)		3,120.00
205 Loan Payable		5,000.00
301 Common Stock		60,000.00
401 Sales		31,140.00
501 Cost of Goods Sold	12,570.00	
601 Advertising	705.00	
603 Bank Charges	60.00	
605 Dues & Subscriptions	275.00	
609 Freight & Delivery	206.45	
619 Meals and Entertainment	282.51	
621 Office Supplies	538.78	
625 Repair & Maintenance	290.00	
627 Shipping and delivery expense	94.00	
629 Stationery & Printing	669.00	
633 Telephone Expense	557.09	
635 Utilities	248.65	
TOTAL	**$99,260.00**	**$99,260.00**

Check the Trial Balance carefully. The December 31 trial balance shows the work completed in Chapters 2 through 6, including the end-of-chapter exercises. Beginning with this chapter, Check Your Data shows the Trial Balance completed at the end of the previous chapter (Exercise 6-2). If necessary, make any needed corrections.

END-OF-QUARTER ADJUSTING ENTRIES

It is the policy of QB Cloud_Student Name to record adjusting entries at the end of the quarter. The accounting records are complete through December 31, 20XX (your current year).

Adjusting entries are recorded in the Journal. Use these steps for entering the three adjusting entries that follow.

1. Select > Journal Entry. The Journal Entry window appears.
2. Type **12/31/20XX** in the Journal date field.
3. Select the appropriate account to Debit. (*Hint:* If you type the account number, the account name automatically appears.)
4. Type the amount in the Debits field.
5. Type a Description.
6. Select the appropriate account to Credit. The credit part of the entry and the description is completed automatically.
7. Select Save and new.

Journalize and post the following December 31, 20XX adjusting entries. To post the transactions to the General Ledger, click <Save and New>. When done, select <Save and Close>.

1. Adjust three months prepaid rent ($2,000 X 3 = $6,000).

Acct. #	Account Name	Description	Debit	Credit
623	Rent or Lease	Adjust prepaid rent	6,000.00	
123	Prepaid Rent	Adjust prepaid rent		6,000.00

2. Adjust prepaid insurance ($3,000 X 3/12 = $750). QB Cloud paid a one year insurance premium on 10/2/20XX.

Acct. #	Account Name	Description	Debit	Credit
611	Insurance	Adjust prepaid insurance	750.00	
125	Prepaid Insurance	Adjust prepaid insurance		750.00

3. Use straight-line depreciation for computer equipment. The computer equipment has a three-year service life and a $400 salvage value. To depreciate computer equipment for the fourth quarter, use this calculation:

   $10,000 - $400 ÷ 3 years X 3/12 = $800.00

Acct. #	Account Name	Description	Debit	Credit
607	Depreciation Expense	Adjust depreciation	800.00	
137	Accumulated Depreciation	Adjust depreciation		800.00

4. Close the Journal Entry window. After journalizing and posting the end-of-quarter adjusting entries, print the Journal for December 31, 20XX.

Reports > type **Journal** in the search field > in the Date fields, type **12/31/20XX >** press <Tab>. *Hint:* The bank statement service charge and the adjusting entries are shown.

If any of your journal entries are incorrect, drill down to the Journal Entry window. Make the appropriate corrections, and then post your revised Journal Entry. Display the Journal report.

5. Display the 12/31/20XX Journal. (*Hint:* Your current year is shown.)

QB Cloud_Student Name

JOURNAL

December 31, 2017

DATE	TRANSACTION TYPE	NUM	NAME	MEMO/DESCRIPTION	ACCOUNT #	ACCOUNT	DEBIT	CREDIT
12/31/2017	Check	SVCCHRG		Service Charge	101	101 Checking		$20.00
					603	603 Bank Charges	$20.00	
							$20.00	**$20.00**
12/31/2017	Journal Entry	2		Adjust prepaid rent	623	623 Rent or Lease	$6,000.00	
				Adjust prepaid rent	123	123 Prepaid Rent		$6,000.00
							$6,000.00	**$6,000.00**
12/31/2017	Journal Entry	3		Adjust prepaid insurance	611	611 Insurance	$750.00	
				Adjust prepaid insurance	125	125 Prepaid Insurance		$750.00
							$750.00	**$750.00**
12/31/2017	Journal Entry	4		Adjust depreciation	607	607 Depreciation Expense	$800.00	
				Adjust depreciation	137	137 Accumulated Depreciation		$800.00
							$800.00	**$800.00**
TOTAL							**$7,570.00**	**$7,570.00**

Troubleshooting: Do your journal entries agree? Check each adjusting entry. If not, drill down > make the necessary changes, <Save and close>. Display the 12/31/20XX journal gain.

- Export the December 31 Journal to Excel and save as a PDF file. Use the file name **Chapter 7_December 31 Journal.**

6. Display the December 31 Transaction Detail by Account report. The Transaction Detail by Account lists transactions subtotaled by each account on the chart of accounts. Credits are shown with the minus sign in front of them.

   The Transaction Detail by Account report is shown below.

QB Cloud_Student Name

TRANSACTION DETAIL BY ACCOUNT

December 31, 2017

DATE	TRANSACTION TYPE	NUM	NAME	MEMO/DESCRIPTION	SPLIT	AMOUNT	BALANCE
101 Checking							
12/31/2017	Check	SVCCHRG		Service Charge	603 Bank Charges	-20.00	-20.00
Total for 101 Checking						**$ -20.00**	
123 Prepaid Rent							
12/31/2017	Journal Entry	2		Adjust prepaid rent	-Split-	-6,000.00	-6,000.00
Total for 123 Prepaid Rent						**$ -6,000.00**	
125 Prepaid Insurance							
12/31/2017	Journal Entry	3		Adjust prepaid insurance	-Split-	-750.00	-750.00
Total for 125 Prepaid Insurance						**$ -750.00**	
137 Accumulated Depreciation							
12/31/2017	Journal Entry	4		Adjust depreciation	-Split-	-800.00	-800.00
Total for 137 Accumulated Depreciation						**$ -800.00**	
603 Bank Charges							
12/31/2017	Check	SVCCHRG			101 Checking	20.00	20.00
Total for 603 Bank Charges						**$20.00**	
607 Depreciation Expense							
12/31/2017	Journal Entry	4		Adjust depreciation	-Split-	800.00	800.00
Total for 607 Depreciation Expense						**$800.00**	
611 Insurance							
12/31/2017	Journal Entry	3		Adjust prepaid insurance	-Split-	750.00	750.00
Total for 611 Insurance						**$750.00**	
623 Rent or Lease							
12/31/2017	Journal Entry	2		Adjust prepaid rent	-Split-	6,000.00	6,000.00
Total for 623 Rent or Lease						**$6,000.00**	

- ➢ Export the December 31 Transaction Detail by Account to Excel and save as PDF file. Use the file name **Chapter 7_December 31 Transaction Detail by Account**.

7. Display the Trial Balance (Adjusted) from 10/1/20XX to 12/31/20XX. Observe that when compared to the December 31 trial balance shown at the beginning of the chapter in the Check Your Data section, the following accounts have different balances or have been added.

Account	Adjusted Balance	Before Adjustment
123 Prepaid Rent	0.00 (Dr.)	6,000.00 (Dr.)
125 Prepaid Insurance	2,250.00 (Dr.)	3,000.00 (Dr.)
137 Accumulated Depreciation	800.00 (Cr.)	0.00
607 Depreciation Expense	800.00 (Dr.)	0.00
611 Insurance	750.00 (Dr.)	0.00
623 Rent or Lease	6,000.00 (Dr.)	0.00

Since three months of prepaid rent and insurance was recorded in October within asset accounts, the Insurance and Rent or Lease expense account needed to be adjusted for these amounts. Computer equipment also needed to be depreciated. That amount is shown on the Accumulated Depreciation and Deprecation Expense accounts. The Adjusted Trial Balance and financial statements will reflect these adjustments.

On page 318, the December 31 trial balance was displayed *before* adjustments were entered in the journal. Also, amounts were filtered so that non-zero amounts were shown. The adjusted trial balance shows also debit and credit balances.

QB Cloud_Student Name

TRIAL BALANCE

As of December 31, 2017

	DEBIT	CREDIT
101 Checking	53,493.52	
105 Accounts Receivable (A/R)	400.00	
115 Merchandise Inventory	9,870.00	
123 Prepaid Rent	0.00	
125 Prepaid Insurance	2,250.00	
130 Undeposited Funds	0.00	
135 Computer Equipment	10,000.00	
137 Accumulated Depreciation		800.00
201 Accounts Payable (A/P)		3,120.00
205 Loan Payable		5,000.00
3000 Opening Balance Equity		0.00
301 Common Stock		60,000.00
401 Sales		31,140.00
501 Cost of Goods Sold	12,570.00	
601 Advertising	705.00	
603 Bank Charges	60.00	
605 Dues & Subscriptions	275.00	
607 Depreciation Expense	800.00	
609 Freight & Delivery	206.45	
611 Insurance	750.00	
619 Meals and Entertainment	282.51	
621 Office Supplies	538.78	
623 Rent or Lease	6,000.00	
625 Repair & Maintenance	290.00	
627 Shipping and delivery expense	94.00	
629 Stationery & Printing	669.00	
633 Telephone Expense	557.09	
635 Utilities	248.65	
TOTAL	**$100,060.00**	**$100,060.00**

- Export the Trial Balance to Excel and save as a PDF file. Change the title to Adjusted Trial Balance. Save as **Chapter 7_Adjusted Trial Balance**.

QB Cloud_Student Name
Adjusted Trial Balance
As of December 31, 2017

- Save the Trial Balance as a PDF file. Use the file name **Chapter 7_Adjusted Trial Balance**.

8. Display the Profit and Loss from 10/1/20XX to 12/31/20XX. Observe that the Net Income amount reflects these expense accounts: Depreciation, Insurance, and Rent or Lease. Those amounts were recorded as adjusting entries.

   When you compare the Profit and Loss *after* adjustments to the P&L saved in Exercise 6-2, observe these differences.

Account	P&L after Adjustments	P&L Before Adjustments
607 Depreciation Expense	800.00 (Dr.)	0.00
611 Insurance	750.00 (Dr.)	0.00
623 Rent or Lease	6,000.00 (Dr.	0.00
Adjusting Entries Total	7,550.00	

Net Income *before* adjusting entries	$14,643.52
Minus adjusting entries total	-7,550.00
Net Income after adjustments	**$7,093.52**

   On the P&L statement, the total amount of journalized and posted adjusting entries equals the difference between the Net Income before adjustments and Net Income after adjustments.

Troubleshooting: Does QBO move slower than usual? For example, you selected Reports and the page doesn't respond? Refer to Appendix A, Troubleshooting, Clearing Temporary Internet Files/Cache.

QB Cloud_Student Name

PROFIT AND LOSS

October - December, 2017

	TOTAL
INCOME	
401 Sales	31,140.00
Total Income	**$31,140.00**
COST OF GOODS SOLD	
501 Cost of Goods Sold	12,570.00
Total Cost of Goods Sold	**$12,570.00**
GROSS PROFIT	**$18,570.00**
EXPENSES	
601 Advertising	705.00
603 Bank Charges	60.00
605 Dues & Subscriptions	275.00
607 Depreciation Expense	800.00
609 Freight & Delivery	206.45
611 Insurance	750.00
619 Meals and Entertainment	282.51
621 Office Supplies	538.78
623 Rent or Lease	6,000.00
625 Repair & Maintenance	290.00
627 Shipping and delivery expense	94.00
629 Stationery & Printing	669.00
633 Telephone Expense	557.09
635 Utilities	248.65
Total Expenses	**$11,476.48**
NET OPERATING INCOME	**$7,093.52**
NET INCOME	**$7,093.52**

- Save the Profit and Loss as a PDF file and export to Excel. Use the file name **Chapter 7_EOY Profit and Loss**. (*Hint:* EOY is an abbreviation of End of Year.) On the Excel file, change the title to End-of-Year Profit and Loss.

QB Cloud_Student Name
End-of-Year Profit and Loss
October - December, 2017

Filter the Profit and Loss

By default the P&L shows all income and expense accounts. Follow these steps to show some accounts instead of all of them.

1. If necessary, display the 10/1/20XX to 12/31/20XX P&L > click <Customize>.
2. On the Customize report page, select Filter > check Distribution Account > All Income Accounts.

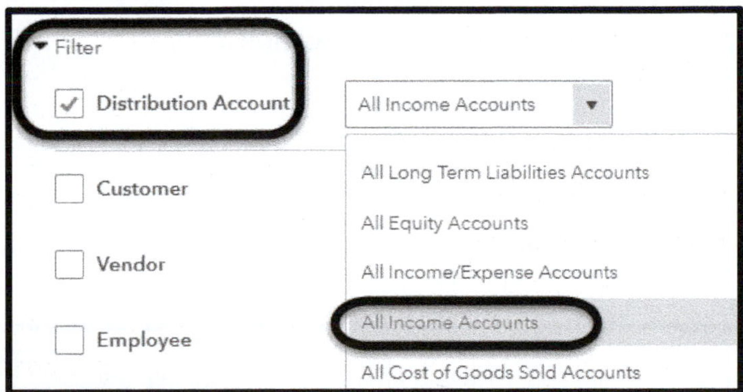

3. **Run report**. Compare your filtered Profit and Loss with the one shown on the next page.

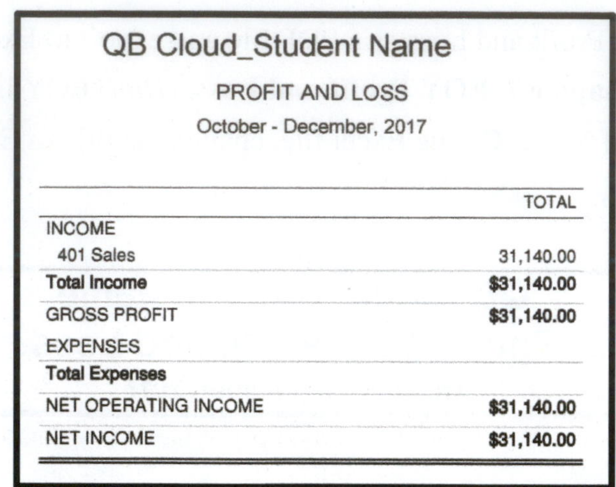

QB Cloud_Student Name

PROFIT AND LOSS

October - December, 2017

	TOTAL
INCOME	
401 Sales	31,140.00
Total Income	**$31,140.00**
GROSS PROFIT	**$31,140.00**
EXPENSES	
Total Expenses	
NET OPERATING INCOME	**$31,140.00**
NET INCOME	**$31,140.00**

4. Use other filter criteria. For example, select All Expenses.

Dashboard

To see the Expenses, Profit and Loss, and Sales graphs on your Dashboard or Home page, select [This year ▾] for Expenses and Profit and Loss, and for Sales This year by quarter. (*Hint:* Amounts are rounded. If your Sales graph does not match, try a different selection.)

- This year Expenses: $24,046
- Profit and Loss, Net Profit for this Year: $7,094
- Sales, This year by quarter: $31,140

Expenses This year ▾ $24,046 THIS YEAR
$12,570 501 Cost of Good...
$6,000 623 Rent or Lease
$800 607 Depreciation...
$4,676 Everything else

Profit and Loss This year ▾ $7,094 NET PROFIT FOR THIS YEAR
$31,140 INCOME
$24,046 EXPENSES

Sales This year by quarter ▾ $31,140 THIS YEAR BY QUARTER
$33K $22K $11K $0
Q1 Q2 Q3 Q4

You can also drill down from the Dashboard's Expenses amount to go to the Transaction Report. Type the appropriate Report period

> Run report. The total at the bottom of the report is the same as the Expenses balance on the Dashboard.

Why are the total Expenses of $24,046 on the Dashboard more than Total Expenses on the Profit and Loss report? The dashboard has a managerial reporting focus that displays the same data in a different way than a standard Profit and Loss financial report.

The display totals include both Reviewed and To Review transactions while the P&L report only shows Reviewed transactions. For example, the Dashboard Expenses shows Total Cost of Goods Sold plus Total Expenses:

Total COGS:	$12,570.00
Total Expenses:	$11,476.48
Dashboard	$24,046.48 (rounded on Dashboard)

QBO reports Expenses and Profit and Loss amounts and graphs based on your computer's system date (current date). If selecting This year does not display the amounts, your entries are probably for a different year than the current one.

1. Display the Balance Sheet from 10/1/20XX to 12/31/20XX. Observe that Accumulated Depreciation is added in the Fixed Assets area — $800.00 with a minus in front of it. The Fixed Assets total is $9,200.00 instead of the $10,000.00 *before* the adjusting entry. The Net Income amount is the same as the P&L, $7,093.52.

QB Cloud_Student Name
BALANCE SHEET
As of December 31, 2017

	TOTAL
ASSETS	
Current Assets	
Bank Accounts	
101 Checking	53,493.52
Total Bank Accounts	**$53,493.52**
Accounts Receivable	
105 Accounts Receivable (A/R)	400.00
Total Accounts Receivable	**$400.00**
Other Current Assets	
115 Merchandise Inventory	9,870.00
123 Prepaid Rent	0.00
125 Prepaid Insurance	2,250.00
130 Undeposited Funds	0.00
Total Other Current Assets	**$12,120.00**
Total Current Assets	**$66,013.52**
Fixed Assets	
135 Computer Equipment	10,000.00
137 Accumulated Depreciation	-800.00
Total Fixed Assets	**$9,200.00**
TOTAL ASSETS	**$75,213.52**
LIABILITIES AND EQUITY	
Liabilities	
Current Liabilities	
Accounts Payable	
201 Accounts Payable (A/P)	3,120.00
Total Accounts Payable	**$3,120.00**
Other Current Liabilities	
205 Loan Payable	5,000.00
Total Other Current Liabilities	**$5,000.00**
Total Current Liabilities	**$8,120.00**
Total Liabilities	**$8,120.00**
Equity	
3000 Opening Balance Equity	0.00
301 Common Stock	60,000.00
318 Retained Earnings	
Net Income	7,093.52
Total Equity	**$67,093.52**
TOTAL LIABILITIES AND EQUITY	**$75,213.52**

- Export the Balance Sheet to Excel and save as a PDF file. Use the file name **Chapter 7_EOY Balance Sheet**. Change the title on the Excel file to End-of-Year Balance Sheet.

QB Cloud_Student Name
End-of-Year Balance Sheet
As of December 31, 2017

2. Display the Statement of Cash Flows from 10/1/20XX to 12/31/20XX. Observe that the Balance Sheet *and* Statement of Cash Flows shows the same Net Income amount. Net Income will be reported as Retained Earnings on the January 1 Balance Sheet. The cash at the end of the period is the same as the Balance Sheet's Total Bank Accounts.

QB Cloud_Student Name

STATEMENT OF CASH FLOWS

October - December, 2017

	TOTAL
OPERATING ACTIVITIES	
Net Income	7,093.52
Adjustments to reconcile Net Income to Net Cash provided by operations:	
105 Accounts Receivable (A/R)	-400.00
115 Merchandise Inventory	-9,870.00
123 Prepaid Rent	0.00
125 Prepaid Insurance	-2,250.00
137 Accumulated Depreciation	800.00
201 Accounts Payable (A/P)	3,120.00
205 Loan Payable	5,000.00
Total Adjustments to reconcile Net Income to Net Cash provided by operations:	**-3,600.00**
Net cash provided by operating activities	**$3,493.52**
INVESTING ACTIVITIES	
135 Computer Equipment	-10,000.00
Net cash provided by investing activities	**$ -10,000.00**
FINANCING ACTIVITIES	
3000 Opening Balance Equity	0.00
301 Common Stock	60,000.00
Net cash provided by financing activities	**$60,000.00**
NET CASH INCREASE FOR PERIOD	**$53,493.52**
CASH AT BEGINNING OF PERIOD	0.00
CASH AT END OF PERIOD	**$53,493.52**

- Export the Statement of Cash Flows to Excel and save as a PDF file. Use the file name **Chapter 7_EOY Statement of Cash Flows**. Change the title on the Excel file to End-of-Year Statement of Cash Flows.

QB Cloud_Student Name
End-of-Year Statement of Cash Flows
October - December, 2017

CLOSING THE FISCAL YEAR

When the date is changed to January 1, 20XX (the next year), Net Income on the Balance Sheet is shown as Retained Earnings and the income and expense accounts have a zero balance.

1. Display the Balance Sheet from 1/1/20XY to 1/1/20XY. (*Hint:* Make sure you are using the next year.) Observe that Account 318 Retained Earnings shows $7,093.52. That's the end-of-year's P&L net income amount.

   In QBO when you change the date to January 1 of the next year, the P&L accounts have zero balances and the net income is transferred to Retained Earnings.

QB Cloud_Student Name
Balance Sheet
As of January 1, 2018

January 1 of the NEXT year.

		Total
ASSETS		
Current Assets		
Bank Accounts		
101 Checking		53,493.52
Total Bank Accounts	$	53,493.52
Accounts Receivable		
105 Accounts Receivable (A/R)		400.00
Total Accounts Receivable	$	400.00
Other Current Assets		
115 Merchandise Inventory		9,870.00
123 Prepaid Rent		0.00
125 Prepaid Insurance		2,250.00
130 Undeposited Funds		0.00
Total Other Current Assets	$	12,120.00
Total Current Assets	$	66,013.52
Fixed Assets		
135 Computer Equipment		10,000.00
137 Accumulated Depreciation		-800.00
Total Fixed Assets	$	9,200.00
TOTAL ASSETS	$	75,213.52
LIABILITIES AND EQUITY		
Liabilities		
Current Liabilities		
Accounts Payable		
201 Accounts Payable (A/P)		3,120.00
Total Accounts Payable	$	3,120.00
Other Current Liabilities		
205 Loan Payable		5,000.00
Total Other Current Liabilities	$	5,000.00
Total Current Liabilities	$	8,120.00
Total Liabilities	$	8,120.00
Equity		
3000 Opening Balance Equity		0.00
301 Common Stock		60,000.00
318 Retained Earnings		7,093.52
Net Income		
Total Equity	$	67,093.52
TOTAL LIABILITIES AND EQUITY	$	75,213.52

- Export the January 1 Balance Sheet to Excel and save as a PDF file. Use the file name **Chapter 7_January 1 Balance Sheet**.

2. To verify, display the Profit and Loss from 1/1/20XY to 1/1/20XY (next year). The P&L shows no data because the ***temporary accounts*** are zeroed when the new year begins.

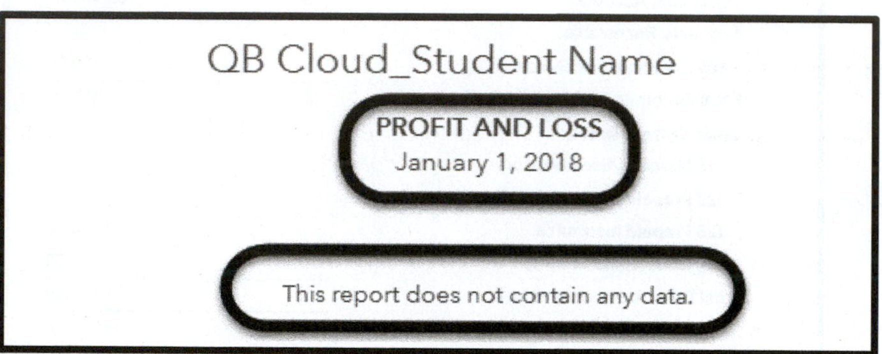

Accounts that are closed at the end of the year are called ***temporary accounts***. Temporary accounts, such as income, cost of goods sold, and expenses, accumulate transactions and balances during one accounting year. In QBO, when January 1 (of the next year) is selected for the Balance Sheet, the balances in the temporary accounts are transferred to the Retained Earnings account and the income and expense accounts have a zero balance.

The asset, liability, and equity accounts shown on the Balance Sheet are called ***permanent accounts***. They do not close at the end of the accounting year. Permanent account balances accumulate month to month and year to year.

POSTCLOSING TRIAL BALANCE

After the fiscal year is closed, a postclosing trial balance is printed. Only permanent accounts appear on the postclosing trial balance. All temporary accounts (income, cost of goods sold, and expenses) have been closed.

Follow these steps to display a postclosing trial balance:

1. Reports > type **trial balance** in the search field > press <Enter>

   1/1/20XY to **1/1/20XY** (next year) > Run report. The author selected Non-zero to show accounts with balances only.

   Observe that the Trial Balance is dated January 1, 20XY (next year). The balance in Account 318 Retained Earnings, $7,093.52, was QB Cloud's end-of-year P&L Net Income.

QB Cloud_Student Name

TRIAL BALANCE

As of January 1, 2018

	DEBIT	CREDIT
101 Checking	53,493.52	
105 Accounts Receivable (A/R)	400.00	
115 Merchandise Inventory	9,870.00	
125 Prepaid Insurance	2,250.00	
135 Computer Equipment	10,000.00	
137 Accumulated Depreciation		800.00
201 Accounts Payable (A/P)		3,120.00
205 Loan Payable		5,000.00
301 Common Stock		60,000.00
318 Retained Earnings		7,093.52
TOTAL	**$76,013.52**	**$76,013.52**

2. Export to Excel and save as a PDF file. Use the file name **Chapter 7_Postclosing Trial Balance**. On the Excel file, change the title to Postclosing Trial Balance.

QB Cloud_Student Name
PostclosingTrial Balance
As of January 1, 2018

ANALYZE REPORTS

QuickBooks Online organizes reports by modules within the accounting system. If you go to the Reports page and then select All Reports, the links shown below are available. Each link includes the reports related to that module. If you select a module, for example, Business Overview, select All Reports to go back to the Reports page.

- Business Overview: These reports show different perspectives of how the business is doing. The reports include Profit and Loss Comparison, Profit and Loss by Month, Profit and Loss % of Total Income, Quarterly Profit and Loss Summary, Profit and Loss YTD Comparison, Profit and Loss by Customer, and Balance Sheet Detail. Company Snapshot (because the system date is used by QBO, only Who Owes Me and Whom I Owe is shown), Profit and Loss, Balance Sheet, Balance Sheet Comparison, Profit and Loss Detail, Statement of Cash Flows, Balance Sheet Summary, and Audit Log.

- Review Sales: These reports group and total sales in different ways to help analyze sales to see how you are doing and where you make money. The reports include Sales by Customer Summary, Sales by Customer Detail, Sales by Product/Service Summary, Sales by Product/Service Detail, Product/Service List, Income by Customer Summary, Customer Contact List, Payment Method List, Terms List, Transaction List by Customer, Time Activities by Customer Detail, Unbilled Time, Unbilled Charges, and Deposit Detail.

- Manage Accounts Receivable: These reports include who owes you money and how much they owe you so you can get paid. The reports include Customer Balance Summary, A/R Aging Summary, Customer Balance Detail, A/R Aging Detail, Collections Reports, Invoice List, and Statement List.

- Review Expenses and Purchases: These reports show expenses and purchases and group them in different ways to help you understand what is being spent. The reports include Expenses by Vendor Summary, Transaction List by Vendor, Vendor Contact List, Open Purchase Order List, Purchases by Vendor Detail, Purchases by Product/Service Detail, and Check Detail.

- Manage Accounts Payable: These reports show what you owe and when payments are due so you can take advantage of the time you have to pay bills but still make payments on time. The reports include A/P Aging Summary, Vendor Balance Detail, Bill Payment List, A/P Aging Detail, Unpaid Bills, and Vendor Balance Summary.

- Manage Sales Tax: These reports help you manage the sales taxes you collect and then pay to tax agencies. These reports include Taxable Sales Summary, Taxable Sales Detail, and Sales Tax Liability Report.

- Accountant Reports: These are reports accountants typically use to drill down into your business details and prepare tax returns. These reports include Account Listing, Reconciliation Reports, Trial Balance, Journal, Profit and Loss, Balance Sheet, Balance Sheet Comparison, Transaction Detail by Account, General Ledger, Transaction List with Splits, Statement of Cash Flows, Transaction List by Date, Recent Transactions, and Recurring Template List.

- Manage Employees: These reports help you manage employee activities and payroll. The reports include Time Activities by Employee Detail, Recent/Edited Time Activities, and Employee Contact List.

- Manage Products and Inventory: These reports help you understand how much inventory you have and how much you are paying and making for each of your inventory items. The reports include Inventory Valuation Summary, Inventory Valuation Detail, Product/Service List, Purchases by Product/Service Detail, Sales by Product/Service Summary, Sales by Product/Service Detail, and Physical Inventory Worksheet.

The default for reports is your current system date, for example, the current year-to-date or today's date. Since not all reports and charts require entering a date range, some of these features may not show data because your system date is different than the dates entered for transactions.

List reports vs. balance or totaled reports

The difference between List reports vs. balance and totaled reports is that the majority of list reports do not show balances or totals, just account information. For example, the Vendor Contact List report shows the vendor name, phone number, full name, and address but does not show vendor balances. There are also other types of reports such as the Transaction List by Date that has list in the title. This report will show an amount column but will not provide a balance column or a total.

So if you ran a report and it has no balance column or total, double check the title at the top of the report. Chances are the report has "List" in the title.

A list report with amounts can be exported and customized in Excel to provide a total. Go to the top left of the report and click on the Excel button to export.

Once you locate the desired report and customize it, QuickBooks Online provides the ability to memorize the report so you will not need to recreate it.

Customize Reports

Sometimes it's helpful to customize reports. You can customize the following reports

- Profit & Loss
- Balance Sheet
- Majority of summary reports

To customize a report:

1. Go to the Reports page.
2. Display the desired report.
3. Once the customize window is open, click Rows/Columns. (You may also want to make other choices: General, Lists, Numbers, Header/Footer).
4. Make preferred selections.
5. Click Run Report.

Memorize a Report

Memorizing a report allows you to save it with its current customization settings.

1. Find and display the report you want to memorize.
2. To change what's in the report, click on the customize icon.
3. Once the report is customized the way you like it, click the Save Customizations button.
4. Enter a descriptive name for the report in the Name of memorized report: field.

Reconciliation Report

The Reconcile Report in QuickBooks Online is one of the few reports that can't be directly exported to Excel. However, there is a simple workaround to accomplish this.

1. Find the reconcile report you want to print:
   - Go to the Reports page.
   - Search Reconciliation Reports.
   - Drill down to 101 Checking.
2. Highlight the information on the report.
3. Right-click and copy the information.
4. Open Excel and paste the information.
5. Adjust the column widths for the format of the Excel report to show all the information.
6. Save the Excel file. Use the file name **Chapter 7_Reconcilation Report**.

CHECK YOUR PROGRESS

1. What is the account balance on 1/1/20XY (next year) in these accounts? Indicate whether these accounts have debit (dr.) or credit (cr.) balances.

   Account 101 Checking ____________________

   Account 105 Accounts Receivable ____________________

   Account 115 Merchandise Inventory ____________________

   Account 123 Prepaid Rent ____________________

   Account 125 Prepaid Insurance ____________________

   Account 137 Accumulated Depreciation ____________________

   Account 603 Bank Charges ____________________

   Account 318 Retained Earnings ____________________

2. What are total current assets? ____________________

3. What are total Liabilities and Equity? ____________________

4. What is the amount owed by customers? ____________________

5. List the customer(s) and due dates that payments are owed to QB Cloud_Student Name.

    ____

6. What is the amount owed by QB Cloud_Student Name to vendors?

    ____

7. List the vendor name, amounts due, and due date.

    ____

SIGN OUT

To sign out of QBO, go to the company settings (click on the company name), link to Sign Out. *Or,* continue.

ONLINE LEARNING CENTER (OLC): www.mhhe.com/qbo2e

The OLC includes additional Chapter 7 resources. Go online to www.mhhe.com/qbo2e > Student Edition > Chapter 7.

1. Narrated PowerPoints.
2. Online quizzes: 10 True or False and 10 multiple-choice questions. The Online quizzes are graded and can be emailed to your instructor.

3. Analysis question: Answer the analysis question, then email to your instructor.
4. Going to the Net

    a. Go to the QuickBooks Learn & Support website at https://community.intuit.com.
    b. Type the Search word, **Customize your Profit and Loss Report**.
    c. Link to Customize your Profit and Loss Report. Select See only some accounts not all of them.

        1) What is the P&L default?
        2) Describe the steps to see some accounts but not all of them.

5. Videos: Go to Prof. Susan Crosson's Financial Accounting videos at http://www.bus.emory.edu/scrosso/FA%20Videos.htm. To review financial accounting principles and procedures, link to a video.

6. Glossary of terms: Words that are italicized and boldfaced are defined in the glossary. The Glossary is also Appendix B.
7. Problem Solving link includes Exercise 7-3.

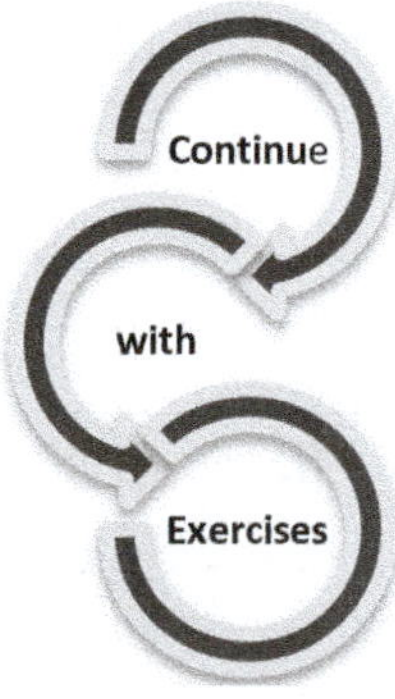

Exercise 7-1: Follow the instructions below to complete Exercise 7-1:

1. If necessary start QBO.
2. Match the Report Description with the Report Name. Write the appropriate letter next to the Report Name column.

Letter	Report Description	Write Letter a. b., etc.	Report Name
a.	Summarizes key information, for example, quantity on hand, value, and average cost of each item.		Expenses by Vendor Summary
b.	Groups purchases by the items in the Product/Service List.		Sales by Customer summary
c.	Allows you to see all activity and transactions related to each customer.		Deposit Detail
d.	Breaks down every transaction into debits and credits and displays them chronologically.		Transaction List by Vendor
e.	Lists individual sales, including dates, types, amounts and totals.		Check Detail
f.	This report shows total expenses for each vendor.		Trial Balance
g.	Lists all transactions so you can view the company's activities with a specific vendor.		Sales by Customer Detail
h.	This report shows which customers generated the most revenue.		Account Listing
i.	Summarizes debit and credit balances for each account.		Journal

j.	Provides detailed information about each check issued.		Purchases by Product/Service Detail
k.	Shows money earned and money spent so you can see if you have a profit or loss. Also called the income statement.		Balance Sheet
l.	Transactions modified within the last 4 days.		Transaction List by Customer
m.	Provides the name, type, and balance for each account listing in your chart of accounts.		Inventory Valuation Summary
n.	Provides detailed information about amounts received, including date, client or vendor, and amount.		Recent Transactions
o.	Lists the permanent accounts: assets, liabilities, and equity.		Profit and Loss

Exercise 7-2: Follow the instructions below to complete Exercise 7-2:

1. Export these reports to Excel and save as PDF files. The dates are not included in the file name; for example, use Exercise 7-2_AR Aging Summary as the file name.

   Manage Accounts Receivable reports:

   - Exercise 7-2_AR Aging Summary (as of 1/1/20XY [next year])
   - Exercise 7-2_Customer Balance Detail (as of 1/1/20XY)

- Exercise 7-2_Invoice List (from 12/1/20XX to 12/31/20XX)

Manage Accounts Payable reports:

- Exercise 7-2_AP Aging Summary (as of 1/1/20XY [next year])
- Exercise 7-2_Vendor Balance Detail (as of 1/1/20XY)
- Exercise 7-2_Unpaid Bills (as of 1/1/20XY). (*Hint:* The past due column computes from the system, or current, date. Depending on the system date of your computer, the Past Due column may not be accurate.)

2. **Check Your Figures, January 1, 20XY** (next year)

    - Account 101 Checking, $53,493.52
    - Account 105 Accounts Receivable, $400.00
    - Account 125 Prepaid Insurance, $2,250.00
    - Account 201 Accounts Payable, $3,120.00
    - Account 137 Accumulated Depreciation, $800.00
    - Account 318 Retained Earnings, $7,093.52
    - Total Liabilities and Equity, $75,213.52

Problem 7-3

The Online Learning Center includes Exercise 7-3 at www.mhhe.com/qbo2e > Student Edition > Chapter 7 > Problem Solving.

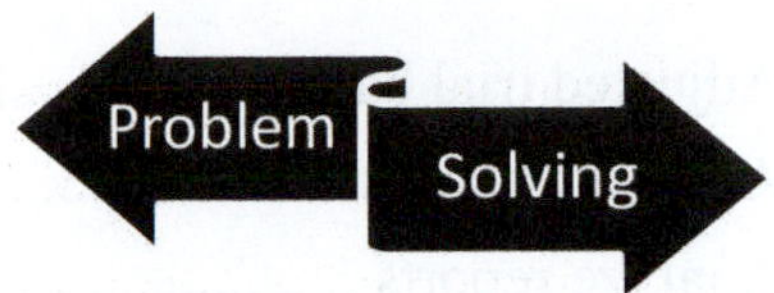

1. Explain why the amounts are different when the Trial Balance on page 318 is compared to the Adjusted Trial Balance on page 324.
2. What are the differences on the Profit and Loss *after* adjustments to the P&L saved in Exercise -2?

CHAPTER 7 INDEX

Chapter 8 January Source Documents

Scenario: In this chapter, start by checking your data with the January 1 Trial Balance. The stop sign reminds you to make sure your debit and credit balances are correct. In Chapter 8, you analyze typical source documents used by businesses. Memos remind you to make customer payments and vendor payments, sales receipts show cash and credit card sales, bills are used for recording purchases on account, and invoices are used for sales on account. You also display reports and complete financial statements. To review what you will do in Chapter 8, read the objectives.

OBJECTIVES

1. Start QuickBooks Online and sign in to QB Cloud_Student Name (your first and last name).
2. To check data, display the January 1 Postclosing Trial Balance.
3. Analyze source documents.
4. Record vendor, customer, cash, and credit card transactions.
5. Export reports to Excel and save as PDF files.
6. Complete Check Your Progress.
7. Go to the Online Learning Center at www.mhhe.com/qbo2e for additional resources.
8. Complete Exercises 8-1, 8-2 and 8-3.

In Chapter 8, January Source Documents, you complete January business transactions for QB Cloud_Student Name. QB Cloud sells computers, data storage, network products, web servers, and webinars.

The source documents shown prompt transaction analysis for issuing checks for expenses, accounts payable (vendors), inventory, accounts receivable (customers), and cash and credit card sales. You also use the January 31 bank statement to reconcile Account 101 Checking.

GETTING STARTED

1. Start your browser. Go online to http://qbo.intuit.com.
2. Sign in to QuickBooks Online with your User ID and Password.

CHECK YOUR DATA

To make sure you are starting in the correct place, display the 1/1/20XY to 1/1/20XY Trial Balance. (*Hint:* Remember to use the next year. For example, if you recorded transactions for the fourth quarter of 2017, the year used in Chapters 8, 9 and 10 is 2018.) The screen images show 2018 because the author recorded fourth quarter transactions in 2017.

QB Cloud_Student Name

TRIAL BALANCE

As of January 1, 2018

	DEBIT	CREDIT
101 Checking	53,493.52	
105 Accounts Receivable (A/R)	400.00	
115 Merchandise Inventory	9,870.00	
123 Prepaid Rent	0.00	
125 Prepaid Insurance	2,250.00	
130 Undeposited Funds	0.00	
135 Computer Equipment	10,000.00	
137 Accumulated Depreciation		800.00
201 Accounts Payable (A/P)		3,120.00
205 Loan Payable		5,000.00
301 Common Stock		60,000.00
305 Opening Balance Equity		0.00
318 Retained Earnings		7,093.52
TOTAL	**$76,013.52**	**$76,013.52**

Comment: What is Account 130 Undeposited Funds? Think of the Undeposited Funds account as an envelope where you keep checks until you take them to the bank. Since QB Cloud_Student Name uses Account 101 Checking for recording checks, Undeposited Funds has a zero balance. QBO automatically sets up an Undeposited Funds account.

Check the January 1, 20XY trial balance *before* recording January transactions. What about account numbers? Do you need to do any editing? For example, the author had two accounts for Opening Balance Equity–Account 3000 Opening Balance Equity and another one for 305 Opening Balance Equity. Once I deleted Account 305 and changed the account number for Account 3000 to 305, the Chart of Accounts shows this for Account 301 Common Stock and 305 Opening Balance Equity.

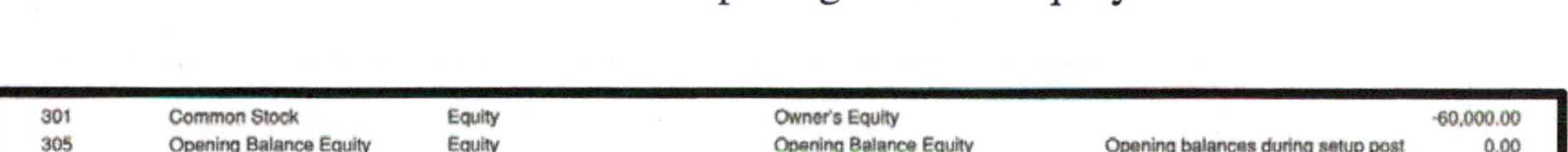

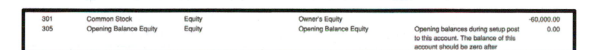

301	Common Stock	Equity	Owner's Equity		-60,000.00
305	Opening Balance Equity	Equity	Opening Balance Equity	Opening balances during setup post to this account. The balance of this account should be zero after	0.00

JANUARY SOURCE DOCUMENTS

After analyzing each source document, record the appropriate transaction. All transactions occurred during January of the year *after* fourth quarter transactions recorded in Chapters 2 through 7.

For January's transactions, use the next year. For example, if you recorded transactions for the fourth quarter of 2015, use 2016 as the year for each source document in Chapter 8.

QB Cloud_Student Name

Memo

Date: 1/2

Re: Vendor Payments

QB Cloud_Student Name pays the following vendors:

Vendor ID	Bill #	Check No.	Amount
AmpleStore	AS42	1065	$300.00
CloudZ Channel	CZ132	1066	$800.00
Conf/Call	143CC	1067	$90.00

REMITTANCE	
Bill #	AS42
Customer ID	QB Cloud_Student Name
Date	1/2/20XY
Amount Enclosed	$300.00
	AmpleStore Inc. 200 West Concord Ave. Palo Alto, CA 94301 650-555-8527

REMITTANCE	
Bill #	CZ132
Customer ID	QB Cloud_Student Name
Date	1/2
Amount Enclosed	$800.00
	CloudZ Channel 110 Merit Street Menlo Park, CA 94025 650-555-3250

REMITTANCE	
Bill #	143CC
Customer ID	QB Cloud_Student Name
Date	1/2
Amount Enclosed	$90.00
	Conf/Call 700 North Prince Street Tempe, AZ 85008 480-555-2411

Transaction Register

Check No.	*Date*	*Description of Transaction*	Debit (-)	Credit (+)	Balance
	1/3	*Balance*			$52,303.52
1068	1/4	Best Cellular	82.13		52,221.39
1069	1/4	Valley News	100.00		52,121.39
1070	1/4	County Telephone	76.19		52,045.20
1071	1/4	Office Suppliers	88.52		51,956.68
1072	1/4	Cays Advertising	125.00		51,831.68
1073	1/4	RSP Gas	90.14		51,741.54
1074	1/4	U.S. Post Office	47.00		51,694.54
1075	1/4	Albert Benson	150.00		51,544.54
1076	1/4	Simon Rentals (Paid rent for 3 months)	6,000.00		45,544.54

QB Cloud_Student Name

Memo

Date: 1/4

Re: Credit Card Receipts

The bank sent verification of credit card receipts in the amount of $3,500.00. Refer to the sales receipts on the next three pages for the products sold and credit cards used.

Checking Account Bank Statement		**Checks**	**Credit Card**	**Amount**
Date: January 4		1	American Express	$300.00
List of Deposits:		2	MasterCard	$1,200.00
Coin	**Totals**	3	Visa	$2,000.00
Quarters:	$	4		
Dimes:	$	5		
Nickels:	$	6		
Pennies	$			
Total				
Cash	**Totals**			
$1	$			
$5	$			
$10	$			
$20	$			
$50	$			
$100	$			
Total	$		**Totals**	$3,500.00
Total Cash			**Total Deposit**	$3,500.00

Hint: On the Sales Receipt page, select the appropriate credit card. Credit Card Sales are deposited to Account 101 Checking.

SALES RECEIPT

QB Cloud_Student Name

Date: 1/4

RECEIPT # 1034

For: **CREDIT CARD**

Payment Method	Type
CREDIT CARD	American Express

Qty	Description	Rate	Amount
10	Data storage	$30.00	$300.00
		Subtotal	300.00
		Total	$300.00

Thank you for your business!

SALES RECEIPT

QB Cloud_Student Name

Date: 1/4
RECEIPT # 1035
For: **CREDIT CARD**

Payment Method	Type
CREDIT CARD	MasterCard

Qty	Description	Rate	Amount
3	Web servers	$400.00	$1,200.00
		Subtotal	1,200.00
		Total	$1,200.00

Thank you for your business!

SALES RECEIPT

QB Cloud_Student Name

Date: 1/4
RECEIPT # 1036
For: **CREDIT CARD**

Payment Method	Type
CREDIT CARD	Visa

Qty	Description	Rate	Amount
2	Computers	$1,000.00	$2,000.00
		Subtotal	2,000.00
		Total	$2,000.00

Thank you for your business!

QB Cloud_Student Name

Memo

Date: 1/5

Re: Customer Payments

QB Cloud_Student Name received the following customer payment.

Received payment from Springfield Unified School District Invoice 1029, $400, customer check 8447. (*Hint:* Use the Reference no. field for the check number.)

BILL #: CZ155 DATE: 1/8 **Customer:**

QB **Cloud_**

Student Name

CloudZ Channel
110 Merit Street
Menlo Park, CA 94025
650-555-3250

Date	Quantity	Description	Unit Price	Amount
1/8	4	Web server	$200.00	$800.00

Remittance

Bill #	CZ155
Date	1/8
Amount Due	$800.00

Thank you for your business!
Make all checks payable to CloudZ Channel.

Date:

1/8 **BILL #: 210C2U**

Computers 2 You

2006 East 14 Avenue

Los Angeles, CA 90046

(213) 555-2300

BILL TO:

QB Cloud_

Student Name

quantity	description	Unit Price	amount
3	Computers	$500.00	$1,500.00

Remittance

Bill #	210C2U
Date	1/8
Amount Due	$1,500.00

QB Cloud_Student Name

Memo

Date: 1/9

Re: Vendor Payments

QB Cloud_Student Name pays the following vendors:

Vendor ID	Bill #	Check No.	Amount
AmpleStore Inc.	AS99	1077	$180.00
Any Time Deployment	ATD460	1078	$250.00
Computers 2 You	190C2U	1079	$1,500.00

REMITTANCE	
Bill #	AS99
Customer ID	QB Cloud_Student Name
Date	1/9
Amount Enclosed	$180.00
	AmpleStore Inc. 200 West Concord Ave. Palo Alto, CA 94301 650-555-8527

REMITTANCE	
Bill #	ATD460
Customer ID	QB Cloud_Student Name
Date	1/9
Amount Enclosed	$250.00
	Any Time Deployment 1189 W. Burnside Lexington, MA 02421 781-555-4671

REMITTANCE	
Bill #	190C2U
Customer ID	QB Cloud_Student Name
Date	1/9
Amount Enclosed	$1,500.00
	Computers 2 You 2006 East 14 Avenue Los Angeles, CA 90046 213-555-2300

Bill: AS144

AmpleStore Inc.

Bill To: QB Cloud_Student Name

Date	Quantity	Description	Unit Price	Amount
1/10	14	Data storage	$15.00	$210.00

Remittance

Bill #	AS144
Date	1/10
Amount Due	$210.00

AmpleStore Inc. 200 West Concord Ave. Palo Alto, CA 94301
(650) 555-8527

QB Cloud_Student Name

Memo

Date: 1/17

Re: Credit Card Receipts

The bank sent verification of credit card receipts in the amount of $2,560.00. Refer to the sales receipts on the next three pages for the products sold and credit cards used.

Checking Account Bank Statement		Checks	Credit Card	Amount
Date: January 17		1	American Express	$380.00
List of Deposits:		2	MasterCard	$1,000.00
Coin	**Totals**	3	Visa	$1,180.00
Quarters:	$	4		
Dimes:	$	5		
Nickels:	$	6		
Pennies	$			
Total				
Cash	**Totals**			
$1	$			
$5	$			
$10	$			
$20	$			
$50	$			
$100	$			
Total	$		**Totals**	$2,560.00
Total Cash			**Total Deposit**	$2,560.00

Hint: Credit Card Sales are deposited to Account 101 Checking.

SALES RECEIPT

QB Cloud_Student Name

Date: 1/17
RECEIPT # 1037
For: **CREDIT CARD**

Payment Method	Type
CREDIT CARD	American Express

Qty	Description	Rate	Amount
6	Data storage	$30.00	$180.00
4	Network products	$50.00	200.00
		Subtotal	380.00
		Total	$380.00

Thank you for your business!

SALES RECEIPT

QB Cloud_Student Name

Date: 1/17
RECEIPT # 1038
For: **CREDIT CARD**

Payment Method	Type
CREDIT CARD	MasterCard

Qty	Description	Rate	Amount
4	Network products	$50.00	$200.00
2	Web server	400.00	800.00
		Subtotal	1,000.00
		Total	$1,000.00

Thank you for your business!

SALES RECEIPT

QB Cloud_Student Name

Date: 1/17
RECEIPT # 1039
For: **CREDIT CARD**

Payment Method	Type
CREDIT CARD	Visa

Qty	Description	Rate	Amount
1	Computer	$1,000.00	$1,000.00
2	Webinars	90.00	180.00
		Subtotal	1,180.00
		Total	$1,180.00

Thank you for your business!

Any Time Deployment
1189 W. Burnside
Lexington, MA 02421
(781) 555-4681

Bill Number: ATD510

Date: 1/18

Ship To:
QB Cloud_Student Name

SHIPPED VIA	TERMS
UPS	Net 30

QTY	DESCRIPTION	UNIT PRICE	TOTAL
20	Network products	25.00	$500.00
		SUBTOTAL	500.00
		TOTAL	$500.00

BILL #: CZ333 **DATE: 1/19**

Customer: QB Cloud_
Student Name

CloudZ Channel
110 Merit Street
Menlo Park, CA 94025
650-555-3250

Date	Quantity	Description	Unit Price	Amount
1/19	4	Web server	$200.00	$800.00

Remittance

Bill #	CZ333
Date	1/19
Amount Due	$800.00

Thank you for your business!

Make all checks payable to CloudZ Channel.

Sales Invoice

TO:

eBiz
800 W. Second Ave.
Durango, CO 81301
(970) 555-2000

SHIP TO: SAME

Date	Invoice Number	Payment Terms	Due Date
1/23	1040	Net 30	2/22

Qty	Product	Description	Rate	Amount
6	Data storage	Data storage	$30.00	$180.00

Make all checks payable to QB Cloud_Student Name

Thank you for your business!

Bill: 246CC

Conf/Call
700 North Prince Street
Tempe, AZ 85008 USA
480-555-2411

Bill to:
QB Cloud_
Student Name

Date	Quantity	Description	Unit Price	Amount
1/23	6	Webinars	$45	$270

Remittance

Bill #	246CC
Date	1/23
Amount Due	$270

Make all checks payable to Conf/Call.
Thank you for your business!

Sales Invoice

TO: **Law Offices of Williamson, Gallagher & Katz**
18 Piedmont Ave. NW
Atlanta, GA 30303
(404) 555-8134

SHIP TO: **SAME**

Date	Invoice Number	Payment Terms	Due Date
1/23	1041	Net 30	2/22

Qty	Product	Description	Rate	Amount
6	Network Products	Network products	$50.00	$300.00

Make all checks payable to QB Cloud_Student Name

Thank you for your business!

Sales Invoice

TO: **Permanente Medical Services**
18771 Ala Moana Blvd.
Honolulu, HI 96815
(808) 555-555-9000

SHIP TO: **SAME**

Date	Invoice Number	Payment Terms	Due Date
1/23	1042	Net 30	2/22

Qty	Product	Description	Rate	Amount
3	Webinars	Webinars	$90	$270.00

Make all checks payable to QB Cloud_Student Name

Thank you for your business!

Bill: AS352

AmpleStore Inc.

Bill to: QB Cloud_
Student Name

Date	Quantity	Description	Unit Price	Amount
1/23	12	Data storage	$15.00	$180.00

Remittance

Bill #	AS352
Date	1/23
Amount Due	$180.00

AmpleStore Inc. 200 West Concord Ave. Palo Alto, CA 94301
(650) 555-8527

Sales Invoice

TO:

WebPro
18 Alameda Road
Santa Fe, NM 87501
(505) 555-5311

SHIP TO: **SAME**

Date	Invoice Number	Payment Terms	Due Date
1/25	1043	Net 30	2/24

Qty	Product	Description	Rate	Amount
1	Web server	Web servers	$400.00	$400.00

Make all checks payable to QB Cloud_Student Name

Thank you for your business!

Date:

1/30 **BILL #: 422C2U**

Computers 2 You
2006 East 14 Avenue
Los Angeles, CA 90046
(213) 555-2300

BILL TO:

QB Cloud_
Student Name

quantity	description	Unit Price	amount
3	Computers	$500.00	$1,500.00

Remittance

Bill #	422C2U
Date	1/30
Amount Due	$1,500.00

Any Time Deployment
1189 W. Burnside
Lexington, MA 02421
(781) 555-4681

Bill Number: ATD592

Date: 1/30

Ship To:
QB Cloud_Student Name

SHIPPED VIA	TERMS
UPS	Net 30

QTY	DESCRIPTION	UNIT PRICE	TOTAL
10	Network products	25.00	$250.00
		SUBTOTAL	$250.00
		TOTAL	$250.00

Remittance

Bill #	ATD592
Date	1/30
Amount Due	$250.00

Sales Invoice

TO: **Springfield Unified School District**
4892 Clear Lake Ave.
Springfield, IL 62703
(217) 555-5500

SHIP TO: **SAME**

Date	Invoice Number	Payment Terms	Due Date
1/30	1044	Net 30	3/1

Qty	Product	Description	Rate	Amount
1	Web server	Web server	$400.00	$400.00

Make all checks payable to QB Cloud_Student Name

Thank you for your business!

SALES RECEIPT

QB Cloud_Student Name

Date: 1/30
RECEIPT # 1045
For: **Cash Sales**

Payment Method	Type
Check	14520

Qty	Description	Rate	Amount
1	Computer	$1,000.00	$1,000.00
		Subtotal	$1,000.00
		Total	$1,000.00

Thank you for your business!

QB Cloud_Student Name

Memo

Date: 1/30

Re: Vendor Payments

QB Cloud_Student Name pays the following vendors:

Vendor ID	Bill #	Check No.	Amount
AmpleStore Inc.	AS144	1080	$210.00
CloudZ Channel	CZ155	1081	$800.00
Computers 2 You	210C2U	1082	$1,500.00

REMITTANCE	
Bill #	AS144
Customer ID	QB Cloud_Student Name
Date	1/30
Amount Enclosed	$210.00
	AmpleStore Inc. 200 West Concord Ave. Palo Alto, CA 94301 (650) 555-8527

REMITTANCE	
Bill #	CZ155
Customer ID	QB Cloud_Student Name
Date	1/30
Amount Enclosed	$800.00
	CloudZ Channel 110 Merit Street Menlo Park, CA 94025 (650) 555-3250

REMITTANCE	
Bill #	210C2U
Customer ID	QB Cloud_Student Name
Date	1/30
Amount Enclosed	$1,500.00
	Computers 2 You 2006 East 14 Avenue Los Angeles, CA 90046 213-555-2300

REPORTS

Display the following reports. The suggested date range is shown for each report.

1. Journal: 1/1/20XY thru 1/30/20XY. The journal report is shown on the next six pages.

QB Cloud_Student Name

JOURNAL

January 1-30, 2018

DATE	TRANSACTION TYPE	NUM	NAME	MEMO/DESCRIPTION	ACCOUNT #	ACCOUNT	DEBIT	CREDIT
01/02/2018	Bill Payment (Check)	1065	AmpleStore Inc.		101	101 Checking		$300.00
					201	201 Accounts Payable (A/P)	$300.00	
							$300.00	**$300.00**
01/02/2018	Bill Payment (Check)	1066	CloudZ Channel		101	101 Checking		$800.00
					201	201 Accounts Payable (A/P)	$800.00	
							$800.00	**$800.00**
01/02/2018	Bill Payment (Check)	1067	Conf/Call		101	101 Checking		$90.00
					201	201 Accounts Payable (A/P)	$90.00	
							$90.00	**$90.00**
01/04/2018	Check	1068	Best Cellular		101	101 Checking		$82.13
				Cell phone service	633	633 Telephone Expense	$82.13	
							$82.13	**$82.13**
01/04/2018	Check	1069	Valley News		101	101 Checking		$100.00
				Subscription	605	605 Dues & Subscriptions	$100.00	
							$100.00	**$100.00**
01/04/2018	Check	1070	County Telephone		101	101 Checking		$76.19
				Paid monthly bill	633	633 Telephone Expense	$76.19	
							$76.19	**$76.19**
01/04/2018	Check	1071	Office Suppliers		101	101 Checking		$88.52
				Supplies	621	621 Office Supplies	$88.52	
							$88.52	**$88.52**
01/04/2018	Check	1072	Cays Advertising		101	101 Checking		$125.00
					601	601 Advertising	$125.00	
							$125.00	**$125.00**
01/04/2018	Check	1073	RSP Gas		101	101 Checking		$90.14
				Paid monthly bill	635	635 Utilities	$90.14	
							$90.14	**$90.14**
01/04/2018	Check	1074	U.S. Post Office		101	101 Checking		$47.00
					627	627 Shipping and delivery expense	$47.00	
							$47.00	**$47.00**
01/04/2018	Check	1075	Albert Benson		101	101 Checking		$150.00
				Maintenance	625	625 Repair & Maintenance	$150.00	
							$150.00	**$150.00**
01/04/2018	Check	1076	Simon Rentals		101	101 Checking		$6,000.00
				Paid rent for 3 months	123	123 Prepaid Rent	$6,000.00	
							$6,000.00	**$6,000.00**
01/04/2018	Sales Receipt	1034	Credit Card Sales		101	101 Checking	$300.00	
				Data storage	115	115 Merchandise Inventory		$150.00
				Data storage	401	401 Sales		$300.00
				Data storage	501	501 Cost of Goods Sold	$150.00	
							$450.00	**$450.00**
01/04/2018	Sales Receipt	1035	Credit Card Sales		101	101 Checking	$1,200.00	

1/4

DATE	TRANSACTION TYPE	NUM	NAME	MEMO/DESCRIPTION	ACCOUNT #	ACCOUNT	DEBIT	CREDIT
				Web server	115	115 Merchandise Inventory		$600.00
				Web server	501	501 Cost of Goods Sold	$600.00	
				Web server	401	401 Sales		$1,200.00
							$1,800.00	**$1,800.00**
01/04/2018	Sales Receipt	1036	Credit Card Sales		101	101 Checking	$2,000.00	
				Computers	501	501 Cost of Goods Sold	$1,000.00	
				Computers	115	115 Merchandise Inventory		$1,000.00
				Computers	401	401 Sales		$2,000.00
							$3,000.00	**$3,000.00**
01/05/2018	Payment	8447	Springfield Unified School District		101	101 Checking	$400.00	
					105	105 Accounts Receivable (A/R)		$400.00
							$400.00	**$400.00**
01/08/2018	Bill	CZ155	CloudZ Channel		201	201 Accounts Payable (A/P)		$800.00
				Web server	115	115 Merchandise Inventory	$800.00	
							$800.00	**$800.00**
01/08/2018	Bill	210C2U	Computers 2 You		201	201 Accounts Payable (A/P)		$1,500.00
				Computers	115	115 Merchandise Inventory	$1,500.00	
							$1,500.00	**$1,500.00**
01/09/2018	Bill Payment (Check)	1077	AmpleStore Inc.		101	101 Checking		$180.00
					201	201 Accounts Payable (A/P)	$180.00	
							$180.00	**$180.00**
01/09/2018	Bill Payment (Check)	1078	Any Time Deployment		101	101 Checking		$250.00
					201	201 Accounts Payable (A/P)	$250.00	
							$250.00	**$250.00**
01/09/2018	Bill Payment (Check)	1079	Computers 2 You		101	101 Checking		$1,500.00
					201	201 Accounts Payable (A/P)	$1,500.00	
							$1,500.00	**$1,500.00**
01/10/2018	Bill	AS144	AmpleStore Inc.		201	201 Accounts Payable (A/P)		$210.00
				Data storage	115	115 Merchandise Inventory	$210.00	
							$210.00	**$210.00**
01/17/2018	Sales Receipt	1037	Credit Card Sales		101	101 Checking	$380.00	
				Data storage	115	115 Merchandise Inventory		$90.00
				Data storage	401	401 Sales		$180.00
				Data storage	501	501 Cost of Goods Sold	$90.00	
				Network products	501	501 Cost of Goods Sold	$100.00	
				Network products	115	115 Merchandise Inventory		$100.00
				Network products	401	401 Sales		$200.00
							$570.00	**$570.00**
01/17/2018	Sales Receipt	1038	Credit Card Sales		101	101 Checking	$1,000.00	
				Network products	501	501 Cost of Goods Sold	$50.00	
				Network products	115	115 Merchandise Inventory		$50.00
				Network products	501	501 Cost of Goods Sold	$50.00	
				Network products	401	401 Sales		$200.00
				Network products	115	115 Merchandise Inventory		$50.00
				Web server	115	115 Merchandise Inventory		$400.00
				Web server	401	401 Sales		$800.00
				Web server	501	501 Cost of Goods Sold	$400.00	

2/4

DATE	TRANSACTION TYPE	NUM	NAME	MEMO/DESCRIPTION	ACCOUNT #	ACCOUNT	DEBIT	CREDIT
							$1,500.00	**$1,500.00**
01/17/2018	Sales Receipt	1039	Credit Card Sales		101	101 Checking	$1,180.00	
				Computers	401	401 Sales		$1,000.00
				Computers	115	115 Merchandise Inventory		$500.00
				Computers	501	501 Cost of Goods Sold	$500.00	
				Webinars	115	115 Merchandise Inventory		$90.00
				Webinars	501	501 Cost of Goods Sold	$90.00	
				Webinars	401	401 Sales		$180.00
							$1,770.00	**$1,770.00**
01/18/2018	Bill	ATD510	Any Time Deployment		201	201 Accounts Payable (A/P)		$500.00
				Network products	115	115 Merchandise Inventory	$500.00	
							$500.00	**$500.00**
01/19/2018	Bill	CZ333	CloudZ Channel		201	201 Accounts Payable (A/P)		$800.00
				Web server	115	115 Merchandise Inventory	$800.00	
							$800.00	**$800.00**
01/23/2018	Invoice	1040	eBiz		105	105 Accounts Receivable (A/R)	$180.00	
				Data storage	115	115 Merchandise Inventory		$45.00
				Data storage	401	401 Sales		$180.00
				Data storage	501	501 Cost of Goods Sold	$45.00	
				Data storage	115	115 Merchandise Inventory		$45.00
				Data storage	501	501 Cost of Goods Sold	$45.00	
							$270.00	**$270.00**
01/23/2018	Bill	246CC	Conf/Call		201	201 Accounts Payable (A/P)		$270.00
				Webinars	115	115 Merchandise Inventory	$270.00	
							$270.00	**$270.00**
01/23/2018	Invoice	1041	Law Offices of Williamson, Gallagher & Katz		105	105 Accounts Receivable (A/R)	$300.00	
				Network products	401	401 Sales		$300.00
				Network products	115	115 Merchandise Inventory		$150.00
				Network products	501	501 Cost of Goods Sold	$150.00	
							$450.00	**$450.00**
01/23/2018	Invoice	1042	Permanente Medical Services		105	105 Accounts Receivable (A/R)	$270.00	
				Webinars	115	115 Merchandise Inventory		$135.00
				Webinars	501	501 Cost of Goods Sold	$135.00	
				Webinars	401	401 Sales		$270.00
							$405.00	**$405.00**
01/23/2018	Bill	AS352	AmpleStore Inc.		201	201 Accounts Payable (A/P)		$180.00
				Data storage	115	115 Merchandise Inventory	$180.00	
							$180.00	**$180.00**
01/25/2018	Invoice	1043	WebPro		105	105 Accounts Receivable (A/R)	$400.00	
				Web server	401	401 Sales		$400.00
				Web server	501	501 Cost of Goods Sold	$200.00	
				Web server	115	115 Merchandise Inventory		$200.00
							$600.00	**$600.00**
01/30/2018	Bill	422C2U	Computers 2 You		201	201 Accounts Payable (A/P)		$1,500.00
				Computers	115	115 Merchandise Inventory	$1,500.00	
							$1,500.00	**$1,500.00**

3/4

DATE	TRANSACTION TYPE	NUM	NAME	MEMO/DESCRIPTION	ACCOUNT #	ACCOUNT	DEBIT	CREDIT
01/30/2018	Bill	ATD592	Any Time Deployment		201	201 Accounts Payable (A/P)		$250.00
				Network products	115	115 Merchandise Inventory	$250.00	
							$250.00	**$250.00**
01/30/2018	Invoice	1044	Springfield Unified School District		105	105 Accounts Receivable (A/R)	$400.00	
				Web server	501	501 Cost of Goods Sold	$200.00	
				Web server	401	401 Sales		$400.00
				Web server	115	115 Merchandise Inventory		$200.00
							$600.00	**$600.00**
01/30/2018	Sales Receipt	1045	Cash Sales		101	101 Checking	$1,000.00	
				Computers	501	501 Cost of Goods Sold	$500.00	
				Computers	115	115 Merchandise Inventory		$500.00
				Computers	401	401 Sales		$1,000.00
							$1,500.00	**$1,500.00**
01/30/2018	Bill Payment (Check)	1080	AmpleStore Inc.		101	101 Checking		$210.00
					201	201 Accounts Payable (A/P)	$210.00	
							$210.00	**$210.00**
01/30/2018	Bill Payment (Check)	1081	CloudZ Channel		101	101 Checking		$800.00
					201	201 Accounts Payable (A/P)	$800.00	
							$800.00	**$800.00**
01/30/2018	Bill Payment (Check)	1082	Computers 2 You		101	101 Checking		$1,500.00
					201	201 Accounts Payable (A/P)	$1,500.00	
							$1,500.00	**$1,500.00**
TOTAL							**$31,713.98**	**$31,713.98**

4/4

➢ Export the Journal to Excel and save as a PDF file. Use the file name, **Chapter 8_Journal**.

2. Trial Balance: 1/1/20XY to 1/30/20XY

QB Cloud_Student Name

TRIAL BALANCE

As of January 30, 2018

	DEBIT	CREDIT
101 Checking	48,564.54	
105 Accounts Receivable (A/R)	1,550.00	
115 Merchandise Inventory	11,575.00	
123 Prepaid Rent	6,000.00	
125 Prepaid Insurance	2,250.00	
130 Undeposited Funds	0.00	
135 Computer Equipment	10,000.00	
137 Accumulated Depreciation		800.00
201 Accounts Payable (A/P)		3,500.00
205 Loan Payable		5,000.00
301 Common Stock		60,000.00
305 Opening Balance Equity		0.00
318 Retained Earnings		7,093.52
401 Sales		8,610.00
501 Cost of Goods Sold	4,305.00	
601 Advertising	125.00	
605 Dues & Subscriptions	100.00	
621 Office Supplies	88.52	
625 Repair & Maintenance	150.00	
627 Shipping and delivery expense	47.00	
633 Telephone Expense	158.32	
635 Utilities	90.14	
TOTAL	$85,003.52	$85,003.52

➢ Export the Trial Balance to Excel and save as a PDF file. Use the file name, **Chapter 8_Trial Balance**.

3. **A/R Aging Summary:** As of 1/30/20XY

QB Cloud_Student Name

A/R AGING SUMMARY

As of January 30, 2018

	CURRENT	1 - 30	31 - 60	61 - 90	91 AND OVER	TOTAL
eBiz	180.00					$180.00
Law Offices of Williamson, Gallagher & Katz	300.00					$300.00
Permanente Medical Services	270.00					$270.00
Springfield Unified School District	400.00					$400.00
WebPro	400.00					$400.00
TOTAL	**$1,550.00**	**$0.00**	**$0.00**	**$0.00**	**$0.00**	**$1,550.00**

- Export the A/R Aging Summary to Excel and save as a PDF file. Use the file name, **Chapter 8_AR Aging Summary.**

4. **Inventory Valuation Summary**: As of 1/30/20XY

QB Cloud_Student Name

INVENTORY VALUATION SUMMARY

As of January 30, 2018

	SKU	QTY	ASSET VALUE	CALC. AVG
Computers		13.00	6,500.00	500.00
Data storage		55.00	825.00	15.00
Network products		32.00	800.00	25.00
Web server		15.00	3,000.00	200.00
Webinars		10.00	450.00	45.00
TOTAL			**$11,575.00**	

- Export to Excel and save as a PDF file. Use the file name **Chapter 8_Inventory Valuation Summary.**

5. **A/P Aging Summary**: As of 1/30/20XY

QB Cloud_Student Name

A/P AGING SUMMARY

As of January 30, 2018

	CURRENT	1 - 30	31 - 60	61 - 90	91 AND OVER	TOTAL
AmpleStore Inc.	180.00					$180.00
Any Time Deployment	750.00					$750.00
CloudZ Channel	800.00					$800.00
Computers 2 You	1,500.00					$1,500.00
Conf/Call	270.00					$270.00
TOTAL	$3,500.00	$0.00	$0.00	$0.00	$0.00	$3,500.00

- Export to Excel and save as a PDF file. Use the file name **Chapter 8_AP Aging Summary.**

6. **Profit and Loss** from 1/1/20XY to 1/30/20XY

QB Cloud_Student Name

PROFIT AND LOSS

January 1-30, 2018

	TOTAL
INCOME	
401 Sales	8,610.00
Total Income	$8,610.00
COST OF GOODS SOLD	
501 Cost of Goods Sold	4,305.00
Total Cost of Goods Sold	$4,305.00
GROSS PROFIT	$4,305.00
EXPENSES	
601 Advertising	125.00
605 Dues & Subscriptions	100.00
621 Office Supplies	88.52
625 Repair & Maintenance	150.00
627 Shipping and delivery expense	47.00
633 Telephone Expense	158.32
635 Utilities	90.14
Total Expenses	$758.98
NET OPERATING INCOME	$3,546.02
NET INCOME	$3,546.02

- Export the Profit and Loss to Excel and save as a PDF file. Use the file name **Chapter 8_Profit and Loss**.

7. **Balance Sheet** from 1/1/20XY to 1/30/20XY

QB Cloud_Student Name

BALANCE SHEET

As of January 30, 2018

	TOTAL
ASSETS	
Current Assets	
Bank Accounts	
101 Checking	48,564.54
Total Bank Accounts	**$48,564.54**
Accounts Receivable	
105 Accounts Receivable (A/R)	1,550.00
Total Accounts Receivable	**$1,550.00**
Other Current Assets	
115 Merchandise Inventory	11,575.00
123 Prepaid Rent	6,000.00
125 Prepaid Insurance	2,250.00
130 Undeposited Funds	0.00
Total Other Current Assets	**$19,825.00**
Total Current Assets	**$69,939.54**
Fixed Assets	
135 Computer Equipment	10,000.00
137 Accumulated Depreciation	-800.00
Total Fixed Assets	**$9,200.00**
TOTAL ASSETS	**$79,139.54**

LIABILITIES AND EQUITY	
Liabilities	
Current Liabilities	
Accounts Payable	
201 Accounts Payable (A/P)	3,500.00
Total Accounts Payable	$3,500.00
Other Current Liabilities	
205 Loan Payable	5,000.00
Total Other Current Liabilities	$5,000.00
Total Current Liabilities	$8,500.00
Total Liabilities	$8,500.00
Equity	
301 Common Stock	60,000.00
305 Opening Balance Equity	
318 Retained Earnings	7,093.52
Net Income	3,546.02
Total Equity	$70,639.54
TOTAL LIABILITIES AND EQUITY	$79,139.54

- Export the Balance Sheet to Excel and save as a PDF file. Use the file name **Chapter 8_Balance Sheet**.

8. **Statement of Cash Flows** from 1/1/20XY to 1/30/20XY

QB Cloud_Student Name

STATEMENT OF CASH FLOWS

January 1-30, 2018

	TOTAL
OPERATING ACTIVITIES	
Net Income	3,546.02
Adjustments to reconcile Net Income to Net Cash provided by operations:	
105 Accounts Receivable (A/R)	-1,150.00
115 Merchandise Inventory	-1,705.00
123 Prepaid Rent	-6,000.00
201 Accounts Payable (A/P)	380.00
Total Adjustments to reconcile Net Income to Net Cash provided by operations:	**-8,475.00**
Net cash provided by operating activities	**$ -4,928.98**
NET CASH INCREASE FOR PERIOD	**$ -4,928.98**
CASH AT BEGINNING OF PERIOD	53,493.52
CASH AT END OF PERIOD	**$48,564.54**

- Export the Statement of Cash Flows to Excel and save as a PDF file. Use the file name **Chapter 8_Statement of Cash Flows.**

CHECK YOUR PROGRESS

1. What is the account balance from 1/1/20XY to 1/30/20XY in these accounts? Indicate whether these accounts have debit (dr.) or credit (cr.) balances.

   Account 101 Checking ____________________

   Account 105 Accounts Receivable ____________________

   Account 115 Merchandise Inventory ____________________

   Account 201 Accounts Payable ____________________

   Net Income ____________________

   Total Liabilities and Equity ____________________

2. What is the quantity, asset value, and average cost of computers?

   ____

3. What is the quantity, asset value, and average cost of data storage?

   ____

4. What is the quantity, asset value, and average cost of network products?

   ____

5. What is the quantity, asset value, and average cost of web servers?

___

6. What is the quantity, asset value, and average cost of webinars?

___

SIGN OUT

To sign out of QBO, go to the company settings (click on the company name), link to Sign Out. *Or,* continue.

ONLINE LEARNING CENTER (OLC): www.mhhe.com/qbo2e

The OLC includes additional Chapter 8 resources. Go online to www.mhhe.com/qbo2e > Student Edition > Chapter 8.

1. Narrated PowerPoints.
2. Online quizzes: 10 True or False and 10 multiple-choice questions. The Online quizzes are graded and can emailed to your instructor.
3. Analysis questions: Answer the analysis questions, then email to your instructor.
4. Going to the Net

    a. Go to the QuickBooks Online support website at https://community.intuit.com/quickbooks-online. In the Ask a question field, type **Take quick action on vendor transactions** > Search > link to Take quick action on vendor transactions.

b. How do you take quick action on vendor transactions?
c. Go back to the QuickBooks Online support website. (*Hint:* Click on the back arrow twice.) Link to related information. In the Ask a question field, type **How do I turn on Billable Expenses** > Search.
d. How do you use the Use Billable Expenses preferences? How does this affect tracking expenses and items by customer?

5. Videos: Go to Prof. Susan Crosson's Financial Accounting videos at http://www.bus.emory.edu/scrosso/FA%20Videos.htm. To review financial accounting principles and procedures, watch videos.
6. Glossary of terms: Words that are italicized and boldfaced are defined in the glossary. The Glossary is also Appendix B.
7. Problem Solving link includes Exercise 8-3.

Exercise 8-1: Follow the instructions below to complete Exercise 8-1:

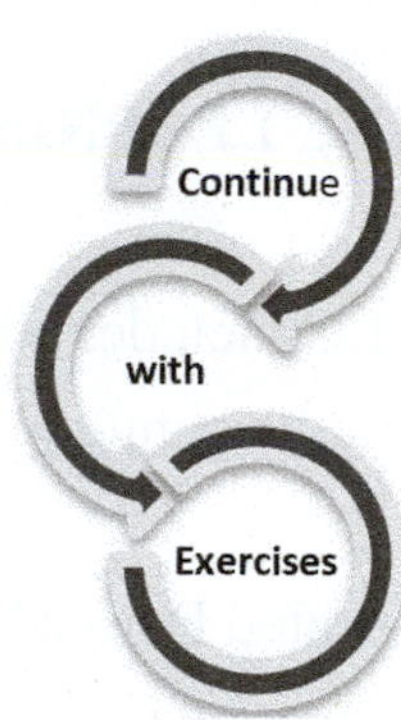

1. Start QBO. Sign into QB Cloud_Student Name.
2. To reconcile Account 101 Checking, use the January 31 bank statement on the next two pages.

Statement of Account Checking Account January 1 to January 31, 20XY		Account No. 7731-2256	QB Cloud_Student Name Your address Your city, state, Zip
REGULAR CHECKING			
Previous Balance	12/31/XX	$ 53,493.52	
8 Deposits (+)		7,460.00	
18 checks (-)		12,388.98	
Other Deductions (-)		0.00	
Service Charge		20.00	
Ending Balance	1/31/XY	**$48,544.54**	

DEPOSITS				
		1/5/XY	300.00	
		1/5/XY	1,200.00	
		1/5/XY	2,000.00	
		1/7/XY	400.00	
		1/17/XY	380.00	
		1/17/XY	1,000.00	
		1/17/XY	1,180.00	
		1/30/XY	1,000.00	
CHECKS (Asterisk * indicates break in check number sequence)				
	1/3/XY	1065	300.00	
	1/3/XY	1066	800.00	
	1/3/XY	1067	90.00	
	1/10/XY	1068	82.13	
	1/10/XY	1069	100.00	
	1/10/XY	1070	76.19	
	1/10/XY	1071	88.52	
	1/10/XY	1072	125.00	*Continued*

	1/10/XY	1073	90.14	
	1/10/XY	1074	47.00	
	1/10/XY	1075	150.00	
	1/12/XY	1076	6,000.00	
	1/12/XY	1077	180.00	
	1/12/XY	1078	250.00	
	1/31/XY	1079	1,500.00	
	1/31/XY	1080	210.00	
	1/31/XY	1081	800.00	
	1/31/XY	1082	1,500.00	

3. Print the Reconciliation Report. Save as a PDF file. Use the file name **Exercise 8-1_Reconciliation Report**.

Exercise 8-2: Follow the instructions below to complete Exercise 8-2:

1. Export to Excel and save as PDF files. Run reports from **1/1/20XY to 1/31/20XY** unless another date range is shown. (*Hint:* When the report needs an As of date, use 1/31/20XY)

   - Exercise 8-2_Journal (from 1/31/20XY to 1/31/20XY)
   - Exercise 8-2_Transaction Detail by Account
   - Exercise 8-2_General Ledger
   - Exercise 8-2_Customer Balance Summary
   - Exercise 8-2_Vendor Balance Summary
   - Exercise 8-2_Trial Balance
   - Exercise 8-2_Profit and Loss
   - Exercise 8-2_Balance Sheet
   - Exercise 8-2_Statement of Cash Flows

2. **Check Your Figures** (from 1/1/201XY to 1/31/XY):

    - Account 101 Checking, $48,544.54
    - Account 105 Accounts Receivable, $1,550.00
    - Account 115 Merchandise Inventory, $11,575.00
    - Account 123 Prepaid Rent, $6,000.00
    - Account 201 Accounts Payable, $3,500.00
    - Account 401 Sales, $8,610.00
    - Account 501, Cost of Goods Sold, $4,305.00
    - Account 621 Office Supplies, $88.52
    - Total Liabilities and Equity, $79,119.54
    - Net Income, $3,526.02
    - Net cash increase (or decrease) for period, $-4,948.98

Exercise 8-3

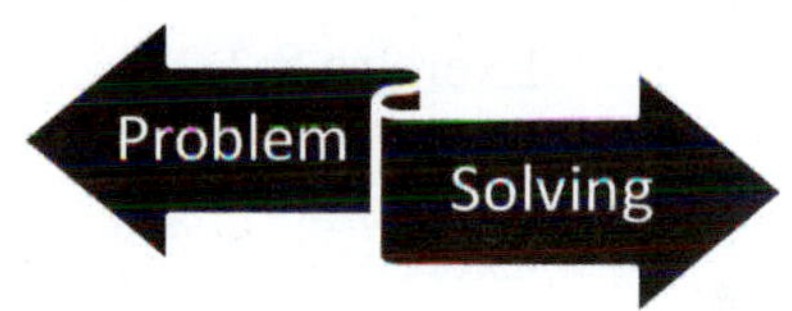

The Online Learning Center includes Exercise 9-3 at www.mhhe.com/qbo2e > Student Edition > Chapter 8 > Problem Solving.

Describe the difference between a Bill and Invoice. Include an example, which QBO module is being used, and the account distribution for a bill and an invoice.

CHAPTER 8 INDEX

Chapter 9 February Source Documents

Scenario: In Chapter 9, start by checking your data with the January 31 Trial Balance. The stop sign reminds you to make sure your debit and credit balances are correct. In Chapter 9, you analyze typical source documents used by businesses. Memos remind you to make customer payments and vendor payments, sales receipts show cash and credit card sales, bills are used for recording purchases on account, and invoices are used for sales on account. You also display reports and complete financial statements. To review what you will do in Chapter 9, read the objectives.

OBJECTIVES

1. Start QuickBooks Online and sign in to QB Cloud_Student Name.
2. To check data, display the January 31 Trial Balance.
3. Analyze source documents.
4. Record vendor, customer, cash, and credit card transactions.
5. Export reports to Excel and save as PDF files.
6. Complete Check Your Progress.
7. Go to the Online Learning Center at www.mhhe.com/qbo2e for additional resources.
8. Complete Exercises 9-1, 9-2 and 9-3.

In Chapter 9, you complete business processes for QB Cloud_Student Name. QB Cloud sells computers, data storage, network products, web servers, and webinars. QB Cloud also purchases products from vendors.

The purpose of Chapter 9 is to review what you have learned in the previous chapters. In this chapter, you analyze source documents, then record transactions. The documents shown trigger transaction analysis for accounts payable (vendors), inventory, accounts receivable (customers), cash and credit card sales. You also use a bank statement to reconcile Account 101 Checking.

The source documents that you analyze include:

- Vendor bills for purchasing inventory.
- Memos include customer payments, vendor payments and remittances.
- Transaction register for issuing checks for expenses and recording ATM withdrawals.
- Sales invoices for credit customers.
- Sales receipts for cash and credit card sales.

GETTING STARTED

1. Start your browser. Go online to http://qbo.intuit.com.
2. Sign in to QuickBooks Online with your User ID and Password.

CHECK YOUR DATA

To make sure you are starting in the correct place, display the 1/1/20XY to 1/31/20XY Trial Balance. This trial balance was also completed in Exercise 8-2.

Check the January 31 trial balance *before* recording February transactions. The trial balance on the next page shows non-zero amounts only.

QB Cloud_Student Name

TRIAL BALANCE

As of January 31, 2018

	DEBIT	CREDIT
101 Checking	48,544.54	
105 Accounts Receivable (A/R)	1,550.00	
115 Merchandise Inventory	11,575.00	
123 Prepaid Rent	6,000.00	
125 Prepaid Insurance	2,250.00	
135 Computer Equipment	10,000.00	
137 Accumulated Depreciation		800.00
201 Accounts Payable (A/P)		3,500.00
205 Loan Payable		5,000.00
301 Common Stock		60,000.00
318 Retained Earnings		7,093.52
401 Sales		8,610.00
501 Cost of Goods Sold	4,305.00	
601 Advertising	125.00	
603 Bank Charges	20.00	
605 Dues & Subscriptions	100.00	
621 Office Supplies	88.52	
625 Repair & Maintenance	150.00	
627 Shipping and delivery expense	47.00	
633 Telephone Expense	158.32	
635 Utilities	90.14	
TOTAL	**$85,003.52**	**$85,003.52**

The trial balance shows non-zero or active accounts only.

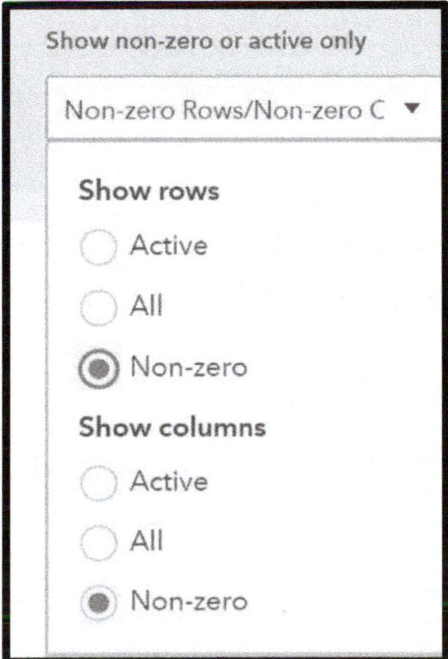

FEBRUARY SOURCE DOCUMENTS

QB Cloud_Student Name

Memo

Date: 2/2

Re: Credit Card Receipts

The bank sent verification of credit card receipts in the amount of $3,900.00. Refer to the sales receipts on the next three pages for the products sold and credit cards used.

Checking Account Bank Statement		Checks	Credit Card	Amount
Date: February 5		1	American Express	$1,450.00
List of Deposits:		2	MasterCard	$1,150.00
Coin	Totals	3	Visa	$1,300.00
Quarters:	$	4		
Dimes:	$	5		
Nickels:	$	6		
Pennies	$			
Total				
Cash	Totals			
$1	$			
$5	$			
$10	$			
$20	$			
$50	$			
$100	$			
Total	$		Totals	$3,900.00
Total Cash			Total Deposit	$3,900.00

SALES RECEIPT

QB Cloud_Student Name

Date: 2/2
RECEIPT # 1046
For: **Credit Card**

Payment Method	Type
CREDIT CARD	American Express

Qty	Description	Rate	Amount
15	Data storage	$30.00	$450.00
1	Computer	$1,000.00	1,000.00
		Subtotal	1,450.00
		Total	$1,450.00

Thank you for your business!

Analyze source document → **Enter date** → **Input transaction**

SALES RECEIPT

QB Cloud_Student Name

Date: 2/2
RECEIPT # 1047
For: **CREDIT CARD**

Payment Method	Type
CREDIT CARD	MasterCard

Qty	Description	Rate	Amount
7	Network products	$50.00	$350.00
2	Web server	400.00	800.00
		Subtotal	1,150.00
		Total	$1,150.00

Thank you for your business!

SALES RECEIPT

QB Cloud_Student Name

Date: 2/2
RECEIPT # 1048
For: **CREDIT CARD**

Payment Method	Type
CREDIT CARD	Visa

Qty	Description	Rate	Amount
1	Computer	$1,000.00	$1,000.00
6	Network products	50.00	300.00
		Subtotal	1,300.00
		Total	$1,300.00

Thank you for your business!

Transaction Register

Check No.	Date	Description of Transaction	Debit (-)	Credit (+)	Balance
	2/2	*Balance*			$52,444.54
1083	2/5	Office Suppliers	91.20		52,353,34
1084	2/5	Cays Advertising	150.00		52,203.34
1085	2/5	County Telephone	76.19		52,127.15
1086	2/5	Best Cellular	82.13		52,045.02
1087	2/6	Journal of Accounting	75.00		51,970.02
1088	2/6	RSP Gas	195.89		51,774.13
ATM	2/7	Cottage Restaurant	55.22		51,718.91
1089	2/7	Albert Benson	150.00		51,568.91
1090	2/7	Hour Deliveries	95.97		51,472.94
1091	2/7	Loan Payable*	5,000.00		46,322.94
		Interest Expense	150.00		

*In Chapter 3, Account 205 Loan Payable was recorded as a transfer of funds. Add the Payee First Trust Bank as a vendor.

Troubleshooting: How can I check that the date and year used for entering transactions is correct? To display recent transactions, click . The Recent Transactions page appears, and each recently recorded transaction is shown. Check the dates and year. To see more transactions, select View more.

From the Recent Transactions window, you can drill down to the original entry. Make any needed changes, then save.

Observe that when you go to the Dashboard, the balance in Account 101 Checking is the same as 2/7 balance in the Transaction Register.

101 Checking
In QuickBooks $46,322.94

BILL #: CZ403 **DATE: 2/7**

Customer: QB Cloud_ Student Name

CloudZ Channel
110 Merit Street
Menlo Park, CA 94025
650-555-3250

Date	Quantity	Description	Unit Price	Amount
2/7	5	Web server	$200.00	$1,000.00

Remittance

Bill #	CZ403
Date	2/7
Amount Due	$1,000.00

Thank you for your business!

Make all checks payable to CloudZ Channel.

Hint: If a prefill this bill pop-up message appears, click <No>. If necessary, click on the down-arrow next to Item details so that the Product/Service field appears.

Sales Invoice

TO:

eBiz
800 W. Second Ave.
Durango, CO 81301
(970) 555-2000

SHIP TO: SAME

Date	Invoice Number	Payment Terms	Due Date
2/7	1049	Net 30	3/9

Qty	Product	Description	Rate	Amount
6	Data storage	Data storage	$30.00	$180.00

Make all checks payable to QB Cloud_Student Name

Thank you for your business!

Bill: AS401

AmpleStore Inc.

Bill To: QB Cloud_Student Name

Date	Quantity	Description	Unit Price	Amount
2/9	20	Data storage	$15.00	$300.00

Remittance

Bill #	AS401
Date	2/9
Amount Due	$300.00

AmpleStore Inc. 200 West Concord Ave. Palo Alto, CA 94301
(650) 555-8527

QB Cloud_Student Name

Memo

Date: 2/15

Re: Vendor Payments

QB Cloud_Student Name pays the following vendors:

Vendor ID	Bill #	Check No.	Amount
AmpleStore	AS352	1092	$180.00
Any Time Deployment	ATD510	1093	$500.00
CloudZ Channel	CZ333	1094	$800.00
Conf/Call	246CC	1095	$270.00

REMITTANCE	
Bill #	AS352
Customer ID	QB Cloud_Student Name
Date	2/15
Amount Enclosed	$180.00
	AmpleStore Inc. 200 West Concord Ave. Palo Alto, CA 94301 650-555-8527

REMITTANCE	
Bill #	ATD510
Customer ID	QB Cloud_Student Name
Date	2/15
Amount Enclosed	$500.00
	Any Time Deployment 1189 W. Burnside Lexington, MA 02421 781-555-4671

REMITTANCE	
Bill #	CZ333
Customer ID	QB Cloud_Student Name
Date	2/15
Amount Enclosed	$800.00
	CloudZ Channel 110 Merit Street Menlo Park, CA 94025 650-555-3250

REMITTANCE	
Bill #	246CC
Customer ID	QB Cloud_Student Name
Date	2/15
Amount Enclosed	$270.00
	Conf/Call 700 North Prince Street Tempe, AZ 85008 (480) 555-2411

Bill: 275CC

Conf/Call
700 North Prince Street
Tempe, AZ 85008 USA
480-555-2411

Bill to: QB Cloud_
Student Name

Date	Quantity	Description	Unit Price	Amount
2/18	3	Webinars	$45	$135.00

Remittance

Bill #	275CC
Date	2/18
Amount Due	$135.00

Make all checks payable to Conf/Call.
Thank you for your business!

Sales Invoice

TO: Law Offices of Williamson,
Gallagher & Katz
18 Piedmont Ave. NW
Atlanta, GA 30303
(404) 555-8134

SHIP TO: SAME

Date	Invoice Number	Payment Terms	Due Date
2/18	1050	Net 30	3/20

Qty	Product	Description	Rate	Amount
6	Network Products	Network products	$50.00	$300.00

Make all checks payable to QB Cloud_Student Name

Thank you for your business!

Sales Invoice

TO: **Permanente Medical Services**
18771 Ala Moana Blvd.
Honolulu, HI 96815
(808) 555-555-9000

SHIP TO: **SAME**

Date	Invoice Number	Payment Terms	Due Date
2/18	1051	Net 30	3/20

Qty	Product	Description	Rate	Amount
3	Webinars	Webinars	$90	$270.00

Make all checks payable to QB Cloud_Student Name

Thank you for your business!

Bill: AS423

AmpleStore Inc.

Bill to: QB Cloud_
Student Name

Date	Quantity	Description	Unit Price	Amount
2/20	12	Data storage	$15.00	$180.00

Remittance

Bill #	AS423
Date	2/20
Amount Due	$180.00

AmpleStore Inc. 200 West Concord Ave. Palo Alto, CA 94301
(650) 555-8527

Sales Invoice

TO:	WebPro 18 Alameda Road Santa Fe, NM 87501 (505) 555-5311	SHIP TO: SAME

Date	Invoice Number	Payment Terms	Due Date
2/20	1052	Net 30	3/22

Qty	Product	Description	Rate	Amount
1	Web server	Web server	$400.00	$400.00

Make all checks payable to QB Cloud_Student Name

Thank you for your business!

QB Cloud_Student Name

Memo

Date: 2/20

Re: Customer Payments

QB Cloud_Student Name received the following customer payments.

1. Received payment from eBiz, Invoice 1040, $180, customer check 10321.
2. Received payment from the Law Offices of Williamson, Gallagher, & Katz, Invoice 1041, $300, customer check 5730.
3. Received payment from Permanente Medical Services, Invoice 1042, $270, customer check 1588.
4. Received payment from Springfield Unified School District, Invoice 1044, $400, Check 9213.
5. Received payment from WebPro Invoice 1043, $400, customer check 802.

Date:

2/25 **BILL #: 492C2U**

Computers 2 You
2006 East 14 Avenue
Los Angeles, CA 90046
(213) 555-2300

BILL TO:

QB Cloud_
Student Name

quantity	description	Unit Price	amount
4	Computers	$500.00	$2,000.00

Remittance

Bill #	492C2U
Date	2/25
Amount Due	$2,000.00

Any Time Deployment
1189 W. Burnside
Lexington, MA 02421
(781) 555-4681

Bill Number: ATD645

Date: 2/25

Ship to: QB Cloud_Student Name

SHIPPED VIA	TERMS
UPS	Net 30

QTY	DESCRIPTION	UNIT PRICE	TOTAL
10	Network products	25.00	$250.00
		SUBTOTAL	$250.00
		TOTAL	$250.00

Remittance

Bill #	ATD645
Date	2/25
Amount Due	$250.00

Sales Invoice

TO:	Springfield Unified School District 4892 Clear Lake Ave. Springfield, IL 62703 (217) 555-555-5500	SHIP TO:	SAME

Date	Invoice Number	Payment Terms	Due Date
2/25	1053	Net 30	3/27

Qty	Product	Description	Rate	Amount
1	Web server	Web server	$400.00	$400.00

Make all checks payable to QB Cloud_Student Name

Thank you for your business!

SALES RECEIPT

QB Cloud_Student Name

Date: 2/25
RECEIPT # 1054
For: **Cash Sales**

Payment Method	Type
Check 406	Cash sales

Qty	Description	Rate	Amount
1	Computer	$1,000.00	$1,000.00
		Subtotal	$1,000.00
		Total	$1,000.00

Thank you for your business!

QB Cloud_Student Name

Memo

Date: 2/27

Re: Credit Card Receipts

The bank sent verification of credit card receipts in the amount of $2,730.00. Refer to the sales receipts on the next three pages for the products sold and credit cards used.

Checking Account Bank Statement		Checks	Credit Card	Amount
Date: February 5		1	American Express	$2,150.00
List of Deposits:		2	MasterCard	150.00
Coin	**Totals**	3	Visa	430.00
Quarters:	$	4		
Dimes:	$	5		
Nickels:	$	6		
Pennies	$			
Total				
Cash	**Totals**			
$1	$			
$5	$			
$10	$			
$20	$			
$50	$			
$100	$			
Total	$		**Totals**	$2,730.00
Total Cash			**Total Deposit**	$2,730.00

Hint: On the Sales Receipts page, select the appropriate credit card.

SALES RECEIPT

QB Cloud_Student Name

Date: 2/27
RECEIPT #1055
For: **CREDIT CARD**

Payment Method	Type
CREDIT CARD	American Express

Qty	Description	Rate	Amount
5	Data storage	$30.00	$150.00
2	Computer	$1,000.00	$2,000.00
		Subtotal	$2,150.00
		Total	$2,150.00

Thank you for your business!

SALES RECEIPT

QB Cloud_Student Name

Date: 2/27
RECEIPT #1056
For: **CREDIT CARD**

Payment Method	Type
CREDIT CARD	MasterCard

Qty	Description	Rate	Amount
3	Network products	$50.00	$150.00
		Subtotal	$150.00
		Total	$150.00

Thank you for your business!

SALES RECEIPT

QB Cloud_Student Name

Date: 2/27
RECEIPT #1057
For: **CREDIT CARD**

Payment Method	Type
CREDIT CARD	Visa

Qty	Description	Rate	Amount
5	Data storage	$30.00	$150.00
2	Network products	$50.00	$100.00
2	Webinars	$90.00	180.00
		Subtotal	$430.00
		Total	$430.00

Thank you for your business!

QB Cloud_Student Name

Memo

Date: 2/27

Re: Vendor Payments

QB Cloud_Student Name pays the following vendors:

Vendor ID	Bill #	Check No.	Amount
Any Time Deployment	ATD592	1096	$250.00
Computers 2 You	422C2U	1097	$1,500.00

REMITTANCE	
Bill #	ATD592
Customer ID	QB Cloud_Student Name
Date	2/27
Amount Enclosed	$250.00
	Any Time Deployment 1189 W. Burnside Lexington, MA 02421 (781) 555-4781

REMITTANCE	
Bill #	422C2U
Customer ID	QB Cloud_Student Name
Date	2/27
Amount Enclosed	$1,500.00
	Computers 2 You 2006 East 14 Avenue Los Angeles, CA 90046 213-555-2300

Bill: 385CC

Conf/Call
700 North Prince Street
Tempe, AZ 85008 USA
480-555-2411

Bill to: QB Cloud_
Student Name

Date	Quantity	Description	Unit Price	Amount
2/27	6	Webinars	$45	$270

Remittance

Bill #	385CC
Date	2/27
Amount Due	$270

Make all checks payable to Conf/Call.
Thank you for your business!

REPORTS

1. Journal: 2/1/20XY thru 2/27/20XY, page 1 of 4

QB Cloud_Student Name

JOURNAL

February 1-27, 2018

DATE	TRANSACTION TYPE	NUM	NAME	MEMO/DESCRIPTION	ACCOUNT #	ACCOUNT	DEBIT	CREDIT
02/02/2018	Sales Receipt	1046	Credit Card Sales		101	101 Checking	$1,450.00	
				Data storage	115	115 Merchandise Inventory		$225.00
				Data storage	501	501 Cost of Goods Sold	$225.00	
				Data storage	401	401 Sales		$450.00
				Computers	115	115 Merchandise Inventory		$500.00
				Computers	501	501 Cost of Goods Sold	$500.00	
				Computers	401	401 Sales		$1,000.00
							$2,175.00	**$2,175.00**
02/02/2018	Sales Receipt	1047	Credit Card Sales		101	101 Checking	$1,150.00	
				Network products	115	115 Merchandise Inventory		$125.00
				Network products	115	115 Merchandise Inventory		$50.00
				Network products	401	401 Sales		$350.00
				Network products	501	501 Cost of Goods Sold	$50.00	
				Network products	501	501 Cost of Goods Sold	$125.00	
				Web server	115	115 Merchandise Inventory		$400.00
				Web server	501	501 Cost of Goods Sold	$400.00	
				Web server	401	401 Sales		$800.00
							$1,725.00	**$1,725.00**
02/02/2018	Sales Receipt	1048	Credit Card Sales		101	101 Checking	$1,300.00	
				Computers	401	401 Sales		$1,000.00
				Computers	115	115 Merchandise Inventory		$500.00
				Computers	501	501 Cost of Goods Sold	$500.00	
				Network products	501	501 Cost of Goods Sold	$150.00	
				Network products	115	115 Merchandise Inventory		$150.00
				Network products	401	401 Sales		$300.00
							$1,950.00	**$1,950.00**
02/05/2018	Check	1083	Office Suppliers		101	101 Checking		$91.20
					621	621 Office Supplies	$91.20	
							$91.20	**$91.20**
02/05/2018	Check	1084	Cays Advertising		101	101 Checking		$150.00
					601	601 Advertising	$150.00	
							$150.00	**$150.00**
02/05/2018	Check	1085	County Telephone		101	101 Checking		$76.19
				paid monthly bill	633	633 Telephone Expense	$76.19	
							$76.19	**$76.19**
02/05/2018	Check	1086	Best Cellular		101	101 Checking		$82.13
				cellular service	633	633 Telephone Expense	$82.13	
							$82.13	**$82.13**
02/06/2018	Check	1087	Journal of Accounting		101	101 Checking		$75.00
				subscription	605	605 Dues & Subscriptions	$75.00	
							$75.00	**$75.00**
02/06/2018	Check	1088	RSP Gas		101	101 Checking		$195.89
				Paid utility bill	635	635 Utilities	$195.89	
							$195.89	**$195.89**
02/07/2018	Check	ATM	Cottage Restaurant		101	101 Checking		$55.22
				Meal with clients	619	619 Meals and Entertainment	$55.22	
							$55.22	**$55.22**
02/07/2018	Check	1089	Albert Benson		101	101 Checking		$150.00
				Repairs and maintenance	625	625 Repair & Maintenance	$150.00	
							$150.00	**$150.00**
02/07/2018	Check	1090	Hour Deliveries		101	101 Checking		$95.97
				Paid for delivery	609	609 Freight & Delivery	$95.97	
							$95.97	**$95.97**

Journal, page 2 of 4

DATE	TRANSACTION TYPE	NUM	NAME	MEMO/DESCRIPTION	ACCOUNT #	ACCOUNT	DEBIT	CREDIT
02/07/2018	Check	1091	First Trust Bank		101	101 Checking		$5,150.00
					205	205 Loan Payable	$5,000.00	
					613	613 Interest Expense	$150.00	
							$5,150.00	**$5,150.00**
02/07/2018	Bill	CZ403	CloudZ Channel		201	201 Accounts Payable (A/P)		$1,000.00
				Web server	115	115 Merchandise Inventory	$1,000.00	
							$1,000.00	**$1,000.00**
02/07/2018	Invoice	1049	eBiz		105	105 Accounts Receivable (A/R)	$180.00	
				Data storage	115	115 Merchandise Inventory		$60.00
				Data storage	501	501 Cost of Goods Sold	$30.00	
				Data storage	401	401 Sales		$180.00
				Data storage	115	115 Merchandise Inventory		$30.00
				Data storage	501	501 Cost of Goods Sold	$60.00	
							$270.00	**$270.00**
02/09/2018	Bill	AS401	AmpleStore Inc.		201	201 Accounts Payable (A/P)		$300.00
				Data storage	115	115 Merchandise Inventory	$300.00	
							$300.00	**$300.00**
02/15/2018	Bill Payment (Check)	1092	AmpleStore Inc.		101	101 Checking		$180.00
					201	201 Accounts Payable (A/P)	$180.00	
							$180.00	**$180.00**
02/15/2018	Bill Payment (Check)	1093	Any Time Deployment		101	101 Checking		$500.00
					201	201 Accounts Payable (A/P)	$500.00	
							$500.00	**$500.00**
02/15/2018	Bill Payment (Check)	1094	CloudZ Channel		101	101 Checking		$800.00
					201	201 Accounts Payable (A/P)	$800.00	
							$800.00	**$800.00**
02/15/2018	Bill Payment (Check)	1095	ContiCall		101	101 Checking		$270.00
					201	201 Accounts Payable (A/P)	$270.00	
							$270.00	**$270.00**
02/18/2018	Bill	275CC	ContiCall		201	201 Accounts Payable (A/P)		$135.00
				Webinars	115	115 Merchandise Inventory	$135.00	
							$135.00	**$135.00**
02/18/2018	Invoice	1050	Law Offices of Williamson, Gallagher & Katz		105	105 Accounts Receivable (A/R)	$300.00	
				Network products	115	115 Merchandise Inventory		$150.00
				Network products	401	401 Sales		$300.00
				Network products	501	501 Cost of Goods Sold	$150.00	
							$450.00	**$450.00**
02/18/2018	Invoice	1051	Permanente Medical Services		105	105 Accounts Receivable (A/R)	$270.00	
				Webinars	115	115 Merchandise Inventory		$90.00
				Webinars	401	401 Sales		$270.00
				Webinars	501	501 Cost of Goods Sold	$45.00	
				Webinars	501	501 Cost of Goods Sold	$90.00	
				Webinars	115	115 Merchandise Inventory		$45.00
							$405.00	**$405.00**
02/20/2018	Bill	AS423	AmpleStore Inc.		201	201 Accounts Payable (A/P)		$180.00
				Data storage	115	115 Merchandise Inventory	$180.00	
							$180.00	**$180.00**
02/20/2018	Invoice	1052	WebPro		105	105 Accounts Receivable (A/R)	$400.00	
				Web server	115	115 Merchandise Inventory		$200.00
				Web server	401	401 Sales		$400.00
				Web server	501	501 Cost of Goods Sold	$200.00	
							$600.00	**$600.00**
02/20/2018	Payment	10321	eBiz		101	101 Checking	$180.00	
					105	105 Accounts Receivable (A/R)		$180.00
							$180.00	**$180.00**
02/20/2018	Payment	5730	Law Offices of Williamson,		101	101 Checking	$300.00	

Journal, page 3 of 4

DATE	TRANSACTION TYPE	NUM	NAME	MEMO/DESCRIPTION	ACCOUNT #	ACCOUNT	DEBIT	CREDIT
			Gallagher & Katz					
					105	105 Accounts Receivable (A/R)		$300.00
							$300.00	**$300.00**
02/20/2018	Payment	1588	Permanente Medical Services		101	101 Checking	$270.00	
					105	105 Accounts Receivable (A/R)		$270.00
							$270.00	**$270.00**
02/20/2018	Payment	9213	Springfield Unified School District		101	101 Checking	$400.00	
					105	105 Accounts Receivable (A/R)		$400.00
							$400.00	**$400.00**
02/20/2018	Payment	802	WebPro		101	101 Checking	$400.00	
					105	105 Accounts Receivable (A/R)		$400.00
							$400.00	**$400.00**
02/25/2018	Bill	492C2U	Computers 2 You		201	201 Accounts Payable (A/P)		$2,000.00
				Computers	115	115 Merchandise Inventory	$2,000.00	
							$2,000.00	**$2,000.00**
02/25/2018	Bill	ATD645	Any Time Deployment		201	201 Accounts Payable (A/P)		$250.00
				Network products	115	115 Merchandise Inventory	$250.00	
							$250.00	**$250.00**
02/25/2018	Invoice	1053	Springfield Unified School District		105	105 Accounts Receivable (A/R)	$400.00	
				Web server	501	501 Cost of Goods Sold	$200.00	
				Web server	115	115 Merchandise Inventory		$200.00
				Web server	401	401 Sales		$400.00
							$600.00	**$600.00**
02/25/2018	Sales Receipt	1054	Cash Sales		101	101 Checking	$1,000.00	
				Computers	501	501 Cost of Goods Sold	$500.00	
				Computers	115	115 Merchandise Inventory		$500.00
				Computers	401	401 Sales		$1,000.00
							$1,500.00	**$1,500.00**
02/27/2018	Sales Receipt	1055	Credit Card Sales		101	101 Checking	$2,150.00	
				Data storage	401	401 Sales		$150.00
				Data storage	115	115 Merchandise Inventory		$75.00
				Data storage	501	501 Cost of Goods Sold	$75.00	
				Computers	115	115 Merchandise Inventory		$500.00
				Computers	115	115 Merchandise Inventory		$500.00
				Computers	501	501 Cost of Goods Sold	$500.00	
				Computers	501	501 Cost of Goods Sold	$500.00	
				Computers	401	401 Sales		$2,000.00
							$3,225.00	**$3,225.00**
02/27/2018	Sales Receipt	1056	Credit Card Sales		101	101 Checking	$150.00	
				Network products	501	501 Cost of Goods Sold	$75.00	
				Network products	401	401 Sales		$150.00
				Network products	115	115 Merchandise Inventory		$75.00
							$225.00	**$225.00**
02/27/2018	Sales Receipt	1057	Credit Card Sales		101	101 Checking	$430.00	
				Data storage	115	115 Merchandise Inventory		$45.00
				Data storage	115	115 Merchandise Inventory		$30.00
				Data storage	501	501 Cost of Goods Sold	$45.00	
				Data storage	501	501 Cost of Goods Sold	$30.00	
				Data storage	401	401 Sales		$150.00
				Network products	501	501 Cost of Goods Sold	$50.00	
				Network products	115	115 Merchandise Inventory		$50.00
				Network products	401	401 Sales		$100.00
				Webinars	115	115 Merchandise Inventory		$45.00
				Webinars	501	501 Cost of Goods Sold	$45.00	
				Webinars	401	401 Sales		$180.00
				Webinars	501	501 Cost of Goods Sold	$45.00	
				Webinars	115	115 Merchandise Inventory		$45.00
							$645.00	**$645.00**

Journal, page 4 of 4

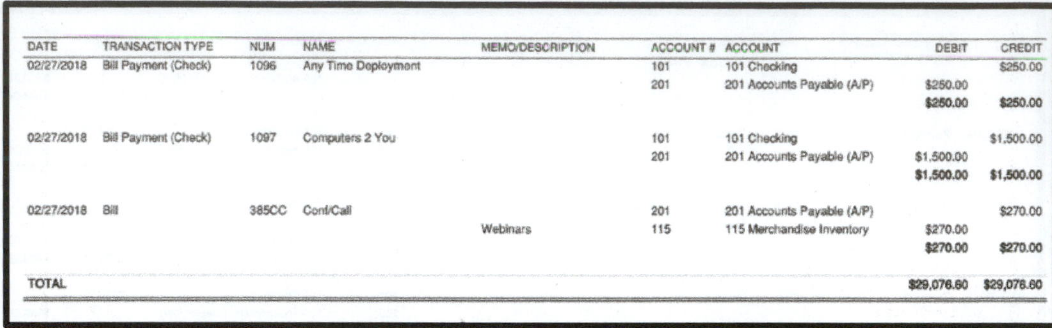

DATE	TRANSACTION TYPE	NUM	NAME	MEMO/DESCRIPTION	ACCOUNT #	ACCOUNT	DEBIT	CREDIT
02/27/2018	Bill Payment (Check)	1096	Any Time Deployment		101	101 Checking		$250.00
					201	201 Accounts Payable (A/P)	$250.00	
							$250.00	**$250.00**
02/27/2018	Bill Payment (Check)	1097	Computers 2 You		101	101 Checking		$1,500.00
					201	201 Accounts Payable (A/P)	$1,500.00	
							$1,500.00	**$1,500.00**
02/27/2018	Bill	385CC	Conf/Call		201	201 Accounts Payable (A/P)		$270.00
				Webinars	115	115 Merchandise Inventory	$270.00	
							$270.00	**$270.00**
TOTAL							**$29,076.60**	**$29,076.60**

- Export the Journal to Excel and save as a PDF file. Use the file name, **Chapter 9_Journal**.

2. Trial Balance: 1/1/20XY to 2/27/20XY

QB Cloud_Student Name

TRIAL BALANCE

As of February 27, 2018

	DEBIT	CREDIT
101 Checking	48,102.94	
105 Accounts Receivable (A/R)	1,550.00	
115 Merchandise Inventory	11,120.00	
123 Prepaid Rent	6,000.00	
125 Prepaid Insurance	2,250.00	
130 Undeposited Funds	0.00	
135 Computer Equipment	10,000.00	
137 Accumulated Depreciation		800.00
201 Accounts Payable (A/P)		4,135.00
205 Loan Payable		0.00
301 Common Stock		60,000.00
305 Opening Balance Equity		0.00
318 Retained Earnings		7,093.52
401 Sales		17,790.00
501 Cost of Goods Sold	8,895.00	
601 Advertising	275.00	
603 Bank Charges	20.00	
605 Dues & Subscriptions	175.00	
609 Freight & Delivery	95.97	
613 Interest Expense	150.00	
619 Meals and Entertainment	55.22	
621 Office Supplies	179.72	
625 Repair & Maintenance	300.00	
627 Shipping and delivery expense	47.00	
633 Telephone Expense	16.64	
635 Utilities	286.03	
TOTAL	**$89,818.52**	**$89,818.52**

➢ Export the Trial Balance to Excel and save as a PDF file. Use the file name, **Chapter 9_Trial Balance**.

3. **A/R Aging Summary:** As of 2/27/20XY

QB Cloud_Student Name

A/R AGING SUMMARY

As of February 27, 2018

	CURRENT	1 - 30	31 - 60	61 - 90	91 AND OVER	TOTAL
eBiz	180.00					$180.00
Law Offices of Williamson, Gallagher & Katz	300.00					$300.00
Permanente Medical Services	270.00					$270.00
Springfield Unified School District	400.00					$400.00
WebPro	400.00					$400.00
TOTAL	**$1,550.00**	**$0.00**	**$0.00**	**$0.00**	**$0.00**	**$1,550.00**

➢ Export the A/R Aging Summary to Excel and save as a PDF file. Use the file name, **Chapter 9_AR Aging Summary.**

4. **Inventory Valuation Summary**: As of 2/27/20XY

QB Cloud_Student Name

INVENTORY VALUATION SUMMARY

As of February 27, 2018

	SKU	QTY	ASSET VALUE	CALC. AVG
Computers		12.00	6,000.00	500.00
Data storage		56.00	840.00	15.00
Network products		18.00	450.00	25.00
Web server		16.00	3,200.00	200.00
Webinars		14.00	630.00	45.00
TOTAL			**$11,120.00**	

➢ Export to Excel and save as a PDF file. Use the file name **Chapter 9_Inventory Valuation Summary.**

5. **A/P Aging Summary**: As of 2/27/20XY

QB Cloud_Student Name

A/P AGING SUMMARY

As of February 27, 2018

	CURRENT	1 - 30	31 - 60	61 - 90	91 AND OVER	TOTAL
AmpleStore Inc.	480.00					$480.00
Any Time Deployment	250.00					$250.00
CloudZ Channel	1,000.00					$1,000.00
Computers 2 You	2,000.00					$2,000.00
Conf/Call	405.00					$405.00
TOTAL	**$4,135.00**	**$0.00**	**$0.00**	**$0.00**	**$0.00**	**$4,135.00**

➢ Export to Excel and save as a PDF file. Use the file name **Chapter 9_AP Aging Summary.**

6. **Profit and Loss** from 1/1/20XY to 2/27/20XY

QB Cloud_Student Name

PROFIT AND LOSS

January 1 - February 27, 2018

	TOTAL
INCOME	
401 Sales	17,790.00
Total Income	**$17,790.00**
COST OF GOODS SOLD	
501 Cost of Goods Sold	8,895.00
Total Cost of Goods Sold	**$8,895.00**
GROSS PROFIT	**$8,895.00**
EXPENSES	
601 Advertising	275.00
603 Bank Charges	20.00
605 Dues & Subscriptions	175.00
609 Freight & Delivery	95.97
613 Interest Expense	150.00
619 Meals and Entertainment	55.22
621 Office Supplies	179.72
625 Repair & Maintenance	300.00
627 Shipping and delivery expense	47.00
633 Telephone Expense	316.64
635 Utilities	286.03
Total Expenses	**$1,900.58**
NET OPERATING INCOME	**$6,994.42**
NET INCOME	**$6,994.42**

- Export the Profit and Loss to Excel and save as a PDF file. Use the file name **Chapter 9_Profit and Loss**.

7. **Balance Sheet** from 1/1/20XY to 2/27/20XY

QB Cloud_Student Name

BALANCE SHEET

As of February 27, 2018

	TOTAL
ASSETS	
Current Assets	
Bank Accounts	
101 Checking	48,102.94
Total Bank Accounts	**$48,102.94**
Accounts Receivable	
105 Accounts Receivable (A/R)	1,550.00
Total Accounts Receivable	**$1,550.00**
Other Current Assets	
115 Merchandise Inventory	11,120.00
123 Prepaid Rent	6,000.00
125 Prepaid Insurance	2,250.00
130 Undeposited Funds	0.00
Total Other Current Assets	**$19,370.00**
Total Current Assets	**$69,022.94**
Fixed Assets	
135 Computer Equipment	10,000.00
137 Accumulated Depreciation	-800.00
Total Fixed Assets	**$9,200.00**
TOTAL ASSETS	**$78,222.94**
LIABILITIES AND EQUITY	
Liabilities	
Current Liabilities	
Accounts Payable	
201 Accounts Payable (A/P)	4,135.00
Total Accounts Payable	**$4,135.00**
Other Current Liabilities	
205 Loan Payable	0.00
Total Other Current Liabilities	**$0.00**
Total Current Liabilities	**$4,135.00**
Total Liabilities	**$4,135.00**
Equity	
301 Common Stock	60,000.00
305 Opening Balance Equity	0.00
318 Retained Earnings	7,093.52
Net Income	6,994.42
Total Equity	**$74,087.94**
TOTAL LIABILITIES AND EQUITY	**$78,222.94**

- Export the Balance Sheet to Excel and save as a PDF file. Use the file name **Chapter 9_Balance Sheet**.

8. **Statement of Cash Flows** from 1/1/20XY to 2/27/20XY

QB Cloud_Student Name

STATEMENT OF CASH FLOWS

January 1 - February 27, 2018

	TOTAL
OPERATING ACTIVITIES	
Net Income	6,994.42
Adjustments to reconcile Net Income to Net Cash provided by operations:	
105 Accounts Receivable (A/R)	-1,150.00
115 Merchandise Inventory	-1,250.00
123 Prepaid Rent	-6,000.00
201 Accounts Payable (A/P)	1,015.00
205 Loan Payable	-5,000.00
Total Adjustments to reconcile Net Income to Net Cash provided by operations:	**-12,385.00**
Net cash provided by operating activities	**$ -5,390.58**
NET CASH INCREASE FOR PERIOD	**$ -5,390.58**
CASH AT BEGINNING OF PERIOD	53,493.52
CASH AT END OF PERIOD	**$48,102.94**

- Export the Statement of Cash Flows to Excel and save as a PDF file. Use the file name **Chapter 9_Statement of Cash Flows.**

CHECK YOUR PROGRESS

1. What is the account balance from 1/1/20XY to 2/27/20XY in these accounts? Indicate whether these accounts have debit (dr.) or credit (cr.) balances.

   Account 101 Checking ____________________

   Account 135 Computer Equipment ____________________

   Account 137 Accumulated Depreciation ____________________

   Account 401 Sales ____________________

   Account 501 Cost of Goods Sold ____________________

2. What is Net Income?

   ____

3. What are the total Liabilities and Equity?

   ____

4. What is the quantity, asset value, and average cost of computers?

   ____

5. What is the quantity, asset value, and average cost of data storage?

   ____

6. What is the quantity, asset value, and average cost of network products?

____

7. What is the quantity, asset value, and average cost of web servers?

____

8. What is the quantity, asset value, and average cost of webinars?

____

SIGN OUT

To sign out of QBO, go to the company settings (click on the company name), link to Sign Out. *Or,* continue.

ONLINE LEARNING CENTER (OLC): www.mhhe.com/qbo2e

The OLC includes additional Chapter 9 resources. Go online to www.mhhe.com/qbo2e > Student Edition > Chapter 9.

1. Narrated PowerPoints.
2. Online quizzes: 10 True or False and 10 multiple-choice questions. The Online quizzes are graded and can be emailed to your instructor.
3. Analysis question: Answer the analysis question, then email to your instructor.

4. Going to the Net

   a. Go to the QuickBooks Online support website at https://community.intuit.com/quickbooks-online. In the Ask a question field, type **More cool things you can do with QuickBooks Online** > Search > link to More cool things you can do with QuickBooks Online.
   b. List 4 cool things you can do with QuickBooks.
   c. What does the Resource Center include?

5. Videos:

   a. Go to Prof. Susan Crosson's Financial Accounting videos at http://www.bus.emory.edu/scrosso/FA%20Videos.htm. To review financial accounting principles and procedures, link to a video.
   b. Watch QuickBooks tutorials at http://quickbooks.intuit.com/tutorials/all-quickbooks-tutorials/.
6. Glossary of terms: Words that are italicized and boldfaced are defined in the glossary. The Glossary is also Appendix B.
7. Problem Solving is exercise 9-3.

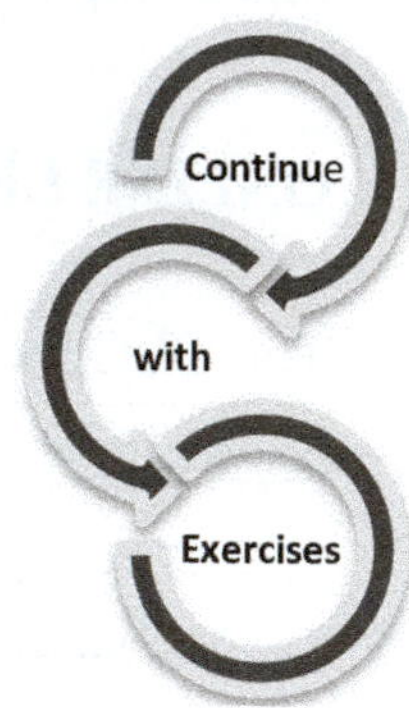

Exercise 9-1: Follow the instructions below to complete Exercise 9-1:

1. Start QBO. Sign into QB Cloud_Student Name.
2. To reconcile Account 101 Checking, use the February 28 bank statement. (*Hint:* The Statement Ending Date is 2/28/20XY.)

Statement of Account		QB Cloud_Student Name	
Checking Account		Your address	
February 1 to February 28, 20XY	Account No. 7731-2256	Your city, state, Zip	
REGULAR CHECKING			
Previous Balance	1/31/XY	$ 48,544.54	
12 Deposits (+)		9,180.00	
15 checks (-)		9,566.38	
1 Other Deductions (-)		55.22	
Service Charge		20.00	
Ending Balance	2/28/XY	**$48,082.94**	
DEPOSITS			
	2/2/XY	1,450.00	
	2/2/XY	1,150.00	
	2/2/XY	1,300.00	
	2/21/XY	180.00	
	2/21/XY	300.00	
	2/21/XY	270.00	
	2/21/XY	400.00	
	2/21/XY	400.00	
	2/24/XY	1,000.00	
	2/27/XY	2,150.00	
	2/27/XY	150.00	
	2/27/XY	430.00	

CHECKS (Asterisk * indicates break in check number sequence)

	Date	Check No.	Amount	
	2/6/XY	1083	91.20	
	2/6/XY	1084	150.00	
	2/6/XY	1085	76.19	
	2/6/XY	1086	82.13	
	2/7/XY	1087	75.00	
	2/7/XY	1088	195.89	
	2/8/XY	1089	150.00	
	2/8/XY	1090	95.97	
	2/8/XY	1091	5,150.00	
	2/10/XY	1092	180.00	*Continued*

	2/17/XY	1093	500.00	
	2/18/XY	1094	800.00	
	2/19/XY	1095	270.00	
	2/28/XY	1096	250.00	
	2/28/XY	1097	1,500.00	
OTHER DEDUCTIONS (ATM's)				
	2/7/XY	ATM	55.22	

3. Print the 2/28/XY Reconciliation Report. Save as a PDF file. Use the file name **Exercise 9-1_Reconciliation Report**.

Exercise 9-2: Follow the instructions below to complete Exercise 9-2:

1. Save these reports as PDF files and export to Excel. Run reports from **1/1/20XY to 2/28/20XY** unless another date is shown. (*Hint:* When the report needs an As of date, use 2/28/20XY.

   - Exercise 9-2_Journal (from 2/28/20XY to 2/28/XY)
   - Exercise 9-2_Transaction Detail by Account (from 2/1/XY to 2/28/XY)
   - Exercise 9-2_General Ledger (from 2/1/XY to 2/28/XY)
   - Exercise 9-2_Customer Balance Summary
   - Exercise 9-2_Vendor Balance Summary
   - Exercise 9-2_Trial Balance
   - Exercise 9-2_Profit and Loss
   - Exercise 9-2_Balance Sheet
   - Exercise 9-2_Statement of Cash Flows

2. **Check Your Figures** (from 1/1/201XX to 2/28/XX):

    - Account 101 Checking, $48,082.94
    - Account 105 Accounts Receivable, $1,550.00
    - Account 115 Merchandise Inventory, $11,120.00
    - Account 201 Accounts Payable, $4,135.00
    - Account 401 Sales, $17,790.00
    - Account 501 Cost of Goods Sold, $8,895.00
    - Account 621 Office Supplies, $179.72
    - Account 318 Retained Earnings $7,093.52
    - Total Liabilities and Equity, $78,202.94
    - Net Income, $6,974.42
    - Net cash increase (or decrease) for period, $-5,410.58

Exercise 9-3: Problem Solving

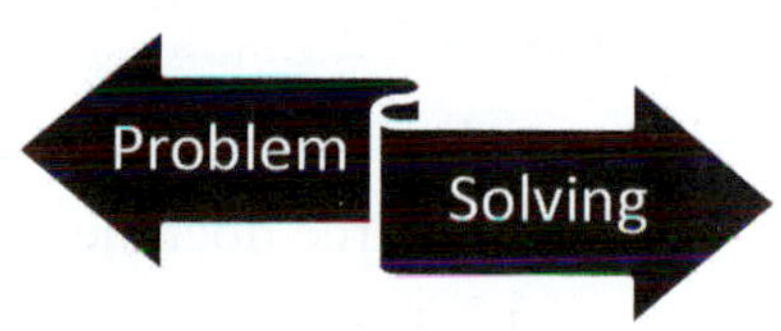

The Online Learning Center includes Exercise 9-3 at www.mhhe.com/qbo2e > Student Edition > Chapter 9 > Problem Solving.

1. What is a module?
2. Organize the following source documents according to the QBO modules used. Define each module.

    - Bills and vendor payments
    - Invoices and customer payments

CHAPTER 9 INDEX

Chapter 10 March Source Documents

Scenario: In Chapter 10, start by checking your data with the February Trial Balance. The stop sign reminds you to make sure your debit and credit balances are correct. In this chapter, you analyze typical source documents used by businesses. Memos remind you to make customer payments and vendor payments, sales receipts show cash and credit card sales, bills are used for recording purchases on account, and invoices are used for sales on account. Then, complete end-of-first-quarter adjusting entries, an adjusted trial balance, and financial statements. To review what you will do in Chapter 10, read the objectives.

OBJECTIVES

1. Start QuickBooks Online and sign in to QB Cloud_Student Name.
2. To check data, display the February 28 Trial Balance.
3. Analyze source documents.
4. Record vendor, customer, cash, and credit card transactions.
5. Record end-of-quarter adjusting entries.
6. Display the adjusted trial balance and financial statements.
7. Save PDF files and export reports to Excel.
8. Complete Check Your Progress.
9. Go to the Online Learning Center at www.mhhe.com/qbo2e for additional resources.
10. Complete Exercises 10-1, 10-2 and 10-3.

In Chapter 10, you complete business processes for QB Cloud_Student Name. QB Cloud sells computers, data storage, network products, web servers, webinars, and purchases inventory on account from vendors. In order to record transactions, analyze source documents. You also use the March 31 bank statement to reconcile Account 101 Checking.

At the end of the first quarter — January, February, and March —adjusting entries and financial statements are completed.

The source documents include:

- Vendor bills for purchasing inventory.
- Memos include customer payments, vendor payments and remittances.
- Transaction register for issuing checks for expenses and recording ATM withdrawals.
- Sales invoices for credit customers.
- Sales receipts for cash and credit card sales.

GETTING STARTED

1. Start your browser. Go online to http://qbo.intuit.com.

2. Sign in to QuickBooks Online with your User ID and Password.

CHECK YOUR DATA

To make sure you are starting in the correct place, display the 01/01/20XY to 2/28/20XY Trial Balance. The Trial Balance was also completed in Exercise 9-2.

QB Cloud_Student Name

TRIAL BALANCE

As of February 28, 2018

	DEBIT	CREDIT
101 Checking	48,082.94	
105 Accounts Receivable (A/R)	1,550.00	
115 Merchandise Inventory	11,120.00	
123 Prepaid Rent	6,000.00	
125 Prepaid Insurance	2,250.00	
130 Undeposited Funds	0.00	
135 Computer Equipment	10,000.00	
137 Accumulated Depreciation		800.00
201 Accounts Payable (A/P)		4,135.00
205 Loan Payable		0.00
301 Common Stock		60,000.00
305 Opening Balance Equity		0.00
318 Retained Earnings		7,093.52
401 Sales		17,790.00
501 Cost of Goods Sold	8,895.00	
601 Advertising	275.00	
603 Bank Charges	40.00	
605 Dues & Subscriptions	175.00	
609 Freight & Delivery	95.97	
613 Interest Expense	150.00	
619 Meals and Entertainment	55.22	
621 Office Supplies	179.72	
625 Repair & Maintenance	300.00	
627 Shipping and delivery expense	47.00	
633 Telephone Expense	316.64	
635 Utilities	286.03	
TOTAL	**$89,818.52**	**$89,818.52**

Before recording March transactions, make sure your February 28 trial balance agrees with the one shown. If editing is needed, drill-down to the Transaction Report > then drill-down to the transaction. *Or,* go to 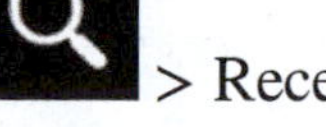 > Recent Transactions; or  > Audit Log.

MARCH SOURCE DOCUMENTS

After analyzing each source document, record the appropriate transaction. All transactions occurred during March.

QB Cloud_Student Name

Memo

Date: 3/6

Re: Customer Payment

QB Cloud_Student Name received the following customer payment.

Received payment from eBiz, Invoice 1049, $180, customer check 10392.

Analyze source document → **Enter date** → **Input transaction**

QB Cloud_Student Name

Memo

Date: 3/6

Re: Credit Card Receipts

The bank sent verification of credit card receipts in the amount of $4,140.00. Refer to the sales receipts on the next three pages for the products sold and credit cards used.

Checking Account Bank Statement		**Checks**	**Credit Card**	**Amount**
Date: March 5		1	American Express	$1,450.00
List of Deposits:		2	MasterCard	$1,540.00
Coin	**Totals**	3	Visa	$1,150.00
Quarters:	$	4		
Dimes:	$	5		
Nickels:	$	6		
Pennies	$			
Total				
Cash	**Totals**			
$1	$			
$5	$			
$10	$			
$20	$			
$50	$			
$100	$			
Total	$		**Totals**	$4,140.00
Total Cash			**Total Deposit**	$4,140.00

SALES RECEIPT

QB Cloud_Student Name

Date: 3/6
RECEIPT # 1058
For: **CREDIT CARD**

Payment Method	Type
CREDIT CARD	American Express

Qty	Description	Rate	Amount
15	Data storage	$30.00	$450.00
1	Computer	$1,000.00	1,000.00
		Subtotal	1,450.00
		Total	$1,450.00

Thank you for your business!

SALES RECEIPT

QB Cloud_Student Name

Date: 3/6
RECEIPT # 1059
For: **CREDIT CARD**

Payment Method	Type
CREDIT CARD	MasterCard

Qty	Description	Rate	Amount
5	Network products	$50.00	$250.00
3	Web server	400.00	1,200.00
1	Webinar	90.00	$90.00
		Subtotal	1,540.00
		Total	$1,540.00

Thank you for your business!

SALES RECEIPT

QB Cloud_Student Name

Date: 3/6
RECEIPT # 1060
For: **CREDIT CARD**

Payment Method	Type
CREDIT CARD	Visa

Qty	Description	Rate	Amount
1	Computer	$1,000.00	$1,000.00
5	Data storage	30.00	150.00
		Subtotal	1,150.00
		Total	$1,150.00

Thank you for your business!

BILL #: CZ459 **DATE: 3/7** Customer:

QB Cloud_
Student Name

CloudZ Channel
110 Merit Street
Menlo Park, CA 94025
650-555-3250

Date	Quantity	Description	Unit Price	Amount
3/7	5	Web server	$200.00	$1,000.00

Remittance

Bill #	CZ459
Date	3/7
Amount Due	$1,000.00

Thank you for your business!

Make all checks payable to CloudZ Channel.

Sales Invoice

TO:

eBiz
800 W. Second Ave.
Durango, CO 81301
(970) 555-2000

SHIP TO: SAME

Date	Invoice Number	Payment Terms	Due Date
3/8	1061	Net 30	4/7

Qty	Product	Description	Rate	Amount
9	Data storage	Data storage	$30.00	$270.00

Make all checks payable to QB Cloud_Student Name

Thank you for your business!

QB Cloud_Student Name

Memo

Date: 3/8

Re: Vendor Payments

QB Cloud_Student Name pays the following vendors:

Vendor ID	Bill #	Check No.	Amount
AmpleStore	AS401	1098	$300.00
CloudZ Channel	CZ403	1099	$1,000.00

REMITTANCE	
Bill #	AS401
Customer ID	QB Cloud_Student Name
Date	3/8
Amount Enclosed	$300.00
	AmpleStore Inc. 200 West Concord Ave. Palo Alto, CA 94301 650-555-8527

REMITTANCE	
Bill #	CZ403
Customer ID	QB Cloud_Student Name
Date	3/8
Amount Enclosed	$1,000.00
	CloudZ Channel 110 Merit Street Menlo Park, CA 94025 650-555-3250

Bill: AS476

AmpleStore Inc.

Bill To: QB Cloud_Student Name

Date	Quantity	Description	Unit Price	Amount
3/12	22	Data storage	$15.00	$330.00

Remittance

Bill #	AS476
Date	3/12
Amount Due	$330.00

AmpleStore Inc. 200 West Concord Ave. Palo Alto, CA 94301

(650) 555-8527

Bill: 431CC

Conf/Call
700 North Prince Street
Tempe, AZ 85008 USA
480-555-2411

Bill to: QB Cloud
Student Name

Date	Quantity	Description	Unit Price	Amount
3/12	3	Webinars	$45	$135.00

Remittance

Bill #	431CC
Date	3/12
Amount Due	$135.00

Make all checks payable to Conf/Call.
Thank you for your business!

Sales Invoice

TO: **Law Offices of Williamson, Gallagher & Katz**
18 Piedmont Ave. NW
Atlanta, GA 30303
(404) 555-8134

SHIP TO: **SAME**

Date	Invoice Number	Payment Terms	Due Date
3/15	1062	Net 30	4/14

Qty	Product	Description	Rate	Amount
6	Network Products	Network products	$50.00	$300.00

Make all checks payable to QB Cloud_Student Name

Thank you for your business!

Sales Invoice

TO:	Permanente Medical Services 18771 Ala Moana Blvd. Honolulu, HI 96815 (808) 555-555-9000	SHIP TO:	SAME

Date	Invoice Number	Payment Terms	Due Date
3/15	1063	Net 30	4/14

Qty	Product	Description	Rate	Amount
4	Webinars	Webinars	$90	$360.00

Make all checks payable to QB Cloud_Student Name

Thank you for your business!

Bill: AS490

AmpleStore Inc.

Bill to: QB Cloud
Student Name

Date	Quantity	Description	Unit Price	Amount
3/17	10	Data storage	$15.00	$150.00

Remittance

Bill #	AS490
Date	3/17
Amount Due	$150.00

AmpleStore Inc. 200 West Concord Ave. Palo Alto, CA 94301
(650) 555-8527

Sales Invoice

TO:

WebPro
18 Alameda Road
Santa Fe, NM 87501
(505) 555-5311

SHIP TO: **SAME**

Date	Invoice Number	Payment Terms	Due Date
3/17	1064	Net 30	4/16

Qty	Product	Description	Rate	Amount
1	Web servers	Web servers	$400.00	$400.00

Make all checks payable to QB Cloud_Student Name

Thank you for your business!

QB Cloud_Student Name

Memo

Date: 3/19

Re: Vendor Payments

QB Cloud_Student Name pays the following vendors:

Vendor ID	Bill #	Check No.	Amount
AmpleStore Inc.	AS423	1100	$180.00
Conf/Call	275CC	1101	$135.00

REMITTANCE	
Bill #	AS423
Customer ID	QB Cloud_Student Name
Date	3/19
Amount Enclosed	$180.00
	AmpleStore Inc. 200 West Concord Ave. Palo Alto, CA 94301 650-555-8527

REMITTANCE	
Bill #	275CC
Customer ID	QB Cloud_Student Name
Date	3/19
Amount Enclosed	$135.00
	Conf/Call 700 North Prince Street Tempe, AZ 85008 (480) 555-2411

QB Cloud_Student Name

Memo

Date: 3/19

Re: Customer Payments

QB Cloud_Student Name received the following customer payments.

1. Received payment from the Law Offices of Williamson, Gallagher & Katz, Invoice 1050, $300, customer check 5911.

2. Received payment from Permanente Medical Services, Invoice 1051, $270, customer check 1794.

Transaction Register

Check No.	*Date*	*Description of Transaction*	Debit (-)	Credit (+)	Balance
	3/19	*Balance*			$51,357.94
1102	3/19	Best Cellular	82.13		51,275.81
1103	3/19	Barber's Paper Supply	150.00		51,125.81
1104	3/19	County Telephone	78.23		51,047.58
1105	3/19	Office Suppliers	132.40		50,915.18
1106	3/19	Cays Advertising	175.00		50,740.18
1107	3/19	RSP Gas	113.25		50,626.93
1108	3/20	Hour Deliveries	60.00		50,566.93
1109	3/20	U.S. Post Office	47.00		50,519.93
1110	3/20	Albert Benson	150.00		50,369.93

Date:

3/21 **BILL #: 501C2U**

Computers 2 You
2006 East 14 Avenue
Los Angeles, CA 90046
(213) 555-2300

BILL TO: QB
Cloud_Student Name

quantity	description	Unit Price	amount
4	Computers	$500.00	$2,000.00

Remittance

Bill #	501C2U
Date	3/21
Amount Due	$2,000.00

Any Time Deployment
1189 W. Burnside
Lexington, MA 02421
(781) 555-4681

Bill Number: ATD694

Date: 3/21

Ship To:

QB Cloud_Student Name

SHIPPED VIA	TERMS
UPS	Net 30

QTY	DESCRIPTION	UNIT PRICE	TOTAL
10	Network products	25.00	$250.00
		SUBTOTAL	$250.00
		TOTAL	$250.00

Remittance

Bill #	ATD694
Date	3/21
Amount Due	$250.00

QB Cloud_Student Name

Memo

Date: 3/21

Re: Customer Payments

QB Cloud_Student Name received the following customer payments.

1. Received payment from Springfield Unified School District, Invoice 1053, $400, customer check 9290.

2. Received payment from WebPro, Invoice 1052, $400, customer check 912.

Sales Invoice

TO: **Springfield Unified School District**
4892 Clear Lake Ave.
Springfield, IL 62703
(217) 555-555-5500

SHIP TO: SAME

Date	Invoice Number	Payment Terms	Due Date
3/25	1065	Net 30	4/24

Qty	Product	Description	Rate	Amount
2	Web server	Web server	$400.00	$800.00

Make all checks payable to QB Cloud_Student Name

Thank you for your business!

SALES RECEIPT

QB Cloud_Student Name

Date: 3/25
RECEIPT # 1066
For: **Cash Sales**

Payment Method	Type
Check 12978	Cash sales

Qty	Description	Rate	Amount
1	Computer	$1,000.00	$1,000.00
		Subtotal	$1,000.00
		Total	$1,000.00

Thank you for your business!

QB Cloud_Student Name

Memo

Date: 3/26

Re: Credit Card Receipts

The bank sent verification of credit card receipts in the amount of $1,910.00. Refer to the sales receipts on the next three pages for the products sold and credit cards used.

Checking Account Bank Statement		Checks	Credit Card	Amount
Date: March 5		1	American Express	$1,240.00
List of Deposits:		2	MasterCard	150.00
Coin	**Totals**	3	Visa	520.00
Quarters:	$	4		
Dimes:	$	5		
Nickels:	$	6		
Pennies	$			
Total				
Cash	**Totals**			
$1	$			
$5	$			
$10	$			
$20	$			
$50	$			
$100	$			
Total	$		**Totals**	$1,910.00
Total Cash			**Total Deposit**	$1,910.00

Hint: On the Sales Receipts page, select the appropriate credit card.

SALES RECEIPT

QB Cloud_Student Name

Date: 3/26

RECEIPT #1067

For: **Credit Card**

Payment Method	Type
CREDIT CARD	American Express

Qty	Description	Rate	Amount
8	Data storage	$30.00	$240.00
1	Computer	$1,000.00	$1,000.00
		Subtotal	1,240.00
		Total	$1,240.00

Thank you for your business!

SALES RECEIPT

QB Cloud_Student Name

Date: 3/26
RECEIPT #1068
For: **Credit Card**

Payment Method	Type
CREDIT CARD	MasterCard

Qty	Description	Rate	Amount
3	Network products	$50.00	$150.00
		Subtotal	$150.00
		Total	$150.00

Thank you for your business!

SALES RECEIPT

QB Cloud_Student Name

Date: 3/26
RECEIPT #1069
For: **Credit Card**

Payment Method	Type
CREDIT CARD	Visa

Qty	Description	Rate	Amount
5	Data storage	$30.00	$150.00
2	Network products	$50.00	$100.00
3	Webinars	$90.00	$270.00
		Subtotal	$520.00
		Total	$520.00

Thank you for your business!

QB Cloud_Student Name

Memo

Date: 3/26

Re: Vendor Payments

QB Cloud_Student Name pays the following vendors:

Vendor ID	Bill #	Check No.	Amount
Any Time Deployment	ATD645	1111	$250.00
Computers 2 You	492C2U	1112	$2,000.00
Conf/Call	385CC	1113	$270.00

REMITTANCE	
Bill #	ATD645
Customer ID	QB Cloud_Student Name
Date	3/26
Amount Enclosed	$250.00
	Any Time Deployment 1189 W. Burnside Lexington, MA 02421 (781) 555-4781

REMITTANCE	
Bill #	492C2U
Customer ID	QB Cloud_Student Name
Date	3/26
Amount Enclosed	$2,000.00
	Computers 2 You 2006 East 14 Avenue Los Angeles, CA 90046 213-555-2300

REMITTANCE	
Bill #	385CC
Customer ID	QB Cloud_Student Name
Date	3/26
Amount Enclosed	$270.00
	Conf/Call 700 North Prince Street Tempe, AZ 85008 Phone: 480-555-2411

BILL #: CZ476 **DATE: 3/30**

Customer:
QB Cloud_
Student Name

CloudZ Channel
110 Merit Street
Menlo Park, CA 94025
650-555-3250

Date	Quantity	Description	Unit Price	Amount
3/30	6	Web server	$200.00	$1,200.00

Remittance

Bill #	CZ476
Date	3/30
Amount Due	$1,200.00

Thank you for your business!

Make all checks payable to CloudZ Channel.

Any Time Deployment
1189 W. Burnside
Lexington, MA 02421
(781) 555-4681

Bill Number: ATD734

Date: 3/30

Ship To:

QB Cloud_Student Name

SHIPPED VIA	TERMS
UPS	Net 30

QTY	DESCRIPTION	UNIT PRICE	TOTAL
11	Network products	25.00	$275.00
		SUBTOTAL	275.00
		TOTAL	$275.00

Remittance

Bill #	ATD734
Date	3/30
Amount Due	$275.00

QB Cloud_Student Name

Memo

Date: 3/30

Re: Credit Card Receipts

The bank sent verification of credit card receipts in the amount of $3,680.00. Refer to the sales receipts on the next three pages for the products sold and credit cards used.

Checking Account Bank Statement		Checks	Credit Card	Amount
Date: March 5		1	American Express	$750.00
List of Deposits:		2	MasterCard	1,450.00
Coin	**Totals**	3	Visa	1,480.00
Quarters:	$	4		
Dimes:	$	5		
Nickels:	$	6		
Pennies	$			
Total				
Cash	**Totals**			
$1	$			
$5	$			
$10	$			
$20	$			
$50	$			
$100	$			
Total	$		**Totals**	$3,680.00
Total Cash			**Total Deposit**	$3,680.00

Hint: On the Sales Receipts page, select the appropriate credit card.

SALES RECEIPT

QB Cloud_Student Name

Date: 3/30

RECEIPT # 1070

For: **Credit Card**

Payment Method	Type
CREDIT CARD	American Express

Qty	Description	Rate	Amount
15	Data storage	$30.00	$450.00
6	Network products	$50.00	$300.00
		Subtotal	750.00
		Total	$750.00

Thank you for your business!

SALES RECEIPT

QB Cloud_Student Name

Date: 3/30
RECEIPT # 1071
For: **Credit Card**

Payment Method	Type
CREDIT CARD	MasterCard

Qty	Description	Rate	Amount
1	Computers	$1,000.00	$1,000.00
6	Network products	50.00	300.00
5	Data storage	30.00	150.00
		Subtotal	1,450.00
		Total	$1,450.00

Thank you for your business!

SALES RECEIPT

QB Cloud_Student Name

Date: 3/30
RECEIPT # 1072
For: **Credit Card**

Payment Method	Type
CREDIT CARD	Visa

Qty	Description	Rate	Amount
16	Data storage	$30.00	$480.00
1	Computer	$1,000.00	1,000.00
		Subtotal	1,480.00
		Total	$1,480.00

Thank you for your business!

UNADJUSTED TRIAL BALANCE AND JOURNAL

1. Trial Balance (unadjusted): 1/1/20XY to 3/30/XY

QB Cloud_Student Name

TRIAL BALANCE

As of March 30, 2018

	DEBIT	CREDIT
101 Checking	55,239.93	
105 Accounts Receivable (A/R)	2,130.00	
115 Merchandise Inventory	10,030.00	
123 Prepaid Rent	6,000.00	
125 Prepaid Insurance	2,250.00	
130 Undeposited Funds	0.00	
135 Computer Equipment	10,000.00	
137 Accumulated Depreciation		800.00
201 Accounts Payable (A/P)		5,340.00
205 Loan Payable		0.00
301 Common Stock		60,000.00
305 Opening Balance Equity		0.00
318 Retained Earnings		7,093.52
401 Sales		30,650.00
501 Cost of Goods Sold	15,325.00	
601 Advertising	450.00	
603 Bank Charges	40.00	
605 Dues & Subscriptions	175.00	
609 Freight & Delivery	155.97	
613 Interest Expense	150.00	
619 Meals and Entertainment	55.22	
621 Office Supplies	312.12	
625 Repair & Maintenance	450.00	
627 Shipping and delivery expense	94.00	
629 Stationery & Printing	150.00	
633 Telephone Expense	477.00	
635 Utilities	399.28	
TOTAL	**$103,883.52**	**$103,883.52**

➢ Export the Trial Balance to Excel and save as a PDF file. Use the file name **Chapter 10_Unadjusted Trial Balance**.

2. Journal: 3/1/20XY to 3/30/XY

Journal, page 1 of 8

QB Cloud_Student Name
Journal
March 1-30, 2018

Date	Transaction Type	Num	Name	Memo/Description	Account #	Account	Debit	Credit
03/06/2018	Payment	10392	eBiz		101	101 Checking	180.00	
					105	105 Accounts Receivable (A/R)		180.00
							$ 180.00	$ 180.00
03/06/2018	Sales Receipt	1058	Credit Card Sales		101	101 Checking	1,450.00	
				Data storage	115	115 Merchandise Inventory		180.00
				Data storage	501	501 Cost of Goods Sold	180.00	
				Data storage	501	501 Cost of Goods Sold	45.00	
				Data storage	401	401 Sales		450.00
				Data storage	115	115 Merchandise Inventory		45.00
				Computers	115	115 Merchandise Inventory		500.00
				Computers	501	501 Cost of Goods Sold	500.00	
				Computers	401	401 Sales		1,000.00
							$ 2,175.00	$ 2,175.00
03/06/2018	Sales Receipt	1059	Credit Card Sales		101	101 Checking	1,540.00	
				Network products	115	115 Merchandise Inventory		125.00
				Network products	501	501 Cost of Goods Sold	125.00	
				Network products	401	401 Sales		250.00
				Web server	501	501 Cost of Goods Sold	600.00	
				Web server	401	401 Sales		1,200.00
				Web server	115	115 Merchandise Inventory		600.00
				Webinars	401	401 Sales		90.00
				Webinars	501	501 Cost of Goods Sold	45.00	
				Webinars	115	115 Merchandise Inventory		45.00
							$2,310.00	$2,310.00

Journal, page 2 of 8

03/06/2018	Sales Receipt	1060	Credit Card Sales		101	101 Checking	1,150.00	
				Computers	401	401 Sales		1,000.00
				Computers	115	115 Merchandise Inventory		500.00
				Computers	501	501 Cost of Goods Sold	500.00	
				Data storage	115	115 Merchandise Inventory		75.00
				Data storage	401	401 Sales		150.00
				Data storage	501	501 Cost of Goods Sold	75.00	
							$ 1,725.00	**$ 1,725.00**
03/07/2018	Bill	CZ459	CloudZ Channel		201	201 Accounts Payable (A/P)		1,000.00
				Web server	115	115 Merchandise Inventory	1,000.00	
							$ 1,000.00	**$ 1,000.00**
03/08/2018	Invoice	1061	eBiz		105	105 Accounts Receivable (A/R)	270.00	
				Data storage	115	115 Merchandise Inventory		60.00
				Data storage	401	401 Sales		270.00
				Data storage	115	115 Merchandise Inventory		75.00
				Data storage	501	501 Cost of Goods Sold	60.00	
				Data storage	501	501 Cost of Goods Sold	75.00	
							$ 405.00	**$ 405.00**
03/08/2018	Bill Payment (Check)	1098	AmpleStore Inc.		101	101 Checking		300.00
					201	201 Accounts Payable (A/P)	300.00	
							$ 300.00	**$ 300.00**
03/08/2018	Bill Payment (Check)	1099	CloudZ Channel		101	101 Checking		1,000.00
					201	201 Accounts Payable (A/P)	1,000.00	
							$ 1,000.00	**$ 1,000.00**
03/12/2018	Bill	AS476	AmpleStore Inc.		201	201 Accounts Payable (A/P)		330.00
				Data storage	115	115 Merchandise Inventory	330.00	
							$ 330.00	**$ 330.00**

Journal, page 3 of 8

Date	Transaction Type	Num	Name	Memo/Description	Account #	Account	Debit	Credit
03/12/2018	Bill	431CC	Conf/Call		201	201 Accounts Payable (A/P)		135.00
				Webinars	115	115 Merchandise Inventory	135.00	
							$ 135.00	**$ 135.00**
03/15/2018	Invoice	1062	Law Offices of Williamson, Gallagher & Katz		105	105 Accounts Receivable (A/R)	300.00	
				Network products	115	115 Merchandise Inventory		75.00
				Network products	501	501 Cost of Goods Sold	75.00	
				Network products	501	501 Cost of Goods Sold	75.00	
				Network products	401	401 Sales		300.00
				Network products	115	115 Merchandise Inventory		75.00
							$ 450.00	**$ 450.00**
03/15/2018	Invoice	1063	Permanente Medical Services		105	105 Accounts Receivable (A/R)	360.00	
				Webinars	501	501 Cost of Goods Sold	180.00	
				Webinars	401	401 Sales		360.00
				Webinars	115	115 Merchandise Inventory		180.00
							$ 540.00	**$ 540.00**
03/17/2018	Bill	AS490	AmpleStore Inc.		201	201 Accounts Payable (A/P)		150.00
				Data storage	115	115 Merchandise Inventory	150.00	
							$ 150.00	**$ 150.00**
03/17/2018	Invoice	1064	WebPro		105	105 Accounts Receivable (A/R)	400.00	
				Web server	501	501 Cost of Goods Sold	200.00	
				Web server	115	115 Merchandise Inventory		200.00
				Web server	401	401 Sales		400.00
							$ 600.00	**$ 600.00**
03/19/2018	Bill Payment (Check)	1100	AmpleStore Inc.		101	101 Checking		180.00
					201	201 Accounts Payable (A/P)	180.00	
							$ 180.00	**$ 180.00**

Journal, page 4 of 8

Date	Transaction Type	Num	Name	Memo/Description	Account #	Account	Debit	Credit
03/19/2018	Bill Payment (Check)	1101	Conf/Call		101	101 Checking		135.00
					201	201 Accounts Payable (A/P)	135.00	
							$ 135.00	$ 135.00
03/19/2018	Payment	5911	Law Offices of Williamson, Gallagher & Katz		101	101 Checking	300.00	
					105	105 Accounts Receivable (A/R)		300.00
							$ 300.00	$ 300.00
03/19/2018	Payment	1794	Permanente Medical Services		101	101 Checking	270.00	
					105	105 Accounts Receivable (A/R)		270.00
							$ 270.00	$ 270.00
03/19/2018	Check	1102	Best Cellular		101	101 Checking		82.13
					633	633 Telephone Expense	82.13	
							$ 82.13	$ 82.13
03/19/2018	Check	1103	Barber's Paper Supply		101	101 Checking		150.00
					629	629 Stationery & Printing	150.00	
							$ 150.00	$ 150.00
03/19/2018	Check	1104	County Telephone		101	101 Checking		78.23
				Paid monthly bill	633	633 Telephone Expense	78.23	
							$ 78.23	$ 78.23
03/19/2018	Check	1105	Office Suppliers		101	101 Checking		132.40
				Bought office supplies	621	621 Office Supplies	132.40	
							$ 132.40	$ 132.40
03/19/2018	Check	1106	Cays Advertising		101	101 Checking		175.00
					601	601 Advertising	175.00	
							$ 175.00	$ 175.00

Journal, page 5 of 8

Date	Type	Num	Name	Memo	Acct #	Account	Debit	Credit
03/19/2018	Check	1107	RSP Gas		101	101 Checking		113.25
				Paid monthly bill	635	635 Utilities	113.25	
							$ 113.25	**$ 113.25**
03/20/2018	Check	1108	Hour Deliveries		101	101 Checking		60.00
				Paid for delivery	609	609 Freight & Delivery	60.00	
							$ 60.00	**$ 60.00**
03/20/2018	Check	1109	U.S. Post Office		101	101 Checking		47.00
					627	627 Shipping and delivery expense	47.00	
							$ 47.00	**$ 47.00**
03/20/2018	Check	1110	Albert Benson		101	101 Checking		150.00
				Repairs and maintenance	625	625 Repair & Maintenance	150.00	
							$ 150.00	**$ 150.00**
03/21/2018	Bill	501C2U	Computers 2 You		201	201 Accounts Payable (A/P)		2,000.00
				Computers	115	115 Merchandise Inventory	2,000.00	
							$ 2,000.00	**$ 2,000.00**
03/21/2018	Bill	ATD694	Any Time Deployment		201	201 Accounts Payable (A/P)		250.00
				Network products	115	115 Merchandise Inventory	250.00	
							$ 250.00	**$ 250.00**
03/21/2018	Payment	9290	Springfield Unified School District		101	101 Checking	400.00	
					105	105 Accounts Receivable (A/R)		400.00
							$ 400.00	**$ 400.00**
03/21/2018	Payment	912	WebPro		101	101 Checking	400.00	
					105	105 Accounts Receivable (A/R)		400.00
							$ 400.00	**$ 400.00**

Journal, page 6 of 8

03/25/2018	Invoice	1065	Springfield Unified School District		105	105 Accounts Receivable (A/R)	800.00	
				Web server	401	401 Sales		800.00
				Web server	115	115 Merchandise Inventory		400.00
				Web server	501	501 Cost of Goods Sold	400.00	
							$ 1,200.00	**$ 1,200.00**
03/25/2018	Sales Receipt	1066	Cash Sales		101	101 Checking	1,000.00	
				Computers	115	115 Merchandise Inventory		500.00
				Computers	401	401 Sales		1,000.00
				Computers	501	501 Cost of Goods Sold	500.00	
							$ 1,500.00	**$ 1,500.00**
03/26/2018	Sales Receipt	1067	Credit Card Sales		101	101 Checking	1,240.00	
				Data storage	501	501 Cost of Goods Sold	120.00	
				Data storage	401	401 Sales		240.00
				Data storage	115	115 Merchandise Inventory		120.00
				Computers	501	501 Cost of Goods Sold	500.00	
				Computers	401	401 Sales		1,000.00
				Computers	115	115 Merchandise Inventory		500.00
							$ 1,860.00	**$ 1,860.00**
03/26/2018	Sales Receipt	1068	Credit Card Sales		101	101 Checking	150.00	
				Network products	115	115 Merchandise Inventory		75.00
				Network products	401	401 Sales		150.00
				Network products	501	501 Cost of Goods Sold	75.00	
							$ 225.00	**$ 225.00**
03/26/2018	Sales Receipt	1069	Credit Card Sales		101	101 Checking	520.00	
				Data storage	401	401 Sales		150.00
				Data storage	501	501 Cost of Goods Sold	75.00	
				Data storage	115	115 Merchandise Inventory		75.00
				Network products	501	501 Cost of Goods Sold	50.00	
				Network products	401	401 Sales		100.00
				Network products	115	115 Merchandise Inventory		50.00

Journal, page 7 of 8

				Webinars	401	401 Sales		270.00
				Webinars	115	115 Merchandise Inventory		135.00
				Webinars	501	501 Cost of Goods Sold	135.00	
							$ 780.00	**$ 780.00**
03/26/2018	Bill Payment (Check)	1111	Any Time Deployment		101	101 Checking		250.00
					201	201 Accounts Payable (A/P)	250.00	
							$ 250.00	**$ 250.00**
03/26/2018	Bill Payment (Check)	1112	Computers 2 You		101	101 Checking		2,000.00
					201	201 Accounts Payable (A/P)	2,000.00	
							$ 2,000.00	**$ 2,000.00**
03/26/2018	Bill Payment (Check)	1113	Conf/Call		101	101 Checking		270.00
					201	201 Accounts Payable (A/P)	270.00	
							$ 270.00	**$ 270.00**
03/30/2018	Bill	CZ476	CloudZ Channel		201	201 Accounts Payable (A/P)		1,200.00
				Web server	115	115 Merchandise Inventory	1,200.00	
							$ 1,200.00	**$ 1,200.00**
03/30/2018	Bill	ATD734	Any Time Deployment		201	201 Accounts Payable (A/P)		275.00
				Network products	115	115 Merchandise Inventory	275.00	
03/30/2018	Sales Receipt	1070	Credit Card Sales		101	101 Checking	750.00	
				Data storage	501	501 Cost of Goods Sold	225.00	
				Data storage	115	115 Merchandise Inventory		225.00
				Data storage	401	401 Sales		450.00
				Network products	501	501 Cost of Goods Sold	100.00	
				Network products	115	115 Merchandise Inventory		100.00
				Network products	501	501 Cost of Goods Sold	50.00	
				Network products	115	115 Merchandise Inventory		50.00
				Network products	401	401 Sales		300.00
							$ 1,125.00	**$ 1,125.00**

Journal, page 8 of 8

03/30/2018	Sales Receipt	1071	Credit Card Sales		101	101 Checking	1,450.00	
				Computers	115	115 Merchandise Inventory		500.00
				Computers	501	501 Cost of Goods Sold	500.00	
				Computers	401	401 Sales		1,000.00
				Network products	501	501 Cost of Goods Sold	150.00	
				Network products	115	115 Merchandise Inventory		150.00
				Network products	401	401 Sales		300.00
				Data storage	501	501 Cost of Goods Sold	75.00	
				Data storage	115	115 Merchandise Inventory		75.00
				Data storage	401	401 Sales		150.00
							$ 2,175.00	$ 2,175.00
03/30/2018	Sales Receipt	1072	Credit Card Sales		101	101 Checking	1,480.00	
				Data storage	115	115 Merchandise Inventory		180.00
				Data storage	115	115 Merchandise Inventory		30.00
				Data storage	501	501 Cost of Goods Sold	30.00	
				Data storage	401	401 Sales		480.00
				Data storage	501	501 Cost of Goods Sold	30.00	
				Data storage	115	115 Merchandise Inventory		30.00
				Data storage	501	501 Cost of Goods Sold	180.00	
				Computers	501	501 Cost of Goods Sold	500.00	
				Computers	401	401 Sales		1,000.00
				Computers	115	115 Merchandise Inventory		500.00
							$ 2,220.00	$ 2,220.00
TOTAL							$ 31,303.01	$ 31,303.01

Export the Journal to Excel and save as a PDF file. Use the file name **Chapter 10_Journal**.

END-OF-QUARTER ADUSTING ENTRIES

It is the policy of QB Cloud to record adjusting entries at the end of the quarter. The accounting records are complete through March 31, the end of the first quarter. Make the following journal entries as of March 31, 20XY. (*Hint:* Refer to end-of-quarter adjusting entries in Chapter 7.)

1. Adjust three months of prepaid rent.
2. Adjust prepaid insurance. QB Cloud paid a one year insurance premium on 10/2/XX. An adjusting entry was recorded on December 31.

3. Adjust accumulated depreciation. Use straight-line depreciation for computer equipment. The computer equipment has a three-year service life and a $400 salvage value.
4. Display the March 31, 20XY journal.

QB Cloud_Student Name

JOURNAL

March 31, 2018

DATE	TRANSACTION TYPE	NUM	NAME	MEMO/DESCRIPTION	ACCOUNT #	ACCOUNT	DEBIT	CREDIT
03/31/2018	Journal Entry	5			623	623 Rent or Lease	$6,000.00	
				Adjust prepaid rent	123	123 Prepaid Rent		$6,000.00
							$6,000.00	**$6,000.00**
03/31/2018	Journal Entry	6			611	611 Insurance	$750.00	
				Adjust prepaid insurance	125	125 Prepaid Insurance		$750.00
							$750.00	**$750.00**
03/31/2018	Journal Entry	7			607	607 Depreciation Expense	$800.00	
				Adjust depreciation	137	137 Accumulated Depreciation		$800.00
							$800.00	**$800.00**
TOTAL							**$7,550.00**	**$7,550.00**

- Export the March 31 Journal to Excel and save as a PDF file. Use the file name **Chapter 10_March 31 Journal**.

Comment: In Chapter 10, the end-of-quarter adjusting entries are journalized and posted before Account 101 Checking is reconciled. This policy change takes affect for the new year. At the end of last year, the adjusting entries were completed after account reconcilation.

The March 31 bank statement is completed in Exercise 10-1.

REPORTS

1. **Trial Balance** (adjusted) from 1/1/XY to 3/31/XY

QB Cloud_Student Name

TRIAL BALANCE

As of March 31, 2018

	DEBIT	CREDIT
101 Checking	55,239.93	
105 Accounts Receivable (A/R)	2,130.00	
115 Merchandise Inventory	10,030.00	
123 Prepaid Rent	0.00	
125 Prepaid Insurance	1,500.00	
130 Undeposited Funds	0.00	
135 Computer Equipment	10,000.00	
137 Accumulated Depreciation		1,600.00
201 Accounts Payable (A/P)		5,340.00
205 Loan Payable		0.00
301 Common Stock		60,000.00
305 Opening Balance Equity		0.00
318 Retained Earnings		7,093.52
401 Sales		30,650.00
501 Cost of Goods Sold	15,325.00	
601 Advertising	450.00	
603 Bank Charges	40.00	
605 Dues & Subscriptions	175.00	
607 Depreciation Expense	800.00	
609 Freight & Delivery	155.97	
611 Insurance	750.00	
613 Interest Expense	150.00	
619 Meals and Entertainment	55.22	
621 Office Supplies	312.12	
623 Rent or Lease	6,000.00	
625 Repair & Maintenance	450.00	
627 Shipping and delivery expense	94.00	
629 Stationery & Printing	150.00	
633 Telephone Expense	477.00	
635 Utilities	399.28	
TOTAL	**$104,683.52**	**$104,683.52**

- Export the Trial Balance to Excel and save as a PDF file. Use the file name **Chapter 10_Adjusted Trial Balance**.

2. **A/R Aging Summary:** As of 3/31/20XY

QB Cloud_Student Name

A/R AGING SUMMARY

As of March 31, 2018

	CURRENT	1 - 30	31 - 60	61 - 90	91 AND OVER	TOTAL
eBiz	270.00					$270.00
Law Offices of Williamson, Gallagher & Katz	300.00					$300.00
Permanente Medical Services	360.00					$360.00
Springfield Unified School District	800.00					$800.00
WebPro	400.00					$400.00
TOTAL	**$2,130.00**	**$0.00**	**$0.00**	**$0.00**	**$0.00**	**$2,130.00**

- Export the A/R Aging Summary to Excel and save as a PDF file. Use the file name, **Chapter 10_AR Aging Summary.**

3. **Inventory Valuation Summary**: As of 3/31/20XY

QB Cloud_Student Name

INVENTORY VALUATION SUMMARY

As of March 31, 2018

	SKU	QTY	ASSET VALUE	CALC. AVG
Computers		10.00	5,000.00	500.00
Data storage		10.00	150.00	15.00
Network products		11.00	275.00	25.00
Web server		21.00	4,200.00	200.00
Webinars		9.00	405.00	45.00
TOTAL			**$10,030.00**	

- Export to Excel and save as a PDF file. Use the file name **Chapter 10_Inventory Valuation Summary.**

4. **A/P Aging Summary**: As of 3/31/20XY

QB Cloud_Student Name

A/P AGING SUMMARY

As of March 31, 2018

	CURRENT	1 - 30	31 - 60	61 - 90	91 AND OVER	TOTAL
AmpleStore Inc.	480.00					$480.00
Any Time Deployment	525.00					$525.00
CloudZ Channel	2,200.00					$2,200.00
Computers 2 You	2,000.00					$2,000.00
Conf/Call	135.00					$135.00
TOTAL	**$5,340.00**	**$0.00**	**$0.00**	**$0.00**	**$0.00**	**$5,340.00**

➤ Export to Excel and save as a PDF file. Use the file name **Chapter 10_AP Aging Summary.**

5. **Profit and Loss** from 1/1/20XY to 3/31/20XY

QB Cloud_Student Name

PROFIT AND LOSS

January - March, 2018

	TOTAL
INCOME	
401 Sales	30,650.00
Total Income	**$30,650.00**
COST OF GOODS SOLD	
501 Cost of Goods Sold	15,325.00
Total Cost of Goods Sold	**$15,325.00**
GROSS PROFIT	**$15,325.00**
EXPENSES	
601 Advertising	450.00
603 Bank Charges	40.00
605 Dues & Subscriptions	175.00
607 Depreciation Expense	800.00
609 Freight & Delivery	155.97
611 Insurance	750.00
613 Interest Expense	150.00
619 Meals and Entertainment	55.22
621 Office Supplies	312.12
623 Rent or Lease	6,000.00
625 Repair & Maintenance	450.00
627 Shipping and delivery expense	94.00
629 Stationery & Printing	150.00
633 Telephone Expense	477.00
635 Utilities	399.28
Total Expenses	**$10,458.59**
NET OPERATING INCOME	**$4,866.41**
NET INCOME	**$4,866.41**

➢ Export the Profit and Loss to Excel and save as a PDF file. Use the file name **Chapter 10_Profit and Loss**.

6. **Profit and Loss by Month** from 1/1/20XY to 3/31/XY

QB Cloud_Student Name

PROFIT AND LOSS BY MONTH

January - March, 2018

	JAN 2018	FEB 2018	MAR 2018	TOTAL
INCOME				
401 Sales	8,610.00	9,180.00	12,860.00	$30,650.00
Total Income	**$8,610.00**	**$9,180.00**	**$12,860.00**	**$30,650.00**
COST OF GOODS SOLD				
501 Cost of Goods Sold	4,305.00	4,590.00	6,430.00	$15,325.00
Total Cost of Goods Sold	**$4,305.00**	**$4,590.00**	**$6,430.00**	**$15,325.00**
GROSS PROFIT	**$4,305.00**	**$4,590.00**	**$6,430.00**	**$15,325.00**
EXPENSES				
601 Advertising	125.00	150.00	175.00	$450.00
603 Bank Charges	20.00	20.00		$40.00
605 Dues & Subscriptions	100.00	75.00		$175.00
607 Depreciation Expense			800.00	$800.00
609 Freight & Delivery		95.97	60.00	$155.97
611 Insurance			750.00	$750.00
613 Interest Expense		150.00		$150.00
619 Meals and Entertainment		55.22		$55.22
621 Office Supplies	88.52	91.20	132.40	$312.12
623 Rent or Lease			6,000.00	$6,000.00
625 Repair & Maintenance	150.00	150.00	150.00	$450.00
627 Shipping and delivery expense	47.00		47.00	$94.00
629 Stationery & Printing			150.00	$150.00
633 Telephone Expense	158.32	158.32	160.36	$477.00
635 Utilities	90.14	195.89	113.25	$399.28
Total Expenses	**$778.98**	**$1,141.60**	**$8,538.01**	**$10,458.59**
NET OPERATING INCOME	**$3,526.02**	**$3,448.40**	**$ -2,108.01**	**$4,866.41**
NET INCOME	**$3,526.02**	**$3,448.40**	**$ -2,108.01**	**$4,866.41**

➢ Export the Profit and Loss by Month to Excel and save as a PDF file. Use the file name **Chapter 10_Profit and Loss by Month.**

7. **Balance Sheet** from 1/1/20XY to 3/31/20XY

QB Cloud_Student Name

BALANCE SHEET

As of March 31, 2018

	TOTAL
ASSETS	
Current Assets	
Bank Accounts	
101 Checking	55,239.93
Total Bank Accounts	**$55,239.93**
Accounts Receivable	
105 Accounts Receivable (A/R)	2,130.00
Total Accounts Receivable	**$2,130.00**
Other Current Assets	
115 Merchandise Inventory	10,030.00
123 Prepaid Rent	0.00
125 Prepaid Insurance	1,500.00
130 Undeposited Funds	0.00
Total Other Current Assets	**$11,530.00**
Total Current Assets	**$68,899.93**
Fixed Assets	
135 Computer Equipment	10,000.00
137 Accumulated Depreciation	-1,600.00
Total Fixed Assets	**$8,400.00**
TOTAL ASSETS	**$77,299.93**
LIABILITIES AND EQUITY	
Liabilities	
Current Liabilities	
Accounts Payable	
201 Accounts Payable (A/P)	5,340.00
Total Accounts Payable	**$5,340.00**
Other Current Liabilities	
205 Loan Payable	0.00
Total Other Current Liabilities	**$0.00**
Total Current Liabilities	**$5,340.00**
Total Liabilities	**$5,340.00**
Equity	
301 Common Stock	60,000.00
305 Opening Balance Equity	0.00
318 Retained Earnings	7,093.52
Net Income	4,866.41
Total Equity	**$71,959.93**
TOTAL LIABILITIES AND EQUITY	**$77,299.93**

- Export the Balance Sheet to Excel and save as a PDF file. Use the file name **Chapter 10_Balance Sheet**.

8. **Statement of Cash Flows** from 1/1/20XY to 3/31/20XY

QB Cloud_Student Name

STATEMENT OF CASH FLOWS

January - March, 2018

	TOTAL
OPERATING ACTIVITIES	
Net Income	4,866.41
Adjustments to reconcile Net Income to Net Cash provided by operations:	
105 Accounts Receivable (A/R)	-1,730.00
115 Merchandise Inventory	-160.00
123 Prepaid Rent	0.00
125 Prepaid Insurance	750.00
137 Accumulated Depreciation	800.00
201 Accounts Payable (A/P)	2,220.00
205 Loan Payable	-5,000.00
Total Adjustments to reconcile Net Income to Net Cash provided by operations:	**-3,120.00**
Net cash provided by operating activities	**$1,746.41**
NET CASH INCREASE FOR PERIOD	**$1,746.41**
CASH AT BEGINNING OF PERIOD	53,493.52
CASH AT END OF PERIOD	**$55,239.93**

- Export the Statement of Cash Flows to Excel and save as a PDF file. Use the file name **Chapter 10_Statement of Cash Flows.**

CHECK YOUR PROGRESS

1. What is the account balance from 1/1/20XY to 3/31/20XY in these accounts? Indicate whether these accounts have debit (dr.) or credit (cr.) balances.

Account 101 Checking ____________________

Account 115 Merchandise Inventory ____________________

Account 123 Prepaid Rent ____________________

Account 401 Sales ____________________

Net Income ____________________

Total Assets ____________________

2. What accounts are debited and credited for the prepaid rent adjustment? Indicate the account type.

____

3. What is the amount of the adjusting entry for prepaid rent?

____

4. What accounts are debited and credited for the prepaid insurance adjustment? Indicate the account type.

____

5. What is the amount of the adjustment entry for prepaid insurance?

____

6. What accounts are debited and credited for the depreciation adjustment? Indicate the account type.

____

7. What is the amount of the adjustment for depreciation?

____

SIGN OUT

To sign out of QBO, go to the company settings (click on the company name), link to Sign Out. *Or,* continue.

ONLINE LEARNING CENTER (OLC): www.mhhe.com/qbo2e

The OLC includes additional Chapter 10 resources. Go online to www.mhhe.com/qbo2e > Student Edition > Chapter 10.

1. Narrated PowerPoints.
2. Online quizzes: 10 True or False and 10 multiple-choice questions. The Online quizzes are graded and can be emailed to your instructor.
3. Analysis question: Answer the analysis question, then email to your instructor.

4. Going to the Net

   a. Go to the QuickBooks Blog. The website is http://quickbooks.intuit.com/blog/. To explore what is included on the Blog, click each selection. As of this writing, the selections are News, Thought Leadership, What's New in QBO, Innovation, Accountant Advice, Customer Profiles, Search.

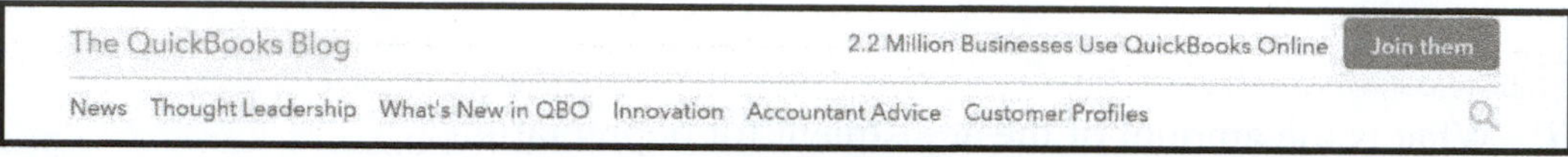

   b. Write a brief summary of what is included within each Blog selection.

5. Videos:

   a. Go to Prof. Susan Crosson's Financial Accounting videos at http://www.bus.emory.edu/scrosso/FA%20Videos.htm. To review financial accounting principles and procedures, link to a video.
   b. Watch QuickBooks tutorials at http://quickbooks.intuit.com/tutorials/all-quickbooks-tutorials/.

6. Glossary of terms: Words that are italicized and boldfaced are defined in the glossary. The Glossary is also Appendix B.
7. Exercise 10-3, Problem Solving.

Exercise 10-1: Follow the instructions below to complete Exercise 10-1:

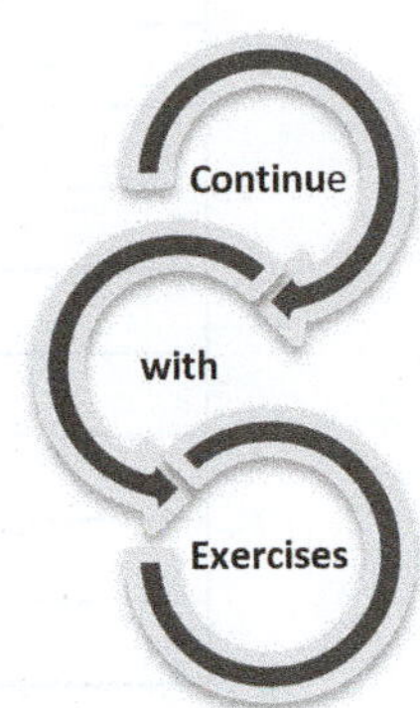

1. Start QBO. Sign into QB Cloud_Student Name.
2. To reconcile Account 101 Checking, use the March 31 bank statement. (*Hint:* The Statement Ending Date is 3/31/20XY.)

Statement of Account Checking Account March 1 to March 31, 20XY	Account No. 7731-2256		QB Cloud_Student Name Your address Your city, state, Zip
	REGULAR CHECKING		
Previous Balance	2/28/XY	$48,082.94	
15 Deposits (+)		12,280.00	
16 checks (-)		5,123.01	
Service Charge		20.00	
Ending Balance	3/31/XY	**$55,219.93**	
	DEPOSITS		
	3/6/XY	180.00	
	3/6/XY	1,450.00	
	3/6/XY	1,540.00	
	3/6/XY	1,150.00	
	3/19/XY	300.00	
	3/19/XY	270.00	
	3/19/XY	400.00	
	3/21/XY	400.00	
	3/25/XY	1,000.00	
	3/26/XY	1,240.00	
	3/26/XY	150.00	
	3/26/XY	520.00	
	3/30/XY	750.00	
	3/30/XY	1,450.00	
	3/30/XY	1,480.00	*Continued*

CHECKS (Asterisk * indicates break in check number sequence)				
	3/9/XY	1098	300.00	
	3/10/XY	1099	1,000.00	
	3/21/XY	1100	180.00	
	3/21/XY	1101	135.00	
	3/21/XY	1102	82.13	
	3/22/XY	1103	150.00	
	3/23/XY	1104	78.23	
	3/23/XY	1105	132.40	
	3/23/XY	1106	175.00	
	3/24/XY	1107	113.25	
	3/24/XY	1108	60.00	
	3/24/XY	1109	47.00	
	3/27XY	1110	150.00	
	3/27/XY	1111	250.00	
	3/28/XY	1112	2,000.00	
	3/28XY	1113	270.00	

3. Save the Reconciliation report as a PDF file. Use the file name **Exercise 10-1_Reconciliation Report**.

Exercise 10-2: Follow the instructions below to complete Exercise 10-2:

1. Save these reports as PDF files and export to Excel. Run reports from **1/1/20XY to 3/31/20XY** unless another date range is shown. (*Hint:* When the report needs as As of date, use 3/31/20XY)

   - Exercise 10-2_Journal (from 3/31/20XY to 3/31/20XY)
   - Exercise 10-2_Trial Balance
   - Exercise 10-2_Transaction Detail by Account (from 3/1/20XY to 3/31/XY)
   - Exercise 10-2_General Ledger (from 3/1/20XY to 3/31/20XY)
   - Exercise 10-2_Customer Balance Summary

- Exercise 10-2_Vendor Balance Summary
- Exercise 10-2_Profit and Loss
- Exercise 10-2_Balance Sheet
- Exercise 10-2_Statement of Cash Flows

2. **Check Your Figures** (from 1/1/201XY to 3/31/XY):

    - Account 125 Prepaid Insurance, $1,500.00
    - Account 137 Accumulated Depreciation, $1,600.00
    - Account 603 Bank Charges, $60.00
    - Account 607 Depreciation Expense, $800.00
    - Account 611 Insurance, $750.00
    - Account 621 Office Supplies, $312.12
    - Cash at end of period, $55,219.93

Exercise 10-3, Problem Solving

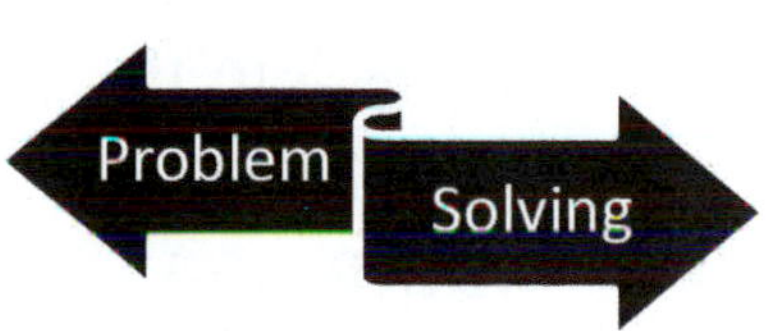

The Online Learning Center includes Exercise 10-3 at www.mhhe.com/qbo2e > Student Edition > Chapter 10 > Problem Solving.

1. What are the similarities and differences between the Transaction Detail by Account and the General Ledger?
2. Why does the Profit and Loss by Month report (page 505) show a Net Loss for March 20XX? Show the calculation.

CHAPTER 10 INDEX

Chapter 11 Certification, Report Customization and QB Labs

Scenario: Chapter 11 focuses on four areas:

- QuickBooks Online Certification includes objectives, what students should know, and grade percentage.
- Report Customization includes settings to help build the report you want to see.
- Management Reports: There are three ready-to-use management reports–Company overview, sales performance, and expenses performance.
- QuickBooks Labs shows some plug-ins that can be used.

To review what you will do in Chapter 12, read the objectives.

OBJECTIVES

1. Learn about QuickBooks Online User Certification and the textbook chapters that coordinate with the certification test.
2. Prepare management reports.
3. Complete report customization.
4. Use QuickBooks Labs.
5. Use the Online Learning Center, www.mhhe.com/qbo2e, for additional resources.
6. Complete Exercises 11-1 and 11-2.

QUICKBOOKS ONLINE USER CERTIFICATION

Students confirm their QuickBooks Online knowledge by passing the QuickBooks Online Certified User test. QuickBooks Online is the leading cloud-based accounting software for small business. QBO provides an easy-to-understand interface for students to grasp accounting concepts while honing cloud computing skills. QuickBooks Online User Certification is managed by Certiport, www.certiport.com.

The chart outlines what the certification test covers in the Certification Objectives column and the chapters within *Computer Accounting with QuickBooks Online* that cover those objectives. A summary of the Certification test, including subtopics, and grade percentage, is shown on the chart.

QuickBooks Online Certification and *Computer Accounting with QuickBooks Online: A Cloud-Based Approach, 2/e*			
Certification Objectives	**Chapters**	**Title**	**Students should know how to:**
	1	QuickBooks Online Test-drive	Use this chapter to learn about QBO's user interface. No questions are on the Certification Test using QBO's sample company (test drive).
QBO Setup **14%**	2	New Company Setup and the Chart of Accounts	• Set up a QBO company. • Complete company settings (preferences for your company) • Set up, add, edit, and save the chart of accounts. • Assign a company administrator. • Export reports to Excel and save as PDF files. • Use the Audit Log. • Sign in and sign out of QBO.

Certification Objectives	Chapter	Title	Student should know how to:
General Knowledge	3	Beginning Balances and October Transaction Register	• Navigate and move around QBO (use home page, navigation bar, add transactions, create menu, view recent transactions, search, etc.) • Set up beginning balances. • Write checks, post to the general ledger, and print reports.
Purchases/ Money-Out **18%**	4	Vendors and Inventory	• Set up and manage lists and items (vendors and inventory). • Edit company settings for expenses. • Navigate and use the vendor pages. • Use the purchases workflow: entering and paying bills (A/P), writing checks, using a credit card, using a debit card. • Add vendor transactions, search transactions, and edit them. • Print reports.

Certification Objectives	Chapter	Title	Students should know how to:
Sales/ Money-In **20%**	5	Customers and Sales	• Set up and manage lists (customers and sales). • Add sales invoices and customer payments. • Navigate and use the customer pages. • Use the sales workflow: Invoicing (A/R) and Sales Receipts (A/R). • Use Undeposited Funds, accounts receivable, and checking accounts in the invoicing system. • Create statements and understand why. • Print reports.
A/P and A/R systems	6	December Source Documents	• Identify general ledger, accounts payable and accounts receivable source documents. • Make the appropriate selections for entering invoices, bills, payments, etc. • Identify and use adjusting entries. • Print the appropriate reports.

Certification Objectives	Chapter	Title	Student should know how to:
List Management **12%**	Chapters 2 through 6		• The names of majors lists in QBO and what information is tracked in each. • How to manage lists (Customers, Chart of Accounts, Products and Services, etc. • Add new list entries.
Reports **8%**	7	Analysis and Reports–End of Fourth Quarter and Year	• Analyze reports. • Process and understand reports. • Send reports to Excel and save as PDF files.
Basic Accounting	8	January Source Documents	• Describe financial statements and understand what they mean. • Describe the difference between cash and accrual reports. • Close the fiscal year. • Print the postclosing trial balance.
Basic Accounting	9	February Source Documents	• Identify general journal, write checks, sales, and purchase documents. • Record transactions on QBO's appropriate pages. • Print reports and why.

Certification Objective	Chapter	Title	Students should know how to:
Basic Accounting 10%	10	March Source Documents and End of First Quarter	• Describe a basic understanding of QB Online features, functions, and navigation. • Identify general journal, write checks, sales documents, purchase documents, and how they are processed within the QBO system. • Record transactions on QBO's appropriate pages. • Print reports and understand why.
Customization/ Saving time 18%	11	Certification, QuickBooks Labs and Report Customization	• Complete report customization exercises. • The time saving benefits of using QBO. • Go online to www.mhhe.com/qbo2e to take practice tests for Certification.
Updates	12	Apps, Updates and QB Blog	• Learn about QB Online updates.

Before taking the Certification Practice Test, complete the quizzes online at www.mhhe.com/qbo2e > Student Edition > select each Chapter > complete the Multiple Choice Quiz and True or False quizzes.

The Online Learning Center at www.mhhe.com/qbo2e > Certification includes this chart and practice tests for QBO Certification. To pass the certification test, you need to be proficient in these software features and functions. The list below expands on the chart.

1. QuickBooks Online Setup

   a. Before setting up a QBO account, what information is required?
   b. How to sign in and sign out.
   c. How to complete company settings.
   d. Customizing the home page.
   e. Setting up lists – customers, vendors, products and services.

2. QBO General Knowledge

   a. User Interface and navigation – familiarity with QBO's home page, menus, navigation bar, etc.
   b. How to save reports in Excel and Adobe PDF.
   c. How to determine the user profile, subscription status, and QBO updates.
   d. How and why to set up a User ID and password.
   e. How and why to complete account settings, including Company, Billing & Subscription, Sales, Expenses, Payments and Advanced.

3. List Management

    a. Management customer, vendor, product and service lists.
    b. Adding new list entries.
    c. Deleting list entries.
    d. Editing list entries.

4. Items or Products and Services

    a. How does QBO use items to perform accounting procedures behind the scenes? For example, what are the appropriate journal entries when recording inventory transactions?
    b. What are the different types of inventory and when to use each type?
    c. How do you use items for different types of situations; for example, products for a specific price; services for a specific price?

5. Sales

    a. Who is listed in the Customer Center?
    b. How to navigate the Customer Center?
    c. How to complete the workflow from the sales to receiving customer payments for Invoicing (A/R) and Sales Receipts (no A/R).
    d. How and why to record a customer credit.
    e. How and why to create statements.
    f. Understand the invoicing cycle.

6. Purchases

    a. Who should be listed in the Vendor Center?
    b. Navigating the Vendor Center.
    c. How to complete the workflows for making purchases, including entering and paying bills (A/P), writing checks, using a credit card, and using a debit card.
    d. How to record purchases transactions.
    e. How and why to record a Vendor credit.
    f. Bank reconciliation.

7. Reports

    a. Why and how to use the Report Center.
    b. How to customize reports.
    c. Understand what each report represents.
    d. How and why to send reports to Excel.
    e. How are reports memorized?

8. Basic Accounting

    a. What the basic financial statements are and what do they mean and represent?
    b. The difference between cash and accrual reports.
    c. How to enter a Journal Entry.

9. Customization

   a. How does QBO memorize transactions?
   b. How to create customize reports.

GETTING STARTED

1. Start your browser. Go online to http://qbo.intuit.com.
2. Sign in to QBO with your User ID and Password.

CHECK YOUR DATA

Make sure you have the data that will be used in this chapter. Display the 10/1/20XX to 11/30/20XX Profit and Loss report.

The October through November 20XX P&L is shown on the next page.

QB Cloud_Student Name

PROFIT AND LOSS

October - November, 2017

	TOTAL
INCOME	
401 Sales	17,920.00
Total Income	**$17,920.00**
COST OF GOODS SOLD	
501 Cost of Goods Sold	5,960.00
Total Cost of Goods Sold	**$5,960.00**
GROSS PROFIT	**$11,960.00**
EXPENSES	
601 Advertising	375.00
603 Bank Charges	40.00
605 Dues & Subscriptions	150.00
609 Freight & Delivery	153.80
619 Meals and Entertainment	172.80
621 Office Supplies	338.67
625 Repair & Maintenance	140.00
627 Shipping and delivery expense	47.00
629 Stationery & Printing	553.18
633 Telephone Expense	316.64
635 Utilities	163.32
Total Expenses	**$2,450.41**
NET OPERATING INCOME	**$9,509.59**
NET INCOME	**$9,509.59**

CUSTOMIZING REPORTS

Reports let you view your company and financial information at a glance. If you don't see the report that you want, simply customize an existing report and memorize it to use later. The Reports page lists the reports that are available.

- Recommended: Reports that QBO recommends you run.
- Frequently Run: Reports that you run most frequently. They are easy to access in this section.
- My Custom Reports: Reports that you have customized and saved.
- Management Reports: Management reports include professional, ready-to-use ***templates*** that contain reports and other customizable content, consolidated into a single document. They can be printed, emailed, or exported.
- All Reports: A list of all available reports, categorized by subject.

Follow these steps to use Management Reports.

Go to the Reports page > click Management Reports.

Management Reports

Follow these steps to look at the Sales Performance report.

1. Go to the Reports page > select Management Reports.

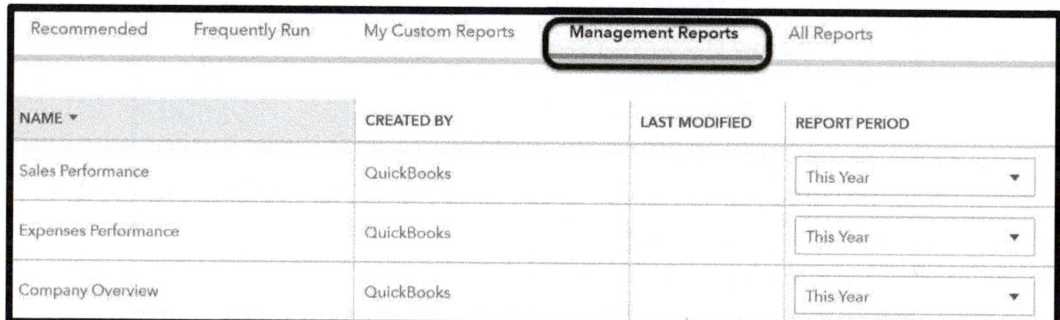

2. On the Sales Performance row, click on the down-arrow next to This Year > select Custom > from 10/1/20XX to 11/30/20XX.

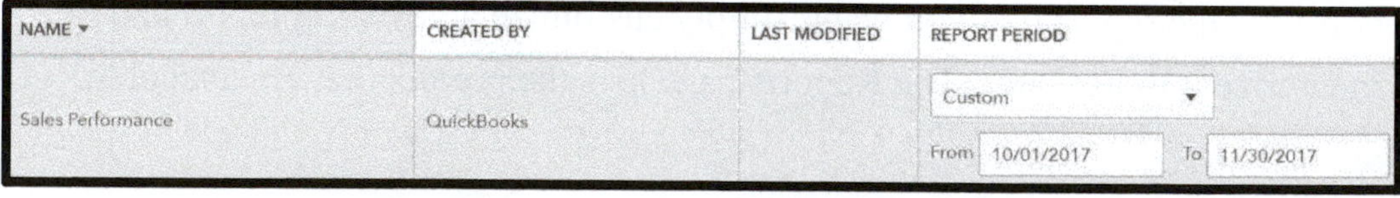

3. Click <View>. The Print preview page appears. Read the information.
4. Click <Print>. If necessary, select <Change>, then <Save as PDF>.
5. Click on the vertical bar to go to page 2 of the 5-page report. Page 2 is the Table of Contents.
6. Go to page 3 to see the Profit and Loss from October – November, 20XX. Compare it to the one shown on page 527.
7. On page 4, the A/R Aging Detail is shown. It is blank because the report contains no date for the specified date range (10/1/20XX to 11/30/20XX).
8. Go to page 5 to see the Sales by Customer Summary, October – November 20XX.

Sales by Customer Summary

October - November, 2017

	Total
Cash Sales	17,030.00
eBiz	120.00
Law Offices of Williamson, Gallagher & Katz	100.00
Permanente Medical Services	270.00
Springfield Unified School District	400.00
TOTAL	**$17,920.00**

9. To save the Management Report as a PDF file, click on the <Save> icon -- Use the file name **Chapter 11_Management Report_Sales Performance.pdf**.
10. When through, click Close.

Edit the Management Report

1. The Sales Performance row, Report Period is Custom, from 10/1/20XX to 11/30/20XX. Click the down-arrow next to <View>, select <Edit>.
2. After selecting <Edit>, the Management Reports page appears. Read the reminder: To customize this report, just scroll through each section here to see the different changes you can make. (*Hint:* Read pop-up messages.)

   Template name: Sales Performance.

   Cover title: Management Report.

   Subtitle" Type **QB Cloud_Student Name** (use your first and last name.)

   Report Period: For the period ended {ReportEndDate}

   Prepared By: Type **your first and last name**

   Prepared date: Current date is shown.

   Disclaimer: For Management use only

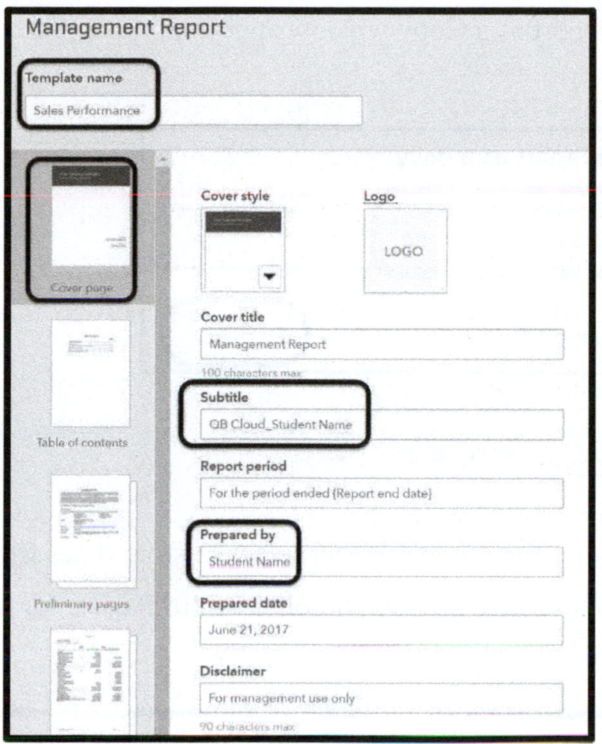

3. Go to page the Reports page > link to Add new report. In the New report area, complete these fields.

    Select a report: Trial Balance

    Period > Custom > From 10/1/20XX to 11/30/20XX.

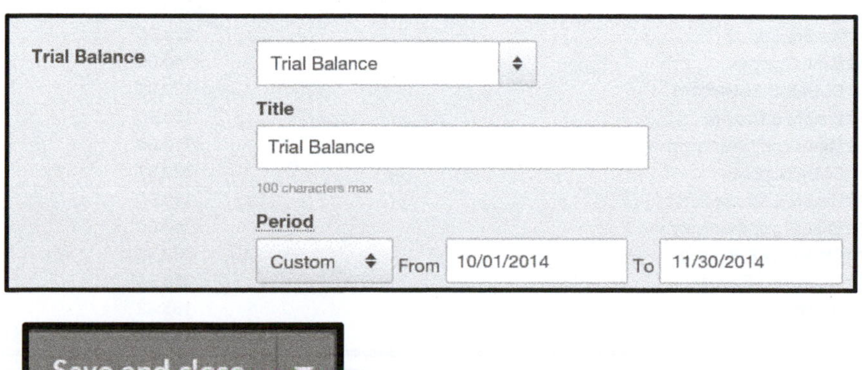

Save and close

When the Save Report as a Copy window appears, type **2_Sales Performance**.

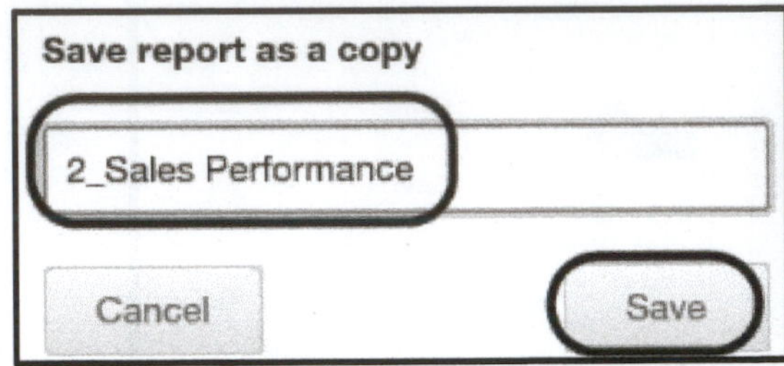

Click <Save>, then <Save and close>.

4. Go to the 2_Sales Performance row and select Custom dates from 10/1/20XX to 11/30/20XX > View. Scroll down to Page 6 for the Trial Balance as of November 30, 20XX.

Trial Balance

As of November 30, 2017

	Debit	Credit
101 Checking	61,469.59	
115 Merchandise Inventory	11,960.00	
123 Prepaid Rent	6,000.00	
125 Prepaid Insurance	3,000.00	
135 Computer Equipment	10,000.00	
201 Accounts Payable (A/P)		17,920.00
205 Loan Payable		5,000.00
301 Common Stock		60,000.00
401 Sales		17,920.00
501 Cost of Goods Sold	5,960.00	
601 Advertising	375.00	
603 Bank Charges	40.00	
605 Dues & Subscriptions	150.00	
609 Freight & Delivery	153.80	
619 Meals and Entertainment	172.80	
621 Office Supplies	338.67	
625 Repair & Maintenance	140.00	
627 Shipping and delivery expense	47.00	
629 Stationery & Printing	553.18	
633 Telephone Expense	316.64	
635 Utilities	163.32	
TOTAL	$100,840.00	$100,840.00

5. Click <Print>. Save as a PDF file. Use the file name, **Chapter 11_2_Sales Performance.pdf.**
6. Close the Print preview page. Observe that that 2_Sales Performance is shown on the Management Reports page.

My Custom Reports

Once you customize a report, the My Custom Reports selection on the Reports page lists the customized reports.

1. If necessary, go to the Reports page > Recommended > Profit and Loss.

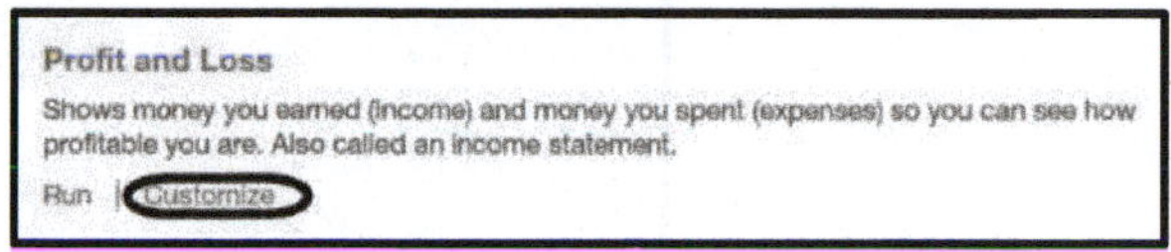

2. Click Customize. A Customize Report window appears. Complete these fields.

Report period: Select Custom, 10/1/20XX to 11/30/20XX
Accounting method: Accrual is selected
Number format: Except zero amount is checked

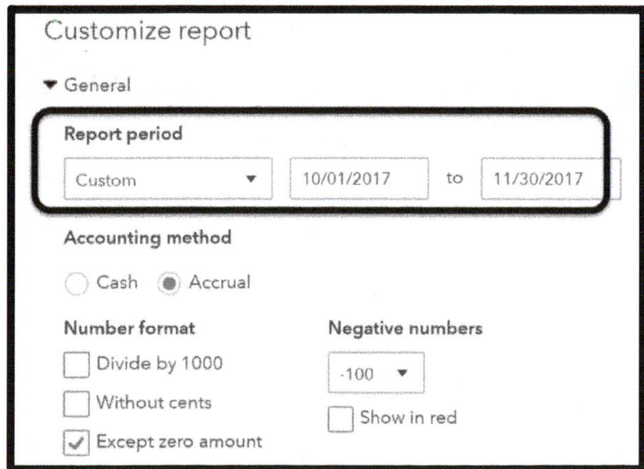

3. Select Rows/Columns. Make these selections:

Columns: Select Months

Place a checkmark next to % of Income

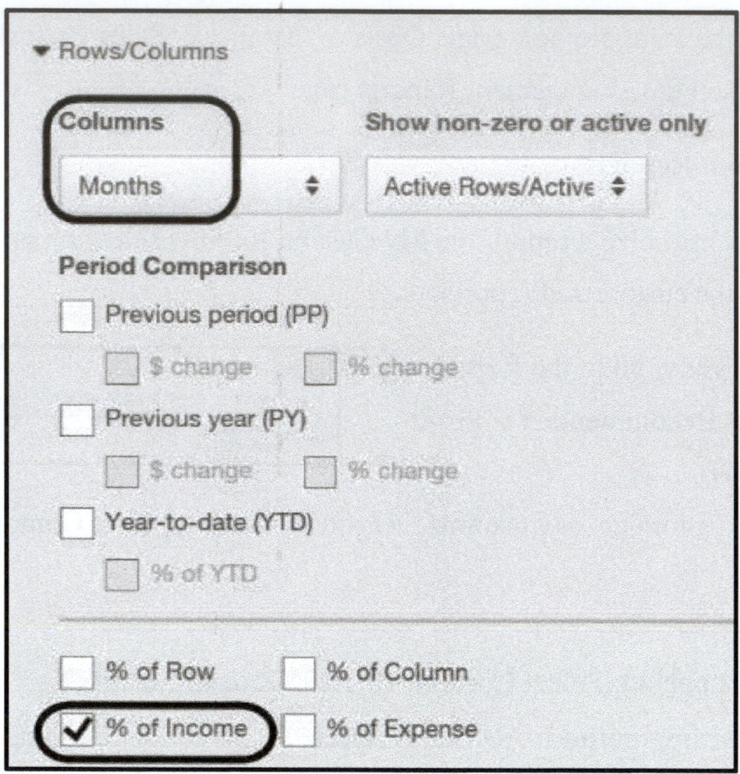

4. Run report. Your customized report appears. The Profit and Loss, October – November, 20XX is shown on the next page.

QB Cloud_Student Name
Profit and Loss
October - November, 2017

	Oct 2017		Nov 2017		Total	
	Current	% of Income	Current	% of Income	Current	% of Income
Income						
401 Sales	6,000.00	100.00%	11,920.00	100.00%	17,920.00	100.00%
Total Income	**$ 6,000.00**	**100.00%**	**$ 11,920.00**	**100.00%**	**$ 17,920.00**	**100.00%**
Cost of Goods Sold						
501 Cost of Goods Sold		0.00%	5,960.00	50.00%	5,960.00	33.26%
Total Cost of Goods Sold	**$ 0.00**	**0.00%**	**$ 5,960.00**	**50.00%**	**$ 5,960.00**	**33.26%**
Gross Profit	**$ 6,000.00**	**100.00%**	**$ 5,960.00**	**50.00%**	**$ 11,960.00**	**66.74%**
Expenses						
601 Advertising	125.00	2.08%	250.00	2.10%	375.00	2.09%
603 Bank Charges	20.00	0.33%	20.00	0.17%	40.00	0.22%
605 Dues & Subscriptions	150.00	2.50%		0.00%	150.00	0.84%
609 Freight & Delivery	64.65	1.08%	89.15	0.75%	153.80	0.86%
619 Meals and Entertainment	126.40	2.11%	46.40	0.39%	172.80	0.96%
621 Office Supplies	226.85	3.78%	111.82	0.94%	338.67	1.89%
625 Repair & Maintenance	140.00	2.33%		0.00%	140.00	0.78%
627 Shipping and delivery expense	47.00	0.78%		0.00%	47.00	0.26%
629 Stationery & Printing	425.22	7.09%	127.96	1.07%	553.18	3.09%
633 Telephone Expense	158.32	2.64%	158.32	1.33%	316.64	1.77%
635 Utilities	79.00	1.32%	84.32	0.71%	163.32	0.91%
Total Expenses	**$ 1,562.44**	**26.04%**	**$ 887.97**	**7.45%**	**$ 2,450.41**	**13.67%**
Net Operating Income	**$ 4,437.56**	**73.96%**	**$ 5,072.03**	**42.55%**	**$ 9,509.59**	**53.07%**
Net Income	**$ 4,437.56**	**73.96%**	**$ 5,072.03**	**42.55%**	**$ 9,509.59**	**53.07%**

5. Save customization. In the Custom report name field, type **Oct_Nov_Profit and Loss** > click <Save>.

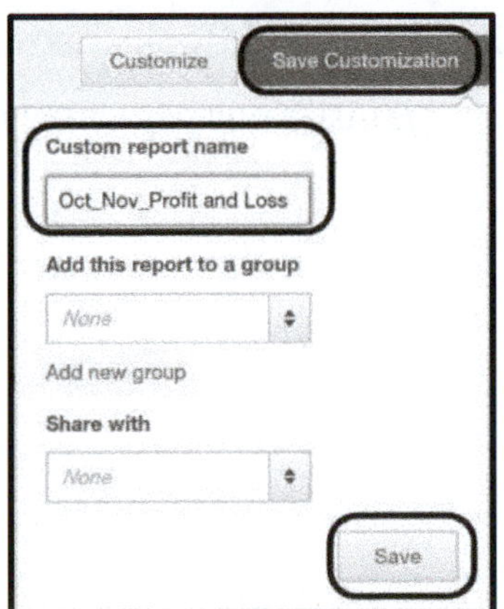

6. On the Reports page > go to My Custom Reports > select Oct_Nov_Profit and Loss. The Oct_Nov_Profit and Loss report is shown. Export to Excel and save as a PDF file. The file name is **Chapter 11_Oct_Nov_Profit and Loss**.

QUICKBOOKS LABS

QuickBooks Labs is like a high-tech playground for QuickBooks experts. It's a place where you can be the first to try experimental plug-ins. Like any good laboratory, QuickBooks Labs is always moving forward. Sometimes experiments break or disappear. And sometimes they evolve into real features. Because the plug-ins are experimental, they are not supported by QB technical support.

Note: Because the QB Labs plug-ins are experimental, they are not supported by Intuit's technical support agents.

1. Go to  > QuickBooks Labs. The QB Labs plug-ins that are shown are as of the author's system date. Your plug-ins may differ.
2. The QuickBooks Labs, Come play in our high-tech playground page appears. (*Hint:* Your page may differ. QuickBooks Labs changes plug-ins regularly.)

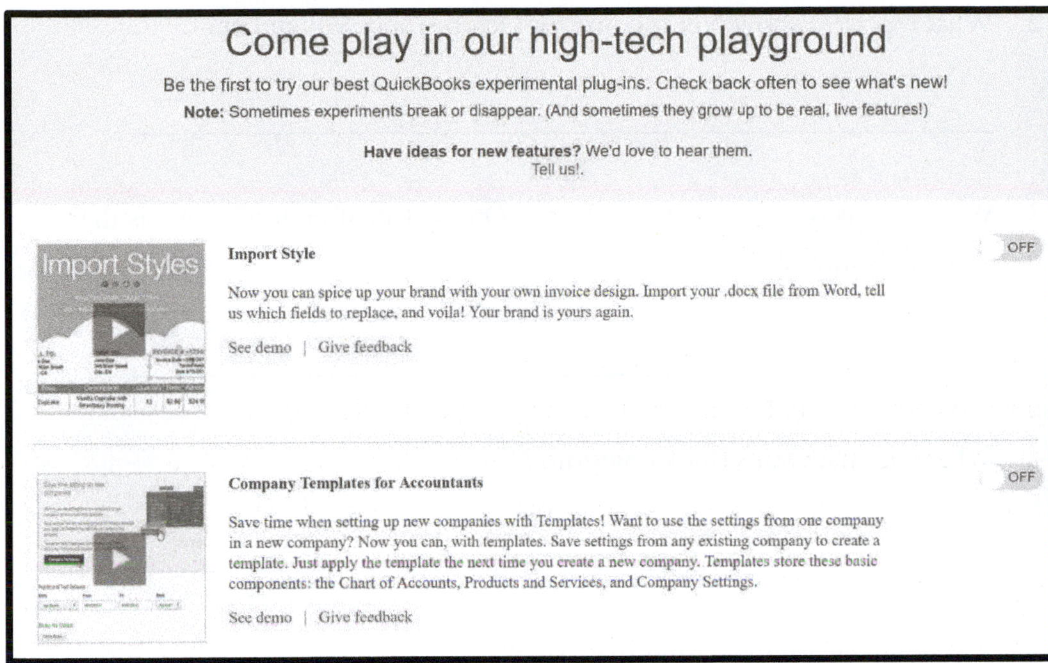

TIP: Click See demo to watch a demo or Give feedback to learn more about what's available on the day that you go to QuickBooks Labs..

3. When you want to learn more, slide the on/off switch to <On>. That's all you need to do.
4. To stop using a plug-in, return to the QuickBooks Lab page and slide its switch to <Off>. You can also send Intuit feedback.

CHECK YOUR PROGRESS

1. What is the Net Income on October 31, 20XX?

____

2. What report(s) show Net Income for October and November?

____

3. What company manages QuickBooks Online Certification? What is their website address?

____

4. Where are the QuickBooks plug-ins?

____

5. Where are customized reports located?

____

SIGN OUT

Sign out of QBO *or,* continue.

ONLINE LEARNING CENTER (OLC): www.mhhe.com/qbo2e

The OLC includes additional Chapter 11 resources. Go online to www.mhhe.com/qbo2e >Student Edition > Chapter 11.

1. Narrated PowerPoints.
2. Online quizzes: 10 True or False and 10 multiple-choice questions. The Online quizzes are graded and can be emailed to your instructor.

3. Analysis question: Answer the analysis question, then email to your instructor.
4. Going to the Net

   a. Go to the QuickBooks Learn & Support website at https://community.intuit.com/. In the Ask a question field, type **Accounting Methods** > Search > link to Accounting methods. The website is https://community.intuit.com/articles/1430710-accounting-methods.
   b. Describe accounting methods, cash basis and accrual basis.

5. Videos: Go to QuickBooks Labs and watch videos of interest to you. To watch Customize Reports and Email, go to http://quickbooks.intuit.com/tutorials/lessons/custom-reports/.
6. Glossary of terms: Words that are italicized and boldfaced are defined in the glossary. The Glossary is also Appendix B.
7. Exercise 11-3, Problem Solving.

Exercise 11-1: Follow the instructions below to complete Exercise 11-1:

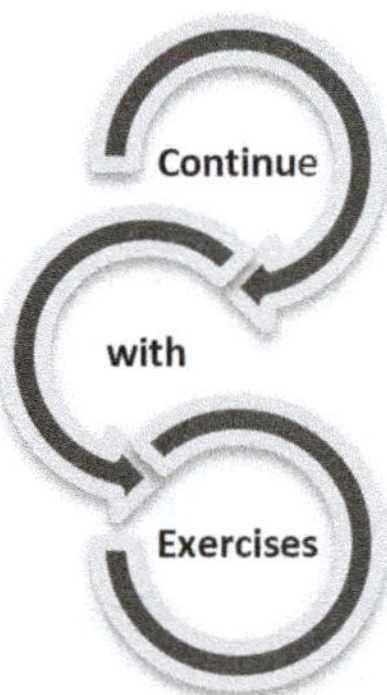

1. Start QBO. Sign into QB Cloud_Student Name.
2. Customize the Balance Sheet to show October and November balances. Change the report title to October and November Balance Sheet.
3. Customize the Statement of Cash Flows to show October and November balances. Change the report title to October and November Statement of Cash Flows.
4. Continue with Exercise 11-2.

Exercise 11-2: Follow the instructions below to complete Exercise 11-2:

1. Save the customized Balance Sheet as Excel and PDF files. Use the file name **Exercise 11-2_Oct_Nov_Balance Sheet**.
2. Save the customized Statement of Cash Flows as Excel and PDF files. Use the file name **Exercise 11-2_Oct_Nov_Statement of Cash Flows**.

Check Your Figures:

- October Total Current Assets, $59,437.56
- November Total Current Assets, $82,429.59
- October Total Current Liabilities, $5,000.00
- November Total Current Liabilities, $22,920.00
- October Total Liabilities and Equity, $69,437.56
- November Total Liabilities and Equity, $92,429.59
- October Cash at end of period, $50,437,56
- November Cash at end of period, $61,469.59

Exercise 11-3: Problem Solving

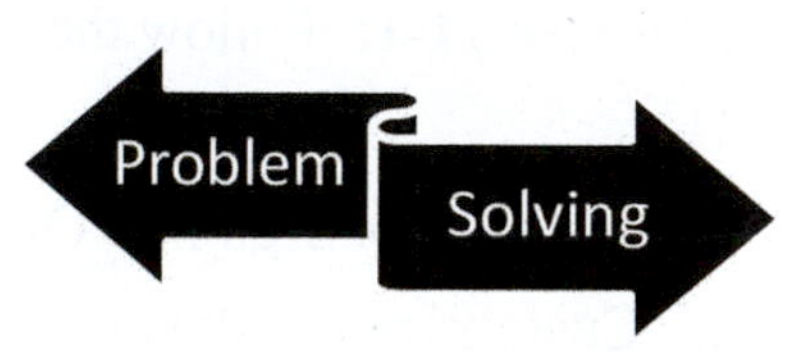

The Online Learning Center includes Exercise 11-3 at www.mhhe.com/qbo2e > Student Edition > Chapter 11 > Problem Solving.

Compare the differences in percent of net income on the October – November Profit and Loss (page 535). Explain why.

CHAPTER 11 INDEX

Chapter 12 Apps, Updates, QuickBooks Blog and Tips

Scenario: Chapter 12 focuses on these areas:

- Apps
- Updates
- QuickBooks Blog
- QBO tips

To review what you will do in Chapter 12, read the objectives.

OBJECTIVES

1. Start QBO and sign into QB Cloud_Student Name.
2. Connect to Apps and search for new ones.
3. Learn about QuickBooks Online updates.
4. Use the QuickBooks blog.
5. Learn about QBO tips.
6. Use the Online Learning Center, www.mhhe.com/qbo2e, for additional resources.
7. Complete Exercises 12-1, 12-2 and 12-3.

GETTING STARTED

1. Start your browser. Go online to http://qbo.intuit.com.
2. Sign into QBO with your User ID and Password.

APPS

1. From the Navigation bar, select Apps > See all apps > click the Browse Category down-arrow > select Account Payable. Periodically check Apps because new ones are regularly added.

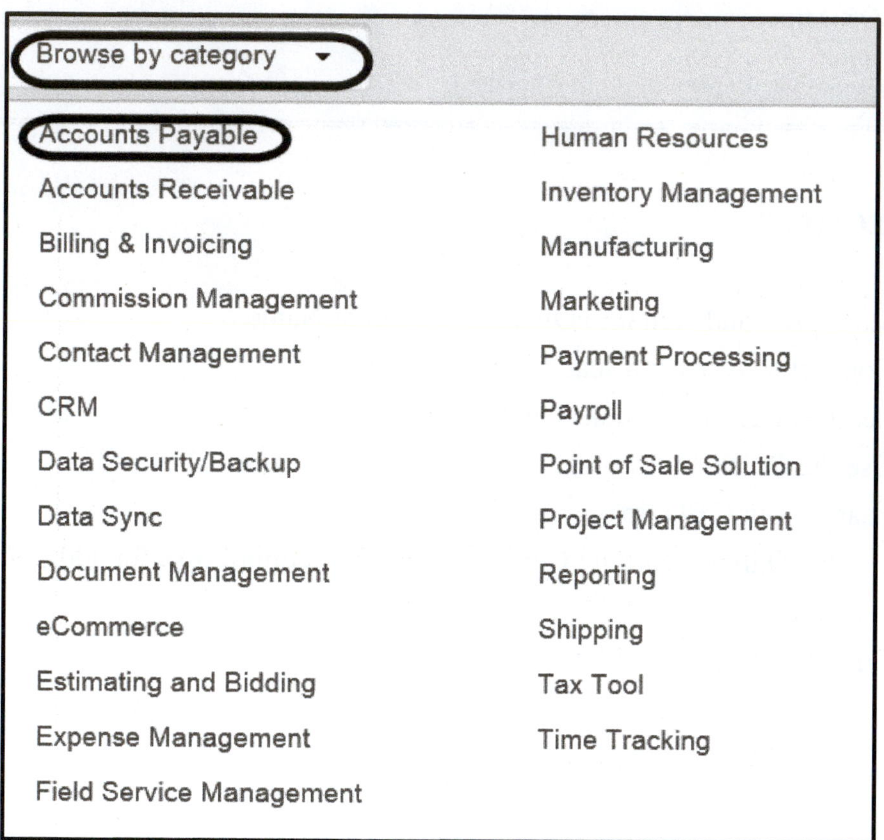

2. Depending on when you go to the Accounts Payable page, your Apps may differ.

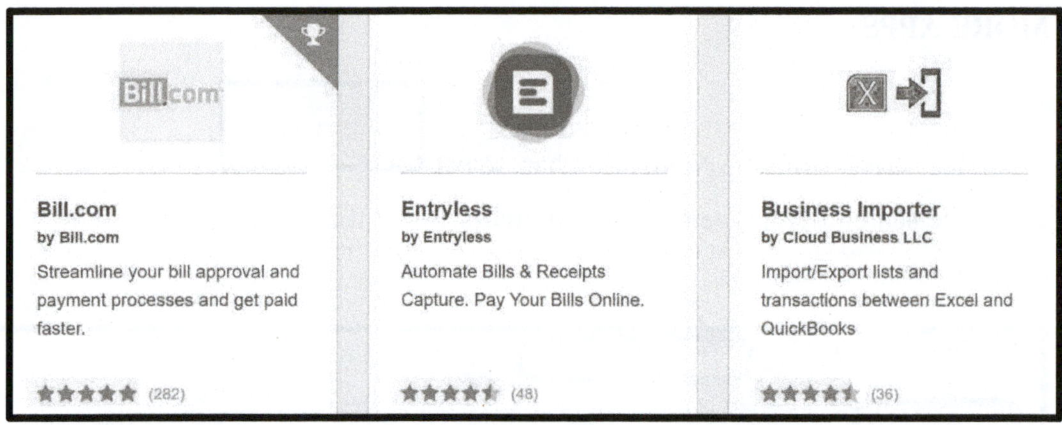

3. Link to Bill.com. Read the information. Watch the Bill.com video. Observe the Overview tab is selected. To learn more, click Reviews, Pricing, Support.
4. Go back to the Apps page. In the Browse Category field, select Reporting > Link to Qvinci. Read the information. Watch the Qvinci for Accountants video. Click on the Reviews, Pricing and Support tabs.
5. Go back to the Apps page. In the Browse Category field, select CRM. ***CRM*** is an abbreviation for Customer Relationship Management. Link to one of the CRM apps. Read the information. Watch the video.
6. Go back to the Apps page. In the Search for an app field, type **ERP**. ***ERP*** is an abbreviation for Enterprise Resource Planning. Link to an ERP app. Read the information. Watch the video.

MORE APPS

1. If necessary, from the Navigation bar, select .

2. In the search field, type **Online payments**. As of this writing, the search results show 100 apps.

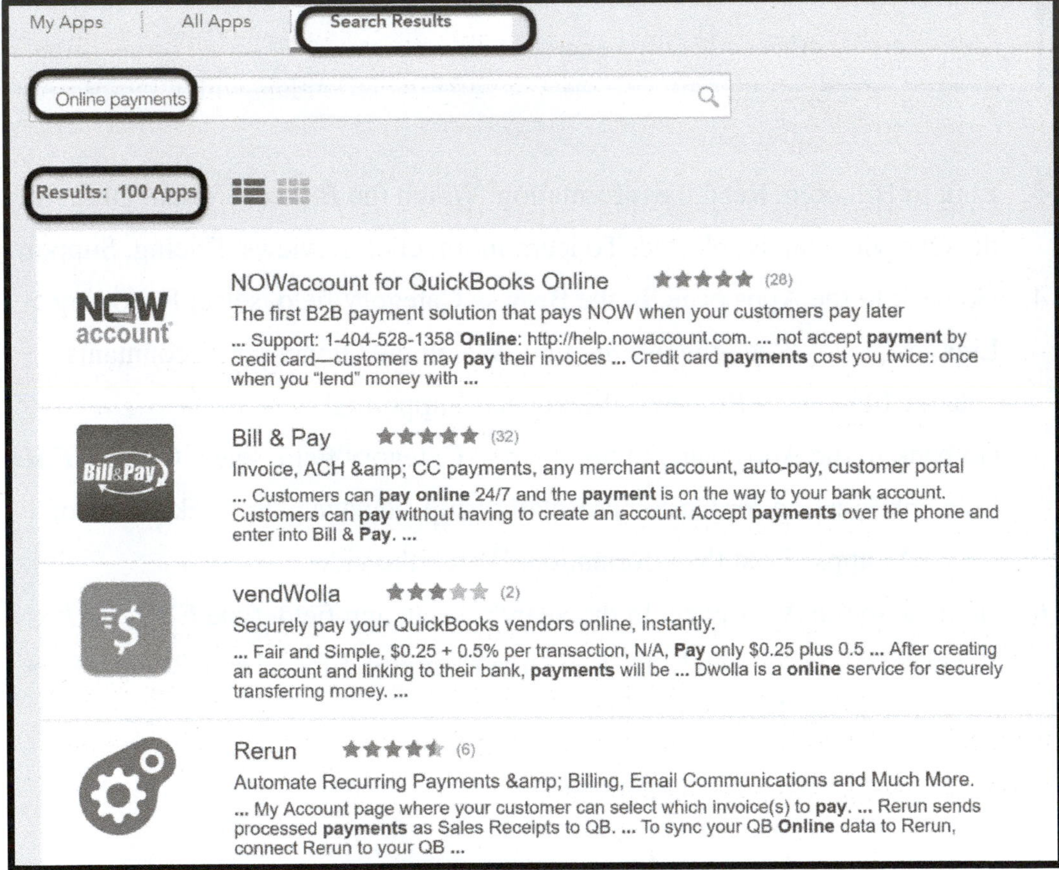

3. To see more apps, scroll down the page. To learn more about the Online payments apps, click on them.
4. Do another search for **QuickBooks mobile apps**. As of this writing, 100 mobile apps are shown.

Troubleshooting: My Navigation Bar does not have an Apps button. What should I do? To see if it's a browser issue, try clearing your temporary internet files/cache (https://community.intuit.com/articles/1145697-how-do-i-clear-the-temporary-internet-files-cache). Once done, close out of the browser completely and open it again. If this does not resolve the issue, try using another supported browser or try another computer.

You can also access the App Center outside of QuickBooks Online by going to https://apps.intuit.com/. Use the same log in credentials with QuickBooks Online when signing in.

5. Experiment. Type searches of interest to you.

SIGN OUT

To sign out of QBO, go to the company settings (click on the company name), link to Sign Out.

UPDATES AND THE QUICKBOOKS BLOG

Updates include various user interface elements, accounting features, and user functions. Sometimes changes are done for specific users or companies so that feedback can be collected. If users like the update, it is changed. When using QBO, be flexible. Updates are inevitable.

QuickBooks Online updates automatically. When you sign in, you are using the most recent version. Sometimes when you select a feature, information about an update appears.

The blog includes the latest information about QuickBooks Online. Information is shared on recent happenings and future developments. The QuickBooks Blog includes News, Thought Leadership, What's New in QBO, Innovation, Account Advice, and Customer Profiles.

1. Go to The QuickBooks Blog at http://quickbooks.intuit.com/blog/ > select What's New in QBO.

2. The What's New in QBO includes links to monthly QBO Features & Improvements along with timely information. Scroll down the page to see what is included. As of this writing, the page looks like this. Your information will differ.

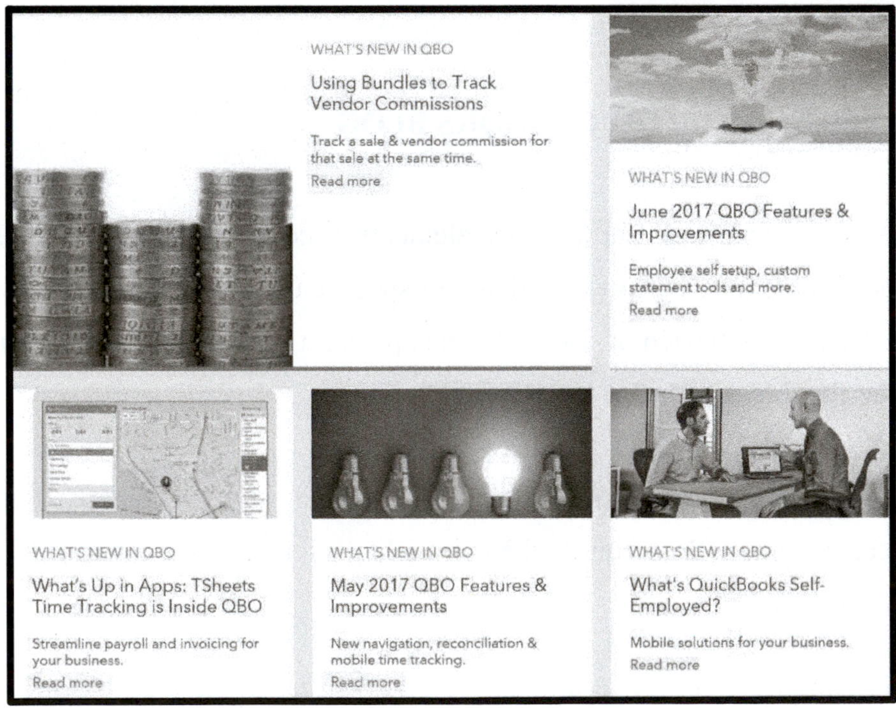

3. Explore the QuickBooks Blog. Select the other links: News, Thought Leadership, Innovation, Accountant Advice, and Customer Profiles.

FIVE QBO TIPS

Tip 1: You can split your QBO screen

While working in QBO if you want to split your screen just press the Windows key and the right arrow for the screen you want right and the Windows key and left arrow for the screen you want left. To reverse the split screen press the Windows key and up arrow.

Tip 2: Duplicate Screen Tabs

There are several ways to duplicate your screen in Chrome but here's one that you don't even need to use your mouse for. <Alt> + <D > grabs the address, then <Alt> + <Enter> opens a new tab with the URL. The trick is you don't have to move your thumb off the <Alt> key – just push down <Alt> then hit D and <Enter> in quick succession to duplicate the current tab.

Tip 3: Go Bold and Send Customer Invoice Reminders

QBO has a default reminder message. When you see overdue Invoices it's easy to hit the Remind button and off goes the email to our clients reminding them to pay. To send reminders: from the QBO Navigation Bar > Select Overdue Invoices to view > Send Reminders.

Tip 4: Trust me baby, it's safe

Transfer secure docs in attachments. For example, say you have Bob Company asking us to reconcile his 2016 bank accounts but he feels uncomfortable emailing bank statements – use QBO attachments. It's totally secure and easy to use because there are no additional portals or passwords. Your client can Export, Download and Delete the file after saving a copy.

Or… In most cases there are only a few hands in the QBO data so some users may want to keep these files here forever as a safe parking spot for this type of shared data.

Here's how it's done:

1. Select the Gear icon > Attachments > Import.
2. Export Zip Attachments: Check-mark the desired file and Export Zip.
3. Download Attachments: In the desired file row. Select <Download>.

Tip 5: Use shortcut keys

QuickBooks Online includes short-cut keys to help you take action faster. To access the list of short-cuts, go to Gear > Account and Settings > Billing & Subscription. Next to your Company ID press <Ctrl> + <Alt> + ? (the question-mark key is also the forward slash key). The dialog box that opens includes shortcut keys

ONLINE LEARNING CENTER (OLC): www.mhhe.com/QBO

The OLC includes additional Chapter 12 resources. Go online to www.mhhe.com/QBO > Student Edition > Chapter 12.

1. Narrated PowerPoints.
2. Online quizzes: 10 True or False and 10 multiple-choice questions. The Online quizzes are graded and can be emailed to your instructor.
3. Analysis question: Answer the analysis question, then email to your instructor.
4. Going to the Net
   a. Go to this Firm of the Future website https://www.firmofthefuture.com/content/3-apps-to-increase-productivity-for-bookkeepers-everywhere/. Read the article 3 Apps to Increase Productivity for Bookkeepers Everywhere.
   b. What are the apps listed in this article? Write a brief explanation of each apps.
   c. In the article, what are the final thoughts?
5. Videos: Watch the QuickBooks Connect 2015 Conference video at https://www.youtube.com/watch?list=PLX0olpXZdQFL_zl2m1wlbx8BACyR1lUv_&v=QwwJV5luCsg. Watch additional videos at https://quickbooks.intuit.com/tutorials/lessons/see-business-health/ and https://quickbooks.intuit.com/tutorials/all-quickbooks-tutorials/.
6. Glossary of terms: Words that are italicized and boldfaced are defined in the glossary. The Glossary is also Appendix B.
7. Exercise 12-3, Problem Solving

Exercise 12-1: Follow the instructions below to complete Exercise 12-1:

1. Start QBO. Sign into QB Cloud_Student Name.
2. Go to the Apps page. Select an App of interest to you. Read about it.
3. Do a search for an App.

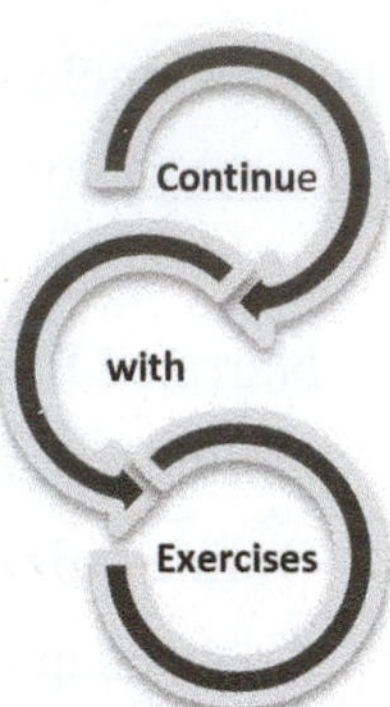

Exercise 12-2 Follow the instructions below to complete Exercise 12-2.

1. Go to the QuickBooks Online blog at http://quickbooks.intuit.com/blog.
2. Select a link. Read more.
3. Link to additional areas of interest.

Exercise 12-3, Problem Solving

Go to The QuickBooks Blog at http://quickbooks.intuit.com/blog/ > link to Innovation. Read an article about Innovation. For example, the author chose Get a New, Special Report on AI (Artificial Intelligence) and Machine Learning at http://quickbooks.intuit.com/blog/innovation/get-a-new-special-report-on-artificial-intelligence-and-machine-learning/. The complete report could be downloaded.

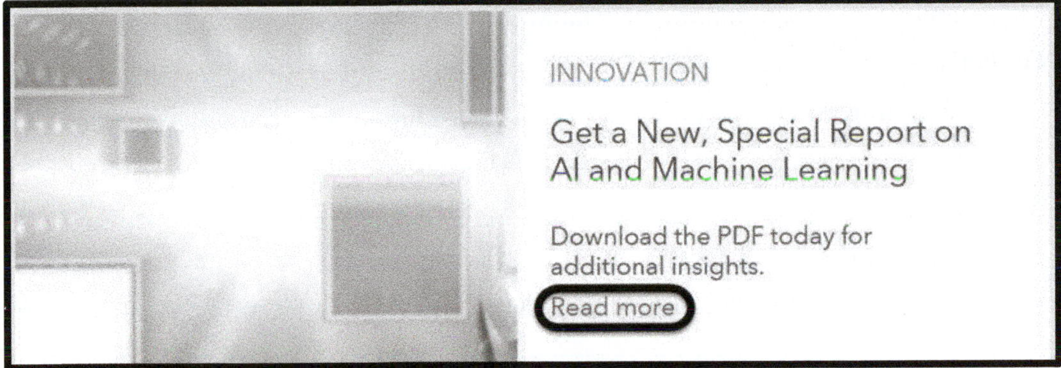

Your Innovation page will differ. Check with your professor to see if he or she would like you to write a brief essay about the innovation article you read.

CHAPTER 12 INDEX

Case Problem 1 — Payroll and Importing Excel Data

To see how Payroll works with QBO, use the sample company data at https://qbo.intuit.com/redir/testdrive. The sample company is Craig's Design and Landscaping Services. This is the company that you used in Chapter 1, QuickBooks Online Test-drive.

QBO payroll is a fee-for-service add-on that requires linking to an online bank account. Using the sample company allows you to see how payroll works without an extra charge. Both Case Problem 1 and Case Problem 2, Budgeting, use the sample company data.

Case Problem 1 also includes importing a Customer file created in Microsoft Excel into the sample company. Once the Excel file is imported, additional customers are added to Craig's Design and Landscaping Services.

TEST-DRIVE SIGN IN

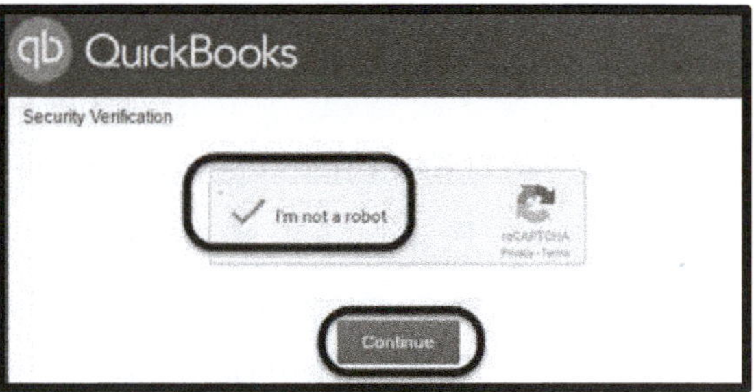

1. Go online to https://qbo.intuit.com/redir/testdrive. **Each time you start the test drive, a new session begins. Data is <u>not</u> saved.**
2. Complete the Security Verification I'm not a robot > click <Continue>. Select images and verify.

In CP1, you use Craig's Design and Landscaping Services' payroll data. The payroll service that QBO offers is fee-based. To learn more about the payroll, go to https://quickbooks.intuit.com/payroll-service/. If the Seamless payroll right inside QuickBooks video is available, watch it. The video is also available on YouTube at https://www.youtube.com/watch?v=bixqocWe_9c. As of this writing, QBO Enhanced Payroll starts at $20/month; Full Service Payroll is $47/month. Case Problem 1's payroll transactions and withholdings are for example purposes only.

PAYROLL OVERVIEW

In QBO, you can run payroll in three easy steps:

1. Pay employees.
2. Pay payroll taxes.
3. File payroll tax forms online.

Payroll Features

QBO's payroll features include:

- Direct bank deposit or pay employees by check.
- Federal and state payroll tax forms are completed for you.
- Free support from payroll experts.
- Run payroll online or from a smartphone.
- Built-in payroll calculator for instant tax calculations.
- Electronically file and pay taxes.
- Pay employees and contractors.

EMPLOYEES

Follow these steps to see Craig's Design and Landscaping Services employees and turn on payroll. To complete payroll work the author used the Chrome browser.

1. On the list next to the Navigation bar, select Pay your employees.

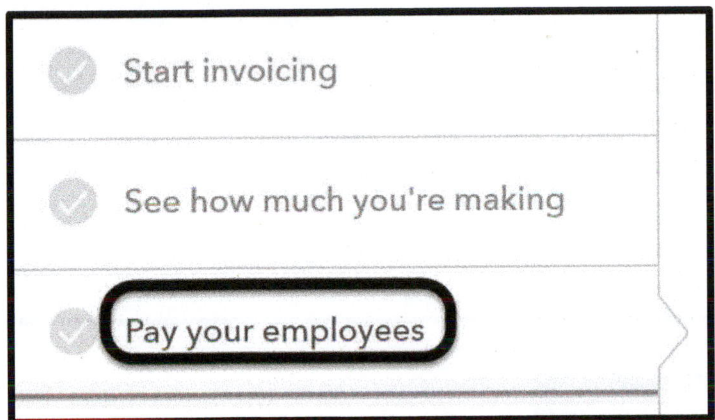

2. In the Your employees are family section, click Get started with payroll. Click <Dashboard>. Select Pay your employees again. Observe there is a checkmark next to Pay your employees. Make sure there is also a checkmark next to Success! You're signed up for payroll.

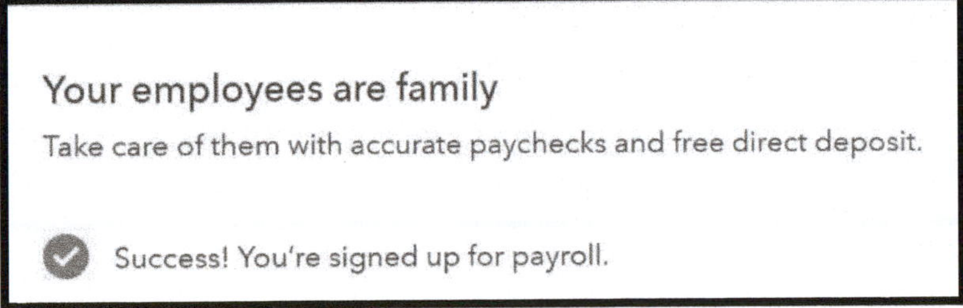

3. From the Navigation bar, select Employees. The Employees page appears.

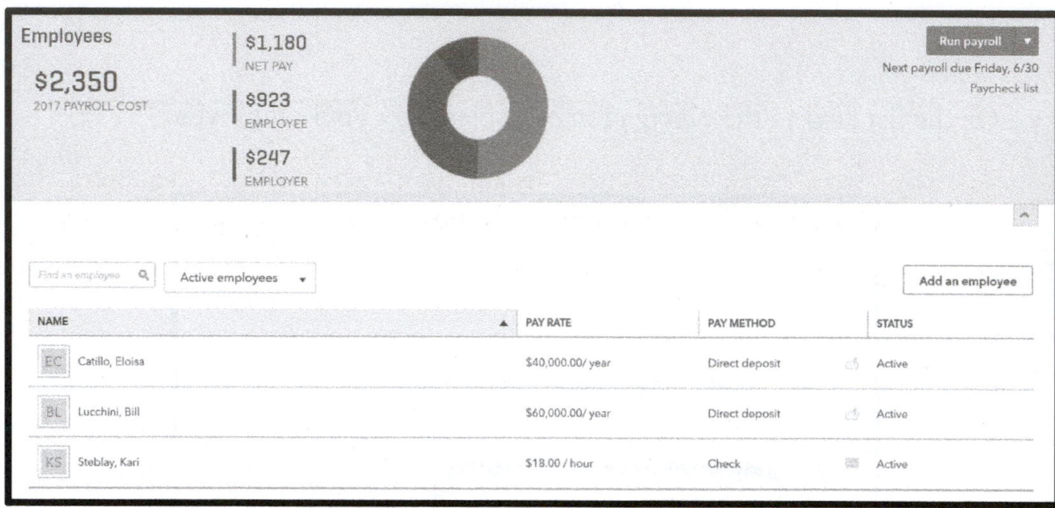

4. Click Run payroll. The Run Payroll: Friday page appears. As of the date the author signed in, the Total Pay for the three employees is $1,923.08. Your Pay period and Pay date will differ. The Total Pay may differ too.

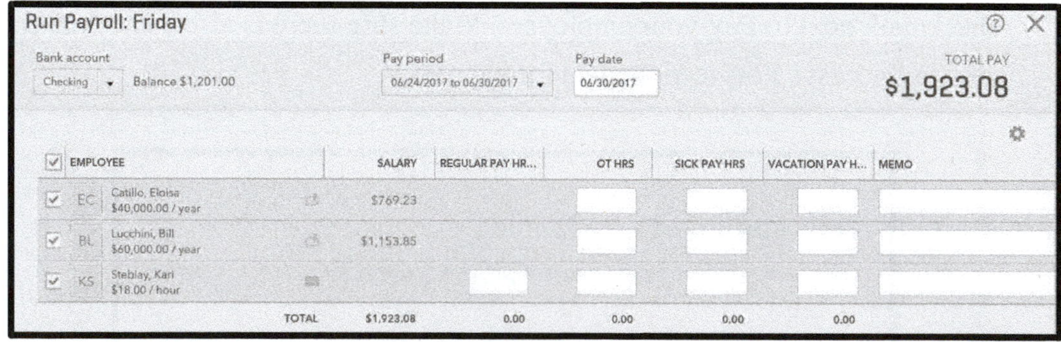

5. Click on the back-arrow. You are returned to the Dashboard. Select <Employees> from the Navigation bar > link to Paycheck list.

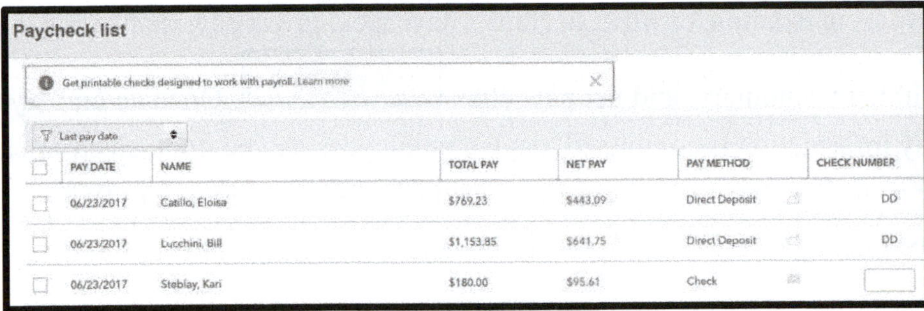
Paycheck list

Get printable checks designed to work with payroll. Learn more

Last pay date

PAY DATE	NAME	TOTAL PAY	NET PAY	PAY METHOD	CHECK NUMBER
06/23/2017	Catillo, Eloisa	$769.23	$443.09	Direct Deposit	DD
06/23/2017	Lucchini, Bill	$1,153.85	$641.75	Direct Deposit	DD
06/23/2017	Steblay, Kari	$180.00	$95.61	Check	

The Pay Dates are determined by the computer's system date, the curernt date. Your Pay Date will differ. The Total Pay and Net Pay may also differ. If a pop-up message appears, close it.

6. Click on the back-arrow to go the Employees page shown below step 3 on the previous page. On the Employees page, click Lucchini, Bill. The Employee Details page appears. Review the information on the Employee details page. A partial page is shown below. Scroll down to see all of it.

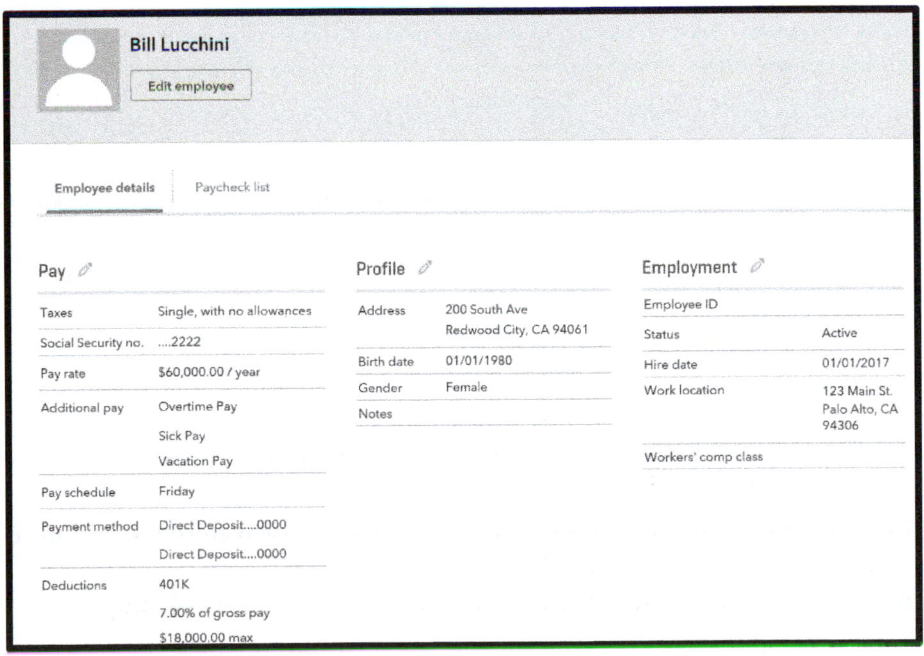

7. To see an example of Mr. Lucchini's paycheck, gross pay, deductions, taxes withheld, summary, and net pay, click Edit employee. Once an employee's pay information is completed, paying employees can be done electronically or manually. Mr. Lucchini's paycheck includes deductions for 401K, Insurance, taxes withheld, and a summary of paycheck information.

   Comment: Your screen(s) may show different information. The test-drive's pay information defaults to the date the you signed in. A partial page is shown. Scroll down to see all of it.

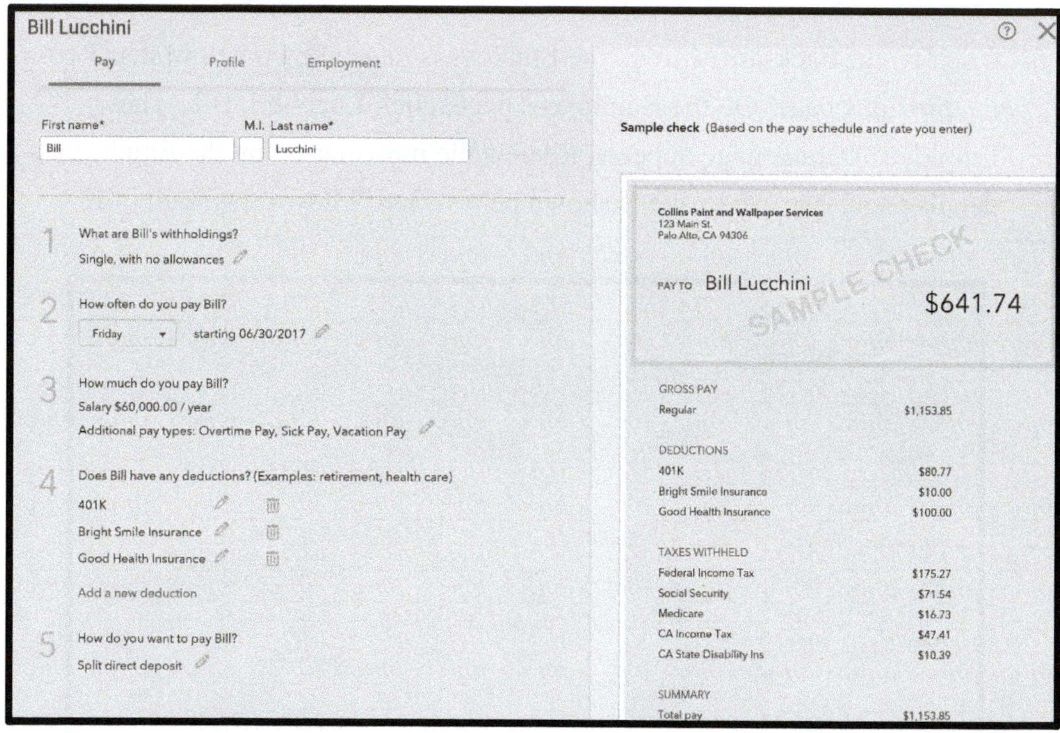

8. Observe the exclamation point next to Enter W-4 form in the What are Bill's withholdings? field. Click Enter W-4 form. Review the W-4 Employees

Withholding Allowance Certificate. Click Done. You are returned to Bill Lucchini's Pay page. Observe there are two other tabs – Profile and Employment. Select them to review the information.

Bill Lucchini's net pay amount is $641.74 as per the author's test-drive information, yours may differ. (*Hint:* Due to yearly changes in federal and state taxes, the amounts shown on your screen may differ from the table below.) QBO calculates payroll withholdings automatically. The table shows the same information as the Summary area on Bill Lucchini's Pay screen above.

Gross Pay			**$1,153.85**
Deductions			
401K	$80.77		
Bright Smile Insurance	10.00		
Good Health Insurance	100.00	$190.77	-190.77
Subtotal			$963.08
Taxes Withheld			
Federal Income Tax	175.27		
Social Security	71.54		
Medicare	16.73		
CA Income Tax	47.41		
CA State Disability Ins.	10.39	$321.34	-321.34
Total Net Pay			**$641.74**

9. Close the Pay screen by clicking <X>.

Ways to Pay Employees

You have four choices:

1. Handwrite a check from your bank account.

    a) Make the check payable to your employee for the net amount from their pay stub.
    b) Give the check to your employee along with a copy of their pay stub, which shows all withholding amounts.

2. Print the paycheck and pay stub on preprinted check stock.

    a) Use check stock that is compatible with QuickBooks or Microsoft Money.
    b) Give the paycheck and pay stub to your employee.

3. Print the paycheck and pay stub on blank check stock.

    - Blank check stock is less expensive than preprinted stock and is especially convenient if you print checks for more than one company.

4. Direct deposit to the employee's bank account.

    a) If your employee chooses direct deposit, we'll electronically transfer the net amount from your bank account to your employee's bank account. Handwrite paychecks if your direct deposit is pending.
    b) Give your employee a copy of their pay stub printed on plain paper. Setting up direct deposit takes about a week. (There's no extra charge for direct deposit.)

PAYROLL TAX

Once payroll is turned on, the Navigation bar includes a Taxes selection.

1. Select Taxes > Payroll Tax.

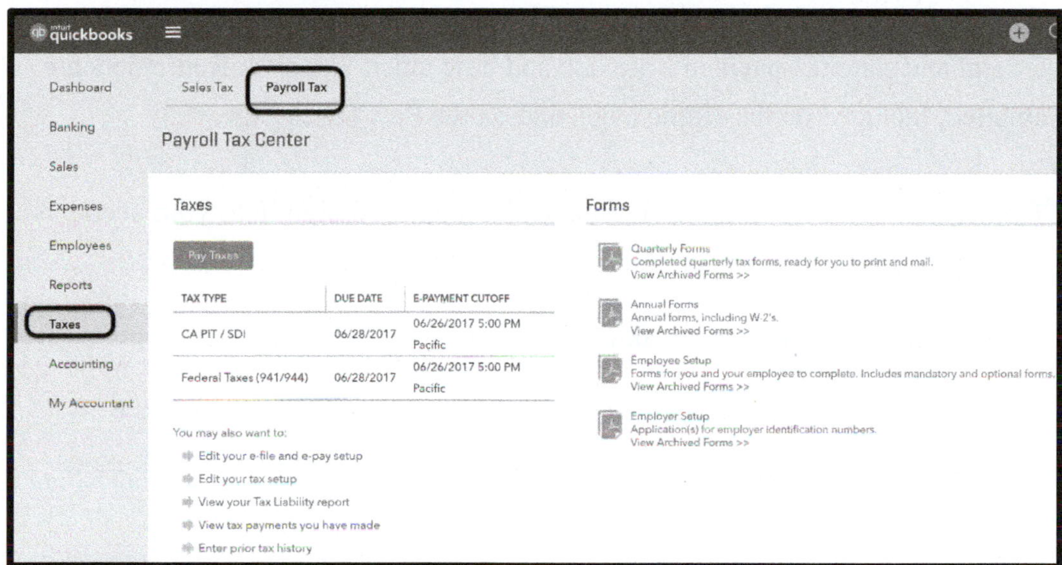

2. The Payroll Tax Center appears. Taxes and Forms are included. Go to the following links:

   Taxes:

   - Edit your e-file and e-pay setup
   - Edit your tax setup
   - View your Tax Liability report
   - View tax payments you have made
   - Enter prior tax history

Forms:

- Quarterly Forms
- Annual Forms
- Employee Setup
- Employer Setup

QBO includes a link for paying taxes. The payroll feature reminds you when federal and state tax payments are due and how much you owe. Reminders are emailed, included on the Home page, and on the Pay Taxes page.

Tax payments are not created automatically. You must sign in to your accounts and approve the payments on the Pay Taxes page.

Read this information about making tax payments. There are several options.

- **If you are signed up for our electronic services**: You must approve all electronic tax payments no later than 5 pm (Pacific Time) two banking days before the payment date.
    - For an electronic **federal tax payment**, the IRS directly withdraws the funds from your bank account on the payment date.
    - For an electronic **state tax payment**, we'll withdraw the funds after 5 pm (Pacific Time) two banking days before the payment date.
- **If you are not signed up for our electronic services**:
    - For **federal tax payments**, the IRS requires that you e-pay, so if you're not signed up for our electronic services, sign up directly with IRS Electronic Federal Tax Payment System (EFTPS). With EFTPS, you approve the payment, and the IRS automatically withdraws the funds from your account.

- If you're not using e-services for **state tax payments**, QBO provides pre-filled payment coupons after you approve the payments. If pre-filled coupons aren't available, you're responsible for getting the payment coupon from the tax agency, completing it, and mailing it to the agency with your payment. In some jurisdictions, you can make the payments directly on the state agency's web site.

E-pay and E-file

Electronic payment (e-pay) and electronic filing (e-file) saves you time. QBO does most of the work and reminds you when tax payments and forms are due. Instead of manually creating a check or filling out a form, you approve payments and forms that we prepare for you.

- E-pay allows you to pay your payroll taxes electronically, without the hassle of transcribing data onto paper coupons or mailing checks.
- E-file allows you to file tax forms electronically, without the hassle of printing forms and mailing them.

Both e-pay and e-file save time and eliminate mistakes.

For states where electronic filing is not available, QBO provides signature-ready forms, or worksheets to assist you in preparing the filings yourself.

Make Tax Payments Electronically

To pay taxes electronically, you need to sign up for QBO's electronic services. After your electronic services enrollment is complete, you can approve payments and the funds are automatically withdrawn from your bank account on or before the payment date (depending on whether it's a federal or state tax).

PAYROLL SETTINGS

To pay taxes, you need to define accounting preferences. Follow these steps to complete payroll settings.

1. Select Gear > Payroll Settings.

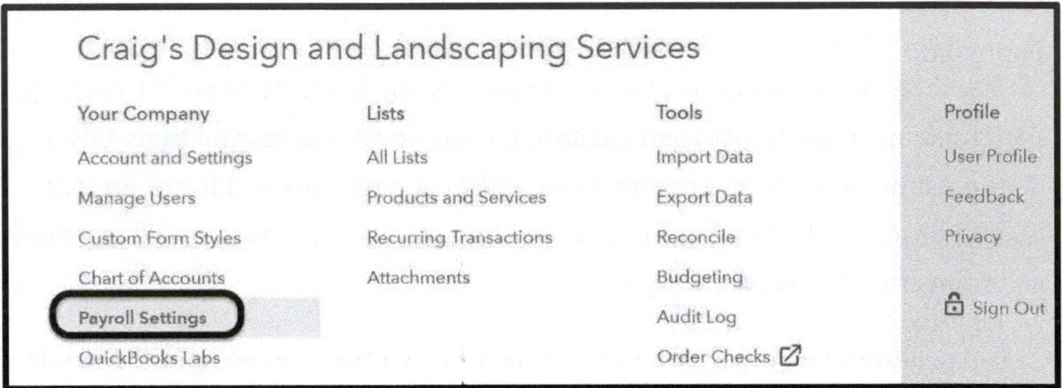

2. The Preferences page appears > select Preferences.

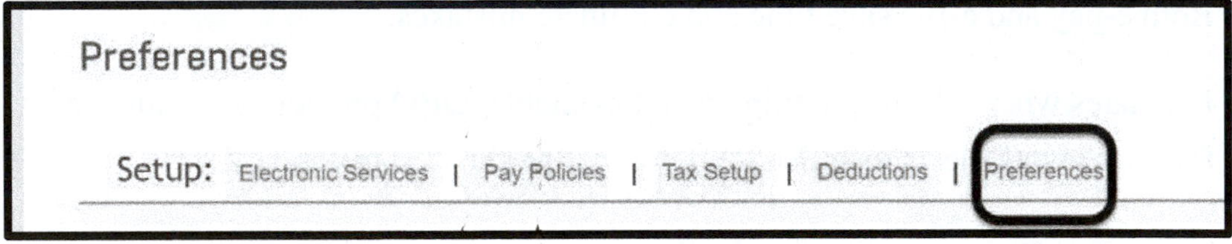

3. In the Preferences area, select Accounting Preferences.

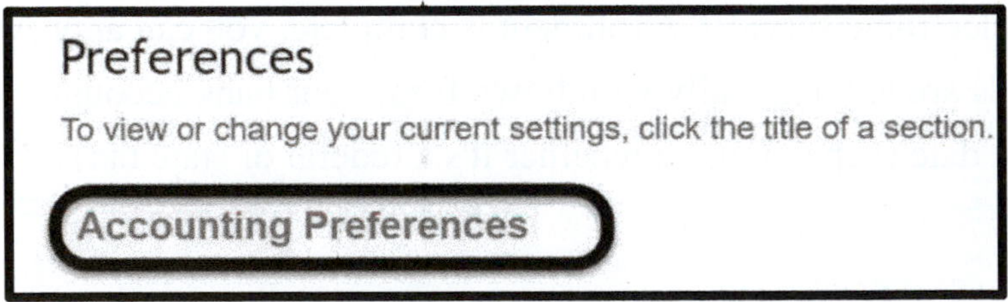

4. Click 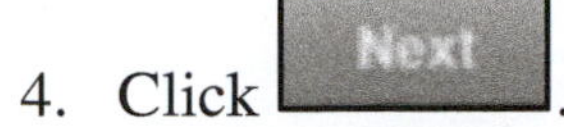

.
5. In the Bank Account Checking Account* field, click on the down arrow. Select Checking – Checking.

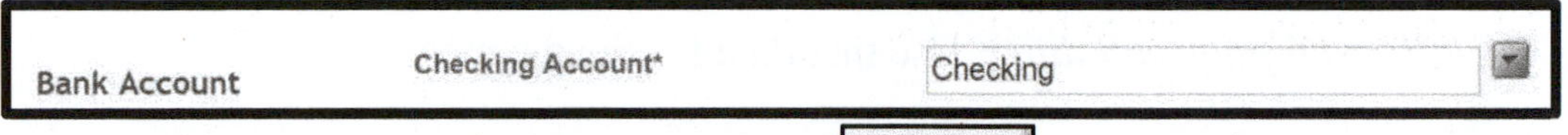

6. To use recommended preferences, click OK. The Accounting Preferences Summary page appears showing the Bank Account is Checking. The Wage Expense Accounts, Tax Expense Accounts, Tax Liability Accounts, and Other Liability and Asset Accounts are also shown. Review this information to familiarize yourself with QBO's accounting preferences summary for payroll.

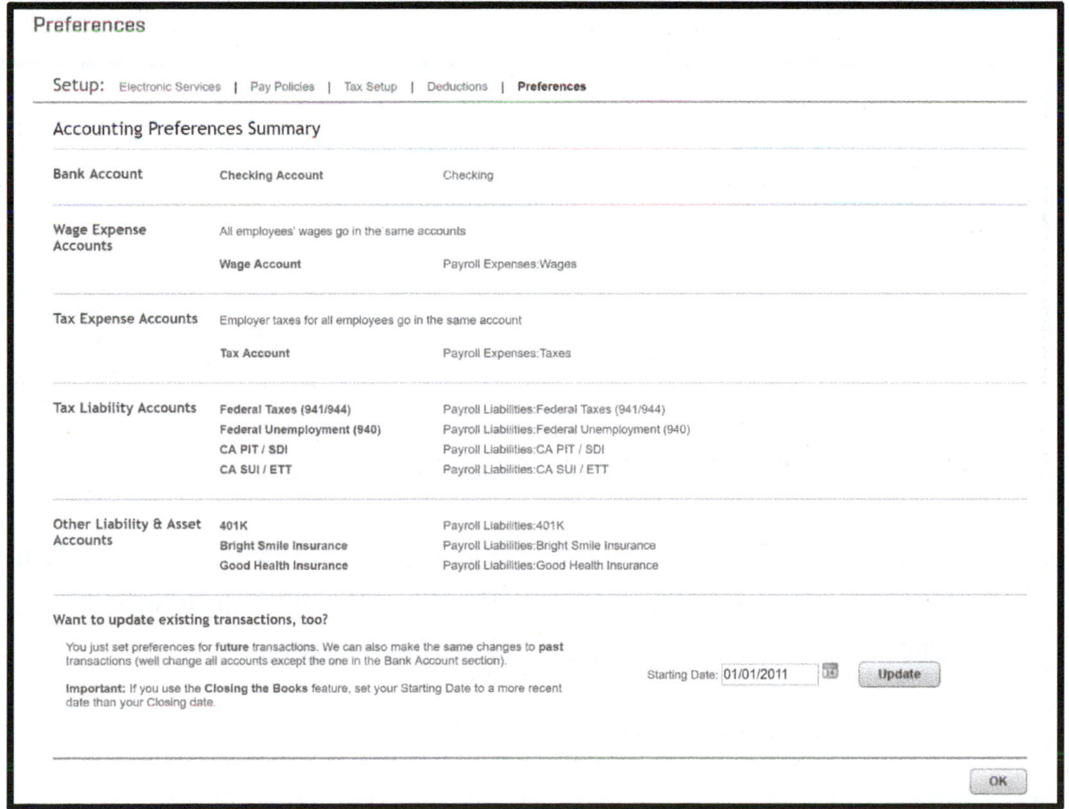

7. Click OK.

Make a Tax Payment

To make a tax payment, complete this transaction. *The Due Date shown on your CA PIT / SDI page will differ.* Use that date for the payments.

Date	*Description of Transaction*
6/28/20XX	Pay the California Employment Development Department (CA EDD) the tax amount owed, $71.33.

1. From the Navigation bar, click Taxes > if necessary, select the Payroll Tax > Pay Taxes. The Pay Taxes page appears showing the taxes that are due. (*Hint:* Your dates will differ.)

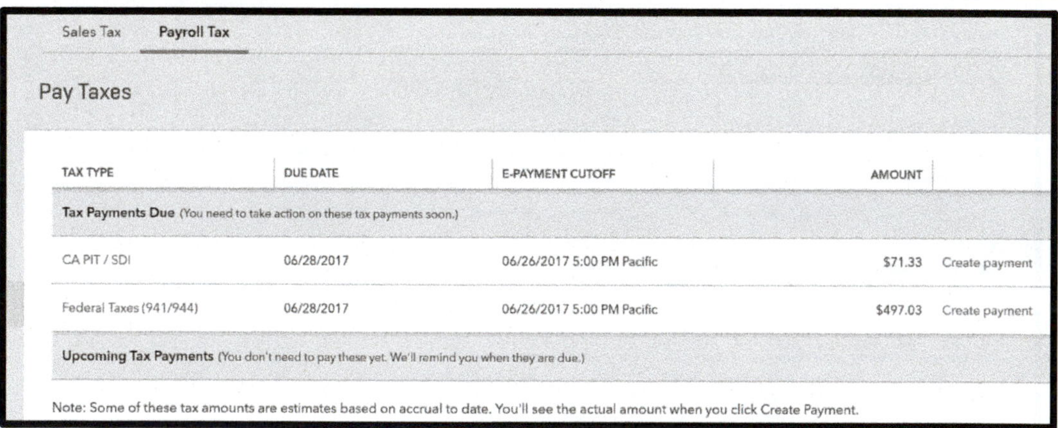

Sales Tax | Payroll Tax

Pay Taxes

TAX TYPE	DUE DATE	E-PAYMENT CUTOFF	AMOUNT	
Tax Payments Due (You need to take action on these tax payments soon.)				
CA PIT / SDI	06/28/2017	06/26/2017 5:00 PM Pacific	$71.33	Create payment
Federal Taxes (941/944)	06/28/2017	06/26/2017 5:00 PM Pacific	$497.03	Create payment
Upcoming Tax Payments (You don't need to pay these yet. We'll remind you when they are due.)				

Note: Some of these tax amounts are estimates based on accrual to date. You'll see the actual amount when you click Create Payment.

2. On the CA PIT /SDI row > click Create payment. CA PIT is an abbreviation for California Personal Income Tax. SDI is State Disability Insurance. The CA PIT / SDI page appears. Make the following selections:

- Select the radio button next to Pay Electronically.
- If necessary, in the Payment Date field select Earliest. Your date and amounts will differ.

3. Click E-pay. (*Hint:* If necessary, select the radio button to Pay Electronically.) The Payment Confirmation page appears. (*Hint:* Since your year differs, the Payment Amount will not be the same.)

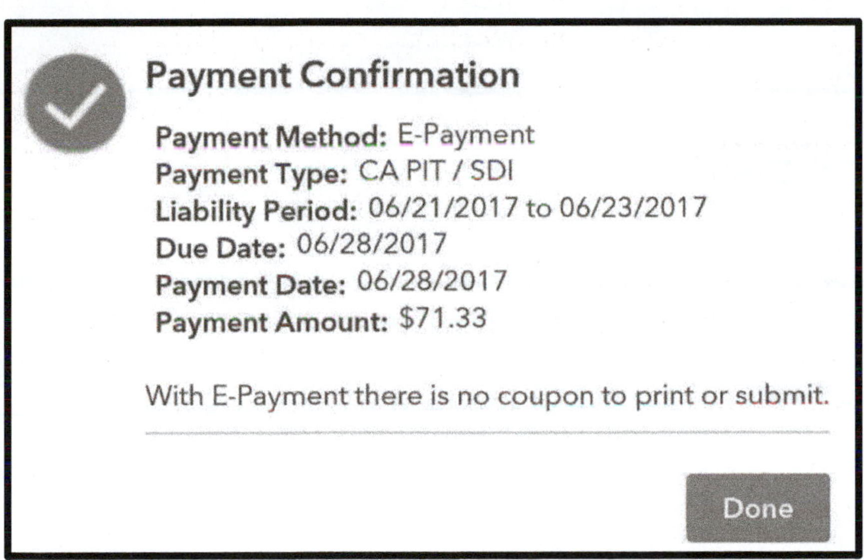

4. Click Done. The Federal Taxes (941/944) page appears > click Create payment > Pay Electronically is automattically selected. If not, select it. The Approve Payment shows the Federal Taxes (941/944) amounts.

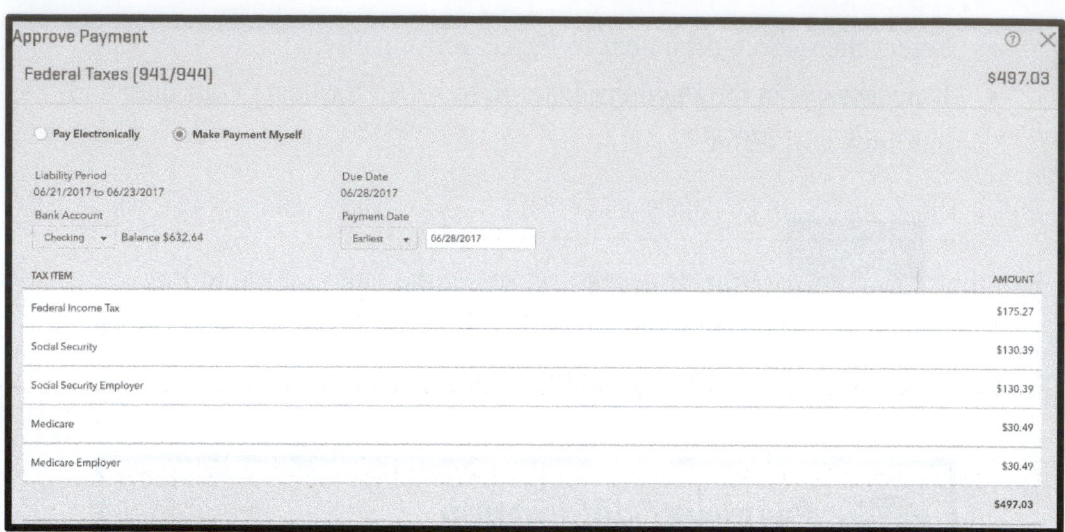

5. Click E-pay. The Payment Confirmation page appears.

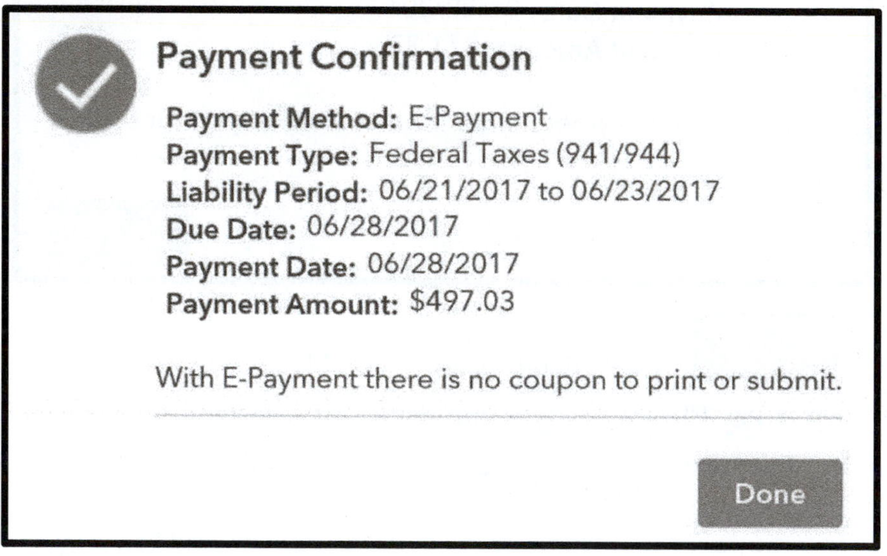

6. Click Done. The Pay Taxes page appears. The Upcoming Tax Payments are shown.

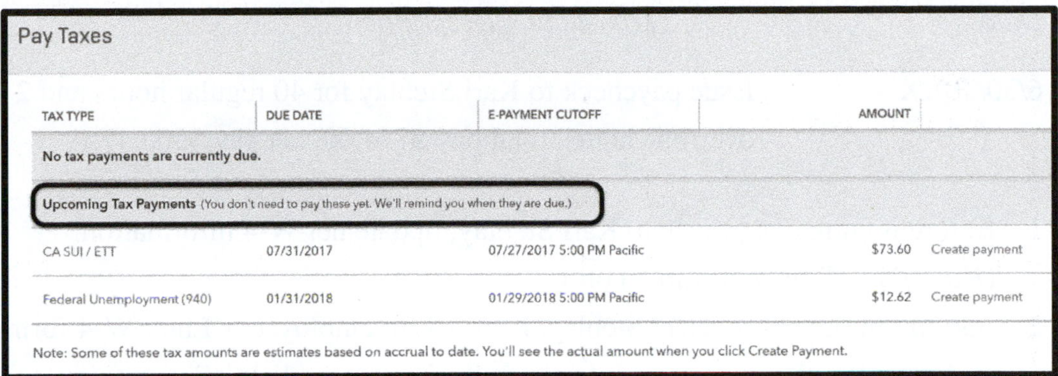

Pay Taxes

TAX TYPE	DUE DATE	E-PAYMENT CUTOFF	AMOUNT	
No tax payments are currently due.				
Upcoming Tax Payments (You don't need to pay these yet. We'll remind you when they are due.)				
CA SUI / ETT	07/31/2017	07/27/2017 5:00 PM Pacific	$73.60	Create payment
Federal Unemployment (940)	01/31/2018	01/29/2018 5:00 PM Pacific	$12.62	Create payment

Note: Some of these tax amounts are estimates based on accrual to date. You'll see the actual amount when you click Create Payment.

7. To see the account distribution for the payroll taxes paid, go Reports > Journal > type the date of the payments > press <Tab>. Your date will differ.

Craig's Design and Landscaping Services

JOURNAL

June 28, 2017

DATE	TRANSACTION TYPE	NUM	NAME	MEMO/DESCRIPTION	ACCOUNT	DEBIT	CREDIT
06/28/2017	Tax Payment		CA EDD	Tax Payment for Period: 06/21/2017-06/23/2017	Checking		$71.33
				CA PIT / SDI	Payroll Liabilities:CA PIT / SDI	$71.33	
						$71.33	**$71.33**
06/28/2017	Tax Payment		IRS	Tax Payment for Period: 06/21/2017-06/23/2017	Checking		$497.03
				Federal Taxes (941/944)	Payroll Liabilities:Federal Taxes (941/944)	$497.03	
						$497.03	**$497.03**
TOTAL						**$568.36**	**$568.36**

PAY AN HOURLY EMPLOYEE

Pay the following employee for regular hours plus 2 overtime hours. The employee information shown for Bill Lucchini was for a salaried employee. To see how an hourly employee is paid, do the following.

Date	*Transaction Description*
6/30/20XX	Issue paycheck to Kari Steblay for 40 regular hours and 2 overtime hours, total pay $774.00; net pay $560.47.

1. Before issuing a paycheck to Kari Steblay, update her W-4 information. (*Hint:* Payroll must be turned on.)
2. Go to Employees > select Steblay, Kari > Edit employee > Enter W-4 form > Done. If a We need more info about Kari appears, click <Finish this later>.
3. To add a transaction, click [+] > Payroll.
4. The Run Payroll: Friday page appears. Uncheck Catillo, Eloisa and Lucchini, Bill. A checkmark should be placed next to Steblay, Kari.

EMPLOYEE
EC Catillo, Eloisa $40,000.00 / year
BL Lucchini, Bill $60,000.00 / year
KS Steblay, Kari $18.00 / hour

5. Complete these fields for Steblay, Kari. (*Hint:* Total pay is gross pay.)

REGULAR PAY HRS: type **40**
OT HRS: type **2**
TOTAL PAY $774.00 completed automatically

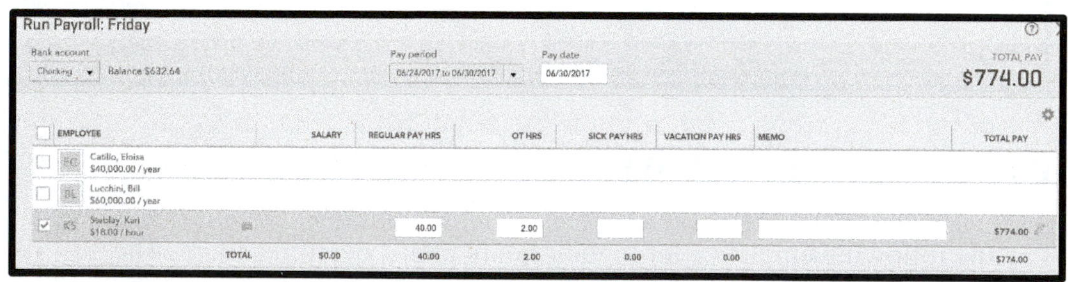

6. Click **Preview payroll**. The Run Payroll: Friday Review and Submit page appears showing the paycheck information for Steblay, Kari. Review the information.

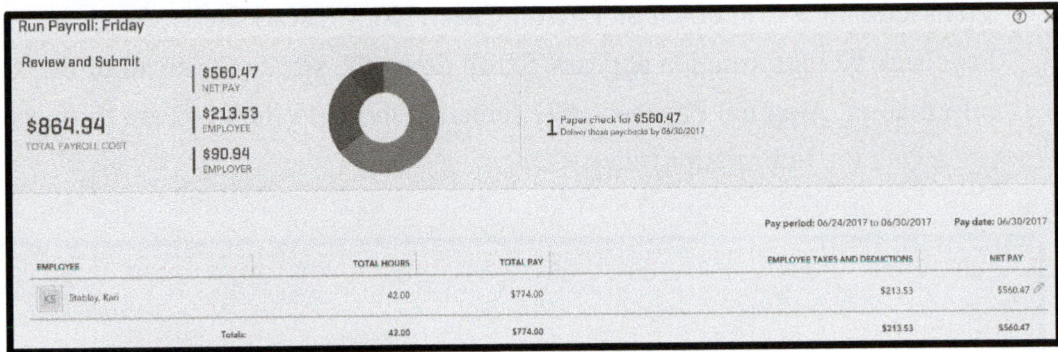

7. Click **Submit payroll**. The Got it! Your payroll is all set page appears. Since Kari Stabley receives a check, type **77** in the CHECK NUMBER field. (Depending on when the paycheck is issued, the Net Pay may differ.)

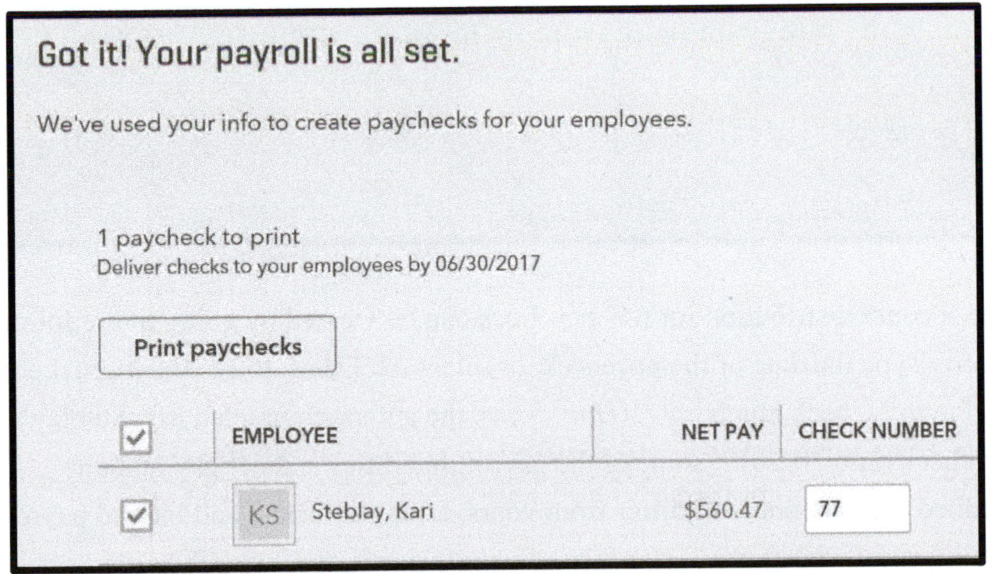

8. Click **Finish payroll**. The Tax payments due page appears. Select <I'll do it later>. To see the transaction you just completed, go to 🔍 (Recent Transactions) > drill down on Payroll Check No. 77. Kari Steblay's Paycheck #77 information appears. Scroll down the screen to see all of the information. A partial Paycheck #77 screen is shown. When you are through reviewing the information, click <OK>.

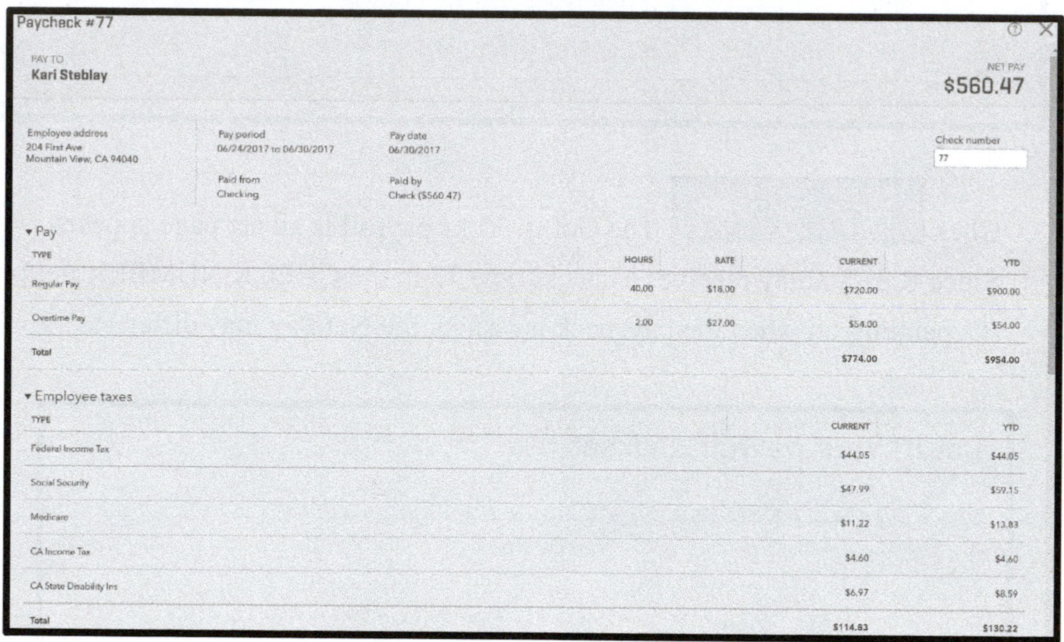

Paycheck #77

PAY TO
Kari Steblay

NET PAY
$560.47

Employee address
204 First Ave
Mountain View, CA 94040

Pay period
06/24/2017 to 06/30/2017

Pay date
06/30/2017

Check number
77

Paid from
Checking

Paid by
Check ($560.47)

▾ Pay

TYPE	HOURS	RATE	CURRENT	YTD
Regular Pay	40.00	$18.00	$720.00	$900.00
Overtime Pay	2.00	$27.00	$54.00	$54.00
Total			**$774.00**	**$954.00**

▾ Employee taxes

TYPE	CURRENT	YTD
Federal Income Tax	$44.05	$44.05
Social Security	$47.99	$59.15
Medicare	$11.22	$13.83
CA Income Tax	$4.60	$4.60
CA State Disability Ins	$6.97	$8.59
Total	**$114.83**	**$130.22**

The account distribution for this paycheck can be viewed by going to the Journal report. Type the date of the paycheck, or select All Dates, to see the journal entry for Payroll Check number 77. (*Hint:* Since the author completed Ms. Steblay's paycheck on 6/30/2017, some of the payroll liabilities and net pay amount credited to Checking will differ from yours. Each year, state and federal payroll liabilities can change.)

Transaction Type	Num	Account	Debit	Credit
Payroll Check	77	Payroll Expenses: Wages	774.00	
		Payroll Expenses: Taxes	90.94	
		Payroll Liabilities: 401K		38.70
		Payroll Liabilities: Bright Smile Insurance		10.00
		Payroll Liabilities: Good Health Insurance		50.00
		Payroll Liabilities: CA SUI / ETT		27.09
		Payroll Liabilities: CA PIT / SDI		11.57
		Payroll Liabilities: Federal Unemployment (940)		4.64
		Payroll Liabilities: Federal Taxes (941/944)		162.47
		Checking		$560.47

The account distribution shows both the amounts withheld from the employee's paycheck and the employer's payroll liabilities. The Checking account is credited for the net pay amount, $560.47.

The payroll liability abbreviations are:

CA SUI / ETT: California State Unemployment Insurance, Employment Training Tax.

CA PIT / SDI: California Personal Income Tax, State Disability Insurance.

Craig's Design and Landscaping Services is located in San Pablo, CA. The sample company's employee withholdings and payroll taxes are for example purposes only. QBO's payroll service includes federal and state tax computations based on the company's location. Kari Steblay's withholdings are based on California state taxes, and the two allowances claimed on her W-4 form.

IMPORT DATA FROM AN EXCEL SPREADSHEET

To import data from Excel into QBO, a sample file is downloaded from within the test-drive company, Craig's Design and Landscaping Services. Once the sample file is downloaded and saved, you import additional customers into Craig's Design and Landscaping Services customer list.

Import adds additional customer names, business names, emails, phone numbers, and address information (street, city, state and zip) into the customer list. Import does <u>not</u> bring in other information such as sales history, balances or notes.

The Excel file that you are going to import looks like this. Nine customers are added to the test-drive company.

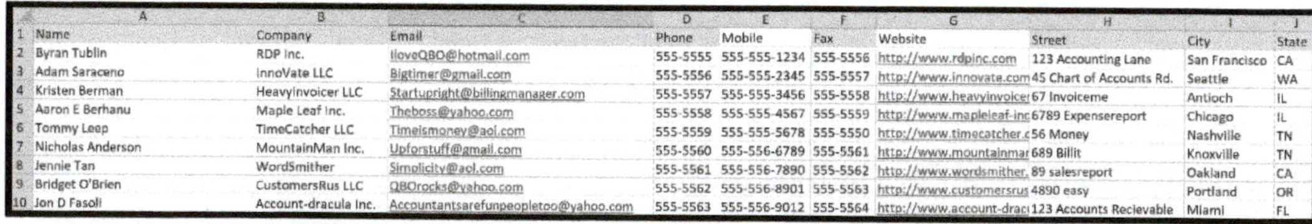

	A	B	C	D	E	F	G	H	I	J
1	Name	Company	Email	Phone	Mobile	Fax	Website	Street	City	State
2	Byran Tublin	RDP Inc.	IloveQBO@hotmail.com	555-5555	555-555-1234	555-5556	http://www.rdpinc.com	123 Accounting Lane	San Francisco	CA
3	Adam Saraceno	InnoVate LLC	Bigtimer@gmail.com	555-5556	555-555-2345	555-5557	http://www.innovate.com	45 Chart of Accounts Rd.	Seattle	WA
4	Kristen Berman	HeavyInvoicer LLC	Startupright@billingmanager.com	555-5557	555-555-3456	555-5558	http://www.heavyinvoicer	67 Invoiceme	Antioch	IL
5	Aaron E Berhanu	Maple Leaf Inc.	Theboss@yahoo.com	555-5558	555-555-4567	555-5559	http://www.mapleleaf-inc	6789 Expensereport	Chicago	IL
6	Tommy Leep	TimeCatcher LLC	Timeismoney@aol.com	555-5559	555-555-5678	555-5550	http://www.timecatcher.c	56 Money	Nashville	TN
7	Nicholas Anderson	MountainMan Inc.	Upforstuff@gmail.com	555-5560	555-556-6789	555-5561	http://www.mountainmar	689 Billit	Knoxville	TN
8	Jennie Tan	WordSmither	Simplicity@aol.com	555-5561	555-556-7890	555-5562	http://www.wordsmither.	89 salesreport	Oakland	CA
9	Bridget O'Brien	CustomersRus LLC	QBOrocks@yahoo.com	555-5562	555-556-8901	555-5563	http://www.customersrus	4890 easy	Portland	OR
10	Jon D Fasoli	Account-dracula Inc.	Accountantsarefunpeopletoo@yahoo.com	555-5563	555-556-9012	555-5564	http://www.account-drac	123 Accounts Recievable	Miami	FL

Before importing additional customers, look at Craig's Design and Landscaping Services Customer Contact list (Reports > type **Customer Contact List.**) Scroll

through the list. Observe that the names on the spreadsheet illustrated above do not appear on the customer contact list. Here's how to add them.
Follow the instructions to download these customers into the Craig's Design and Landscaping Services.

1. If needed, start the test-drive at https://qbo.intuit.com/redir/testdrive. These steps are consistent with Chrome.
2. Go to Gear > Import Data. The Import Data page appears. Observe that you can import the following: Customers, Vendors, Accounts, and Products and Services. In this example, the Customers list will be imported.

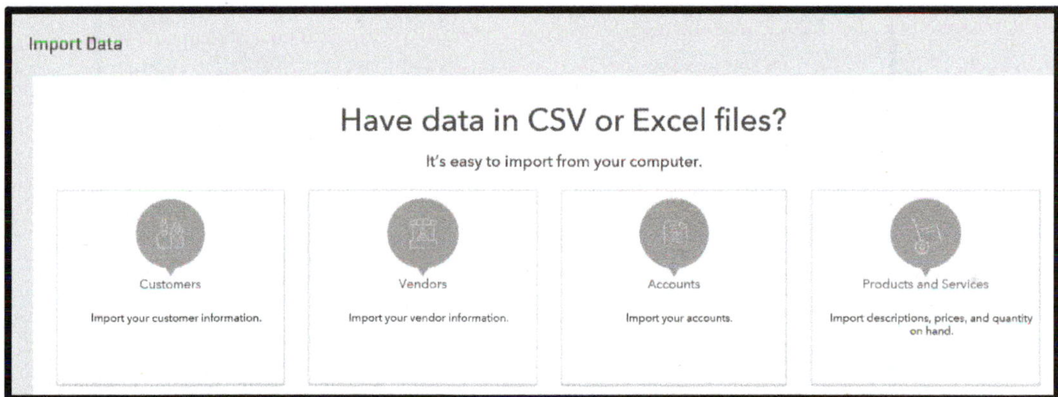

3. Link to Customers. The Import Customers page appears > link to Download a sample file ↓.
4. At the bottom of your screen, there is a QuickBooks_Online…xls selection > click on it. When the file opens > select Enable Editing. Save the file to your desktop or USB flash drive.
5. From the Import Customers page, browse to the location of the QuickBooks_Online_Customer_Sample_File file > click Open. You are returned to the Import Customers page. Observe that the Select a CSV or Excel file to upload field shows the file name > click 
.

6. A Map your fields to QuickBooks fields page appears with checkmarks next to each field.

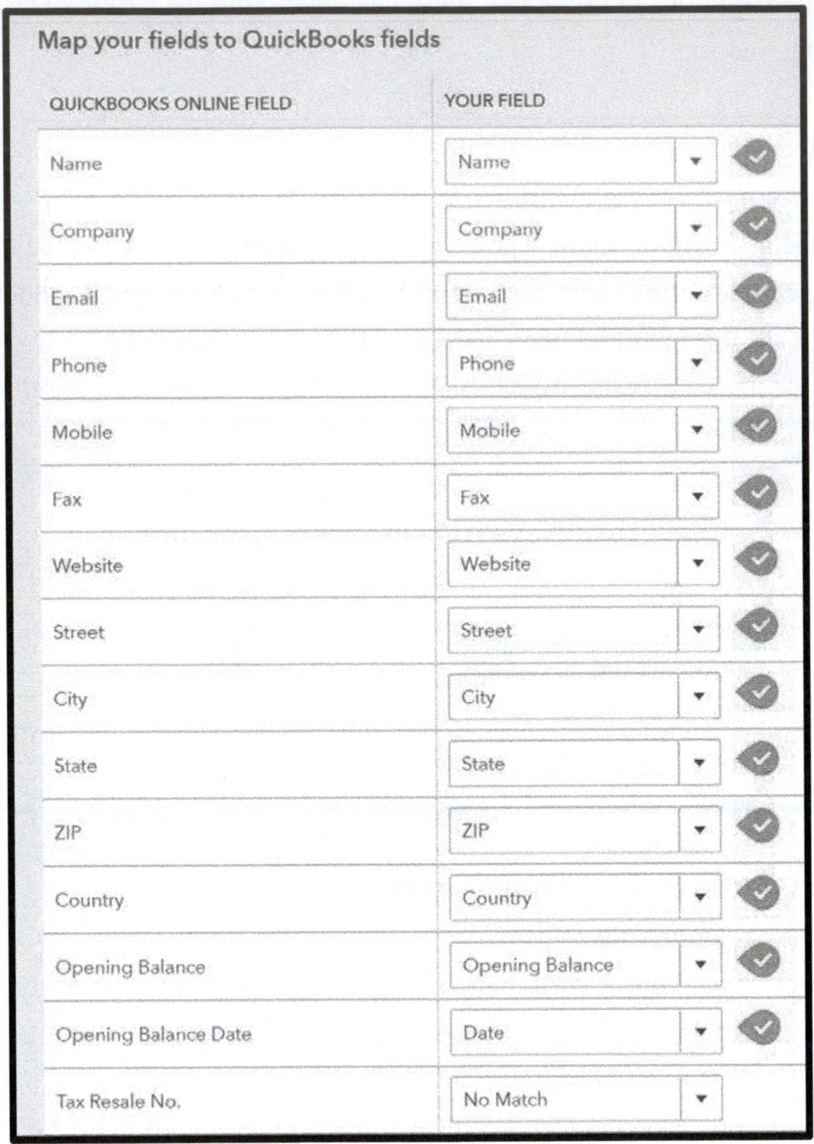

Map your fields to QuickBooks fields

QUICKBOOKS ONLINE FIELD	YOUR FIELD
Name	Name
Company	Company
Email	Email
Phone	Phone
Mobile	Mobile
Fax	Fax
Website	Website
Street	Street
City	City
State	State
ZIP	ZIP
Country	Country
Opening Balance	Opening Balance
Opening Balance Date	Date
Tax Resale No.	No Match

7. Click <Next>. The Import Customers page says **10 records are ready to be imported**. There are 9 customers – Byran Tublin to Jon

D. Fasoli. If necessary, scroll down and **UNCHECK** the last cell, "All data is for sample purposes only."

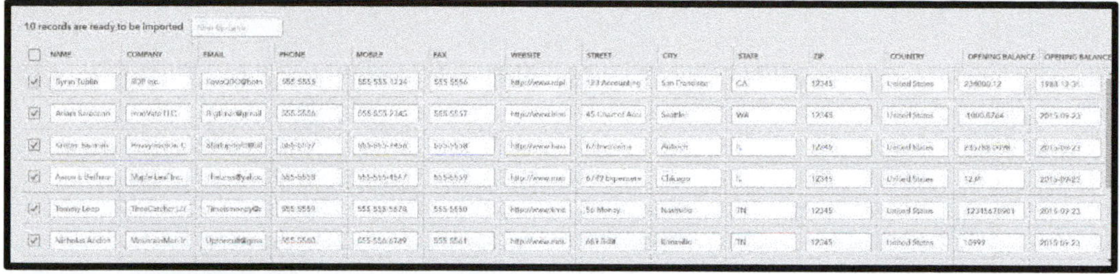

8. Click [Import] A message prompts "9 of 9 customers successfully imported."
9. From the Navigation bar, select Sales > Customers. The additional customers are imported. *Or,* go to Reports and display the Customer Contact List. Scroll through the customers. The customers shown below were added from the Excel file imported into Craig's Design and Landscaping Services.

A partial Customer Contact List is shown. Adam Saraceno is one of the customers imported from the Excel file.

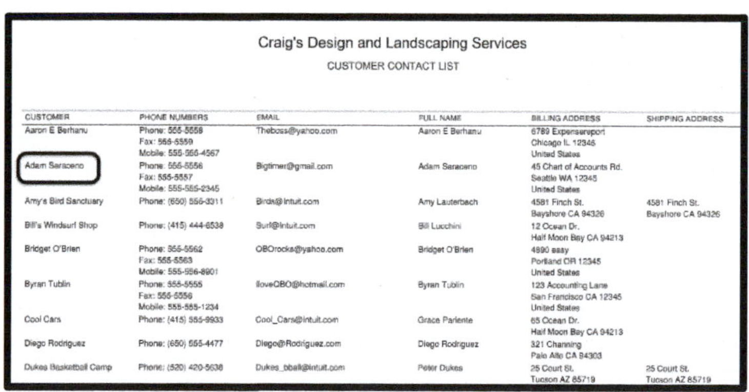

Craig's Design and Landscaping Services

CUSTOMER CONTACT LIST

CUSTOMER	PHONE NUMBERS	EMAIL	FULL NAME	BILLING ADDRESS	SHIPPING ADDRESS
Aaron E Berhanu	Phone: 555-5558 Fax: 555-5559 Mobile: 555-555-4567	Theboss@yahoo.com	Aaron E Berhanu	6789 Expensereport Chicago IL 12345 United States	
Adam Saraceno	Phone: 555-5556 Fax: 555-5557 Mobile: 555-555-2345	Bigtimer@gmail.com	Adam Saraceno	45 Chart of Accounts Rd. Seattle WA 12345 United States	
Amy's Bird Sanctuary	Phone: (650) 555-3311	Birds@intuit.com	Amy Lauterbach	4581 Finch St. Bayshore CA 94326	4581 Finch St. Bayshore CA 94326
Bill's Windsurf Shop	Phone: (415) 444-6538	Surf@intuit.com	Bill Lucchini	12 Ocean Dr. Half Moon Bay CA 94213	
Bridget O'Brien	Phone: 555-5562 Fax: 555-5563 Mobile: 555-556-8901	OBOrocks@yahoo.com	Bridget O'Brien	4890 easy Portland OR 12345 United States	
Byran Tublin	Phone: 555-5555 Fax: 555-5556 Mobile: 555-555-1234	IloveQBO@hotmail.com	Byran Tublin	123 Accounting Lane San Francisco CA 12345 United States	
Cool Cars	Phone: (415) 555-9933	Cool_Cars@intuit.com	Grace Pariente	65 Ocean Dr. Half Moon Bay CA 94213	
Diego Rodriguez	Phone: (650) 555-4477	Diego@Rodriguez.com	Diego Rodriguez	321 Channing Palo Alto CA 94303	
Dukes Basketball Camp	Phone: (520) 420-5638	Dukes_bball@intuit.com	Peter Dukes	25 Court St. Tucson AZ 85719	25 Court St. Tucson AZ 85719

Case Problem 2 Budgeting

To see how QBO's budgeting feature works, use the sample company data at https://qbo.intuit.com/redir/testdrive. You can use a budget to estimate future income and expenses. Then, as time goes by, compare actual income and expense activity with the budget.

In QBO, you can create a Profit and Loss budget which tracks amounts in income and expense accounts. The basic budget design includes a row for each of your income and expense accounts. There is a column for each month. You can track an amount in the intersection of each row and column, and track monthly account amounts for each class, each business, or each customer.

There are several ways to enter Budget data:

- Base the budget on historical data.
- Enter annual or quarterly amounts and calculate a monthly average from them.
- Enter an amount and copy it across the remainder of a row.

ENABLE POP-UPS

Budgeting requires enabling your browser's pop-ups. To enable pop-ups, follow these steps.

1. In this example, the author used Chrome.

2. At the top right of Chrome, click ⋮ > Settings > select the Advanced down-arrow > under Privacy and security, click the Content settings right-arrow > select Popups > move the Blocked slider to allowed.
3. In the Allow field, click ADD > type **[*.]Intuit.com** in Site field.

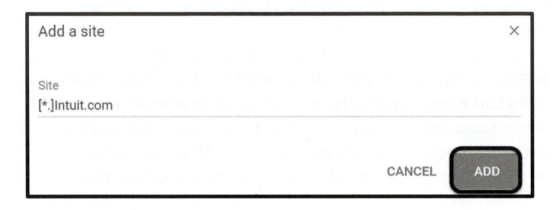

4. Click ADD.
5. Exit your browser.

If you are using another browser, for example, Microsoft Edge, Internet Explorer, or Firefox, different steps are used for allowing popup. If you are unsure how to turn on popups, do an Internet search. For example, type How do I turn on popups in Internet Explorer.

CREATE A BUDGET

1. Go online to https://qbo.intuit.com/redir/testdrive. In this example, Chrome is used.

2. To make sure your Fiscal year starts in January, go to > Accounts and Settings > Advanced. In the Accounting field, the first month of fiscal year shows January. (If not, edit it by selecting the pencil icon.)

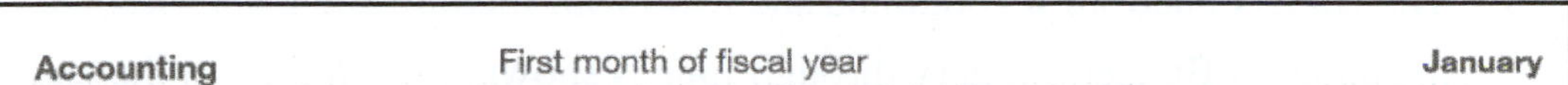

3. Close the Account and Settings page by clicking on its <X>.
4. Print the This Year-to-date Profit and Loss Statement. You can print the P&L from the Company Snapshot (Reports > Recommended > Company Snapshot > Profit and Loss > Run Report > Print.). After completing the budget, a Budget vs. Actuals report is printed. The year-to-date P&L amounts will be shown for comparison purposes. In Case Problem 2, the P&L used for the Budget is from January 1, 2017 to June 25, 2017. Your ending date and year will differ. Amounts may also differ.
5. Select > Budgeting. The Add your first budget page appears. Read the information. Click Add budget. The New Budget page appears.
6. In the Name field, type **Budget your initials** > the Fiscal Year shows FY2017 (Jan 2017 – Dec 2017) – your year may differ > the Interval is Monthly. In the Pre-fill data? Field, select Actual data – 20XX (current year). When Actual data is selected, data populates.

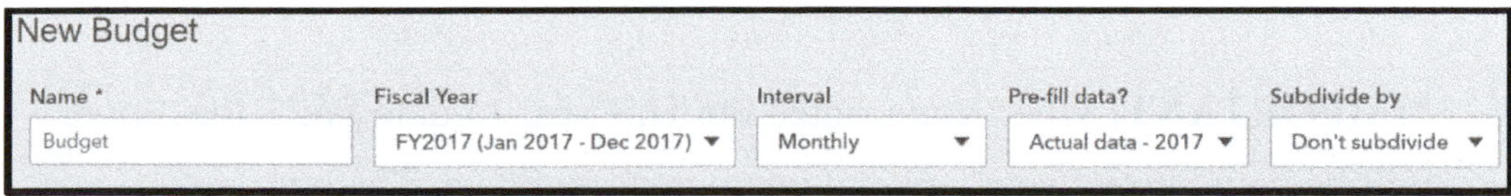

7. Click **Create Budget**. If a field needs to be closed, click on its <X>. Scroll through the Budget to see all the fields.
8. Click **Save**. Budget (your initials) saved appears.
9. The Budget page shows columns and rows with Income and Expenses. On the author's Budget, January through June is shown. Depending on the date you started the test-drive, your months will differ. A partial page is shown.

ACCOUNTS	JAN	FEB	MAR	APR	MAY	JUN	JUL	AUG	SEP	OCT	NOV	DEC	TOT
- INCOME													
Billable Expense Income													
Design income	0.00	0.00	0.00	0.00	2,250.00	0.00	0.00	0.00	0.00	0.00	0.00	0.00	2,250.00
Discounts given	0.00	0.00	0.00	0.00	-89.50	0.00	0.00	0.00	0.00	0.00	0.00	0.00	-89.50
Fees Billed													
- Landscaping Services	0.00	190.00	90.00	400.00	797.50	0.00	0.00	0.00	0.00	0.00	0.00	0.00	1,477.50

Add Budget Projections

You are going to change the budget to add amounts for the month after your This Year-to-date P&L report. The author's P&L report was from January 1 to June 2017. You should look on your This Year-to-date P&L and see what dates are shown. Then, use the next month for the following budget projects.

1. Type **3,000** in the Design income row for the month *after* your P&L > press <Tab>. Since the author's P&L report is from Jan 1 – June 25, 2017, 3,000 is typed in the JUL column. You should type 3,000 in the appropriate month *after your P&L report.*

   ***IMPORTANT:** When you printed the This year-to-date P&L, the report will be your current year and end on your current date. The budget illustration shows amounts entered for July because the author's P&L ended on June 25, 2017. Your month for entering budget amounts will differ. Enter budget amounts for the month *after* the ending date of your P&L. For example, if your year-to-date P&L ends in March, type amounts for April.

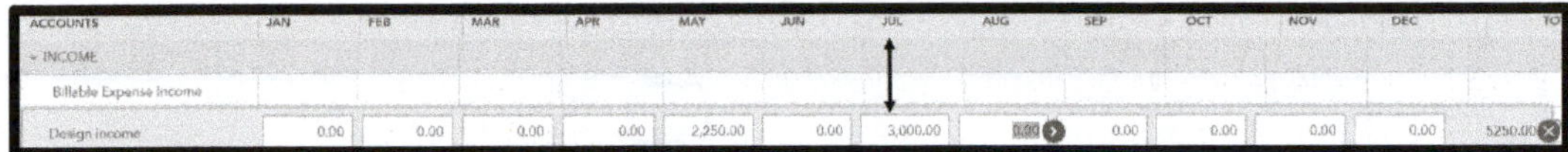

ACCOUNTS	JAN	FEB	MAR	APR	MAY	JUN	JUL	AUG	SEP	OCT	NOV	DEC	TO
▾ INCOME													
Billable Expense Income													
Design income	0.00	0.00	0.00	0.00	2,250.00	0.00	3,000.00	0.00	0.00	0.00	0.00	0.00	5250.00

2. Edit the following budget fields.

3. Complete these amounts for October *for your appropriate month.*

    a. Go to the Landscaping Services row. In the month after your P&L, type **1,250** <Tab>.

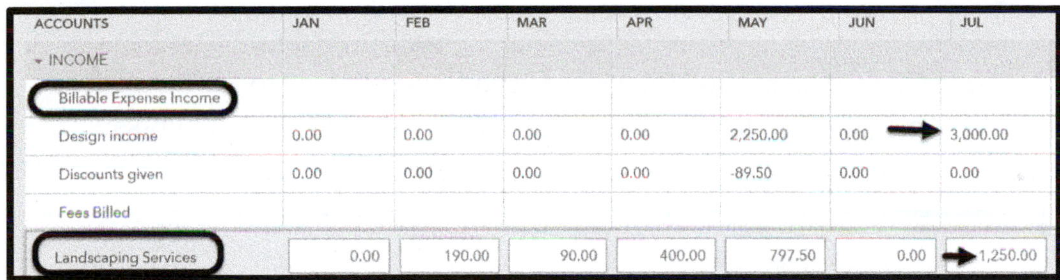

ACCOUNTS	JAN	FEB	MAR	APR	MAY	JUN	JUL
▾ INCOME							
Billable Expense Income							
Design income	0.00	0.00	0.00	0.00	2,250.00	0.00	3,000.00
Discounts given	0.00	0.00	0.00	0.00	-89.50	0.00	0.00
Fees Billed							
Landscaping Services	0.00	190.00	90.00	400.00	797.50	0.00	1,250.00

    b. Below Labor, go to Installation. In the appropriate month *after* your P&L, type **300** <Tab>.

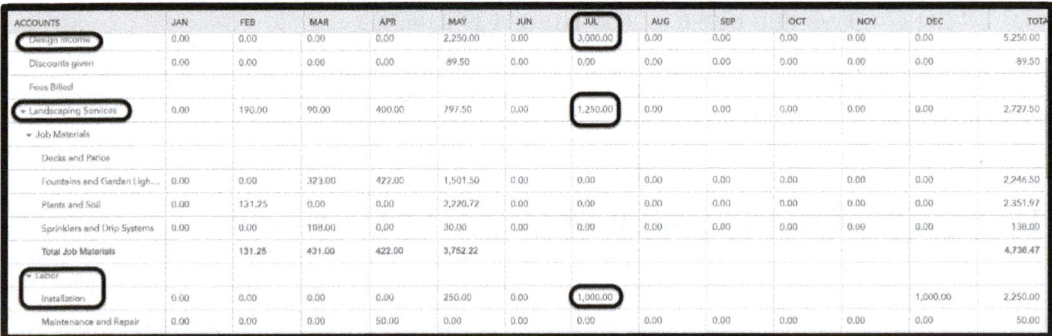

ACCOUNTS	JAN	FEB	MAR	APR	MAY	JUN	JUL	AUG	SEP	OCT	NOV	DEC	TOTA
Design income	0.00	0.00	0.00	0.00	2,250.00	0.00	3,000.00	0.00	0.00	0.00	0.00	0.00	5,250.00
Discounts given	0.00	0.00	0.00	0.00	-89.50	0.00	0.00	0.00	0.00	0.00	0.00	0.00	-89.50
Fees Billed													
▾ Landscaping Services	0.00	190.00	90.00	400.00	797.50	0.00	1,250.00	0.00	0.00	0.00	0.00	0.00	2,727.50
▾ Job Materials													
Decks and Patios													
Fountains and Garden Ligh...	0.00	0.00	323.00	422.00	1,501.50	0.00	0.00	0.00	0.00	0.00	0.00	0.00	2,246.50
Plants and Soil	0.00	131.25	0.00	0.00	2,220.72	0.00	0.00	0.00	0.00	0.00	0.00	0.00	2,351.97
Sprinklers and Drip Systems	0.00	0.00	108.00	0.00	30.00	0.00	0.00	0.00	0.00	0.00	0.00	0.00	138.00
Total Job Materials		131.25	431.00	422.00	3,752.22								4,736.47
▾ Labor													
Installation	0.00	0.00	0.00	0.00	250.00	0.00	1,000.00					1,000.00	2,250.00
Maintenance and Repair	0.00	0.00	0.00	50.00	0.00	0.00	0.00	0.00	0.00	0.00	0.00	0.00	50.00

c. Click <Save>. Go to Sales of Product Income. In the appropriate month, type **1,000** <Tab> >. (*Hint:* You may need to expand the Income rows by clicking in the INCOME down-arrow).

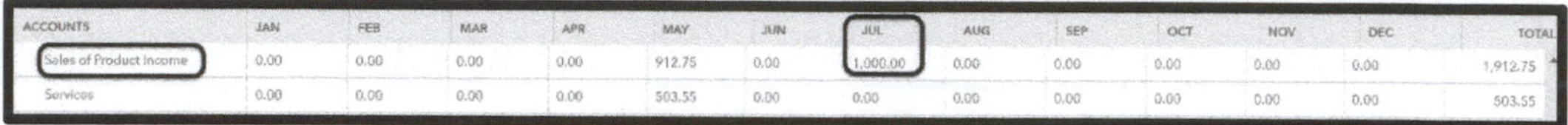

ACCOUNTS	JAN	FEB	MAR	APR	MAY	JUN	JUL	AUG	SEP	OCT	NOV	DEC	TOTAL
Sales of Product Income	0.00	0.00	0.00	0.00	912.75	0.00	1,000.00	0.00	0.00	0.00	0.00	0.00	1,912.75
Services	0.00	0.00	0.00	0.00	503.55	0.00	0.00	0.00	0.00	0.00	0.00	0.00	503.55

d. Click <Save>. Go to Expenses for Automobile > select the Fuel row. In appropriate month's field, type **450** <Tab>, click <Save>.

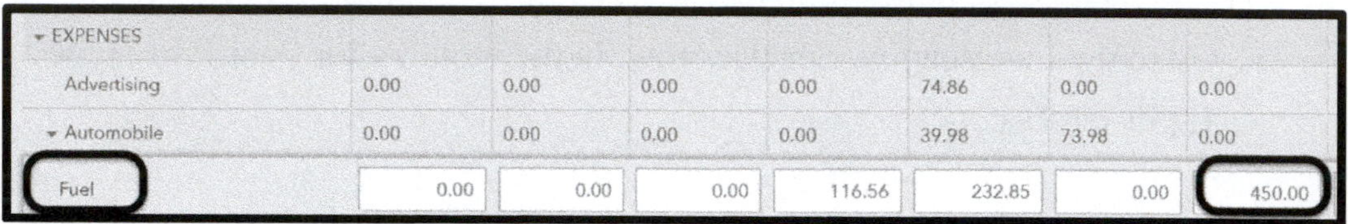

▾ EXPENSES							
Advertising	0.00	0.00	0.00	0.00	74.86	0.00	0.00
▾ Automobile	0.00	0.00	0.00	0.00	39.98	73.98	0.00
Fuel	0.00	0.00	0.00	116.56	232.85	0.00	450.00

e. Click <Save>. In Maintenance and Repair list, go to the Equipment Repairs row. In the appropriate month, type **700** > press <Tab>.

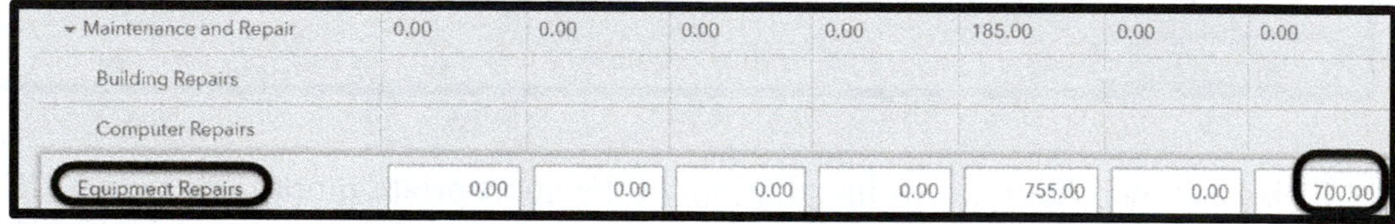

▾ Maintenance and Repair	0.00	0.00	0.00	0.00	185.00	0.00	0.00
Building Repairs							
Computer Repairs							
Equipment Repairs	0.00	0.00	0.00	0.00	755.00	0.00	700.00

4. Click <Save and close>. The Budget is saved.

REPORTS

Display the Budget vs. Actuals and the Budget Overview reports.

1. Select **Reports** > in the search field, type **Budget vs. Actuals**. For the month you typed budget amounts, observe if the amount is over or under budget. For example, for July 2017 the author added $3,000 for Design income. When compard to June's Design income budget which was 0.00, the July budget was $3,000 over budget. Scroll through the Budget to budget projections to earlier months. The Actual amounts are the account balances on your year-to-date Profit and Loss statement.

   The Budget vs. Actuals compares your budgeted income and expenses to the actual amounts so you can tell whether you are over or under budget. A partial Budget vs. Actuals report is shown.

2. In the Report period field, type three months. For example, the author typed 5/1/2017 to 7/31/2017. Include the month that your entered budget projections. A partial report is shown.

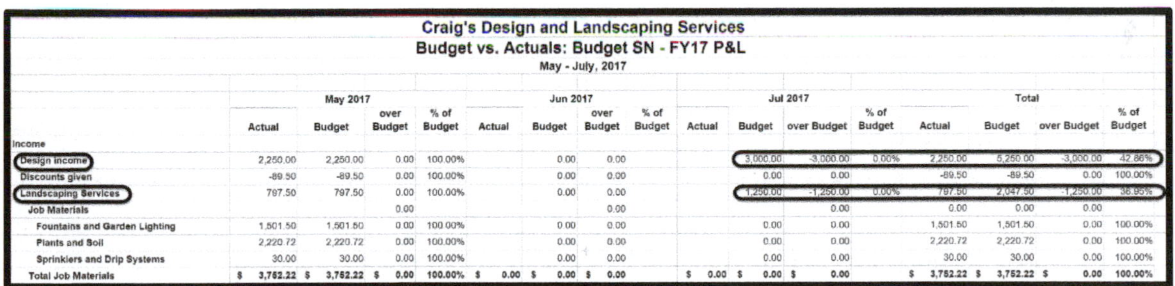

Craig's Design and Landscaping Services
Budget vs. Actuals: Budget SN - FY17 P&L
May - July, 2017

	May 2017				Jun 2017				Jul 2017				Total			
	Actual	Budget	over Budget	% of Budget	Actual	Budget	over Budget	% of Budget	Actual	Budget	over Budget	% of Budget	Actual	Budget	over Budget	% of Budget
Income																
Design income	2,250.00	2,250.00	0.00	100.00%		0.00	0.00			3,000.00	-3,000.00	0.00%	2,250.00	5,250.00	-3,000.00	42.86%
Discounts given	-89.50	-89.50	0.00	100.00%		0.00	0.00			0.00	0.00		-89.50	-89.50	0.00	100.00%
Landscaping Services	797.50	797.50	0.00	100.00%		0.00	0.00			1,250.00	-1,250.00	0.00%	797.50	2,047.50	-1,250.00	38.95%
Job Materials			0.00				0.00				0.00		0.00	0.00	0.00	
Fountains and Garden Lighting	1,501.50	1,501.50	0.00	100.00%		0.00	0.00			0.00	0.00		1,501.50	1,501.50	0.00	100.00%
Plants and Soil	2,220.72	2,220.72	0.00	100.00%		0.00	0.00			0.00	0.00		2,220.72	2,220.72	0.00	100.00%
Sprinklers and Drip Systems	30.00	30.00	0.00	100.00%		0.00	0.00			0.00	0.00		30.00	30.00	0.00	100.00%
Total Job Materials	$ 3,752.22	$ 3,752.22	$ 0.00	100.00%	$ 0.00	$ 0.00	$ 0.00		$ 0.00	$ 0.00	$ 0.00		$ 3,752.22	$ 3,752.22	$ 0.00	100.00%

3. Go to Reports > display the Budget Overview. The Budget Overview shows a summary of budgeted amounts for your budget. A partial report is shown.

Craig's Design and Landscaping Services

BUDGET OVERVIEW: BUDGET SN - FY17 P&L

January - December 2017

	JAN 2017	FEB 2017	MAR 2017	APR 2017	MAY 2017	JUN 2017	JUL 2017	AUG 2017	SEP 2017	OCT 2017	NOV 2017	DEC 2017	TOTAL
INCOME													
Design income	0.00	0.00	0.00	0.00	2,250.00	0.00	3,000.00	0.00	0.00	0.00	0.00	0.00	$5,250.00
Discounts given	0.00	0.00	0.00	0.00	-89.50	0.00	0.00	0.00	0.00	0.00	0.00	0.00	$ -89.50
Landscaping Services	0.00	190.00	90.00	400.00	797.50	0.00	1,250.00	0.00	0.00	0.00	0.00	0.00	$2,727.50
Job Materials													$0.00
Fountains and Garden Lighting	0.00	0.00	323.00	422.00	1,501.50	0.00	0.00	0.00	0.00	0.00	0.00	0.00	$2,246.50
Plants and Soil	0.00	131.25	0.00	0.00	2,220.72	0.00	0.00	0.00	0.00	0.00	0.00	0.00	$2,351.97
Sprinklers and Drip Systems	0.00	0.00	108.00	0.00	30.00	0.00	0.00	0.00	0.00	0.00	0.00	0.00	$138.00
Total Job Materials	**0.00**	**131.25**	**431.00**	**422.00**	**3,752.22**	**0.00**	**0.00**	**0.00**	**0.00**	**0.00**	**0.00**	**0.00**	**$4,736.47**
Labor													$0.00
Installation	0.00	0.00	0.00	0.00	250.00	0.00	1,000.00	0.00	0.00	0.00	0.00	1,000.00	$2,250.00
Maintenance and Repair	0.00	0.00	0.00	50.00	0.00	0.00	0.00	0.00	0.00	0.00	0.00	0.00	$50.00
Total Labor	**0.00**	**0.00**	**0.00**	**50.00**	**250.00**	**0.00**	**1,000.00**	**0.00**	**0.00**	**0.00**	**0.00**	**1,000.00**	**$2,300.00**
Total Landscaping Services	**0.00**	**321.25**	**521.00**	**872.00**	**4,799.72**	**0.00**	**2,250.00**	**0.00**	**0.00**	**0.00**	**0.00**	**1,000.00**	**$9,763.97**
Pest Control Services	0.00	70.00	0.00	70.00	-30.00	0.00	0.00	0.00	0.00	0.00	0.00	0.00	$110.00
Sales of Product Income	0.00	0.00	0.00	0.00	912.75	0.00	1,000.00	0.00	0.00	0.00	0.00	0.00	$1,912.75
Services	0.00	0.00	0.00	0.00	503.55	0.00	0.00	0.00	0.00	0.00	0.00	0.00	$503.55
Total Income	**$0.00**	**$391.25**	**$521.00**	**$942.00**	**$8,346.52**	**$0.00**	**$6,250.00**	**$0.00**	**$0.00**	**$0.00**	**$0.00**	**$1,000.00**	**$17,450.77**

Comment: Because your dates on the Year-to-Date P&L report differs, your reports will also differ.

Case Problem 3 Your Name Accounting

Your Name Accounting is a service business project. There are two ways to complete Your Name Accounting.

1. Using the 30-day free trial version of QuickBooks Online Plus at http://quickbooks.intuit.com, complete Your Name Accounting. The instructions that follow show you how to do that.
2. If you have QuickBooks Desktop software available, go online to www.mhhe.com/qbo2e > Student Edition > CP3. Use the QuickBooks Desktop company file, Your Name Accounting.qbw, to convert a QuickBooks Desktop company to QuickBooks Online. To convert the company file from QB Desktop to QBO Online, QuickBooks Desktop 2014 or higher should already be installed locally on the hard-drive of your computer. The Your Name Accounting.qbw file is compatible with Microsoft Windows 7, 8, and 10. If you do not have QB Desktop software available, complete Case Problem 3 on pages 589 – 605.

SETTING UP A QUICKBOOKS ONLINE COMPANY

Go online to the website shown on the next page, to set up a new QB Online Plus company using the free trial version. It can be used for 30 days or less and then it expires. Follow these steps to set up a trial version.

Set up another email address, for example, a Gmail or Yahoo email address. A new User ID and Password will also be set up. (Do not use the same email and

Password used with QB Cloud_Student Name.) This distinguishes Your Name Accounting from QB Cloud (company used in Chapters 2-10).

Tip: You must use a valid email address.

1. Go online to http://quickbooks.intuit.com.
2. Select Free Trial. As of this writing, it is next to Sign In. When the next page appears, click Free Trial again. In the Most Popular Plus column, click Try it free.

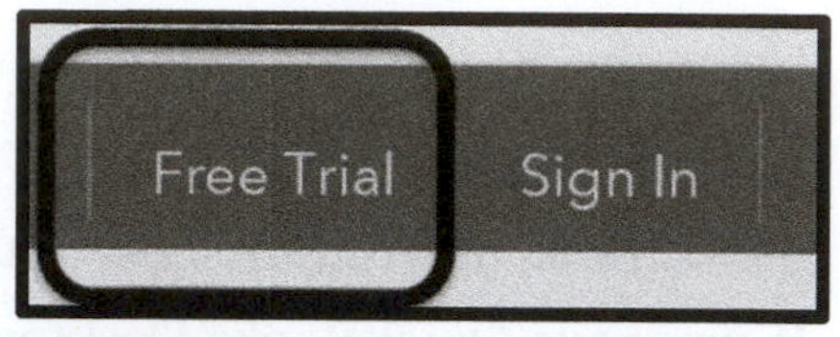

Tip: Steps for obtaining the 30-day free trial version change. You may need to make different selections. For example, select Plans & Pricing > FREE TRIAL for 30 days > Plus Try it free. Make sure when you select the Plus version, that Try it free *or* Continue with trial is shown. You should not enter credit card information. If that page appears, start step 1 again.

3. The Try QuickBooks for free for 30 days page appears. Type a valid email address and password.

IMPORTANT: Do **not** use the same email or password that you used with QB Cloud_Student Name in Chapters 2 through 10. Write down your User ID and Password.

User ID ____

Password ____

4. If a page appears asking for a phone number, it's optional > click <Continue>.
5. The Signing In page appears with your User ID shown. Read the information. Select <Yes, that's correct>, then <Continue with trial>.
6. As of this writing, complete fields for the name of the business and length of time for the business. (Field names may differ.)

   What's your business called: **Your Name Accounting** (use your first and last name Accounting)
   How long have you been in business: select Less than 1 year.

   Do not put a checkmark next to I've been using QuickBooks Desktop and want to bring in my data.

7. Click Next to go to the next page. Read the information. If All set appears, select it (or select the button on your page).

> fyi You can access the Trial Version for **30 days**, then it will expire. If you do not complete Your Name Accounting within 30 days, monthly subscription fees apply in order to continue.

BILLING & SUBSCRIPTION

To see when your subscription to QB Online Plus's free trial ends, select Gear > Account and Settings > Billing & Subscription. These fields appears:

Subscription status: Trial ends in 30 days! Subscribe now or Cancel trial.
Plan details: QuickBooks Plus
Next Charge: Free through – date is shown

ENABLE CHART OF ACCOUNTS NUMBERS

Go to Gear > Account and Settings > Advanced > Chart of accounts > Edit > Enable and Show account numbers > Save > Done.

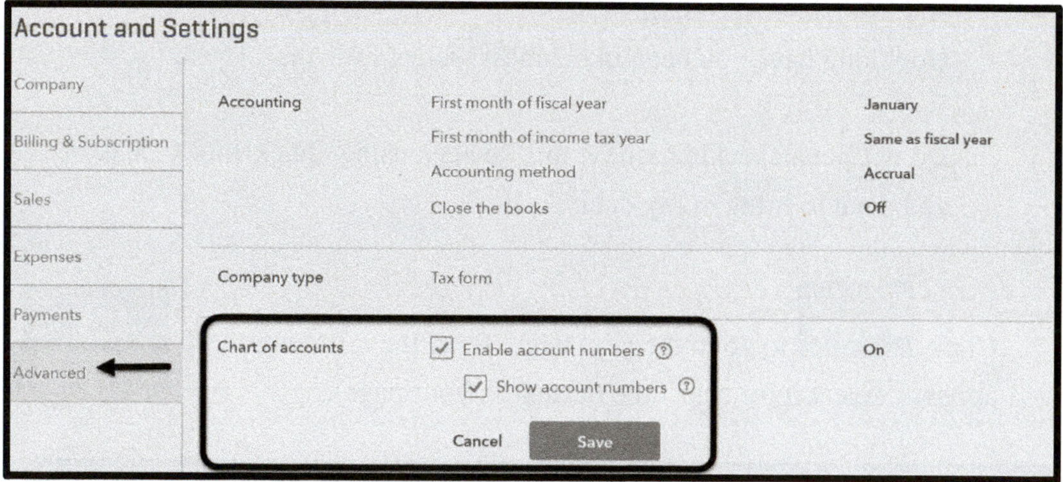

CHART OF ACCOUNTS AND BEGINNING BALANCES

Set up the following Chart of Accounts and Beginning Balances as of 11/30/20XX. Use your curent year.

The accounts to be added or edited are shown below and on the next two pages. Remember to select the appropriate Detail Type and Category Type.

Number	Name	Category Type	Detail Type	QuickBooks Balance
10000	Glendale Bank	Bank	Checking	50,000.00
11000	Accounts Receivable	Other Current Assets	Other Curent Assets	0.00
14000	Prepaid Rent	Other Current Assets	Prepaid Expenses	2,000.00
14500	Supplies	Other Current Assets	Other Curent Assets	2,500.00
15000	Furniture and Equipment	Fixed Assets	Other fixed assets	4,000.00
15500	Computer Equipment	Fixed Assets	Other fixed assets	1,000.00
17000	Accum Depr-Furn&Eq	Fixed Assets	Accumulated Depreciation	0.00
17500	Accum Depr-Computer Equip	Fixed Assets	Accumulated Depreciation	0.00
20000	Accounts Payable	Other Current Liabilities	Other Current Liabilities	0.00
24000	Payroll Tax Payable	Other Current Liabilities	Other Current Liabilities	0.00
25000	Notes Payable	Other Curent Liabilities	Other Current Liabilities	20,000.00
30000	Your Name, Capital *(Edit Opening Balance Equity)*	Equity	Opening Balance Equity	39,500.00 *(Completed automatically)*
30800	Your Name, Draw	Equity	Owner's Equity	0.00

Number	Name	Category Type	Detail Type	QuickBooks Balance
32000	Owner's Equity *(Edit Retained Earnings)*	Equity	Retained Earnings	0.00
41000	Accounting Services Income	Income	Service/Fee Income	0.00
42700	Consulting Income	Income	Service/Fee Income	0.00
60000	Advertising Expense	Expenses	Advertising/Promotional	0.00
60400	Bank Service Charges	Expenses	Bank Charges	0.00
61550	Wages Expense-Adm Asst	Expenses	Office/General Administrative Expenses	0.00
61600	Wages Expense-Acctg Tech	Expenses	Office/General Administrative Expenses	0.00
62400	Depr Exp-Furn&Eq	Expenses	Office/General Administrative Expenses	0.00
62450	Depr Exp-Computer Equip	Expenses	Office/General Administrative Expenses	0.00
62500	Subscriptions Expense	Expenses	Dues & subscriptions	0.00
63400	Interest Expense	Expenses	Interest Paid	0.00
64900	Supplies Expense	Expenses	Supplies & Material	0.00
66500	Postage Expense	Expenses	Other Miscellaneous Service Cost	0.00

Number	Name	Category Type	Detail Type	QuickBooks Balance
67100	Rent Expense	Expenses	Rent or Lease of Buildings	0.00
67200	Repairs & Maintenance	Expenses	Repair & Maintenance	0.00
68100	Telephone Expense	Expensess	Office/General Administrative Expenses	0.00
68600	Utilities Expense	Expenses	Utilities	0.00

- Export the Chart of Accounts to Excel and save as a PDF file. Use the file name **Case Problem 3_Chart of Accounts**.

DECEMBER 1, 20XX BALANCE SHEET

1. Display the December 1 balance sheet: Reports > Balance Sheet > 12/1/20XX to 12/1/20XX > Run Report. The Balance Sheet is shown on the next page. O Observe that two months' rent was prepaid on December 1 (Account 14000 Prepaid Rent).

   Hint: To make sure you entered beginning balances as of November 30, 20XX, display the November 30 balance sheet. If you did not enter beginning balances as of 11/30/20XX, go to the Journal report, drill down, then edit the Opening Balance dates.

Your Name Accounting
BALANCE SHEET
As of December 1, 2017

	TOTAL
ASSETS	
Current Assets	
Bank Accounts	
10000 Glendale Bank	50,000.00
Total Bank Accounts	**$50,000.00**
Other Current Assets	
14000 Prepaid Rent	2,000.00
14500 Supplies	2,500.00
Total Other Current Assets	**$4,500.00**
Total Current Assets	**$54,500.00**
Fixed Assets	
15000 Furniture and Equipment	4,000.00
15500 Computer Equipment	1,000.00
Total Fixed Assets	**$5,000.00**
TOTAL ASSETS	**$59,500.00**
LIABILITIES AND EQUITY	
Liabilities	
Current Liabilities	
Other Current Liabilities	
25000 Notes Payable	20,000.00
Total Other Current Liabilities	**$20,000.00**
Total Current Liabilities	**$20,000.00**
Total Liabilities	**$20,000.00**
Equity	
30000 Student Name, Capital	39,500.00
32000 Retained Earnings	
Net Income	
Total Equity	**$39,500.00**
TOTAL LIABILITIES AND EQUITY	**$59,500.00**

2. Export the December 1 Balance Sheet to Excel and save as a PDF file. Use the file name **Case Problem 3_December 1 Balance Sheet**. (You may want to use Your Name Accounting in the file name. Check with your instructor.)

ACCOUNT AND SETTINGS

If necessary, make the following changes.

1. Select Gear > Account and Settings.
2. In the Company name field, select the pencil icon to edit. In the Company Name field, add your first and last name. The Company name should be Your first and last name Accounting.
3. Edit the Address information with your name and address.
4. Edit the Tax form field. Select Sole proprietor (Form 1040) > Save.

5. Select Advanced. Edit the Customer label field. Select Clients

6. From the Navigation bar, select Sales. Clients replaces Customers.

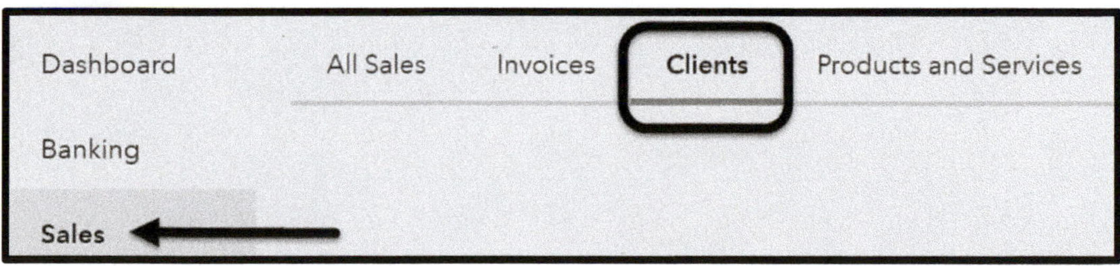

7. Return to the Dashboard.

DECEMBER 20XX TRANSACTIONS

Complete the accounting cycle for your accounting company. Use the current year. You employ two independent contractors: an Accounting Technician and an Administrative Assistant. They are paid at the end of the month.

Use the Transaction Register on the next page to complete December 20XX entries. When recording checks, add vendors. For deposits, do this:

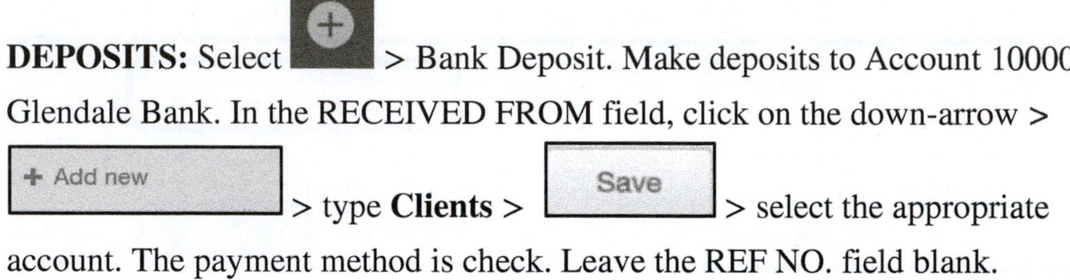

DEPOSITS: Select > Bank Deposit. Make deposits to Account 10000 Glendale Bank. In the RECEIVED FROM field, click on the down-arrow > > type **Clients** > > select the appropriate account. The payment method is check. Leave the REF NO. field blank.

Transaction Register

Check No.	*Date*	*Description of Transaction*	Debit (-)	Credit (+)	Balance
	11/30	*Balance*			$50,000.00
	12/1	Deposit (accounting services)		4,000.00	54,000.00
9001	12/1	Second Bank (Notes Payable) Interest Expense	2,000.00 85.00		51,915.00
9002	12/12	Office Staples; Account 14500 Supplies	259.75		51,655.25
	12/16	Deposit (accounting services)		5,500.00	57,155.25
9003	12/17	Southwest Telephone	109.35		57,045.90
9004	12/17	U.S. Post Office	49.00		56,996.90
9005	12/17	Accounting Online Journal	125.00		56,871.90
9006	12/20	Rosa's Repairs	75.00		56,796.90
	12/22	Deposit (consulting)		2,500.00	59,296.90
9007	12/24	Moss Advertising	120.00		59,176.90
	12/24	Deposit (accounting services)		4,800.00	63,976.90
9008	12/24	City Utilities	63.23		63,913.67
	12/24	Deposit (consulting)		4,500.00	68,413.67
9009	12/27	Wages-Admin Asst	1,500.00		66,913.97
9010	12/27	Wages-Acctg Tech	1,200.00		65,713.67
9011	12/27	Owner's Draw	5,000.00		60,713.67

UNADJUSTED TRIAL BALANCE AND JOURNAL

Export the Trial Balance to Excel and save as a PDF file. Use the file name **Case Problem 3_Unadjusted Trial Balance**. (*Hint:* Use the date range shown on the Transaction Register. Change the title to Unadjusted Trial Balance.)

END-OF-YEAR ADJUSTING ENTRIES

1. At the end of December, the supplies on hand are $1,550.00.
2. Depreciation for Computer Equipment: $41.67.
3. Depreciation for Furniture and Equipment: $66.67.
4. Adjust one month's rent. Refer to the December 1 Balance Sheet. (*Hint:* Two months' rent was prepaid on December 1.)
5. Export the Journal to Excel and save as a PDF file. Use the file name **Case Problem 3_Journal**. (*Hint:* From 12/1/20XX to 12/31/20XX.)

ADJUSTED TRIAL BALANCE AND DECEMBER BANK STATEMENT

1. Export the Adjusted Trial Balance to Excel and save as a PDF file. Use the file name **Case Problem 3_Adjusted Trial Balance**. Change the title to Adjusted Trial Balance.
2. The December 31 bank statement is shown on the next page.

Statement of Account			Your Name Accounting
Glendale Bank			Your address
December1 - 31, 20XX	Account No. 980-22-1122		Your City, State, Zip
REGULAR CHECKING			
Previous Balance	11/30	$50,000.00	
5 Deposits (+)		21,300.00	
11 checks (-)		10,586.33	
Service Charge		18.00	
Ending Balance	12/31	**$60,695.67**	
DEPOSITS			
	12/2	4,000.00	
	12/17	5,500.00	
	12/23	2,500.00	
	12/26	4,800.00	
	12/27	4,500.00	
CHECKS (Asterisk * indicates break in check number sequence)			
9001	12/3	2,085.00	
9002	12/14	259.75	
9003	12/19	109.35	
9004	12/20	49.00	
9005	12/20	125.00	
9006	12/22	75.00	
9007	12/24	120.00	
9008	12/26	63.23	
9009	12/28	1,500.00	
9010	12/28	1,200.00	
9011	12/28	5,000.00	

3. Save the Reconciliation report as a PDF file. Use the file name **Case Probem 3_Reconciliation Report**.

FINANCIAL STATEMENTS

1. Export the Profit and Loss to Excel and save as a PDF file. Use the file name **Case Problem 3_Profit and Loss**.
2. Export the Balance Sheet to Excel and save as a PDF file. Use the file name **Case Problem 3_Balance Sheet**.
3. Export the Statement of Cash Flows to Excel and save as a PDF file. Use the file name **Case Problem 3_Statement of Cash Flows**.

Tip: If you completed the OLC's Case Problem 3, Convert QB Desktop to QB Online, the Statement of Cash Flows may differ. When compared to QuickBooks Desktop, QuickBooks Online has additional Chart of Accounts Detail Types. For example, with QB Online Accumulated Depreciation can be selected as a Detail Type. QB Desktop includes Account Types and Accumulated Depreciation is a Fixed Asset. Unlike QB Online, there is not a specific QB Desktop category for Accumulated Depreciation. This affects the Statement of Cash Flow sections. The Cash at End of Period is the same but Accumulated Depreciation is shown in the Adjustments section of the Statement of Cash Flows.

CLOSE THE BOOKS

1. On December 31, 20XX, close the balance in the drawing account to capital. Record this journal entry.

Account	Description	Debit	Credit
Your Name, Capital	Close the drawing account	5,000.00	
Your Name, Draw	Close the drawing account		5,000.00

2. Export the January 1, 20XY Balance Sheet to Excel and save as a PDF file. Use the file name **Case Problem 3_January 1 Balance Sheet**.
3. Export the January 1, 20XY Trial Balance to Excel and save as a PDF file. Use the file name **Case Problem 3_Postclosing Trial Balance**.
4. Export the December 1, 20XX to January 1, 20XY Transaction Detail by Account to Excel and save as a PDF file. Use the file name **Case Problem 3_Transaction Detail by Account**.

CHECK YOUR PROGRESS: Your Name Accounting

1. What are the total debit and credit balances on the unadjusted trial balance? ____________________

2. What are the total debit and credit balances on your Adjusted trial balance? ____________________

3. What is the Statement Ending Balance on the reconciliation report? ____________________

4. What is the rent expense balance? ____________________

5. What is the depreciation expense for computer equipment? ____________________

6. What is the depreciation expense for furniture and equipment? ____________________

7. What is the amount of total income? ____________________

8. How much net income (or net loss) is reported on December 31? ____________________

9. What is the account balance in the Notes Payable account? ____________________

10. What is the total assets balance on December 31? ____________________

11. Is there an increase or decrease in Cash for the month of December? ____________________

12. What is the balance in the Owner's Equity account? ____________________

Appendix A Troubleshooting

The screens that are shown in the textbook may differ from what you see. Each time you sign in to QBO, the software is the most current version. If you notice changes, go online to www.mhhe.com/qbo2e > Text Updates.

There are additional Troubleshooting tips in each chapter. To see the Troubleshooting information within each chapter, refer to the end-of-chapter index.

Appendix A, Troubleshooting, includes the following topics.

WHY DO MY SCREENS LOOK DIFFERENT?

The screens shown in the textbook may differ from what you see. Each time you sign on, QuickBooks Online is the most current version. When QBO updates, sometimes screens change. The screen changes are usually minor and do not affect the features and functions of the software.

In most chapters, FYI boxes remind you that updates are automatic. To learn more about updates, to the QuickBooks Blog at http://quickbooks.intuit.com/blog/ > What's New in QBO.

CHART OF ACCOUNTS OR ACCOUNT LIST

Does your Account List show an account with 4 digits, for example, Account 3000 Opening Balance Equity? QBO creates Account 3000 the first time you enter an opening balance for a balance sheet account. For purposes of completing QB Cloud_Student Name, Account 3000 can be ignored.

When preferences or Account and Settings are changed, the selections add accounts to the Chart of Accounts or Account List. Settings also impact the user interface. For example, making products and services selections, also changes fields that are available on QBO transaction pages (bills, sales receipts, invoices, etc.).

The Merchandise Inventory account is Account 115 Merchandise Inventory. Your chart of accounts must include these accounts for purchasing and selling inventory on account.

Account #	Account	Type	Detail Type
105	Accounts Receivable (A/R)	Accounts receivable (A/R)	Account Receivable (A/R)
115	Merchandise Inventory	Other Current Assets	Inventory
401	Sales	Income	Sales of Product Income
501	Cost of Goods Sold	Cost of Goods Sold	Supplies & Materials - COGS

Troubleshooting: Inventory items

What if I have the wrong Product/Service Type?
What if my Inventory Valuation Summary is wrong?

When checking your Inventory Valuation Summary, you may notice the quantity or asset value is wrong. First check to make sure all inventory items are listed, then run a Product/Service list. (Shown on page 225)

Under "Type" you will see Non-inventory, Inventory and Service items. Are these correct? If not, refer to page 163 select Change type. If you are changing your type to "Inventory" be sure all fields shown on page 163 are correct.

If you made purchases or had sales, prior to changing the type, Journal entries will be required to correct your Trial Balance and Balance Sheet.

HOW TO VIDEOS

You can watch short videos about some of the top activities in QuickBooks at http://quickbooks.intuit.com/tutorials/. As of this writing the following videos are included:

1. Create an Invoice
2. See Your Business Health
3. Inventory
4. How to Set Up and Use QuickBooks Payments
5. Create Sales Receipts
6. Time Tracking Invoices

To see all the QuickBooks tutorials, go to http://quickbooks.intuit.com/tutorials/all-quickbooks-tutorials/.

CLEARING TEMPORARY INTERNET FILES/CACHE

Clearing the browser cache (deleting temporary internet files) is a good way to start the browser with a clean slate. The steps are different depending on which browser you're using.

Internet Explorer: https://support.microsoft.com/en-us/help/17438/windows-internet-explorer-view-delete-browsing-history#ie=ie-11
Firefox: https://support.mozilla.org/en-US/kb/how-clear-firefox-cache

Google Chrome: https://support.google.com/chrome/answer/2392709?hl=en&visit_id=0-636286617483735526-488028326&rd=1

Safari: https://support.apple.com/kb/PH19215?locale=en_US

Safari (for iPad/iPhone): https://support.apple.com/en-us/HT201265

QuickBooks Windows App: For information to clear cache in the Windows App, see https://community.intuit.com/articles/1458875-quickbooks-windows-app-general-support

SPREADSHEET COMPARE

Office Professional 2016: "Compare two versions of a workbook by using Spreadsheet Compare" at https://support.office.com/en-US/article/Compare-two-versions-of-a-workbook-by-using-Spreadsheet-Compare-0E1627FD-CE14-4C33-9AB1-8EA82C6A5A7E

"What can you do with Spreadsheet Inquire in Excel 2016 for Windows," at https://support.office.com/en-US/article/what-you-can-do-with-spreadsheet-inquire-in-excel-2016-for-windows-5444eb12-14a2-4d82-b527-45b9884f98cf.

For **Office Professional 2013**, go to https://technet.microsoft.com/en-us/library/dn205148.aspx.

UNDEPOSITED FUNDS

Either Account 101 Checking *or* Undeposited Funds can be used for deposits. QuickBooks Online includes a default account called Undeposited Funds. Your journal may show an Undeposited Funds entry for the current date. The Memo/Description shows Blank and the Debits are zero.

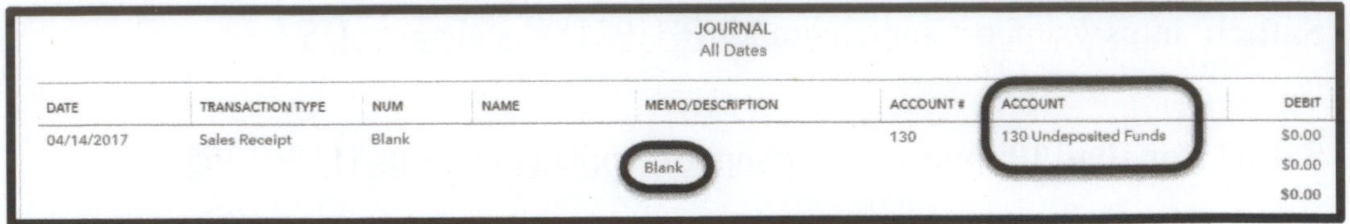

DATE	TRANSACTION TYPE	NUM	NAME	MEMO/DESCRIPTION	ACCOUNT #	ACCOUNT	DEBIT
04/14/2017	Sales Receipt	Blank			130	130 Undeposited Funds	$0.00
				Blank			$0.00
							$0.00

The Undeposited Funds account is like an envelope where you keep checks until you take them to the bank. If you receive more than one check or payment in a day, they could be grouped as one deposit.

SWITCHING FROM QUICKBOOKS DESKTOP

To learn about how to import QuickBooks Desktop data to QuickBooks Online, go to http://quickbooks.intuit.com/move-from-desktop-to-online/. Watch a video or choose your desktop product for a step-by-step guide that shows you how to make a copy of your data and import it into QuickBooks Online. The products include QB desktop Pro or Premier, QB desktop for Mac, and QB Enterprise.

SAVE EXCEL FILE AS ADOBE PDF FILE

After exporting a report to Excel, save the file. Your Excel file should be open.

1. On Excel's menu bar, select File > Save as Adobe PDF.
2. An Adobe PDFMaker window appears > select Convert to PDF.

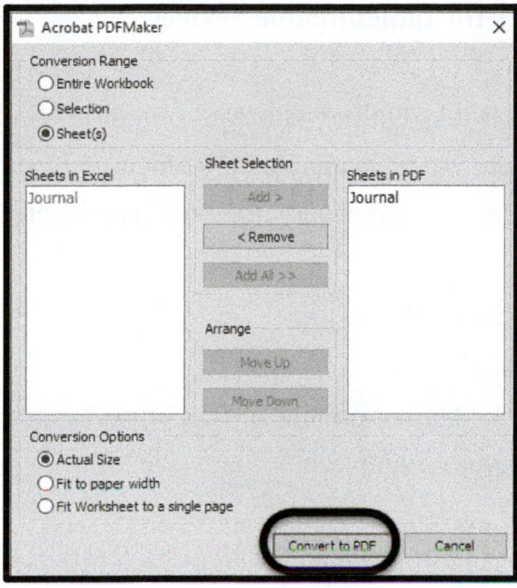

3. After selecting <Convert to PDF>, go to the location to save the file, The PDF file has the same file name as the Excel file. Click <Save>.

WHAT BROWSERS CAN I USE?

Recommended browsers:

Chrome (current stable release): https://www.google.com/chrome/browser/

Firefox (current stable release): https://www.mozilla.org/en-US/firefox/new/?utm_source=firefox-com&utm_medium=referral

Internet Explorer: http://windows.microsoft.com/en-gb/internet-explorer/browser-ie#touchweb=touchvidtab1. To complete the textbook, the author used Internet Explorer 11 with QBO.

Compatible browsers for tablet/mobile devices:

You can access QuickBooks Online with Android, or a Windows 10 device. Some QuickBooks features are available only when viewed from computers (Windows or Mac). Other features may not work as expected.

Looking for an app instead?

Read about QuickBooks Online mobile apps at https://apps.intuit.com/ for more information about what is available.

For best results on your mobile device when using a browser, use the following:

iPhone / iPad

- iOS 6.1 or newer
- Safari browser (recommended)
- Other browsers such as Chrome, Atomic, and Dolphin are not supported on iOS

Android smartphones and tablets

- Jelly Bean 4.2.2 or newer
- Chrome browser (recommended)
- Other browsers such as Firefox, Opera, and Dolphin are not supported, but may work

Surface: Internet Explorer 10 or higher (recommended)

COMPARE QUICKBOOKS ONLINE PLUS VS. QUICKBOOKS ONLINE ACCOUNTANT

QuickBooks Online Plus is included with the textbook. The Plus version includes a one year subscription. Educators can register for an unlimited version, QB Online Accountant, www.mhhe.com/qbo2e > Instructor Edition > Educator Registration.

Tasks	**Plus** Included with textbook	**Accountant** Educator registration
Track your income and expenses	✓	✓
Download transactions from your bank and credit card accounts	✓	✓
Back up your data online automatically	✓	✓
Same security and encryption as banks	✓	✓
Access your data from a tablet or smartphone	✓	✓
Send unlimited estimates and invoices	✓	✓
Print checks and record transactions	✓	✓
Import data from Excel or QuickBooks desktop	✓	✓
Invite up to two accountants to access your data	✓	✓
Integrate with available applications	✓	✓
Set up invoices to automatically bill on a recurring schedule	✓	✓

Manage and pay bills from vendors	✓	✓
Enter bills and schedule payments for later	✓	✓
Compare your sales and profitability with industry trends	✓	✓
Control what your users can access	✓	✓
Create and send purchase orders	✓	✓
Track inventory	✓	✓
Prepare and print 1099s	✓	✓
Give employees and subcontractors limited access to enter time worked	✓	✓
Track billable hours by customer	✓	✓
Create budgets to estimate future income and expenses	✓	✓
Categorize your income and expenses using class tracking	✓	✓
Track sales and profitability for each of your locations	✓	✓
Client Manager to organize and allow access to Multiple QBO companies		✓
Accountant Center to access clean-up and reporting tools		✓
Undo previous reconciliation tool for correcting cleared balances		✓
Write off customer balances in batches		✓
Reclassify transactions in batches		✓
Integration with ProConnect Tax Online		✓
Number of people who can access QuickBooks Online	5	Unlimited

Number of built-in business reports	65+	70+
Pay employees and file payroll taxes. Fees apply with payroll service.		
Receive ACH and Credit Card payments: Transaction fees apply.		

COMPARE QUICKBOOKS ONLINE TO QUICKBOOKS DESKTOP

Go online to http://quickbooks.intuit.com/move-to-quickbooks-online/ to compare QuickBooks Desktop to QuickBooks Online. To see this chart, click <Compare>.

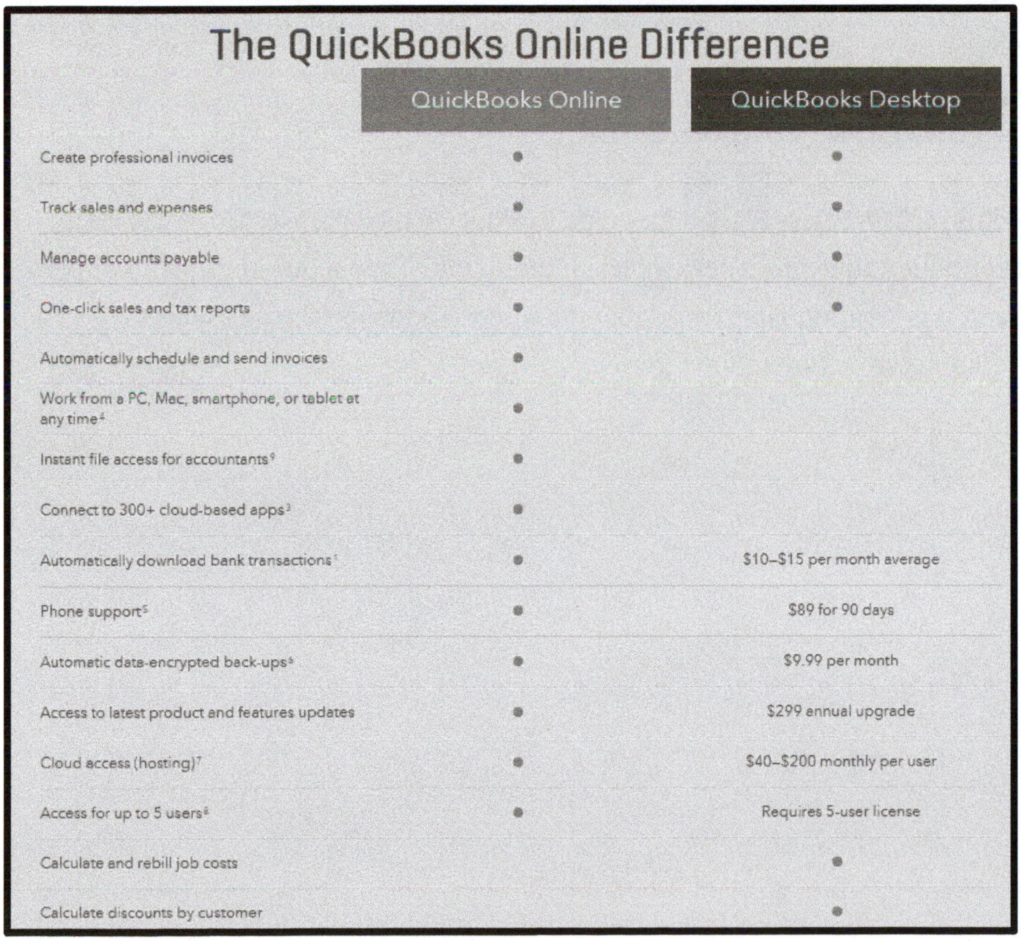

The QuickBooks Online Difference

	QuickBooks Online	QuickBooks Desktop
Create professional invoices	•	•
Track sales and expenses	•	•
Manage accounts payable	•	•
One-click sales and tax reports	•	•
Automatically schedule and send invoices	•	
Work from a PC, Mac, smartphone, or tablet at any time[4]	•	
Instant file access for accountants[9]	•	
Connect to 300+ cloud-based apps[3]	•	
Automatically download bank transactions[1]	•	$10–$15 per month average
Phone support[5]	•	$89 for 90 days
Automatic data-encrypted back-ups[6]	•	$9.99 per month
Access to latest product and features updates	•	$299 annual upgrade
Cloud access (hosting)[7]	•	$40–$200 monthly per user
Access for up to 5 users[8]	•	Requires 5-user license
Calculate and rebill job costs		•
Calculate discounts by customer		•

MULTI-FACTOR AUTHENTICATION (MFA)

Intuit has implemented multi-factor authentication across all of their products to protect your account and ensure only you have access to your data. As part of this, when you sign-in or when you make a change to your account information (such as email, password, user ID) you may be required to use a one-time confirmation code to complete the process.

To learn more about MFA, go online to https://community.intuit.com/articles/1164912-multi-factor-authentication-mfa-faq.

QUICKBOOKS ONLINE HELP

Within QBO, select ? and type in a question or phrase. Go to the Help information to explore help topics. Experiment. Type a question, word or phrase. As of this writing, Help looks like the screen shown on the next page.

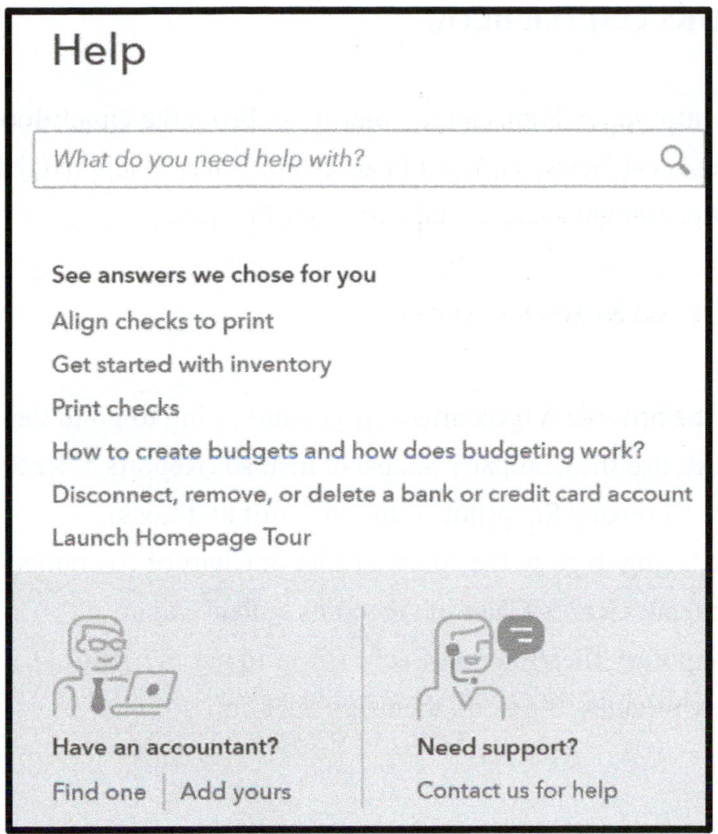

QUICKBOOKS ONLINE SUPPORT

To get help while signed in to your company, click the Help link at the top right which will load the QuickBooks Online Support page. If you are not signed in to your QBO company, you can access support by going to https://community.intuit.com/quickbooks-online. On this page, questions are answered 24/7.

QUICKBOOKS ONLINE BLOG

Go online to http://quickbooks.intuit.com/blog/. From the QuickBooks Blog, you can obtain the latest News, Thought Leadership, What's New in QBO, Innovation, Accountant Advice, and Customer Profiles.

WORKAROUND SUGGESTIONS

1. Click on the browser's back arrow. If you are trying to go to the Profit and Loss report, use the Company Snapshot instead (Reports > Recommended Reports > Company Snapshot > link to Profit and Loss).
2. If you are trying to go to the Account List or Chart of Accounts, use the Settings menu: Gear > Chart of Accounts > Run Report.
3. Clear Temporary files/Internet Cache (refer to pages 610-611).
4. Wait a few minutes. Sign out, then sign back in.

Appendix B Glossary

Appendix B lists the glossary of terms used in *Computer Accounting in the Cloud with QuickBooks Online, 2e*. Within the textbook, words that are boldfaced and italicized are defined in the Glossary. The glossary is also included on the Online Learning Center at www.mhhe.com/qbo2e.

account list — The account list shows the chart of accounts. See chart of accounts. (p. 79)

accounting equation — The balance sheet shows the accounting equation — Assets = Liabilities + Equity. (p. 177)

accounts payable — The money a company owes to a supplier or vendor. (p. 148)

accounts payable transactions — Purchases on account from vendors. Transactions that affect accounts payable appear in the Transaction List by Vendor. The Transaction List by Vendor shows the bill, vendor credit, and bill payment transactions that make up vendors' balances. (p. 148)

accounts receivable Accounts receivable are what customers owe your business. (p. 208)

accounts receivable transactions Credit transactions from customers. (p. 208)

adjusting entries Adjusting journal entries are recorded to correct account balances. Adjusting entries are created for a variety of reasons, including booking depreciation, reallocating accruals, and reversing accruals of prepaid income or expenses. (p. 316)

audit log The audit log contains a list of all the changes that have ever been made to your company data and by whom. By default, the Audit Log displays the 200 most recent events. Dates and Times in the Audit Log and Audit History reflect when events occurred, displayed in your local time. (p. 45 and 86)

balance sheet The balance sheet lists what you own (assets), what your debts are (liabilities), and what you've invested in your company (equity). (p. 16)

bank reconciliation The process of bringing the balance of the bank statement and the balance of the checking account into agreement. (p. 144)

bill A bill posts to Accounts Payable and the vendor with the appropriate expense or account. You enter a bill (payable to a vendor) to record the expense or purchase of assets. (p. 166)

business processes A collection of related, structured activities or tasks that produce a specific service, product, transaction, or report. (p. xxii)

chart of accounts A complete list of a business's accounts and their balances. The chart of accounts includes two categories of accounts — Balance Sheet accounts and Income and Expense accounts. (p. 16)

cloud Data is stored on web servers instead of your computer. Cloud software is always accessible and up to date. (p. xviii)

cloud computing Enables ubiquitous, convenient, on-demand network access to a shared pool of computing resources (for example, applications, servers, and services) that can be rapidly delivered with minimal management effort or server interaction. Examples include Software as a service, QuickBooks Online and NetSuite; Infrastructure as a service, Amazon Web Services and Dropbox; Platform as a service, Windows Azure. More information at http://www.nist.gov/itl/cloud/ (p. 54)

cloudware Refers to software that is built, installed, delivered and accessed entirely from a remote Web server, also called the cloud. Cloudware is a software delivery method that provides software over the Internet. (p. 53)

company administrator Company Administrators have all access rights within QBO. They also have all access rights for every other service to which the company subscribes. (p. 82)

confirmation code
When signing in, multi-factor authentication using a 6-digit confirmation code is required. Each sign is authenticated via the computers IP address. IP address is defined on page 512. For more information refer to https://community.intuit.com/articles/1164912-multi-factor-authentication-faq. (page 83)

credit memo
Refunds for merchandise that is returned by a customer. A credit memo affects the customers balance. (p. 210)

customer relationship management (CRM)
Customer relationship management practices, strategies and technologies that companies use to manage and analyze customer interactions and data throughout the customer lifecycle, with the goal of improving business relationships, assisting in customer retention and driving sales growth. CRM systems are designed to compile information on customers across different channels or points of contact between the customer and the company. (p. 545)

customers
A customer is a person or organization that buys goods or services from a store or business; for example, a consumer, buyer, subscriber, shopper. The Sales page manages your customer list and transactions. (p. 198)

dashboard	The dashboard is a current snapshot of the business as of the day you sign in. For example, the test-drive's dashboard shows profit and loss, how much as spent, the income and sales summary, and bank accounts for Craig's Design and Landscaping Services. The Dashboard is also called the Home page. (p. 3)
default	A setting or a value automatically assigned to a software application, computer program or device, without user intervention. For example, the Dashboard shows software presets. (p. 4)
enterprise resource planning (ERP)	Enterprise resource planning systems are company-wide software products that coordinate all the resources, information, and functions of a business from shared data sources. (p. 545)
financial statements	The financial statements report economic information about the business. (p. 176)

fiscal year

The fiscal year is a period that the company (or government) uses for accounting purposes and preparing financial statements. The fiscal year may or may not be the same as the calendar year. For tax purposes, companies can choose to be calendar-year taxpayers or fiscal-year taxpayers. The default Internal Revenue Service system is based on the calendar year. (p. 316)

generally accepted accounting principles (GAAP)

A common set of accounting principles, standards, and procedures that companies use to compile financial statements. GAAP are a combination of standards set by policy boards and the commonly accepted way of recording and reporting accounting information. (p. 20)

home page

The QBO Home page is the central place for getting an overview of the company. The Home page is also called the Dashboard. (p. 3)

income and expense accounts

Categories of accounts for tracking how money flows in and out of your company. (p. 17)

income statement In QBO, the income statement is the same as the Profit and Loss report. Refer to the glossary definition of Profit and Loss. (p. 20)

internal controls An integrated system of people, processes, and procedures that minimize or eliminate business risks, protect assets, ensure reliable accounting, and promote efficient operations. (p. 86)

inventory item A product that is purchased from vendors for sale to customers. (p. 156)

IP address An Internet Protocol address is a unique address that personal computers, tablets, and smartphones use for identification. (p. 84)

journal entry A journal entry is a transaction in which there are at least two parts – a Debit and a Credit – called distribution lines. Each distribution line has an account from the Chart of Accounts. The total of the Debit column equals the total of the Credit column. (p. 98)

keyboard shortcuts Instead of using the mouse or trackpad, a combination of keys are pressed to complete common tasks and workflows. (p. xxxiv)

modules

A software design that emphasizes separating the functions of a program into independent, interchangeable modules, so that each contains everything necessary to execute only one aspect of the desired function. QBO organizes reports by modules or components within the accounting system. On the Reports page, the link to <All Reports>, shows how QBO organizes each module. (p. 315)

multi-factor authentication MFA

Multi-factor authentication (MFA), also called multi-level authentication, is an internet security method. MFA is a method of computer access in which a user is granted access only after presenting several separate pieces of evidence. An example of MFA is two-factor authentication (2FA). When access is granted to the professor, 2FA is a method of confirming the professor's identity. For more information, read this article at https://community.intuit.com/articles/1164912-multi-factor-authentication-faq (p. 83)

navigation bar

On the left side of the screen, QBO includes a Navigation bar where you access different pages. (p. 4)

permanent accounts

The asset, liability, and equity accounts shown on the Balance Sheet are called permanent accounts. They do not close at the end of the accounting year. Permanent account balances accumulate month to month and year to year. (p. 334)

perpetual inventory When products are set up, general ledger accounts are updated when purchases and sales are recorded. QBO tracks cost of goods sold, stock levels, sales prices, and inventory. In a perpetual inventory system, an up-to-date record of inventory is maintained and the inventory account is revised each time a purchase or sale is made. (p. 159)

products and services Use products and services to enter consistent transaction descriptions, prices or rates. (p. 157)

profit and loss The profit and loss report shows money you earned (income) and money you spent (expenses) so that you can see how profitable your company is. The report shows subtotals for each income or expense account in your chart of accounts. The last line shows your net income (or loss). If you want to focus on a particular week, month, quarter or year, set the date range to that time period. (p.10)

QBO An abbreviation for QuickBooks Online. The version used in Chapter 1 with the sample company is QBO Plus. (p. xvii)

record keeping The process of recording transactions and events in an accounting system. Since the principles of accounting rely on accurate and thorough records, record keeping is the foundation accounting. An example of an accounting transaction is the sales to a customer on account. (p. 315)

refund — When a refund is issued, you write a check or pay out cash to the customer. (p. 210)

remittances — The action of sending money in payment of a bill. (p. 254)

Software as a Service (SaaS) — QBO is an example of Software as a Service. SaaS is a way of delivering applications over the Internet—as a service—instead of installing and maintaining software locally on your hard drive. You access the software through your Internet browser. (p. 54)

source document — Written evidence of a business transaction. Examples of source documents are sales invoices, sales receipts, bills, transaction register, and a bank statement. (p. 96)

specialized screens — Examples of specialized screens are checks, receive payments, bill, bank deposit, and transfers. (p. 99)

statement of cash flows — A report that shows how your cash position changed over time. It shows the amount of cash earned from profit, where you received additional cash and where your cash was spent. It uses all the Bank-type accounts from your chart of accounts. The SCF assumes that all activity within current assets and current liabilities are operating activities. Entries that affect fixed assets are investing activities. Entries that affect long-term liabilities and equity are financing activities. (p. 177)

templates	A document or transaction pattern that is stored so that it can be used again. In QBO, recurring transactions can also be set up (Gear > Recurring Transactions). (p. 528)
temporary accounts	Accounts that are closed at the end of the year are called temporary accounts. Temporary accounts, such as income, cost of goods sold, and expenses, accumulate transactions and balances during one accounting year. In QBO, temporary account balances are transferred to the Retained Earnings account on the first day of the new year, and the income and expense accounts have a zero balance. (p. 334)
transaction register	A term used to identify checking account activity. (p. 96)
trial balance	This report summarizes the debit and credit balances of each account on the chart of accounts for a period of time. (p. 36 and 123)
undeposited funds	The Undeposited Funds account is like an envelope where you keep checks until you take them to the bank. If you receive more than one check or payment in a day, they could be grouped as one deposit. (p. 134)
updates	Next to links that have changed, reminder information is shown. (p. 61)
user interface (UI)	The user interface is the link between the user and the software. The QBO user interface includes links for software navigation. (p. 4)

vendors	The Expenses page is where you keep track of the suppliers you work with. Vendors are people or companies that you pay money to, such as a store, utility, or landlord. (p. 140)
workflow	The sequence of processes through which work passes from initiation to completion. (p. xxiii)

Index